Publication Number 28

Duke University Commonwealth-Studies Center

*Asian Bureaucratic Systems Emergent from
the British Imperial Tradition*

Duke University Commonwealth-Studies Center Publications

1. The British Commonwealth: An Experiment in Co-operation among Nations, by Frank H. Underhill   2. South Africa: Economic and Political Aspects, by Hector Menteith Robertson   3. Some Comparative Aspects of Irish Law, by Alfred Gaston Donaldson   4. Economic Analysis and Policy in Underdeveloped Countries, by P. T. Bauer   5. The Higher Public Service of the Commonwealth of Australia, by Howard A. Scarrow   6. Economic Opinion and Policy in Ceylon, by Henry M. Oliver, Jr.   7. Problems of the New Commonwealth, by Sir Ivor Jennings   8. Commonwealth Perspectives, by Nicholas Mansergh, et al.   9. Evolving Canadian Federalism, by A. R. M. Lower, F. R. Scott, et al.   10. The Commonwealth Economy in Southeast Asia, by T. H. Silcock   11. Public Expenditures in Australia, by B. U. Ratchford   12. The American Economic Impact on Canada, by Hugh G. J. Aitken, John J. Deutsch, W. A. Mackintosh, et al. 13. Tradition, Values, and Socio-Economic Development, edited by Ralph Braibanti and Joseph J. Spengler   14. The Growth of Canadian Policies in External Affairs, by Hugh L. Keenleyside, et al.   15. Canadian Economic Thought: The Political Economy of a Developing Nation, 1814–1914, by Craufurd D. W. Goodwin   16. Economic Systems of the Commonwealth, edited by Calvin B. Hoover   17. The Nigerian Political Scene, edited by Robert O. Tilman and Taylor Cole   18. Administration and Economic Development in India, edited by Ralph Braibanti and Joseph J. Spengler   19. Canada–United States Treaty Relations, edited by David R. Deener   20. Post-primary Education and Political and Economic Development, edited by Don C. Piper and Taylor Cole   21. Bureaucratic Transition in Malaya, by Robert O. Tilman   22. The West African Commonwealth, by C. W. Newbury   23. The Transfer of Institutions, edited by William B. Hamilton   24. Economic Enquiry in Australia, by Craufurd D. W. Goodwin   25. A Decade of the Commonwealth, 1955–1964, edited by W. B. Hamilton, Kenneth Robinson, and C. D. W. Goodwin   26. Research on the Bureaucracy of Pakistan,* by Ralph Braibanti   27. The International Law Standard and Commonwealth Developments, by Robert R. Wilson, et al.

* Program in Comparative Studies on Southern Asia publication.

Asian Bureaucratic Systems Emergent from the British Imperial Tradition

Ralph Braibanti
Hugh Tinker   Bernard S. Cohn
David C. Potter   James F. Guyot
Sir Charles Collins   Robert N. Kearney
Robert O. Tilman   Merrill Goodall

Edited by Ralph Braibanti

Published for the
Duke University Commonwealth-Studies Center
Duke University Press, Durham, N. C.
1966

Printed in the United States of America
by Kingsport Press, Inc., Kingsport, Tenn.

Foreword

This series of integrated studies, *Asian Bureaucratic Systems*, is a substantial addition to the literature on comparative administration. Its central focus on bureaucracy opens one avenue for insight into the functioning of the several political systems. The countries of Southern Asia constitute collectively a populous, territorially contiguous, and strategically located area of the world. The uniformities, evidenced by a common British imperial heritage, underdeveloped economies, and relatively low civic cultures, are offset by the substantial differences which religion, environment, and history have provided. The resulting cultural diversities of these states provide the justification for the self-contained and discrete studies which have been made by authors who have combined high academic attainment with substantial professional involvement and field experience. They have indeed brought together an impressive amount of bibliographical material and empirical data.

The volume has two recurrent themes. The first of these is the impact and resiliency of the British bureaucratic heritage, with its special organizational features, its elitist aspects associated with a generalist educational background, and its behavioral characteristics which included a stress on personal integrity and political neutrality. Historical circumstance, environment, and indigenous factors have resulted in some variance among themselves and between these bureaucracies and those of the Western states, including members of the "Old Commonwealth" which have borrowed heavily from British precedent. A careful reading of the chapters will offer a good description of this degree of differentiation.

The second of these themes is the pervasiveness of the elitist tradition, which incorporates elements of careful selectivity, prestige, a corporate identity, common objectives, and substantial discretion in the choice of means to attain them. One of the authors, James F. Guyot, has chosen to refer to these members of the higher civil services as the "guardian class." The qualities of these elitist groups, most clearly typified by the ICS, provide one answer to the query—raised in this volume by David Potter—as to how so few could rule so many for such a long period of time.

These studies also provide several pertinent case studies of the transfer of power from the British to independent governments and of office from British to indigenous personnel. The Indian case provides the heart of this story; the Nepal case is the major variant. This final British "withdrawal," which has been nearly completed in all countries, occurred too rapidly in Burma, says Hugh Tinker, where there was "little to take its place." The heritage was greater in other countries. The materials are here available for some comparisons with the bureaucratic evolution in other parts of the British Commonwealth, especially in Africa, where the elitist tradition for lack of time and encouragement never was as deeply implanted.

Among the many important matters which receive attention in these studies, the problem of the responsibility of the bureaucracy is an especially intriguing one. How and why did Pakistan's courts, Ceylon's trade unions, Malaya's Whitley Councils, and India's dominant party acquire special roles? What were some of the particular characteristics of the respective political cultures that determined the contours of responsibility within which these bureaucracies function?

Ralph Braibanti has noted in his Introduction that three agencies, the United States Agency for International Development, the United Nations Technical Assistance Programme, and the Ford Foundation during the period from 1951 to 1962 have spent "throughout the world at least a quarter of a billion dollars in administrative modernization, supported some seventy-five training institutions and trained at least seven thousand persons in public administration." These massive efforts in the transnational inducement of administrative reform have encountered many obstacles. To take one extreme case, Merrill Goodall records that of OPEX officials in Nepal: "some have been dismissed by the host country, two have died in service, others have experienced severe health problems, and one resigned having found it impossible to harmonize the conflicting purposes of rival aid agencies." In consequence, one might ask with Professor Braibanti whether the emphasis on administrative change has sometimes been stressed without adequate attention to its relevancy to and dependence upon other aspects of the political process. Further, in terms of which goals and by which criteria has the "effectiveness" of these efforts to procure administrative "modernization" been measured? At the least, the chapters in this volume contain pertinent data on which some answers can be based.

In sum, *Asian Bureaucratic Systems* is a welcome addition to the professional literature on comparative administration in general and on bureaucracy in particular. With its different geographical coverage and its heavier historical orientation, this collection of studies provides a valuable companion symposium to Joseph LaPalombara (ed.), *Bureaucracy and Political Development*. The volume will contribute to our beginning efforts not only to analyze political systems but also to compare them.

TAYLOR COLE

Duke University

Acknowledgments

The studies in this volume were completed at various times from the spring of 1963 through the summer of 1965, each being revised, modified, and in some cases brought up to date during that period.

Research on which the various chapters are based has been made possible through grants or fellowships awarded the authors quite independently of this project. Separate acknowledgment for such support is made, where appropriate, at the beginning of each chapter. Among such sources of research support are the American Council of Learned Societies, the American Society of International Law, the Asia Foundation, the University of California at Los Angeles, the Carnegie Corporation, the Duke University Commonwealth-Studies Center, the Ford Foundation, the Fulbright Program, the Guggenheim Foundation, the Human Ecology Fund, the University of London, the University of Rochester, and the Social Science Research Council. Final preparation of the research for these studies was facilitated by a grant from the Program in Comparative Studies on Southern Asia, supported by the Ford Foundation as an activity of the Commonwealth-Studies Center. I am grateful to my colleagues in the program for making such help available. Publication of the volume was made possible by financial support from Carnegie Corporation to the Commonwealth-Studies Center of Duke University. The indebtedness of all the authors for support by these organizations is hereby gratefully acknowledged. None of the organizations mentioned above is responsible for data or conclusion presented in this volume. Such responsibility rests solely with the authors.

I am grateful to my colleagues on the Commonwealth-Studies

Committee, especially to Professor R. Taylor Cole whose foresight in the organizational period of the committee ultimately made this volume possible, and to Professor Calvin B. Hoover whose *Economic Systems of the Commonwealth* served as a model and inspiration. Professor Alan K. Manchester, who handled the financial arrangements for these studies with his usual efficiency, is also due my gratitude.

My thanks also go to the collaborating authors whose enthusiastic participation in this project was one of its most satisfying outcomes. They exhibited uncommon patience and generosity as we sought together to forge a series of distinctly individual yet not unrelated studies.

Finally, I am grateful to Mrs. Mary Ellen Earp who handled the administrative details connected with this project, typed all the tables, and typed many successive revisions of research notes as well as drafts and final copy of the manuscript.

RALPH BRAIBANTI

Durham, North Carolina
February, 1966

Contributors

Ralph Braibanti was born in Danbury, Connecticut, in 1920 and received his doctorate from Syracuse University in 1949. His service in World War II included two years as a military government officer in Japan for which he was decorated for meritorious achievement. In the summer of 1952 he was in Okinawa as political adviser to the Civil Administrator for the Ryukyu Islands. He held a Ford Foundation Foreign Area Training and Research Fellowship in 1954, and under auspices of a Social Science Research Council postdoctoral fellowship and a Commonwealth-Studies Center grant did research in Pakistan in 1957, and in India and Pakistan in 1958 and 1959. He returned for shorter visits during that period as a consultant for the United States Agency for International Development. From 1960–1962 he was chief adviser to the Civil Service Academy in Lahore and returned to Pakistan on three subsequent occasions. He is the author of *Research on the Bureaucracy of Pakistan* (1966) and of various studies in learned journals. He is co-editor (with J. J. Spengler) and a contributor to *Tradition, Values and Socio-Economic Development* (1961), *Administration and Economic Development in India* (1962), and is a contributing author to such volumes as Joseph LaPalombara (ed.), *Bureaucracy and Political Development* (1963), John D. Montgomery and William D. Siffin (eds.), *Approaches to Development: Politics, Administration and Change* (1966), and Myron Weiner (ed.), *Modernization* (1966). He is professor of political science at Duke University where he has been a member of the faculty since 1953.

Bernard S. Cohn, born in Brooklyn, New York, in 1928, received his doctorate in anthropology from Cornell University in 1954. He has carried out anthropological field work in a North Indian village, 1952–1953, archival research on legal and administrative change in India, 1958–1959, and in Great Britain and India. His chapter in this volume is based on research carried out in London in 1962 supported by the Social Science Research Council, the American Council of Learned Societies, and the Arts College of the University of Rochester.

He has published articles on anthropology and history of nineteenth-century India in various learned journals. Formerly on the faculty of the University of Rochester, he is at present associate professor of anthropology and history at the University of Chicago.

Sir Charles Henry Collins was born in London in 1887. He received the Bachelor of Arts degree from King's College, University of London, entered the Ceylon Civil Service in November, 1910, and spent some thirty-eight years in the island, retiring in 1948. Roughly half this period was spent in secretariat positions in Colombo, where he officiated frequently as chief secretary and financial secretary. Latterly he was responsible for advising the government on the administrative changes necessitated by the introduction of a cabinet form of government in 1947. The earlier part of his service was spent mainly in provincial administration. He was created C.M.G. in 1941 and Knight Bachelor in 1947. The history of Ceylon and particularly of the British period was always a special interest, and he found opportunities for research in the archives in Ceylon and in London. His major publications are *Public Administration in Ceylon* (1951) and *Public Administration in Hong Kong* (1952).

Merrill R. Goodall was born in San Francisco in 1917. He served in the China-Burma-India theater during the war and subsequently was awarded a pre-doctoral Social Science Research Council fellowship in 1947–1948, a Social Science Research Council area travel grant for India, 1951–1952, and an American Council of Learned Societies–Social Science Research Council Asia research grant in 1960–1961. He received the doctorate from the Johns Hopkins University. He has been a Fulbright professor at Delhi University, a professor at Lucknow University, and executive director of the Cornell India Program. In 1952 he was adviser on administration to the prime minister of Nepal and in other years a short-term consultant to the Government of Nepal. From March, 1962, to September, 1963, he was senior United Nations adviser in public administration to His Majesty's Government of Nepal. He is author of *Administration and Planning for Economic Development* (1952), *The Political System of India 1865–70* (1958), and a contributor to Richard L. Park and Irene D. Tinker (eds.), *Leadership and Political Institutions in India* (1959). Since 1955 he has been professor of government and Asian studies at the Claremont Graduate School.

James F. Guyot was born in Detroit, Michigan, in 1932. While working as a management intern and later as an examiner for the United States Civil Service Commission in Boston, he began a study of motivational and sociological differences between governmental and corporate middle managers. His major interests center on the social factors active in the recruitment of administrative elites and the patterns of bureaucratic survival during political change. Research in the latter area began during several summers of travel in the Soviet Union with the Yale Russian Chorus. After receiving his doctor's degree from Yale University he spent a year and a half in Burma under grants from the Fulbright Program and the Human Ecology Fund studying the impact of independence on the Civil Service and observing the early months of the second army government. He returned to Southeast Asia for field research in Singapore and Malaysia during 1966–67. He has contributed to professional journals and is presently assistant professor of political science at the University of California at Los Angeles.

Robert N. Kearney, born in 1930 in Exira, Iowa, holds the doctorate from the University of California, Los Angeles. During 1960–1962, as a Fellow in the Ford Foundation Foreign Area Training and Research Program, he studied at the School of Oriental and African Studies of the University of London and engaged in field research on contemporary politics and political change in Ceylon. Supported by a grant from the American Council of Learned Societies, during the summer of 1965 he was in Ceylon doing research on problems of communalism. His primary interest is in the study of comparative politics and administration in South Asia. Author of several articles on Ceylonese politics and bureaucracy in various learned journals and a contributor to such volumes as Robert Scalapino (ed.), *The Communist Revolution in Asia* (1966), he was formerly on the faculty of Duke University and is presently assistant professor of political science at the University of California at Santa Barbara.

David C. Potter, born in Berkeley, California, in 1931, received the doctorate from the University of London in 1962. His first field research in India was carried on as a Fulbright student from the University of California (Berkeley) in 1958–1959. He again studied in India in 1960–1961 as a Research Fellow in public law and government in the Commonwealth at the London School of Economics and Political Science, an appointment held from 1960 through 1962. He continued his research in England during the summer of 1965 and 1966 and returned to India in 1966–67 under auspices of an American Institute of Indian Studies Research Grant. He is the author of *Government in Rural India* (1964) and of several articles in learned journals. Formerly on the faculty at Oakland University in Rochester, Michigan, he is now assistant professor of political science at Simon Fraser University in British Columbia.

Robert O. Tilman was born in 1929 at Caruthersville, Missouri, and was awarded the doctorate by Duke University in 1961. Grants from the Social Science Research Council, the Duke University Commonwealth-Studies Center, the American Society of International Law, and the American Council of Learned Societies permitted him to undertake field research in the Malaysian area on three occasions during the period 1959–1963 and again in the summer of 1966. He is author of *Bureaucratic Transition in Malaya* (1964), co-editor (with Taylor Cole) of *The Nigerian Political Scene* (1962), and the contributor of a number of essays to learned journals and to such symposium volumes as Wang Gungwu (ed.), *Malaysia: A Survey* (1964). The author's principal research interests lie in the fields of Southeast Asian politics and administraton. Formerly a member of the department of political science at Tulane University, he has been assistant professor of political science at Yale University since 1965.

Hugh Tinker, born in 1921 in Westcliff, England, was graduated from Sidney Sussex College, Cambridge, in 1948. He pursued graduate studies at the University of London where he earned the diploma in public administration in 1948 and the doctorate in 1951. After serving as an officer in the Armored Corps of the Indian Army from 1941 to 1945, he was appointed to the Indian Civil Service in which he remained until 1946. He studied in Asia in several capacities: as a visiting professor at the University of Rangoon, 1954–1955, Southeast Asia Treaty Organization traveling lecturer in 1960, and in 1963 as a Commonwealth Relations Office lecturer. In 1959 he was visiting professor of government at Cornell University. His research interests have been in local government, politics, and administration of several Asian states, particularly Burma, India, and Pakistan. He is the author of *Foundations of Local Self-Government in India, Pakistan and Burma* (1954); *The Union of Burma* (1957); *India and Pakistan: A Political Analysis* (1962); *Ballot Box and Bayonet; People and Government in Emergent Asian Countries* (1964); *Reorientations* (1965); and *South Asia, a Short History* (1966). He has written for various learned journals and is a contributing author to such symposium volumes as D. G. E. Hall (ed.), *Historians of Southeast Asia* (1961), and Ralph Braibanti and J. J. Spengler (eds.), *Administration and Economic Development in India* (1963). In 1963 he was appointed professor of government and politics with reference to Asia in the University of London.

Contents

Tables and Charts

Recruitment and Training of British Civil Servants in India 1600–1860

Bureaucratic Change in India

The Higher Bureaucracy of Pakistan

Administrative Change in Nepal

Concluding Observations

*Asian Bureaucratic Systems Emergent from
the British Imperial Tradition*

Introduction

Ralph Braibanti

I. Bureaucracy in Developing Systems

The comparative analysis of bureaucratic systems is one of the most dynamic research specialties in contemporary political studies. Analytically, administration—the cutting edge of government—is a departure from the study of formal institutions embodied in constitutional formularies, statutory law, and legislative process. When as early as 1887 Woodrow Wilson called attention to administration as a valid field of inquiry, he was identifying the importance of the behavior of administrators filling in the generality of statute with interpretation forged both by presidential impulse and by the accretion of successive administrative actions. In relation to earlier developments in political science this type of analysis had essentially a behavioral emphasis, although the study of administration itself quickly embraced and emphasized elements which focused on institutional and legal aspects of government as well. Subsequently, there was a resurgence of the behavioral dimension as attention was given to the interaction of statutory and administrative law with discretionary behavior controlled within a matrix of politics. This development was enriched by the application of psychology and sociology to political conduct and especially to the emotional, intellectual, and environmental components of the decision-making process.

More recently, analysis of bureaucracies has been quickened by large-scale efforts at transnational inducement of administrative reform in the newly independent states. This has been facilitated by codification of doctrine generated by organized institutional forces such as the United Nations Technical Assistance Programme, the United States Agency for International Development, and various philanthropic enterprises such as the Ford Foundation. These two official agencies and the Ford Foundation together spent throughout the world in the decade 1951–1962 at least a quarter of a billion dollars in administrative modernization, supported some seventy-five training institutions, and trained at least seven thousand persons in public administration. These figures are minimal, and if local currency expenditures and foreign and local currency costs of related activities such as community development, welfare, agricultural, and educational administration were included, the expenditure might approach half a billion dollars. Efforts of such magnitude have shifted attention to the cultural and historical forces deemed to impede or facilitate reform. In consequence we have been led to a concern for not only the ideological and institutional content of the legacy of imperial rule but also for the style by which the transition to independence has been accomplished. Finally, an interest in the larger sphere of political modernization, of which administrative reform is but a segment, has rightly directed attention to the means of rendering bureaucracy responsible to some element or sets of elements in the political process. Thus, such issues as the quality of the representativeness of bureaucrats, the synaptic relations developed with the public, legislative oversight, judicial review of administrative discretion, and infra-bureaucratic institutional responsibility to the chief executive become subjects illuminating the pattern of such responsibility.

The issues raised by bureaucratic systems in political orders—both the highly developed orders and the emerging ones—are essentially the same. The principal distinction is that older constitutional orders have evolved formularies and to a lesser extent patterns of behavior resolving these issues. In the older orders, the bureaucratic function has been fitted into a political system, not permanently to be sure, but in a manner allowing for articulation with other functions in the order. For convenience of exposition, the theoretical issues raised by bureaucracy can be arranged in three categories:

(1) The first of these is the maintenance of compatibility between the spirit and substance of statutory law and administrative discretion. This involves the compatibility of substance and procedure with canons of due process of law. This relationship must be achieved without negating the operation of expertise and flexibility which the administrative process is designed to achieve.

(2) The determination of the role of bureaucracy as an institution with the capability of converting political and social demands into programs and action is the second category. This problem is different from the first. The first problem assumes that the demands converted are exclusively statutory and politically tempered by an executive style. The second problem assumes that statutory origins are only one of many sources of demands, which vary in proportion from one political system to another. Other sources of demands are the internal resources of the bureaucratic system, including its own conception of its role in the political order and its capability of converting the consequence of that role into some form of action in the political process. Another extra-statutory source of demand is the public mass itself, either segmentally organized or as a totality. The synapses between such segments and the bureaucratic system, both conditioned by and isolated from statutory and other executive influences are of critical significance. In newly developing states, this second problem is more important than in older constitutional systems. Bureaucratic systems, long accustomed to near paramountcy under imperial rule, may rely less on the statutory source of their programs and actions and much more on their internal resources and on synaptic relations with extra-statutory sources for the generation of action. As a political system matures and the institutional performance of various functions becomes progressively more symmetrical, the sphere of bureaucratic action which is statutorily derived is likely to expand and the sphere which is otherwise derived is likely to shrink. Included under this second category is the bureaucracy's capability of infusing qualities of

rationality and innovation in the political process, both as bureaucratic refinements of qualities derived from statutory sources or as spontaneous qualities generated from within the system. Again, in developing states, the generation of such qualities internally, within a larger political context of relevance to statutory and non-statutory sources, is likely to be far more critical than in established systems. This is essentially the problem of a bureaucratic system developing autonomous political orientations, with minimal synaptic connections with other sources of polity.

(3) The third theoretical issue in which we are interested is the bureaucracy as a social institution for a large segment of employed population. The bureaucratic system as a more or less closed arena conditions personality, affects individual behavior, and becomes both a source of norms and a means of re-diffusing both personal and bureaucratic norms. Here we are concerned with the internal structure and operation of the bureaucratic apparatus, the extent to which it reflects the total social order or is insulated from it, and especially the extent to which it diffuses the same or different norms as those of the total social order. In developing states this aspect of bureaucracy as a way of life is important as a powerful conditioner of the human spirit in assisting the state to achieve an ultimate moral purpose of moving toward noble ends. But it is even more important as a factor conditioning the values and behavior which are ultimately brought to bear in the application of discretion in decision-making. The greater the size and the autonomy of the sphere of discretion, and the greater the reliance on infra-bureaucratic generation of norms, the more critical the intrinsic ethos of the bureaucratic apparatus as a life pattern is likely to become.

While, in general, these three issues are involved in the political evolution of both well-established and new states, there are special considerations in developing states which must be taken into account. In older states, the context in which bureaucracy functions is already politicized, and the likelihood is that it was politicized before the emergence of a significant and powerful bureaucratic system. But in the new states, the context is quite different, with the elements being reversed. Bureaucratization has usually occurred first, accelerated by colonial or imperial rule; and politicization, long sedated by colonial or imperial rule, is only now gathering momentum. We are led by this juxtaposition of conditions to consider the relationship of administrative modernization with the broader aspect of political growth and with the role of foreign technical assistance in the growth process.

It is sometimes said that foreign aid should be specifically directed at hastening politicization rather than at administrative reform alone. The effect of administrative reform on the larger activity of politicization appears somewhat more complex than such criticism would suggest. Political modernity embraces four qualities: (1) The establishment of an institutional apparatus which has the potential for conversion of valid expressions of popular will into actions fairly predictable and consistent with the fundamental polity of the state. This potential may not always equal present capability; indeed, the gap between potential and capability is one means of determining the effectiveness of this aspect of modernity. (2) The expansion of popular participation in the political process and the enrichment of the quality of such participation in terms of popular comprehension of issues, acceptance of personal responsibility, and commitment to orderly pursuit of change. Judged in the context of established constitutional systems, it is easy to overlook the significance of this qualitative dimension. (3) The capability of maintaining national integration through orderly and just accommodation of cultural, religious, and similar divisive forces. (4) The capacity to blend elements of the popular will in markedly disparate stages of development into an aggregate and to make that aggregated will effective and subject ultimately (though not necessarily immediately) to neutrally imposed canons of equity and justice. Thus, the rationality of bureaucracy, which Weber so well described as becoming cumulatively more rational with experience, must be blended with the comprehension of norms of justice manifested by the judiciary, with sacerdotal norms of religious institutions, and with the popular will into an aggregated pattern.

It is apparent that these four attributes of political modernization are achieved at an unequal or asymmetrical pace in most emerging states. Much emphasis is given to the first half of the second attribute above, that is, the quantitative dimension of popular participation in and control of the political process. This emphasis is understandable, especially because determinations of qualitative participation have been used in the past as justification for colonial rule, or in sovereign systems for non-participative authoritarianism. It is also the consequence of Western liberal zeal applied to emerging societies whose pattern of development is far less symmetrical than that experienced by most Western nations.

The emphasis given this quantitative aspect of participation, or "popularity," neglects some very important characteristics of most developing societies. The first of these, and the most important, is the bifurcated nature of the social order. Politicization proceeds on the basis of Western ideological and constitutional norms which are divorced—sometimes even in language—from the mainstream of the social order. Thus, the ideological cohesion of the social order is badly disturbed, and even minimal popular comprehension of polity may not exist. Most developing states have faced this problem in one way or another by seeking to unite the bifurcated strata of the social order through mediational processes such as rural development, direct or indirect elections, or ideological indoctrination. Nevertheless, and to a greater extent than is commonly supposed, such bifurcation affects the nature of popular participation and renders it a less effective vehicle for the attainment of a just society. In assessing this participative element it is also common to overlook the relationship of the masses to the manipulators of lawlessness: thus, mass agitational behavior is wrongly assessed as a valid expression of popular will. Nor can earlier experiences in the political development of the United States emerging from colonial rule—however intriguing in terms of comparable experience—be of much help in terms of contextual equivalence. The extent of understanding of issues and the relationship between leaders and the led were qualitatively different in the uprisings preceding the American Revolution than they are in many comparable behaviors in developing states. To transfer the same criteria of validity from the American Revolution to the uprisings in younger nations is to reflect a curious ethnocentrism and a misconception of the nature of developing political systems. While systems and perhaps even the process of political growth may be the same, the qualitative fiber of the context both affects and creates conditions of dissimilarity vitiating relevance of other experience. In short, the extent and quality of popular knowledge and responsibility and the low state of civic culture prevailing in most new states suggest an interpretation of "participation" somewhat at variance from that commonly held. It is an implicit comprehension of this reality, or at least a vital political response to the problems created by it, that has led state after state to evolve distinctive transitional systems, whether tutelary democracies, basic democracies, indirect elections, military rule, suspension of popular liberties, or even moratoria on the political process, in an effort to seek a means that will accommodate these otherwise sharply separated conditions of the social order in some form of unity.

The bureaucratic systems of developing states must be viewed in the context of such issues of political modernization. Such contextual analysis suggests that the impact of administrative modernization may not always be detrimental to the participative aspect of politicization. It further suggests that if it is detrimental, such an effect may not necessarily be a deterrent to politicization broadly conceived as including the four aspects described earlier. It is doubtful if administrative modernization can wait for the maturation of the political process; on the contrary, it must proceed irrespective of it. This appears necessary because an expanding capability for converting political demands into administrative actions is a fundamental state function, the technological complexities of which are such that only a modernized administrative apparatus can cope with them effectively. Such capability improvement may make even more asymmetrical the already uneven development of the four characteristics of political development outlined above. This is especially true if the administrative apparatus is already superior to the other segments and can therefore improve at a much faster rate. It is also likely that a rapidly improving bureaucracy can concentrate power more effectively, and by virtue of a monopoly of the skills, attitudes, and technology of modernization can overwhelm the political process, delay its maturation, and thus aggravate the asymmetry of the growth process. This is especially likely to occur when the social order is bifurcated and foreign technical assistance and support play a major role in political and economic development. In such an instance the linguistic-cultural differential and the distribution of negotiating and technological skills significantly enhance bureaucratic power. Correlatively, massive foreign technical assistance may also change the balance in distribution of powers within the political system, compelling greater centralization and assumption by the central government of powers otherwise traditionally regarded as local. While these influences further distort symmetrical political development, it may also be argued that the effect may not be as detrimental as is often supposed.

In the first place, even if the effect were markedly detrimental, the distorting influence on theoretical symmetry would be manifestly impossible to control. It would not be possible to hold back administrative modernization so as to allow other sectors of political development to catch up. Such restraint of modernization is especially unlikely in the face of external technical assistance made contingent upon rapid improvement in the capability of bureaucracy. Secondly, while rapid administrative modernization is likely to be accomplished at the expense of improving other characteristics of political growth, the over-all effect is likely to have many more dimensions than that. For example, the modernization of administration may set in motion forces which activate modernizing irritants in the political realm. Thus, the establishment in universities of courses in administration and politics tends to break the monopoly of a bureaucratic elite on administrative learning by diffusing throughout the body politic what were formerly secrets of the trade. The extent to which these irritants may operate effectively depends, of course, on the existence and viability of at least embryonic political institutions. This diffusion may not be effective for some time, but if other changes occur in the social order which even gradually induce politicization, such dissemination of ideas and skills may become influential. Thirdly, the rapid modernization of administration may not only increase the capability of bureaucracy in converting demands, as was earlier stated, but may also improve the quality of administrative decision-making by enlarging the component of rationality. Fourthly, almost all aspects of administrative modernization carry certain implicit ideological assumptions, however much effort is made to separate such assumptions from technique. Though the technical skills may be record-keeping, efficiency, work analysis, or financial controls, they are premised on such concepts as accountability to the public, equality of opportunity within the bureaucracy, or intra-bureaucratic participation in decision-making. To be sure, the technical skills can be separated from the ideological tissue and used for purposes antithetical to the underlying concepts. In fact, this has often occurred. But little is known about this process of transfer, and it is possible that unless politicization is completely suppressed even sedated politicization will react with latent ideological premises of administrative modernization in a manner enhancing the diffusion of both. Another possible advantage extracted when the pace of administrative modernization exceeds that of other growth components is the effectiveness of the bureaucracy as a social matrix for the diffusion of ideology and technology. The hierarchical and disciplined nature of the structure coupled with respect shown and inclination to emulate super-elites within it are powerful forces by which ideology and technology to some extent can be controlled, either by indigenous means or by adaptation of another kind. This is particularly so in the bureaucracies of former British imperial systems in which a small super-elite of former ICS officers are in a powerful position to influence the larger bureaucratic apparatus. This possibility is enhanced further when formal training institutions exist for the molding of new ideologies infused into the system.

Even if these advantages do not result from administrative modernization, partial containment of the political process is not, per se, a disadvantage. By one means or another, most developing states have, in fact, depressed the vigor of politicization to allow a bureaucracy to convert demands with minimum political harassment. This appears to be necessary and even desirable. The difficulty in reconciling this fact with certain preconceptions of political development lies in denial of the validity of the qualitative dimension of public participation or in ignoring it as a factor of relevance. Once its validity and relevance are accepted, the acceleration of administrative modernization, with its possible concomitant of deceleration of other aspects of politicization, is not unacceptable either analytically or as a political stratagem. On the other hand, this argument cannot be carried too far. The asymmetrical evolution of the four characteristics of political development can probably be only a transitional phenomenon. A system in which the bureaucracy is vastly superior to the political process cannot long maintain such imbalance without the risk of tyranny and eventual collapse. Eventually, some force must contain bureaucratic discretion. It may be the tempering effect of an ideology of humaneness, compassion, and stewardship to the public. This is the least likely and the least effective, since men are no more seraphim now than they were the angels of which Madison spoke. The application of law by the judiciary may also be a temporary restraint, but in the long run the risk here is great, for the burden on the judiciary may cause internal imbalance in the administration of justice, and it may be difficult to prevent a steadily expanding encroachment of the judiciary in the administrative realm. Inevitably, the judiciary will more and more substitute its judgment for administrative expertness and in so doing will stretch its own competence. The consequence of this approach may be a diminution in respect for the judiciary and a loss in its status in the social order. In the final analysis, the rise of countervailing elites and a vigorous political process seem to be the most promising restraints on administrative behavior. There must be a synaptic network connecting the bureaucratic system with the total social order. In a political context premised on popular sovereignty, a bureaucracy which remains autonomous, generating its own norms of behavior, is not likely long to endure.

The position of bureaucracies in new states inheriting the

British imperial tradition appears to have certain distinctive advantages in the context of political modernization as described above. In that context, bureaucracy exercising broad discretion has the transitional function of carrying on in a social order whose quantitative aspects have outpaced the qualitative aspects of the political growth process. It must, therefore, accommodate itself to political demands while yet infusing the polity with a quality of rationality far greater than that of the aggregated public will. All bureaucratic systems face this task of accommodation, but in the emerging states considered in this volume the hiatus is widened by an unusually well-trained bureaucracy and an unusually low state of civic culture.

From what sources can the bureaucracy derive the ideology and the rationality necessary to infuse the national polity with a sense of higher purpose? It cannot derive such sustenance entirely from the public will, or the legislature, or even from its indigenous cultural tradition to the same degree that this is possible in most Western systems. This is so not only because of the quality of civic culture but also because the political and bureaucratic norms are not diffused through and shared by the whole social order. The ideological motivations of the bureaucracy can come from three sources. (1) The first of these is a reconstructed indigenous tradition in which strands of thought equivalent to the assumptions underlying Western constitutional systems have been identified, elucidated, and woven into a cohesive doctrine. This essentially is the concept behind Pyidawtha in Burma, Panchayati Raj in India, and Basic Democracies in Pakistan. But such doctrine usually must be infused by contrived means into the bureaucratic ideology; rarely does a bureaucracy with external orientation absorb such ideology osmotically. This accounts for bureaucratic resistance to all community development movements and for the perennial political efforts to involve the bureaucracy in them in the hope that the ideology will be contagious. (2) The wellsprings of British doctrine as embodied in the ICS tradition form a second source of ideological motivation for the bureaucracy. But unless such doctrine is refurbished constantly, it fades as the physical presence of its agents vanishes. The autonarcotic effect of living exclusively on fading standards of the past is not likely to be a sufficient generative impulse for an action both philosophically based and articulated to the dynamics of the times. Atrophy is likely to be the consequence. (3) Thirdly, the bureaucracy can be motivated by the creation of a dynamic institutional medium for the diffusion of an ideology and technology of administration. This can be augmented by bringing into the bureaucracy older recruits from other sectors of society who carry with them the modernizing ferment of those sectors. It can best be accomplished by vigorous training programs in which new doctrine is diffused and made indigenous. These three sources are available in varying degrees of effectiveness in each of the six states considered in this volume. In most, principal reliance is placed on the British tradition. But in time this will fade and be overwhelmed by indigenous ideology. The elucidation of this ideology and its integration with past British traditions is a peculiar function of the British-trained bureaucracy. In the larger transitional phase in which bureaucracy must infuse the polity with a rationality not yet characteristic of the political process—essentially a tutelary or educative role—the ICS tradition with its ethos of platonic guardianship, however tarnished it may now be, would seem to enhance the possibility that this transitional responsibility will be effectively met.

II. Comparative Political Analytics

Since Max Weber's studies of bureaucracy in *Wirtschaft und Gesellschaft* in 1920, significant advances in both research method and accretion of data have been made within what is generally known as comparative administration. Two decades ago it was common and to some extent justifiable to criticize comparative political studies as being excessively descriptive, unrelated to the larger forces of the total social order implicated, and deficient in scientific rigor with respect to typology and method. As the effect of this criticism converged with a rather massive infusion of radical empiricism in the method of political science, a consequence was fairly rapid development of a corpus of research attempting to frame typologies at various levels of abstraction. Such typological experimentation was more or less evenly balanced with the accretion of substantive knowledge derived predominantly from established constitutional systems. The sudden rise of new political systems from imperial and colonial rule shifted attention from established systems to the new states. The balance between knowledge and methodology which was at least beginning to emerge in the study of older systems did not characterize subsequent analysis of the new states. By now methodological advances and typology construction had exceeded in quantity and sophistication the universe of empirical data necessary to sustain them. This was stimulated by extensive experience in the transnational inducement of administrative reform as well as by private research, both of which yielded enough data to accelerate crude research design. The time appeared ripe for extensive multi-system efforts to test hypotheses which emerged.

Curiously, such empirical verification was rendered difficult by various internal and external conditions. Foremost was the fact that typology and research design were not sufficiently seated in the analytics of political comparability to be accorded wide acceptance by researchers. Common terminology, agreement on priorities and on strategies were argued and re-argued. By no stretch of the imagination can it be said that the same degree of common acceptance which characterized economics and sociology in these matters had then been attained in comparative politics. Secondly, the research apparatus was not structured or financed in such a way as to facilitate large-scale study in several countries simultaneously by mature scholars, who were committed to a common typology and intimately acquainted with the total social order being studied. Thirdly, documentation and field work became accessible at different times in different countries, thus making it impossible to carry on simultaneous studies of several national systems. External conditions made further field studies difficult, if not impossible. In Burma, Indonesia, Vietnam,

Laos, and Cambodia, research has been virtually impossible for Western scholars, and research in Pakistan has been made difficult by deteriorating relations with the United States. Although research conditions seem to be improving in some states, such as India, Ceylon, and Malaya, comparably stable conditions in an unchanging group of systems have not lasted long enough to permit sustained, multi-system research.

Students of political growth thus find themselves in a dilemma. Having seen their conceptual apparatus constructed from limited empirical evidence, and having themselves stimulated the accretion of further evidence, they are now frustrated by lack of data of acceptable refinement and uniformity to give the apparatus the necessary push to finality. One solution appears to be the rapid ordering of refined empirical data by use of computer technology from which will emerge a rigorously defined classificatory scheme. But the dilemma here is that a classificatory scheme is too easily divorced from reality: it mutes the subtleties of distinctions and compels nuances to become sharpened shadows cast in "proper" places in contrived schema. This obscures new and more subtle classifications which are continually being formed and which can rarely be identified or comprehended by systems analysis divorced from detailed cultural or institutional studies. For example, until the last decade or so the salient characteristics of parliamentary and presidential, unitary and federal, forms of government have been isolated, classified, and fairly well seated in the body of political analytics. But in the newly emerging states, permutations of these classic designs have occurred in various relations to such a variety of existing ideological dispositions and social facts that these classic designs now have little or no significance in political analysis except as base points from which deviations may be measured. The formulation of a classificatory scheme makes accommodation to the continually shifting pattern of classes extremely difficult. If the scheme does not incorporate the kaleidoscopic movement and subtle cultural tones beneath and even within the formal institutions, it rivets attention on systems analysis per se and detracts from the reconstruction of reality which is the ultimate purpose of the scheme. To put it another way, we are faced with the classic dilemma of all scholarship, namely, the necessity for conjoining three elements: the perspective of generalization, the precision of empirical detail, and the leavening of cultural analysis which gives qualitative meaning to the detail. Each of these elements chastens and disciplines the other two. Rarely can expertise in all three dimensions be found in a single person. Indeed, this combination is likely to be even rarer, if not nonexistent, as the demands of radical empiricism force ever greater precision in data accretion and simultaneously expand almost infinitely the universe of relevant data to be accreted. The ultimate solution probably lies in data ordered by computer technology but submitted to the chastening revision of cultural analysis. This would mean, in effect, the concurrent application of two research modes: the one scientific, the other non-scientific and impressionistic.

The studies of bureaucratic systems which follow in this volume are affected by the dilemmas, uncertainties, and adverse conditions which have been discussed above. The systems examined are in various stages of development. We cannot venture to say whether one system is more highly developed than another, since subsectors within the bureaucratic system are themselves undergoing different rates of development. It is also true that research on these systems has been unevenly pursued and developed. In some instances, scarcely any research has been done; in others the volume of published research approaches that done on certain Western systems. All the studies are plagued by unevenness of data and the dubious reliability of those data which are available. This is especially true with respect to time periods of validity. Data on public employment may be available for one period in one country, but for another period in other countries. While some transfer of validity can be made by extrapolation and plain guessing, the aim of rigorous comparative analysis is thereby defeated. In fact, so simple a bit of knowledge as a census of total government employment, on which so much subsequent analysis depends, is one of the most elusive and unreliable findings in studies of developing bureaucracies. These difficulties are suggested in the notes to Table 4 in the final chapter of this volume. This unevenness exists not only from country to country but within a given national system as well. Thus, we find a fairly reliable census of government employment for the province of West Pakistan, but none for East Pakistan. We find a careful study of the background of IAS probationers in India, but only for those recruited from 1948 to 1961, although in Pakistan a similar survey has been made for CSP officers recruited from 1948 to 1964. These are merely illustrative of many such disparities in data. As a consequence, the emphasis and format which these studies have assumed were determined in large measure by these conditions. They are not designed as uniform studies within the context of this volume, for while uniformity for its own sake might serve a pedagogical purpose, it would not well serve further research aims. The separate country studies have been based on these general principles:

(1) Each study is intended to be partly self-contained bibliographically and analytically, except that it bears a relationship to the state of research already done on the subject. Thus, for example, the study on Burma, which is virtually the first of its kind, is somewhat more comprehensive in scope than the others. The same is true for the study on Nepal which, however, is necessarily shorter because of the paucity of written documentation. On the other hand, since more research has been published for India than for any other country considered in this volume, many issues have deliberately been left untouched in the chapter on that country. The existence of a comprehensive study of the Indian Parliament and studies on federalism and on the background of the elite cadre, for example, make it feasible either to omit or hurriedly to pass over these subjects here. Similarly, certain aspects of the bureaucratic systems of other states, such as judicial review and Basic Democracies in Pakistan, have already been extensively studied and are given minimal attention here.

(2) An effort has been made to provide as much bibliographical guidance, especially in documentary materials, as is possible within this format. Again, this is adjusted to the state of research for each country. Hence, the documentation for India is not as comprehensive as for Burma or Nepal. Each of the contributors, keenly aware of the bibliographical deficiencies in research of this kind, has tried to incorporate bibliographic guidance which may be of some subsequent usefulness.

(3) Although the chapters on each country follow the loose outline described below, the individuality of the author's style, his approach, and the characteristic emphases of the system under study have been retained. This framework has the disadvantage of the absence of standardized terminology and uniform treatment of particular phenomena. It has also meant some overlap of analysis, some duplication, and some disagreement as to analysis. No effort was made to accept a common point of view, to agree upon a set of conclusions, or to interpret data in the same manner. The alternative to nurturing such individuality would have been prior agreement on a rigorously conceived typology, followed by simultaneous field work in which the concepts of the typology would have been tested against rigorously collected empirical data. This is an intriguing possibility and may well be the ultimately satisfying design for comparative political analysis. Here, for several reasons, it was not possible to pursue such a plan. First, the physical and financial problems involved in having eight or ten experienced scholars pursue field research simultaneously could not be surmounted. Methodological standardization and intimacy with the total social order in which the system being studied is implicated are rarely found in combination. If a choice between these two expertnesses must be made, it is perhaps as appropriate at this stage in the development of comparative studies to concentrate on intimacy with the total system as it is to insist on methodological uniformity. It is not suggested here that either competence is more important than the other. On the contrary, it is clear that activity generated by both competences must develop simultaneously, each acting as a catalyst upon the other and causing the scholar to strive for greater precision in observation and larger generality of perspective. The balance in this volume is weighted by circumstances and not by doctrinaire preconceptions on the side of discrete country analysis rather than on the side of methodology. Nearly all the authors have had a minimum of two years of field work in

the country studied. Every author has had at least one year in the field, and one author spent his entire professional career in the bureaucracy of one of the states. At least three of the authors have played not insignificant roles in the administrative reforms of the countries of which they write. It appeared that we could profit by encouraging each author to develop, within broad limits, a theme reflecting the peculiarities of his experience.

(4) It has also seemed desirable to allow the individual character of each nation's bureaucratic development to emerge in the study of each country. Such individuality might have been lost in a rigid format allocating uniform space to common topics. It is worthy of note that the major interest and speciality of each author seems to coincide with the dominant characteristics of the bureaucratic system studied. Thus, foreign technical assistance is given more attention in Nepal than in India. In India, on the other hand, the dominant motif is a relatively evenly paced political development slowly reducing the power and role of bureaucracy. This is accurately reflected in the chapter on India by the emphasis given the rural development movement and political parties. In Pakistan, the emphasis is appropriately juridical and institutional, for politicization has proceeded in that state at a different pace than in others. In Ceylon, communal difficulties, of more importance relatively than in other states, are given commensurate attention.

Despite the looseness of organization and individuality of treatment which necessarily results from the application of the four general principles outlined above, a certain degree of minimal uniformity of objective underlies the writing of each chapter. The issues the authors sought to explore were these:

(1) Five of the countries studied inherited basically the same ideology and structure of bureaucracy, as embodied in the Indian Civil Service. Nepal, never under foreign rule, inherited some of these traditions only indirectly, through intermediary contacts such as with India and foreign aid programs. Our attempt to describe the structure and its permutations in the various states, undertaken by Tinker, was designed as an overview followed by more detailed analysis in each chapter.

(2) Since British imperial rule was essentially rule by administrative discretion, relatively unchecked by political or other countervailing forces, it appeared crucial to examine the ideology of British officers of the Indian Civil Service. This ideology is not codified or otherwise made explicit, but it emerges from British training and culture in the application of discretionary power. It therefore appeared significant to examine the antecedents and education of officers of the ICS, a task performed by Cohn for officers recruited from 1600 to 1860.

(3) In the chapters on individual countries the authors sought to examine the condition of the British legacy at independence in terms of such questions as these: To what extent did British officers remain after independence? Did the break with British rule also result in an ideological and institutional severance with the imperial past? To what extent and in what ways did the British tradition endure in the new independent states?

(4) Since one of the distinctive legacies of British imperial rule was the elite cadre as an institution, each of the chapters on individual countries, except for Nepal which never experienced such rule, and where the elite cadre is not so important, emphasizes this institution. We are concerned here with changes made in the concept, adaptations in structural loci of power, and reorientation of attitudes.

(5) The impact of foreign technical assistance on bureaucratic modernization is also considered. Has such influence displaced or reinforced British values? Has it compelled the new governments to move in directions of greater centralization in order to manage the intrusion of foreign aid? If there has been no such aid, what have been the sources of administrative modernization?

(6) The changes in administration which have been programmed and accomplished is the next major issue developed. Here we have attempted to review the key reform efforts and to indicate changes in structure and attitude. The extent of egalitarian leavening in the elite cadre as indicated by mode of entry, composition of the services, and disparity in salary scales is also analyzed. We are also concerned with structural changes in deeply rooted institutions such as the omnicompetent generalist, secretariat organization, planning, financial controls, and trade unionism.

(7) How and to what extent are these bureaucratic systems amenable to control? In developing this issue, we have sought to give emphasis to the classic institutional restraints such as legislative oversight and judicial review, since in embryonic constitutional orders with well-developed juridical systems, institutional restraints may be more effective than behavioral or other restraints premised on attitudes of responsibility and political participation. The rise of competing elites and the political process are also analyzed in states such as India, Ceylon, and Malaya where they are highly developed.

(8) Each author has tried to enrich his findings with as much detailed empirical data as is possible under the circumstances. Again marked disparity is noted. A list of government corporations, for example, may be available for some states but not for others. Despite such inevitable unevenness, it must be remarked that one of the concomitant advantages of British imperial rule is the propensity to publish government documents. Considering the trauma of independence and the political uncertainties of its aftermath, the state of documentation in the former imperial states is not completely unimpressive. We have sought to tabulate much of that documentation in an orderly way.

(9) Finally, it must be said that these studies do not result in a series of carefully developed hypotheses closely correlated with the data. Such an undertaking would be premature, since the data are not sufficiently refined. Nor is any effort made to predict what future developments will do to bureaucratic systems or what the evolution of these systems may mean for the Commonwealth or for the English-speaking world.

In sum, the succeeding chapters present a series of preliminary studies, as carefully integrated as research conditions permit, in five different states in Asia inheriting the bureaucratic traditions of British imperial rule, and in one state, Nepal, which was indirectly influenced by British norms.

2

Structure of the British Imperial Heritage

Hugh Tinker

The legacy of British administration in the empire which once straddled the Indian Ocean area has created a common pattern in the civil services of India, Pakistan, Ceylon, Burma, and Malaysia quite distinct from those in other Commonwealth countries such as Canada, Australia, and the West Indies—or even from the civil service in the United Kingdom. Comparisons have been made with the imperial Chinese mandarinate; but though there are interesting parallels, no serious scholar has been able to show that the British-Asian bureaucracy consciously adapted features from China. Rather, the first administrators were drawn from the merchants and factors of the East India Company, and they attempted to apply the technique of the ledger, of profit over loss, to the management of cities and countries. As will be seen, the unexpected inheritance of Mughal India, together with other kingdoms and principalities of the Eastern Seas, led the "writers" and "factors" sent out from Leadenhall Street in the City of London to undertake the Oriental role of hakim, or lawgiver. But at first they were reluctant to take on the actual task of administration. Ten years after Plassey, Clive wrote to the directors of the company, urging a policy of non-intervention: "To do any act by an exertion of the English power which can be equally done by the nabob, would be throwing off the mask and declaring the Company soubah [governor] of the province." Because of the failure of all attempts to rule Bengal by indirect means more than from any positive impulse, the servants of the company were sent into the districts as collectors of the revenue and incidentally as the guardians of the public good. Still, for some decades, the outlook of the company and its servants was determined by the ethos of trade. *The Annals of Rural Bengal*[1] shows clearly how this was reflected in the comparative status of the administrator and the merchant in an up-country district:

Of longer standing in the service than the Collector, and less liable to be transferred, the Commercial Resident formed the real head of the district. His gains were unlimited; for besides his official pay he carried on an enormous business on his own account. We find Mr. Keating [the Collector] complaining that he can barely subsist on his salary; that the mud tenement in which the collectors lived was letting in water, and tumbling down upon his head. . . . Mr. Cheape [the Commercial Resident] on the other hand not only made a fortune, and bequeathed the largest indigo plantation in Bengal, but meanwhile lived sumptuously in a pile of building surrounded by artificial lakes and spacious gardens. . . .

In the backwaters of the British territories in Asia, administrators continued to deal profitably in trade and plantations for many years yet; but in India, at the center of the system, a new, professional, "career" Civil Service emerged before the end of the eighteenth century.

I. Framework of the Service

The principal features which distinguished the modern British Civil Service are open entry based on academic competition; permanency of tenure irrespective of party political change; a division into grades or classes according to whether the function is responsible or merely routine; a regular, graduated scale of pay; and a system of promotion based on a combination of seniority and selection by merit. None of these features could be detected, even in embryo, in the "Civil Service" in the United Kingdom of the eighteenth century. Whitehall functionaries

1. W. W. Hunter, *The Annals of Rural Bengal* (London, 1868), pp. 353 ff. This work provides much valuable evidence about the genesis of British district administration in Bengal.

moved from party political appointments into "administrative" office and back into politics. Appointment was by patronage. Salary was attached to a specific appointment, some of the most lucrative being posts in the West Indies. Frequently, an ill-paid deputy discharged the duties of the post. No clear distinction was drawn between purely clerical posts, which might be ill paid or richly paid, and higher positions of responsibility. Not until after 1870 did the "Home" Civil Service begin to assume its present pattern. This pattern was largely derived from the evolution of a superior civil service in India, but the middle years of the eighteenth century, the time of the Nabobs and the shaking of the pagoda tree, merely reproduced in a more crude and lush guise the habits of contemporary England.

Indeed, the motive for reform was mainly a determination that the power generated by the cornucopia of Indian patronage should not become the means of dominating the political life of England. Pitt's India Act of 1784 extended the authority of the governor general of Bengal over the other two presidencies (thus promoting uniformity), provided for definite scales of pay and emoluments, laid down the principle of promotion by seniority, and fixed the age of admission to the service of writers or military cadets at fifteen to eighteen years.[2] The renewal of the company's charter in 1793 further defined the position: to members of the "covenanted" civil service were reserved the principal civil offices of India below the rank of member of council.[3] Appointments to this service were made in London by the Court of Directors. The 1784 Act had also vested in the court the nomination to the offices of governor general, governor, and high military command; but in practice these nominations were usually made by the British government of the day. The directors' own patronage covered an annual average (from 1793 to 1812) of about forty writers and 240 cadets. A director might expect to have at his disposal some

2. This was raised to twenty-two years in 1793.
3. The name "covenanted civilian" arose from the covenant into which superior servants of the company were required to enter, undertaking such pledges as not to trade and not to receive presents or to subscribe for pensions. The covenant continued to be required until the end of British rule in India. The form of covenants can be seen in Akshoy Kumar Ghosal, *Civil Service in India Under the East India Company* (Calcutta, 1944), Appendix B, pp. 415–436.

six or seven appointments every year. In an age when every public appointment, civil or military, had its price, the value of a writership was about £3,500. Secret inquiries by the Court of Directors disclosed that some nominations were sold in 1790 and 1799, and as a consequence the offenders were compelled to resign.[4] However, most directors exercised their patronage conscientiously, often to provide places for the sons of deserving servants of the company. The few but most highly prized writerships at Canton, the company's outpost in the lucrative China trade, were usually reserved for sons of directors. Trade still glittered more brightly than administration. On the other hand, some public-spirited directors reserved their nominations for exceptionally brilliant boys from ancient schools belonging to the City of London, such as Christ's Hospital and Charterhouse. The principle of merit was partially recognized.

By restricting all senior positions to the covenanted service, the British effectively eliminated the adventurers who had battened on Indian administration; this restriction also sowed the seeds of a professional *esprit de corps,* while the changing spirit of the age —fed by the humanitarian zeal of evangelical Christianity and the reforming, scientific sense of Benthamite Utilitarianism—was elevating the tone of government service. But the exclusiveness inherent in the new system also had the effect of eliminating Indians from posts of administrative and judicial esteem throughout the British territories in India.

As will be related below, the almost continuous territorial expansion during the period 1800–1850 created such a demand for senior officials that the covenanted service was unable to meet all needs from its own cadre. After the transfer of India to the Crown in 1858, the situation was regularized by the Indian Civil Service Act, 1861.[5] This act validated certain irregular appoint-

---

4. See C. H. Philips, *The East India Company, 1784–1834* (Manchester, 1940), pp. 14–16.

5. This may be the first example of the term "Indian Civil Service" being used. Following the division of British India into Presidencies, men called themselves members of the Bengal, Madras, Bombay, or Penang Civil Service. This continued until late in the nineteenth century. It is not, however, the first instance of use of the term "civil service" in relation to administration in India. Ghosal reports use of the term in manuscript records of John Company as early as 1706 and conjectures that the term became current toward the end of the seventeenth century. Ghosal, *op. cit.,* p. 18, n. 1.

ments made in the past, but it expressly reserved to members of the covenanted service for the future all the more important civil posts below the rank of member of council in the "regulation" provinces. A schedule of reserved posts was appended to the act. The right of the covenanted service to a monopoly of higher administration was adhered to tenaciously at all times.

The expansion of British power during the early nineteenth century led to the annexation of areas less amenable to rule by ledger and law book than Bengal or Madras. Such areas were excluded from the "regulations" or laws of the Presidencies. Instead of the separation of judicial and executive functions between district judge and collector which became the rule in the regulation provinces, in the non-regulation areas there was a concentration of powers at the district level in the hands of a deputy commissioner, who exercised all the functions of government—executive, magisterial, and judicial. This system was extended to the Punjab, Oudh, the Central Provinces, and Burma. It was also applied in certain backward areas within the regulation provinces: for example, the Chittagong Hill Tracts in Bengal. Gradually, these non-regulation provinces and districts were assimilated to the regulation model, although even after independence in 1947 the distinction in the title of the head of the district as between collector or deputy commissioner was retained. Of more substantive significance is the fact that the covenanted monopoly of the higher administration did not apply in these areas. This was partly because the cadre of the covenanted service, with its carefully controlled recruitment, could not cope with the demands of the newly annexed provinces and districts. Some appointments in the non-regulation provinces went to "uncovenanted civilians"; that is, to men who came to the front in a time of unrest and challenge. Occasionally, these were men of mixed blood—Eurasians. For example, Henry Charles Van Cortlandt (1814–1888), an officer in the service of the Sikh Darbar, stood by Herbert Edwardes in the siege of Multan and ended his days as a deputy commissioner of the Montgomery (then Gujaira) district in the Punjab.[6] Thomas Henry Kavanagh,

6. For an account see C. Grey, *European Adventurers of Northern India 1785 to 1849*, ed. H. L. O. Garrett (Lahore, 1929), pp. 303–307.

the Eurasian telegraph clerk who won the Victoria Cross at Lucknow, became an assistant commissioner in Oudh.[7] But the major source of personnel for the administration of the non-regulation provinces was the military establishment of the company. The first great "military civilian"—the man who has a claim to be also called the first district officer in the new tradition—was Sir Thomas Munro, an officer of the Madras army. Munro ended his days as governor of Madras, but his great work was the creation of peasant prosperity in Baramahal and Kanara districts. His contemporary, Sir John Malcolm, by his work in central India laid down the pattern for the military-political officer.

A generation later, when British rule came to the Punjab, the young deputy commissioners for the Land of Five Rivers were drawn equally from the covenanted civilians of the frontier districts of the Bengal Presidency, and officers of the Bengal army. This dualism continued in the higher administration of the Punjab, Assam, and Burma into the first years of the twentieth century. Military recruitment ended for the administration of Oudh, the Central Provinces, and non-regulation areas of Bengal and the North-Western Provinces (later United Provinces) in 1876. Sind followed suit in 1885, the Punjab in 1903, and Assam in 1907. But after World War I, the military civilian continued to be recruited only into the administration of Burma and the North-West Frontier Province. The Corps of Indian Engineers supplied not only technical officers, who built many of India's roads, canals, and public buildings, but also senior administrators. Henry Yule, Mortimer Durand, Richard Strachey, and James Browne—all military engineers—rose to the heights in departmental administration and frontier governance.[8] When the Indian police was remodeled in the 1860's on the lines of the Irish constabulary, its superintendents were drawn from the military.

The covenanted civilian, however, remained the principal

7. Kavanagh, disguised as an Indian, escaped the siege of Lucknow, joined Sir Colin Campbell's forces, and guided them into Lucknow. See Thomas Henry Kavanagh, *How I Won the Victoria Cross* (London, 1860).

8. For example, Major General Sir James Browne, who built portions of the Grand Trunk Road and the North-Western Railway, was chief commissioner of Baluchistan, 1891–1896, before his early death.

element in higher administration, and to Englishmen of the age of the Great Reform Bill it was increasingly intolerable that any system of monopoly or oligarchy should continue. Movements to reform the Home Civil Service were confronted by the aristocracy, still largely unbending, but the middle class directors of the East India Company were another matter. Some even preached reform themselves. Reformers sought to ameliorate restrictions on recruitment of civilians in two ways. First, an attempt was made to end the exclusion of Indians. Into the Act of 1833, which renewed the company's charter, was inserted a declaration that "No native of the said territories [of British India] . . . shall by reason only of his religion, place of birth, descent, colour, or any of them, be disabled from holding any place, office, or employment of the Company." The interpretation placed on this act by the directors was that "Fitness is henceforth to be the criterion of eligibility." As we shall see, Indians thereby gained a greater share of the middle ranks of administration, but they were still not taken into the covenanted service. After the Mutiny of 1857, Queen Victoria's Proclamation to India included this passage: "It is our further will that, so far as may be, our subjects of whatever race or creed, be freely and impartially admitted to offices in our service." This proclamation was hailed by Indian leaders as a definite pledge to throw open the higher administration to Indians; the paltry manner in which it was implemented provided the early Indian nationalists with one of their main grievances.

The second desired reform was the introduction of the principle of entry by open competition. C. W. Wynn, a former president of the Board of Control, in the parliamentary debate on the 1833 bill advocated entry by competition; he received the sympathetic support of Macaulay, then a junior minister—secretary of the Board of Control. The act provided that the directors were to nominate four times the required number of candidates: the actual appointees would be chosen by examination from this group. Subsequently, the directors succeeded in nullifying the act and in retaining their patronage for two more decades.[9] However,

9. Philips, *op. cit.*, pp. 294–297.

the next time the charter was renewed, entry into the civil service by competition became mandatory, although the directors continued to nominate to military cadetships for the brief remainder of the company's rule. A committee was appointed, with Macaulay as chairman, to draft examination rules. Among the members, only Macaulay himself had a brief experience of Indian service.[10] The committee looked to Oxford and Cambridge which were then newly experiencing the reforming impulse of the Prince Consort, and provided for a purely academic examination, designed to attract the intellectual who might otherwise compete for a college fellowship. Among the wide range of subjects which candidates could offer, English history and mathematics scored the highest rating (a maximum of one thousand marks each), while Sanskrit and Arabic, admitted on sufferance, could only yield a maximum of 375 marks. The Indian vernaculars were totally excluded as "of no value except for the purpose of communication with natives of India." The first examinations took place in 1855.

II. The System and Its Hierarchy

Amid the changing pageant of British rule, one office, that of the governor general, remained almost unchanged. From 1774 to 1947, "the Governor General in Council" *was* the Government of India. From 1774 to 1833 he was "the Governor General of Fort William in Bengal"; he then became governor general of India, though still charged with the special responsibility of administering Bengal.[11] When India came under the direct rule of the Crown, he became one of the two officials in the British Empire officially designated viceroy (the other viceroy reigned at

10. Other members were Lord Ashburton, a banker; Rev. Henry Melvill, principal of Haileybury College; Benjamin Jowett, tutor of Balliol College, Oxford; and Sir John Shaw Lefevre, a Liberal politician and vice chancellor of the University of London, 1842–1862.

11. From 1833 to 1853 the governor general was still titular governor of Bengal, though he delegated this function to the senior member of the Executive Council (who might well be the commander in chief) when away from Calcutta. In the period 1838–1850 there were nine governors or deputy governors. Under the 1853 Act, Bengal became the separate responsibility of a lieutenant governor.

Dublin). But apart from these purely stylistic changes, the position of the governor general remained constant; even under the Government of India Act, 1935, the viceroy remained the ultimate reservoir of power. It has often been argued that after the completion of the cable-link between Britain and India in 1865, the viceroy's authority was effectively subordinated to that of the secretary of state, with whom he was henceforward in close communication. Yet it is possible to argue that a strong viceroy could initiate policy (as did Ripon, Curzon, or Irwin) and that in these circumstances the secretary of state would only acquiesce. Indeed, it appears that one of the most momentous decisions ever made—to advance the date for independence from June, 1948, to August, 1947—was presented by the viceroy as an ultimatum to the British cabinet. The Simon Commission Report aptly observed that the viceroy could "in cases of emergency and stress completely over-ride [the Executive] Council and disregard the most carefully considered expression of [the central] Legislature."[12]

The masterful rule of Warren Hastings served to convince British politicians that this supremely important office should never again be held by a man who had passed his life in Indian administration. It is true that had he wished, Elphinstone could have become governor general while Charles Metcalfe was provisional governor general for one year (1835–1836) and John Lawrence served the full term as viceroy, 1864–1869.[13] But these experiences only seemed to underline the principle that the governor general should be drawn from the public and political life of Britain. Only a handful of viceroys were politicians of the first quality: Ripon, Curzon, Irwin. Most were of cabinet rank, but some were not. Two viceroys were professional diplomats (Dufferin and the second Hardinge). No professional soldier occupied the position between Sir Henry Hardinge (1844–1848)

---

12. *Report of the Indian Statutory Commission,* Cmd. 3568 (1930), I, 177. Hereinafter cited as Simon Commission Report.
13. Metcalfe's biographer observes that "It would have been better for him if he had gone home sooner and never attained it [the governor generalship]." Edward Thompson, *The Life of Charles Lord Metcalfe* (London, 1937), p. 313. Many would apply the same verdict to Lawrence's viceroyalty.

and Lord Wavell (1943–1947), although Kitchener desperately desired to become viceroy. Lord Reading (1921–1926) came from humble origins, but most viceroys were members of the lesser landed aristocracy; numerically, Scottish peers were given preference.[14]

The governors of Madras and Bombay were also chosen from British public life, and more for their social than their administrative brilliance. As Harvey observed, "the title [of governor] was as sacrosanct in the Indian as it is common in the colonial empire."[15] Until the introduction of the Reforms (1920), the major provinces were governed by lieutenant governors, and the minor provinces by chief commissioners. Because Penang was raised to the dignity of a fourth Presidency in 1805, the Straits Settlements qualified for a governor. This status continued even after Penang was derated as an economy measure in 1829 until the Straits Settlements were transferred from India to the Colonial Office in 1867. Ceylon, which escaped in 1802 from the trammels of the East India Company to become a Crown colony, qualified for a colonial governor.

Almost without exception, the Indian lieutenant governors were covenanted civilians. They were required by statute to have at least ten years' Indian service. Whereas governors were appointed by the Crown, lieutenant governors were appointed by the governor general. The first lieutenant governorship was created for the North-Western Provinces in 1835; these later became the United Provinces, and their charge was regarded as the foremost appointment to which a civilian could attain. The United Provinces and the Punjab were usually given to civilians

14. In 1833–1834 when the future of the East India Company was widely discussed in Great Britain, these aristocratic gubernatorial appointments were commonly characterized as being "a vast system of outdoor relief for the English upper classes." Although the origins of this quip are not known, it is commonly associated with John Bright, who on at least one occasion used it in referring to diplomatic appointments in Europe. See, for example, a speech printed in James E. Thorold Rogers (ed.), *Speeches on Questions of Public Policy by the Rt. Hon. John Bright, M.P.* (London, 1878), p. 470.

15. G. E. Harvey, *British Rule in Burma* (London, 1946), p. 77. However, an Indian lieutenant governor drew an annual salary of Rs. 100,000 (about $20,000), while the governor of Ceylon (the premier appointment under the Colonial Office) received only Rs. 80,000 (about $18,000) a year.

who had passed all their earlier careers in these provinces. Normally the other posts went to officials who had shown ability, regardless of their earlier service. Most lieutenant governors were appointed after a period of membership on the viceroy's Executive Council. While the Straits Settlements were a part of the Indian Empire, their governors were almost always drawn from the Penang Civil Service. The first two chief commissioners of British Burma, Sir Arthur Phayre and General A. Fytche, had passed the greater part of their careers in Burma and were recognized Burmese scholars. But all their successors came from India, after a lifetime spent in a different culture. This was a prime cause of the lack of sureness of touch in British policy in Burma.

Ceylon, and the Straits Settlements after 1867, were governed by appointees sent out from Britain. Many were retired military officers. Because Singapore was regarded as a military outpost, a "fortress," several of its governors were military engineers. Only occasionally (as in the case of Sir Frank Swettenham, governor of the Straits Settlements, 1901–1903) did a local official attract sufficient attention in Whitehall to be deemed worthy of the governorship.[16] The virtual exclusion from the highest office had some effect on the morale of the Civil Service in Ceylon and Malaya.[17]

As an exception to the ICS monopoly of all governorships in India outside the Presidencies, Lord Sinha was briefly governor of Bihar in 1920–1921. In Burma, Sir Joseph A. Maung Gyee, a Burmese minister, officiated as governor from 1930 to 1931.

The head of a province governed strictly within the oversight of the viceroy and the secretary of state. His freedom to initiate policy was limited, but he enjoyed considerable freedom to render higher initiative nugatory by interpreting and implement-

16. Swettenham left Malaya in October, 1903; he lived until 1946, drawing his governor's pension for forty-three years. This is supposed to be a Colonial Service record.

17. S. A. Pakeman states that the last colonial governor of Ceylon, Sir Henry Monck-Mason Moore, was the only governor to have begun his career in the Ceylon Civil Service. See S. A. Pakeman, *Ceylon* (London, 1964), p. 155.

ing policy in his own style. Few governors were removed from office. Following the Amritsar massacre in April, 1919, the lieutenant governor of the Punjab, Sir Michael O'Dwyer, who firmly indorsed Brigadier General R. E. H. Dyer's action in shooting, quit his post one month later; but he had already completed six years in the governorship. After the activities of Sir William Jervois, governor of the Straits, had resulted in two revolts in western Malaya, he directed a dispatch to the secretary of state, the Earl of Carnarvon, which the latter described as "One of the least satisfactory that I have read. . . . Unscrupulous in argument, unbecoming in tone and very disingenuous in character." But Jervois was not dismissed; instead, he was subsequently appointed governor of South Australia.[18] Sir Robert Chalmers, as governor of Ceylon, was held responsible for the disturbances in Kandy in 1915, which led to martial law. Chalmers consented to relinquish his governorship, but he was reinstated in the Home Civil Service from which he had come and on retirement received a peerage. Few governors failed badly, for most were men of outstanding ability. But equally, few left their stamp on a province so as to alter the course of development to any marked degree. Even Lord Hailey, who governed the Punjab for four years and the United Provinces for six years, cannot be said to have left his mark in the same way as the pioneers—men like Munro, Elphinstone, Thomason, the Lawrences. "It was a curiously impersonal system," observed Harvey, meaning that men might come and go; the government endured.[19] But it was a system deriving from very high standards, and it is not a matter of

18. See C. Northcote Parkinson, *British Intervention in Malaya* (Singapore, 1960), p. 321, and C. D. Cowan, *Nineteenth Century Malaya* (London, 1961), p. 243. These two authors are not quite in agreement. Parkinson talks about the removal of Jervois. Cowan suggests that the secretary of state was "willing to wound, and yet afraid to strike."

19. Harvey, *op. cit.*, p. 30 and n. 1. Here is the verdict of a Victorian Radical politician with a deep knowledge of the British Empire: "Persons do not count for much in India. The Indian governmental system is too regular, the codes are too complete, traditions too strong to give much room to human personality. No one man can really change the policy, and the greatest alterations of recent times have taken place gradually by the help of scores of distinguished men. While in young colonies a single governor or a single minister may bring about a change which will alter the whole future of the country, in India talent can expect no such results." Sir Charles Wentworth Dilke, *Problems of Greater Britain* (London, 1890), pp. 434–435.

surprise that the ICS was frequently drawn upon as a source for governors of the British Colonial Empire.[20]

The governor general, the governors of Madras and Bombay, and, after 1920, the governors of all the Indian provinces and Burma, were joined in the decision-making process by an Executive Council. Each of these councils originally consisted of three members, but from 1833 the councils of Madras and Bombay were limited to two (the number at which they remained thereafter). The governor general's council was slowly expanded, and in the 1920's it reached six members, together with the commander in chief. The three members required by statute to be persons with ten years' service in India were usually from the ICS, while the law member was required to be a barrister. Macaulay became the first law member (1834–1838); and Sinha, the first Indian law member, was appointed in 1909. By the 1920's three of the six members were Indians, and in 1946 when the council had been increased by wartime needs to fourteen, all of its members were Indians.

The viceroy's council met as a corporate body to register decisions already agreed upon, rather than to debate and determine policy. It resembled the cabinet of the United States president much more closely than that of a British prime minister. Each member of the council was in charge of one or two of the departments. The viceroy himself held the portfolio of the foreign and political department, which after 1935 was divided into the external affairs department and the political department. Because members of the council were mainly civil servants, they discharged the role of departmental chief, supervisor of day-to-day administration, rather than acting as co-ordinators of policy.

20. Metcalfe was appointed governor of Jamaica and then governor general of Canada; Sir George Anderson of Bombay became governor of Mauritius and Ceylon; two other governors of Jamaica, Sir J. P. Grant and Sir William Grey, were Indian civilians; Sir Bartle Frere, commissioner in Sind and governor of Bombay, became governor of Cape Colony; Sir Arthur Phayre, chief commissioner of Burma, became governor of Mauritius; and Sir H. B. Bourdillon of the United Provinces became governor of Uganda. After independence, the last of the ICS kept up this tradition. Sir Michael Nethersole of the United Provinces, as chief secretary of the Gold Coast, played a major role in creating Ghana. Sir Humphrey Trevelyan, British ambassador at Cairo, Peking, and Moscow, is only one of several ICS officers who have made a second career in the British Foreign Service.

This precedent has exercised a strong influence upon the manner in which cabinet ministers have interpreted their function in post-independence southern Asia.

In Ceylon, the Executive Council dates from 1833, and consisted of the governor and five officials.[21] From 1924, four non-officials were added to the council, and under the Donoughmore Reforms, the council was replaced by a Board of Ministers. The Straits Settlements, under the East India Company, possessed its own Executive Council, though as a measure of economy two members were assigned to administrative duties as resident councilors of Penang and Malacca. After transfer to the Colonial Office, the Executive Council was expanded. For a time, the resident councilors were advanced to the rank of lieutenant governor; but in the 1880's they reverted to their earlier title. Finally, in the twentieth century, they became resident commissioners.[22]

The system whereby the viceroy was assisted by executive councilors, who supervised departments, was followed at the provincial level at a later period. Before the Mutiny the main function of the provincial government was to act as tax-gatherer in chief, and for this purpose most governments were equipped with a board of revenue. From the 1850's, welfare functions were added, and the first departments of public works and of public instruction were set up. Gradually, a whole range of functions developed: police, irrigation, public health, and many others.[23] These were all under departmental heads, some of whom were ICS men, others technicians or specialists. To coordinate departmental activities on behalf of the head of the province was a secretary to government. The office in which the various provincial departments were housed became known as the secretariat.

21. The Ceylon Executive Council comprised the governor, the officer commanding the troops, the chief secretary, the queen's advocate, the treasurer, and the government agent of the Central Provinces. See Lennox A. Mills, *Ceylon Under British Rule* (London, 1933), p. 72.

22. After Merdeka the chief administrators of Penang and Malacca were accorded the title of governor.

23. In the 1880's, the North-Western Provinces (United Provinces) contained the following provincial departments: police, jails, education, medical services, public health and vaccination, agriculture and commerce, forests, meteorology, registration, stamps and excise, public works.

Writing of provincial secretariats in 1890, Sir William Hunter says "the Secretaries are only from one to three or four in number."[24] By 1914, the secretariat of Bombay Presidency comprised five secretaries (of whom the senior was styled chief secretary) together with five undersecretaries and eight assistant secretaries. Of the secretaries, four were covenanted civilians and one (in charge of public works and railways) a military engineer. The Civil List of the United Provinces for 1945 shows fourteen secretaries (eleven ICS men), sixteen deputy secretaries (nine ICS men), three undersecretaries, and thirteen assistant secretaries (nine being temporary).

The belief that the technical expert should be subordinated to the administrator was usually sustained in the secretariat, and transfers between offices were frequent. A tendency for officials to become "secretariat wallahs" was noticed by Curzon, and he insisted that service in the secretariat, whether at Simla or at a provincial headquarters, must be interspersed with postings in district work. However, just as staff duty is the main ladder to high military command, so selection for the secretariat was the main ladder to civil preferment. Several chief secretaries were appointed governors.

The secretariat in Colombo evolved on much the same lines as an Indian provincial secretariat. The governor's "chief of staff" was called the colonial secretary, and beside him sat the principal assistant colonial secretary and the second assistant colonial secretary. The Straits' government organization was similar, with a colonial secretary at its head, but the formation of a departmental structure in Malaya proceeded on somewhat original lines. As we shall shortly discover, the first British experiments in administration in the Malay States were highly eclectic. Gradually, a centralized pattern was evolved and in 1895 four of the states were persuaded to unite in a federation. The driving force toward centralization and standardization was Sir Frank Swettenham, who in July, 1896, was established as resident general at Kuala Lumpur with a federal secretariat which included

24. W. W. Hunter, *The Indian Empire: Its People, History and Products* (London, 1890), p. 438.

the departments of legal adviser, judicial commissioner, the secretary for Chinese affairs, the commissioner of police, the commandant of the Malay States Guides, the commissioner of lands and mines, and others. Some of the departmental heads were civil servants; some were not; but none had any real standing beside the resident general. Indeed, Swettenham towered over the governor. A later governor, Sir John Anderson, described Swettenham as "the final authority, to all intents and purposes." When Swettenham himself became governor, the picture changed. His resident general, William Treacher, was shy and retiring, and the focus of power shifted upward. When the secretary of state consulted Swettenham on the future of the office of resident general, he advised that it be abolished. This was done in 1910, and the head of the secretariat was henceforth called chief secretary.

From the earliest times, local and district administration in India has taken its stamp from the basic function of land revenue collection. Sher Shah (1529–1545) set the seal of Muslim revenue administration by dividing his empire into forty-seven divisions, or sarkar, and subdivided into some 113,000 pargana (the ancient Hindu revenue unit). Sher Shah established a hierarchy of revenue officials, and each sarkar was headed by a military supervisor (shiqdar-i-shiqdaran) and a civil head (munsif-i-munsifan). However, throughout the empire there were many who were outside the system, enjoying quasi-autonomous powers, in return for discharging certain duties to the state. Under various titles, there were zamindars, or revenue-farmers; these might be rajas with ancient hereditary rights over their subjects, or—at the other end of the scale—parvenu land contractors who had bought their way into power. When the East India Company assumed the diwani, or governorship, of Bengal, it found a powerful group of these zamindars in control of the countryside, such as the huge Rajshahi zamindari, extending over 13,000 miles and paying a revenue of Rs. 25 lakhs.[25] When, after several false starts, the company decided to appoint its servants as collectors, their districts frequently coincided with the boundaries of these zamin-

25. One lakh equals 100,000.

daris. These were vast areas, with teeming populations; Mymen-singh, even in the nineteenth century, was a district of over three million souls. After considerable debate, the directors of the company ordered in a dispatch of March 20, 1793, that a permanent settlement be concluded, apportioning the liabilities of the zamindars for land revenue throughout Bengal and Bihar for all time. This permanent settlement was subsequently applied to the Benares and Mirzapur districts (United Provinces) and to the Northern Sircars (Madras, now Andhra). The directors pressed for the extension of this system to all their territories, but as we shall see they were induced to revise their policy.

Within the area of the permanent settlement, the pattern of district administration was thereby immutably established. There was no motive to extend the tentacles of administration beyond district headquarters. The responsibility of the collector was limited to insuring that the zamindar remitted his revenue at the due date; if he failed, then his estate would be sold under the "Sunset Law." This restricted concept of district administration, despite certain reforms, dominated Bengal and Bihar to the close of British rule. The isolation of the collector from the life of his district was accentuated in eastern Bengal by the poorness of communications, especially when the great rivers were running high. There was the paradoxical situation that where communi-cation was most difficult, the deployment of administrators was most inadequate. Early in the twentieth century, in the Dacca and Chittagong divisions, there were twenty-one British cove-nanted civil servants and twelve British police officers to supervise a population of seventeen and a half million.[26] Not surprisingly, this lack of effective administration permitted the growth of a revolutionary movement during the early twentieth century, con-tributed to the virtual collapse of British rule in Bihar during the "August disturbances" of 1942, allowed the spread of the Bengal famine of 1943, and failed to anticipate the holocaust of Noahkali and of Patna in 1946.

26. Sir H. Verney Lovett, "District Administration in Bengal, 1858–1918," chap. xiii in H. H. Dodwell (ed.), *The Cambridge History of India* (Cambridge, 1932), VI, 252.

However, this "extensive" pattern of district administration did not, ultimately, provide the model for India or her neighbors; the general pattern derives from the "intensive" system, first evolved by Sir Thomas Munro in Madras. The original Madras districts were even more vast than those in Bengal; if the population of Mymensingh exceeded that of Switzerland, Vizagapatam was larger than Denmark in both population and area. During and after the wars with Tipu Sultan, the company acquired new tracts of territory. The first acquisition, the Baramahal, was placed under the administration of a soldier, Colonel Alexander Read, whose assistant was Thomas Munro. Their administration was utterly different from the Bengal mode. Munro lived for eight or nine months in every year under the fly of a tent, touring throughout his district; he traveled over a thousand miles during the year. By listening to cultivators, holy men, local leaders, he rediscovered the ancient pattern of landed tenure in the south. Munro concluded that for centuries the land revenue had been paid to the sovereign by the individual cultivator. In time, he succeeded in impressing the directors with his views. He gave evidence in the great inquiry which preceded the Fifth Report of the House of Commons Select Committee on the East India Company, 1812, and the process of extending the Bengal system to the other provinces was halted and reversed. Of Munro's victory in the settlement controversy, Woodruff has said,

Munro had had the backing of most of the district officers, many of whom had been trained under himself and Read, and his victory was the triumph of the district officer. It was more; it precipitated, it crystallized, the idea of a district officer; henceforward he was not to be a distant guide, but in close contact with the peasant, the father and mother of his people, controlling everything that happened so completely that a time came when the child felt the control irksome and wanted his own way.[27]

In 1814, Munro was appointed to undertake an inquiry into the judicial system. Following the reorganization of the Cornwallis period, all responsibility for law and order had been allocated to

27. For an account of Munro see Philip Woodruff, *The Men Who Ruled India: The Founders of Modern India* (New York, 1954), pp. 183–198.

the zila judge, leaving only revenue functions with the collector. Munro recommended that police and magisterial responsibilities be handed over to the collector. He made further suggestions designed to rehabilitate village life. The activities of the irregular Faujdari district police should be curtailed in favor of the village patel and a village network. He urged that "village panchayats be authorised to hear and determine suits." Two years later, these reforms were adopted in Madras and were imitated in Bombay Presidency in 1818. When Munro returned to Madras as governor, he showed impatience with the elaborate correspondence favored by government: "a mass of useless trash" was his verdict. He entertained little respect for the pedantic type of official, urging the vital necessity for a living knowledge of the language among British officials. There were to be many such as Munro in the next half-century.

The next important development in the evolution of the "code" of the British-Indian district officer was the settlement of the North-Western Provinces. The argument over the value of a Permanent Settlement was not yet concluded, but under the influence of Robert Bird, and then of James Thomason (first lieutenant governor of the Agra Provinces), settlement operations were directed toward discovering and recording the actual rights to ownership or occupation of the peasantry, here organized mainly under the so-called joint village system. This settlement entailed a painstaking inquiry into peasant rights, and a careful survey, leading to preparation of detailed field-maps. This settlement work made British officials much more closely aware of the nature of rural Indian society and gave them a livelier concern for rural welfare. The first civil appointment held by Henry Lawrence (then a lieutenant in the Bengal artillery) was that of assistant revenue surveyor in the North-Western Provinces.

The Lawrence brothers, Henry and John, set the seal on district administration by their pioneering in the Punjab. Both brothers were merciless to themselves and to subordinates, driving body and mind to the limit of endurance. Their outlook, it must be said, was philistine. Though Henry was a writer of distinction, his pen was employed upon political and economic subjects; there was no place for literary or philosophical speculation. And this was very much the tone of succeeding scholar-civilians, from S. S. Thorburn to W. H. Moreland and M. L. Darling. The Lawrences chose their subordinates with care, tested them to the limit, and then either discarded them or gave them absolute trust and support. In return, the men who served the Lawrences either loathed them or loved them. This was, perhaps, the greatest of the great ICS traditions—one that was not successfully transplanted in the counterpart services in neighboring lands, and one that has not really survived independence—from above, trust, and a complete readiness to allow the junior man initiative, backing him up if his initiative should lead him into trouble; from below, loyalty to one's chief, and confidence that whatever befall, one could see it through.[28]

Henry Lawrence's "young men" (as he called them) were drawn equally from the army and the civilian cadre of the North-Western Provinces. The keynote was action. Of John Nicholson, the Pathans of Peshawar District used to say, "The sound of his horse's hoofs was heard from the Attock to the Khyber." But these district officers of the Lawrence school were not mere troubleshooters, men of action; they were also men with a sense of mission. Here are the thoughts of Herbert Edwardes, a young infantry officer turned deputy commissioner, at this time:

To be flung into a country where anarchy prevails, and introduce the rights of man to man and all to Government is doubtless high employ. But to succeed this rough pioneering, and build on the space that has been cleared . . . to lay broad foundations of national prosperity by limiting taxation . . . , to open schools and dream of plans for education; to effect, in short, a social change which the missionary alone can crown, must be allowed to be a lot of exceeding great utility, such as the largest heart might be occupied in filling.[29]

28. Philip Woodruff cites an incident from the life of Lord Hailey: " 'You will have a trying day tomorrow,' he said when chief commissioner of Delhi to the district magistrate. 'You will be on the alert all day and will probably have a riot. But I have discussed all your arrangements and I approve of them. One embarrassment at least you shall be spared. I am going fishing.' " Of this trust, this rejection of any tendency to breathe over the neck of one's subordinate, Woodruff rightly concludes: "This could have been said in no other service." *The Men Who Ruled India: The Guardians* (London, 1954), p. 290.

29. *Memorials of the Life and Letters of Sir Herbert Benjamin Edwardes by His Wife* (2 vols.; London, 1886), I, 210.

Not all Victorian civilians were possessed of a social conscience, but most were—whether they were conservative and conformist or radical and non-conformist.

By the time of the Mutiny, the district was established as the key administrative unit and the district officer as the key figure in administration. Above, there was the commissioner, exercising supervision over a division, a collection of districts which varied according to their size. Thus, in Bengal, each division contained only three or four districts of enormous size; in United Provinces, with its more compact districts, there were an average of five or six to a division. Occasionally, because of geographical isolation, a commissioner exercised real powers, as did the commissioner in Sind in the days when Sind formed part of the Bombay Presidency. In general, however, as communications improved, the commissioner became little more than an intermediary, a "post office," as he was often called. He heard appeals in revenue cases, and he was empowered to make certain transfers in his division and to appoint certain subordinate staff. But, in general, a commissioner's appointment was a form of consolation prize for the ICS man who had just failed to attain the heights. Madras managed to do without commissioners at all, but an attempt to do likewise in Upper Burma after its annexation (when a chief commissioner at Mandalay dealt with his fourteen district officers) was deemed unsuccessful because of the isolation of much of the country.

Within the district, the highest administrative unit was the subdivision, which was designed for purposes of general administration and magisterial control. In the rambling Bengal districts, the subdivisional magistrate lived away from headquarters in the depths of his subdivision. This was also the custom in the Punjab, with its Lawrence tradition of mingling with the people. But in United Provinces and most other provinces, the subdivisional officer lived at district headquarters except when he was on tour.[30] A subdivisional officer (SDO) was usually a young civilian of

30. In United Provinces the immense size of the district of Gorakhpur necessitated the post of additional district magistrate and additional collector for Deoria-Kasia.

some four or five years' service, exercising his first independent responsibilities; alternatively, he would be a senior officer of the provincial service.

Within the area of the Permanent Settlement, revenue administration was centralized at district headquarters, and as previously noted there was virtually no infrastructure of district administration in Bengal, Bihar, and Orissa apart from the thanas, or police circles. Elsewhere, the districts were divided, for revenue purposes, into three, four, or five sub-units called tehsils in northern India and taluks in Madras and Bombay (also townships in Burma). The tehsildar, or his equivalent (mamlatdar, etc.), was a member of the subordinate Civil Service, the lowest level of gazetted officer. Endowed with class-two magisterial and revenue powers, he was responsible for the actual collection of the land revenue. On the revenue side, the tehsil was divided into circles, the responsibility of the kanungo. The title of kanungo (whose office dates from the time of Akbar and Todar Mal) comes from Persian, "law utterer." He maintained revenue registers based upon the reports of the village accountant, the patwari. About thirty patwaris were under each kanungo, and at this village level the district administration merged into village administration, the patwari being a hereditary official and a member of the village community.

Burma, as a province of India, followed the standard pattern, except in the outer, border regions. The deputy commissioners of frontier districts, such as Myitkyina or the Upper Chindwin, were much more wardens of the marches than regular collectors. District administration was sketchy, consisting mainly of showing the flag and carrying out long expeditions through remote jungle and mountain regions to remind the unruly tribesmen (and the long-range agents of China) that this was a corner of the British Empire.[31] About one-third of the area of Burma was without even a minimal system of district administration. Although the Shan States were technically part of British Burma, they remained

31. Until 1914 British administration stopped a dozen miles north of Myitkyina. To check Chinese intrusion, a police post (Fort Hertz) was established at Putao. See Hugh Tinker, "Burma's Northeast Borderland Problems," *Pacific Affairs*, XXIX (1956), 324–346.

under the rule of their own chiefs. Unlike the Indian princes, these chiefs (known, according to rank, as sawbwa, myosa, or ngwegunhmu) were not merely under the protection of a paramount power: they were specifically brought under the British Crown. However, British influence was limited to the appointment of two senior officials as superintendents.

The superintendent of the Northern Shan States exercised control over six states; his colleague for the Southern group was concerned with thirty-two states and sub-states. Assistant superintendents were stationed in the major states such as Kengtung. From October, 1922, all these states were brought into a federation on the Malayan model. A federal council of Shan chiefs was created without legislative powers under a commissioner of the Federated Shan States—the office being held by the Southern superintendent. Certain federal departments such as public works, forests, and education were created.[32]

Burma covers an area of about 240,000 square miles, of which about 102,000 square miles were not under regular administration in 1930. The area of Ceylon is only 25,332 square miles, but following the Colonial Office and not the Indian model, its administrative structure was much more imposing. The Kandyan kings, the Portuguese, and the Dutch all left their mark; but the present structure came into being in 1833, when the island was divided into five provinces. These were later redistributed into nine provinces. At the head of each was the government agent, a civil servant of twenty years' service or more. Each province was itself divided into two or more districts. There were nineteen districts in all, and each was supervised by an assistant government agent, usually an officer of six to twenty years' service. The extent to which decision-making was abrogated by the government agent himself was partly dependent on his own personality. Many government agents were content to leave all initiative to their juniors.[33]

32. See *Memoranda Submitted to the Statutory Commission by the Government of Burma* (Rangoon, 1930), Simon Commission Report, IX, 559–562.

33. For an account of district administration in Ceylon in the early twentieth century, which is also a superb literary work, see Leonard Woolf, *Growing: An Autobiography of the Years 1904 to 1911* (London, 1961). Further references to Woolf can be found in Collins' chapter (Chapter 7), p. 446, n. 1, in this volume.

The infrastructure of administration in Ceylon was a duplicate in miniature of the Indian revenue system. Districts were divided into chief headman's divisions (110 in all); under these were 613 subdivisions under superior headmen and four thousand villages and hamlets under village headmen. The chief headmen and superior headmen were civil servants of considerable standing. They enjoyed such titles as mudaliyar and rate mahatmaya, and wore splendid uniforms. Although civil servants, their office was largely hereditary, following the pattern established under the ancient Ceylonese kings.

The British genius for creating an empire in a fit of absence of mind was never better exemplified than in Malaya: all one can say in elucidation of Malayan district administration is that it "just growed." In Singapore, Malacca, and Penang (or rather Georgetown, on Prince of Wales Island) administration was municipal, on the original lines of the company's Indian settlements. In the small areas of paddy and coconut plantations beyond the ports, the Indian district system was reproduced in miniature, with a collector of land revenue for Penang and Province Wellesley, for example. As British activity in the hinterland developed in the 1870's, so began a gradual movement toward centralization and uniformity throughout the peninsula. This centralization was not yet complete by the time of Merdeka, and during the nineteenth century it is easier to describe differences than similarities.

When following the Pangkor Treaty in 1874, a resident was placed in Perak—and subsequently in Selangor and Sungai Ujong —the stated intention was to appoint an adviser with functions similar to those of residents in the Indian princely states.[34] The

34. The so-called Pangkor Treaty provided that the advice of the resident "must be asked and acted upon on all questions other than those touching Malay Religion and Custom." It was further laid down that "the collection and control of all Revenues and the general administration of the country be regulated under the advice of these Residents." The chiefs were awarded incomes from a Civil List and ceased to collect their own taxes. It will be seen that even initially the residents in Malaya were endowed with powers far beyond what is usually covered by the term "advice." Text of the Pangkor Treaty is accessible in W. G. Maxwell and W. S. Gibson (eds.), *Treaties and Engagements Affecting the Malay States and Borneo* (London, 1924), pp. 28–30. This treaty (or "Pangkor Engagement," as it is officially known) has recently been reprinted in Parkinson, *op. cit.*, Appendix A.

Malay rulers governed through chiefs of aristocratic lineage. In accordance with a hierarchy based on astrological computation, the ruler's court or concilium was normally headed by four superior officials and by eight of lesser rank. The ministers were collectively known as the mentri, and one of the superior four was "secretary of state," or mentri besar. The Malay States were an aggregation of districts (daerah) ruled by chiefs. Frequently, these daerah were semi-independent. In Perak, the rich tin-mining area of Larut was from the 1850's the fief of the mentri of Larut. The "nine states" of Negri Sembilan comprised a loose confederacy of clans and chiefs. This decentralized, even anarchic, policy was now brought within an administrative system which cannot properly be characterized as extending either "direct" or "indirect" rule.

After certain unhappy first experiences, including the murder of J. W. W. Birch, the first British resident in Perak,[35] the residents in the western states settled down to long periods of power: Hugh Low, for instance, remained in Perak from 1877 to 1889. They interpreted their duties in the direction of substituting a bureaucracy, largely British-directed, for a semi-feudal, semi-clan nexus of control. The first additions were the assistant residents, who were frequently made responsible for supervising a section of the state. Then, police forces, frequently recruited from Sikhs or Gurkhas, were organized. These forces were led by British officers, and thereby the basic instrument of public order was placed under British control. Finally, British officials were posted as district officers, responsible for revenue collection, law and order, and public welfare throughout the western states. These district appointments began about 1885, and by 1890 British district officers were functioning throughout western Malaya.

The trend toward centralization was furthered by the bringing together of the petty Menangkabau states in the hinterland of Malacca, first in the Sri Menanti Confederacy (1887), and then into a coagulated state to which the traditional name of Negri

35. See comments on Birch in Robert O. Tilman, *Bureaucratic Transition in Malaya* (Durham, N. C., 1964), p. 26, n. 56. See also Tilman's chapter (Chapter 9) in this volume, esp. p. 551, n. 2.

Sembilan was applied in 1889. Uniformity further resulted from the Agreement of 1895, whereby Perak, Selangor, Negri Sembilan, and Pahang came together in a federation. The legal fiction that the residents were "advisers" only was now abandoned, and it was overtly accepted that the resident general was the chief executive officer at the head of a unified administration of the Federated Malay States.

However, the peculiar characteristic of Malayan administration, which to some extent remains after independence, is the persistence of local variants.[36] Pahang, the least "assimilated" of the Federated Malay States, lagged behind the western states in conforming to their pattern. Johore, the largest of the states and also the most open to European influence from Singapore, steadfastly resisted all attempts by the governor and resident general to bring it into line. A treaty was concluded in December, 1885, whereby the sultan of Johore undertook to accept a British official as agent, "having functions similar to those of a Consular officer"; but even this limited extension of British control was not put into effect. The sultan had his own advisory board, composed of retired British colonial officials who were "contact men" rather than overseers. The office of agent was not filled until 1909. And not until 1914 did the sultan consent to accept a general adviser, "whose advice must be asked and acted upon on all matters affecting the general administration of the country." Similarly, those Malay states subject to Thai influence or domination only gradually came into the British administrative orbit. When by 1904 Kedah had virtually became bankrupt, the state was compelled to accept outside interference: Siam provided a substantial loan in 1905 on the condition that G. C. Hart, an ICS officer seconded to the Thai service, would be appointed financial adviser. Kelantan, the state most affected by Thai cultural and political influence, also received two British advisers appointed by Siam in 1903: W. A. Graham of the ICS and H. W. Thompson. Then, in 1909 Siam concluded a treaty with Britain, whereby in

---

36. One scholar describes the Malayan administrative patchwork as "this ultra-Parkinsonian organisation." See Sir Charles Jeffries, *Transfer of Power* (London, 1960), p. 83.

return for the abolition of extra-territorial rights, railway concessions, and a loan, Siamese rights over Kedah, Trengganu, Kelantan, and Perlis were transferred to Britain. The sultan of Kelantan undertook in 1910 to follow the advice of his British adviser; Trengganu accepted an adviser only in 1919, while Kedah followed suit in 1923, and Perlis did not formally accept British advice until 1930.

Before World War II, a district system had been extended to the whole of Malaya: in 1931, there were fifty-five administrative districts (outside Penang, Malacca, and Singapore).[37] In the Federated Malay States all district officers were members of the Malayan Civil Service. In the non-federated states, they were (and are) mainly or entirely members of the state civil service. While in the Federated Malay States the head of the state administration was the British resident, functioning with a secretariat staffed by Europeans, in the other states the head of the actual administration was the mentri besar, with the British adviser fulfilling an admonitory role only. Alongside the district and state administrative hierarchy, there was another hierarchy designed to deal with Malaya's "plural society." From 1877 there was a Chinese protectorate, headed by the secretary for Chinese affairs, while later the Labour Department fulfilled a similar function for the Indian community.

A feature of British administration in Asia was the blending and blurring of the executive and judicial functions of government. This represented a recognition of the pull of circumstances rather than any deliberate extension of policy. Within the Mughal system, there was a separation of the judicial function from those of revenue collection and the enforcement of order. From the chief judge of the realm, qazi-ul-quzat, the chain extended through the qazi-i-subah at provincial level to the district judge, or shariat panah. Yet, in practice, these judges had a lesser authority than that of the nizamat, the chain of enforcement in which was invested the power of criminal justice. In Burma, the royal council (hlut-daw) was both the king's executive and the

37. Perlis—called by Sir Gerald Templer, when high commissioner, "piddling Perlis"—is so small that it is governed directly from its capital, Kangar.

highest court in the land. Provincial courts, known as khon-taw, were found in large towns, but they had no criminal jurisdiction. Old Malaya knew no separate judiciary: "sultans and chiefs administered the law as part of their function of preserving order."[38]

When the East India Company "stood forth as Dewan," it was specifically reluctant to alter the indigenous system of justice. Gradually—and then rapidly, as the impetus of reform quickened —the system was Anglicized, although not till 1864 was the office of Qazi finally abolished. From 1793, covenanted servants were appointed to the post of district judge. There followed a series of compromise adjustments between the collector and the judge, whereby revenue, police, and magisterial powers were passed from one to the other. Finally, the district judge emerged as the tribunal in civil cases and in the more serious criminal cases, but the collector as district magistrate retained a plenitude of justiciary power. And as the border regions—the Punjab, the Central Provinces, Burma, etc.—were placed under "non-regulation" rule, so the deputy commissioner was invested with dual authority as collector and judge; the divisional commissioner served as a Court of Appeal.[39]

Gradually, even in non-regulation provinces, a separate organization of district and sessions judges was created, and appeals lay to a Chief Court or High Court. These reforms, however, did not remove the courts from contact with the ICS. The Act of 1861, establishing the high courts, provided that at least one-third of the judges must be barristers or advocates of the United King-

---

38. J. M. Gullick, *Indigenous Political Systems of Western Malaya* (London, 1958), p. 115. For Burma, see Maung Htin Aung, *Burmese Law Tales* (London, 1962), p. 21.

39. Divisional commissioners in the Punjab were relieved of all civil and criminal appellate work in 1884. From 1853, the highest judicial authority in the Punjab was a judicial commissioner who was both sessions judge and head of the provincial police. This institution was replaced by a Chief Court in 1866. The office of judicial commissioner was established in most non-regulation provinces as a "halfway house" to a High Court. For an historical survey of these developments in the Punjab, see Ram Lal Handa, *A History of the Development of the Judiciary in the Punjab (1846–1884)* (Lahore, 1927), and Daya Krishna Kapur, *A History of the Development of the Judiciary in the Punjab (1884–1926)* (Lahore, 1928). Both of these are monographs in the Punjab Government Records Office Publication Series.

dom, and at least one-third Indian civilians of not less than ten years' service, having three years' experience as a district judge. Originally, all district judges were civilians. Toward the end of the nineteenth century, members of the provincial judicial services were being appointed to a few district judgeships. But this did not alter the "official" character of the judiciary, although in practice most civilians who opted to become members of the "judgee" were of an independent and sometimes contumacious frame of mind.[40]

The pattern in Ceylon was similar. In the early days of British rule, there were four provincial judges. A "charter of justice" of 1833 instituted a system of district courts and a Supreme Court with appellate jurisdiction. The district judges, without exception, were civil servants with no previous legal training. In 1856, the Colonial Office ordered that the district judgeship of Colombo must be held by a member of the Ceylon bar. Subsequently, the important judgeship of Kandy District was also usually held by a barrister, and this was confirmed by a Colonial Office order of 1872. Separation between the judiciary and the executive existed, except in four of the most remote districts where the assistant government agent was also district judge.[41] Whereas in India the civilian was entitled to make his choice between the executive or the judicial line, in Ceylon it appears that there was no such choice, and the less able (or socially acceptable) are said to have been most often appointed judges.[42]

As in the Presidency towns in India, so in the Straits Settlements; British judicial institutions were transplanted with little modification. The legal profession played a leading part in the life of Singapore, and the recorder and other judges were almost all barristers or advocates. When control over the Straits Settlements

40. For example, Henry Beveridge as district judge was often at odds with the Government of Bengal. He had a notable tussle with the High Court at Calcutta over the succession to a large estate, the Jalpaiguri Raj. Beveridge's judgment was overturned by the High Court, but on appeal to the Privy Council in London, Beveridge's decision was upheld. Lord Beveridge, *India Called Them* (London, 1947), pp. 185–186, 272.

41. These four districts were Anuradhapura, Trincomalee, Vavuniya Vilankulam, and Mannar. See Mills, *op. cit.*, pp. 91, 97. Late in the nineteenth century these districts also obtained separate district judges.

42. Woolf, *op. cit.*, pp. 35–36.

passed to the Colonial Office in 1867, a Supreme Court was established at Singapore. In the hinterland, officials of the Straits Settlements Civil Service fulfilled dual functions, as in India and Ceylon, and moved frequently between executive and judicial posts. As residents and assistant residents were established in the Malay States, courts of law, which administered the Indian Penal Code imported via the Straits Settlements, came into being.

To the ordinary people, the new legal systems impressed them as an incalculable importation, quite distinct and different from their own systems of authority and of customary law. To the Westernized, educated Asian, on the other hand, the courts were not sufficiently separated from the influences of those who governed.

III. Indianization and the Civil Services in India

The Indian Civil Service was foreshadowed in the mansabdari imperial service of Akbar. This was an aristocracy of service. It was not at all an aristocracy of noble blood, or of feudal strength, and not even an indigenous aristocracy. Some 70 per cent of Akbar's chief officers were of central Asian origin: Turks, Afghans, and Persians. Yet, alongside this Islamic elite there were Hindu leaders. Raja Todar Mal, architect of Akbar's revenue system, was a Kayastha of the clerical caste. Of the 416 mansabdars of Akbar's empire, forty-seven were Rajputs. Above them all, Raja Man Singh of Ambar had the supreme dignity of five thousand horses, was brother-in-law to the emperor, and was given the posts of greatest trust and danger—such as governor of Kabul and of Bengal.

The enforcement of the covenanted monopoly virtually deprived Indians of any hope of rising to the higher levels of administration. As long as entry into the covenanted service was dependent upon the chance of obtaining one of the directors' precious nominations, Indians were virtually excluded, whatever the 1833 Act might state. One director conceived the plan of nominating the adopted son of Ram Mohan Ray to a writership, but this came to nothing.[43]

If the new Western-educated middle class was debarred from obtaining an equal footing with the British middle class covenanted civilians, to an increasing extent the members of the traditional official families were seeing the prospects of employment wither away. Persian was the language of the courts and of administration throughout all areas which had come under Muslim rule. From the late 1830's, Persian began to give way to English as the language of the courts, and it was generally abolished by 1845. On the revenue side of the administration, Persian was discarded in Madras and the North-Western Provinces in favor of the vernaculars, and later Urdu and Bengali were substituted in Bihar and Bengal for Persian. Kayasthas and Brahmins of the official classes very soon acquired a knowledge of English, just as earlier they had mastered Persian, as a necessary qualification for employment. Muslims of the official classes clung to their Persian and Arabic as the foundation of their culture and so began that shift in the balance of strength among the official families, Hindu and Muslim, which was to have such incalculable consequences in the twentieth century.

Lord William Bentinck, who told Jeremy Bentham that as governor general he intended to put Philosophical Radicalism into practice, gave some relief to the new Western-educated class. In 1831 a higher grade of Indian civil judge, that of principal sadr amin, was created, while the office of deputy collector was opened to Indians. At first these grades were filled by promotion, but within a short time appointments were being made on the basis of the records of the candidates in public examinations—largely, examinations conducted in English. Because of the concentration of colleges on the Western model in Calcutta and its suburbs, the capital began to attain a near-monopoly in entry into the services. For example, in 1841, among those successful in the munsif's

43. See K. A. Ballhatchet, "Raja Ram Roy's Visit to England," *Bulletin of the School of Oriental and African Studies*, XX (1957), 69–71. Ram Mohan Ray's son, Rama Prasad Ray, became one of the first Indian judges of the Calcutta High Court.

examination, three came from Dacca, four from Murshidabad, seven from Patna, and forty from Calcutta. Of even greater significance is the fact that of the seventy candidates who gained the munsif diploma in 1841, only three were Muslims.

While the urban Hindu middle class were quick to take advantage of such changes, the situation did not satisfy the leaders of the new Westernized classes. Largely in response to the pleas of Dwarkanath Tagore, the new post of deputy magistrate was created in the Bengal Presidency in 1843, having parity (supposedly) with the junior covenanted civilians. The first appointment went to Chandra Mohan Chaterjea, a nephew of Dwarkanath who had accompanied him to England. But the monthly salary was only Rs. 400 (soon reduced to Rs. 350), and genuine parity of esteem was lacking. Chandra Mohan resigned within three years.

As soon as the covenanted service was opened to competition, it became a prime object of the reformers to promote Indian candidates. Because of fear of the loss of caste involved in crossing the Black Water, the majority of the pioneer candidates were members of "fringe" communities, especially members of the Brahmo Samaj, the reformist neo-Hindu church founded by Ram Mohan Ray and revivified by Maharshi Debendranath Tagore and Keshub Chandra Sen. The first successful Indian candidate, Satyendranath Tagore, who gained his place in 1864, was the second son of the Maharshi.[44] In 1869, four Brahmo candidates, Surendranath Banerjea, Romesh Chandra Dutt, Bihari Lal Gupta, and S. B. Thakur, competed and all were successful.

The opening of the ICS to competition coincided with the reform of Oxford and Cambridge and a marked expansion in the numbers of young Englishmen working for honors degrees. There was a rapid increase among numbers of candidates for the ICS (the Home Civil Service did not attract middle-class intellectuals until a later period). In 1857 there were sixty candidates for twelve places. In 1870 there were 327 candidates for forty-three

44. Of the first twelve Indians appointed to the ICS between 1864–1886, eight were Hindus (almost all Brahmos), three were Parsis, and one was a Christian. The first successful Muslim candidate, the son of Badruddin Tyabji, third president of the Congress and a wealthy lawyer, joined the service in 1888.

places. From 1871 an entrance fee of £5 was charged, and thereafter numbers remained just under 200. But the quality of the candidates rose even higher.

The leaders of the Indian middle class emphasized how difficult it was, under these conditions, for Indian youth to compete successfully. John Lawrence, as viceroy, initiated a scheme for the annual award of nine Queen's Scholarships, tenable for three years in England, to encourage promising Indian candidates. Instituted in 1868, the scholarships were suspended in the following year and were never actually awarded again. The reason for this curtailment, although not precisely stated, was the growing prejudice against the "educated native," who it was alleged did not make a satisfactory leader and governor of his countrymen. The next step after withdrawing financial aid was the deliberate creation of barriers to entrance into the service. In 1876, the upper age limit for competing was lowered from twenty-one to nineteen years.[45] Unless an Indian boy was sent to Britain to be educated from about the age of fifteen—then still an almost unknown occurrence—he stood little chance of success. The impact of the lower age limit was soon seen in the results. Between 1868 and 1875, fourteen Indian candidates appeared for the exam and eleven passed. Between 1876 and 1883, twenty-eight sat for the exam and one passed.

The injustice naturally incensed the reformers. Surendranath Banerjea had been dismissed from the ICS during his first year for an offense that was technical rather than culpable.[46] In 1877 and 1878 he launched his Civil Service movement as the first phase of a long campaign of popular political agitation. With the creation of the Congress in 1885, Indianization of the ICS became one of its main features.

The Liberal party, and its radical wing in particular, showed a concern for the reform of administration in India from the 1850's

---

45. Macaulay and his committee laid down a maximum age for candidates of twenty-three years. After six years, this was reduced to twenty-two, and in 1866 the upper age limit was lowered to twenty-one.

46. For an explanation of this action, see his autobiography, *A Nation in the Making; Being the Reminiscences of Fifty Years of Public Life* (London, 1925), p. 30.

onward. Henry Fawcett, often called "the Member for India," secured a considerable measure of support in Parliament for a motion, debated in 1868, to introduce a simultaneous examination for the ICS in India as well as England. Largely because of his efforts, an act was passed in 1870 to provide "additional facilities for the employment of Natives of India of proved merit and ability in the Civil Service of Her Majesty in India."[47] After several years, rules were framed to implement these provisions, but only two or three appointments were made. The whole question of Indianization was examined by Lord Lytton as viceroy. He favored the creation of a service open only to Indians and filled by nomination. This service was to be recruited by nomination, and for the criteria of "merit and ability" was substituted the test of family and social position. The Statutory Rules of 1879 provide for "employment in Her Majesty's Covenanted Civil Service," but the combination of the English sense of class distinction and the Indian sense of caste differentiation at once served to separate the "statutory civilians" from the competition wallahs. Lytton was intoxicated with the notion of aristocracy (he devoted much time and trouble to devising heraldic insignia for the Indian princes), and he endeavored to appoint aristocrats to his statutory service. Unfortunately, few of these had the necessary English and other qualifications, and the few who were appointed soon became bored with the routine and were piqued by the obvious refusal of their British colleagues to treat them as equals. They soon withdrew. Some statutory appointments went to meritorious serving officials. For example, Muhammad Hyat Khan, once orderly to John Nicholson, became a deputy commissioner in the Punjab (his grandson became chief minister of the province). Some statutory civilians were even appointed on a competitive basis. The scheme was generally disliked, and although the declared intention was to fix the strength of the statutory civilians at one-fifth of the competitive entry, in the end only sixty-nine statutory appointments were made.

47. Government of India Act, 1870, 33 Vict., cap. 3, sec. 6.

The leaders of the Muslim community generally favored the statutory scheme, because experience had shown that Muslims stood only a meager chance of entering government service when they had to compete against Hindus. Sir William Hunter has been widely quoted as making a case to show that by about 1870 the Muslims had lost their earlier ascendancy in the public services.[48] Where entry was by competition, this assertion was true. Bengal and Bihar provided the most striking evidence of change. In 1838 of the nine principal sadr amins in Bengal Presidency, eight were Muslims, while twenty-one of the forty-four munsifs were Muslims. By 1871 there were seventy-eight Hindu munsifs in Bengal and only thirty-seven Muslims. But a survey of the whole field of Indian administration showed that in the 1880's Muslims retained 20 per cent of all posts in the executive and judicial gazetted services, which was roughly equivalent to their proportion of the general population. While in Bengal and Bombay Presidencies the Muslims were at a grave disadvantage, and in Punjab were somewhat under-represented, in the North-Western Provinces, Central Provinces, and Berar they enjoyed a share of the services out of all proportion to their communal strength.[49] In these areas, appointment generally was still by nomination. Sir Sayyid Ahmad Khan and other Muslim leaders strongly urged the need to maintain appointment by nomination until such time as the Muslims had drawn level with the Hindus in acquiring advanced Western education. This argument for special treatment remained the basis of the Muslim case down to 1947.

The viceroyalty of Lord Ripon (1880–1884) was one of the few

48. W. W. Hunter, *The Indian Musalmans* (London, 1871); see esp. chap. iv, "Wrongs of the Muhammadans under British Rule," pp. 143–213.

49. In the Bengal Presidency, Muslims formed 31 per cent of the population but held only 8 per cent of gazetted executive and judicial posts. In Bombay Presidency and Sind, 18 per cent of the population was Muslim, but they held only 5 per cent of such posts. In the Punjab, Muslims made up 51 per cent of the population and held 39 per cent of the posts. By contrast, in the North-Western Provinces and Oudh, Muslims comprised 13 per cent of the population and held 45 per cent of the posts, and in Central Provinces, Muslims formed only 2 per cent of the population but held 18 per cent of such posts. *Report of the Public Service Commission—1886–87*, Cd. 5327 (Calcutta: Superintendent of Government Printing, 1888), chap. iv., p. 31. Hereinafter cited as Aitchison Commission Report.

periods when Liberal influence was directly felt in the Government of India. It was clear that the statutory scheme fell short of its promises, especially in giving Indians a guaranteed share of one-sixth of the higher civil service. Ripon secured certain small improvements, such as the raising of the examination age limit to twenty-one, and he set in motion a full-scale inquiry into the future of the civil service in India.[50] This Public Service Commission is usually known by the name of its chairman, Sir Charles Aitchison, a former lieutenant governor of the Punjab.[51] One innovation of the commission was the inclusion of six Indian members, representing the major regions of India. The terms of reference of the commission required it "to do full justice to the claims of natives of India to higher and more extensive employment in the public service." The commission held sittings in the chief towns of India and recorded the evidence of all leading Indians of the day. The recommendations of the commission followed the usual *festina lente* pattern. They rejected any rule or practice based on racial difference: the "only just criterion is that of fitness ascertained, where it is possible, by adequate tests." The commission strongly supported the retention of the London examination as the sole means of entrance to the covenanted service, but recommended adopting age limits of nineteen to twenty-three and raising of the marks which might be earned by Sanskrit and Arabic. The Statutory Service was to be ended, and in its place would be a Provincial Civil Service with a similar status. The cadre of the covenanted service would be reduced, and 108 reserved posts (including one-third of all district judges, one-sixth of all joint magistrates, and one-tenth of all collectors) were handed over to the Provincial Service.

These proposals did not satisfy educated Indians: nor did they go far enough, in the view of the radical wing of the Liberal party. An Indian parliamentary committee of 154 members was pledged to press for reform. On June 2, 1893, one of the members

50. For a general survey of the contribution of Ripon toward Indianization of the services, see Hira Lal Singh, *Problems and Policies of the British in India, 1885–1898* (London, 1963), chap. i, "Problems of Indianisation in the Civil Services."

51. Cited above, n. 49.

of this committee, H. W. Paul, introduced a motion in the House of Commons, calling for simultaneous examinations for the covenanted service in England and in India; the resolution was passed, by eighty-four to seventy-six votes. Gladstone, as prime minister, indicated that the Government of India would be called upon to indicate how the resolution should be put into effect. In a reply in November, 1893, the Government of India pointed out that the Civil Service of India contained in its cadre 898 posts, of which 731 were reserved for covenanted civilians and "military civilians." This, it was argued, already cut the number of Europeans in higher administration to the minimum. The new proposal was characterized as "ill-advised and dangerous."[52] This view was accepted by Kimberley, the secretary of state, who had differed with Gladstone all along. Soon after, the Liberal government was ousted, and Britain entered twenty years of Conservative rule. The position of Indians in the administration remained virtually unchanged.

The Provincial Service was expanded to almost double the numbers of the covenanted civilians. In 1893 there were 1,030 in the executive branch and 797 in the judicial branch of the Provincial Service, as compared to a total of 898 covenanted civilians. Outside of Bengal, where the Provincial Service was entered only by examination, recruitment was a mixture of examination entry and entry under the nomination of the governor or other head of the province. The original intention to give the Provincial Service parity of esteem with the Civil Service of India was not realized. The Islington Commission, which carried out its inquiry on the eve of World War I (though its report was not published until 1917), stated firmly: "The expectations formed as to the status which these officers would enjoy have to a great extent been falsified."[53] More specifically, the Islington Commission noted that out of ninety-three superior posts provided for the Provincial Service, only fifty-one had actually been filled by them.

---

52. Quoted by Singh, *op. cit.*, p. 68.
53. *Report of the Royal Commission on the Public Services in India*, Cd. 8382 (1917), I, 11. Hereinafter cited as Islington Commission Report.

Meanwhile, the process of Indianization in the ICS had been equally disappointing. In part this was due to keen competition from the intellectual elite of the British universities, with Oxford maintaining the lead. (In 1910, thirty-six of the fifty-eight successful candidates were Oxford men.) From 1895 the ICS examination was also the entrance examination for the Home Civil Service and from 1896 for the Eastern Cadetships of the Colonial Service and from 1924 for the Foreign Service. Yet such was the reputation of the ICS that—to quote a highly qualified professional commentator—"many of the best candidates chose it" in preference to the Home Service or Foreign Service.[54] After the raising of the age of entry in 1892, the Indian rate of successes was doubled. Even so, by 1909, out of 1,142 members of the ICS, only about sixty were Indians; ten years later their total had risen to seventy-eight.[55] Most Indians in the ICS found life on the executive side frustrating and even humiliating. A Bengali member of the ICS said to a French administrative expert: "They treat me as an inferior and patronise me. The only man who has really

54. C. J. Hayes, "Report on the Public Service Commissions of British Commonwealth Countries," unpublished report of the Civil Service Commission (London, 1955), p. 142. Hereinafter cited as Hayes Report. In the combined ICS, Home Service, and Colonial Service examination of 1905, first place was taken by John Anderson, later governor of Bengal. His biographer notes: "The choice now lay open to him of appointment to either the Indian Civil or the Home Civil Service. It was customary in those days for most leading candidates to give preference to India. . . . It was an alluring prospect to young bachelors. But with an eye to imminent matrimony John [Anderson] eschewed the fleshpots of the East." See J. W. Wheeler-Bennett, *John Anderson, Viscount Waverley* (London, 1962), p. 19.

55. There are discrepancies in the reported number of Indian members of the ICS. Woodruff, *The Guardians*, p. 363, reports sixty in 1909 and seventy-eight in 1919. These figures were, respectively, 5 per cent and 6 per cent of the total ICS strength for those years. Singh, *op. cit.*, p. 74, reports sixty-five in 1909, and Sir Edward A. H. Blunt, *The I.C.S.: The Indian Civil Service* (London, 1937), p. 52, reports sixty-three in 1915. The Islington Commission Report lists a total strength of 1,371 members of the ICS on April 1, 1913. Of these, 1,305 were Europeans, three Eurasians, forty-one Hindus, six Parsis, nine Muslims, and seven Indian Christians. Excluding Eurasians and Indian Christians, this gives a total of sixty-three Indian members (4.5 per cent of the total strength) (Islington Commission Report, Appendix VII, p. 511). The proportion of Indian members steadily increased so that at independence in 1947, 48 per cent of the total strength of 1,157 were Indian. See Ralph Braibanti, "Public Bureaucracy and Judiciary in Pakistan," in Joseph LaPalombara (ed.), *Bureaucracy and Political Development* (Princeton, N. J., 1963), p. 365, for distribution of British, Hindu (and other), and Muslim ICS officers by province.

treated me as an equal is an Irishman."[56] Many Indians chose to enter the "judgee" where they were relatively aloof from the trammels of British higher officialdom.

During World War I, British entry into the ICS came to a stop. After 1918 many senior officials who had been retained in the service due for retirement and a massive new recruitment was needed. Yet the introduction of dyarchy, followed by the distressing upheavals of Amritsar in 1918 and Gandhi's first civil disobedience campaign, presented a new picture of India to the interested British candidate. There was no longer security and unchallenged dominion, but uncertainty and civil strife. All this combined to create in the ICS a condition characterized by one of its members as "dry rot."[57] During the period 1918–1923, 150 British candidates, most of whom were veterans of World War I, were selected by nomination. This was the first departure from competitive entry for almost sixty years. The regular examination was resumed, but British university candidates were few and of uneven quality: in 1921, three were chosen by competition; in 1922, six; and in 1923, seven. Also during the early 1920's, some senior civilians claimed that the famous covenant between the secretary of state and the civilian had been breached by the introduction of dyarchy, so that there was no longer absolute security of tenure. Accordingly, the right to retire prematurely on a pension proportionate to length of service was claimed and was accepted.[58] Under these provisions, about 350 senior British officials retired prematurely in the 1920's.

Meanwhile, one of the principal points of contention for Indians had been quietly conceded after seventy years of bitter opposition. In 1922, the Civil Service commissioners, responsible for holding all British public service examinations, supervised the holding of the ICS examination in Allahabad. Thus, the principle

56. Joseph Chailley, *Administrative Problems of British India* (London, 1910), p. 193.

57. *Report of the Royal Commission on the Superior Civil Services in India,* Cmd. 2128 (1924), p. 181. Hereinafter cited as the Lee Commission Report.

58. The analysis here is expanded in Hugh Tinker, "New Lamps for Old" (a review article of Kenneth Younger's *The Public Service in the New States*), *International Affairs*, XXXVI (1960), 489–494.

of simultaneous examinations was at last accepted. Whereas candidates who passed the London examination were required to spend one probationary year at Oxford, Cambridge, or London universities, the Allahabad entrants were required to spend two years at a British university.[59]

It was against this background that another royal commission, under the chairmanship of Lord Lee of Fareham, was asked to make recommendations on the future of the services in India.[60] Lord Lee and his colleagues, four of whom were British and four Indian, recommended that the all-India services, concerned with subjects now wholly transferred to ministerial control under dyarchy, should no longer be recruited on an all-India basis, and that the British entry should be restricted to persons engaged by the provinces on short-term contracts.[61] The only all-India services in which a British element should continue as a permanent feature were the ICS, the Indian Police, and the Indian Medical Service. The latter was included because it provided a war reserve of medical officers for the Indian army.

With regard to the ICS, the Lee Commission proposed that future direct recruitment by competition should be on a basis of parity between British and Indian entry. Although this was intended to accelerate Indianization, this proposal in a sense revived the concept of a racial quota. The Lee Commission also proposed that 20 per cent of the superior posts should be filled by the appointment of provincial service officers to "listed posts." The effect of these dual proposals, it was calculated, would be to make the ICS half-Indian and half-British by 1939. Thereafter, the British component would wither away, but no terminal date was set for complete Indianization.

The Indian Police Service had lagged behind the ICS in Indianization. Indeed, there had long been a definite restriction

59. As ICS men took their seniority in the service from the first forenoon in which they actually began duty, this gave the London entrant a year's head start.

60. Complete citation to the Lee Commission Report can be found above, n. 57.

61. The services for which all-India (and British) recruitment ceased after 1924 were Indian Forest Service, Indian Service of Engineers (except for the Irrigation Branch), Indian Educational Service, Indian Agricultural Service, and Indian Veterinary Service.

upon entry to British (i.e., United Kingdom) candidates. The Lee Commission's recommendation of future entry on a basis of five British to three Indian was calculated to achieve parity by 1949.

These and other recommendations by the Lee Commission were accepted in full by the secretary of state. The procedure for appointing provincial service officers to the ICS by the "listed posts" formula anticipated the method whereby independent India made up the strength of the Indian Administrative Service after 1947. The effect of the change may be illustrated from one province. Previously in the United Provinces all forty-eight district officers had been included among the superior reserved posts, although twenty-one district and sessions judges had been drawn from the provincial judicial service. Henceforward, fifteen district officers were provincial Civil Service men holding ICS posts and promoted to the ICS pay scale, while an additional nine of the district judges were drawn from the United Provinces judicial service and were brought into the ICS pay scale. Another important innovation was the creation of a Public Service Commission for India. The 1919 Government of India Act had authorized the establishment of such a body; the Lee Commission recommended that this provision now be implemented; and in 1926 it came into being. In 1928 the Public Service Commission (India) held the ICS examination at Delhi on behalf of the (British) Civil Service Commission. Renamed the Federal Public Service Commission in 1937, this body now took over responsibility for recruitment to the all-India services for which entry was by examination.[62]

The numbers of British and Indians in the ICS or holding ICS posts were, in 1929, 894 British and 367 Indians; by 1939 the figures were 759 British and 625 Indians. Because professional opportunities, both in Britain and in India, were severely limited from about 1929 with the onset of the depression, competition among able young university graduates was again as intense during the 1930's as it had been in the great days of the 1880's and 1890's. The strikingly high quality of entrants during this

62. See the Hayes Report, pp. 143 ff.

decade was a factor of some significance in viewing the impressive performance of India's top-level administrators of the 1960's, who entered service during this period. Entry on the "parity" basis continued until 1939. After the outbreak of World War II, examinations for the Home Civil Service were suspended, but the ICS examination was held in London and in India until 1943. A sizable number of Indians entered the service up to 1943. Thereafter, all vacancies were reserved for war-service candidates, of whom a number were selected by the new, so-called country house examination.[63] In 1947, independent India's first competition for the new Indian Administrative Service (IAS), which replaced the ICS, was held by the Federal Public Service Commission.

During the first twenty years of the Congress, a considerable proportion of its endeavors were devoted toward opening up the ICS to Indians. Even up to the years just before World War I, Indian nationalists regarded a career in the ICS as a legitimate and indeed an honorable field of service. India's first president, Rajendra Prasad, relates in his autobiography that he "began to be obsessed by a new idea: to go to England somehow and pass the I.C.S. examination," but family circumstances closed the door.[64] Subhas Chandra Bose sat for the examination and actually spent a year as a probationer before failure in the riding test led to his rejection and so launched him on a career of violent revolt against British rule.[65] Yet even from the early days of Indian nationalism there was a conviction among the Indian leaders that British officialdom in India was the real barrier to the attainment of India's legitimate aspirations to become a self-governing

63. Early in 1945 the present writer took part in an examination by a board at Dehra Dun. The examination comprised physical tests, tests of mental agility, intellectual exercises, and "situation" tests which were supposedly designed to assess powers of decision. The proceedings ended with interviews by a psychiatrist and a distinguished member of the ICS. The writer was then appointed to a temporary cadre of "Civil Administrative Officers" and took over a post from an ICS officer. In 1946 he again went through a "country house" examination in England and was appointed to the ICS, being almost the last entrant into the service. Because of the decision to advance the date of independence he did not, in fact, return to India.

64. *Autobiography* (Bombay, 1957), p. 52.

65. The riding test still forms part of the training of the IAS probationer, though horses are rarely used in the districts today.

community within the British Empire. So long as the moderates retained control, the Congress tactics were to appeal to the English people over the barrier of the Government of India.

Because the early Indian nationalists were only claiming their rights as British subjects, and because so many of them were steeped in the English common law tradition, they concentrated their attack on the Government of India on the issue of the separation of the judiciary from the executive. The new Indian middle class took to the law above every other profession.[66] The first Indian to be called to the bar was G. M. Tagore (1862); the first Indian judge to sit on the High Court was Sambu Nath Pandit (1863–1867). The Congress was virtually created by lawyers. The first Congress president, W. C. Bonnerjea, was one of the four Indians who practiced in the old Supreme Court at Calcutta. Among the delegates to annual sessions of the Congress from 1892 to 1909, 40 per cent were members of the legal profession. It was not surprising, therefore, that the Congress devoted so much energy to attempting to abolish the conjunction of executive and magisterial power in the person of the district officer.[67] Resolution after resolution was devoted to this purpose. In 1898 a memorial in favor of separation was signed by a number of distinguished retired civilians. Finally, in 1908, as an experiment, collectors and their assistants were disassociated from criminal case work in Bengal and East Bengal, though they retained police and preventative powers.[68] This experiment was not extended, and when the question was reviewed by the Simon Commission, no recommendation for further change was made.[69]

However, by this time Indian nationalism had passed beyond the reform of the administration and was concerned only with

66. For an account of the mushroom growth of the legal fraternity, see B. B. Misra, *The Indian Middle Classes* (London, 1961), esp. pp. 324–332.

67. See Minute of Dissent by Abdur Rahim in Islington Commission Report, I, 394–488, esp. 444–452. In this Minute, the text of the Memorial to the secretary of state for India, dated July, 1899, by Lord Hobhouse and others is included. The Memorial refers to resolutions passed by the Congress each year from 1886 to 1896 on the question of separation of executive and judicial powers, and quotes a portion of the 1893 resolution (p. 450). For a brief account of these resolutions, see B. Pattabhai Sitaramayya, *The History of the Indian National Congress* (Bombay, 1935), I, 35–36.

68. See Chailley, *op. cit.*, pp. 442–455.

69. Simon Commission Report, I, 288–289.

condemning the "Satanic Government." Nehru, for example, in his autobiography expresses a certain grudging admiration for the ICS, but he concludes: "I am quite sure that no new order can be built up in India so long as the spirit of the I.C.S. pervades our administration and our public services. That spirit of authoritarianism . . . cannot co-exist with freedom. . . . Therefore it seems to be essential that the I.C.S. and similar services must disappear completely, as such, before we can start real work on a new order."[70] This mistrust of the ICS—embracing the Indian members of the service, which included some members of the Nehru family—became general among the Congress leaders. The only major politician to resist this mistrust was Sardar Patel, who was himself an administrator rather than an ideologue or demagogue. This division between the politicians and the administrators continues in independent India. The senior administrator is vulnerable and becomes the scapegoat whenever one is required. An instance of this trend was the scalping after the Life Insurance Corporation scandal.[71] And yet, by a curious paradox, the Nehru policy of centralized planning and control has made the administrators more numerous, more powerful, with more wide-reaching responsibilities than was the case in British times.[72]

IV. The Civil Service in Burma

For a long time, the administration of Burma drew upon Bengal and the Straits Settlements for its personnel: as late as 1857, the resident councilor, Malacca, was transferred as commis-

70. Jawaharlal Nehru, *An Autobiography* (London, 1936; new ed. 1953), p. 445.
71. A forthright account of this incident is given by Taya Zinkin, *Reporting India* (London, 1962), pp. 126–147. Mrs. Zinkin calls the scandal "the Mundhra Affair," after Haridas Mundhra, the owner of a group of firms in which the Life Insurance Corporation had purchased £1 million worth of shares. This affair, she says, "marks a turning point in India's administrative history" because it revealed the dangers of untrammeled power wielded by administrators and because the subsequent inquiries "damaged the relationship between Ministers and civil servants and between civil servants themselves." For further discussion, see Potter's chapter (Chapter 4) in this volume, pp. 173 ff.
72. See, for example, Government of India, *Third Five Year Plan* (New Delhi, 1961), which states: "It is indeed inevitable that each Plan should not only lead to substantial increase in the numbers [of public service employees] needed, but should also place challenging burdens and responsibilities on the administrative as well as technical services. Thus, over the past decade, the authorised strength of the Indian Administrative Service has risen from about 1,200 to well over 2,000."

sioner of Moulmein. Military civilians, such as the scholarly Sir Arthur Phayre, played a leading part in building the foundations of British rule.[73] The infrastructure of administration drew heavily upon the minority peoples, the Mons and Arakanese. For example, Maung Tawle was a Mon who was Myowun, or governor, of Dallah under the Burmese kings; he threw in his lot with the British and fled to Moulmein in 1827. Thereafter, he became a sitke, or judge. His descendants included a member of the Governor's Council in the 1920's.

After the annexation of Upper Burma in 1886, expansion of the administration became necessary. Young civilians and army officers were encouraged to transfer to Burma, but in addition uncovenanted Englishmen had to be taken into the administration. One such was J. G. Scott, who had been journalist and schoolmaster in Burma. He now became assistant to Ney Elias (an ICS man who had explored the borders of Tibet) in pacifying the Shan States. Another was W. A. Hertz, who became deputy commissioner of Myitkyina, with his brother as his superintendent of police. These men, together with the ICS and military component (one-third of the total), formed the Burma Commission. So far as the ICS was concerned, Burma came at the bottom of the list in terms of attractiveness. Those who came out at the top of the ICS exam could expect, if they wished, to be posted to the United Provinces or the Punjab, the two provinces from which the future governors and members of council were most frequently drawn. Other provinces were rated in descending order, with Bihar and Bengal fairly low on the list and Burma at the bottom.[74] Of course, there were men of high quality in the Burma Commission.[75] But there were also persons who com-

73. See Hugh Tinker, "Arthur Phayre and Henry Yule: Two Soldier-Administrator Historians," in D. G. E. Hall (ed.), *Historians of South-East Asia* (London, 1961), pp. 467–478.

74. This is illustrated by the autobiography of Maurice Collis, *The Journey Outward* (London, 1952). He reveals that after leaving Oxford he went to a London crammer and sat for the ICS examination. He was not successful, but he topped the list of failures. One of those chosen decided to withdraw, so Collis was taken. However, in fairness, it should be added that Collis had gained first-class honors at Oxford and had been considered for an All Souls Fellowship.

75. As one example of a man who never rose higher than divisional commissioner: J. A. Stewart. He gained the highest honors as a classical scholar at a Scottish university, and after a most humane career in Burma he became professor of Burmese in the University of London and the originator of Southeast Asian studies in the university.

manded a mechanical ability to attain a given standard, but who lacked the vital spark. The constitutional and political development of modern Burma was partially marred by such disparity in high-level competence.

There was no systematic evolution of a provincial civil service in Burma. This was because until 1920 there was no university in Burma to create a middle class. Such Burmans as rose toward the top in the Civil Service were mainly the scions of those official families who had formed the court of the Burmese kings. For example, Po Hla was descended from a myosa (town-governor) of Henzada. Po Hla started as a clerk in the office of a Divisional Commissioner; after a few years became a myook, or township officer (equivalent to a tehsildar); and about 1918 he became a deputy commissioner, one of the two or three Burmese district officers at that time.[76]

With the establishment of the University of Rangoon in 1920, a source for the recruitment of a provincial service existed. During the 1920's a few young Burmans were given places in the ICS by nomination. The first place went to Tin Tut, son of a Burmese deputy commissioner, who had been educated at an English boarding school and at Cambridge. Only one Burman was ever successful in gaining a place in the ICS by the open door of competition: Kyaw Min, member of a wealthy Arakanese banking family, who had been educated in England.

When the dyarchical system was applied to Burma two years later than in India, almost half the area of the country was excluded from the new reformed Constitution and continued under direct governor's rule. For these excluded areas (the Shan States, and the Kachin, Chin, and Karen hills) a Burma Frontier Service was constituted in December, 1922. Because the Burma Civil Service operated only in the plains, and the Frontier Service operated only in the hills, a sense of difference, and indeed of division, was fostered. This was to produce evil political consequences.

76. Po Hla was made Commander of the Indian Empire and deputy president of the Senate in 1939. His son, Dr. U Ba U, became chief justice and then second president of the Union of Burma.

Finally, with the separation of Burma from India in 1937, a substitute for the ICS had to be produced. In its place came the Burma Civil Service, Class I, or BCS (I); the provincial service became the Burma Civil Service, Class II BCS—(II). The process of Burmanization was more complicated than that of Indianization. There was the same problem of the replacement of the British element, but there was the further problem of the plural society in which non-Burmese Asians were in government employment. This situation arose partly from the lateness of the Burmese in absorbing Western higher education (as late as 1937, out of 138 students graduating from Rangoon University, only sixty were Burmese). It was also partly due to the alienation of the Burmese from the minority peoples in Burma. Thus, in 1940 in the BCS (I), out of a total strength of 162 officers, Burmans numbered sixty-two, Anglo-Burmans three, Indians two, and British ninety-five. In the BCS (II), out of a total of 221 officers, 207 were Burmans and fourteen Anglo-Burmans. In the much smaller Burma Frontier Service with a strength of sixty, Burmese numbered less than one-fifth; the remainder were Karens, Shans, and other hill peoples, including a high proportion of Christians and some Anglo-Burmans.

When the Japanese invaded Burma, most of the British and Indian officials followed their orders to accompany the retreating army. By June, 1942, only the extreme north, the Chin hills, and a small part of Arakan was still under British rule. The great majority of Burmese officials remained at their posts or retired to their villages. The Japanese, and then the Japanese-sponsored Ba Maw government, appointed these officials as commissioners and deputy commissioners and retained the British structure of government. From the British BCS men in India and the personnel of trading companies, a Civil Affairs Service (Burma), or CASB, was formed to provide a framework of military government.[77] By early 1945, the CASB was responsible for the whole administration of Burma, with the exception of the extreme eastern border. The Burmese officials who had stayed behind

77. See F. S. V. Donnison, *British Military Administration in the Far East* (London, 1956). See also Guyot's chapter (Chapter 6) in this volume.

were taken into the administration, but not always at the same level of seniority they had enjoyed from 1942–1945, and only after a security clearance which in some cases left bitterness behind.

Postwar recruitment for the BCS (I) drew upon war-service candidates, as in India, and a number of former military officers were selected. Because the Burmese elite, in general, had not rallied to the Allied cause, most of the non-British officers selected were Karens, Kachins, or other minority peoples.

The chief administrator of CASB, Major General Hubert Rance, by a queer twist of circumstances returned later as civil governor, with a virtual mandate to transfer power to Aung San and the Thakins (now called the Anti-Fascist Freedom League). The new leaders made it clear that they intended to force a break with the past. All British officials came under immediate notice of dismissal. Most of the Indians, who were prominent in the technical, medical, and education services, were also offered impossible terms and so left the service. The Burma Frontier Service was summarily brought to an end. Whereas in India and Pakistan the senior civil servants provided the main element of continuity in the transfer of power, in Burma there was an almost complete break with the past.[78]

V. The Civil Service in Ceylon

Although the British administration in Ceylon really began with a Madras civilian, Robert Andrews, his methods were so disastrous that within a short while a revolt broke out among the Sinhalese. Andrews was withdrawn and Ceylon became a Crown Colony.

To assist Frederick North, the first governor, eight young men were sent out from England in 1798, and twenty-four more in 1801. Recruited at the ages of fifteen to seventeen, these youths

78. For the role of the Civil Service in Burma today, see Hugh Tinker, *The Union of Burma: A Study of the First Years of Independence* (3rd ed.; London, 1961), pp. 129–165.

retired on pension after twelve years' service. After the initial appointments from England, all places were to be filled by promotions within the service—usually on the basis of seniority. Most of these civil servants retired as soon as they became pensionable. Only a handful bothered to learn Sinhalese; indeed, the only scholar of this group was Sir John D'Oyly.[79]

After the conquest of the hill kingdom of Kandy, military civilians were largely employed in its administration, although this was contrary to the orders of the Colonial Office. Sir Edward Barnes, governor in the 1820's, and a former general, actually proposed that the Ceylon Civil Service be abolished and all existing positions in Ceylon be filled by military officers at about half the existing rates of pay. He pointed out that eight of the twelve British officials in the Kandyan Provinces were military men and that the system worked well. The Colonial Office was not impressed. Governor Barnes in 1822 also laid down the restriction that no civil servant would be promoted beyond the grade of assistant until he had "attained a tolerable proficiency" in Tamil or Sinhalese.

The infrastructure of administration was staffed mainly by the Burghers, or persons of Eurasian descent. The situation came under review in the 1830's by means of the Commission of Inquiry to the Eastern Colonies, usually known from the names of its two principal members as the Colebrooke-Cameron Commission. Their aims were economy and social justice. For both these reasons, the wider employment of Ceylonese in the higher administration and in the courts was advocated. Measures were proposed to overcome the domination of the higher over the lower castes in district and village administration, as elsewhere. The key to progress was conceived to be the English language, and the commission proposed the establishment of a university college at Colombo. These proposals had a mixed reception. For example, Ceylon had to wait for its university college for another ninety years. On the other hand, the secretary of state agreed and said: "The civil situations in the island will henceforth be open to

79. See Collins' chapter (Chapter 7) in this volume, esp. n. 1 and p. 450.

all classes of the native community." Also, salaries in the higher administration were reduced, the over-all reduction being from £43,976 to £24,985. Pensions were abolished. The effect of these changes was to lower the morale of the British civil servants. Sir Emmerson Tennent, who came from Whitehall to be colonial secretary from 1846 to 1851, compared the Civil Service of Ceylon most unfavorably with that of India. It failed, he suggested, because of its "circumscribed area" of opportunity: "Like the miniature oak which the Chinese can raise in a flower pot, the dwarfed plant had every characteristic of the great tree, except its strength and solidity."[80] Against this judgment should be set the hostility which grew up between Tennent and the Civil Service. Alleging that he ran away from a crowd in Galle, they christened him Sir Timorsome Emmit.

Colebrooke's wish to see Ceylonese taken into the higher Civil Service was partially realized. The first two Ceylonese members of the Ceylon Civil Service were chosen by nomination in 1844, twenty years before the first Indian gained entry into the covenanted service. The first Ceylonese to be nominated by the governor was Simon Casie Chitty (a member of the Hindu chettyar caste). The other was Frederick de Livera, a mudaliyar who became district judge of Matara until his death in 1854. Livera was educated in Calcutta; after 1857 many of the Tamils who entered service were educated at Madras University. The best-remembered of these Tamil civilians was Sir Ponnambalam Arunachalam, later a political leader. Their advantage in being able to obtain a university education among their own language group partly accounted for their early ascendancy in the higher administration. A few Indians, and two West Indians were also appointed to the Ceylon Civil Service.

Because of their relatively meager salaries, many officials, including the government agents, took to growing coffee and acquired extensive plantations. Many devoted more attention to their plantations than to their official duties. Most of these abuses were brought to an end when in 1845 the secretary of state forbade the acquisition of plantations by officials, at the same time restoring adequate salaries. From 1845, candidates for

80. Sir J. E. Tennent, *Ceylon* (London, 1859), I, 173.

Ceylon were required to be from sixteen to twenty-two years of age and to pass the Haileybury entrance examination, while from 1856 the open competitive examination instituted by the Macaulay Committee was applied to Ceylon. No such examination was required of the candidates nominated by the governor; these numbered one-half of the entry and included domiciled Europeans, Burghers, and Ceylonese. From 1863 these governor's candidates were required to sit for a local test on "general attainments," and from 1870 they had to sit for the same examination in Colombo as did the candidates in London. From 1880 the dual entry was abolished: all candidates were required to compete in open competition in London. The purpose of this change was, explicitly, to compel all candidates to obtain their education in England. To some extent, the injustice of this requirement was palliated by the award from 1870 of Queen's Scholarships for study in British universities.[81] The age limits for the examination were fixed in 1878 at twenty-one to twenty-four years; these limits were not so stringent as those prevailing for young Indians.

Because of these changes to their disadvantage, the numbers of Ceylonese in the Civil Service actually declined. An analysis made in 1868 showed that throughout the public services in Ceylon there were 1,084 appointments, of which 894 were held by natives of Ceylon. In the Civil Service proper, there were seventy-four British and ten Ceylonese and Burghers. By 1881 the Civil Service was composed of eighty-four British and seven Ceylonese and Burghers. This situation was met by a device similar to that employed in India: a "local division" was created in 1891, with supposedly similar prospects but undeniably inferior status.[82]

81. See Collins' chapter in this volume and Tennent, *op. cit.*, chap. vi, for accounts of the evolution of the Ceylon Civil Service. The first students from Ceylon to be educated in England were the sons of a mudaliyar, and they entered Trinity Hall, Cambridge, in 1812, almost half a century before the pioneer Indian students came to England.

82. The Ceylon Civil Service (CCS) was divided into five classes. Class I comprised the government agents and heads of non-technical departments. Classes II and III included assistant government agents, district judges, municipal police magistrates, and the principal assistants in the secretariat. Officers of the "local division" seldom rose beyond Class III. The first Ceylonese was appointed assistant government agent in charge of a district in 1923. This was C. L. Wickremasinghe, who in 1931 became the first Ceylonese government agent.

Toward the end of the century, the role of the Ceylon Civil Service became involved in a general review of colonial administration. In 1895, Joseph Chamberlain, a dynamic politician of industrial stock and radical views, was appointed as secretary of state for the colonies, a post usually reserved for a member of the aristocracy. He ordered a junior minister, Lord Selborne, to prepare a survey of the system of appointments in the colonial empire. Selborne's report showed that out of a total of 434 higher administrative officers, about one hundred were employed in the Eastern Cadet Services (Ceylon, Malaya, Hong Kong). The Eastern Cadet Services could not be drawn upon for selection of governors or colonial secretaries in Africa or the West Indies because the terms of service were more attractive in the East. Chamberlain sought for a means whereby a wider service might be created, and he studied the possibility of combining the colonial services with the ICS. Finally, it was decided to create a unified Colonial Service, to be recruited by examination as in the case of the Eastern Cadets and to be interchangeable between the various colonies. However, Chamberlain's scheme proved premature; a unified Colonial Service had to wait for another thirty years.[83]

While the dyarchy experiment in India was coming up against the fixed opposition of Gandhi, the nationalist movement in Ceylon was making its protest. There were considerable constitutional changes between 1920 and 1924, with repercussions on the Civil Service. As in India, there was a great reluctance on the part of senior civil servants to adjust themselves to the changed circumstances of ministerial government—a "legacy of discontent," it was called.[84] Following the Indian pattern, the right to retire on proportionate pension was granted to civil servants recruited in the former period of "absolute" rule. Also as in India, the "nationalization" of the Civil Service was accelerated. The

83. Selborne's report was not published, but a summary of his findings and Chamberlain's proposals is given by Sir Charles Jeffries, *The Colonial Empire and Its Civil Service* (Cambridge, 1938), pp. 8–14.

84. *Ceylon: Report of the Special Commission on the Constitution*, Cmd. 3131 (London; 1928), p. 127. Hereinafter cited as Donoughmore Report. See also Collins' chapter in this volume, p. 463, n. 21.

decision was made in 1919 that one-third of the service ought to be Ceylonese. From 1923, recruitment was on a basis of parity between British and Ceylonese.

The Donoughmore Commission (1927–1928) made proposals which resulted in a new Constitution in 1931 which transferred most of the internal affairs of the island to a Board of Ministers. With a greater sense of logic than was shown in India, it was recognized that this was the moment to cease British recruitment to the services. In 1931 this recruitment was halted, and although a few British candidates entered the Civil Service in 1935–1937, all entrants after 1937 were natives of Ceylon. From 1924, the entrance examination was again held in Colombo, simultaneously with the London examination. From 1932 the Colombo examination was restricted to candidates who were graduates. The London entry was closed with the outbreak of the war. During, and shortly after World War II, the CCS examination was controlled by the Civil Service Commission in Ceylon, with examiners mainly drawn from the Indian universities. This body was absorbed in 1947 into the Public Service Commission of Ceylon which had been established in 1931 on the recommendation of the Donoughmore Commission.

Before independence the Ceylon Civil Service had become very nearly an indigenous service, but already the shadow of communal tension was being cast. When the Soulbury Commission took evidence 1946–1947), they heard many complaints from the Ceylon Tamils about the threats to their position in the public services. Because of their educational advancement, the Tamils in 1938 had about twice the number of posts in the public services which they would have enjoyed on a basis of communal strength: 1,164 out of a total of six thousand pensionable posts. But the Sinhalese were rapidly increasing their representation; they were doing this by sharp practice, the Tamils alleged. The Soulbury Commission concluded that the real cause was the spread of education among the Sinhalese.

As in India, there was a certain amount of feeling against the CCS as the watchdogs of imperialism. The senior administrators were able to ally themselves skilfully with Don Senanayake and the United National party; but in the end they felt the whiplash of the more radical Sri Lanka Freedom party government.

VI. The Civil Service in Malaya

The Penang Civil Service began with an elaborate establishment befitting the fourth Presidency, but from 1816 the directors of the East India Company began to cut back the Penang establishment. Soon after, the rendition of Bencoolen to the Dutch added a further surplus of redundant officials to the Penang cadre. In consequence, between 1826 and 1845 recruitment was virtually at a standstill, as was promotion for the unhappy officials who idled out the long years in minor offices. Many devoted their main energies to commerce and plantation agriculture: Robert Ibbetson (governor, 1830–1833), for instance, possessed nutmeg plantations. Even when this practice was suppressed among the Civil Service, the company's medical officers and police continued to grow coconuts and coffees. Any Penang civilian with ambition strained his utmost to obtain a posting to India; those who remained were discontented or listless. Few took pains to acquire a deep knowledge of Asian languages. James Law knew Thai, and Governor Sir Samuel G. Bonham knew Chinese, while most officials were fluent in bazaar Malay. Even those who rose to the top had largely lost all vital spark during the years of waiting. E. A. Blundell came out as a writer in 1820. He was commissioner of Tenasserim in Burma from 1833 to 1843, and from 1848–1855 he was resident councilor at Malacca. When at last he became governor of the Straits from 1855 to 1861, he was content to do little.

Some military civilians were numbered among the Straits officials; the most outstanding was Lieutenant Colonel Henry Burney, who acquired a knowledge of Southeast Asian languages, negotiated a treaty with Siam in 1826, and was British resident at the Burmese court from 1830 to 1837.

After the transfer of the Straits Settlements to the Colonial Office, a conscious attempt was made to sever the Indian connection. New recruits came via the Eastern Cadetships and became members of the Straits Civil Service. Senior positions were filled from the Colonial Service. J. W. W. Birch, the first resident in Perak, had been a member of the Ceylon Civil Service from 1852 to 1870, and Hugh Low, his successor, had accompanied Raja Brooke to Sarawak as a botanist, subsequently spending twenty-nine years in Labuan and holding office as chief secretary and acting governor before going to Perak. As British activity in Malaya intensified, so British officials were required in greater numbers, and their recruitment was sometimes haphazard.[85] The first collector and magistrate at Kuala Pilah, Negri Sembilan, was Leo Cazalas, a clerk of works (i.e., public works overseer); his successor, R. N. Bland, was a Straits Settlements cadet; and Bland's successor, the Hon. Martin Lister, was a former planter.

Entry into the Straits Settlements Civil Service was via the London competitive examination, which was introduced in 1869; but appointments in the Malay States were filled by nomination until 1896, when the Federated Malay States cadets were also selected by means of the joint London examination. In 1932 separate recruitment to the Eastern Cadetships was terminated. Thenceforward, as part of the process of creating a unified Colonial Service, candidates for Malaya were appointed to the Colonial Administrative Service and were liable for transfer to other parts of the British Empire. In practice, however, this did not occur except at the higher levels. Because the examination system of entry had not prevailed in recruitment to the remainder of the Colonial Service, Malaya was required to fall into line. After 1932, candidates were appointed on the basis of their record at the university or in the field and by the selection of the Appointments Board of the Colonial Office. After appointment, successful candidates were required to spend a year at Oxford, Cambridge,

85. According to one account, a certain pioneer district officer was a former Royal Navy midshipman and settled disputes by holding cockfights. Another was an Italian of dubious morals. See Sir Richard Winstedt, *Malaya and Its History* (London, 1948), p. 88.

or London University, in the same manner as ICS probation-ers.[86]

The term "Malayan Civil Service" came into use early in the twentieth century, and the old name of Straits Settlements Civil Service was revived between the two world wars for a locally recruited administrative cadre (corresponding to the Provincial Service in India) for Singapore, Penang, and Malacca. Eurasians, particularly from the Portuguese community, and the long-resident Chinese families (the so-called Babas) were recruited, along with some Malays. A Malay Administrative Service was formed in 1910 to provide a middle-rank service for the Federated Malay States. Its members were recruited largely from the Malay aristocracy and could expect to attain the position of assistant district officer. By the late 1920's six Malays had been accepted into the Malayan Civil Service by selection from outstanding younger officials of the junior services; the total strength of the MCS was then about 250.[87]

Malayanization was not considered on a broad basis until the eve of independence. As late as 1956 there were only 122 Malayans in the MCS beside 222 British officers. Of the Malayans, only thirty came into the MCS before 1951.[88] Few candidates from the Malay community possessed a B.A. honors degree, the necessary entrance qualification; while those of Chinese blood, many of whom were properly qualified, were only accepted into the administrative service on a quota basis after 1953. By inter-communal agreement, the Chinese were thereafter permitted to take one vacancy in five. In consequence, the main

86. See Jeffries, *Colonial Empire and Its Civil Service,* esp. pp. 74, 128 ff. The argument against entry by examination gained force because "The Eastern Cadetship services took mainly those passing lowest in the [combined] civil service examinations": Robert Heussler, *Yesterday's Rulers; the Making of the British Colonial Service* (Syracuse, 1963), p. 66.

87. See C. W. Harrison, *Some Notes on the Government Services in British Malaya* (London, 1929), p. 65. One of the early entrants to the MCS was Raja Tun Uda Al-Haj bin Raja Muhammad. Born in 1894, he joined government service in 1910. He was promoted to the Malay Administrative Service in 1914 and appointed to the MCS in 1924. The Raja was Speaker of the Federal Legislative Council in 1955 and governor of Penang from 1957.

88. For example, the present deputy prime minister, Tun Abdul Razak, joined the Malay Administrative Service in 1939 at the age of seventeen. After World War II he came to Britain as a state scholar and was appointed to the MCS in 1949.

avenue of entry into the MCS was via the Malay Administrative Service. A few entrants were taken from the various state civil services (only sixteen before 1956).[89] Some were promoted from the Straits Civil Service. By 1956, only forty Malayans had entered the MCS direct from college. Thereafter, about twenty-five direct entrants were accepted each year: qualifications for entry were broadened to include candidates with first- or second-class honors in the bar final examination.[90]

VII. The Approach to Independence

Some of the issues relating to the Civil Service in the last days of imperial rule have already become apparent. We have seen that the need to transform the public service from an imperial to a national elite (the process known in these days as "-ization") was nowhere anticipated sufficiently early—although Ceylon came very near to attaining a wholly national bureaucracy before independence. Equally, however, it may be argued that nowhere in Southern Asia did Britain utterly fail to leave as part of the imperial legacy the nucleus of a capable national Civil Service. In Burma and Malaya, Britain came closer to leaving an inadequate apparatus than elsewhere. It has been suggested that in Burma the British did not really train an adequate cadre of responsible Burmese officials but were content to create a corps of administrative helots.[91] Such an argument overlooks the speed at which Burma was plucked out of the Middle Ages and thrust into the

89. Total numbers of state service officers on the eve of independence were about two hundred. Many state administrators were distant relatives of the rulers, distinguished by the honorific *tunku*, or *nik*, denoting descent from royalty in the male or female line. One of the best-known of the state officials was Dato Onn bin Ja'afar (1895–1962), a member of the Johore aristocracy, son of the Mentri Besar of Johore, and for thirty years a member of the Johore Civil Service, who himself became Mentri Besar. Dato Onn is mainly remembered, however, as the first president of the United Malay National Organization, successor to the Pan-Malayan Congress.

90. Federation of Malaya, *Report of the Committee on the Malayanisation of the Public Service* (Kuala Lumpur, 1956), pp. 38–39.

91. So argues Lucian Pye in *Politics, Personality, and Nation Building* (New Haven, 1962). "In sum," Pye says, "the Burmese were trained in the spirit of the clerk" (p. 216).

twentieth century. It also does not take account of the pressure exerted by politics and the politicians. In prewar Burma these factors introduced the solvent of wholesale corruption, and in postwar Burma they contributed to the denigration and collapse of the whole concept of an administrative elite.[92] Things were managed better in Malaya. Although the need to create a national bureaucracy was realized only on the threshold of the transfer of power, by the combination of a crash program of training for responsibility and a phased program of withdrawal of British officials, a most effective superior civil service was brought into being. But perhaps more important, the relationship between the ruling political party and the senior administrators in independent Malaya was exceptionally cordial and close. Both the prime minister and his deputy had been professional administrators, and giving loyal trust to their officials they received loyal service in return.

The clash between politicians and administrators is one of the most general features of the process of "decolonization." In some cases the main struggle came before, in some cases after, the formal transfer of power. British policy, although far from consistent, made a fairly general effort to provide a bridge between foreign "absolute" rule and national "popular" rule by a partial transfer of authority, both at the upper levels of power by some form of dyarchy, and at the lower levels by the gradual development of institutions of local self-government.

At the upper levels, senior officials dealt with the politicians on a footing of equality. As departmental heads, they represented their departments in the legislatures: the Donoughmore Report describes the colonial secretary in Ceylon as "in the position of a Minister in charge of some forty Departments of Government."[93] It was at this stage that the tension between politicians and officials became most acute. When political control was trans-

---

92. *Report of the Bribery and Corruption Committee* (Rangoon, 1941) gives many cases of corruption among lower- and middle-rank officials. The multitude of examples of corruption among legislators and ministers is indicated in the published report only by a large number of blank spaces where the original findings of the committee were omitted by ministerial order.
93. Donoughmore Report, p. 29.

ferred from the officials to the nationalist leaders (as happened in India at the provincial level in 1937), some of the tension disappeared. At this stage, the nationalist politicians revealed their underlying attitudes to government, whatever banner they had been marching under before. Some now emerged as essentially (in English eighteenth-century political parlance) men of business, men of affairs; such were Sardar Patel or C. Rajagopalachari in the Congress. Others remained men of an idea: the idea of Freedom. The men of affairs naturally made common cause with the professional administrators; the men of an idea persisted in regarding the administrators as enemies. This cleavage among the politicians persisted long after independence.

At the level of local government, there was not even this modified rapprochement between official and non-official. Part of the cause for this lies in the essential differences between the actual operation of local government, as compared to government at higher levels. At the higher levels there is a clear differentiation of function between creating and implementing policy. We have seen that tension existed between nationalists and officials, when at the dyarchy stage the senior official subsumed the policy-making function into his executive function. When politicians were recognized as policy-makers, then their resentment of the senior official largely disappeared. Tension persisted only where it was suspected that the official was using his position to obstruct the politician's purpose. But in local government it is much more difficult to separate policy-making and executive action into two different compartments.[94] In India and in most emergent countries immediately before independence, administrators of the superior government in the field still held reserve powers, which gave them the negative power to check abuses, though not the positive power to stimulate action. The actual officials of the local authorities were petty functionaries who possessed no authority

94. In the United States there are examples where city bosses have manipulated city government for political purposes, turning the professional administrators into their puppets. The reformers have often countered by installing a city manager, thus negating the concept of local self-government. For a discussion of these problems, see the present writer's "Local Government in Developing Countries," *Journal of Local Administration Overseas*, II (1963), 170–174.

other than that allowed them by their elected bosses. Thus, politicians in the local authorities in many cases exercised power without a sense of responsibility. Ceylon provides the only example of a country where some solution was found for the dilemma of handing over power from the superior official to the local politicians without giving the latter a license to meddle in routine administration.

Municipalities in Ceylon have a long history, originating in Colombo, Galle, and Kandy in 1865. From 1920 a much wider scheme of local self-government began, with the formation of urban district councils for suburban and semi-rural areas. The Donoughmore Commission reported that the achievements in the first years of these local authorities had not come up to expectations. Among other reforms, they urged the need "To provide in Colombo a cadre of technical experts, the members of which would be available on loan at the demand of any local board or council which had need of them."[95] This suggestion was not immediately implemented, but gradually a unified local government service came into being, to which belong all employees of local authorities except those paid on a daily basis. The service came to number about 7,500 persons. A Local Government Service Commission was established in December, 1945, and its first main task was to draw up schedules of grades, salary scales, and terms of service for all local employees. This involved replacing some four hundred different grades by one unified form. The commission recruits to the clerical grade by examination. Appointments to scheduled posts (with salaries over Rs. 1,200) are made by the commission by advertisement and interview; posts may be filled by competitive selection. "The Commission claims that as a result of centralised recruitment, and its insistence on high qualifications, recruits are now the equals of those . . . in central government service. . . . The value of the Commission in discipline cases is that these are removed from the elected members if an authority and handled by a body with no local interests."[96] The Ceylon pattern provides a model to neigh-

95. Donoughmore Report, chap. vii, "Local Administration," esp. p. 115.
96. Hayes Report, pp. 197–198.

boring countries for the creation of genuine local self-government while still insuring recognized standards of bureaucratic efficiency.

Ceylon was also unique in Southern Asia in that it made the transfer into independence with nothing more serious than a passing difference over details between the nationalist leaders and the imperial power.[97] Every other country witnessed a final period of acute bitterness, and indeed of violence, before independence was realized. The "August Disturbances" of 1942 for the areas within the Gangetic plain were virtually a civil war, with all the extra horror and cruelty which civil war always brings. The administration of eastern United Provinces was stretched to the limit; the administration of Bihar almost entirely collapsed. When Congress was permitted to resume activity in 1945, one of its first measures was the preparation of a black list of the names of those civil servants and police officers, British and Indian, who were alleged to have dealt severely with the Congress mobs in 1942. A clear warning was served that any official desirous of promotion under a nationalist government must in future abstain from such action. Then, in 1946 and 1947 there followed the chain of murder and arson which ended in the great Punjab killings. Officials had to make decisions, in isolation, with no expectation of support from above.[98] Not surprisingly, most decided to leave the service at the earliest possible moment. This trend was accelerated by the excellent conditions which the secretary of state's services were able to negotiate. It will be remembered that in the 1920's officers in the ICS and subse-

97. Jeffries shows that a leading part in winning advantageous conditions for independence in Ceylon was actually played by a senior official, the financial secretary, Sir Oliver Goonetilleke, who became the emissary of the nationalist politicians. Sir Oliver went on to become governor general of Ceylon from 1954 to 1962 and its preserver during the emergency of 1958. Jeffries, *Transfer of Power*, pp. 60–64.

98. It is salutary to turn to the debates of the Indian Constituent Assembly for the summer of 1947 and read the statements of politicians, abusing the civil servants and accusing them of provoking the very atrocities which they—the politicians—had helped to bring about by their irresponsible mob oratory. Later, Sardar Patel was to say of this period that "if, during the last two or three years, most of the members of the services had not behaved patriotically and with loyalty, the Union would have collapsed." Government of India, *Constituent Assembly Debates*, X (October 10, 1949), 50.

quently the Ceylon Civil Service were given the option to retire, under the changed constitutional conditions, on proportionate pension. It will also be recalled that candidates for the ICS were selected from veterans of World War II. It was clearly impossible under the conditions of 1945–1946 to guarantee a life career to these new men; and so they were accepted on terms which envisaged possible premature termination of service at the time of independence. These terms provided for the payment of compensation for loss of career: retirement after the first few years' service yielded only a small sum, but this scale rose like a fever patient's graph until between ages forty and forty-five it reached a maximum,[99] and then fell rapidly until the official who retired with full service would draw only his normal pension. The ICS members who had entered service before the war now advanced a claim to the benefit of both these schemes: proportionate pension and lump-sum payment in compensation. Both the British government and the successor states were ready to agree. Having gained such advantageous terms for retirement, and having become sickened at the prospect of continuing service under the same politicians who had heaped abuse on them, most ICS men chose to leave India at or soon after the transfer of power. The Indian members of the ICS had also received compensation, but (by agreement) it was on less generous terms since their expectations of continuing service and, indeed, of rapid promotion were not prejudiced by the advent of independence. Most of these Indian ICS men now opted to serve either the new India, or Pakistan, although a few of the senior Indians also decided to retire prematurely.

Although Ceylon achieved independence by consent, and British members of the CCS were invited to stay in service, the attractions of the terms of compensation which almost automatically followed the ICS pattern led most of the small surviving band of British officials to retire. Burma arrived at independence through a struggle which outdid that of India in bitterness. After

99. The justification was that at this age men had given India almost twenty years of service, yet they were still young enough to need a second career at a time of life when they would find difficulty in obtaining suitable employment.

the experience of a "scorched earth" invasion, Burma was the scene of the most widespread and bitter fighting in World War II between the Japanese and the Allies before final liberation. Then came a struggle between the British and the forces of Aung San which almost reached the point of a full-scale guerrilla war. British and other foreign civil servants received little encouragement to continue in service from the new nationalist government, and the combination of adverse circumstances precipitated a withdrawal of the British officials. Other than a remnant in the Frontier Service, most had left a full year before independence. The Frontier Service officials also departed in 1948. The scene was set for administrative chaos.

Malaya's independence came about under very different circumstances. The British government actually advanced the date of the transfer of power two years ahead of the target fixed by the leaders of the majority Alliance party. The utmost cordiality surrounded the British departure. Nevertheless, British officials in Malaya had undergone enormous tensions. The senior men had undergone the horrors of three and a half years in Japanese prison camps. All officials, senior and junior, had experienced the strain of twelve years of guerrilla war, which went under the euphemism of the Emergency.[100] Moreover, the same excellent compensation terms as for the ICS were offered. In fact, the terms were rather better, and many MCS men sought the first opportunity of leaving Malaya. Of the 1,579 British officials of all grades who were serving Malaya on the eve of independence (August, 1957), only 722 remained in service by April, 1959.

The Indian precedent set the pattern of British decolonization. Whereas in the African states of the former French Union a great majority of the French officials still remain at their old posts despite the formal dissolution of the old ties with France, in the former British colonies in Africa independence has entailed the exodus of all but a handful of British officials. In West Africa, a nucleus of African administrators stood ready to take over; but, to

100. One of the by-products of the Emergency was the recruitment of two women into the MCS for work in the secretariat to release men for field operations. One of these unique pioneers in British imperial administration, Dr. Mary Turnbull, stayed on to teach in the University of Malaya.

quote a well-qualified observer, "notoriously, none of the East and Central African territories has even a skeleton body of African trainees ready and able to take over from those now in charge."[101] But the British exodus has been almost complete. Even when a moderate leader such as President Julius Nyerere wishes to retain British officers in the knowledge that there are no competent Africans to replace them, his hand is forced by the extremists and the British have to go.

Time alone will show whether the gradual French method or the sudden British method of withdrawal has served best to stimulate the growth of a competent and responsible national bureaucracy. Experience in Southern Asia has demonstrated that where the imperial tradition of service has been casually discarded (as in Burma), there is little to take its place. Other new nations in Southern Asia have been almost too careful to maintain the form of British administrative practice with its hierarchy and precedent. It is doubtful whether in any of the former British colonies in Africa any prolonged effort will be made to keep up the British pattern. In Southern Asia, the British imperial administrative legacy is impressive and substantial; it seems highly unlikely that the same conclusion can be predicted in Africa.[102]

101. Letter to *The Times,* June 3, 1960, from W. M. Macmillan.
102. Written in 1963.

3

Recruitment and Training of British Civil Servants in India, 1600–1860*

Bernard S. Cohn

The first British contacts with India were in the last decades of the sixteenth century when a few merchant adventurers, interested in establishing trade connections, were successful in reaching India and in returning home. On December 31, 1600, the British Crown granted to a group of merchants a monopoly over the trade in Eastern Waters. Forming the East India Company, the merchants' first two expeditions took them to Sumatra, Java, and the Moluccas. One of the ships of the third expedition in 1607–1608, under William Hawkins, went to Surat, the most important Mughal port on the West Coast of India. Hawkins went overland to Agra to the Court of Jahangir to get permission for the company to trade in his domain.[1] For the first one hundred and fifty years thereafter the British had little direct interest in political development in India. Their servants were commercial agents. In the generation which spans Robert Clive's time in India (1744–1767), the company emerged as a predominant political power; and in the next forty years, down to the end of

* The research on which this chapter is based was carried out in 1962 at the India Office Library of the Commonwealth Relations Office, London, and was supported by grants from the Asian Studies Committee of the American Council of Learned Societies, the Social Science Research Council, and the Arts College of the University of Rochester. A fellowship from the Guggenheim Foundation provided the time necessary for the final writing of the chapter. I am grateful to Professors F. G. Bailey of the University of Sussex and Edward Shils of the University of Chicago for their comments and suggestions.

1. Sir William Foster, "The East India Company," chap. iv in H. H. Dodwell (ed.), *The Cambridge History of India* (Cambridge, 1929), V, 76–116.

Wellesley's governor generalship in 1805, a Civil Service was created to administer the company's expanding territory.

This chapter focuses on those who became civil servants and the ways in which they were trained. Although there is a large literature on nineteenth-century administration in India, it is either anecdotal in nature or largely summaries of the development of regulations under which the administration functioned. There is little systematic description or analysis of the Civil Service as such. A topic of such complexity can only be outlined in this chapter.

I. Civil Servants as Merchants, 1600–1740

William Hawkins, the first servant of the East India Company in India, appears to be typical of its earliest employees. He was a merchant who had extensive experience in the Levant trade, and his ability to speak Turkish was a key to his getting this important job.[2] By 1615 the company had four trading posts or factories in India employing thirty-two Europeans, of whom twenty-one were designated as factors, the name applied to the company's mercantile agents.[3] In 1647 the number of factories had grown to twenty-three and employed ninety men.[4] As with Hawkins, the social origins of the earliest owners and servants of the company were mercantile. When in 1617 the East India Company raised £1,600,000 from 954 individuals, the owners of the stock included 313 merchants, 214 tradesmen, twenty-five foreign merchants, fifteen dukes and earls, eighty-two knights, twenty-six doctors of divinity and medicine, thirteen "ladies of title," eighty "widows and virgins," and 248 others.[5] Thompson and Garratt, writing about the early company, stated: "A resolution was passed [by the owners] 'not to employ any gentlemen in any

2. *Ibid.*, p. 77.
3. John W. Kaye, *The Administration of the East India Company: A History of Indian Progress* (2nd ed.; London, 1853), p. 417.
4. Philip Woodruff, *The Men Who Ruled India: The Founders of Modern India* (New York, 1954), p. 55.
5. Sir George Birdwood, *Report on the Records* (London, 1891), p. 46.

place of charge.' "[6] In addition, according to Thompson and Garratt, the owners were allowed by the Crown to "sort their business with men of their own quality."[7] Many of the early factors, for example, Sir Edward Winter, Sir John Child, Justinian Offley, and Gregory Clement came from merchant families. Others such as William Finch "began life as the private servant of a cheapside merchant."[8] Others were recruited in India from crews of East Indian merchantships.[9]

In the middle of the seventeenth century the company's affairs in India were gaining in scope and complexity, and there emerged a recognition of varying levels of responsibility and seniority among the company's servants in India. "Assistants" or "writers" were responsible for routine work. Factors were of a more senior rank and responsibility. For a period in the mid-seventeenth century, "apprentices" in their teens were recruited, many of whom came from Christ's Hospital, an orphanage and charity school founded by Edward VI in an expropriated monastery of the Grey Friars.[10] In addition to orphans, the school educated children of Freemen of London who could not otherwise educate their children. Christ's Hospital appears to have been one of the few schools which offered instruction in commercial accounts, a prime skill for the company's servants. In 1694 the East India Company offered service as writers to ten youths from Christ's Hospital and in addition to their salaries agreed to pay their passage to India.[11] Even in the middle of the eighteenth century some of the youths going into company service received their commercial training at Christ's Hospital.[12]

Until the middle of the eighteenth century the company did not have civil servants but commercial agents in name and in fact.

6. Edward Thompson and G. T. Garratt, *Rise and Fulfillment of British Rule in India* (London, 1935), p. 6.
7. *Ibid.*
8. Sir Edward A. H. Blunt, *The I.C.S.: The Indian Civil Service* (London, 1937), p. 12.
9. Sir William Foster, *John Company* (London, 1926), p. 211.
10. On Christ's Hospital, see Edward C. Mack, *Public Schools and British Opinion: 1780–1860* (New York, 1939), p. 10, n. 3; also G. A. T. Allan, *Christ's Hospital* (London, 1937), p. 9.
11. Allan, *op. cit.*, p. 135.
12. Foster, *John Company*, pp. 221–222.

These agents spent their working time doing accounts, copying bills of lading and sale, arranging for the acquisition of country products for export to England, and in maintaining the company's warehouses in India. The factories were organized almost along collegiate or monastic lines with the senior merchant, or in the case of a Presidency town, the governor, acting as the head of the community. The younger servants' lives were almost completely governed by the rules of the settlement. There was a communal table, and attendance at Sunday services was compulsory. There were strict rules governing drinking and gambling.[13] Few of the English were married, and until the end of the seventeenth century those who were rarely had their wives with them.

In 1678, there were seventy-four Company servants in Madras, only six were married of which five had their wives with them. One of the wives was English, one Dutch, two English half-castes, and two Portuguese. . . . In 1699 of 119 recorded Englishmen on the Coromandel Coast, twenty-six had English wives, fourteen "Castee" [a person of pure Portuguese descent] wives, four Mustees [a person of mixed Indian and Portuguese descent] two French and one a Georgian wife.[14]

The business of the company was conducted through Indian middlemen and brokers (banyan).[15] It was the banyan who collected from Indian cultivators or farmers the goods and raw materials which were to be shipped to England. They also disposed of the English trade goods in the Indian markets.[16] By the very early eighteenth century through a system of the payment of advances, the company was beginning to direct and control the production of finished textile goods—their main

13. For good summaries of the structure and culture of the company's factories until the middle of the eighteenth century, see Percival Spear, *The Nabobs* (London, 1932), pp. 1–22; for Madras, H. H. Dodwell, *The Nabobs of Madras* (London, 1926), pp. 1–30; for Surat and Western India, H. G. Rawlinson, *British Beginnings in Western India* (Oxford, 1920), pp. 118–134.

14. Spear, *op. cit.*, p. 13.

15. Henry Yule traces this important term from an adaptation of vaniva, a man of the trading caste, which was derived from the Sanskrit vanij, a merchant. It is probable, says Yule, that the Portuguese found the term already in use by Arab traders. Henry Yule and A. C. Burnwell, *Hobson-Jobson: A Glossary of Colloquial Anglo-Indian Words* . . . , ed. William Crooke (new ed.; London, 1903), p. 63.

16. Blunt, *op. cit.*, p. 17; L. S. S. O'Malley, *The Indian Civil Service* (London, 1931), p. 10.

export to Europe.[17] Not only was the trade of the company carried on through banyans, but each civil servant had his Indian broker to conduct his own private trading operation. William Bolts, a civil servant in Bengal in the eighteenth century, described the banyan and his functions:

> He is interpreter, head bookkeeper, head secretary, head broker, the supplier of cash, cash-keeper. . . . He conducts all the trade of his master, to whom, unless pretty well acquainted with the country languages, it is difficult for any native to obtain access.[18]

The corporate living, the screening effect of the Indian middlemen, the concentration on commercial activity—all tended to restrict contact with or knowledge of a broad spectrum of Indian life. Few English appear to have known any Indian language well. Conversely, there appears to have been little prejudice against Indians in the period from 1600 to 1750. The English "had developed no contempt for Indian social customs or political power."[19]

The pay of the company's servants was low, even when allowances for room and board are taken into account. In 1674 the Court of Directors fixed the following as the pay scale:

Table 1. *Pay Scale of East India Company Servants in 1674 (in English pounds)*

Rank	First five years (annual)	Next two years (annual)	Next three years (annual)
Apprentice	5	10	20
Writer	10	—	20
Junior factor	20	—	30
Senior factor	30	—	40

Source: Sir Edward Blunt, *The I.C.S.: The Indian Civil Service* (London, 1937), p. 15.

In 1680, the chief agent in Surat received £300 per year, the second in council £89, the lowest rank in the Council £40 a

17. Sukumar Bhattacharya, *The East India Company and the Economy of Bengal from 1704–1740* (London, 1954), p. 137.
18. Quoted in Rawlinson, *op. cit.*, p. 127.
19. Spear, *op. cit.*, p. 22.

year.[20] The same general low rate of pay was followed in Bengal in 1706: chairman and cartuer, £100; accountant, £40; import warehouse keeper, £40; buxie (paymaster), £40; senior merchant, £40; junior merchant, £30.[21] These low rates continued until the late eighteenth century.[22] The company assumed that its servants could engage in private trade to make their living.

The appointment of a company servant was generally made in London by the "Court of Committees" as the Court of Directors, the governing body of the East India Company, was then called. A person seeking employment in the East applied and his application was accepted or rejected. From 1682 a person applying for a writership had to give evidence that he was skilled in keeping accounts. It was not until 1714, though, that an application for appointment had to be accompanied by the indorsement of a member of the Court of Directors. It was then laid down in a Court of Directors minute "that in future all petitions for employments in the Company service, either at home or abroad, be presented by some gentleman in the Direction, and that they speak to the same."[23] By the middle of the eighteenth century, company appointments began to be eagerly sought, and there were more demands for posts than there were positions. The Court of Directors developed a system for dividing the patronage among themselves.

Between 1608 and 1740, the East India Company had firmly established itself in India as a commercial enterprise. Its servants were primarily commercial. The company had some territorial rights, as on the Coromandel Coast where the descendants of the Rajas of Vijayanagar had granted them a strip of land one mile wide and six miles long in 1639. This became the city of Madras. In 1661, when the Portuguese Princess Catherine of Braganza married Charles II, Bombay became English as part of her dowry. In the 1690's Job Charnock on behalf of the company

20. R. Grant quoted in Akshoy Kumar Ghosal, *Civil Service in India Under the East India Company* (Calcutta, 1944), p. 39.
21. *Ibid.*, p. 437, based on India Office Library, *Bengal Civil Servants*, Vol. I (1706–1760).
22. Ghosal, *op. cit.*, Appendices C and D.
23. Foster, *John Company*, p. 212.

obtained the right of zamindari (landlord) over three Bengal villages; these grew into Calcutta. The three territories which were fortified in the beginning of the eighteenth century soon grew into the three great commercial cites and ports of the eighteenth and nineteenth centuries.

Until the 1740's, though, what territorial rights were acquired were as part of the company's commercial activities. The company on occasion did engage in military and political activities to safeguard their trade. Company servants on occasion acted in diplomatic and military roles, but these were secondary to their other roles. Within their limited territories, the Company servants acted as municipal judges and local administrators. A few of the servants of the period were able to retire after their years in India with small fortunes built up through private trade, but the amassing of great fortunes and the English Nabob were phenomena of the mid- and late eighteenth century.

II. The Transition from Merchants to Governors

The East India Company emerged from the tangled political and military maneuvers of the period 1740–1760 as a major political power in India with control over large parts of the subcontinent. In the first half of the eighteenth century the Mughal empire ended as an imperial system, as it could not check external military powers such as those marshaled by the Afghan and Nadir Shah, nor internal ones such as the Sikhs and Marathas. During this period the French and British fought for the trade of the Carnatic and Bengal through local dynasties and adventurers. The Anglo-French rivalry was an expression of their antagonisms in Europe as well as in India.[24]

The Europeans discovered their commercial activities could be furthered through trade monopolies by intervening in Indian politics and military affairs. The servants of the European companies found Indian politics highly profitable in the receipts, bribes,

24. The narrative of the complicated rivalries can be followed in H. H. Dodwell, *Dupleix and Clive: The Beginning of Empire* (London, 1920).

prize money, and utilization of their employer's commercial rights for their own private trade. By 1765 some British civil servants had made huge fortunes, and the prospects seemed limitless.

The most famous example of the "get rich" technique of the time were the payments Robert Clive and other British officers, civil and military, received for their support of Mir Jaffar in replacing Siraj-ud-daula as Nawab of Bengal. Clive is reputed to have received £234,000, and other payments to company officials ranged from £117,000 to £12,000.[25] It is in describing these payments that Clive made his famous defense of his actions before Parliament.

Am I not rather deserving of praise for the moderation which marked my proceedings? Consider the situation in which I found myself after the victory at Plassey. A great Prince was dependent upon my pleasure; an oppulant city lay at my mercy; its richest bankers bid against each other for my smiles; I walked through vaults which were thrown open to me alone, piled on each hand with gold and jewels! Mr. Chairman, at this moment I stand astonished at my own moderation.[26]

In South India in addition to private trade, moneylending and the providing of troops to princes became a quick way to wealth. John Holland, who became governor of Madras in 1789, sold potentially lucrative posts in the government to the highest bidder. He employed English troops in unauthorized expeditions on behalf of those holding the Nawab of Arcot's debts. When ordered by his superiors to support the state of Travancore, he tried to make the Raja pay for the assistance, and he ended his career by absconding with funds of the Nawab of Arcot intrusted to him for payment to the East India Company.[27]

It was during the period after 1750 that positions in India became highly sought after. "The East Indies were not 'til of late years, considered a quick road to wealth; formerly, appointments in the Company's service were not objects of general solicitation,"[28] wrote a pamphleteer in 1772. Advertisements appeared in

25. A. Mervyn Davies, *Clive of Plassey* (London, 1939), p. 238.
26. *Ibid.*, p. 234.
27. Dodwell, *The Nabobs of Madras*, p. 26.
28. Quoted in James M. Holzman, *The Nabobs in England: A Study of the Returned Anglo-Indians, 1760–1785* (New York, 1926), p. 8.

the *Public Advertiser* offering one to three thousand pounds for writerships to India.[29]

Outright purchase, although a spectacular indication of the demand, appears to have been comparatively rare, but all manner of personal influence and connection were used to try to secure appointments in the East. Lord Cornwallis, governor general from 1786–1793 who specifically was sent to India to try to regulate the corruption, was besieged with requests from friends and politicians to provide posts for their dependents.[30] Members of royalty seem to have been the most persistent demanders of favor. A Mr. Ritso was sent out to India with a recommendation from the Queen, and although in 1787 Cornwallis refused an appointment by saying, "I cannot desert the only system that can save this country, even for sacred Majesty,"[31] a few month later he nevertheless wrote to Lord Sydney: "He [Mr. Ritso] is now writing in the Secretary's office for 200 or 250 rupees a month, and I do not see the probability of my being able to give him anything better without deserving to be impeached."[32] On another occasion, after the Prince of Wales was particularly demanding, Cornwallis wrote to a friend:

If I was to create offices, or extra offices . . . I would not only disgrace myself and undo everything I have been doing since I have landed in Bengal, but I should render a very short-lived service to the person for whom they were created. . . . I must beg of you, my dear Lord, to state what I have said, in the strongest, most respectful terms to the Prince of Wales. . . . he would not desire that I should set an example that would prove ruinous to the public interests, and lay a foundation for the renewal of those abuses that had well might overset our Indian Empire.[33]

Notwithstanding Lord Cornwallis' difficulties over patronage, it was during his governor generalship that there began to emerge

---

29. *Ibid.*, p. 22.
30. Charles Ross (ed.), *Correspondence of Charles, First Marquis Cornwallis* (London, 1859), Vols. I, II. See I, Cornwallis to Fox, 260–261; Cornwallis to Lord Sydney, 284–285; Cornwallis to Charles Stuart, 296–297; Cornwallis to Sydney, 321–322; Marquis of Lansdowne to Cornwallis, 371; Cornwallis to Lord Southampton, 450; II, H.R.H. The Prince of Wales to Cornwallis, 28.
31. Ross, *op. cit.*, I, 285.
32. *Ibid.*, I, 322.
33. *Ibid.*, I, 458–459; also see the case of Pelegrine Treves, II, 29, 35–36.

the system of administration by which India was and to some extent still is governed. Warren Hastings had tried to establish a workable system of administration, but he lacked clear authority over officials in Calcutta and was bound too tightly by the Court of Directors at home to effect the radical changes that were necessary.[34] Cornwallis arrived in India with strong backing from the Court of Directors and Parliament to establish an efficient and honest administration for the company's territories. He was authorized to raise salaries and to root out corruption. Cornwallis often operated on the basis of his prejudices and on too hastily or ill-assembled information, but in retrospect, despite all the faults in his administrative reforms, much of his influence has lasted through today.[35] The next generation of Malcolm, Elphinstone, Munro, and Metcalf are better known and more widely respected than the Cornwallis men—Sir John Shore, Charles Grant, Sir George Barlow, Jonathan Duncan, and James Grant, who nevertheless were for their time equally impressive.

Cornwallis' underlying assumption that Indians were dishonest and hence incapable of ruling in their own best interests,[36] combined with the orientation of an English Whig, led him to try to build a government "reduced to the minimal functions of justice and protection from violence."[37] Through his land policies

34. Hastings' plans can be followed best in G. W. Forrest (ed.), *Selections from the State Papers of the Governors-General of India: Warren Hastings* (2 vols.; London, 1910).

35. There is an extensive literature on the consolidation of the administration under Hastings, Cornwallis, and Wellesley (1774–1805). The most useful is B. B. Misra, *The Central Administration of the East India Company, 1773–1834* (Manchester, 1959). A good brief introduction is Lillian M. Penson, "The Bengal Administrative System, 1786–1818," chap. xxvi in *Cambridge History of India*, Vol. V. For a recent critical Indian review, see R. C. Majumdar and K. K. Data, "Administrative System," chap. xii in B. C. Majumdar (ed.), *British Paramountcy and Indian Renaissance* (Bombay, 1963), Vol. I, Part I; on Cornwallis, see Ross, *op. cit.*; A. Aspinall, *Cornwallis in Bengal* (Manchester, 1931); George Forrest (ed.), *Selections from the State Papers of the Governors-General of India: Lord Cornwallis* (2 vols.; Oxford, 1926). The best criticism of the Cornwallis system was that of Samuel Davis who wrote the Bengal part of the Fifth Report. See Kenneth Ballhatchet, "The Authors of the Fifth Report of 1812," *Notes and Queries*, CCII (1957), 477–478; K. Firminger, *5th Report from the Select Committee of the House of Commons on the Affairs of the East India Company . . . 1812* (3 vols.; Calcutta, 1917–1918), p. 36; George Bearce, *British Attitudes Towards India, 1784–1858* (Oxford, 1961), p. 46.

36. Bearce, *op. cit.*, p. 46.

37. Eric Stokes, *English Utilitarians and India* (Oxford, 1959), p. 26.

in Bengal which would be extended to the Presidencies of Madras and Bombay, he hoped to develop an Indian landed aristocracy to stabilize the country. Cornwallis' plan for administration was embodied in the Code of Regulations of 1793. The role of the district collector was stabilized into an office whose responsibility was overseeing the collection of revenue due from the landholders, who were newly regularized by law into being responsible for direct payment of the land taxes. As the revenue obligation of the landowner was permanently fixed, it was assumed the job of collector was a supervisory one. The number of collectorships was reduced to less than they had been under Hastings. In some areas such as Banaras where today there are five district collectors, in the beginning of the nineteenth century there was only one collector. Collectors had no responsibility for administration of law, whether civil, criminal, or revenue. This was to be under the civil judge and magistrate. Under the code, the judge/magistrate tried all suits, civil, criminal, and revenue. Cornwallis assumed that by providing the Indians with a court system manned by "impartial" European officers, citizens who felt themselves disadvantaged by other citizens or government officials would be free to sue for their rights in the courts. Sir George Barlow, one of Cornwallis' trusted assistants and advisers, saw the administrative system as "giving security to those rights [of person and property] by affording to our native subjects the means of obtaining redress against any infringement of them, by the Government itself, its officers, or individuals of any character or description."[38]

The work of the collectors was to be supervised by the Board of Revenue in Calcutta. The work of judge/magistrates was supervised by the provincial courts of appeals, of which originally there were five, and the sadr dewani and nizamat adalat in Calcutta. There were still the company's commercial residents in those districts in which the company had trade or manufacturing interests. They were supervised by the Board of Trade. Where there were independent or semi-independent Indian states, there

38. Quoted in Sir John Kaye, *Lives of Indian Officers* (new ed.: London, 1904), I, 153.

were quasi-diplomatic officers or residents supervised by the Political and Secret Department in Calcutta. In Calcutta there was the Military Board subject to the governor general. Also in Calcutta there was a secretariat responsible to the boards and to the governor general and his council.

From 1793 until the annexation of Oudh in 1856 the company's territory grew extensively until it covered three-fifths of the land area of pre-partition India. Cornwallis' hope of a minimal government proved illusory. The assessment and collection of taxes alone led to the development of an extensive bureaucracy, and these tax duties, combined with the administration of justice, accounted for much of the work of the civil servants.

There were extensive changes in Cornwallis' system from 1793 to 1859. The separation of judicial and supervisory functions regarding land-revenue assessment and collection proved unworkable, and in the newly acquired territories the district officer more and more had judicial functions as well. With the annexation of the Punjab in 1849, the district officer was ma-bap (mother and father) to the residents of his district, and rather than a functionary bound by regulations, he was a paternal autocrat. Police functions, originally rudimentary and in the hands of subordinate Indian revenue officials, developed into a separate service manned by Europeans at top posts. Provincial boards of revenue for each major territory emerged, and each Presidency developed its own hierarchy of courts. With the end of its trade monopoly in 1813 and abolition of its commercial function altogether in 1834, the commercial line of the East India Company's service declined.

Ultimate supervision, control, and what was in effect the legislative function of the governing system were all centered in London, where there was dual control exercised by the company and by the Board of Control, which had been established by Parliament. Theoretically, ultimate authority in the company rested with the proprietors of East India Company stock:

Any person who bought shares in the capital stock of the East India Company was denominated a proprietor, and was permitted to attend the meetings of the General Court of Proprietors. The possession of £600 of stock entitled the holder to vote "in a show of hands;" possession of £1,000 of stock gave the proprietor one vote in a ballot, £3,000 two votes, £6,000 three votes and £10,000 and upwards four votes, which was the maximum.[39]

There were 2,163 proprietors in 1800 and 2,140 in 1831.[40] Philips, whose work on the management of the East India Company is the standard one, does not give numbers of potential votes in any given year but notes, "there were rarely more than 50 holders of four votes."[41] The major function of the proprietors was the election of the twenty-four directors, who were collectively known as the Court of Directors. The Court of Directors was the executive and decision-making body of the company. Parliament in 1773 had established that each year six directors were to be elected for a four-year term; after being out of office for a year, a director could be and most frequently was re-elected. Therefore, there were in reality thirty directors, twenty-four of whom were serving at any one time. The direction of the company was essentially a self-perpetuating oligarchy. To be elected the first time was an expensive and arduous task, but once elected a man served for life.[42]

The work of the Court of Directors was done by committees, of which the most important were those on correspondence, secret, political, and shipping affairs. Decisions were first made in committees and then had to be approved by vote of the Court of Directors. The two most important positions in the court were the chairman and the deputy chairman, who served one-year terms. The court and company had their own secretariat in which the higher posts were significant for making policy on administration in India. The crucial office was that of the examiner of Indian correspondence. Here all non-secret reports, minutes, and letters from India were read and digested for the members of the Court

39. C. H. Philips, *The East India Company 1784–1834* (Manchester, 1940), p. 2.
40. *Ibid.*, p. 2, n. 2.
41. *Ibid.*, p. 2, n. 3.
42. *Ibid.*, pp. 4–8.

of Directors. In this office dispatches which approved, disapproved, commented on, or innovated new policies were drawn up to be sent to India over the name of the Court of Directors.[43]

James Mill, who was appointed assistant examiner in charge of revenue matters in 1819 and who in 1830 became chief examiner, described his life in a letter:

as you know that the government of India is carried on by correspondence; and that I am the only man whose business it is, or who has the time to make himself master of the facts scattered in a most voluminous correspondence, on which a just decision must rest, you will conceive to what an extent the real decision on matters belonging to my Department rests with the man who is in my situation.[44]

The control over policy in India exercised in London could and often was very direct and specific.

In addition to the sources of control represented by the proprietors, the directors, and the examiner's office, there were the Commissioners for India Affairs, or the Board of Control, a body appointed by Parliament. The president of the board served in the cabinet. Theoretically, since the Board of Control was the superior of the Court of Directors, conflict between the board and the court was possible, but actually it was surprisingly infrequent. When disputes arose between the two bodies, policy appears to have been determined by compromise, "just as in the matter of appointments [governor generals, governors of Presidencies, chiefs of army commands] both sides had in effect a power of veto. So also, in discussion about policy, neither body cared to provoke the other over much save in exceptional circumstances."[45] Many of the influential stockholders and directors of the company were also important in politics. In the Parliament of 1780–1784, thirty-five members had served as king's officers or in company service in India. In 1802–1806 this number rose to sixty-six, and in 1830–1831 it was thirty-one.[46] In addition, there were those in

43. *Ibid.*, pp. 16–18; John Foster, *The East India House* (London, 1924), pp. 193–225.

44. Quoted in Stokes, *op. cit.*, p. 48.

45. H. H. Dodwell, "Legislation and Governments, 1786–1818," chap. xviii in *Cambridge History of India*, p. 315.

46. Philips, *op. cit.*, Appendix I.

Parliament who had financial interests in the company. Given the kind of political interconnections existing between Parliament and the company, it is not difficult to see that compromises could usually be worked out if there were any conflicts between the two.[47] Commissioners on the Board of Control frequently had extensive Indian experience. For example, the board included Lord Teignmouth, who had been governor general and served on the board from 1807 to 1828; Sir James Mackintosh, who was a former Bombay judge; and Holt Mackenzie, an important revenue official.[48] The India board had a permanent secretariat, but with exceptions such as James Cumming, they were not of the caliber nor had they the influence that the personnel in the examiner's office exercised.[49]

In the first half of the nineteenth century, then, a civil servant at the district level had a large but somewhat attenuated formal superstructure over him. His actions were subject to question and revision at any of the following levels: regional, provincial, at the Presidency, and in London at the Court of Directors and the Board of Control and ultimately at Parliament. Policy affecting a civil servant's actions could be set at any one of these levels. However, given the difficulties of communication and the sheer bulk of information and correspondence which had to pass between India and London, it often took two or three years for matters originating in a district to be commented on in London. In reality there was a considerable amount of autonomy for the civil servant in the field.

Two parliamentary acts established the rules governing appointment and promotion in the Civil Service in India. The India Act of 1784 and the Charter Act of 1793 established the following principles:[50]

(1) Nomination to be writers, cadets, surgeons, and chaplains was vested in the Court of Directors;

(2) Promotion to all civil service positions in India, except the Governor-Generalship, Governorships, and high army commands,

47. *Ibid.*, p. 307.
48. Foster, *John Company*, pp. 249–250.
49. Philips, *op. cit.*, pp. 19, 202; Ballhatchet, *op. cit.*, p. 478.
50. H. H. Dodwell as cited in n. 45 above, pp. 318–319.

were to be filled from the covenanted servants of the Company, generally following the principle of seniority.

(3) Posts paying £500 a year to £1500 were to be filled with officers actually resident in India for at least three years; those posts paying £1500–£3000 a minimum of six years; £3,000–£4,000 a minimum of nine years; and £4,000 and above a minimum of 12 years.

These regulations, combined with Cornwallis' determination to enforce them, meant that, once appointed, a civil official's future progress was mainly determined in India. Within the acts no Indian could hold a post paying more than £500 a year, since no Indian was a company servant within the meaning of the acts. No adequate work has been done to see if the connections of civil servants external to their roles in India were crucial to their promotion within the Civil Service, nor has material of a statistical nature been compiled regarding career lines of civil servants. Except for biographical studies we do not know on what basis other than seniority men were actually picked for promotion by their superiors or the governor general. The impression that connections did help, especially in relation to first and second postings, does not seem unwarranted. Mountstuart Elphinstone, for example, came from a family that was powerful in the company; his father's brother was a director over a forty-year period. When Elphinstone was appointed to the Civil Service in 1795, his uncle wrote to the governor general, and as a result of the governor general's interest, Elphinstone received a posting to Banaras which was then considered one of the plums in the service.[51]

III. Recruitment and Social Background of the Company's Civil Servants

By 1793 a regular system for the distribution of appointments to the East India Company's service had been established among

51. S. Cotton, *Mountstuart Elphinstone* (Oxford, 1892), chap. i. Also see letter of April 22, 1796, from Elphinstone's brother to his mother in T. F. Colebrooke, *Life of the Honorable Mountstuart Elphinstone* (London, 1884), I, 12.

the members of the Court of Directors. Appointments to the Civil Service, and after 1806 nomination to the East India Company's Training College at Haileybury, were the most valued. In 1808–1809, there was a parliamentary committee appointed to investigate rumors that writerships and cadetships were being sold by members of the Court of Directors. At least two cases of sale of civil offices appear to have been substantiated. A writership for Bengal was sold for £3,500, and a writership for Madras for £3,000; cadetships sold for £150 to £320.[52] The sale of appointments was not direct; the committee found that there was "throughout the whole of the evidence nothing which traces any one of these corrupt or improper bargains to any director, or induces in a reasonable suspicion that it was done with connivance by any member of that Court."[53] But as appointments could be given from one person to another, or even willed by a director to be honored by the court after his death as in the case of Thomas Monsell,[54] the possibility of sale for money existed.

The system of division of the patronage followed lines of seniority on the court, and chairman and deputy chairman had a double allocation. The president of the Board of Control received the same allocation as the chairman. The number of appointments varied from year to year. In the period from 1802 to 1833, 1,190 writers were sent to the three Presidencies in India.[55] The range was from seven sent in 1814 to sixty-nine sent in 1828. The average was thirty-seven a year. During the same period, 7,727 military cadets were sent, an average of 258 per year.[56] For the period from 1825–1826 to 1830–1831, the appointments were divided in the following fashion.

52. *House of Commons, Parliamentary Papers,* 1809, "Report from the Committee Appointed to Inquire into the Existence of any Abuses in the Disposal of the Patronage of the East India Company," Vol. 2, Paper 91, pp. 3–12. *House of Commons, Parliamentary Papers* are hereinafter cited as *HCPP.*
53. *Ibid.,* p. 12.
54. Commonwealth Relations Office, *Committee on College References,* Vol. 24, 1811, No. 25, "Thomas Monsell." Documents from the Commonwealth Relations Office are hereinafter cited as *CRO.* Documents of the Committee on College References are hereinafter cited as *CRO, CCR.* See below, n. 57.
55. *HCPP,* 1812–13, "East India Accounts," Vol. 8, Paper 171, p. 493; *HCPP,* 1833, "Writers and Cadets, India," Vol. 26, Paper 536, p. 87.
56. *Ibid.*

Table 2. *Appointments of Civil Servants by Board of Control and Court of Directors, East India Company, 1825–1831*

Position	Average number each year	Chairman, deputy chairman (each)	Board of Control	Directors (each)
Writers	39.2	2.8	2.8	1.40
Cadets—engineers and artillery	67.2	4.8	4.8	2.40
Cadets—cavalry	15.2	1.6	1.6	.47
Cadets—infantry	124.8	8.4	8.4	4.52
Assistant surgeons	56.0	4.0	4.0	2.00
Chaplains		{ 2.8 { 3.0		

Source: HCPP, 1831–32, "Statement Showing Number of Appointments to India . . . ," Vol. 9, Paper 735, p. 326.

In an average year for this period a director had close to eleven positions to which he could nominate young men. Table 3, which is based on compilations made from "Writer's Petitions," shows a director's possible reasons for giving an appointment. These reasons were stated on an official document that each director had to sign. It set forth his connections with the person being appointed, his reason for making the appointment, and a sworn statement that he (the director) had received no money for the appointment.[57]

Of the 426 appointees (during the period described, it was appointment to Haileybury rather than directly to the Civil Service), about 23 per cent were relatives of members of the

57. Tables 3, 4, 5, and 6 are based on material found in what are conventionally called "Writer's Petitions" and in the series called *Committee on College References*, 88 volumes, in the Commonwealth Relations Office Library, formerly the India Office Library. This series is hereinafter cited as *CRO, CCR*. The volumes used were Vol. 19 (1806) to Vol. 88 (1858). From 1806 on these volumes contain documents which each civilian appointee had to submit or have on record at the time of his actual appointment, and in the majority of instances these documents contain a birth certificate or other official statement of his age, a questionnaire (which asked among other things father's occupation and relation to the directors and/or reason for his appointment), a certificate from the last school he attended, and the above-mentioned statements by the director who appointed him. These records for each individual are by no means always complete, nor is every single individual who went to India as a covenanted servant listed, although the vast bulk do appear in these records.

Table 3. *Reason Given for Appointment of Civil Servants by Directors, East India Company, 1809–1850*

	1809-1810		1819-1820		1829-1830		1839-1840		1849-1850		Total	Percentage
	No.	Pct.	No.	Pct.	No.	Pct.	No.	Pct.	No.	Pct.		
Friendship	38	57	45	51	56	59	56	56	38	50	233	54.69
Kinship connections	12	18	20	23	15	16	29	29	22	29	98	23.00
Business relationships	3	4	1	1	—	—	3	3	—	—	7	1.64
Company service	2	3	3	3	8	8	3	3	4	5	20	4.69
Political recommendation	2	3	1	1	—	—	—	—	—	—	3	0.70
Recommendation of Board of Control	5	7	8	9	6	6	6	6	3	4	28	6.57
No information	5	7	10	11	10	10	3	3	9	12	37	8.69
Totals	67		88		95		100		76		426	

Source: See p. 104, n. 57, in text.

Court of Directors. Data do not permit an analysis of what the category "friendship" means. It appears to have been the standard answer given by a director when asked his reason for giving an appointment to a particular individual. It may have been friendship for the boy's father or for another relative. Many friendships were based on service together in India. Of the 110 directors who served between 1784 and 1834, "well over half had resided in India."[58] From 1834 to 1854 "the Court of Directors became entirely Anglo-Indian."[59] The significance of a director's direct connection to India is seen in Table 4 which follows. Over the forty-year period almost 35 per cent of those entering the East India Company's Civil Service had fathers who served in either the company's Military Service or Civil Service. In 1839–1840 when the membership of the Court of Directors appears to have been almost exclusively Anglo-Indian, this number reached 45 per cent. During this last period of the company's rule in particular, the number of appointees from families with Indian experience would be much higher if uncles, grandfathers, mothers' families, and those persons with commercial experience had been included.

In addition to providing posts for their sons and other relatives and for the sons of friends, political considerations were important in the allocation of patronage, both in maintaining "friendly relations with members of his Majesty's government,"[60] and in getting members of the Court of Directors elected to the House of Commons. From 1784 to 1834, forty-five of the 110 directors served in the House of Commons.[61]

The key to the selection of the civil servants in India from 1793 to 1854 was the Court of Directors of the East India Company. Other than Philips' work there is little systematically known about the directors. During the period down to 1834 they were divided

58. Philips, *op. cit.*, p. 8.

59. H. Morse Stephens, "An Account of the East India College at Haileybury (1806–1857)," in A. Lawrence Lowell (ed.), *Colonial Civil Service* (New York, 1900), p. 250. "Anglo-Indian" is used in the nineteenth-century sense as a Britisher who had lived and worked in India rather than in the twentieth-century sense as the offspring of a European and Indian marriage.

60. See Charles Grant's remarks in *Asiatic Annual Register*, XI (1809), 232.

61. Philips, *op. cit.*, p. 16, n. 1.

Table 4. *Occupation of Fathers of Appointees to Haileybury, 1809–1850*

	1809–1810		1819–1820		1829–1830		1839–1840		1849–1850		Total	Percentage
	No.	Pct.	No.	Pct.	No.	Pct.	No.	Pct.	No.	Pct.		
Company service	18	27	26	29	25	26	46	46	33	43	148	34.74
Gentlemen	12	18	7	8	12	13	3	3	5	7	39	9.15
Merchant, manufacturing, banking	9	13	10	11	15	15	10	10	9	12	53	12.44
Clergy	6	9	7	8	10	11	10	10	7	9	40	9.39
Royal military and naval service	4	6	8	9	11	12	8	8	5	7	36	8.45
Civil Service	3	4	2	2	4	4	—	—	2	3	11	2.58
Medical	2	3	2	2	4	4	5	5	1	1	14	3.29
Legal	—	—	4	5	3	3	5	5	3	4	15	3.52
Member of Parliament	1	1	—	—	1	1	1	1	—	—	3	.70
No information	12	18	22	25	10	11	12	12	10	13	66	15.49
Farmer	—	—	—	—	—	—	—	—	1	1	1	.23
Totals	67		88		95		100		76		426	

Source: See p. 104, n. 57, in text.

Table 5. Place of Birth or Place of Residence of Parents of Appointees to Haileybury, 1809–1850

	1809–1810 No.	1809–1810 Pct.	1819–1820 No.	1819–1820 Pct.	1829–1830 No.	1829–1830 Pct.	1838–1840 No.	1838–1840 Pct.	1849–1850 No.	1849–1850 Pct.	Total	Percentage
London	20	30	27	31	28	29	22	22	19	25	116	27.23
Rest of England	26	39	19	22	31	33	22	22	17	22	115	27.00
Scotland	10	15	11	13	9	9	15	15	9	12	54	12.68
Ireland	2	3	7	8	3	3	4	4	4	5	20	4.69
Wales	—	—	—	—	1	1	1	1	—	—	2	.47
India	4	6	21	24	18	19	34	34	22	29	99	23.24
Other	4	6	1	1	3	3	2	2	4	5	14	3.29
No information	1	1	2	2	2	2	—	—	1	1	6	1.41
Totals	67		88		95		100		76		426	

Source: See p. 104, n. 57, in text.

into several "interests," of which three were of persistent importance. The "Indian" interest was made up of returned company
servants; "City interests" represented some major London financial and commercial groups; and the "shipping interests"
represented companies and individuals under contract to provide the ships which carried the trade of the East India
Company. Of the thirty directors (twenty-four in office and six
out in rotation) in 1831, thirteen were former company officers,
eight were London merchants and bankers, five retired com-
manders of East Indiamen, and four in other professions or
activities.[62]

It would appear that the directors were connected in a number
of ways. Most of them resided in London. Of the thirty directors
of the company in 1816, twenty-four lived in London; of these
twenty-four, fourteen lived within an area one mile by one-half
mile in Marylebonne, on Baker Street, Harley Street, and the
squares of this area.[63] Nineteen of the twenty-four, including the
above mentioned fourteen, lived within a mile and a half of
Regents Park. Those six who lived out of London all lived in the
surrounding counties: Surrey, Essex, Hertfordshire, and Kent.
Many may have been born elsewhere, but increasingly through
the first half of the nineteenth century London and a particular
neighborhood was the residential locus of the direction of the
company.

In view of such residential propinquity and assuming that
people in the particular neighborhood lived or aspired to a
particular style of life, intermarriage among the offspring and
relatives of the directors would seem to be inevitable. The
directors formed a tight society, bound by culture, economic
interest, and social relations. It would also seem inevitable that
those they appointed to serve in India would have some affinities
with this tight segment of upper-middle-class English society.

62. "Analysis of the Court of Directors as it stood on 31 December 1831,
including Directors out by Rotation," *HCPP*, 1831–1832, Vol. 9, Paper 735, p.
325.
63. For listing of addresses, see *Asiatic Journal*, I (1816), 523. Some insight into
the culture of this area of London at the time is conveyed in William M.
Thackeray's *Vanity Fair*. Thackeray himself was of a distinguished Anglo-Indian
family.

This is not to say that the group was totally homogeneous in outlook or in social interrelations. In the early nineteenth century within the direction of the company, the Evangelicals were a small but important group representing somewhat different social values. The Evangelicals looked to a moral and social revolution in behavior and attitude at home and the proselytizing of Christianity overseas, and particularly in India. Men like Charles Grant saw India's problems as stemming from its wickedness and immorality and argued that Christianity was its only salvation. In addition to Charles Grant, W. Thornton Astell, W. T. Money, Hugh Inglis, Robert Thornton, and Francis Baring were active Evangelicals and were important directors of the company in the first two decades of the nineteenth century.[64] It is difficult, though, to determine how much conscious and direct Evangelical influence there was in selection or training for the company's service. The obvious separateness of the directors from other crucial groups in the middle and upper classes of Great Britain of the period was as significant as the unifying characteristics. In the Civil Service, for the periods 1809–1810, 1819–1820, 1829–1830, about 12 per cent of the students described their fathers as gentlemen.[65] For the periods 1839–1840 and 1849–1850, the figure dropped to around 4 per cent. In addition, it is likely that those students who were the sons of clergy also had landed connections, since so many of the clergy were second sons of landed families. The same is true of some sons of civil servants, since they too may have come from landed families. My impression is that the aristocracy by and large did not contribute much to the direction of the company or the Civil Service. Small-scale businessmen and artisans are not represented in the directors or in the Civil Service, nor are the new middle class of industrial and commercial entrepreneurs of the Midlands.

To summarize, the directors of the East India Company, and

64. For identification of the "Evangelicals," see lists in Ford K. Brown, *Fathers of the Victorians* (Cambridge, 1961), pp. 351–360. For Charles Grant, see Ainslee Embree, *Charles Grant and British Rule in India* (London, 1962), pp. 239–241, and for the influence of the Evangelicals, Stokes, *op. cit.*, pp. 27–37; Bearce, *op. cit.*, pp. 78–86; and Ernest M. Howse, *Saints in Politics* (London, 1953), pp. 68–94.

65. See above, Table 4, p. 107.

by extension the Civil Service, were recruited from a very restricted group in English society centered essentially in London and drawn from banking and commercial families and landed groups in Scotland and the southeast of England. Cultural and economic ties of these groups were very much buttressed by ties of descent and affinity. It is likely that from 1840 to 1860 fifty or sixty interconnected extended families contributed the vast majority of the civil servants who governed India. And these civil servants certainly had crucial administrative roles until the 1870's when those selected through open competition had enough seniority to begin to rise high in the bureaucracy.

IV. Training of the Civil Servants, 1800–1859

The College at Fort William

Lord Wellesley in a famous dispatch to the Court of Directors in 1800 gave expression to the changed reality of the functions of the East India Company's servants in India. No longer were they commercial agents but governors expected

To dispense justice to millions of people of various languages, manners, usages, and religions; to administer a vast and complicated system of revenue throughout districts equal in extent to some of the most considerable Kingdoms in Europe; to maintain civil order in one of the most populous and litigious regions of the world.[66]

To carry on their work in the judicial, revenue, political, and financial departments, the company's servants needed a new range of skills in languages and law in addition to a broad education to help them develop standards of judgment.

Their education should be founded in a general knowledge of those branches of literature and science, which form the basis of the education of persons destined to similar occupations in Europe; to this

66. "Extracts from the Governor-General's Notes for an official despatch, to be forwarded to the Court of Directors, with Respect to the Foundation of a College at Fort William," July 10, 1800. Reproduced in Ghosal, *op. cit.*, Appendix I, pp. 469–486 (quotation at p. 470).

foundation should be added an intimate acquaintance with the history, languages, customs and manners of the people of India; with the Mohammedan and Hindoo codes of law and religion. . . . their early habits should be so formed, as to establish in their minds such solid foundations of industry, prudence, integrity and religion, as should effectually guard them against those temptations, with which the nature of this climate, and peculiar depravity of the people of India, will surround and assail them in every station, especially upon their first arrival in India.[67]

An education necessary for service in the East did not exist anywhere in England, Wellesley argued. Under the system in use at Wellesley's time, he contended, the civil servants were too young and either ill-educated or their education was stopped too soon for them to adequately do anything beyond the menial, laborious, unwholesome, and unprofitable duty of a mere copying clerk.[68] According to Wellesley, the difficulties of the civil servants could be found in their inadequate education, lack of discipline in their early careers, and the lack of relationship "between promotion in the civil service and the possession of those qualifications requisite for the due discharge of the several civil stations."[69]

Wellesley, under Regulation IX of 1800, set about to remedy these lacks in the Civil Service by establishing a College of Fort William in Calcutta. The college was to instruct the junior civil servants "in such branches of literature, science, and knowledge as may be deemed necessary to qualify them for the discharge of the duties of the different offices constituted for the administration of the government of British possessions in the East Indies."[70]

The college was to be housed in its own building. The provost, a clergyman of the Church of England, would regulate the students in general morals and conduct, and "instruct them in the principles of the Christian religion, according to the doctrine,

67. *Ibid.*, p. 474.
68. *Ibid.*, p. 476.
69. *Ibid.*, p. 482.
70. The full text of Regulation IX (1800) is accessible in *ibid.*, Appendix J, pp. 487–493. See also David Kopf, *Orientalism and the Bengal Renaissance*, unpublished doctoral dissertation, University of Chicago, 1964, pp. 5–39, 70–120.

discipline, and rites of the Church of England." The first provost was David Brown. A friend of missionaries, he owed his concurrent position as Presidency chaplain to Charles Grant.[71] Vice provost was to be Claudius Buchanan, an Evangelical chaplain in Calcutta,[72] who had this view of Indians: "Their general character is imbecility of body and imbecility of mind. Their moral powers are, and have been for ages in a profound stupor. . . . The Hindoo mind seems at present to be bound by a Satanic spell."[73] The governor general was to be patron and visitor of the college, and the members of the Supreme Council and the judges of sadr dewani adalat were to be the governors of the colleges. Hence, the governor general made faculty appointments and the higher civil administrators were responsible for overseeing the running of the college.

It was expected that instruction would be offered in Arabic, Persian, Sanskrit, Hindustani, Bengali, Telugu, Maharathi, Tamil, and Kenarese. In addition to language work, there were courses in Hindu and Mohammedan law, jurisprudence, English law and the regulations of the East India Company. For general education, students were to receive instruction in political economy, geography, mathematics, Latin and Greek and modern European languages, and European and Indian history.[74] Students would be expected to spend three years at the college and to be examined regularly. Civil servants for all three Presidencies were to be trained at the college, and successful completion of the course was to be a prerequisite for civil appointments.

Distinguished civil servants were appointed to the faculty: George Barlow lectured on government regulations; H. T. Colebrooke was professor of Hindu laws and Sanskrit; and John Baillie, who later was a distinguished political officer and a director of the East India Company, was first professor of Arabic, Persian, and Mohammedan law. The erratic and brilliant J. B.

71. Embree, *op. cit.*, p. 189.
72. Brown, *op. cit.*, p. 279.
73. Hugh Pearson, *Memoirs of the Life and Writings of the Rev. Claudius Buchanan* (London, 1834), pp. 114–115.
74. Regulation IX (1800), Article XV, as reproduced in Ghosal, *op. cit.*, p. 491.

Gilchrist was the first professor of Hindustani, and the great Baptist missionary, William Carey, the first teacher of Bengali.[75]

The college did not function for as long as Wellesley had intended. At this time Wellesley was somewhat out of favor with the Court of Directors for his championing of private trade interests, his policy of military expansion, and his general attitude of superiority to his colleagues.[76] At first the court wanted to abolish the college, but under pressure it was maintained as essentially a language training school. And as a language school it had great significance on the development of modern Indian languages and modern forms of scholarship in India. Although language teaching was under the direction of Europeans, distinguished Indian scholars were appointed as tutors and to produce materials for the students. In the budget of the college there was provision for thirty-three munshis in the Persian department; forty in the Hindustani department, including four translators; fourteen in Bengali; four maulavis in the Arabic department; and five pandits in Sanskrit. The college also had a fund of Rs. 40,000 to encourage Oriental literature. The monthly salaries for the Indian heads and assistant heads were set at Rs. 200 and Rs. 100, respectively.[77] The Indians wrote examination questions, historical, biographical, and geographical works in Bengali, and were instrumental in turning Bengali from a Persianized into a Sanskritized language.[78]

Even though Wellesley's early plan did not succeed, it did give an added professionalism to the service, and it would appear that there was some correlation between success in the language school and in service. Such men as W. B. Bayley, who rose to be

75. For a list of the teaching staff down to 1818, see Thomas Roebuck, *The Annals of the College of Fort William* (Calcutta, 1819), Appendix IV.

76. The conflict over the college is discussed in detail in Ghosal, *op. cit.*, pp. 125–130; Embree, *op. cit.*, pp. 187–194; and Paul E. Roberts, *India Under Wellesley* (London, 1929), pp. 155–165.

77. "Copy of General Letter from the Governor General in Council in the Public Department to Court of Directors, 5 June 1805, Relative to Reform of the Expenditures and Establishment of the College of Ft. William," *HCPP*, 1806, Vol. 16, Paper 307, No. 2, p. 33.

78. Romesh Chandra Majumdar, "The Fort William College and Historical and Geographical Studies in Bengal," *Bengal Past and Present*, LXVII (1946), 40–45. Also see Kopf, *op. cit., passim.*

acting governor general; Holt Mackenzie, who was a member of the governor general's council and who worked out the revenue settlement of the North-Western Provinces; R. M. Bird, another great settlement officer; and H. T. Prinsep, who was chief secretary and member of the governor general's council—all achieved top honors at Fort William in the first eight years of the college.

Students in Calcutta, though, appear to have led a rather lazy and pleasant life while attending to their language learning. Calcutta had a flourishing and rather formal social life, with an active racing season, dances, and dinners. Many careers appear to have been somewhat damaged by the heavy debts which some students incurred in order to maintain their social position. In 1802, out of sixteen students in the college, four had no debts; five were in debt up to Rs. 1,000; six owed Rs. 2,000 to 3,999; and one owed over Rs. 4,000.[79] Henry T. Prinsep, who was a most successful civil servant, in later life could defend the spending of the two or three years at Calcutta:

For in this association they [the young civilians] acquired a knowledge of each other's character and formed their friendships and their habits of life in a manner that influenced their future career most advantageously. I deem myself to have been very fortunate in the associates with whom I was thrown at this period. [These friendships] were the bright spot in my life and a source of happiness that made me almost cease to regret the exile from country and family in which I was compelled to pass my days.[80]

In a letter on the departure of his son to take a post, a civil servant in Bengal, Lord Teignmouth (John Shore), described in the bleakest of tones the life a wastrel could live in Calcutta and its disastrous consequences. He describes the activities of Indolens, the bad boy:

On his arrival, new temptations occur, and his disposition to yield to them is strengthened. He has reached the land of promise, and eagerly seizes the enjoyments which he had anticipated. Without adverting to want of means, he adopted the luxuries and indulgences of the

79. *CRO*, Personal Records, XII, 613–614.
80. James Prinseps, "Three Generations in India," *CRO* MS. Eur. c 97/1; I, 62–63.

country; sets up the establishment of a Hookah; purchases a horse and equipage; receives and gives entertainments; and plunges into luxury, vice and extravagance. The natives supply money for his use, which he borrows at an exorbitant interest.[81]

Our hero, according to Lord Teignmouth, through his wasting ways fails his language examinations and falls deeper into debt. He finally succeeds, and now heavily in debt and in order to appease his creditors "he is perhaps seduced into illegal and dishonest compliances."[82] His creditors continue to press through his career preventing him from taking leave or returning to England. "A debt of £ 1000 contracted during his first two years of a writer's residence in India will hang like a millstone around his neck for many."[83]

It was likely that the first two or three years in Calcutta set the tone for the subsequent career a person had in India. At one extreme were those who did brilliantly at the College of Fort William and who received good first appointments, either in the secretariat in Calcutta as assistant Persian translators, or assistants to secretaries, or posts in newly acquired territories under the company's rule. At the other extreme were those who did poorly and became indebted. There were those also who avoided the worst excesses, and being well introduced into Calcutta society, used their time to build effective social connections which could help their careers at a later date.

The pattern of education which Wellesley tried to establish—language training and legal training with "good Christian overtones"—reappeared in the curriculum at Haileybury.

The East India Company's Training College at Haileybury

In the summer of 1804 the Court of Directors decided to explore the question of a training college in Great Britain[84] and on

---

81. Lord Teignmouth, *Memoir of the Life and Correspondence of John Lord Teignmouth* (London, 1843), II, 310–311.
82. *Ibid.*, II, 312.
83. *Ibid.*, II, 313.
84. CRO, *Minutes and Reports of the Committee of Haileybury College*, Vol. I, Minutes of October 26, 1804. This series is hereinafter cited as *CRO, MRCH.*

September 19 of that year agreed to form "some establishment at home for the education of young men intended for the civil service of the Company."[85] The Committee on Correspondence was given the responsibility of drawing up the plan for education. Charles Grant, who was then deputy chairman, appears to have written the report.[86] The report stressed the need for a classical education, good command of English composition, European literature and science, political economy, and Oriental learning. In addition, the servants should be "good subjects and enlightened Patriots . . . and imbued with reverence and love for the religion, the Constitution and laws of their own Country." Their education should be such that they will be fortified against "erroneous and dangerous opinions."[87] It was felt that no institution then existing in England could impart the knowledge of political economy or of Oriental languages necessary for the company's servants, and in order to have the excellent training in European subjects, India would not be the appropriate place for the college. A site twenty miles from London, Hertford Castle, was decided on as a temporary quarters, and plans were made for the erection of permanent buildings.[88]

In the spring of 1805, the Reverend H. Samuel Henley (1740–1815) was appointed principal. Henley had gone to America to teach moral philosophy at William and Mary College. At the beginning of the American Revolution he returned to England and taught at Harrow. He then was curate at Northall in Middlesex. He published several works on theological and classical subjects, such as "A dissertation on the passages in St. Peter and St. Jude concerning the Fallen Angels," "Observation on the Pallas of Vergil." He was well regarded by several scholars at Cambridge[89] and also thought of himself as something of an Orientalist.

The College Committee of the Court of Directors outlined the

85. *Ibid.*
86. Embree, *op. cit.*, p. 195.
87. *CRO, MRCH*, minute, Oct. 26, 1804.
88. The college opened in February, 1806, at the Hertford Castle and in 1809 moved to its own buildings at Haileybury two miles away.
89. *CRO, MRCH*, Vol. I, April 9, 1805; *CRO, CCR*, Vol. 18, Henley to Committee, n.d. (probably April, 1805).

responsibilities of the staff of the college as follows:[90] The principal was to supervise the college and to lecture on moral conduct and theology. There was to be a professor of humanity and philology to teach classical composition "and all that is commonly comprehended under the name Belles Lettres"; a professor of history, political economy, and finance who was to provide instruction in ancient and modern history, "also the sources and wealth arising from natural production which modified by the mechanic arts through the intervention of commerce became perpetual objects of finance, and funds of revenue and gain. These topics to be more especially insisted upon in their relation to India." The professor of mathematics, in addition to mathematics, was to offer some instruction in land-surveying elements of geography and astronomy. The professor of natural philosophy was to cover physics, chemistry, and botany. The Oriental professor was to teach "the Oriental languages and, with Indian History in particular, whatever relates to the government, laws, policies, produce, commerce and affairs of India. . . ." The professor of civil polity was to teach "The Elements of General Law, and the Law of England and the British Constitution." There was to be a French master and a drawing master.

In addition to Samuel Henley, the original faculty included as professor of classical and general literature, the Reverend Edward Lewton, who had been vice-principal and tutor of St. Alban's Hall, Oxford. Joseph Batten, who became the second principal of the college in 1815, was appointed the additional professor of classical and general literature. He was a graduate of Trinity College, Cambridge. The first professor of general polity and the laws of England was Edward Christian, who served until 1818. Also a graduate of Cambridge, he was a lawyer, but one of little distinction. He appears to have been incompetent, and on his death it was remarked that he had died "in full vigor of his incapacity."[91]

T. R. Malthus, the first professor of history and political economy, a post in which he served until 1834, was undoubt-

90. *CRO, MRCH*, Vol. I, June 13, 1805.
91. *Dictionary of National Biography*, IV, 276. Hereinafter cited as *DNB*.

edly the most distinguished member of the staff. He reputedly received his appointment through the influence of Pitt.[92] This was after he published his famous work on population, and many of his later works were first delivered as lectures at Haileybury.[93] Malthus took a major part in the life of the college, both with students and as part of an intellectual circle within the staff which later included Mackintosh, Dealtry, and Charles LeBas.

The first two mathematics and science professors were William Dealtry and Berwick Bridge. Dealtry was another Cambridge graduate, a fellow of the Royal Society, who had published several works on mathematics. He was, however, most famous as a clergyman, and he resigned his professorship to succeed John Venn, the famous Evangelical rector of Clapham. He was hand-picked by Venn and Charles Simeon, one of the major figures in the Evangelical Movement, to succeed Venn.[94] Bridge was a graduate of St. Peter's College, Cambridge, and published several textbooks on mathematics. He retired in 1816.

The staff had a distinct religious orientation: most were ordained as Anglican priests, and some, such as Dealtry, were active and noted Evangelicals. The Evangelical tone of the staff reflected the interest of Charles Grant and other "Saints" who were active in the direction of the company; it also reflected the Court of Directors' objective to instil in their servants Christian principles.

Jonathan Scott was appointed the first professor of Oriental languages. He conceived the teaching of Oriental languages as part of the general study of Indian history and culture and considered that this should be central to work in the college. He planned that the students in their language work should read Persian historians, not "Tales of a Parrot" and other novels lightly esteemed by the Asiatics.[95] He felt that the company's servants were ignorant of the better class of Indians and that this could

92. James Bonar, *Malthus and His Work* (New York, 1924), p. 240.
93. *Ibid.*, pp. 214, 222, 229.
94. Charles James Hoare, *The Blessed Death of the Righteous: A Funeral Sermon After the Death of Venn* (London, 1847), p. 18.
95. Jonathan Scott, "Observation on the Oriental Department of the Honourable East India Company's College at Hertford," *CRO, Home Miscellaneous Series*, Vol. 488, 1805. This series is hereinafter cited as *CRO, HMS*.

lead to a prejudice against Indians on the part of the British and in turn to dissatisfaction among the company's Indian subjects. Scott argued that it should be the goal of the civil servants' education to remove their prejudices, and this could be accomplished through instructing them in the laws, history, and customs of India. Then the company's servants would view "the respectable natives worthy of higher consideration rather than as mere mediums of procuring money."[96] Scott resigned his appointment without ever teaching at the college. He complained that he was not paid enough, as Oriental professors were scarce and entitled to more money than other professors on the staff.[97] He also saw the company's unwillingness to pay him a higher salary as symbolic of the subordination of Oriental subjects to the European curriculum.[98]

John B. Gilchrist was temporarily appointed to teach Hindi when Scott resigned, and in 1807 Alexander Hamilton, a former company employee in Bengal who had returned and studied Sanskrit in England and France, was appointed to teach Sanskrit and Bengali. Hamilton was one of the pioneer Sanskritists in Europe and taught Sanskrit to Frederick Schlegel and Claude Fauriel and other early European comparative philologists. He published a text of the Hitopedesa, a famous catalogue of Sanskrit manuscripts in France, and works on Sanskrit grammar and Hindu chronology. Charles Stewart was appointed to teach Persian and Hindustani.[99]

In addition to the two European professors of Oriental languages, Gulam Hyder, an Indian from Patna, was appointed Persian writing master.[100] Mir Abdul Ali was appointed maulvi of the college to help in the teaching of Hindustani.[101] A short while later a third Indian, Mirza Khuleel of Calcutta, was added. Ali and Khuleel had been recruited by the Bengal government at the

96. *CRO*, Vol. 19, 1806, Scott to Committee L.S., July 25, 1806.
97. The principal received £1,000 a year and each professor £500; in addition, each received housing or a housing allowance.
98. *CRO, HMS*, Vol. 488, 1805; *CRO, CCR*, Vol. 18, Scott to Committee, L.S., December 3, 1805.
99. *CRO, MRCH*, Vol. K, minutes of August 6, 1806, p. 151; *DNB*, VIII, 1018; *CRO, CCR*, Vol. 19, Wilkins to Committee, April 7, 1806.
100. *CRO, MRCH*, Vol. I, minutes of August 20, 1806, p. 154.
101. *CRO, MRCH*, Vol. I, minutes of May, 18, 1808, p. 235.

request of the Court of Directors for the college.[102] Their salaries ranged from £200 to £600 a year plus housing allowances. A short time after joining the staff both Gulam Hyder and Mir Abdul Ali married Englishwomen and settled near the college. Ali died leaving a widow and several children, but not enough money to pay his funeral and medical expenses.[103] Mir Abdul Ali was replaced on his death by Mir Hasan Ali, who was assistant to the professor of Oriental languages at Addiscombe, the company's military college.[104]

Instruction was offered initially in Sanskrit, Persian, Arabic, Hindi (Hindustani), and Bengali. The teaching of these languages was severely handicapped in the beginning by lack of text materials. Stewart, professor of Persian, complained that "many of the writers [students] attached to this College, who have been studying the Oriental Languages for more than twelve months, have never yet seen an Arabic or Persian manuscript."[105] Hamilton and Stewart wanted the East India Company to import books published for the College of Fort William. Hamilton stressed the need for Sanskrit as the basis for study of Indian languages. On the basis of a study of Malabar (Malayalam) and Maratta grammar, he believed "the languages of the peninsula to be as nearly affiliated with Sanskrit as that of Bengal."[106] Hamilton apparently confused the number of Sanskrit-derived words in Malayalam with affiliation or structural relationship with other Dravidian languages.

For the first few years the only books available were Richardson's *Dictionary of Persian;* copies of *The Gulistan,* a series of Persian tales; the *Hitopedesa,* a collection of Sanskrit tales; and William Carey's *Dialogues Intended to Facilitate the Acquiring of the Bengali Language.*[107] The latter work is reminiscent of kinds of language texts still in use for the study of the spoken

102. *CRO, MRCH,* Vol. I, minutes of September 21, 1808, p. 244.
103. *CRO, CCR,* Vol. 25, 1812, Henley to Committee, October 14, 1812; "Petition of Moonshee Ghoolam Hydor," September 4, 1812; Dr. Samuel Jones to Committee, November 24, 1812, "Petition of Elizabeth Moolvey" (n.d.).
104. *CRO, CCR,* Vol. 25, 1812, "Petition of Mir Hasan Ali."
105. *CRO, CCR,* Vol. 21, 1808, Stewart to Wilkins, L.S., September 30, 1807.
106. *CRO, CCR,* Vol. 22, 1809, Hamilton to Grant, L.S., December 24, 1808.
107. Published in Serampore, 1801.

vernaculars. It is set up as a series of typical conversations "to shew the difference of idiom among the lower orders of people in different situations."[108] There was some rivalry between the College of Fort William and Haileybury over the teaching of Oriental languages. Increasingly, Fort William stressed the vernaculars and Haileybury the "classical languages," Sanskrit, Persian, and Arabic, the rationale for this being that they were basic to all the vernaculars. The emphasis may also have been in emulation of the English liberal education of the time which stressed Greek and Latin.[109] The second generation of Oriental language teachers at the college were Graves C. Houghton, 1818–1827, Sanskrit and Bengali, H. G. Keene, 1824–1834, Francis Johnson, 1825–1855, Sanskrit, Bengali, and Telugu, and Mirza Mohammad Ibrahiann, 1826–1844, Persian and Arabic. They appear to have been more efficient and better equipped with experience and materials.

Houghton distinguished himself early at the College of Fort William as a gifted linguist. He produced several works specifically as class books: *Bengali Selections with Translations and a Vocabulary* (London, 1822), for example, contained simple graded stories and vocabularies; he also published texts of *Tota Itihas* and *Balris and Vicramadetya*. He did glossaries for works of fiction, history, and biography, which were published in Bengali by the pandits at Fort William College to facilitate their use by students at Haileybury, and *Rudiments of Bengali Grammar* (London, 1821). His major work was a Bengali, Sanskrit, and English dictionary, published after he left the college. Houghton felt that the learning of language was the key to success of every company servant; otherwise, they would be cut off by "venal interpreters" from communication with Indians. In addition, Indian morality could not be raised unless Indians could freely communicate with the British, and hence they would have the

---

108. *Ibid.,* p. v.
109. *Public Disputation of the Students of the College of Fort William in Bengal before the Rt. Hon. Lord Minto, Together with His Lordship's Discourse,* September 15, 1810, London, 1811 (*CRO P/T* 3890); CRO, CCR, Vol. 24, 1811. Stewart to Grant, L.S., March 20, 1871; Hamilton to Wilkins, L.S., April 6, 1811.

"opportunity of seeing practical examples of the advantage of that system of morality which we are anxious to impart to them."[110]

H. G. Keene described the teaching of Persian and Hindustani in 1821 as follows:

The plan pursued in the College is this: The students on their first arrival, are taught by the Professor the peculiar form and sound of each letter; and those particulars in which the alphabet and the mode of writing in the Oriental Language differs from those to which the student has become accustomed are carefully explained. The pronunciation is taught by the pupils continuing to repeat the sounds uttered by the Professor until by practice they gradually acquire as much facility and correctness as can be reasonably expected. . . . At the same time that the Professor is thus employed, the students attend the Munshi (or writing master), who is a native of Bengal and who is teaching them to write the characters, and takes pains to correct their pronunciation. As soon as they are sufficiently familiar with the characters and the common rules of the grammar, they proceed to read and translate easy passages: The Professor reading every word distinctly and explaining the whole grammatical construction. They are at the same time encouraged to make translations from English, which they bring to the Professor, in the character peculiar to the language, which gives him an opportunity of correcting the errors in grammar and spelling.[111]

Students took instruction in three or four Oriental languages. Sanskrit and Persian were required of everyone. In addition, students received instruction in a vernacular of the Presidency to which they were appointed. Some took Arabic as well, and if they were assigned to Bengal, they took Hindi and Bengali. Instruction in Oriental languages by modern standards was not very intensive. A senior in 1823 took two hours of Persian, two hours of Sanskrit, and two hours of Bengali or Hindustani per week.[112] A total of thirty-six hours of language instruction a term for the four classes in the college were offered by Professors Stewart, Hough-

110. G. C. Houghton, *Rudiments of Bengali Grammar* (London, 1821), p. xi and entire preface.
111. East India Company Proprietors, *General Court Papers Respecting the System of Education in the Oriental Languages Adopted at the East India Company's College and Seminary in England* (London: Printed by Order of the General Court of Proprietors, December 19, 1821). H. G. Keene to Wilkins, December 10, 1821, p. 10.
112. *CRO, CCR,* Vol. 36, 1823, "Class Schedule in Senior Term."

ton, Keene, and Anderson, and there were twelve hours offered by Munshis in 1823.[113]

In order to obtain the certificates necessary to receive their appointments, students had to pass an examination in Sanskrit. This appears to have been the only language course which they were required to pass. Sir George Campbell described Sanskrit as *the* great study at Haileybury, but after ten years of working in India he concluded that it was as useful to an Indian magistrate "as a knowledge of ancient German would be to an English Commissioner of Police."[114] A few students such as Sir William Muir or Sir Monier Monier-Williams became distinguished Orientalists, but most learned their Sanskrit as did J. H. Rivett-Carnac by having his fellow student, Chester Bernard, cram him with enough to "just scrape through the examination."[115]

The centrality of Sanskrit and Oriental languages was maintained by two powerful figures who were not on the faculty but were the Oriental visitors. Sir Charles Wilkins, who acted as visitor from 1806 to 1836, and H. H. Wilson, 1836–1851. In their time both were thought to be among the foremost Oriental scholars, and both were librarians for the East India Company. As they lived in London and were close to the College Committee, they were asked for their formal opinion on any matter regarding the teaching of Oriental languages at Haileybury. They examined all candidates for posts in Oriental languages at the college and recommended which Oriental publications were to receive company subsidy and which were to be used for texts at Haileybury. Their role in the life of Haileybury was crucial. Twice a year they journeyed to Haileybury to examine the students in Oriental languages.

Charles Wilkins had gone to India in the 1770's as a writer. He was one of the first Englishmen "to acquire a thorough knowledge

113. *Ibid.,* "Lectures Given."
114. George Campbell, *Modern India* (London, 1852), p. 265. In retrospect, even Monier-Williams, one of the professors of Sanskrit, doubted its value as a compulsory subject. M. Monier Williams, "My Student Days," in F. D. Danvers *et al., Memorials of Old Haileybury* (Westminster, 1892), p. 52, n. 4.
115. J. H. Rivett-Carnac, *Many Memories of Life in India, At Home and Abroad* (Edinburgh and London, 1910), p. 14.

of Sanskrit,"[116] and Wilkins and N. B. Halhead published in English the first systematic compilation of Hindu law and wrote the first Bengali grammar. Wilkins cast the first type font of Bengali and did much to establish printing in Oriental languages in India.[117] He also published a Sanskrit grammar in 1808, which although inaccurate provided a beginning place for several generations of Sanskritists.[118]

H. H. Wilson stands with Sir William Jones, H. C. Colebrooke, and James Prinsep among the founders of Oriental studies in Great Britain. He went to India in 1808 as an assistant surgeon. When a post as assay master of the Calcutta Mine became open, he took it, using a knowledge of chemistry learned as a boy from an uncle who was in the Assay Department of the Government Mint in London. He began his study of Indian languages by learning Hindustani from an Indian while en route to India by ship. His career in India was mainly in Calcutta. Monier-Williams described his scholarship in this way: "He was never great as a scholar (in its restricted sense) or as a grammarian, and was quite untrained in the scientific methods of the German School of Philology."[119] It was rather his breadth of scholarship and his zeal to promote Indian studies on which his fame rests. In addition to a Sanskrit grammar, he published a translation of the *Rig Veda*, a study of the Vishnu Purana, and studies of the religion and philosophy of the Hindus. Modern historians of India continue to rely heavily on his *A Glossary of Judicial and Revenue Terms . . . of British India*. Although Monier-Williams denigrates his knowledge of Indian languages, Lutfullah, an Indian who met Wilson in London in 1844, was impressed by his attainments.[120]

It was assumed that students would come to Haileybury well grounded in the classics, the Bible, and with some rudiments of

116. E. Buchland, *A Dictionary of Indian Biography* (London, 1906), p. 451.
117. M. Siddig Khan, "William Carey and the Serampore Books," *Libri*, XI (1961), 202–203; Anant K. Priorkar, *The Printing Press in India: Its Beginning and Early Development* (Bombay, 1958), p. 51.
118. Monier-Williams, *op. cit.*, p. 208.
119. *Ibid.*, p. 212.
120. *Autobiography of Lutfullah* (London, 1858), p. 389.

modern history and moral philosophy. From the beginning of the college in 1806, there was an entrance examination given by a professor and the principal.[121] This appears to have been *pro forma,* but by the 1830's it had become a formidable examination in which a student had to present evidence that he knew the Four Gospels of the Greek Testament and had to translate portions of Homer, Herodotus, Xenophon, Thucydides, Sophocles, and Euripides, as well as the Latin authors Terence, Cicero, Tacitus, Vergil and Horace. Paley's *Evidence of the Christian Religion* was also an important work for the examination.[122] After 1836 outside examiners paid by the company were employed to administer the entrance examination and were drawn from Oxford, Cambridge, and King's College, London. The passing rate in the late 1830's appears to have been about 75 per cent.[123]

With the stiffening of the entrance requirements, special tutors, schools, and crammers developed. The examination may have deterred some directors from wasting their patronage on a totally incompetent candidate, but as Campbell observed:

Still the art of cramming is, like other modern science, carried to such a pitch of refinement (being quite a profession), that most young men of decent education can be crammed into passing without remarkable talent or acquirement.[124]

Most of the crammers were clergymen, such as C. Yeatman, M. Barnard, Rolfe, and Peters.[125] One, at least, James Morris of London, was a retired Madras civil servant; E. E. Rowsell appears to have been one of the most popular crammers.[126] He

121. T. R. Malthus, "Statement Respecting the East India College with an Appeal to Facts in Refutation of the Charges Lately Brought Against It in the Court of Proprietors (London, 1817) (seen in India Office Library, *Fort William College,* Vol. XXV).

122. "Rules and Regulations to be Observed with Respect to the Examination of Candidates for Admission into the East India College at Haileybury," British Museum, *Add. MS* 36,470 F. 341, n.d. (after 1836).

123. British Museum, *Add. MS* 36,470 F. 45.

124. Campbell, *op. cit.,* p. 264.

125. Little information on the crammers is available. This discussion, unless otherwise noted, is derived from information in the educational certificates submitted by candidates and found in volumes of the *Committee on College Reference* in the *CRO.*

126. H. G. Keene, *Here and There: Memories Indian and Other* (London, 1906), p. 21.

had expected as a young man to receive an appointment to India and had by the time he was eighteen studied Persian and Hindustani, but he did not get his appointment and instead went to St. John's College, Cambridge, from which he received an M.A. In the early 1830's he began training students for the entrance examination and was active into the next decade.[127]

For fifteen years there was a special preparatory school called the East India Company College School. It was headed by the Rev. M. H. Luscombe for a period starting in 1806 and was established mainly but not exclusively for boys going to Haileybury.[128] As can be seen from Table 6, only eight boys in 1809 and 1810 and six boys in 1819 and 1820 presented educational certificates from the school.

In addition to the crammers, there were a few language schools which students attended to get a head start on the learning of Oriental languages before entering the college. The most important of these was the London Oriental Institution of Sanford Arnot and Duncan Forbes in Leicester Square. The school had been founded by John B. Gilchrist. Gilchrist, who was one of the original professors at Fort William and who taught briefly at Haileybury, believed he should have been a permanent member of the staff and was a constant critic of the company and its college. He thought there was little point for those going into company service to study the classical languages of India. In addition, he believed that the vernaculars should be taught through romanized script. When Gilchrist ran the London Oriental Institution he did not take fees, but he did charge fifteen guineas for the textbooks used at the institution, of which he was the sole author. Arnot and Forbes followed the more conventional system and claimed to be able to teach their pupils the Arabic and Nagri script, to translate and speak simple Hindustani in three months, and to master Persian and Hindustani in six months.[129] Duncan Forbes was later appointed first professor of

127. *CRO, Financial and Home Correspondence,* Vol. 79(2), E. E. Rowsell to Committee, L.S., November 21, 1843; British Museum, *Add. MS* 36,408, Rowsell to Hobhouse, L.S., November 21, 1853.
128. Danvers *et al., op. cit.,* p. 252.
129. John B. Gilchrist, *The Oriental-Occidental Tuitionary Pioneer to . . .*

Oriental languages at King's College, London, in 1837, a post he held until 1861. He published a number of Persian, Hindustani, and Bengali dictionaries and grammars.[130] Even after this appointment he continued to coach students in Sanskrit before they entered Haileybury.[131]

Table 6 ("Educational Institutions from which Students Presented Certificates Before Entering Haileybury") does not give a complete summary of the educational background of the students, since they were required minimally to present a certificate of education and good character from only their last place of study. It is likely that more attended the public schools at one time or other than is recorded here. But it is still interesting to note that certainly less than one-third of the students went to the public schools. Because of the age requirements, few had been to the universities. Generally speaking, students entering Haileybury through this period had to be more than seventeen years old and less than twenty or twenty-one. The majority of those presenting college or university certificates had gone to Edinburgh University, which apparently took students at a younger age than did the English universities. A few had transferred from Addiscombe, the company's military college. Although well over one-quarter of the students at Haileybury were from London, even these often had had their education privately with clergymen in small towns or rural areas. There also were several academies in the suburbs of London—Stanton and Mayors and the Manor House of Finchley were the most popular—to which some of the students went.

The assumption often made then, about Britain's overseas rulers having had a common secondary education in the public schools, does not hold for the company's civil servants of this period. Of course, down until the 1840's, the public schools were not in a very flourishing state, and their great period was still to come. Even though over the period about one-quarter of the

Literary Pursuits (London, n.d. [1826 or 1827]); *Annual Report of the London Oriental Institution* (London, 1829), II, 4–7; East India Company Proprietors, *op. cit.*

130. *DNB*, XIX, 387–388.
131. Danvers *et al.*, *op. cit.*, pp. 44–45.

Table 6. Educational Institutions from which Students Presented Certificates Before Entering Haileybury, 1809–1850

	1809–1810		1819–1820		1829–1830		1839–1840		1849–1850		Total	Percentage
	No.	Pct.	No.	Pct.	No.	Pct.	No.	Pct.	No.	Pct.		
Clergy	9	13	31	35	32	33	23	17	18	20	113	23.99
Grammar schools and academies	17	25	16	18	2	2	23	17	17	20	75	15.92
Public schools	13	19	10	11	13	14	11	11	17	18	64	13.59
East India School	8	12	6	7	—	—	—	—	—	—	14	2.97
Private tutor	2	3	5	6	8	8	1	1	1	1	17	3.61
Colleges	—	—	4	5	1	1	18	13	2	2	25	5.28
Addiscombe	—	—	5	6	3	3	4	3	2	2	14	2.97
Special crammers	—	—	—	—	26	27	47	35	33	36	106	22.51
Abroad	—	—	—	—	2	2	1	1	1	1	4	.85
No information	18	27	11	13	9	9	1	1	—	—	39	8.28
Totals	67		88		96		129		91		471	

Source: See p. 104, n. 57, in text.

students at Haileybury were born in India (see Table 5), none of them were educated there, as from the middle of the eighteenth century the British rulers in India sent their children home by the age of seven or eight to be brought up and educated in Great Britain.

Even with the stricter administration of the entrance examination, the educational preparation of the new students continued to be uneven. Throughout the period of the college, 1806–1859, its supporters and critics saw that Haileybury functioned to give the students a common background and culture and direct ties to each other. Because of the unevenness of their previous education and the variety of institutions they had previously attended, they did not have and could not establish direct ties with the men with whom they were to spend their working lives. Joseph Batten, the principal, in his defense of the college in 1833 before the Parliamentary Select Committee on the East India Company stated:

The College, by giving what may be called a public school feeling to persons previously educated in private or at inferior seminaries operate to render that portion of the students more like English gentlemen educated at our great national schools and universities, while at the same time it corrects the separate partisanships of those schools, and sends out, not so much Etonians or Westminsters, as Englishmen.[132]

John Sullivan, a retired Madras civil servant, agreed with Batten on the effects of the college but evaluated them differently:

The collection of a number of young men of the same age, and destined for the same scene in the same college, has always appeared to me a capital mistake in the existing plan of education. It deprives young men of the opportunity of forming a general acquaintance with the men who are hereafter to figure upon the public stage in this country. To rivet the affection of those who go early in life to India to persons and things in England should, always I imagine, be a main object of their education. . . . [Going to Haileybury] cuts them off from all society except what is to be found within the walls of the college, until they embark for India . . . and upon arrival in India

132. Joseph Batten, "Testimony," *HCPP*, 1831–1832, Vol. 9, Paper 735 I, Answer 1833.

they again associate almost exclusively with those who were their fellow collegians at Hertford.[133]

James Mill and Mountstuart Elphinstone agreed with Sullivan's view of the college, Mills feeling that the corporate life led to habits of profligacy and Elphinstone to prejudice against India and Indians.[134] In the original plan as discussed above, stress on the European side was placed on mathematics, moral philosophy, classics, history, political economy, and law. One of the first changes in the European part of the curriculum was the dropping of the principal's formal lectures on theology on the ground that they produced no effect. In the Greek course "a portion of the Greek Testament was assigned with appropriate collateral readings."[135] Batten, the principal from 1815 to 1835, also gave lectures to the Senior class on Christians of eminence, notably Paley and his works, "A View of the Evidence of Christianity."[136]

The instruction was in the form of lectures and set questions in class on lectures and readings. On the material they were learning, the students had to prepare notebooks of questions and answers to be inspected and graded by the instructor. J. H. Rivett-Carnac, a student from 1855 to 1857, described the system as it applied to the law class as follows:

We were supposed to make full notes in a "rough notebook" of the words of wisdom that fell from the lips of our legal lecturer. Then we were required in the solitude of our chambers to proceed, with the assistance of certain law books that were prescribed for us, to elaborate valuable treatises on these legal subjects, taking our rough lecture-notes as guides. At the close of the month these fair notes, as the elaborated treatises were termed, had to be handed into the "legislator" who having inspected them returned the books a few days later to us in class with his remarks, complimentary or otherwise.[137]

As in most educational institutions not all the students appear

133. "Letter from John Sullivan, February 21, 1832," *HCPP*, 1831–1832, Vol. 9, Paper 735 I, Appendix I, pp. 265–266.
134. *Ibid.*, p. 54, Question 38; p. 64, Question 475.
135. Batten, *op. cit.*, Vol. 9, Answer 1831.
136. Paley's work was the standard answer to the Deism of the eighteenth century. On Paley, see "Defender of the Faith: William Paley," *Times Literary Supplement*, XLII (July 3, 1943), 318.
137. Rivett-Carnac, *op. cit.*, p. 17. There exists a copy of such a notebook in the Commonwealth Relations Office Library, "Reade Notebooks," MS. Eur. 10/52.

to have been interested in learning what was taught them. In order to obtain the certificates stating they had been through Haileybury, the students had to pass an examination in one of the Oriental languages, usually Sanskrit. In 1819 under a parliamentary act (Act 53, Geo. 3, C. 155) it was established that in addition to the language requirement, a student needed a "good proficiency" (a high pass) in one European department (of these there were four), or two "proficiencies" (a pass) in two European departments.[138]

Many of the teachers appear to have had strong religiously orthodox positions. William Dealtry, Henry Walter, and W. E. Buckley were noted Anglican theologians. Henry Melville, the principal from 1848 to 1857, was thought to be one of the greatest preachers of his day.[139] There was strong Utilitarian influence as well. Eric Stokes has recently pointed out that "Bentham's ideas were being disseminated amongst the young Indian civilians at the East India Company's College at Haileybury"[140] via William Empson, a strong Utilitarian, who lectured there for over thirty years.

At this date there is no way of measuring how much of what was taught was retained in any fashion by the students, nor is it possible to determine how the teaching affected their behavior in India. There is little evidence in the *Haileybury Observer*, the student magazine published from 1839 to 1858, that students were given much to serious social and political thought or for that matter that they were very interested in their future in India. Other than in their language classes, there was little direct teaching about India. Few of the European subject professors had direct experience in India. Sir James Mackintosh, professor of law from 1818 to 1824, had held a judicial post in Bombay from 1804 to 1811, but in his courses it would appear there was little thought about Indian law. His aim was to impart

---

138. Batten, *op. cit.*, Vol. 9, Question 1831.
139. *DNB*, XXXVII, 229; Cornelia E. Stephen, *The Right Honorable Sir James Stephen: Letters with Biographic Notes* (London, 1906), pp. 217–218; Danvers *et al.*, *op. cit*, pp. 153–162.
140. Stokes, *op. cit.*, p. 52.

as much as possible of that kind of information which every English gentleman ought to possess . . . to elevate the minds of his youthful hearers to the principles of a high toned morality, and to imbue them with a love and veneration for all the social and active virtues which must enoble the minds of man.[141]

J. F. Leith, last professor of law, had practiced law in India, and many of the Oriental professors had spent part of their lives there as well. As far as interest on the part of the students in first-hand knowledge, though, Beames in his frank memoir seems to sum up the prevailing attitude:

If at any time one wanted to know what sort of a place India was, or what one's future life or work there was to be like, it was impossible to find anyone who could give the requisite information. . . . All we knew was that it was "beastly hot" and that there were "niggers" there, and that it would be time enough to bother about it when you got there.[142]

In addition to the few Europeans with direct knowledge of India, there were in the early years a few Indians attached to the college as language teaching assistants. This practice was dropped after fifteen years, however, as there was considerable difficulty with pensions for widows of these men and also because of "the too frequently observed irregularity or rather immorality of conduct in Mussulmans residing in this country which is injurious to the discipline of the College."[143] Even in the face of this attitude, Mirz Ibrahim, who was appointed in 1826 as assistant professor of Persian, was a Persian whose manners, dress, and command of English were highly admired.[144]

Neither the students nor the faculty were overburdened with class work. A professor of European subjects lectured on the average of four hours a week and the Oriental professor nine hours a week. There appears to have been little out-of-class

141. Robert James Mackintosh (ed.), *Memoirs of the Life of the Right Honourable Sir James Mackintosh* (London, 1835), pp. 357–358; also see outline of his course, "Moral Science-General Principles," *ibid.*, pp. 358–367.
142. John Beames, *Memoirs of a Bengal Civilian* (London, 1961), p. 64.
143. "Memorandum of N. B. Edmonstone and J. Ballie," July 19, 1826, *CRO, MRCH*, Vol. 5, 1826.
144. Danvers *et al., op. cit.*, pp. 186–188.

contact between students and teachers, and a few professors such as William Empson lived in London and commuted to Hailey-bury for his two days a week. Students were in class ten to twelve hours a week, usually from 10 A.M. to 12 noon Monday through Saturday. Their afternoons were free for amusements in the countryside:

The great charm of Haileybury was its thoroughly rural surround-ings. . . . Bathing on the Lea in the Rye House meadows was a great amusement in the summer (football in the winter). . . . But in all seasons we used to take long walks in every direction.[145]

Originally there were two terms a year: February 2 to June 19, then a vacation until August 1, and then a term to December 21. In 1835 there was a change from two to three terms a year on the grounds that it would bring the college into line with other collegiate institutions and would make the students work harder since there would not be so much time in the term before examinations.[146] At the end of each term there were examinations, followed by the visit of the College Committee of the Court of Directors. The committee assembled in private with the faculty to hear the principal's report and then met with the students to distribute prizes of medals and books and to hear the reading of the prize essays. The chairman of the committee who was always chairman of the Court of Directors would deliver a speech. Everyone appears to have enjoyed these visits.

Most contemporary evaluators of the college, former students, and subsequent scholars may not agree with Sir Alfred Lyall who saw Haileybury as "one well organized humbug."[147] Few thought the contribution to the Civil Service was found in its academic instruction, distinguished as its faculty may have been, or in the fact that it was the first institution to offer training in Oriental languages in Great Britain, or that it offered instruction in law

---

145. Sir Charles Trevelyan, quoted in R. Bosworth Smith, *Life of Lord Lawrence* (New York, 1883), I, 28.

146. C.R.O., *Letters from the Board of Control to the East India Company*, Vol. 10, No. 2884, September 17, 1834, September 27, 1834, No. 3053, March 13, 1835.

147. Quoted in Sir Mortimer Durand, *Life of the Right Honorable Sir Alfred Comyn Lyall* (Edinburgh, 1913), p. 21.

and political economy before these subjects became courses of study at Oxford and Cambridge.[148] There was a general feeling, though, that the college did instil "a spirit of camaraderie" in the students,[149] and "the friendships and associations formed at the College constituted one of the several bonds of comradeship among all the civil servants during their administrative careers, and helped to maintain an elevated standard of thought and feeling in the service as a corps d'elite."[150] This feeling of camaraderie would appear to have had several sources: the isolation of Haileybury; the relative smallness of the student body, which totaled 1,985 over its fifty-two years, an average of thirty-eight per year, or seventy-six students in residence in the college at any given time;[151] and a common bond of opposition to the college authorities and a distaste which many apparently had for their projected career in India.

The official records of the college are filled with accounts of riotous behavior by the students. There were riots in 1808,[152] 1809,[153] 1810,[154] 1815,[155] 1822,[156] and 1837.[157] On occasion students threw rocks through classroom windows, tore tiles off the roofs of some of the faculty houses, shot off guns in the quadrangle, destroyed the college back gate, attacked the college watchman, abused faculty members, shot the dogs of some of the local

---

148. The distinction of the faculty is indicated by the fact that out of thirty-one professors at the college, the biographies of nineteen appear in the *DNB*.

149. H. Morse Stephens, "An Account of the East India College at Haileybury, 1805–1857," in Lowell (ed.), *op. cit.*, pp. 233–345. This is the only lengthy analytical study of the school, and even after sixty years it stands as the most useful work on the subject.

150. Sir Richard Temple, *Men and Events of My Time in India* (London, 1882), p. 19. For similar statements, see Robert Grant, *A View of the Systems and Merits of the East India College at Haileybury . . .* (London, 1826), p. 40; Smith, *op. cit.*, p. 24; Rivett-Carnac, *op. cit.*, p. 15; and Keene, *op. cit.*, p. 20. Danvers *et al.*, *op. cit.*, is one long salute to his idea of the *esprit de corps* of the Haileybury men.

151. Stephens, in Lowell (ed.), *op. cit.*, p. 279.

152. *CRO, MRCH*, Vol. I, "At a Secret Committee of the College at Hertford," November 17, 1808.

153. *Ibid.*, "Committee Meetings at College," October 27, 1809, and November 29, 1809.

154. *Ibid.*, "Committee Meetings at College," minutes of September 7, 1810.

155. *Ibid.*, Vol. II, Part I, minutes of May 17, 1815.

156. *Ibid.*, Vol. IV, minutes of October 2, 1822; December 17, 1822.

157. *CRO, Financial Department and Home Correspondence*, Vol. 24, November, 1837, Le Bas to Committee, November 13, 1837.

gentry, and generally "raised hell" in the college and in the local countryside. Although the college was several miles from the nearest towns, Ware and Hertford, students frequented these towns, and drunkenness and gambling were activities for which the students were frequently admonished. Punishment of individual offenders was met frequently by widespread insubordination, and students as a point of honor protected offenders against college regulations.[158] Down to the end of the college, students took delight in evading the regulations established to govern their activities.[159]

The bond which commentators frequently mentioned as being formed at Haileybury came from these extracurricular activities rather than from lectures in classes or sermons in chapel. Even though one might argue that the values were false which motivated the students to act as they did, the ability to organize pranks and to individually and corporately flaunt authority may have been good training for men whose lives were to be governed by stringent regulations but who needed on occasion to act on their own.

The college faculty was in a difficult position in maintaining academic standards and discipline. By carrying out what they felt should be done, they could come into conflict with the Court of Directors who had the final say on the college and who also through their patronage were appointing the students. If a student failed for academic inadequacies or was dismissed for misbehavior, the appointing director lost as well, since to him each student represented a very valuable appointment. On occasion the principal and the faculty would dismiss a student, only to have a powerful director intervene on the student's behalf and have the College Committee of the Court of Directors overrule the action of the faculty.[160]

The number of withdrawals for all reasons, including health, change of plans, academic failure, and misconduct, appears to

158. *CRO, CCR*, Vol. 36, 1823, "Letter of Sir Charles Flint to Dr. Batten," *MRCH*, Vol. I, minutes of November 17, 1808.
159. Beames, *op. cit.*, p. 67.
160. *CRO, CCR*, Vol. 21, 1808, Thomas Parry to Court of Directors, January 4, 1809, and *MRCH*, Vol. I, minutes of January 27, 1809.

have been very low. Out of 1,985 students who are listed as having attended the college, only 281, or 12 per cent, did not graduate; of these 12 per cent, many went to India in the army after withdrawing from Haileybury.

In 1832 William Empson, professor of law, testified before the parliamentary committee that there was felt to be "a moral obligation" on the part of the faculty to send out men who in their opinion were not qualified. He said that when he joined the college and spoke to some of the professors of long standing—to "get as it were a map of the country"—they told him the faculty had been trying to raise standards of both conduct and academic attainment and that the "situation was much better than at the beginning of the College." If they did drop a student, Empson stated, they faced a great outcry from the public, since people felt it was very hard that a young man should lose his valuable appointment for some indiscretion or because of idleness.[161]

Many of the parents of students felt the college was an unnecessary delay in the careers of their sons and a financial burden, since they had to pay fifty pounds a year in fees. Questions about the college were frequently raised at meetings of the Court of Proprietors, and the college was threatened with extinction in 1813 and 1833.[162] In the face of parliamentary questions, concern of some of the stockholders, and the fact that the running of the college cost the company considerable money —over £363,000 between 1805–1806 and 1830–1831, or £267 for each writer produced[163]—it is a wonder that the Court of Directors maintained the college at all.

In 1826, faced with the need for a large number of writers, Parliament passed an act (7 Geo. IV, c. 56) allowing a director to make direct appointment of writers to go to India after passing an examination, but without having to go through Haileybury. Appointment by the London Board of Examiners lasted a little

---

161. *HCPP*, 1831–32, Vol. 12, Paper 735 IV, "Testimony of William Empson," p. 131.

162. The faculty was not above lobbying with important politicians on behalf of the college on occasion. See British Museum, *Add. MS* 40,226, F. 259. Bridge to Peel, April 29, 1813, and October 10, 1813.

163. *HCPP*, 1831–32, Vol. 9, Paper 735 I, "Testimony of Peter Auber," March 29, 1832, p. 181.

over three years, and Stephens estimates about one hundred men went to India via this method.[164] Under the company's new charter of 1833 an attempt was made to introduce a form of limited competition for an appointment to Haileybury. Under this system the Court of Directors was to appoint four times the number of applicants as there were places at the school, and these appointees were to compete for the positions through an examination. Apparently the Court of Directors never appointed the necessary number, for the competition and this plan were suspended after a two-year trial.[165] The India Act of 1853, in clauses 36 and 37, established a system of open competition for appointment to the Indian Civil Service. This, however, did not end Haileybury College outright since for a few years there were still patronage appointments to be made. After January, 1856, no more students were to be admitted to the college, and it closed in December, 1857.[166]

As has been suggested, the value of Haileybury to the students does not appear to have been in its training in any direct sense for the job they had to carry out in India. The British in India, as with their contemporary Civil Service, worked with a generalist notion of a civil servant: a man broadly educated and able on the basis of background, general knowledge, and manly virtues to carry out manifold duties. Students learned a smattering of Oriental languages, of highly dubious value to them; they learned nothing about India per se, except perhaps to pick up or confirm some prejudices; and what they knew of European learning probably was largely acquired during their pre-Haileybury education. Since only a minority appears to have matriculated in the better schools of the time, this knowledge too was in most cases slight. The students developed peer relations with a group with whom they were to spend their lives working; they also assimilated a set of values relating them to their fellow students rather than to India, or even to Britain, or to the service of which they were members. Sir George Trevelyan, son of Sir Charles Treve-

---

164. Stephens, in Lowell (ed.), *op. cit.*, p. 230.
165. *CRO, Letters from the Board of Control to the East India Company*, Vol. II, No. 3945, July 25, 1837.
166. *Ibid.*

lyan and nephew of Lord Macaulay, the two men most responsible for the system of open competition, saw this clearly when he wrote in 1863:

Haileybury formed a tie which the vicissitudes of official life could never break. In the swamps of Dacca, in the deserts of Rajpootana . . . wherever the Haileybury men met they had at least one set of associations in common. What matter if one wore the frock-coat of the Board of Revenue while the other sported the jackboots and solar topee of the Muffasil Commissioner. . . . Had they not rowed together on the Lea? Had they not larked together in Hertford . . . ? This strong *esprit de corps* had its drawbacks. The interests of the country were too often postponed to the interests of the service. But the advantages of Haileybury outweighed the defects.[167]

The British officials in India formed a most unusual kind of society with a fossil culture, cut off from close contact with home, recruited from several groups in English middle- and upper-class society, and with diverse educations. Cut off also from most real contact with Indian society, they had to carry out complex administrative tasks and constantly had to make decisions. It would seem axiomatic that in India they needed an understanding of the values and culture of their peers, superiors, and subordinates which the common experience of Haileybury gave them.[168]

The life of Haileybury spanned a period of great social and cultural change in England. It was founded during the Napoleonic Wars when England and Wales had a population of less than ten million, a figure which was to double by 1861. During the period Greater London's population grew from around 1,200,-000 to over three million, and the number of people engaged in trade and manufacturing almost tripled.[169] During this time the political weight and the attraction of the cultural ideal of the landed gentry shifted to other groups; new values began to

---

167. Sir George Trevelyan, *The Competition Wallah* (2nd ed.; London, 1907), pp. 6–7. See pp. 52 ff., in Tinker's chapter (Chapter 2) in this volume.
168. On the formation and nature of the fossil culture, see Bernard S. Cohn, "The British in Banaras: A Nineteenth Century Colonial Society," *Comparative Studies in Society and History*, IV (1962), 169–199.
169. B. R. Mitchell, *Abstract of British Historical Statistics* (Cambridge, 1962), pp. 5–6, 19, 60.

dominate British political, social, and economic life. England was changing into an industrial society during the period. The Civil Service in India, and to some extent its training, did not reflect these shifts. From 1830 the civil servants were selected more and more from a narrowing group of "old-service" families, who at one time may have been a key group in the social structure but now were really a throwback to an eighteenth-century society.

In addition to structural and cultural change at home, the tasks of the Civil Service in India were changing as well. The administration of justice and the collection of land revenue continued to be important jobs, but many new skills and jobs were to be added. Large-scale public works, railroads, canals, and roads were begun. Public health and famine control began to be important considerations, and in the late 1870's with the beginnings of political activity among the Indian elite, new attitudes and relations between the civil servants and Indians began to develop. In 1859 the constitutional basis of government in India became completely imperial. As far as the government in India was concerned, the East India Company ceased to exist, and new methods of training and recruitment for the Civil Service were begun.

· 4 ·

Bureaucratic Change in India

David C. Potter

A chaos of fact and conflicting interpretation characterizes the subject to which this chapter is addressed—the Indian bureaucracy which is emerging from the British imperial tradition. A theoretical perspective has therefore been adopted in an effort to bring order and coherence where none otherwise exists. This may be stated in the form of two propositions: (1) the Indian bureaucracy today interacts with and forms part of a developing political system;[1] and (2) a necessary although not sufficient condition for political development in India is the growth of non-bureaucratic political entities capable of holding the bureaucracy responsible for its behavior. In this chapter this perspective will be sharpened to include only the question of bureaucratic responsibility. Bureaucratic responsibility refers in this context to being both accountable to and amenable to control by non-bureaucratic political institutions, with accountability referring to regular reporting and control, meaning the ability to alter behavior. The question of bureaucratic responsibility in this chapter

1. The "one-party dominance system" model for political development in India provides the context for this chapter. Recent analyses by political scientists in terms of this model are Rajni Kothari, "The Congress 'System' in India," *Asian Survey,* IV (1964), 1161–1173; W. H. Morris-Jones, "Parliament and Dominant Party: Indian Experience," *Parliamentary Affairs,* XVII (1964), 296–307; Paul Brass, "Factionalism and the Congress Party in Uttar Pradesh," *Asian Survey,* IV (1964), 1037–1047. They argue that a comprehensive mechanism of change and a system of conflict articulation and resolution are provided by the system; that communication between society and the political system increases as a result of the working of the extensive factional network within the Congress party (at least in Uttar Pradesh); and that the tension set up between the organizational and ministerial wings of the Congress party is compatible with strong parliamentary institutions.

will be addressed specifically to government officials in the elite cadre, in public enterprises, and in local government.

I. The Elite Cadre[2]

The presence of an elite cadre of civil servants, much like the ICS in the bureaucracy of pre-independence India, today is easily the most striking instance of the structural influence of the British imperial tradition. Tinker's chapter (Chapter 2) in this volume has indicated various features of this structural legacy: open entry based on academic achievement; elaborate training arrangements; permanency of tenure; responsible, generalist posts at central, provincial, and district levels reserved for members of the elite cadre alone; a regular, graduated scale of pay with pension and other benefits; and a system of promotion and frequent transfers based predominantly on seniority and partly on merit. Certain modifications in detail have been made in this pattern since independence, but the essentials have come forward to the present day.

The legacy also contained a functional orientation, or a set of priorities, as guides to administrative behavior. This orientation is difficult to summarize, in part because it is imperfectly understood. One difficulty in such a summary is that the British imperial tradition was not static. The functional orientation of an ICS district officer[3] in the 1890's differed in emphasis from that of his counterpart in the 1930's, not only because of changed social and political conditions in India, but also because of the changing composition of the ICS itself.[4] In addition to the problem of

2. A full-length study of India's elite cadre today has still to be written. In the view of this author the best single analysis and one which also gives a lead to the literature on the subject is Ralph Braibanti, "Reflections on Bureaucratic Reform in India," in Braibanti and J. J. Spengler (eds.), *Administration and Economic Development in India* (Durham, N. C., 1963), pp. 3–68.

3. As in the chapters in this volume on Burma, Pakistan, Ceylon, and Malaya, the generic term "district officer" is used. The district officer bears the official title of collector in Andhra Pradesh, Bihar, Gujarat, Kerala, Madhya Pradesh, Madras, Maharashtra, Orissa, and Rajasthan; of deputy commissioner in Assam, Jammu and Kashmir, Mysore, the Punjab, and Uttar Pradesh; and of district magistrate in West Bengal.

4. Both these points are developed in Tinker's chapter (Chapter 2) in this volume.

summarizing a changing tradition, there are regional variations to contend with; a district officer in the Madras "intensive" system behaved differently from his counterpart in the Bengal "extensive" system. Finally, there is a lack of clear understanding as to the precise nature of the imperial authority which the members of the ICS wielded. Low has recently reminded us that historians still have to explain satisfactorily how it was that so few were able to rule so many for so long.[5] Without intending to dodge the difficulties here, for the purpose of this chapter it is sufficient to suggest two general functional orientations as part of the imperial tradition. Baldly stated, they are (1) that in exercising imperial authority the maintenance of law and order enjoyed absolute priority attention, and (2) that the members of the ICS were responsible, and considered themselves responsible, to themselves.[6] Tinker's chapter in this volume suggests these hypotheses with the following scattered comments: "The governor general in council *was* the Government of India"; "centralization of power"; emphasis on "negative power to check abuses, not positive power to stimulate action"; "loyalty to one's chief"; "self-confidence." It will be the chief concern of this section on the contemporary elite cadre to suggest that, while the maintenance of law and order is still the first priority, the members of the elite cadre are responsible to others as well as to themselves.

The present elite cadre, the Indian Administrative Service (IAS),[7] came into existence in 1947. Rapid recruitment was essential as the bulk of the British ICS officers retired immediately after independence (see Tables 1 and 2 in Braibanti's concluding chapter [Chapter 11] in this volume), and virtually all Muslim officers moved to Pakistan. Almost all of the initial

5. D. A. Low, "Lion Rampant," *Journal of Commonwealth Political Studies,* II (November, 1964); "How is it that 760 British members of the ruling Indian civil service could as late as 1939, in the face of the massive force of the Indian nationalist movement led by Gandhi, *hold down* 378 million Indians?" Quotation is on p. 235.
6. There was some undermining of this latter orientation toward the end of imperial rule.
7. The Indian Police Service (IPS), sometimes considered with the IAS as an elite, is excluded from the present discussion. No detailed study of the IPS exists, although the need for such a study is great. The former Indian Political Service, also abbreviated IPS, which saw service in the princely states and was recruited from both the ICS and the Indian army, was abolished at independence.

appointments to the IAS were made under emergency recruitment orders, in which the ordinary competitive examination was
dispensed with. Table 5 in Braibanti's concluding chapter shows
that the cadre has grown rapidly to its present strength of 1,974, a
growth of about 337 per cent over 1947. Despite this growth, the
IAS today is still a very small group of civil servants in the
bureaucratic system, much as its predecessor, the ICS, was in that
system. Table 4 in Braibanti's concluding chapter shows that the
IAS comprises .0002 per cent of the approximately nine million
government employees in India.

These nine million government employees are organized into
numerous distinct and unequal (in terms of status) services. There
are three categories. First, each of the sixteen[8] state government
bureaucracies in the Indian federation consists of dozens of
separate services; these include state administrative and secretariat services, technical services (e.g., medical officers), and local
government services. Second, there are more than twenty strictly
central government services, of which the Foreign Service, Audit
and Accounts, Customs, Income Tax, and the Central Secretariat
Services are the more important examples.[9] Third, there are five[10]

8. The names of all the states in India are given in several tables below. The
figure sixteen includes the new state of Nagaland, formally established on
December 1, 1963. General elections for the Nagaland legislative assembly were
held in January, 1964, and a new ministry was sworn in by the governor of
Nagaland on January 25, 1964. For a detailed description of the constitutional
history of Nagaland, see *The Times of India Directory and Year Book including
Who's Who, 1964–65* (Bombay, 1964), pp. 960–961. The figure sixteen does not
include Himachal Pradesh; although listed in several tables in this chapter under
"state," it is in fact a Union territory, not a state.

9. In 1962 the All India Services were the (1) Administrative Service and (2)
the Police Service. The Central Services were the (1) Foreign Service, (2) Audit
and Accounts Service, (3) Customs and Central Excise Service, (4) Defense
Accounts Service, (5) Income Tax Service, Class I, (6) Postal Service, Class I,
(7) Railway Accounts Service, (8) Transportation (Traffic) and Commercial
Departments of Superior Revenue, Establishment of Indian Railways, (9)
Ordnance Factories Service, Class I, (10) Military Lands and Cantonments
Service, Classes I and II, (11) Central Secretariat Service, Section Officers' Grade,
(12) Railway Board Secretariat Service, (13) Custom Appraisers' Service, Class
II, (14) Delhi and Himachal Pradesh Civil Service, Class II, and (15) Delhi and
Himachal Pradesh Police Service, Class II. The services listed as (14) and (15) in
this list warrant some explanation. They are small, separate cadres for the
metropolitan area embracing the city of Delhi and for the territory of Himachal
Pradesh. The cadre for the city of Delhi should not be confused with the
government of the Union of India located in Delhi and staffed by All India and
Central Services. The above list is derived from the Union Public Service
Commission, *Twelfth Report for April 1, 1961 to March 31, 1962* (New Delhi,

All India Services; the IAS, the members of which enjoy exceptional status, is the leading example. The all-India feature is a direct carry-over from the ICS structural arrangement. The IAS as a whole, in fact, is made up of sixteen cadres, one for each state. In other words, there is no central government cadre of the IAS. When each new recruit is confirmed in the service, he is allocated permanently by the central government to a particular state cadre.[11] What makes the IAS all-India is that during the course of an officer's career, he may, and many of his colleagues certainly will, work from time to time for the central government; if he does this, he is placed on deputation to the central government for not more than five years, and except in very unusual circumstances he reverts at the end of the deputation period to the state of his cadre. Approximately 70 per cent of the members of the IAS at any time are working for a state government, not the central government.[12] While serving under a state government, an IAS officer comes under the administrative

1962), p. 23, and hereinafter cited as *Twelfth Report*. Since then the three new All India Services mentioned in n. 10 below have been added. (The similarity of these cadres to those of Pakistan can be seen by referring to the list of Central Services in Braibanti's chapter (Chapter 5) in this volume, p. 258, n. 93.) The annual competitive examination for recruitment to these services is a single combined examination for All India and Central Services listed above. Separate interview boards, however, are used for the All India and Central Services, although membership is rotated between the two boards to maintain uniformity of standards.

10. Detailed descriptions of the All India Services, including composition, salary scales, and retirement provisions, are conveniently accessible in a 499-page compilation, Government of India, Ministry of Home Affairs, *Handbook of Rules and Regulations for the All India Services* (2nd ed.; 2 vols.; New Delhi, 1960). These services are established by the All India Services Act, No. LXI of 1951 with amendments. In addition to the IAS and the IPS, action has been taken to form three new All India Services: (1) Indian Services of Engineers (Irrigation, Power, Buildings, and Roads), (2) Indian Forest Service, (3) Indian Medical and Health Service. There is a tendency to think of structural reform in terms of establishing new discrete cadres based on professional specialties. In 1962 the Indian Economic Service and the Indian Statistical Service were established (*Twelfth Report*, p. 12). These were Central Services rather than All India Services. From time to time, proposals to establish other separate cadres are made. See, for example, the proposal to create an Indian Management Service for staffing of public undertakings, in S. T. Raja, "Middle and Higher Management Personnel in Public Sector," *The Indian Journal of Public Administration*, XI (January-March, 1965), 19–26.

11. There have been occasional instances of IAS officers being transferred to another state cadre.

12. *Indian Administrative Service (Fixation of Cadre Strength) Regulations*, 1955, *Handbook of Rules and Regulations for the All India Services*, Vol. 2, pp. 1–17.

control of the state government, that is, his postings and transfers and other ancillary matters are controlled by the state government. However, and this is another aspect of the all-India arrangement, he is governed by rules made by the central government, and these cannot be altered or interpreted to his disadvantage except by or with the approval of that government. Also he can appeal to the central government and the Union Public Service Commission in cases where he considers his service rights to have been infringed by an order of the state government. In this very interesting arrangement India's federal system is straddled and yet not violated.[13]

The IAS is also an elite in the sense that the top generalist posts in the bureaucracy as a whole are reserved for members of this service alone. The ICS tradition is very strong here. Table 1 of this chapter, elaborating comparative Table 4 in Braibanti's concluding chapter (Chapter 11) in this volume, reveals that nineteen of the twenty-three ministries (83 per cent) in the central government are headed by secretaries drawn from the IAS. All of these nineteen secretaries are veteran ICS officers in the IAS. Of equal importance is the fact that IAS officers staff the key positions close to the president and the prime minister as well as the highest-level positions charged with co-ordinating cabinet policy, controlling the recruitment, training, and discipline of the upper reaches of the Civil Service, and formulating the policies of administrative reform. In state and local governments the same pattern of IAS paramountcy is found. Table 2 shows that about 86

13. The subject of Indian federalism, particularly its structure, is well represented in the literature on Indian government. It has also been the subject of much judicial interpretation by the Supreme Court of India; hence, a rich and significant body of case law has developed. Federal distribution of powers and consequent structure have an important basic influence in determining the scope of bureaucratic behavior. The subject is not treated in this chapter, however, because of the relatively adequate attention it has been given in published analyses elsewhere. For a detailed discussion of the whole subject, including a comprehensive review of the literature, see T. J. Leonard's long bibliographical essay, "Federalism in India," in William S. Livingston (ed.), *Federalism in the Commonwealth: A Bibliographical Commentary* (London, 1963), pp. 87–143. See also M. P. Jain, *Indian Constitutional Law* (Delhi, 1962), pp. 225–333. The Indian Law Institute has recently undertaken a comprehensive study of Indian federalism. For an analysis of the topic designed to stimulate a research strategy for this project, see M. P. Jain, "Federalism in India," *Journal of the Indian Law Institute*, VI (1965), 355–379.

Table 1. *Government of the Union of India Secretariat and Ministries Showing ICS-IAS Officers Assigned as Secretaries, 1963*

Government entity	Post held by ICS or IAS officer[a]
Secretariats	
Secretary to the president	ICS
Secretary to the prime minister	ICS
Cabinet Secretariat	
Cabinet secretary	ICS
Additional cabinet secretary	ICS
Joint cabinet secretary	ICS
Director, Organization and Methods	IAS
Planning Commission secretary	ICS
Ministries	
1. Atomic Energy	—
2. Commerce and Industry	ICS
3. Community Development	ICS
4. Defense	ICS
5. Economic Defense and Coordination	ICS
6. Education	—
7. External Affairs	ICS
8. Finance	ICS
9. Food and Agriculture	ICS
10. Health	ICS
11. Home Affairs[b]	ICS
Director, National Academy of Administration	ICS
Chairman, Union Public Service Commission	ICS
Secretary, Union Public Service Commission	ICS
Joint secretary, Establishments Office	ICS
12. Information and Broadcasting	ICS
13. Irrigation and Power	ICS
14. Labour and Employment	ICS
15. Law	—
16. Mines and Fuels	ICS
17. Parliamentary Affairs	—
18. Railways	ICS
19. Scientific and Industrial Research	ICS
20. Scientific Research and Cultural Affairs	ICS
21. Steel and Heavy Industries	ICS
22. Transport and Communications	ICS
23. Works, Housing, and Rehabilitation	ICS

[a] The distinction between ICS and IAS is, in a sense, an arbitrary one made for purposes of this table, since ICS officers are actually in the IAS. On the other hand, the official Civil Lists continue to make this distinction.

[b] More detailed analysis is given for the Ministry of Home Affairs because these positions deal directly and crucially with policy matters re-

Table 2. *Secretariats*[a] *of Fifteen State Govern-ments in India Showing ICS-IAS Officers Assigned as Secretaries, 1963*

Name of state[b]	Number of secretariat departments[c]	Number of IAS (ICS) officers[d]
Andhra Pradesh	12	11 (1)
Assam	12	11 (1)
Bihar	20	19 (2)
Gujarat	14	10 (4)
Himachal Pradesh[e]	15	9 (1)
Kerala	10	7 (0)
Madhya Pradesh	14	13 (2)
Madras	12	12 (1)
Maharashtra	12	11 (6)
Mysore	14	11 (1)
Orissa	18	17 (1)
Punjab	12	11 (3)
Rajasthan	15	12 (0)
Uttar Pradesh	19	19 (3)
West Bengal	17	13 (3)
Totals	216	186 (29)

[a] Attached, or operation, technical departments are not meant to be included in this survey. Unfortunately, in the Civil List used, the distinction between secretariat depart-ments (corresponding to ministries in the central govern-ment) and attached departments is not clearly made in a uniform manner for all fifteen states. Hence, some inac-curacy in classifying departments may be expected. Such inaccuracy probably does not exceed two departments for each state.
[b] Information for Nagaland and Jammu and Kashmir not available.
[c] This figure includes the chief secretary.
[d] Number of ICS officers is shown in parentheses. They are included in the IAS figure.
[e] Not yet a state.
Source: Compiled from *All India Civil List, corrected as of July, 1963.*

lating to administration and with recruitment, training, and discipline of the superior civil service. Similar analysis for other ministries would reveal a large number of ICS officers in positions below that of secretary to the ministry.

Source: All India Civil List, corrected as of July, 1963 (Bombay: Asso-ciated Advertisers and Printers, February, 1964). This is not the official Civil List, although it is authorized by the Government of India.

per cent of the secretaries to major departments in the state governments are IAS officers. Of this number, 16 per cent are ICS veterans. Typically, the departments headed by non-IAS officers are law, education, and health. If these departments were ex-

Table 3. *Divisions in States Showing Commissionerships Held by IAS Officers, 1964*

Name of state	Number of divisions	Number of divisions headed by IAS officer[a]
Andhra Pradesh	0	0
Assam	2	2 (0)
Bihar	4	4 (2)
Gujarat	0	0
Jammu and Kashmir[b]	2	NA
Kerala	0	0
Madhya Pradesh	7	7 (0)
Madras	0	0
Maharashtra	4	4 (0)
Mysore	4	4 (0)
Nagaland	0	0
Orissa	0	0
Punjab	3	3 (0)
Rajasthan	0	0
Uttar Pradesh	11	11 (8)
West Bengal	2	2 (0)
Totals	39	37 (10)

[a] ICS incumbents shown in parentheses and included in the larger IAS figure.
[b] Includes districts or parts thereof claimed and presently occupied by Pakistan and China. In Jammu and Kashmir, divisions are known as provinces.
NA: Information not available.
Sources: Compiled from Government of India, Ministry of Information and Broadcasting, *India, A Reference Annual, 1964* (New Delhi, 1964), pp. 7–13, and from *The Civil List of the Indian Administrative Service (as on 1st January, 1964)* (Delhi, 1964), pp. 1–237.

cluded from consideration, the proportion of IAS-headed departments would approximate 100 per cent. Table 3 shows that about 95 per cent of the commissioners of divisions are IAS officers, of whom 27 per cent are ICS veterans. The proportion diminishes somewhat in the districts. Table 4 shows that about 78 per cent of the district officers are members of the IAS. None of these is an ICS officer, since ICS officers would be too senior for district posts. The proportion of IAS officers holding district posts would be considerably higher if special conditions did not obtain in Jammu and Kashmir, Maharashtra, and Uttar Pradesh. Thus, the

Table 4. *Districts in States Showing District Officers' Positions Held by IAS Officers, 1964*

Name of state	Number of districts	Number of districts headed by IAS officer[a]
Andhra Pradesh	20	18
Assam	11	11
Bihar	17	16
Gujarat	17	13
Himachal Pradesh[a]	6	4
Jammu and Kashmir[b]	9	NA
Kerala	9	9
Madhya Pradesh	43	42
Madras	13	13
Maharashtra	26	15
Mysore	20	12
Nagaland	3	NA
Orissa	13	13
Punjab	20	14
Rajasthan	26	25
Uttar Pradesh	54	31
West Bengal	16	15
Totals	**323**	**251**

[a] Not yet a state.
[b] Includes districts or parts thereof claimed and presently occupied by Pakistan and China. In Jammu and Kashmir, divisions are known as provinces.
NA: Information not available.
Sources: Compiled from *India, A Reference Annual, 1964,* pp. 7–13, and from *Civil List of the Indian Administrative Service (as on 1st January, 1964),* pp. 1–237.

most important executive positions in local government throughout India are dominated by IAS officers.

Other structural features of the IAS reinforce its elite character following from the reserved-posts arrangement. One is an elaborate and separate training system for direct recruits to the service.

Such recruits are sent initially to the National Academy of Administration at Mussoorie, a lovely hill station in Uttar Pradesh, for a year; then they are sent out to the states of their assigned cadres for practical, on-the-job training which varies in duration from ten to twenty months, depending on the particular state.[14] The details of the system need not detain us here.[15] It is useful, however, to indicate the general content of the present "foundational course"[16] which has been summarized as follows:

The idea underlying the course is that officers of the higher services should acquire an understanding of the constitutional, economic and social framework within which they have to function, as these largely determine the policies and programmes towards the framing and execution of which they will have to make their contribution. They should, further, acquaint themselves with the machinery of Government and the broad principles of public administration. For civil servants in the higher grades, knowledge and understanding of their individual departments is not enough; they should have an understanding of the machinery of Government as a whole and the interrelationship of its different parts. Civil servants should also have a clear appreciation of the role of the civil service in a parliamentary democracy. The foundational course is also intended to cover such matters as aims and obligations of the civil service, and the ethics of the profession—objectivity, integrity, thoroughness, impartiality, etc.[17]

It is during the foundational course that the direct recruits first learn, in the words of the summary above, "the ethics of the profession in a parliamentary democracy" which may influence them subsequently on the job. The ethics of the profession owe a great deal to the ICS tradition; the role in a parliamentary

14. The IAS Training School, Metcalfe House, Delhi, was converted into the National Academy of Administration in 1959 and moved to more spacious quarters in Mussoorie.
15. For an account, see S. P. Jagota, "Training of Public Servants in India," in Braibanti and Spengler (eds.), *Administration and Economic Development in India*, pp. 69–93. See also a description of the IAS training system in Government of India, Planning Commission, *Report on Indian and State Administrative Services and Problems of District Administration* (by V. T. Krishnamachari) (New Delhi, 1962), pp. 14–19. Hereinafter cited as Krishnamachari Report.
16. The foundational course occurs during the first five months of a trainee's tenure at the National Academy; probationers of the IPS, the Indian Foreign Service, and Class I Central Service also attend this course; then they disperse to the respective departments of training institutions, while the IAS probationers continue separately at the academy for an additional seven months.
17. Krishnamachari Report, p. 14.

democracy is new, for the IAS officers are formally public servants, whereas their predecessors were themselves the government. This changed behavioral orientation of direct recruits leaving the National Academy of Administration today has been observed by Morris-Jones: "the young IAS seems to accept the challenge [of serving rather than ruling]; they see their role as still crucial but to be played in a new style; they go from Mussoorie willing to learn that style."[18]

Another feature which supports elitism in the IAS is high salary, which again following ICS precedent is far above that received by any other group of civil servants in India, a fact revealed by Braibanti's comparative Table 7 in the concluding chapter of this volume. This factor along with others—social prestige attaching to the IAS, for example—draws many of India's brightest college graduates into the service by way of the Union Public Service Commission's annual examination.[19] The education required to compete successfully in the examination costs money, and it is not surprising that the direct recruits tend to come from high-income families. A recent analysis of 615 direct recruits as of 1960 tells us that 33 per cent came from families with salaries in excess of Rs. 900 per month, 58 per cent from families with salaries between Rs. 300 and Rs. 900 per month, and only 9 per cent from families with incomes below Rs. 300

18. W. H. Morris–Jones, *The Government and Politics of India* (London, 1964), p. 124.

19. The latest available report of the Union Public Service Commission for the period April 1, 1961, to March 31, 1962, shows 9,182 applicants for the combined All India–Central Services examination held in October and November, 1961. Of this number, 5,659 took and 1,047 passed the written examination; 872 were declared successful in the entire examination (written and viva voce); 112 applicants were recommended for appointment to the IAS; and ninety-nine were actually appointed to the IAS (*Twelfth Report*, p. 23). The number of university bachelor's degrees conferred that year is not precisely known, but the Krishnamachari Report (p. 10), completed in August, 1962, states that the annual number of university graduates approximates 105,000. Assuming this to be roughly correct, some revealing percentages can be computed. We find .09 per cent of university graduates in 1962 were actually appointed to the IAS; 1.1 per cent of those who applied for the examination were appointed; and 9.3 per cent of those who passed the entire examination were appointed. Of those who took the written examination, 18.4 per cent passed. These figures suggest very high selectivity among applicants ultimately appointed to the IAS. These percentages do not vary much from those for Pakistan. See Braibanti's Table 8 (p. 262) in his chapter on Pakistan (Chapter 5) in this volume and comments in his concluding chapter, esp. p. 644.

per month.[20] Of particular interest, however, is a recent leveling down in composition; the seventy-two recruits undergoing training at the National Academy of Administration in 1960 divided fairly evenly on this scale between high, middle, and low family income groups—37 per cent, 39 per cent, and 24 per cent, respectively. Of further interest is the recent, dramatic increase in the representation of scheduled castes and tribes, formerly called untouchables: 26.2 per cent of the total batch of direct recruits in 1962 came from this background. These two sets of figures suggest a perceptible change in the social background of the IAS which may be changing the power relationship between the service and other groups in the bureaucracy, on the one hand, and the service and other non-bureaucratic groups in society, on the other. We shall return to this point later in this section.

Further data on the social composition of direct recruits are available; for example, Trivedi and Rao,[21] in a study of direct recruits between 1948 and 1960, show that nearly 90 per cent are Hindus (4.4 per cent are Sikhs, 2.9 per cent Christians, and 1.9 per cent Muslims) and that 44.5 per cent are sons[22] of government officials. Fathers of the remainder are teachers (14.3 per cent), lawyers (10.6 per cent), businessmen (9.9 per cent), agriculturists (8.0 per cent), and physicians (4.9 per cent). Roughly 75 per cent of India's population are agriculturists. Regional biases in composition have also been noted, with certain states providing a disproportionate number of direct recruits to the IAS. Madras leads the way with 23 per cent, followed by Uttar Pradesh, 16 per cent, the Punjab, 12 per cent, and the city of Delhi, 8 per cent. This can be contrasted with West Bengal, 7 per cent, Andhra Pradesh, 4 per cent, and Rajasthan, 3 per cent. It is a striking fact that half of the states in the Indian federation provide fewer direct recruits than the state of Madras.

Unfortunately, all these data, valuable as they are, give only a

20. D. N. Rao, "Disparities of Representation Among the Direct Recruits to the I.A.S.," *Indian Journal of Public Administration,* IX (January–March 1963), 91.
21. R. K. Trivedi and D. N. Rao, "Regular Recruits to the I.A.S.—A Study," *Journal of the National Academy of Administration,* V (1960), 50–80.
22. It should be recorded that twenty-one women have also been recruited to the IAS (although one has recently resigned the service). This is a striking departure from the ICS tradition.

partial picture of the social composition of the IAS as a whole. The problem is that only 41 per cent of the members of the IAS are in fact direct recruits—that is, directly recruited between the ages of twenty-one and twenty-four (up to twenty-nine in the case of scheduled castes and tribes) as a result of the Union Public Service Commission's annual examination. We know nothing about the remaining 59 per cent. Of the total cadre strength, 33 per cent have been promoted or recruited from state civil services; 15 per cent either have been selected as a result of special recruitment since 1947 or are former World War II officers for whom certain vacancies in the IAS were reserved; and the remaining 11 per cent are in fact those remaining ICS officers, only three of whom are British (see Braibanti's Table 3 in Chapter 11), who are included in most computations and totals for the IAS. Table 5 shows in somewhat more detail the composition of the IAS in 1963. It should be kept in mind that the percentages shown in Table 5 change each year. The figure of 40.8 per cent for recruits who have entered by regular competition will continually increase, and unless large numbers of officers are promoted from the state services or otherwise appointed, all the other proportions will decrease.

The All India Services Act, 1951, provides for filling some vacancies in the IAS and IPS by promotion of officers employed in the state services. Persons so recruited must not exceed 25 per cent of the senior duty posts borne on the cadre of any state or group of states. This means that at any given time approximately 25 per cent of the IAS cadre will be made up of officers promoted from the state services. If this policy continues, and if no new direct recruitment by methods other than the regular competitive examination is used, the composition by mode of entry will have shifted in a few decades so that about 75 per cent of the cadre instead of the present 41 per cent, will have been recruited by competitive examination. This may affect the cohesion of the cadre as a group, for three-fourths will have entered between the ages of twenty-one and twenty-four years, will have had the same training at the National Academy of Administration, and will have had the same kind of pre-entry university education. Yet this homogeneity, while it may be partially restored, may never be quite as complete as in the pre-independence ICS because of the influx of other types of lateral entrants and their influence in the

Table 5. *Composition of IAS by Mode of Recruitment, 1963*

Mode of recruitment	Number of officers	Percentage
1. Members of the former ICS	206	10.8
2. War-service recruits appointed in 1947	90	4.7
3. Appointed on results of regular annual competitive examinations from 1948–1961	783	40.8
4. Appointed from "Open Market" emergency recruitment in 1948	96	5.0
5. Appointed on results of special recruitment examination in 1956	91	4.7
6. Appointed from state services under Special Recruitment Scheme in 1956	134	7.0
7. Appointed from state services under Emergency Recruitment Scheme in 1948	63	3.3
8. Promoted from state services	328	17.1
9. Appointed from state services under Extension to States Scheme, 1949	108	5.6
10. Appointed to Delhi and Himachal Pradesh, Jammu and Kashmir cadres under "Initial Constitution" Scheme	17	0.9
Total	1,916	

Source: Compiled from Government of India, Ministry of Home Affairs, *The Civil List of the Indian Administrative Service (as on 1st January, 1963)* (New Delhi, 1964), pp. 238–283. Percentages have been added.

cadre for two or three decades. It is not known whether lateral entry or entry into the IAS from other sources will again be resumed. The Krishnamachari Report discussed this matter rather thoroughly and submitted to the state governments a suggestion earlier made by the Second Pay (Das) Commission which called for recruitment into the IAS of other government servants up to age thirty by a separate competitive examination in which the interview would count for half the total grade. The state governments apparently did not favor this plan and no decision was made on it.[23] It appears that principal reliance will be placed on

23. Krishnamachari Report, pp. 10–13.

recruitment by competitive examination of persons between the ages of twenty-one and twenty-four in the traditional method as well as by promotion from the state services within the 25 per cent limit. Whatever the future of lateral entry or emergency recruitment may be, the figures for 1963 dramatically contradict the commonly held view that most IAS officers have been and are now recruited between the ages of twenty-one and twenty-four on the basis of a competitive annual examination. They suggest further, and more importantly, that as regards composition there is a departure from the ICS tradition. The high degree of exclusiveness and internal coherence within the old ICS, stemming largely from a common recruitment and training background, is not shared in the same degree by its successor, as composed in 1963. The IAS, it can be suggested, is a looser organization holding a more disparate collection of civil servants with different backgrounds and experience. This consideration reinforces the contention above as to the social composition of the direct recruits to the IAS; but since nothing is known about the social composition of 59 per cent of the service, we must admit that we have only a very partial understanding of the nature and extent of that change. And, of course, as was indicated above, a complete termination of recruitment other than by the traditional direct mode may restore some of the old homogeneity.

With the exception of this changing composition, the picture of the IAS structure which emerges from the analysis so far—very select, all-India, elite, specially trained, highly paid—suggests a considerable degree of continuity with the British imperial tradition. Before turning to the changed functional orientation of the IAS, however, it is worth pausing briefly to consider another element of continuity which the account as presented so far has obscured.

Those few ICS officers who did not retire directly after independence and who remain on active duty today are usually lumped together with the IAS in Government of India computations and scholarly analyses relating to the elite cadre. It is useful, however, in understanding continuity to distinguish between the two and to discuss separately that dwindling group (recruitment to the ICS ceased in 1944) of ICS officers who remain on active duty in India today.

The rapid growth of the IAS, noted earlier in this essay, has been accompanied by the gradual decline in strength of the ICS, as year by year ICS officers either die or are retired. And yet, sixteen years after independence, there were still 206 ICS officers on active duty in India. Table 6 suggests that the number of ICS

Table 6. *Estimated Annual Retirement of Former ICS Officers in the IAS, Projected through 1982*[a]

Year	Estimated projected strength of total IAS cadre[b]	Number of former ICS officers remaining[c]	Percentage of ICS officers in total estimated IAS cadre
1965	2,252	206	9.1
1966	2,320	193	8.3
1967	2,400	183	7.6
1968	2,480	168	6.8
1969	2,500	159	6.3
1970	2,500	149	6.0
1971	2,500	132	5.3
1972	2,500	125	5.0
1973	2,500	109	4.4
1974	2,500	90	3.6
1975	2,500	79	3.2
1976	2,500	64	2.6
1977	2,500	51	2.0
1978	2,500	39	1.6
1979	2,500	23	0.9
1980	2,500	14	0.6
1981	2,500	4	0.2
1982	2,500	2	0.1

[a] Only anticipated retirement at sixty years of age is calculated in this table. No attrition due to death or other causes has been estimated.

[b] The official estimate of revised strength is 2,252 in 1962; annual intake is projected at eighty to eighty-five; total strength is expected to stabilize at 2,400. (*Report on Indian and State Administrative Services and Problems of District Administration*) (New Delhi, August, 1962) (V. T. Krishnamachari Report), pp. 8–9. This projection is arbitrarily increased to 2,500, and the probability is that it will be even higher.

[c] This has been determined from date of birth of officers as shown in *Civil List of the Indian Administrative Service* (*as on 1st January, 1963*).

Source: Compiled from list cited in note [c], above.

officers will continue to decline gradually, although, fascinatingly, it is possible that there may be a few in service in 1980. Table 7 shows that ICS officers occupy posts throughout the country, with 34 per cent in state government. A perusal of the actual posts held instantly makes clear that the ICS is today the elite of the elite.[24] In the central government, as Table 1 above makes clear, ICS officers hold key positions—e.g., secretary to the cabinet, principal secretary to the prime minister, secretary to the president, and secretary to most ministries in the Government of India—most of

Table 7. *Distribution by Position of 206 Former ICS Officers in the IAS, 1963*

Category of position	Number of officers	Percentage of officers
(Central) Government of India secretariat and related positions	101	49.0
State government secretariats and related position	72	35.0
Diplomatic assignments abroad	26	12.6
On leave	6	2.9
Under suspension	1	0 5

Source: Compiled from *Civil List of Indian Administrative Service* (*as on 1st January, 1963*).

which pay Rs. 4,000 to ICS occupants. The state government ICS officers head the bureaucratic system as chief secretaries with three exceptions: Kerala, Orissa, and Rajasthan (which has no ICS in its cadre). More than twenty are serving abroad in the capacity of ambassador or in other foreign posts; two well-known examples are C. V. Narasimhan (Madras cadre), at the United Nations, and B. K. Nehru (Uttar Pradesh cadre), ambassador to the United States. Finally, two ICS officers hold important training

24. The position is comparable in the case of those remaining sixty-two members of the Indian Police (IP) (recruited before 1947) as distinct from the 1,002 members of the Indian Police Service (IPS) (recruited after 1947). Twenty-one are on deputation to the Government of India and the remaining forty-one are in state government, with IP officers holding the post of inspector general of police in every state government that has such officers in its IPS cadre. For details, see Government of India, Ministry of Home Affairs, *The Civil List of the Indian Police Service* (*as on 1st January 1963*) (Delhi, 1963).

posts, one as director of the National Academy of Administration, the other as principal of the Central Institute for Training and Research in Community Development, also at Mussoorie. In short, ICS officers have held, and will hold for some years to come, those posts in which the occupants are able to set the tone of administrative behavior for the IAS, both under training and on the job. That the IAS on the whole is carrying forward the ICS tradition is noted by most observers: e.g., "The valuable part of the ICS 'ethos' has been astonishingly preserved [in the IAS]."[25] The separate analysis of the position of the ICS, coupled with the analysis of the IAS structure above, suggests that the fact that the ICS "ethos" has been preserved is perhaps not so astonishing after all.

The analysis now joins the ICS and the IAS together again in the form of an elite cadre in which the ICS "ethos," the heart of the British imperial tradition, continues to exercise a profound influence. That ethos includes not only structural form but also functional orientations. Two orientations which influenced administrative behavior in the ICS were singled out at the outset of this chapter in fairly rough and tentative form: a sense of the primacy of law and order, and a sense of responsibility for administrative action to the bureaucracy itself. In considering the difficult question of the influence of these two orientations on IAS behavior today, the remainder of this section will come to the general conclusion that while the "law and order orientation" (definitely part of the ICS ethos) is still prominent, the "exclusive responsibility orientation" has changed.

Taking the primacy of law and order first, it must be allowed that the maintenance of internal order is the first concern of any civil bureaucracy in a viable state. In India, the need to maintain order was a particularly compelling one in the years directly after independence. The new government was faced with communal chaos in the Punjab, military clashes in Kashmir and Hyderabad, and governmental disarray or chaos in two-fifths of its territory following the annexation of the former princely states. These and

25. Morris-Jones, *Government and Politics of India*, p. 123.

other problems influenced sufficient numbers of Congress party leaders to resist the voices raised against the imperial bureaucratic mechanism, which without much discussion in the Constituent Assembly was allowed to survive largely intact.

That mechanism, as we have seen, placed directly in charge of law and order in each district of British India an elite ICS officer. The system both stressed that charge and was particularly suited to carrying it out, although perhaps for motives other than those which now obtain. That mechanism is in place today. The IAS officer today takes with him to his district officer's post a rather definite set of priorities as guides to conduct inherited from his ICS predecessor. It is not difficult to predict the behavior of an experienced IAS district officer in deciding between the alternatives of (1) moving quickly to pacify an imminent riot in his district town, or (2) keeping an appointment with his chief minister who has just arrived at the train station, or (3) attending a scheduled meeting with important district politicians, or (4) signing papers that are essential to the success of the district development program and which must be sent with the jeep leaving now for the state capital—confronted with all these alternatives, his behavior is predictable. He will move to the scene of the imminent riot and attempt to pacify it, or if need be, to quell it. The maintenance of order in a district enjoyed absolute priority during ICS days; it is so today. The training of IAS officers both at the National Academy and later in the states, as well as the influence of more seasoned officers under whom young recruits work, stresses this priority; although at the same time his training broadens the orientation to include the importance of development work as well.[26] The IAS district officer's all-India status and prestige and his known conviction as to the importance of internal peace are crucial in the securing of it by the district police and subordinate district magistrates. This is an exceedingly difficult thing to manage; there have been faulty decisions by district officers and breakdowns here and there from time to time since independence; but the

26. S. S. Khera's recent book, *District Administration in India* (London, 1964), makes it clear that law and order is the first priority for a district officer. The author, an ICS officer of the Uttar Pradesh cadre, was secretary to the cabinet of the Government of India and secretary to the Planning Commission.

over-all record is good and the reason for it can be traced in part to the "law and order orientation" inherent in the British imperial tradition.

A related aspect of the law and order orientation in India's democracy is the conduct of elections which is fair and is believed to be fair by the electorate. The chief election commissioner appointed by the president of India is generally responsible for elections throughout the country, but the actual conduct of balloting is done in each of the 323 districts in the country by the district administration, with the IAS district officer centrally involved in each case as the election administrator. Generally speaking, Indians have gone to the polls peacefully in three general elections and numerous local ones to the pleasant surprise of many foreign observers. That the interested electorate believes the elections to be fairly conducted is suggested by the fact that "complaints of partiality on the part of election administrators have been rare and their substantiation rarer."[27] An explanation for this phenomenon is to be found in the imperial tradition, which enables a state government to place able and disinterested (all-India) officers directly in charge. In Rajasthan, for example, the state government was able to place very seasoned IAS officers in many districts in 1961 so that they would be on hand for the general election of 1962.

The maintenance of internal peace by legitimate civil authority and the conduct of fair and orderly elections in a democratic polity are two elements of government action which conduce to political stability. Another related aspect is the preservation of the state in terms of national unity. Here again, the imperial legacy with its all-India functional orientation is of value. National unity is important for at least two reasons. One is the need for internal unity in terms of effective, national communication through a disparate bureaucracy, which numbers nine million government officials organized into a bewildering quantity of separate services. This is a condition necessary to implement effectively the political aspirations of the national leadership, thereby contrib-

27. Morris-Jones, *Government and Politics of India*, p. 194.

uting to its legitimacy. The second reason for the importance of national unity is the need to build and reinforce commonly accepted norms of behavior in a more general sense. No one acquainted with India will question that the building of this kind of national unity is important for reasons beyond the sheer need for survival, which is characteristically a first priority to a newly independent nation and government. Divisive tendencies which spring from linguistic profusion, marked social stratification, regional separateness, and the general lack of value consensus on the part of much of the population make the building of national unity an especially difficult and important objective. The broad national stance of the Congress party, the comparatively large group of Indian intellectuals, the apolitical coherence of the armed forces, and to some extent the disparate bureaucracy—all of these contribute to India's fragile unity. With reference to the disparate bureaucracy, the IAS, with its all-India features, straddles it from the office of the secretary to the cabinet of the Government of India, to the secretariats of each of the sixteen state governments, to the district officer in his tent on tour in a distant part of his rural district. A hypothesis can be advanced that informal communication within the IAS is effective in terms of quick transmission of signals and fairly extensive agreement as to appropriate responses. The internal unity of the disparate bureaucracy is thereby enhanced. Also, the IAS officer, all-India in his functional orientation, carries national ideology with him into every district, where he articulates it constantly in his exposed position before the district population. His behavior reinforces the national consensus spreading through India's developing political system.

National unity and internal order, then, are two aspects of political stability to which the IAS is able to make an important contribution. The power to maintain order is one of the particularly important resources available to the Indian government to alter behavior in society. One is forced to the question: are those IAS officers who exercise that power responsible (as defined at the outset of this chapter) to non-bureaucratic political institutions? The question is a particularly insistent one in an India now emerging from the British imperial experience. For if the "exclusive responsibility orientation" is another legacy bequeathed to the IAS along with the law and order orientation and the imperial structure, then a necessary condition for political development in India is absent.

It is useful at this point to distinguish between those IAS officers holding the post of district officer and those who hold key posts in the state and central secretariats. We address the question of responsibility first to the district officer.

Whether or not district officers are accountable to non-bureaucratic political institutions in the states is a question which is easily answered: they are. Reports flow regularly (endlessly) from district headquarters to the state secretariat where they are compiled by various departments and "laid on the table of the House[s]" of the state legislature for those MLA's[28] who feel so inclined to plow through them. The ICS legacy of the "exclusive accountability orientation" helps to confirm the IAS district officer in his practice of accounting regularly to his administrative superior (the chief secretary directly, although the general position is rather complex), who in turn accounts through the chief minister to the state legislature. An analysis some years ago of the district officer's work load in the former Bombay state indicated that he spent 54 per cent of his time reading and signing papers, most of which were going to the state secretariat.[29] The time spent on reporting to state headquarters is not necessarily wasted on empty formality. MLA's can and do raise questions based on the reports and accounts sent up by the district officers, and action can follow.

At this point one encounters the rest of the question of responsibility. We must inquire whether or not non-bureaucratic institutions, in this case the state legislatures, are able to control the IAS district officers, that is, to alter their behavior. This is, of course, a much more difficult and important part of the question. A complete answer cannot be attempted here; a short answer

28. Members of the Legislative Assembly; refers to those popularly elected members of the state legislatures in India.
29. Government of Bombay, *Revenue Department Manual* (compiled by M. K. Deshpande) (Poona, 1954), p. 169.

would have to be: not directly. District officers are controlled by their chief secretary, not directly by their chief minister and state legislature. Is the district officer controlled by non-bureaucratic institutions in his district? The answer again must be: not directly. The MLA's elected from a particular district will be men whose views the district officer will respect. They sit in the legislature, and if they hold substantial power in that institution, they can indirectly through the chief minister and the chief secretary have that particular IAS district officer transferred and another IAS officer, say one recently promoted to the post from the state administrative service, put in his place. They are able therefore to alter indirectly the behavior of the district officer in that district. Other non-bureaucratic institutions in the district may influence the district officer, but the number of variables here defy a short treatment of the subject. One might attempt to test Weiner's hypothesis that in states where the Congress party is strong, district officers and other state government officers "tend to be sensitive and responsible to local pressures."[30] One might look at the different local government arrangements in each state, some of which are in a position to be more influential vis-à-vis the district officer than others. And so on. It is true that the district officer is exposed to the public in his district. A crucial part of his job is to hear, either at his office or while on tour in his district, the petitions of leaders of various non-bureaucratic groups in the district affected by his work. The more informed a district officer is regarding the public opinion in a district, the better able he is to perform effectively his functions of maintaining order and directing development programs. Beyond being exposed and accessible, however, the district officer is basically authoritarian regarding the essentials of his job. The maintenance of law and order is not a negotiable commodity in his eyes beyond a certain minimal point, and development programs, designed at the state secretariat or in New Delhi, must be carried out. To put a complex subject shortly, the district officer must be viewed as directly responsible to the state government and not necessarily responsive to his district public as far as the essentials of his job

30. Myron Weiner, *Politics of Scarcity: Public Pressure and Political Response in India* (Chicago, 1962), p. 213.

are concerned. From this point of view, the IAS district officer can be dysfunctional for political development.

To answer the question of whether or not district officers are responsible, we are therefore forced to assess the responsibility of those IAS officers in the state secretariat who supervise district officers. This brings us to the second half of our initial distinction between IAS district officers, on the one hand, and state and central secretariat IAS officers, on the other. Once again the question is: Are IAS secretariat officers responsible to non-bureaucratic political institutions?

An IAS secretary to a state or central government department or ministry accounts to the individual minister who holds that portfolio. Important files are always "put up" to the minister for signature or for other reasons, and there is almost daily personal contact between minister and secretary on ministerial or departmental activities and problems. Furthermore, although funds voted by a state legislature, or Parliament, are placed at the disposal of the IAS secretary (not the minister), the secretary renders an account to the accountant general (auditor general) and through him to the Public Accounts Committee and the legislature (Parliament).

The question of whether non-bureaucratic political institutions are able to control IAS secretariat personnel is not quite so easily disposed. The relations between ministers and civil servants, with which we are faced, has been admirably discussed elsewhere in a general way in terms of the weight of the secretary in the policy decisions of government.[31] Other promising approaches need to be explored if we are to extend our knowledge of this important question for political development.

One approach is to examine the social backgrounds and sets of values of the persons involved. Some data on the social composition of direct recruits to the IAS were presented earlier in this section, suggesting that the service draws upon an elite in Indian society, although there is lately evidence of a leveling downward. The values of these direct recruits—e.g., what they see their role to be as civil servants—need to be analyzed. The content of the

31. For further analysis from this point of view, see Morris-Jones, *Government and Politics of India*, pp. 132–134.

"foundational course" is suggestive here; the more important question is: do these direct recruits carry that set of values to their assignments in the field? In other words, we need to go beyond questioning direct recruits while they are at the National Academy of Administration. Even more important, we know nothing about the social composition and values of the bulk of the IAS who, as we have seen, are not direct recruits. Furthermore, central government ministers tend to work with those remaining ICS officers who hold most posts of secretary to government; no attempt has yet been made empirically to analyze that group in the IAS. Finally, political scientists have only recently begun to look closely at the Congress party leadership, which includes ministers in both state and central government. Once such analyses are made, we may begin to understand more clearly the power relationships between ministers and secretaries. For the present, we must rely on non-empirical observations. One is that all IAS officers have been recruited since 1947 to fill senior posts in a political system dominated by one political party since 1947. Looked at in this way, the world of the IAS officer has always been the world of one-party dominance. The individual ministers may come and go frequently, as they certainly do in many state governments, thereby increasing during periods of change the weight of the more permanent secretary to the ministry. But thus far almost all the ministers have been members of the Congress party, although there have been several exceptions such as the government in Kerala from 1957 to 1959. We would expect the IAS officers, in varying degrees, to be both responsive and responsible to Congress party ideology and national leadership. And during this special post-independence period of national growth, this attitude may not be unfavorable to political development.

A second approach is to examine the influence of ministers on important service matters. The Congress party leadership has ultimate control in that it can abolish the IAS by amending the Constitution or altering its features by legislation. But there is also suggestive evidence in Table 8 below that the Congress party leadership may control postings in the IAS. A full analysis of this table cannot be attempted here, but the most striking single point to emerge from the data is the exceptional favor given to ICS-IAS officers in the Uttar Pradesh cadre. The data show that the Uttar Pradesh cadre is authorized to have fifty senior postings in the central government, but, in fact, ninety officers from this cadre were actually in such posts in 1963. The comparative data further show that all other state cadres approximate with small variation their authorized strength in central government. The reason for this is not to be found in the fact that the Uttar Pradesh cadre is the largest in the IAS-ICS. The data show that the Maharashtra cadre had almost as many ICS officers in state government as the Uttar Pradesh cadre (Maharashtra, eleven; Uttar Pradesh, twelve); but the former had only the same number in central government posts, while the latter had almost three times as many (Maharashtra, eleven; Uttar Pradesh, thirty-four). For the IAS the data show that the Madhya Pradesh cadre has almost as many officers in state government as the Uttar Pradesh cadre (Madhya Pradesh, 138; Uttar Pradesh, 154), but whereas 14 per cent of the Madhya Pradesh IAS cadre were in central government posts, 27 per cent of the Uttar Pradesh IAS cadre were there (Madhya Pradesh, twenty-seven; Uttar Pradesh, fifty-six). The Uttar Pradesh bias can be pushed even further. For example, a breakdown by state cadre of ICS officers holding posts paying Rs. 4,000 (the most highly paid) in central government in 1961 is as follows: Bihar and Mysore cadres—information not available; Assam, Kerala, Madhya Pradesh, Orissa, and the Punjab cadres—none; Gujarat, Madras, Maharashtra, and West Bengal cadres—one; Andhra Pradesh cadre—three; Uttar Pradesh cadre—eleven.[32] The dominant position of the Uttar Pradesh cadre in the most

32. The figures have been compiled from *All-India Civil List* (*as corrected up to 1st July 1961*) (Bombay, 1961), pp. 183–323. The Rs. 4,000 posts held by Uttar Pradesh cadre ICS officers at that time were secretary to the cabinet cum secretary to the Planning Commission; secretary, Ministry of Home Affairs; secretary, Ministry of Steel, Mines and Fuel; secretary, Ministry of Food and Agriculture; secretary, Ministry of Rehabilitation; secretary, Kashmir Affairs (in the Ministry of Home Affairs); special secretary, Government of India; secretary, Ministry of Community Development and Co-operation; secretary, Ministry of Commerce and Industry; chairman, Life Insurance Corporation; India's alternate governor, International Bank of Reconstruction and Development. Length of time in service does not explain the bias.

Table 8. *Postings (Actual) of ICS-IAS Officers in Union and State Governments of India, 1963*

1	2	3	4	5	6	7	8
	State government			On deputation to central government			
State cadre	ICS (actual)	IAS (actual)	Total (actual)	ICS (actual)	IAS (actual)	Total (actual)	Total authorized postings in central government
Andhra Pradesh	5	101	106	6	38	44	36
Assam	4	64	68	6	10	16	20
Bihar	9	127	136	12	24	36	36
Delhi and Himachal Pradesh[a]	0	14	14	0	2	2	13
Gujarat	5	73	78	5	12	17	28
Jammu and Kashmir[a]	0	18	18	0	0	0	6
Kerala	0	48	48	3	13	16	14
Madhya Pradesh	4	138	142	10	22	32	38
Madras	9	74	83	8	24	32	27
Maharashtra	11	105	116	11	24	35	38
Mysore	0	53	53	4	25	29	20
Orissa	3	78	81	0	25	25	29
Punjab	7	69	76	14	21	35	32
Rajasthan	0	87	87	0	27	27	25
Uttar Pradesh	12	154	166	34	56	90	50
West Bengal	9	76	85	15	24	39	31
Totals	78	1,279	1,357	128	347	475	443

[a] Cadre being formed.

Sources: Columns 2 through 7 have been compiled from *Civil List of Indian Administrative Service (as on 1st January, 1963)*, pp. 1–233; column 8 has been compiled from *Indian Administrative Service (Fixation of Cadre Strength) Regulations, 1955 (as corrected up to 1962)*, in Government of India, Ministry of Home Affairs, *Handbook of Rules and Regulations for the All-India Services (corrected up to 1st September, 1962)* (3rd ed.; Delhi, 1962), II, 1–20.

powerful bureaucratic posts in the central government is emphatically confirmed by these data. Although there are several possible explanations, the most attractive, based upon present knowledge, is that a causal connection may exist between Uttar Pradesh bias in elite cadre postings in central government, on the one hand, and Uttar Pradesh bias in Congress party national leadership, on the other. If confirmed (and motives aside), then one could say that the elite service as a whole is amenable to control by a non-bureaucratic political institution in the important matter of intra-service postings and salary. Furthermore, if the regional bases of power in the Congress party national leadership begin to shift away from north-central India to Madras, Maharashtra, and West Bengal (and there is perceptible indication that this is beginning to occur), then we can look for similar changes in the regional composition of elite cadre occupants of senior posts in central government. One could then much more convincingly advance the argument that the IAS is responsible to a non-bureaucratic political institution, rather than relying only on statements to that effect by secretaries and ministers.

The issue of responsibility, therefore, is posed in this analysis generally as follows. On the one hand, the value of an elite cadre in terms of national unity and internal stability is considerable for a newly independent nation. On the other hand, the elite cadre as an institution is reserved space, so to speak, at the top of the bureaucracy in district, state, and central governments, and although it is amenable to control in that it can be abolished, it is not definitely and clearly amenable to continuous control so far as our present knowledge is concerned. The power to control postings is an important one, however, for it can influence an individual officer's career expectations and other gratifications. We can suggest, therefore, that elite cadre behavior in the central government today is influenced by others as well as the elite cadre itself. We pursue further this temporary conclusion in the following section. The position of elite cadres in each state government remains unexplored and will require a separate analysis at a later date.

II. Public Enterprises

Indian public enterprises are those undertakings of a business nature which are owned and/or controlled by the state, almost all of which were initiated (not nationalized) by the central or state governments, or by both. Public enterprises take various forms,[33] although the government corporations and companies are the most important ones. A recent all-India list shows fifty-nine corporations and 119 companies as follows:

Table 9. *Classification of Government Corporations and Companies, 1964*

Corporations	
Central government	13
State governments	46
All-India Total	59

Companies	
Exclusively incorporated and managed by the central government	30
Belonging jointly to the central and state governments	5
With both central government and private interests' participation	4
With central government, state government, and private interests' participation	6
State government companies	74
All-India Total	119

Source: Derived from V. V. Ramanadham, *The Control of Public Enterprises in India* (London, 1964), Appendix I, pp. 247–252. All of these corporations and companies are listed by name in his Appendix, along with a list of central and state departmental undertakings.

33. Om Prakash, *The Theory and Working of State Corporations* (London, 1962), p. 37, distinguishes nine forms: statutory corporations, limited companies, quasi-corporations, departmental undertakings, control boards, commodity boards, commissions, port trusts, and local authorities. Paul Appleby's second report contains many of the guidelines for the subsequent development of public enterprises; see Government of India, Cabinet Secretariat, *Re-examination of India's Administrative System with Special Reference to Administration of Government's Industrial and Commercial Enterprises, by Paul H. Appleby* (New Delhi, 1956).

This chapter does not enter into the large and important general subject of public enterprises in India.[34] Following our theoretical perspective, the discussion here is confined to two problems: (1) the responsibility of those elite cadre officers involved with central government public enterprises to the ministers concerned, and (2) the responsibility of those officers and ministers to the Lok Sabha (popular House of the national Parliament) as a non-bureaucratic, political institution.

Elite cadre officers dominate the boards of directors of the central government companies and corporations. The evidence for this assertion is extensive. One study in 1957 found that senior officers of the Ministry of Finance were members, and in some cases chairmen, of thirty-five company boards and nine corporation boards in the public sector.[35] A study in 1959 showed that thirty-eight government companies had secretaries to the Government of India on their boards of directors.[36] Two years later it was found again that secretaries and deputy secretaries to ministries dominated the composition of company boards in the public sector.[37] Many of the elite cadre officers assigned to public undertakings had been previously grouped into an Industrial Management Pool (IMP) which drew upon officers of the IAS, the Audit and Accounts Service, and similar Central Superior Services with an economic orientation. Some thought has been given by S. T. Raja, managing director of the National Coal Development Corporation, Ranchi, for establishment of a new cadre to be called the Indian Management Service, analogous in scales of pay and status to the IAS.[38] Raja proposes that recruit-

---

34. Four good studies which have recently appeared are Prakash, *op. cit.; S. S. Khera, Government in Business* (London, 1963); and two books by V. V. Ramanadham, *The Structure of Public Enterprise in India* (London, 1961), and *The Control of Public Enterprises in India* (London, 1964).

35. Indian Institute of Public Administration, *Administrative Problems of State Enterprises in India* (report of a seminar, December, 1957) (New Delhi, 1958), Appendices 4 and 5.

36. Ramanadham, *Structure of Public Enterprise in India*, pp. 194–195.

37. Ramanadham, *The Control of Public Enterprises in India*, Appendix 5. Twelve ministries were responsible for forty-eight corporations and companies in 1957; the leading examples were the Ministry of Commerce and Industry with eighteen; Ministry of Transport and Communications, seven; Ministry of Steel, Mines and Fuel, six; and Ministry of Finance, five.

38. Raja, "Middle and Higher Management Personnel in Public Sector," *loc. cit.,* 23.

ment be done by the Union Public Service Commission, with executives from public undertakings participating in the viva-voce test. Training would be carried on at one of the management training institutes at Calcutta or Ahmedabad and at the Administrative Staff College at Hyderabad. This proposal is unofficial and has not been commented on by the government. Ministerial control of public enterprises is established in this way, although it seriously compromises any pretense of the enterprises being "autonomous." This control is mainly exercised in informal ways. A former minister of finance, on the floor of the Lok Sabha, quite frankly admitted his financial control over the decisions of the boards of public enterprises:

Certain patterns are being evolved and where for the sake of facility of administration or for the elimination of red tape, we invest that body, it may be a company or a corporation, with financial powers, certain precautions are taken. One precaution which is invariably taken is that the financial representative at a very high level is attached to that concern as a director. Now when he exercises his powers, *although it is not said so in so many words that everything shall be done with his concurrence, in practice that result is bound to follow*. Because, if he is overruled, well, then he can report the matter to the Ministry of Finance and the Minister of Finance can take up the matter with the corporations and move Government to make the necessary changes which will ensure that financial advice is taken [emphasis supplied].[39]

The justification for maintaining this arrangement was stated by the Ministry of Finance some years later in reply to parliamentary criticism: "It is clearly not feasible to give a completely free hand to the management in view of the responsibility and accountability of the Minister to Parliament."[40]

The celebrated Life Insurance Corporation (LIC) "scandal" of 1957[41] suddenly and briefly shed a shaft of light on the ordinarily

39. C. D. Deshmukh made this statement during the course of the debate in the Lok Sabha on "Parliamentary Control of Public Corporations," House of the People, *Parliamentary Debates*, Part II, Vol. X (December 10, 1953), col. 1922.

40. Ministry of Finance, Department of Economic Affairs, Office Memorandum No. F.20(79)-P/55 (dated March 13, 1957) as recorded in Estimates Committee (Second Lok Sabha), *Nineteenth Report* (New Delhi, 1958), p. 25, col. 4.

41. Life insurance was nationalized on January 19, 1956. The LIC Act, setting up the public corporation, came into effect on September 1 of that year.

unpublicized relations between board chairmen of public enterprises, secretaries and ministers concerned with the enterprises, and Parliament. This affair involved the purchase by the LIC of more than ten million rupees of stock in six business concerns controlled by a financial adventurer named Haridas Mundhra.[42] The main purchase by the LIC took place on the Calcutta Stock Exchange on June 24, 1957; two other smaller transactions with Mundhra concerns also occurred in April and September of 1957. Several of Mundhra's concerns were later found to be financially unsound. Indeed, there appears to have been grave suspicion in the Calcutta Stock Exchange at that time that the shareholders of one (F. C. Osler, Ltd.) had been defrauded of about Rs. 600,000. The main purchase of stock in June was the largest single transaction that the LIC had made since its creation as a public corporation in 1956. There is still some dispute as to what actually occurred; there is no dispute as to how the affair was brought to public attention. A parliamentary question on the matter was addressed on September 4, 1957, to the minister of finance (T. T. Krishnamachari), who was responsible for the LIC. The question was both poorly worded and based on insufficient information, and the minister "did not think it proper to place all the facts fully and frankly before the Lok Sabha."[43] The questioner (Dr. Ram Subhag Singh, M.P.), obviously after obtaining more information about the transaction, pressed the matter further by way of a parliamentary question on November 29, 1957. This resulted in a debate in the Lok Sabha (December 16, 1957), the publication of the Chagla Commission Report (February 10, 1958), the resignation of the finance minister (February 18, 1958), an inquiry *in camera* into the charges against the two ICS officers involved

42. This account of the "Mundhra Affair" is based on the following two documents: *Report of the Honourable Mr. M. C. Chagla, Chairman of the Commission of Inquiry into the Affairs of the Life Insurance Corporation of India* (signed February 10, 1958) (privately printed). Mr. Chagla was the sole member of the Commission; hereinafter cited as Chagla Report. Ministry of Home Affairs, *Resolution No. F.15/HS,* dated May 27, 1959, and published in the *Gazette of India Extraordinary,* Part I, Section I, June 1, 1959 (pp. 733–736). See also a detailed account in Taya Zinkin, *Reporting India* (London, 1962), chap. ix. Mrs. Zinkin knew personally all the principal actors involved. See also comments in Tinker's chapter (Chapter 2) in this volume, p. 66, n. 71.
43. Chagla Report, p. 22.

(Vivian Bose Board, reported September 21, 1958), and consideration of the charges by the Union Public Service Commission in 1959. This is a clear instance in which Parliament, with the assistance of the Indian press, held the minister responsible for his behavior. Whether the minister was in fact aware of the details of the transaction has never been clearly established, although Chagla thought so.

One of a number of questions considered by Chagla was whether one of the ICS officers involved "was acting on his own responsibility or whether he was giving effect to ministerial policy or ministerial direction."[44] The issue of elite cadre responsibility to non-bureaucratic control is neatly posed in this case.

H. M. Patel, ICS (Bombay cadre),[45] was the principal finance secretary to the Ministry of Finance as well as chairman of the LIC Board of Directors when the April transaction took place, and he remained principal secretary during the other transactions after G. R. Kamat, ICS (Assam cadre), became chairman in June, 1957. The heart of the "scandal" was the charge, never proved (or disproved), that the transactions were accomplished at the urging of Haridas Mundhra on the principal finance secretary, who then "advised" the corporation to make the purchases. Disciplinary proceedings were instituted against Patel (and Kamat, although we do not pursue his case here). Charges of improper conduct were framed against him and notice was issued to him to show cause why the penalty of removal from service should not be imposed. As required under his service rules, the case was referred in January, 1959, to the Union Public Service

44. *Ibid.*, p. 19.
45. Born in Baroda, 1904; B.A. (Oxon.), B. Com. (Lond.); joined service 1927; Hindu; mother tongue Gujarati; Patidar caste; decorated with Companion of the Order of the Indian Empire (C.I.E.); formerly secretary to the cabinet of the Government of India (September 30, 1946 to October 7, 1947); left service before partition of former Bombay State. Compiled by the author from Government of India, *History of Service of Officers Holding Gazetted Appointments in Cabinet, Cabinet Secretariat, Home, Education, Health, etc.* (corrected up to 1st July 1947) (Delhi, 1952), p. 6; Government of India, Ministry of Finance, *Supplement to the History of Services of Officers Holding Gazetted Appointments in the Cabinet Secretariat, Home, Education, Health, etc.* (corrected up to 1st July 1951) (Delhi, 1957), p. 13; Government of Bombay, *History of Services, State of Bombay*, Part I, "General Administration" (corrected up to 1st July 1956) (Bombay, 1956), pp. 108–110.

Commission. The commission came to the conclusion that he was blameless and advised the Government of India—more precisely, the Ministry of Home Affairs—that he be exonerated. The final conclusion reached by the government, after considering the evidence obtained by Chagla, Bose, and the Public Service Commission, was that:

whilst Government feel that there is some force in . . . the criticism of Shri Patel, in view of the long and distinguished record of Shri Patel in service, the complicated post-budget economic situation in 1957, the absence of any *mala fides* and the weight which, according to convention, attaches to the advice of the Union Public Service Commission in such matters, the Government of India have decided to drop the charges against him.[46]

It should be added that T. T. Krishnamachari returned several years later to a cabinet post in New Delhi.

In his report, Chagla attempted to summarize the relationship which he considered ought to subsist between a secretary and his minister:

Administration would become impossible if a secretary has to hold his hands until he has received the formal consent or approval of his minister. In day to day administration, in cases of emergency, the secretary must take the responsibility and must act in a manner which according to him would ultimately meet with the approval of the minister.[47]

Chagla then argued that "this was neither a case of day-to-day administration nor a case of emergency . . ." (p. 20) and went on to place constitutional responsibility for the action on the minister. Three rough categories of decisions which a secretary makes in his official capacity are revealed here: (1) routine, day-to-day decisions, (2) emergency decisions, and (3) decisions which are neither (1) nor (2). Chagla argued that the LIC transactions involved a decision of major policy which was not of

46. Ministry of Home Affairs, Resolution No. F. 15/58-HS, dated May 27, 1959. Signed by B. N. Jha, ICS (Uttar Pradesh cadre), secretary to the Ministry of Home Affairs at that time.
47. Chagla Report, p. 20.

an emergency character, thereby throwing it into category (3). Decisions of major policy are reserved for the minister, whom Patel must have consulted, said Chagla. Patel, in explaining his behavior to Chagla, contended that "obviously he would not have advised the Corporation to go into the matter if *he felt* that his view of the matter was not acceptable to the minister."[48] Even in this major decision of policy, then, an informal understanding between the two men was of critical importance, with Patel very close to the point of acting as he thought best for the ministry. That point is reached in categories (1) and (2), where "the secretary must take responsibility and must act in a manner which *according to him* would ultimately meet with the approval of his minister." It is a short step from this position to the one observed by Mr. A. Subbiah, who on resigning from the membership of the investment committee of the LIC in 1959 is reported to have said that he had found "too much uncontrolled concentration of power without responsibility in the hands of top executives."[49]

The informal nature of power shared by secretaries and ministers, which the LIC case exemplifies, adds force to the suggestion made earlier in this essay that a helpful approach to understanding this relationship would be to study the social background and ideological orientations of the parties concerned. For if the parties concerned share in particular a similar ideological orientation, then bureaucratic responsibility is reasonably assured, even though no formal and continuous control is exercised by the minister. Furthermore, if control over ICS-IAS postings does in fact rest with the political leadership (ministers included), as seems likely, then this element may be a major factor sustaining the responsibility of secretaries to ministers.

This section on public enterprises now turns more generally to the question of the responsibility of central government officers (including ICS-IAS) and ministers involved to the Indian

---

48. *Ibid.* Emphasis supplied. The author has transposed Chagla's sentence, in which "if he felt . . ." precedes "obviously he would. . . ."
49. Quoted, without reference, in Prakash, *op. cit.*, p. 235.

Parliament (the Lok Sabha particularly), which represents the non-bureaucratic institution ultimately responsible for these enterprises. The analysis of the question proceeds in terms of the following model:

Parliament has an unlimited general power of control in that it can alter the law; but it has no specific power of control, as distinct from its right to receive an account. On the other hand, it has far more opportunity than a body of shareholders to express its views, its criticisms, its apprehensions, even its confidence and satisfaction if it should come to entertain these feelings; and it would be wrong to suppose that such expressions have no influence, merely because the sanction behind them is an unwieldy one.[50]

Every central government corporation or company has been either established by an act of Parliament or is regulated by the provisions of the Companies Act, 1956.[51] The power of Parliament to pass or amend such acts assures that ultimate control of the public enterprises rests in the hands of that body. Once the enterprises have been established by or have become subject to an act of Parliament, it is essential, in lieu of the very meaning of accountability, that Parliament be continually cognizant of the working of the enterprises in order to be assured that they are acting in accordance with the provisions of the act and in the interest of national policy. In short, if public enterprises are to be accountable to Parliament, that body must be continuously well-informed about them.

Members of Parliament were not well-informed about the

50. Sir Joeffrey Vickers, "The Accountability of Nationalised Industry," *Public Administration,* XXX (1952), 80.

51. The text of this act is available in Government of India, Ministry of Law, *The Companies Act, 1956 (as modified up to the 1st May 1961)* (Delhi, 1961). See also Government of India, Ministry of Commerce and Industry, Department of Company Law Administration, Research and Statistics Division, *A Brochure on Promotion of Research on Matters Relating to the Corporate Sector in India* (2nd ed.; New Delhi, 1964); this includes particulars of relevant research being undertaken in Indian universities, and a note in the second edition indicates that this is intended to be an annual publication. Also useful are the annual reports on the working of the Companies Act by the Department of Company Law Administration in the Ministry of Commerce and Industry as well as the Company Law pamphlet series and *Company Notes and News* (fortnightly), both issued from the same organization.

public enterprises in 1958.[52] There were three main avenues of accountability at that time: budget documents, annual reports from the enterprises, and the annual reports of the ministries responsible for the enterprises. Each will be analyzed briefly in turn.

Most government companies and public corporations are financed initially by money drawn against the Consolidated Fund of India. Parliament must sanction the disbursement of money from this fund[53] and should have all the information necessary to exercise that responsibility effectively. The situation in 1958, however, was that the Explanatory Memoranda gave accounts for seventeen enterprises, although the number at that time exceeded forty-five.[54] The inadequacy of the budget documents on the public enterprises found expression in several recommendations by the Estimates Committee in 1958:

Industrial undertakings should prepare a performance and programme statement for the budget year together with the previous year's statement and it should be made available to Parliament at the time of the annual budget.

These bodies might also be encouraged to prepare business-type budgets which would be of use to Parliament at the time of the budget discussions.

The latest accounts and balance sheets as well as the annual reports should be made available to Parliament at the same time.

The separate volume for each Ministry and Department, incorporating the budget and portions from the Explanatory Memoranda and Annual Reports, should also include a separate chapter containing the above information and documents in respect of all undertakings which are related to the Ministry concerned.

52. The following analysis of the accountability of public enterprises to Parliament relates to the position in 1958, when the author made a study of the problem. Portions of the remainder of this section on public enterprises were published in the author's article, "Public Enterprises: Parliamentary Control or Accountability?" *Indian Journal of Public Administration*, V (1959), 320–332.

53. *Constitution of India (as modified up to 1st March, 1963)* (Delhi, 1963), Article 283, read with Article 112.

54. Government of India, *Explanatory Memorandum on the Budget of the Central Government for 1958–59 (as laid before Parliament)*, Appendix to Section III, ii–clxxxix.

It would be desirable to bring out a consolidated volume containing the documents mentioned above for all the statutory bodies and private limited companies of Government containing an appreciation of their working and their net result on the budget.

To facilitate the understanding of all the activities of the public enterprises it would be desirable that they should have a common financial year, namely the same as that of the Government.[55]

These recommendations serve to underscore the fact that the presentation and organization of data on public enterprises in the budget documents were not conducive to informed debate on the public enterprises except by those few MP's who either already possessed knowledge of the enterprises or who had developed an appetite for detailed study of them. The paucity of direct references to the public enterprises in the 1958–1959 budget session supports this contention. For example, the six demands for grants in respect of the Ministry of Commerce and Industry were debated for more than six hours.[56] This ministry was responsible at the time for eighteen government companies, and yet almost no mention was made of those companies in the debate. The reason for this oversight was that the budgets of these companies were not made available to parliamentarians. Furthermore, the administrative report of the Ministry of Commerce and Industry was still at the printers when the demands for grants were debated.[57]

Every public enterprise is required by law to submit annual reports to Parliament. The government companies are obliged to perform this function under Article 639(1) of the Companies Act, and each statute establishing a public corporation contains a clause requiring the submission of annual reports. In 1958 all the public corporations and all but one of the government companies were forwarding annual reports or statements to Parliament.[58]

55. Estimates Committee (Second Lok Sabha). *Twentieth Report* (1958), p. 30.
56. *Lok Sabha Debates*, Vol. XIII, March 19, 1958, cols. 5633–5758; *ibid.*, cols. 5842–5986.
57. *Ibid.*, cols. 5634–5635.
58. The author found them on a shelf in the parliamentary library.

These are all "laid on the table of the House," and copies therefore are available at the publications desk for scrutiny by members. Few reports are discussed on the floor of the House. Interested members may read them, though, and bring matters in connection with them before the House by asking parliamentary questions, by introducing motions and resolutions, and while debating relevant bills. The tendency, however, is for the reports to circulate closely within governmental circles and eventually to gather dust in the parliamentary library. The majority are printed, although in most cases they are not on public sale.

The annual reports of the ministries directly responsible for public enterprises are easily accessible and more widely used by parliamentarians. If the annual reports of the ministry responsible for the two airlines corporations are representative examples, then this avenue of accountability of public enterprises to Parliament is unusually deficient. Four consecutive reports,[59] in the section on civil aviation, have essentially the same first sentence: "Civil aviation in India maintained steady progress during 1953–54"; "Civil aviation in India continued to make steady progress during 1954–55"; "Civil aviation in India registered good progress during 1955–56"; "Civil aviation in India continued to make steady progress during 1956–57." In the 1955–1956 report there is no mention of the known fact that the Indian Airlines Corporation lost a substantial amount of money, although the report sets down the fact that the Air-India International made a nice profit. The 1956–1957 report does not even refer to two important reports done that year by the Estimates Committee on these two airlines corporations. One periodical commented: "As the investigations carried out by the Estimates Committee during the period under review must be regarded as an event of vital importance to civil aviation in India, it is remarkable that the Minister has passed this civil aviation report for publication with such a glaring and obvious omission."[60]

One final example shows gross carelessness in reporting at that

59. Ministry of Communications, *Report, 1954–55;* Ministry of Communications, *Report, 1955–56;* Ministry of Transport and Communications, *Report, 1956–57;* Ministry of Transport and Communications, *Report, 1957–58.*
60. *Indian Skyways* (Bombay) (July, 1957), p. 9.

time. The following paragraph appeared in the Ministry of Transport and Communications' annual report for 1956–1957:

Two meetings of the Facilitation Committee, a committee for simplifying procedure and formalities with a view to facilitating air transport, established by the Civil Aviation Department were held during 1956–57. Representatives of foreign airlines, the A.I.I., the I.A.S., the Ministries of Communications, Finance (Revenue Department), Health and Transport and of the D.G. of C.A. participated in these meetings. Problems relating to health, immigration and customs clearance were discussed at the meetings with a view to simplifying the procedure and eliminating avoidable formalities.

If one merely changes the dates in the above paragraph from "1956–57" to "1957–58," one has the ministry's report on this committee for the following year. In addition, both the Ministry of Communications and the Ministry of Transport did not even exist when these two reports were published; they had previously been combined into the Ministry of Transport and Communications, as the titles of the two reports clearly indicate.

It is impossible to discover whether this defective accounting to Parliament is by design or through neglect. Nevertheless, the reaction, commendable in many ways, has been that MP's have actively sought information through other channels and have attempted to maintain more than "ultimate" control. The two financial committees of Parliament have been particularly effective in maintaining extensive scrutiny of the officers and ministers responsible for the public enterprises.

The Public Accounts Committee is unambiguously a committee of Parliament, none of its members being allowed to hold a ministerial post and its secretariat needs being performed by the Lok Sabha Secretariat.[61] The committee acts upon information supplied by the comptroller and auditor general.[62] Among other

---

61. Before 1950 the chairman of the committee was the finance minister, and secretarial assistance was performed by the Finance Department. This had been the state of affairs since the first Public Accounts Committee was established under the Montagu-Chelmsford Reforms in 1921. Since 1950 the committee has been able, in the words of its chairman in 1951, "to offer its criticisms in an unrestricted manner." Speech of Mr. B. Das (*Provisional*) *Parliamentary Debates*, Part II, Vol. IX (March 29, 1951), col. 5330.

62. The Constitution of India devotes a whole chapter to this office; see Articles 148–151.

things, its functions include examination of the accounts of the "autonomous and semi-autonomous bodies."[63] The history of the committee is studded with pronouncements on the need to insure parliamentary audit of the accounts of all the public enterprises. In 1952 the comptroller and auditor general claimed that the formation of private, limited companies from government funds by executive decree was "a fraud on the Companies Act and also on the Constitution."[64] He argued at that time that since he had no automatic right to audit the accounts of government companies, Parliament was being bypassed in their constitutional right to supervise expenditure of public funds. The committee indorsed this view.[65] The new Companies Act of 1956, therefore, gave extensive powers to the auditor general as regards the audit of companies.[66] Similarly, all the acts establishing public corporations provide for audit as designated by the central government or on the advice of the auditor general. The committee concentrates on those accounts to which the auditor general draws particular attention. Meetings are held regularly from July each year, and on the basis of the accounts, members of the committee question ministers and senior officials for further details. The oral exchanges between committee members and government officials can become highly charged. One minister remarked in 1958 that government officers in his ministry "trembled" and were "very apprehensive and afraid of the Public Accounts Committee."[67] On the basis of the accounts and oral evidence given by the ministries concerned, the committee formulates its recommendations and findings as periodical reports to Parliament. An effort is made by the committee to curb the "tendency to wander from technical examination of financial administration into the realm of execu-

---

63. *Rules of Procedure and Conduct of Business in Lok Sabha* (New Delhi, 1957), sec. 308.
64. Public Accounts Committee, *Third Report* (New Delhi, 1952), Appendix I.
65. *Ibid.*, pp. 3–4.
66. *The Companies Act 1956*, sec. 619.
67. This statement was made by the railways minister during a debate on excess grants for railways. It was reported in *The Times of India* (August 13, 1958), p. 10. The minister added "that he had always impressed on his officers to try to give the fullest details whenever queries were received from the committee of the House."

tive responsibilities,"[68] but the committee has often failed to remain within this more limited area. For example, in examining the accounts of one government company (Indian Telephone Industries, Ltd.) for the year 1950–1951 in their Tenth Report (1951), the committee found among other things that over nine million rupees of public funds had been spent indiscriminately on stock which was not being used. The members of the committee argued that this showed lack of proper planning and foresight, and they moved out of their province to recommend that disciplinary action be taken against the official at fault. Parliament does not discuss the committee's reports. However, these reports are published and are on public sale. Also they are publicized in the Indian press. Members of Parliament quickly learn of the major findings of the committee and can press committee recommendations further on the floor of the House through questions and during debates.

The Estimates Committee is also completely independent of the ministries which it examines. This committee does not (and obviously could not) examine the entire estimates of any given year, and the demands for grants are eventually voted by Parliament even though the committee has not made a report. The practice of the Estimates Committee has been to examine either certain projects within a given ministry or certain topics common to several ministries. On its own initiative, the committee procures information from the ministry it has decided to examine; this information includes organization charts, detailed statements of activities undertaken, financial statistics, and so forth. The committee makes use of questionnaires and examines witnesses from the ministries in much the same manner as does the Public Accounts Committee. The proceedings, however, are confidential. Before a report by the committee is "laid on the Table of the House," it is sent to the minister concerned as a "secret" document. If a substantial gap exists between the opinions of the ministry and those of the committee, an attempt is made to bridge it through informal discussion. However, a running dialogue is maintained between various ministries and the Estimates Com-

68. Asok Chanda, *Indian Administration* (London, 1958), p. 182.

mittee, and some of this exchange is published in the form of reports which inquire into actions taken by the ministries on recommendations made by the committee in earlier reports. This procedure of the committee undoubtedly discourages evasive replies to initial recommendations. In Table 10 below, there is an analysis of four "follow-up" reports of this type which suggest the nature of the continuous dialogue that has been mentioned.

Table 10. *Analysis of Government Action on Recommendations in Four Reports of the Estimates Committee of the First Lok Sabha on Public Enterprises, 1957–1958*

Results of inquiry	13th report	16th report	22nd report	27th report
Total number of recommendations made	50	23	30	40
Recommendations accepted fully by the government:				
number	20	6	9	13
percentage	40	26.1	30	32.5
Recommendations accepted by the government partly or with some modifications:				
number	4	7	3	4
percentage	8	30.4	10	10
Recommendations not accepted by the government but replies concerning them accepted by the committee:				
number	18	—	6	4
percentage	36	—	20	10
Recommendations not accepted by the government and pursued by the committee (including those which are still under consideration by government:				
number	8	10	12	19
percentage	16	43.5	40	47.5

Sources: Compiled from data found in Estimates Committee (Second Lok Sabha), *First Report,* Action Taken by Government on the Recommendations Contained in the Thirteenth Report of the Estimates Committee (First Lok Sabha, 1957), Appendix VII; Estimates Committee (Second Lok Sabha), *Nineteenth Report,* Action Taken by Government on the Recommendations Contained in the Sixteenth Report of the Estimates Committee (First Lok Sabha, 1958), Appendix IV; Estimates Committee (Second Lok Sabha), *Twelfth Report,* Action Taken by Government on the Recommendations Contained in the Twenty-second Report of the Estimates Committee (First Lok Sabha, 1958), Appendix V; Estimates Committee (Second Lok Sabha), *Thirteenth Report,* Action Taken by Government on the Recommendations Contained in the Twenty-seventh Report of the Estimates Committee (First Lok Sabha, 1958), Appendix IV.

The data suggest that over 30 per cent of the committee's recommendations on public enterprises are generally accepted by the ministries concerned, yet a substantial number of such recommendations are not accepted; thus, there is real and continuous discussion and argument about the enterprises between the ministries concerned and the committee. Formally, the committee merely possesses the power of recommendation, and many of the responses by the ministries to recommendations are vague. One favorite is the assurance: "Directives have been issued."[69] Yet clearly the ministries find it impossible to ignore committee recommendations. Numerous examples could be cited to show that ministerial action followed committee recommendation, or at least that committee recommendation hastened reform which may have been under consideration within the ministries. One reported example is the response to the Fifth Report (First Lok Sabha) which dealt with River Valley Schemes in general:

The Committee attacked a complicated question with enthusiasm and skill and did so at the right time. The Government was *forced* to appoint the high-level Rau Committee to examine some of the criticisms and recommendations relating to the Damodar Valley Corporation, and the improvement which subsequently took place in the administration of that scheme and others owes a great deal to this Fifth Report.[70]

A similar content analysis of 2,172 recommendations contained in forty-two reports of the Estimates Committee on public enterprises shows that 55.8 per cent of the recommendations were accepted by government, 22.4 per cent were answered (but not accepted) by government to the committee's satisfaction, and 21.8 per cent were either unanswered or did not otherwise satisfy the committee.[71]

69. The Estimates Committee has complained that "the reply [of the ministries] simply states that 'there is no objection to the above suggestion' or that 'it is unexceptionable' or that 'Government is in agreement with the recommendation.'" See Estimates Committee (Second Lok Sabha), *Nineteenth Report* (1958), p. 4.

70. W. H. Morris-Jones, *Parliament in India* (London, 1958), p. 305 (emphasis supplied). This is the standard work on the Indian Parliament.

71. J. P. Sharma, "Estimates Committee Report on Public Enterprises," *The Indian Journal of Public Administration*, XI (January–March, 1965), 83–118; figures at 111.

A parliamentary Committee on Public Undertakings was established on May 1, 1964, solely to keep under constant scrutiny the various public enterprises at the central government level. It consists of fifteen members and appears to operate in much the same way as the Estimates Committee, obtaining both written and oral evidence from the ministry and public enterprise under examination. Its terms of reference, however, differ from those of the Estimates Committee. The first report of the Committee on Public Undertakings appeared in 1965.[72] It seems clear that this committee will quickly relieve the Estimates Committee of almost all of its activities in connection with public enterprises: for example, the new committee has assumed responsibility for the follow-up reports.[73]

In addition to being scrutinized by parliamentary committees, ministers are held responsible for the public enterprises through regular parliamentary methods. The question hour has been used with considerable effect from time to time, as the LIC affair clearly demonstrates.

A general conclusion from the foregoing analysis of the relations between secretaries, ministers, and Parliament vis-à-vis the public enterprises is that ultimate control of the ministries rests with Parliament, although there is a tendency for MP's, particularly in the committees of the House, to inquire regularly and in detail into the activities of the ministries. It is suggested that the effect of this scrutiny—particularly on secretaries and other senior officials regularly being called to Parliament to answer for their behavior before the committees—is to alter the functional orientation of the IAS-ICS officers in central government ministries in that they consider themselves responsible not only to the service itself but also to a non-bureaucratic political institution.

---

72. Committee on Public Undertakings (Third Lok Sabha), *First Report,* "National Buildings Construction Corporation, Ltd., New Delhi (Ministry of Works and Housing)," (New Delhi, 1965).

73. Committee on Public Undertakings (Third Lok Sabha), *Seventh Report,* "Action Taken by Government on the Recommendations Contained in the Thirty-second Report of the Estimates Committee (Third Lok Sabha), National Coal Development Corporation, Ltd., Ranchi (Ministry of Steel and Mines)," (New Delhi, 1965).

III. Local Government[74]

The organization of contemporary local government for rural development purposes (to which we confine our attention) owes little to the British imperial tradition. Yet the "exclusive responsibility orientation" may be said to have influenced the behavior of those government officials who took part in rural development administration in the 1950's. Following a brief summary of the background of rural development administration, this section will examine some of the problems encountered in one state during the changeover from the arrangements of the 1950's to the present arrangement, which was designed partly to secure the responsibility of those government officers involved to non-bureaucratic village leaders.

The general purpose of rural development administration has been to induce village communities to participate actively, and to take initiative ultimately, in matters which directly concern their welfare. The means to this goal have been extension methods and offers of financial and technical assistance. The administrative approach was to create within each district separate administrative units (blocks) for rural planning and development; to give each block a unified organization consisting of government personnel specially trained to work with village people; to provide each block with assured funds according to the provisions of schematic budgets formulated by the Government of India; to establish the block as the common agency for all development departments working in rural India; and to insure its efficient working through a series of co-ordinating committees and controlling authorities at the district, state, and national levels.

Seen in broad perspective, the story of rural or community development falls into two parts. In the first part (1952–1956), a

74. The following section is based partly on field research conducted mainly in four districts in the state of Rajasthan during 1960 and 1961. For a general description of rural local government in India, see David C. Potter, *Government in Rural India: An Introduction to Contemporary District Administration* (London, 1964).

program and administrative technique were introduced in selected rural areas by the Indian government. This was done
primarily because local government, necessary to carry out rural
development work, was weak or non-existent.[75] Actual work
started on October 2, 1952 (appropriately Gandhi's birthday), in
only seventy-seven blocks scattered across the country. By the
end of the first year 165 blocks, containing eighteen million
village people, were in operation.[76] The physical achievements in
these first blocks were fairly impressive, particularly in view of
the fact that the first six months were spent mostly in conducting
surveys, formulating programs, having programs approved by
higher authorities, and allowing time for trained personnel to
arrive at the block site for work. Experience during the first year
also showed that many extension staff members had been quickly
trained, an error which had resulted in misconceptions about
extension techniques. During one of his tours in the block areas,
S. K. Dey, the community projects administrator, found a neatly
dressed man with a notebook under his arm standing on a bank
watching one thousand men, women, and children working on an
irrigation project. "Who are you?" S. K. Dey asked him. "I am
your extension worker, Sir." Dey further inquired: "What sort of
extension work are you engaged in here?" "I am inspiring the
people, Sir."[77] In another block, the following dialogue ensued
between Dey and a village level worker:

> DEY: How long have you been here?
> V.L.W.: Four months, Sir.

75. It would serve no useful purpose here to review the history of local
government; the standard work on the subject is Hugh Tinker, *The Foundations of
Local Self-Government in India, Pakistan, and Burma* (London, 1954).

76. Planning Commission, Community Projects Administration, *Report, 1953–54*
(Delhi, 1954), p. 5.

77. *Kurukshetra* (June, 1953), p. 42. *Kurukshetra* is an important monthly
journal issued since 1953 by the Ministry of Community Development and Co-
operation, which until 1956 was known as the Community Projects Administration.
Special issues of the journal are also published from time to time. Each regular
issue contains a number of short essays by political leaders, administrators,
scholars, foreign observers, and others on subjects relating to community
development in India and occasionally in other countries as well. Most of these
essays are descriptive and friendly in nature, although a surprising number have
analyzed critically various aspects of the program. *Kurukshetra* also contains notes
on community development in each state, reviews of books and government
reports dealing with community development, statistical tables, and photographs
of high quality.

DEY: What have you been doing?
V.L.W.: Collecting data.
DEY: What about?
V.L.W.: Felt needs, Sir.
DEY: What do you mean by felt needs?
V.L.W.: Mass Approach Method, Sir.
DEY: Mass Approach Method!
V.L.W.: Yes, psychological approach, Sir.[78]

Government expenditure during this period actually fell far short of the targets established.[79] This experience was contrary to expectations, for it was thought that shortage of funds rather than shortfalls in expenditure would characterize the program. One reason for this unusual experience was that people's participation was required for most schemes in the program, and it was taking time to mobilize this participation and create organizations for it before release of funds. Initial apathy and suspicion were encountered in many places, which also slowed up work. In one state an eloquent and enthusiastic extension worker was quietly asked at the end of his talk: "But is the Government serious this time?"[80] It is clear from S. K. Dey's correspondence at the time that the solution to this shortfall in expenditure was to press ahead with the program at a much more rapid pace, opening more and more blocks to absorb the total allocation for the program. He appreciated the danger involved in this solution: "We seem destined for an expansion faster than we like. There are too many forces about. These will not let us sit down and consolidate."[81] What followed was rapid expansion of the program and a rash of letters imploring the state governments to spend the allotted funds. Administrative innovations were put into effect to facilitate this process. The program began quietly to stress amenities and construction activities which ate up funds more quickly, while the slower and less expensive extension work took second place.

78. *Ibid.*, p. 20.
79. Community Projects Administration, *Report, 1953–54*, p. 9.
80. Planning Commission, Programme Evaluation Organization, *Evaluation Report on First Year's Working of Community Projects* (May, 1954) (Delhi, 1954), p. 8.
81. Letter from S. K. Dey to development commissioners in all states, dated January 1, 1954; this letter was later published in Government of India, Community Projects Administration, *Random Thoughts* (Delhi, 1956), I, 6.

Nevertheless, evidence of enthusiasm for the program continued to appear through 1955. A veteran social worker (not part of the government program) in Madras state over a period of months asked people at bus stops in one project area what was being done by the block staff. At first the reply was usually "nothing!" But gradually this changed until the villagers were answering, "Good work is being done."[82] "Send me a Project by the next mail" came a desperate demand from someone who had vaguely heard about them.[83] There was caution, too. The annual reports of the Programme Evaluation Organization of the Planning Commission offered constructive criticism,[84] and an American observer who had been associated with the program from its inception claimed in 1956 that "far greater progress has been made on the building of physical targets than has been made in penetrating the inner minds of the village people," and he added that "too many village people look upon the village improvement programme as being of Government origin and direction."[85] The program, of course, was of government origin and direction, one in which the village people were asked to participate. It was this weakness which resulted in the momentous changes in the second part of the community development story.[86]

From 1956 increasing criticism of the community development program became evident.[87] It was led by the critical report—

82. *Kurukshetra* (September, 1954), p. 15. The project was an administrative unit containing three blocks; it was abolished after the first few years of the program.

83. *Ibid.* (January, 1954), p. 21.

84. The third report, *Evaluation Report on Working of Community Projects and N.E.S. Blocks, April 1956,* is a particularly fine example of their work. All of their reports are remarkable evaluations (sometimes very critical) of a government program by a unit of that government.

85. Douglas Ensminger, "Training of Gram Sevaks and Gram Sevikas," *Kurukshetra* (October 2, 1956), pp. 17–21.

86. S. K. Dey predicted the direction of this change in a letter to development commissioners in the states, dated May 31, 1955; see *Random Thoughts,* I, 111: "I have never been convinced more than I am today that success or failure of our programme *eventually* will be judged only by one factor—the extent to which we have been able to transform the 'Government programme with people's participation' to one of 'People's programme with Government participation.' The key to this change-over lies in the creation of statutory village bodies which can be trained to take over initiative from the Government before the expiry of the Programme."

87. See reports of the Programme Evaluation Organization of the Planning Commission for the years 1956–1961; Committee on Plan Projects, *Report of the Team for the Study of Community Projects and National Extension Service* (3

perhaps the most important piece of literature on community development in India—of the Committee on Plan Projects in late 1957.[88] The committee's two most important criticisms were (1) that the expansion of the program in terms of the number of blocks opened each year was proceeding too fast, and (2) that the program generally speaking had failed to evoke popular initiative and interest on the part of the village people. The committee recommended (1) that this rapid expansion should be slowed down, and (2) that a system of local self-government should be introduced in rural India and the responsibility for the program transferred to the villagers themselves. These recommendations were accepted by the Government of India. They resulted in the complete coverage of rural India with over five thousand blocks being delayed from 1961 to 1963 (later extended to 1965).[89] They also engendered a request to each state government to establish a system of local self-government generally along the lines recommended by the committee—a system which quickly came to be called Panchayati Raj. Future historians will undoubtedly be struck by the swiftness with which Panchayati Raj swept the field. Andhra Pradesh, Assam, and Rajasthan led the way with Panchayati Raj schemes in 1959, and other states have quickly followed suit. By October, 1964, ten states had implemented legislation setting up the system; Bihar, Madhya Pradesh, and West Bengal were implementing legislation; in Kerala a draft Panchayati Raj bill had been introduced in the

vols.; New Delhi, 1957). Hereinafter cited, after the name of its chairman, as the Balvantray Mehta Report. See also articles in the press during this period, e.g., "CD Movement a Flop says Mysore Report," *Hindustan Times*, December 5, 1960; "Slow Pace of Progress in Community Development," report of the Reserve Bank Review, as reported in the *Times of India*, February 8, 1961; and Jawaharlal Nehru, "Trust the Peasant," *Kurukshetra* (December, 1958), p. 262, in which he said: "I regret to say that the Community Development Movement has only very partially succeeded. Why is it so? Why?"

88. In September, 1956, the National Development Council constituted a Committee on Plan Projects, with the union minister for home affairs as chairman. The committee was to assess the question of the growing financial outlay in the Second Five Year Plan in order to see if higher levels of economy and efficiency could be attained. This committee appointed a special "team" in January, 1957, headed by Balvantray Mehta, chairman of the Estimates Committee of the Lok Sabha, to study community development. Following extensive visits to every state in India, the team submitted its findings in the 742-page Balvantray Mehta Report, cited above, n. 87.

89. *Kurukshetra* (October 2, 1964), p. 76.

state legislature; and in Jammu and Kashmir a committee had been set up to work out the details of such a scheme which would meet the special conditions obtaining there.[90] Change is everywhere apparent today in rural development administration, with the community development program and Panchayati Raj existing and operating side by side.

Three features broadly distinguish the rural development story to date: (1) The community development program was introduced in India because it was felt that local government was either weak or non-existent; (2) initial experience with community development showed that continuing success was difficult without local government; (3) Panchayati Raj was introduced in order to fill this need and to strengthen community development.

In the first period, government officials were not responsible, nor did they consider themselves responsible, to the village people whose behavior they were attempting to change. The "exclusive responsibility orientation" was characteristic of the behavior of community development personnel in the early blocks in that they were basically responsible to their bureaucratic superiors alone. The remainder of this section on local government will analyze the changing nature of that orientation accompanying the introduction of Panchayati Raj and some of the problems encountered during that change. Since it is frankly impossible to synthesize the different Panchayati Raj systems in each state into a coherent, all-India pattern for analytical purposes, we therefore confine the analysis to one state.

Panchayati Raj went into effect in the state of Rajasthan on October 2, 1959 (Gandhi's birthday again; most things associated with rural development appropriately start on Gandhi's birthday).[91] The Rajasthan Panchayat Samitis and Zila Parishads Act,

90. Two spurs drove the states to consider and to implement the recommendations. One was the mounting criticism of the community development program (which we have noted), to which Panchayati Raj provided a nice rejoinder. The second, a consequence of the first, was the active support given to Panchayati Raj by the Congress party. On the latter point, see, e.g., the resolutions drafted and accepted at the annual Congress party session at Bhavnagar in January, 1961, as reported in the press at the time; *Evening News of India* (Bombay) (January, 1961) had a two-inch headline on the front page entitled: "Motion on *Panchayati Raj* adopted at Congress Session."

91. Besides the numerous official publications of the Government of Rajasthan on the subject, there are several independent studies: e.g., Congress Party in

1959 (hereinafter called the 1959 Act),[92] and the Rajasthan Panchayat Act, 1953 (as amended in 1959),[93] set up three layers of local self-government in each of the twenty-six districts in the state. The basic aim of the legislation was to create representative institutions in each district directly responsible for rural development work.

In the first layer, rural Rajasthan is divided into 7,395 panchayats, each embracing about one thousand to three thousand persons in one or several villages. A panchayat in Rajasthan is an elected, statutory body consisting of twelve to fifteen members: one sarpanch (elected by the entire panchayat), eight to ten panches (one panch is elected from each ward), and several co-opted members. Elections take place every three years. Panchayats may impose certain taxes to carry out their prescribed functions, although few have done so; they rely mainly on grants from the next layer in the structure.

A number of panchayats are grouped into 232 panchayat samitis (the second layer) throughout Rajasthan.[94] Samitis correspond precisely in area to each of the 232 community development blocks in Rajasthan. A samiti is a statutory body comprising primarily all the sarpanches elected to the panchayats in the samiti area; these sarpanch members then co-opt additional members. MLA's whose constituency falls within the samiti area are associate members of the samiti. An average samiti consists of forty-two members, eight of whom are co-opted. They elect a pradhan (chairman) from among themselves. The chief executive officer of the samiti is the block development officer (called

Parliament, *Study Team's Report on Panchayati Raj in Rajasthan* (New Delhi, 1960); Association of Voluntary Agencies, *Report of a Study Team on Democratic Decentralization in Rajasthan* (New Delhi, 1961); Ralph H. Retzlaff, "Panchayati Raj in Rajasthan," *Indian Journal of Public Administration*, VI (1960), 141–158; Potter, *Government in Rural India*, chap. viii. See also B. Maheshwari, *Studies in Panchayati Raj* (Delhi, 1963), which, although all-Indian in orientation, provides extensive comment on the Rajasthan scheme.

92. Government of Rajasthan, The Rajasthan Panchayat Samitis and Zila Parishads Act, 1959 (Jaipur, 1959).

93. Government of Rajasthan, The Rajasthan Panchayat Act, 1953 (as amended) (Jaipur, 1960).

94. Samiti populations vary between 30,000 and 100,000; Government of Rajasthan, Letter No. F 156 (Gen) QPR/Stat/DD/60/27859–999, dated February 10, 1961 (unpublished), to be read with the understanding that the 1961 census figures put population in Rajasthan up 26 per cent over the 1951 totals.

under Panchayati Raj a vikas adhikari); other community development personnel working under the samiti are eight extension officers (one each for agriculture, animal husbandry, rural engineering, social education, the program for women and children, co-operation, rural industries, and panchayats), a medical officer, ten gram sevaks (village level workers), and other supporting staff. These personnel in the samiti are still to administer the community development program as before, but with the important difference that the samiti is held responsible for its over-all administration.[95] Samitis have three sources of revenue: community development funds, other rural development funds transferred from development departments in the state, and funds raised by taxation.[96]

There are twenty-six zila parishads (the third layer) in Rajasthan, one for each district. A zila parishad is a statutory body consisting of the pradhans of all the samitis in the district, MLA's and MP's elected from (or residing in) the district, and others. The members elect a pramukh (chairman) from among themselves. A zila parishad has co-ordinating, supervising, and reporting functions; it possesses no executive functions and has no independent source of income.[97] "Its decision can, therefore, be treated as pious wishes which may safely be disregarded," as one zila parishad member from Rajasthan rather strongly put it, "and there is reason to believe that they have begun to be so treated by the Pradhans and the Panchayat Samitis."[98]

The IAS district officer is an "ex-officio member of the zila parishad," which means that he attends its meetings but does not vote on its resolutions. He effectively presides from without over the decisions of the samitis and zila parishad in the district, and he retains distinct powers of intervention to insure that these new

95. Government of Rajasthan, Letter No. F 149(33)Demo.D/Coord/DD/59 /27155–765, dated October 1, 1959 (unpublished).
96. For an analysis of these funds in terms of samiti planning, see the author's "Area Planning in Rajasthan," *Journal of Asian Studies*, XXIII (1964), 571–579.
97. The 1959 Act, secs. 57 and 63(1).
98. Mukut Behari Lal, M.P., "Democratic Decentralization in Rajasthan," *Kurukshetra* (July 1961), p. 23. See also complaints of pramukhs and members of at least four zila parishads about their lack of power over state funds allocated to samitis, in Congress Party in Parliament, *Study Team's Report* . . . (1960), pp. 22–23.

local authorities do not deviate from their prescribed functions.[99]

The principal reason for placing responsibility for community development with the samiti, rather than the zila parishad, was the recognition by the Government of Rajasthan that any decentralization of responsibility for the community development program should be placed exclusively with village leaders, and that while the samiti would probably represent these exclusively rural interests, the zila parishad would certainly represent not only rural interests but also wider political alignments in the district towns and beyond. Also the block was recognized as a viable unit of administration for community development purposes, especially in Rajasthan which was and still is in a fairly elementary stage of development in comparison to other states in India. Samitis, therefore, are the principal authorities in rural development administration in Rajasthan, and we proceed now to analyze the changing behavior of government officials in that organization.

If one were forced to single out the most important element of community development block administration during the 1950's, the selection would have to be continuous contact—contact between trained personnel and village communities. The villagers of Rajasthan were chary of accepting good advice unless its usefulness to their circumstances was demonstrated. Furthermore, more than 85 per cent of the villagers were illiterate. It was largely for these reasons that the spoken word and more especially visual demonstrations undertaken in village conditions were particularly suited to securing maximum acceptance of improved practices. For example, however effectively specialists in the Agriculture Department administered technical services, their objective of increased agricultural production could not be secured unless the Rajasthan farmer accepted the services being offered. Block personnel thus toured extensively in the block area in order to maintain this continuous contact. BDO's, extension officers, and gram sevaks were required to tour for a certain proportion of the total month. They were also asked to spend a minimum number of nights (called night halts) in villages in the

99. The 1959 Act, secs. 59, 66(3), 67, 68, 69, 91.

block each month.[100] The reason for insisting on night halts was that most block personnel were more effective when villagers were concentrated in the village at night rather than scattered in their fields during the day.

The BDO and the extension officers toured throughout a block in support of the gram sevaks, and the gram sevaks toured in their respective circles, dealing with the village people directly. From block headquarters, officers sometimes moved out together in the block jeep, each getting off at the particular gram sevak circle where he would be touring for a day or two. Usually, officers were on tour in the block, visiting several adjacent circles, for four or five consecutive days. Officers also moved alone by bus to a particular circle, then by bicycle, horseback, camel, or on foot within the circle. They took their own bedding and food with them if they were planning to make a night halt at the gram sevak's house or at the panchayat headquarters.

Touring arrangements were made at the monthly staff meeting, the one occasion when the entire block team was present at block headquarters. At this meeting each extension officer informed the gram sevaks concerned of his projected visit in the ensuing month and also submitted his touring plan to the BDO. These arrangements were sometimes embodied in a staff working plan; occasionally attempts were made to maintain a touring register. Usually, however, alterations in projected touring schedules were necessary due to unforeseen circumstances, such as a sudden call to a particular village to assist a villager with a fresh problem beyond the competence of the gram sevak, surprise visits by higher officials or non-official visitors (most visitors and some officials had an unhelpful habit of giving staff only a few days' advance notice of their intention to visit a block), the breakdown of the block jeep, or a sudden change in the weather making village tracks impassable. There was nothing particularly difficult about altering touring schedules as far as the block officers were

100. Monthly touring requirements were as follows: BDO's, twelve days, eight nights; extension officers, fifteen days, ten nights; and gram sevaks, twenty days, fifteen nights. Some staff were constantly on tour; others barely managed to fulfil the minimum requirements. Night halts presented problems, e.g., involvement in village politics by halting for the night with the family of one faction, thereby losing the support and trust of other factions.

concerned, for they lived mostly in contiguous staff housing and saw a great deal of each other in the block office. It was more difficult to inform the gram sevaks of a sudden change in plan, for once they left the monthly staff meeting to return to their respective villages, they naturally could not be contacted by telephone and they frequently resided in villages which saw the postman only once or twice a week. Co-ordination of work in blocks necessarily relied primarily on informal arrangements.

This informality in block administration was valuable considering the nature of community development. Village communities in Rajasthan, as elsewhere, would exhibit enthusiasm for development work some of the time, but they would lie dormant or the villagers would be interested in different activities at other times. It was simply impossible to sustain the villagers' enthusiasm for all aspects of community development all the time. Thus, when a particular village was aroused by a particular program, all available staff would quickly desert their job description and move to meet and encourage that enthusiasm. One found, for example, that the BDO, several extension officers, and a gram sevak were usually on hand when a village play depicting the advantages of clean houses was presented, or when a village shramdan (voluntary labor on works) was offered. Nehru's birthday signaled "Children's Day," and all staff members confined their functions accordingly. "Drives," "campaigns," village fairs, census work, elections, inspections by higher officials, visitations of parliamentary study teams, of newsmen, and of foreign students—all required curtailment of regular duties and attention to new responsibilities. Community development administration was not unlike a series of crash programs, where the important consideration was to have as many bodies as possible on hand at a given time.

The heart of block administration can be characterized, then, as government officials attempting—in some instances with impressive results—to change practices in rural Rajasthan by maintaining direct contact with village people by means of touring. It was an approach by the government to which the villagers were expected to respond. As was noted earlier in this section, the response was judged unsatisfactory by the Committee on Plan Projects and by others. The answer was Panchayati Raj.

The introduction of Panchayati Raj in Rajasthan has increased direct contact between block personnel and village leaders, and in many places it appears to have developed a sense of interest and willingness to participate in rural development which previously did not exist. The major innovation assisting these developments was, and is, the presence of a new procedure in the blocks which may be summarized as follows. Samitis meet regularly on a fixed day of the first week of every month. To this meeting are brought problems of village panchayats, suggestions from the block staff, and new ideas and schemes from higher authorities; from this meeting all the sarpanches, armed with samiti decisions and community development information, go to their respective panchayats, which meet during the following week. At each panchayat meeting, the panches are informed by the sarpanch of the decisions taken by the samiti. The approved monthly programs of the samiti are then explained to the village people, each panch being responsible for informing the villagers in his ward. About the twentieth day of the month, the samiti members and block officers concerned attend meetings of the standing committees of the samiti, which are held at samiti headquarters. Sanction of grants and loans and discussion of detailed matters relating to the subject matter of the committee take place at these meetings. At the end of the month the panchayat meets again in order to discuss matters which the sarpanch will bring up at the samiti meeting the following week. On the day before the samiti is due to meet, the gram sevaks arrive at headquarters, and a staff meeting is held with them and other block personnel. The BDO presides at this meeting, which usually lasts well into the night. The gram sevaks stay the night at headquarters in order to be on hand for the samiti meeting convened by the pradhan the following day.

Apart from the regularity and frequency of direct contact which this new procedure insures, a continuous two-way channel of communications has been created. Every month throughout Rajasthan, sarpanches travel from their villages to samiti meetings, where block officers answer questions, give advice, and encourage action. Most sarpanches will also attempt to push along applications from their constituents for grants and loans; many can be relied upon to make vigorous complaint to the block staff if their constituents are not receiving the service they deserve. Also every month these sarpanches return to their respective panchayats and pass along information and answers to questions to the panches. And every month these panches dispense this information, variously interpreted to them by the sarpanches, to their friends in panchayat ward. The effectiveness of this procedure will depend on the attendance at the meetings, the quality of the block personnel, the retentive power and leadership qualities of the village leaders involved, and the degree of support which the panches have in their wards.[101] Nevertheless, the procedure is working smoothly in many places.

In setting up this procedure, Panchayati Raj appears to be a process full of promise, bringing directly and continuously into rural development administration village leaders who share responsibility for the program. Initial results, however, have been disappointing. The figures in Table 11 suggest clearly that the community development program has suffered a setback since the introduction of Panchayati Raj.[102] But these particular figures were selected out of a larger group of possible figures because

101. It is asserted in Government of Rajasthan, Evaluation Organization, *A Report of the Panchayat Elections in Rajasthan, 1960* (Jaipur, 1961), p. 33, that on the basis of a sample survey of 1,873 heads of households throughout rural Rajasthan, 92 per cent explicitly expressed confidence in their panch. This seems an unusually high figure, although other data to refute it are lacking.

102. A complete list of more than thirty indices of community development program performance can be found in Ministry of Community Development and Co-operation, Department of Community Development, *Report 1960–61* (Delhi, 1961), Annexure IV (43–50). This particular report includes the annual, per-block figures for the year ending September, 1959 (the last year of blocks under community development in Rajasthan), as well as the figures for the year ending September, 1960 (the first year of Panchayati Raj in Rajasthan). The complete picture in terms of these indices is one of decline: e.g., chemical fertilizers distributed, 1,096 maunds in 1959 down to 885 maunds in 1960; rural latrines constructed, 16 down to 6.7; drinking water wells constructed, 14 down to 10; number of children attending rural nurseries, 78 down to 12; new tannery pits started, 4.2 down to 2.5. There are only a few items moving in the opposite direction: e.g., improved seeds distributed, 3,950 maunds up to 4,250 maunds; improved implements (agricultural) distributed, 116 up to 123. An unpublished index found by the author in the Development Department's figures in this same category is animals artificially inseminated, 123 down to 67.

they show quite strikingly that there has been a decline in extension activity by the block staff members. Fewer agricultural demonstrations are held by block personnel under Panchayati Raj. The number of compost pits dug, which depends entirely on the extension work and persuasive ability of the block staff (no funds are available for this in the program), has declined significantly. The mileage of new village roads built by voluntary

Table 11. *Selected Items of Relative Performance in Community Development Areas in Quarters Ending December, 1958, December, 1959, and December, 1960, in Rajasthan (average per block)*[a]

	Relative per-block performance in quarters ending:		
	Dec., 1958	Dec., 1959	Dec., 1960
Item	Community development	Panchayati Raj	Panchayati Raj
1. Number of agricultural demonstrations held	69	52	41
2. Number of compost pits dug	80	87	59
3. Miles of new kachcha roads constructed	1.1	.9	.7
4. Number of adults made literate	180	82	85
5. Number of village leaders' training camps held	2.3	.1	.1
6. Number of village leaders trained	114	3	3

[a] The figures are relative and by no means represent absolute achievement for the period indicated. Nevertheless, they do suggest a comparative trend. At least one-third of the blocks are not reporting regularly, although the author was told (Jaipur, March, 1961) by the chief statistician, Development Department, that the blocks which do not report regularly are in most cases those which are less successful.

Source: Compiled from unpublished data given the author by the Development Department, Government of Rajasthan, in March 1961.

labor has dropped by more than half. Particularly disturbing is the decline in the adult literacy program and the number of village leaders' camps held, for this is happening precisely at the time when such programs have a vital bearing on the success of Panchayati Raj.

There are many possible explanations for this distressing and unexpected occurrence.[103] One explanation, extremely difficult to corroborate, may be simply that the performance figures were inflated in the years prior to Panchayati Raj, but that now with village leaders closely watching the reporting process and block personnel able to share responsibility for program results with village leaders, the figures are more accurate. There are other possibilities. The one explored in the remainder of this section is the effect of the introduction of Panchayati Raj on the relations between different categories of block personnel, on the one hand, and relations between block personnel and the non-bureaucratic members of the samitis, on the other.

Before the introduction of Panchayati Raj and at the present time, block personnel were placed in the administrative organization of the community development block and asked to work together "as a team." By block teamwork is meant the joint effort of qualified personnel working in mutual confidence for the purpose of community development. That teamwork is important in block administration is clear on consideration of the nature of touring as described earlier. That teamwork is difficult to achieve is clear when one considers the diversity of the participants. For block officers are placed on deputation to a block from different government departments, and each officer possesses a different background, different loyalties, different professional standards. To transform these diverse individuals into a team is asking a great deal of any BDO, who is to head that team. Success is undoubtedly the exception.

With the introduction of Panchayati Raj, the BDO's and extension officers are placed on deputation to the samiti from the Government of Rajasthan according to the provisions of the *Rajasthan Panchayat Samitis (Terms and Conditions of Deputation of Vikas Adhikaris, Extension Officers and Other Officers) Rules, 1959.* The period of deputation is two years in the first instance, but this can be extended by the state government (more

103. "Unexpected" by the minister of community development, Government of India (S. K. Dey to the author in a personal interview at New Delhi, April 4, 1961), and the joint development commissioner, Government of Rajasthan (Ram Singh, IAS, to the author in a personal interview at Jaipur, March 26, 1961).

precisely, the district officer in this case) in consultation with the pradhan of the samiti. During this period of deputation, the officers continue to earn increments and promotion in their present cadres as usual. They continue to draw pay in the scale they would have drawn but for their deputation.[104] They continue to be governed by the rules applicable to the service to which they belong. They continue to be under the administrative and disciplinary control of the Government of Rajasthan, except that during the period of deputation the pradhan has power to sanction casual leave to the BDO. They can be transferred by the government in consultation with the pradhan, and they can be withdrawn by the government at any time if they become due for promotion in their parent cadres or for "other administrative reasons." A samiti cannot refuse to accept an officer for any reason. In short, the formal position is that the officers of the samiti belong to the Government of Rajasthan.

Gram sevaks are encadred, along with various other categories of personnel,[105] in the Rajasthan Panchayat Samitis and Zila Parishads Service (hereinafter abridged and capitalized as the Service). The position of the personnel in the Service is defined in provisions contained in the 1959 Act and the Rajasthan Panchayat Samitis and Zila Parishads Service Rules, 1959 (hereinafter abridged and capitalized as the Rules). The Government of Rajasthan fixes the strength of each category of post "which it may consider necessary for each panchayat samiti."[106] It may also

104. The Deputation Rules, section 5. Pay scales of samiti officers are fixed by the government. The samiti has no power over these salaries. Further, should there be a deficit toward the end of the year, additional funds must be provided by the samiti to meet staff salaries.

105. The Service consists of the following categories of posts: (1) gram sevaks; (2) gram sevikas; (3) primary school teachers; (4) field men; (5) stock men; (6) stock assistants; (7) veterinary compounders; (8) sheep and wool demonstrators; (9) dressers; (10) vaccinators; (11) ministerial establishment (except accounts clerks); (12) drivers; (13) project operators; (14) skilled workers, including demonstrators, designers, dye masters, blacksmiths, mechanics, welders, and carpenters; (15) mates; (16) welfare workers; and (17) hostel superintendents. Source: compiled from Development Department, "Notification No. F. 45 (173) (221) Coord/DD/59," dated September 28, 1959 (unpublished); The 1959 Act, sec. 86(2) as amended by the *Rajasthan Panchayat Samitis and Zila Parishads* [*Second Amendment Ordinance, 1960,* sec. 27(i); The Rules, sec. 4(1)].

106. The 1959 Act, sec. 31(1). The samiti may create additional posts only under the fixed government categories, subject to the condition that prior approval is obtained.

"prescribe the duties, functions and powers of each grade and each category of officers and employees encadred in the service."[107] All matters involving conditions of service such as pay and allowances, qualifications for recruitment, leave, seniority, and pension are fixed and regulated by the Government of Rajasthan.[108] Vacancies in Service posts are filled by direct recruitment in the lowest grade of each category of post, by promotion from a lower to a higher grade in the same category, and by transfer of persons holding the same post in another samiti. The procedure for direct recruitment is as follows: samitis send a requisition for direct recruits to a Selection Commission, especially constituted for the Service, which consists of two persons appointed by the Government of Rajasthan and the pramukh of the zila parishad concerned. One of the two government appointees is nominated as chairman by the government.[109] On receipt of a requisition, the commission invites applications through employment exhanges. For each district the commission selects persons for posts in the Service. Then they prepare a list of candidates considered suitable for appointment to each category of post, and this is sent to a District Establishment Committee, one of which has been created for the Service in each district. Each committee is composed of one of the government-nominated members of the commission as chairman and the district officer and pramukh of the district concerned. The committee merely allots candidates to each samiti from the list sent to it from the commission in the order in which the names appear on the list.[110] Finally, the samiti formally appoints the candidates allotted to them by the committee.[111] Selection of Service personnel by promotion or transfer is made by the committee.[112] Whenever vacancies are to be filled by promotion, the committee invites recommendations for the grade and category of post concerned from the samitis in its district, considers the recommendations on

107. *Ibid.*, sec. 86(4).
108. The Rules, secs. 4, 6, 11, 20, 31, 34.
109. The 1959 Act, sec. 86(7).
110. The Rules, sec. 18(2).
111. *Ibid.*, sec. 19.
112. Transfers outside the district, which are rare, are attended to by the commission. See *ibid.*, sec. 29.

the basis of confidential reports and service records of the candidates, prepares a list of suitable candidates for each grade and category according to seniority, and allots persons to each samiti in the order in which the names appear on the list. For transfers within each district, the names of employees desiring transfer or desired to be transferred are sent to the committee by the samiti, and the committee arranges the transfer after consultation with the two samitis involved. In both instances (promotion and transfer), the samiti merely appoints the employees allotted to a particular post by the committee.[113] The Service was formed on October 2, 1959 (Gandhi's birthday again), and all persons holding the various categories of posts included in the Service immediately prior to that date were deemed to have been appointed to it, unless they exercised their option under the Rules not to become a member.[114]

Gram sevaks, as members of the Service, are selected initially by a special committee for that purpose in each district under the chairmanship of the district officer. They are then sent for two years of training at one of several extension training centers in Rajasthan. On completion of training, however, they are assigned to a particular district (if possible, their own) by the Selection Commission of the Service, and then they are allotted to a particular samiti by the District Establishment Committee.

It has been shown that the officers on deputation to the samitis belong formally to the Government of Rajasthan. Likewise, in the case of the Service, the government creates the posts, recruits the personnel through a commission which it dominates, prescribes the functions and powers of each grade and category of employees encadred in it, and determines and regulates all matters involving conditions of service. Finally, Class IV servants, such as peons and sweepers, are regulated by government rules; to clinch the position, the BDO is the appointing authority.[115] The question

113. *Ibid.*, secs. 22(2), 28(2).
114. Some persons did exercise this option and were either absorbed in another post of the former appointing authority or served with a notice of discharge. Figures for the number who left and the number who remained are not available.
115. The 1959 Act, sec. 30(3).

can legitimately be raised: does the samiti possess its own staff? Formally, no—and this should be taken into account when considering to what extent Panchayati Raj, as presently consti- tuted in Rajasthan, is a system of local self-government.

In practice, however, some samitis have been able to modify this rather rigid framework. Categorical statements are impos- sible to make about the hurly-burly of the first eighteen months of Panchayati Raj, but if the author may be permitted to cite an impression gathered during his field studies in Rajasthan at this time, it is that toward the end of 1960 a number of Service staff (as distinct from officers on deputation) owed allegiance of one sort or another to the leading group in the samiti membership. There are three reasons which lend support to this impression.

In the first place, a number of vacancies in Service posts were created at the outset of Panchayati Raj, requiring immediate occupancy. The Rules allow temporary employment not exceed- ing six months to be filled by the appointing authority, which for the Service is the samiti.[116] At least some of the Service personnel in each samiti have been temporarily appointed in this manner and are waiting for permanent appointment from the commission. In a subtle way, these personnel are samiti personnel.

Secondly, disciplinary proceedings can be started against Serv- ice personnel by the samiti's Standing Committee for Finance, Taxation, and Administration with the prior approval of the District Establishment Committee.[117] Even more, the samiti has full power to withhold one increment of salary from any member of the Service.[118] The loss or delay of one increment of salary for such personnel as gram sevaks, primary school teachers, clerks, and others working on similar pay scales can create hardship for the individual and his family, as anyone conversant with Indian rural life will readily understand. Such disciplinary proceedings have been rare, but the potential use of this power and not

116. The Rules, sec. 23, read with sec. 19. This period can be extended up to twelve months with the concurrence of the committee.
117. The 1959 Act, sec. 89(4). The BDO has power only to censure Service staff [sec. 89(2Bi)].
118. *Ibid.*, sec. 89(3).

necessarily the exercise of it has served to assist allegiance of Service personnel to samiti members.

Thirdly, Service staff are invariably residents of the samiti area or the district (it will be recalled that the commission recruits by district). Most gram sevaks work in their home district, many primary school teachers teach in their home village, and clerks tend to be from the large village or small town in which the samiti office is located. Since local leaders elected or co-opted to the samiti membership also reside in the samiti area or in the district, they tend to know personally many Service personnel. This is so because members and Service personnel grew up in the same town or village, because they went to the same school, because they belong to the same caste association, or because they are related in other ways; even if they do not know each other initially, an easy alliance between them is possible because they speak the same dialect, or simply because they live in the same area and tend, as is true in most rural situations, to possess fairly circumscribed area loyalties.

These three factors—temporary employment, possible disciplinary action, and local allegiance—have helped to create a bond between Service personnel and samiti members. Such factors, however, do not apply to the officers on deputation, who cannot be temporarily employed by the samiti, who are not subject to disciplinary action from it, and who almost always come from other districts of Rajasthan or other states of India. Moreover, the frequent rotation[119] of these officers deputed to the samiti serves

119. Frequent rotation of officers was a problem before Panchayati Raj, as it is today. BDO's and extension officers are normally transferred to another block or elsewhere in the government every two or three years. When every one of the ten officers in a block is transferred every two years at different times, it becomes exceedingly difficult to maintain informal relations which seem essential to block teamwork. At the same time, to ask officers to remain indefinitely in one block is to ask too much. The justification for three-year transfers is found in this type of comment made to the author by an able and successful BDO. "In the first year, I'm making contact with the village people, learning their dialect and becoming acquainted with the pecularities of the block area; in the second year, I can do good work; in the third year, I'm growing stale and need a change." Nevertheless, the case for allowing an officer to remain longer than three years in a block, if he desires it, is strong. For example, one BDO, after working two years in a block and then being transferred, was quickly returned to that block, not only because he wished it, but also because a deputation of village leaders from that area traveled to Jaipur and demanded of the joint development commissioner that he be returned.

to accentuate their orientation to the Government of Rajasthan. Gram sevaks, on the other hand, now placed in the Service, find their allegiance going to the members of the samiti. These factors combine to split the gram sevaks away from the BDO and the extension officers within the samiti. This is unfortunate, because, as has been explained, block teamwork is important to successful community development administration.

Another perhaps temporary factor is working to aggravate the situation in the samiti. The gram sevak's role in Panchayati Raj is not defined; it is now the sarpanch who obtains the attention of the village community by bringing news from samiti meetings, sanctioning grants and loans (with the gram sevak and the patwari of the village), and taking credit for the results (thus destroying one of the gram sevak's very few positive incentives). "It is the responsibility of the panchayat" was the familiar response of many gram sevaks to the author's questions about his work. Similarly, "it is the samiti's job now" was the common reply from extension officers to similar questions. These answers underline the fundamental change which is taking place in rural Rajasthan; they also suggest the danger in not fixing responsibility during this transition period when a transfer of power is taking place. What follows from this temporary impasse is that everybody's responsibility in theory becomes nobody's duty in practice.

The introduction of Panchayati Raj in Rajasthan has altered the entire concept of the block team, for it consists now of the officers, the Service staff, and the samiti members. A general conclusion from the preceding analysis, viewed in this larger sense, would be that the block team is in a state of disarray while new relationships among the three components of the team are being built. The confusion as to responsibilities and the growth of divergent allegiances were perhaps to be expected with the introduction of a new organization (the samiti) into an already existing institutional framework (the block administration). It is not so surprising, therefore, that extension work and program performance declined temporarily as a result of the introduction of Panchayati Raj.

IV. Conclusion

The Indian bureaucracy today is influenced partly by the British imperial tradition and partly by certain post-independence phenomena. Insofar as the ICS was concerned, two features of that tradition have been singled out in this chapter in fairly rough and tentative form and have been labeled "the law and order orientation" and "the exclusive responsibility orientation." It has been contended here that these bureaucratic orientations in their successor institution, the IAS, have contributed to political stability in terms of the maintenance of internal peace, the conduct of fair elections, and the preservation of the unity of the nation. The bureaucracy also forms part of and interacts with a developing political system. It is contended here that one aspect of this developing political system is the changing behavior of government officials from the "exclusive responsibility orientation" toward one in which they are and believe themselves to be amenable to control by non-bureaucratic political institutions. And finally, the bureaucracy has been active since independence in the initiation of public enterprises and rural development, both of which conduce to economic development. On the basis of the experience with rural development in one state, it is contended here that the changing behavior of government officials in terms of bureaucratic responsibility (an aspect of political development) results temporarily in less effective bureaucratic performance (an aspect of economic development).

· 5 ·

The Higher Bureaucracy of Pakistan*

Ralph Braibanti

This chapter is based on the assumption that the administrative process remains the paramount manifestation of political power in Pakistan, challenged to some degree by a strong judicial order and to a lesser extent by a slowing emerging political process. Despite these challenges to administrative pre-eminence, the pace of politicization has been checked by a variety of institutional devices which are here described.

The governmental idiom of modernization has been one primarily of attitudinal change rather than of drastic structural renovation. Such attitudinal change has been integrated into an administrative apparatus which bears strong similarity to the pre-independence pattern. The constitutional framework, however,

* The author wishes to record his indebtedness to various officials of the Government of Pakistan whose unfailing courtesy and co-operation made much of this study possible during a series of sojourns in Pakistan starting in 1957 and continuing through 1965. He is grateful also to former colleagues on the faculty of the School of Public Administration, University of Southern California, under whose auspices he served as chief adviser to the Civil Service Academy in Lahore from 1960 to 1962. For other research visits to Pakistan he is indebted to the Social Science Research Council, the Asia Foundation, and the Duke University Commonwealth-Studies Center. The research assistance of Zahid Shariff in the preparation of Tables 9 through 17 and of S. M. Haider and A. T. R. Rahman in the preparation of Tables 6 and 23 is also gratefully acknowledged.

This chapter is designed to complement the author's *Research on the Bureaucracy of Pakistan* (Durham, N. C., 1966). While some of the issues analyzed in that study are mentioned in this chapter as well, they are here either quickly passed over or treated from a different point of view. Functional and sociological dimensions of bureaucracy and the role of the judiciary as an agency of internal control are omitted from this chapter because of published analysis in the author's "Public Bureaucracy and Judiciary in Pakistan," in Joseph La Palombara (ed.), *Bureaucracy and Political Development* (Princeton, N. J., 1963), pp. 360–441. These studies are hereinafter cited as *Research on the Bureaucracy of Pakistan* and "Public Bureaucracy and Judiciary."

has undergone fundamental change from a parliamentary to a presidential system, although the behavior within that framework is molded somewhat by the earlier system. As administration is pre-eminent, so within administration is the role of the elite cadre paramount. The scope of its discretion is remarkably broad, being controlled mainly by judicial review. For this reason, this chapter includes a full-scale analysis of the background of the elite cadre using data not hitherto available.

Omitted from consideration in this chapter is the very important "non-bureaucratic" bureaucracy, namely, the rural development movement manifest in the Basic Democracies Scheme. In a sense, this movement is a substitute for a vigorous political process in that it seeks to provide within the orthodox bureaucratic apparatus the institutional and attitudinal means for the aggregation and articulation of political group interests. Much has been written on this movement; hence, there is some justification for passing over it entirely here rather than surveying it cursorily. Similarly, there has been omitted discussion of the slowing emerging political process, visible since the Combined Opposition party contested so effectively for the presidency in 1965. The omission of these two considerations should in no way be construed as implying their unimportance. On the contrary, they may be more significant aspects of political development than those analyzed here. The design of this chapter, however, is to develop in some detail the juridical, institutional, and internal elements affecting modernization of the higher bureaucracy.

I. Institutional Determinants of Administrative Behavior

The struggle to achieve control of a vigorous bureaucratic system necessarily begins in the structural loci of power as determined in constitutional polity. The same structure which enables the achievement of control also determines the contours and content of administrative action. Juridically, administrative behavior in a constitutional system derives its breath of life from the delegation of power by the law-making authority. In an embryonic constitutional system emergent from an earlier system of near-bureaucratic paramountcy, the interstices into which delegation imperceptibly flows and the points of countervailing force which determine and regulate such flow are questions of crucial importance.

The (Second) Constitution of 1962, still in malleable form, provides for a significant devolution of legislative powers to the two provincial governments. This appeared essential, particularly to satisfy East Pakistan which toward the end of martial law in 1961 and 1962 was becoming increasingly restive about Bengali interests and representation. On the other hand, the 1962 Constitution is amply endowed with provisions to make possible a vigorous administrative state with both leadership and action emanating from the central government. During the three years since the Constitution has been in effect, some power seems to have moved to the center, but perhaps not as quickly as provincial political leaders had feared. The contours of provincial and central powers are very much in flux, and both political pressures and judicial construction are affecting the pattern in a highly dynamic matrix of interaction.

Central-Provincial Distribution of Legislative Powers

Since bureaucratic behavior is juridically only the filling in of the skeletal generality of the statute, the ultimate contours of administrative discretion at various levels are necessarily determined by the scope of legislative powers. The fluidity of the situation in contemporary Pakistan leaves little room for definitive generalization. One attribute, however, is clear. The 1962 Constitution in allocating powers between levels of government departs significantly from the format of the 1956 Constitution, which in this respect had retained the formula of the 1935 Government of India Act. The (First) Constitution of 1956 had enumerated legislative powers in three separate lists: thirty items were included in the federal list, nineteen in the concurrent list, and ninety-four in the provincial list.[1] This scheme under the 1956

1. First (1956) Constitution of Pakistan, Articles 106, 110, and Fifth Schedule.

Constitution was in effect only from March 23, 1956, to October 7, 1958, a period of thirty-one months. A significant corpus of case law interpreting this allocation did not have a chance to develop,[2] in part because of the short time the 1956 Constitution was in force, but more because the nation was preoccupied with even more fundamental constitutional crises[3] and was plagued by serious political instability. During the forty-four months of martial law, this allocation underwent a significant shift toward greater power for the central government. For nearly a year after martial law was proclaimed, the legal pattern was unchanged, but in September, 1959, subjects in the provincial list and subjects assumed to be residual in the provinces were transferred to the concurrent list. This new allocation was given retrospective effect, with the consequence that law made by the president could void conflicting provincial laws.[4]

When the 1962 Constitution was being formulated, the issue of allocation of powers was given considerable attention. Since there was no constituent assembly or constitutional convention, the nearest equivalent was public opinion solicited and recorded by the Constitution Commission, the opinion of the commission itself, and the ultimate Constitution promulgated by the Presi-

2. In the only five reported cases interpreting central-provincial allocation of powers, the issue was dealt with in an ancillary way. In *Lt. Col. Nawabzada Muhammad Amir Khan* v. *Controller of Estate Duty*, PLD 1957 Lah. 706, the court merely confirmed that the distribution of legislative powers under the 1956 Constitution followed the pattern of the Government of India Act, 1935. In *Sui Gas Transmission Co., Ltd.* v. *Islamic Republic of Pakistan* [1959] 1 P.S.C.R. 1, it was held that the provincial legislature could legislate concurrently with the Parliament in matters in the concurrent list "as far as the Province was concerned." The vexing problem facing most federal systems, namely, the reconciliation of competing federal and provincial interests in matters of repugnancy and pre-emption of fields in concurrent jurisdiction, was dealt with by the Supreme Court briefly in *Chief Secretary to the Government of East Pakistan* v. *Moslemuddin Sikdar* [1956] 1 P.S.C.R. 246. See also *Progress of Pakistan Co., Ltd.*, v. *Registrar, Joint Stock Companies*, Karachi, PLD 1958 Lah. 887; *Khaliq and Najam Co.* v. *Sales-Tax Officer*, PLD 1959 Lah. 915. The lengthy exposition and evolution of guidelines found in several Indian cases, especially in *Atiabari Tea Co., Ltd.,* v. *State of Assam*, AIR 1961 SC 232, *Automobile Transport Co., Ltd.,* v. *State of Rajasthan*, AIR 1962 SC 1406, and *State of West Bengal* v. *Union of India*, AIR 1963 SC 1241, is not to be found in Pakistan law for this period.
3. The very juridical foundations of the state were shaken by the crisis which was adjudicated in *Federation of Pakistan and others* v. *Moulvi Tamizuddin Khan* [1955] 1 F.C.R. 155.
4. President's Order No. 17 of 1959 (Legislative Powers [Amendment] Order, 1959). *Gazette of Pakistan, Extraordinary*, September 23, 1959.

dent.[5] The commission examined 6,269 completed questionnaires and interviewed 565 persons. It found that 65.5 per cent of those answering its questionnaires favored a federal form and 34.5 per cent a unitary form of government. Some 61.5 per cent of the answers favored a central government stronger than under the 1956 Constitution, and 38.5 per cent wanted autonomous provinces. The commission itself proposed a triadic allocation of powers similar to the federal, concurrent, and provincial lists of the 1956 Constitution, but with two major departures.[6] Residual powers were to rest with the central government, and the central legislature would be able under certain circumstances to preempt provincial legislative powers. Minor changes included a shift of some subjects from the provincial to the concurrent or federal lists, thus somewhat increasing central government power. Whatever merit the scheme proposed by the Shahabuddin Commission may have had, it was not accepted by the President. Instead, the 1962 Constitution has one list of forty-nine central government powers including such subjects as defense, foreign affairs, inter-provincial and foreign trade and commerce, insurance, posts, telecommunications, and tourism.[7] All other powers are presumed to be reserved to the provinces.

There is, however, a very significant exception under Article 131(2) which empowers the central government to enact legislation when the national interest requires it in relation to security, financial stability, planning or co-ordination or achievement of uniformity in different parts of the nation. Explaining Article 131(2), the President said occasions for its use "should be rare . . ." and "[e]ven in these cases, execution will rest with the provinces. The underlying theme is that what can be done on a Provincial basis ought to be done on that basis."[8] Notwithstanding

5. *Report of the Constitution Commission, Pakistan, 1961* (Karachi: Government of Pakistan Press, 1961). Hereinafter cited as Shahabuddin Report, after the name of its chairman, retired Supreme Court Justice Muhammad Shahabuddin.
6. Shahabuddin Report, p. 42.
7. Second (1962) Constitution of Pakistan, Third Schedule.
8. President Mohammad Ayub Khan in an address to the nation, "The New Constitution: Its Outline and Salient Points." Full text accessible in *Speeches and Statements, Field Marshal Mohammad Ayub Khan* (Karachi: Pakistan Publications, 1962), IV, 169–179, quotation at 171. Hereinafter cited as *President's Speeches and Statements.*

the President's explanation or even what might have been the intent of the new Constitution, the authority implicit in Article 131(2) can change the very nature of central-provincial relations and shift the balance of power markedly to the center. This authority of Article 131(2) is given to the central legislature for the enactment of statutes, but it extends also to the president whose power to promulgate ordinances is derivative from that of the legislature and therefore shares almost the same scope and limitations. It is appropriate to examine the extent to which the central government has legislated in matters otherwise regarded as provincial under the authority of Article 131(2). Table 1 shows that during the thirty-five and a half months from June, 1962, the effective date of the 1962 Constitution, until September 8, 1965, fourteen acts and ordinances were enacted or promulgated under the authority of Article 131(2).[9] Twelve of these invoked the "achievement of uniformity" clause; the remaining two were based on the "economic and financial stability" provision of clause (a). The significant finding of Table 1 is that, excluding item 5 which has always been a central power, ten instruments displace a power formerly regarded under the 1956 Constitution as belonging to the province, and three instruments displace a power formerly on the concurrent list. To be sure, the provincial and concurrent lists of the 1956 Constitution no longer have validity. But it is not unreasonable to assume that powers on the provincial list, not now enumerated in the federal list of the 1962 Constitution, would continue to be reserved for the provinces. Thus, by invoking Article 131(a), governmental action under at least nine rubrics of power have been shifted to the central government. There has been resistance in the legislatures to this centripetal shift in power, but the opposition appears to be based on political expediency rather than on consistency of constitutional principle. Both the Jute Amendment Ordinance and the Censorship of Films Bill (Table 1, items 2, 9) were vigorously attacked in the

9. It is possible but not likely that somewhat more than fourteen acts and ordinances were issued during this period. See limitations of data described in Table 1 under "Sources."

National Assembly as interfering with provincial autonomy.[10] On the other hand, the Indecent Advertisements Prohibition Bill (Table 1, item 8), for which a similar case of interference might have been made, was passed with little discussion and without serious mention of provincial-central powers.[11] In the case of the Elective Bodies Disqualification Ordinance (Table 1, item 6), by which the central government assumed jurisdiction over the prohibition on former politicians running for office, the issue is not clear. This ordinance amends a power which originated under martial law as a central power. Under the 1956 Constitution the determination of qualifications of persons elected to local bodies was generally thought to be a provincial power. But the role of local elective bodies has changed, for they are now charged with local government responsibilities and, as elements of the Basic Democracies Scheme, constitute an electoral college for members of the national and provincial legislatures. Hence, continued central government action in this sphere might be justified by Entry 35 of the Third Schedule of the 1962 Constitution, which like its predecessor clearly lists such elections as a central government power. Whatever the constitutional justification, it appears that at least the determination of some qualifications for the election of local officials has moved into the ambit of the central government.

If Article 131(a) continues to be invoked at roughly the same pace as during this period and the powers thus shifted are of considerable scope and importance, the pattern of central-provincial relations may be changed. The consequence for administration is not yet clear. Theoretically, the province may be more and more concerned with execution of centrally conceived and centrally supervised policy. This, perhaps, is what President Ayub had in mind in his 1962 message on the Constitution.[12] There is a question as to how much provincial "execution" is possible in

10. National Assembly of Pakistan, *Debates*, December 7, 1962, pp. 621–622; December 8, 1962, pp. 640–679; April 5, 1963, pp. 1377–1384; April 8, 1963, pp. 1467–1476; April 9, 1963, pp. 1507–1528; April 11, 1963, pp. 1683–1737.
11. *Ibid.*, May 29, 1963, pp. 62, 67–74; May 31, 1963, pp. 179–185.
12. See above, n. 8.

Table 1. *Acts and Ordinances Invoking Power of Article 131 of the Second (1962) Constitution*

Act or ordinance	Authority under 1962 Constitution		Equivalent power in Fifth Schedule of 1956 Constitution
	Provision of Article 131 invoked, para. (2)[a]	Assumed relevant residual power displaced or Third Schedule central powers invoked[b]	
1. Political Parties Act III, 1962	(c)	Incorporation of societies and associations	provincial list, entry 9
2. Jute Ordinance LXXIV, 1962	(a)	Agriculture, industries (P)	provincial list, entries 14, 39, 43
3. Pakistan Penal Code (Third Amendment) Ordinance LXXVI, 1962	(c)	Criminal law (C)	concurrent list, entry 1
4. Industrial Disputes (Amendment) Ordinance LXXIX, 1962	(c)	Labor relations (C)	concurrent list, entry 5
5. Military Court Sentences (Supplementary Provisions) Ordinance LXXVIII, 1962	(c)	Central power, Third Schedule, item 1	federal list, entry 1
6. Elective Bodies Disqualification (Removal and Remission) Ordinance II, 1963		Constitution of local government authorities (P)	provincial list, entry 15
7. Appellate Jurisdiction (High Courts and Supreme Courts) (Repeal) Act IV, 1963	(c)	Affairs of high courts (P)	provincial list, entry 2
8. Indecent Advertisements Prohibition Act XII, 1963	(c)	Newspapers (C) or Public order (P)	concurrent list, entry 4, or provincial list, entry 1
9. Censorship of Films Act XVIII, 1963	(b) (c)	Sanctioning of films (P)	provincial list, entry 25
10. Jute (Amendment) Ordinance VII, 1963	(a)	Agriculture, industries (P)	provincial list, entries 14, 39, 43

11. Legal Practice (Disqualifications) Ordinance II 1964	(c)	Regulation of professions (P)	provincial list, entry 58
12. Code of Criminal Procedure (Amendment) Ordinance V, 1964	(c)	Criminal law (C)	concurrent list, entry 1
13. Unani, Ayurvedic, and Homoeopathic Practitioners Act II, 1965	(c)	Public health (P)	provincial list, entry 26
14. Basic Democracies Order (Amendment) Ordinance II, 1965	(c)	Local government (P)	provincial list, entry 15

[a] Letters in parentheses in this column refer to clauses of para. (2) of Article 131, which empower the central legislature to make laws on any matter not listed in the list of federal powers where required by the national interest in relation to (a) security, economic and financial stability, (b) planning or co-ordination, (c) achievement, in respect of any matter, of uniformity in different parts of Pakistan.

[b] Capital letters in parentheses in this column refer to a power assumed from tradition of the 1956 Constitution, read with the residuary power doctrine of the 1962 Constitution to be either provincial (P) or concurrent (C).

Source: Central and provincial statutes sections of *All-Pakistan Legal Decisions* (PLD) for 1962, 1963, 1964, and January through October, 1965. This is an unofficial source and may not be complete. Likelihood of completeness, however, is very high. The period covered is thirty-five and one-half months from the end of martial law, June 8, 1962, to the Proclamation of Emergency, September 8, 1965.

the context of other centripetal tendencies, such as a centrally recruited elite cadre and centrally appointed provincial governors.

Another significant potential for shifting power from the provincial to the central government might have been the provision of Article 133 of the 1962 Constitution, which presumably ousted jurisdiction of the courts for ruling on the validity of a law by declaring that the responsibility for deciding if a legislature has power to make a law rests with the legislature itself. Resolution of conflicts in jurisdiction between levels of government was not to be made by the judiciary but by the legislatures. Since under martial law the President had suspended this power of the judiciary, it cannot be said to have been completely an innovation in the 1962 Constitution. But so far as "normal" constitutionalism goes, it was a novel inclusion, for it was well-settled doctrine, both under the Government of India Act of 1935 and under the 1956 Constitution, that courts could determine if legislation was within the competence of the legislature concerned.[13] Nevertheless, it appeared to be the intent of the President as expressed both by him and by Manzur Qadir (said to be the draftsman of the 1962 Constitution) that there was to be no judicial review of legislation.[14] This position was rejected with considerable vigor, first by the East Pakistan High Court and later by the Supreme Court in two unanimous decisions. In the latter, Chief Justice Cornelius and three other judges unequivocally established the principle of the inherent prerogative of the courts to interpret the Constitution and to review legislation for its constitutionality.[15] In the classic Fazlul Quader case, the courts had to deal with Article 133 of the 1962 Constitution which was intended to "oust" their

13. It was on the legal premise that the judiciary had such power that the five decisions cited above, n. 3, were made. A general review of the existence of this power and comment on it may be found in *Chief Administrator of Auqaf, West Pakistan* v. *Rashidud Daula*, PLD 1961 Lah. 990. This judgment is useful also because it includes the full text of President's Order No. 17 of 1959 which suspended that power.

14. See the address of President Ayub before the West Pakistan High Court Bar Association on April 27, 1962, in *President's Speeches and Statements*, IV, 211–219.

15. *Mohd. Abdul Haque* v. *Fazlul Quader Chowdhury*, PLD 1963 Dacca 669; *Mr. Fazlul Quader Chowdhury* v. *Mohd. Abdul Haque*, PLD 1963 SC 486. These two decisions can rightly be said to be the equivalent of *Marbury* v. *Madison* in the development of the United States Constitution.

jurisdiction with respect to the allocation of powers between the central government and the provinces. In this the courts faced a troublesome line of reasoning, for they based the existence of the general power of judicial review on the view that Article 133 was limited in its meaning to the allocation of central-provincial powers. In the Supreme Court decision, Cornelius and Hamoodur Rahman did not deal directly with whether or not the court was rightly denied jurisdiction even in matters of allocation of powers. But the remaining three justices, S. A. Rahman, Fazle Akbar, and B. Z. Kaikaus, asserted with some vigor that Article 133 did not necessarily deny the right of judicial review in allocation of powers, for as Kaikaus reasoned, some forum must decide which law is to prevail if two legislatures legislate on the same subject.[16] Since the views of Justices Rahman, Fazle Akbar, and Kaikaus were not part of the major opinion, it is not clear whether this interpretation of Article 133 is official Supreme Court doctrine or not. It is clear, however, that the High Court of West Pakistan regards the judiciary as the rightful authority to settle conflicting claims to central-provincial legislative powers. In two cases decided after the Supreme Court handed down the Fazlul Quader judgment, the High Court assumed validity of this authority by ruling on conflicting jurisdiction.[17]

The importance of this issue to administration lies in the fact that no unequivocal position has yet been taken by the Supreme Court to restrain the power of the central government in deciding for itself what its legislative powers are. It does not seem probable that the Supreme Court will long maintain this stance, for the logic of the Kaikaus view is likely to prevail, i.e., if the two legislatures disagree as to their competence, a third entity must decide. That entity can hardly be any other than the Supreme Court. Even without such an actual deadlock, this line of reasoning has already been set by three of the five Supreme Court judges in what can be regarded either as a majority opinion or as

16. *Mr. Fazlul Quader Chowdhury* v. *Mohd. Abdul Haque,* at 529.
17. *Chittagong Mercantile Employee's Association* v. *Chairman, Industrial Court of East Pakistan,* PLD 1963 Dacca 856; *Manzoor Ahmad* v. *Commissioner, Lahore Division,* PLD 1964 Lah. 194. These cases were decided on August 2, 1963, and January 24, 1964, respectively. The Fazlul Quader Judgment had been handed down by the Supreme Court on May 13, 1963.

strong obiter dicta. This legislative power, if continued unrestrained and combined with the potential of Article 131, may shift the balance even more to the center, whose authority will be controlled, if at all, by political rather than legal forces. On the other hand, if the judiciary follows the Kaikaus doctrine and the precedent of the High Court of West Pakistan, there is a likelihood of an unstable equilibrium in allocation of central and provincial powers in which the provinces may emerge as stronger rather than weaker.

Executive-Legislative Powers

Although Pakistan now has a presidential form of government, the 1962 Constitution was not designed in a pattern in which legislative and executive powers were clearly separated. Executive power is vested in the president, and the parliamentary system as it was known under the 1956 Constitution has been abandoned. Since Pakistan was the first major nation inheriting the British imperial tradition to depart in such a calculated way from the parliamentary pattern, President Ayub's justification for this step is not without value.[18] In his official announcement of the new Constitution broadcast on March 1, 1962, he said:

We have adopted the Presidential System as it is simpler to work, more akin to our genius and history and less liable to lead to instability —a luxury that a developing country like ours cannot afford. The other alternative was the Parliamentary System. This we tried and it failed. Not that there is anything inherently wrong with it. The trouble is that we have not yet attained several sophistications that are necessary for its successful operation. For it to work, you need democratic institutions right down to villages, trade unions and cooperatives on a large scale to give people training in the spirit of give and take, and dispassionate consideration of problems. You need much higher level

18. The relative suitability of parliamentary and presidential forms to the conditions and needs of new states is a subject of importance in political science. No comparative analysis of the two systems in this new context has yet emerged. The Laski-Price correspondence on the merits of these two forms in established systems might well serve as a basis for relating such institutional forms to the requirements of emerging states. See Don K. Price and Harold J. Laski, "The Parliamentary and Presidential Systems," *Public Administration Review*, III (Autumn, 1943), 317–335, and IV (Autumn, 1944), 347–359.

of education, prosperity, public spirit and integrity. Above all, you need really cool and phlegmatic temperament which only people living in cool climates seem to have. Also it requires long periods of probation. For instance, the British took 600 years of trial and tribulations to reach this stage. Looking around the world you notice that this system has only worked successfully in Britain and the Scandinavian countries. Elsewhere it has not taken real roots. Even France which gave birth to liberal philosophy has not been able to work it. So, don't let us kid ourselves and cling to clichés and assume that we are ready to work such a refined system knowing the failure of earlier attempts.

In that system, the Chief Executive—the Prime Minister—must have the support of a majority of the members of the House, at all times. If Parliamentary traditions have taken root in a country, any member of the House, who withdraws his support, after pledging it, will have to account for it before the bar of public opinion.

In our conditions, however, there is no mechanism which will automatically operate to prevent members from selling their support or from charging a price for continuing to give support. The whole process of Government thus becomes liable to be subverted in the first instance, to placating those members without whose support the government in power would fall. The only insurance against such an eventuality in our conditions is to release the Chief Executive from the obligation of having to be sustained artificially so as to enable him to get on with the functions entrusted to him for the benefit of the people at large.[19]

In establishing presidential government, President Ayub accepted the recommendation of the Constitution Commission which had noted that 47 per cent of opinion solicited preferred that form to a parliamentary system.[20] The commission's recommendation, however, was premised on the concomitant adoption of a system of checks and balances, to which a separate chapter of its report was devoted, and on the creation of a bicameral legislature.[21] In the system actually put into effect, however, the

19. *President's Speeches and Statements*, IV, 176.
20. Shahabuddin Report, pp. 19–31.
21. *Ibid.*, chap. vi, pp. 52–63. This is not the only instance of partial acceptance or total rejection of the commission's recommendations. For example, the commission rather reluctantly conceded the need for a presidential ordinance-making power but advised (p. 62) against giving similar powers to provincial governors. Such power, however, was included in Article 79 of the 1962 Constitution. The commission also recommended bicameral legislatures, but the Constitution prescribes unicameral bodies. President Ayub's rejection of the

presidency as an office was plucked out of the larger concept of the presidential system as an institution and was established devoid of its supporting apparatus. At the time of the deliberations of the Constitution Commission and even after the 1962 Constitution came into force, a significant segment of the Western-oriented elite, particularly the legal community, held a different view of the parliamentary system. In 1960, in response to the Constitution Commission's questionnaire, Chaudhry Mohamad Ali, former prime minister, argued cogently that the parliamentary system should be retained.[22] In the subsequent campaign before the presidential election of January, 1962, he continued to hold this view and the Nizam-i-Islami party, which he headed, joined with four other groups to form the Combined Opposition party (COP) against Ayub. The COP was heavily influenced by eminent lawyers such as Mahmud Ali Qasuri, A. K. Brohi, and Z. H. Lari, who also favored parliamentary government. It was,

---

Constitution Commission's recommendations was not limited to these aspects of a presidential system. On the questions of executive veto, legislative confirmation of executive appointments and dismissals, impeachment of ministers and governors, suspension of the Constitution in emergency, direct elections, separate electorates, separation of the judiciary, justiciability of fundamental rights, and retention of certain Islamic provisions, the 1962 Constitution departs from the commission's recommendations. While fundamental rights were made justiciable and some Islamic provisions restored by the first amendment, the other departures remain.

22. Mohamad Ali's answers reached the press by some means other than official transmittal and were published in their entirety in the *Pakistan Times*, June 13, 1960, pp. 1 ff. A little-known document, it is a vigorous exposition in defense of the parliamentary system in Pakistan. This statement and Ayub's defense of the presidential system are perhaps the nearest equivalent to the Price-Laski dialogue yet made. While both the Ayub and the Mohamad Ali statements are framed within the particular circumstances of Pakistan rather than within the context of the generic problem of political development, the Mohamad Ali statement is somewhat generalized by reference to Latin-American and United States experience. The essence of his argument is that a presidential system is likely to produce deadlock between legislature and president, the resolution of which leads to dictatorship. "Indeed," Mohamad Ali argues, "the main danger of the presidential form is in the rise of a personal dictatorship; and the main objection against this form of government is the ease with which a strong Executive can be converted into a tyranny as the history of Latin-American countries so amply demonstrates. The most recent illustration is South Korea where also the presidential form of government prevailed. . . . If there is a serious deadlock between the Executive and the Legislature, the Executive may feel it incumbent in the national interest to ride roughshod over the legislature and that is the first step on the road to despotism. . . ." In an earlier passage of the same questionnaire, Mohamad Ali had said, "This leaves us with the parliamentary form of government. It is by no means perfect, even as no human institution is perfect, but it is the one best suited to our experience and circumstances and the one most likely to evolve in the direction of true democracy."

therefore, not unexpected that a return to the parliamentary form became one of the major planks in the COP platform.[23]

Despite these declarations clearly labeling the form of government under the 1962 Constitution as presidential, the practice which began to evolve when the legislatures convened in 1962 appeared to be ambiguous. The experience of both the legislature and the executive was exclusively with British parliamentary practice. Legislative sessions were attended by cabinet ministers who submitted to questions during the question period. Each of the ministries had a parliamentary secretary appointed from among the legislators. The most ambivalent practice was the dual appointment of members serving in the National Assembly to positions on the Council of Ministers, which was the president's cabinet. Thus, one of the distinctive attributes of parliamentary government was grafted onto the presidential system. In Article 104, the 1962 Constitution had prohibited a legislator who might be appointed a minister from continuing to serve in the legislature. The President nevertheless issued Order No. 37 allowing ministers appointed from the National Assembly to retain their legislative posts.[24] Presumably he found such action necessary because members of the National Assembly from East Pakistan refused to serve as ministers unless they could also retain their seats in the legislature.[25] This was done under authority of Article 224 of the Constitution which permitted the president to make adaptations "for the purpose of removing difficulties" impeding implementation of the new Constitution. In what is clearly one of the classic decisions in the development of constitutional law in

---

23. *Nine Point Manifesto and Joint Declaration of the Combined Opposition Party* (Dacca, July 14, 1964), Point 1(c).

24. President's Order No. 37 of 1962. Removal of Difficulties (Appointment of Ministers) Order, 1962. Text in *Gazette of Pakistan, Extraordinary*, June 12, 1962.

25. This was the reason given on the floor of the National Assembly by A. K. M. Fazlul Quader Chowdhury, one of five East Pakistani members of the National Assembly who, having been appointed to the Council of Ministers, asked the East Pakistan High Court for an interpretation of their dual status. National Assembly of Pakistan, *Debates*, June 19, 1962, p. 145. This predicament was mentioned, though without specific reference to East Pakistan, in the text of President's Order No. 37, "whereas members of the Assembly have expressed unwillingness to accept the office of the President's Council of Ministers if they thereupon cease to be members of the Assembly."

Pakistan, the High Court of East Pakistan invalidated the President's order.[26] This decision was sustained by the Supreme Court. The courts asserted that a presidential form of government in which the legislature was separated from the executive was clearly the intention of the Constitution, and that the President's "amendment," instead of being mere "adaptation" of a technical nature, would have altered the very essence of the Constitution. "By one sweep of the pen," wrote Justice S. M. Murshed of the East Pakistan High Court, "a vital provision of the Constitution has been wiped out without resorting to the special and massive machinery of amendment. . . ."[27]

In the Fazlul Quader Chowdhury judgments still another attribute of the presidential form was dealt with, namely, the relationship of the president to the Council of Ministers. Article 33 of the Constitution provides that the president *may* appoint a Council of Ministers. This ambiguity as to whether the president is thus obligated or not was mentioned by A. K. Brohi who argued the High Court case against the government. Brohi called attention to the 1956 Constitution which made appointment of a Council of Ministers obligatory. The government argued that the 1962 Constitution conferred discretion coupled with duty in this matter. The High Court dismissed this issue as irrelevant, but Chief Justice Cornelius in the Supreme Court judgment wrote an obiter dictum which may have subsequent significance should this issue arise judicially again:

I think I may here express my opinion that Article 33 requires that the President *shall* act with a Council of Ministers, rather than that there should be complete discretion left to him, in this respect, of which he may make use or not as he pleases. It seems perfectly clear that the Constitution as originally drafted was intended to introduce a Presidential form of Government and in that form, the President most generally is assisted as Chief Executive, by a Council or Cabinet of

26. These were the decisions in the Fazlul Quader Chowdhury cases, cited above, n. 15, which had to clear a way to the issue of the validity of President's Order No. 37 by establishing jurisdiction. This was done by asserting the prerogative of judicial review. Thus, in two decisions relating to one case, the judiciary established two basic principles of government under the 1962 Constitution.

27. *Mohd. Abdul Haque* v. *Fazlul Quader Chowdhury*, PLD 1963 Dacca 669, quotation at 703.

Secretaries or Ministers, according to the designation employed. Therefore, although Article 33 says that the President may appoint persons to be members of his Council of Ministers, I am inclined to regard that in the light of a requirement that the President shall form, for his assistance, a Council of Ministers. For it is abundantly clear that the Constitution was not intended to, and its provisions do not enable, the establishment of rule by a single person, either at the Centre or in the Provinces.[28]

This obiter dictum is especially noteworthy because Article 33 which it interprets does not refer to the president *acting* with his ministers; it refers merely to the president's *appointing* ministers *to assist him*. Moreover, the dictum does not reconcile its cautionary remark on rule by a single person with Article 31 which vests the executive authority in the president to be "exercised by him, either directly or through officers subordinate to him." Thus, it appears that the nature of the relationship of the president to his cabinet yet remains to be juridically determined.

Ambiguity as to central and provincial government subjects is reflected in the proceedings of the National Assembly. Questions involving public liberties under various preventive detention laws have been especially frustrating. It has been assumed that "public order" is now a provincial subject since under the 1956 Constitution it was in the provincial list. On the other hand, civil and criminal law were on the concurrent list, and some matters relating to this subject have been pre-empted by the central government under Article 131 of the 1962 Constitution.[29] Moreover, it is well known that the provincial governors who are appointed by the president often have identical provincial statutes enacted and act in concert under presidential direction in implementing terms of the statute. For example, in the case of Maulana Maudoodi, leader of the Jamaat-e-Islami, notices outlawing the Jamaat were served in West Pakistan and East Pakistan on January 6, 1964, although the action was taken under different statutes. In West Pakistan, the law invoked was the West Pakistan Maintenance of Public Order Ordinance XXI of

28. *Mr. Fazlul Quader Chowdhury* v. *Mr. Mohd. Abdul Haque*, quotation at 509–510.
29. See above, Table 1, items 3, 7, 11, 12.

1960 as amended. In this instance, confusion as to central-provincial jurisdiction is increased further by the fact that in East Pakistan, where there is not an equivalent Public Order Ordinance, the action was taken under a central government statute, the Criminal Law (Amendment) Act, 1908, as amended by Ordinance XXI of 1960.[30] Further, although in West Pakistan a provincial statute alone was involved, the deputy attorney general for the central government appeared with the advocate general of the provincial government in arguing the government's case. Within such an unsettled mixture of responsibilities, the central government has been able to forestall discussion on political arrests by urging the National Assembly not to trespass on the rights of the provincial governments.[31] Begum Shamsun Nahar Mahmood described this predicament aptly when she said, "if some question about preventive detention is asked . . . the Central Government refer it to the provincial government . . . if provincial authorities are approached they in turn refer it to the Central Government."[32]

Nor was this issue clarified by the speaker of the National Assembly who ruled that preventive detention was the concern of both the central and provincial governments. "The Provincial field is quite different from the Central field . . . our purpose is to see whether a subject is primarily the concern of the Central Government. It may be indirectly the concern of the Central Government but that is not what our rules say."[33] Preventive detention is, in fact, the concern of both levels of government, both as to constitutional allocation of legislative powers and as to statutory enactments in force. The Security of Pakistan Act of 1952 is a central government statute[34] which authorizes detention

---

30. See *Abul A'la Maudoodi v. Government of West Pakistan*, PLD 1964 Kar. 478, and *Abul A'la Maudoodi v. Government of West Pakistan*, PLD 1964 SC 673.

31. So argued Zulfikar Bhutto, the foreign minister, in discussions of the arrest of Khan Abdul Qayyum Khan. See Pakistan National Assembly, *Debates*, July 6, 1962, pp. 1112–1113.

32. *Ibid.*, July 5, 1962, p. 1066.

33. *Ibid.*, July 6, 1962, p. 1119.

34. Security of Pakistan Act XXV of 1952 as amended by Preventive Detention Laws Amendment Act IV of 1962. *Gazette of Pakistan, Extraordinary,* July 24, 1962.

of persons acting in a "manner prejudicial to the defence or external affairs or the security of Pakistan." This power is derived unambiguously from Entry 34 of the central list in the Third Schedule of the 1962 Constitution, which mentions the same three categories of prejudicial acts described in the statute. There is also the West Pakistan Maintenance of Public Order Ordinance[35] authorizing detention of persons acting in a "manner prejudicial to public safety or the maintenance of public order." This power is apparently derived from the assumption that since public order was on the provincial list (Entry 1) of the 1956 Constitution and is not on the central list of the 1962 Constitution, it is a residual power of the provinces. While the statutory distinctions and constitutional sources of authority appear to be clear, ambiguity in application can result, since the distinction between safeguarding "security" of the country and maintaining public order, each of which comes under a different statute and hence a different level of government, can easily be blurred.

Another difficulty lies in the constitutional relations of the president and the two provincial governors. Articles 66 and 82 of the 1962 Constitution specify that the governor in the performance of his functions shall be subject to the directions of the president. The president, therefore, may ask the governors to act in concert in implementing either central or provincial statutes. Such action might be deemed exclusively a provincial rather than a central government action and would be subject to review by the provincial rather than the central legislature. Yet since the president is under no obligation to make public his informal understanding with the governors, there would be no proof that such provincial actions emanated from the single will of the central government. This was precisely the kind of ambiguity which was alluded to in the preventive detention cases of Maulana Maudoodi. In East Pakistan a central statute (Criminal Law [Amendment] Act of 1908) was invoked to disband the Jamaat-e-Islami. Although this action was taken by the provincial

---

35. West Pakistan Maintenance of Public Order Ordinance XXXI of 1960 as amended by West Pakistan Maintenance of Public Order (Amendment) Ordinance XLVII of 1962. *Gazette of West Pakistan Extraordinary*, December 2, 1960, and September 25, 1962.

governor, the defendant's attorney, A. K. Brohi, contended that it was really an action of the central rather than the provincial government.[36] The East Pakistan High Court necessarily avoided this issue. The Supreme Court regarded the action "an act of the Governor."[37] Presumably it derived this view from the well-settled doctrine that the governor acts as an agent of the president in executing central statutes. But in the Maudoodi cases, there is a mixture of actions: (*a*) In East Pakistan the governor acted under terms of a central statute; (*b*) in West Pakistan the governor acted under the same central statute but arrested members of the banned organization under a provincial statute, the West Pakistan Maintenance of Public Order Ordinance. The Supreme Court judgment stated: "It was admitted before us by Mr. Manzur Qadir, appearing for the Central Government that the action had been taken simultaneously by the Governments after consultation with the Central Government."[38] This admixture of actions renders improbable any focused accountability to the legislatures. In the Maudoodi cases, for example, the West Pakistan Assembly presumably could not discuss the dissolution of the Jamaat but could discuss the arrest of members. The East Pakistan Assembly presumably could not discuss the dissolution. The National Assembly could presumably discuss dissolution but not the arrest. Criticism of the total government action in the entire case is hence almost impossible to achieve, since each legislature could rightly rule out discussion of crucial aspects of the case. In the context of such ambiguity of responsibility, the role of the high Courts and the Supreme Court as agencies capable of dealing with the totality of such actions is crucial. The courts have responded with speed and responsibility in such matters.[39] An umbrella of juridical uniformity is thus

36. *Tamizuddin Ahmed* v. *Government of East Pakistan*, PLD 1964 Dacca 795.
37. *Abul A'la Maudoodi* v. *Government of West Pakistan*, PLD 1964 SC 673, quotation at 689.
38. *Ibid.*, quotation at 687.
39. In the Maudoodi cases, the two provincial governments acted against the Jamaat-e-Islami on January 6, 1964. The Karachi bench of the West Pakistan High Court decided the appeal on June 16, 1964, and the East Pakistan High Court rendered its decision July 13, 1964. Both judgments were brought to the Supreme Court, which heard the appeals from August 27 through September 2, 1964, and handed down its 159-page judgment on September 25, 1964.

spread over an assortment of provincial and central government actions. But public accountability through the legislatures and effective legislative review and control of executive action are not likely to be easily achieved.

This ambivalence is again well illustrated by the effort to establish a central medical service equivalent in status to the Civil Service of Pakistan. The Medical Reforms Commission in 1960 had advised establishment of a strengthened central medical service,[40] and in 1962 establishment of such a service was authorized by the central government.[41] This was praised in the National Assembly, one member stating that this enactment "lifted [doctors] from the status of scheduled cast[e]s to the class of Brahmins—in the class of Brahmins like C.S.P. [Civil Service of Pakistan] officers or P.S.P. [Police Service of Pakistan] and P.F.S. [Pakistan Foreign Service] officers."[42] The provincial governments had urged creation of a central service, and even the most vigorous proponents of provincial autonomy favored it—an irony not unnoticed by several members of the National Assembly.[43] Even before the new medical service was organized, the central government asked for repeal of the order[44] allegedly on the ground that under the 1962 Constitution health was thought to be a provincial rather than a central subject.[45] To be sure, public health under the 1956 Constitution was on the provincial list, hence may be assumed to be a residuary power left to the provinces under the 1962 Constitution. Yet as Table 1, item 12, shows, in regulating unani, ayurvedic, and homœopathic medicine, the central government pre-empted this public health function under the "achievement of uniformity" provision of Article 131. It can be argued that the creation of a central medical

40. Government of Pakistan, *Report of the Medical Reforms Commission* (Karachi, 1960), p. 10.
41. President's Order No. 15, Medical Service of Pakistan Order, 1962. *Gazette of Pakistan, Extraordinary,* May 12, 1962.
42. National Assembly of Pakistan, *Debates,* March 30, 1963, p. 1051. This entire debate on medical services, extending from p. 1049 to p. 1069, is especially revealing of the difficulty faced by the legislature in assessing its own powers.
43. *Ibid.,* pp. 1062–1064.
44. Medical Service of Pakistan (Repeal) Act XX of 1963. *Gazette of Pakistan, Extraordinary,* September 14, 1963.
45. This is the ground said by Mahbubul Huq to have been used by the central government law minister. See National Assembly of Pakistan, *Debates,* May 29, 1963, p. 59.

service, requested by the medical profession and by the provinces, and consistent with the public service structure generally, is not less essential to the "achievement of uniformity" than the regulation of non-allopathic medical systems.

Ordinance-Making Power

Executive ordinance-making power assigned to the president and governors by Articles 29, 30, and 79 of the 1962 Constitution is substantially the same as it was under the 1956 Constitution. There is provision for the proclamation of emergency and for the issuance of ordinances, valid only during the emergency and exempt from veto by the National Assembly. This provision, contained in Article 30, is an extraordinary power, which was invoked only once, during September, 1965, as a consequence of hostilities with India over Kashmir. At the beginning of 1966 the emergency was still in effect. This emergency power under Article 30 is not the subject of discussion here. The more important power, which can affect the locus of impetus in the making of policy, is the power to issue ordinances when the legislature is not in session. In transitional systems of government in which politicization is minimal, the possibility of the executive branch bypassing the legislature through the use of ordinances is always imminent. The extensive experience which Pakistan had with "government by ordinance" was perhaps a factor in the reluctant concession which the Constitution Commission made to the need for the president's having such power and in its unequivocal warning that provincial governors should not retain such power. Notwithstanding such caution, Article 29 allows the president to promulgate ordinances he thinks may be required under two conditions—when the legislature is not in session and when he "is satisfied that circumstances exist which render immediate legislation necessary." Such ordinances must be submitted to the National Assembly either forty-two days after its first meeting or 180 days after their promulgation. These ordinances have the same legal force as acts of the central legislature. As was pointed out earlier, the subjects on which ordinances can be made are of the same scope as possessed by the legislature; hence, they are cloaked by Article 131(2). If the National Assembly does not approve the ordinance, it shall cease to have effect. Governors of provinces have comparable power under similar limitations with respect to provincial matters.

To ascertain the potential use of ordinances as an executive

Table 2. *Annual Incidence of Ordinances and Acts of Central and West Pakistan Governments*

Year	Central government		West Pakistan government	
	Ordinances	Acts	Ordinances	Acts
1947	6	1	—	48
1948	27	20	9	43
1949	18	16	12	36
1950	6	52	8	82
1951	9	44	15	43
1952	10	63	6	66
1953	6	41	12	45
1954	4	20	10	36
1955	36	9	6	2
1956	25	47	35	10
1957	18	45	21	—
1958	17[a]	47	34[c]	48
1959	61	—	53	—
1960	43	—	29	—
1961	48	—	31	—
1962	80[b]	5	49[d]	5
1963	9	23	45	17
1964	13	9	26	34
1965	23[e]	12[e]	25[e]	4
Totals	459	454	426	519

[a] This is an uncertain figure. Proclamation of martial law on October 7, 1958, resulted in some confusion in numbering and in use of instruments other than ordinances.
[b] Seventy-two of these were promulgated during martial law which ended June 8, 1962.
[c] Twenty of these were promulgated during martial law.
[d] Forty-four of these were promulgated during martial law.
[e] Incomplete count based on statutes printed through October, 1965, issue of *All-Pakistan Legal Decisions.*

Source: Compiled from lists in central and provincial statutes section of *PLD* for 1947 through October, 1965. This is an unofficial source but probably does not vary from official lists which are unavailable.

device for promulgating legislation, it is instructive first to examine the use of ordinances from 1947 to the beginning of martial law in October, 1958—somewhat more than a decade. It appears quite clear that during this period ordinances were used far less than regular acts of the legislature. Tables 2 and 3 reveal

Table 3. *Incidence of Ordinances and Acts of Central and West Pakistan Governments by Major Time Periods*

Column	Unit of government	Before martial law[a]	During martial law[b]	After martial law[c]	Totals
		Central government			
A	Ordinances	165	241	53	459
B	Acts	405	0	49	454
C	Total	570	241	102	913
D	Pct. A of C	29	100	52	50
E	Pct. B of C	71	0	48	50
		West Pakistan government			
F	Ordinances	148	177	101	426
G	Acts	459	0	60	519
H	Total	607	177	161	945
I	Pct. F of H	24	100	63	46
J	Pct. G of H	76	0	37	54
		Total for Central and West Pakistan governments			
K	Ordinances	313	418	154	885
L	Acts	864	0	109	973
M	Total	1,177	418	263	1,858
N	Pct. K of M	26	100	60	49
O	Pct. L of M	74	0	40	51

[a] August 15, 1947, to October 7, 1958.
[b] October 7, 1958, to June 8, 1962.
[c] June 8, 1962, to September 6, 1965, when the Proclamation of Emergency under Article 30 of the 1962 Constitution put emergency rule into effect.
Source: See above, Table 2.

that the President issued about 165 ordinances while the central legislature passed about 405 acts during this period. Data are not available for East Pakistan, but in West Pakistan about 148 ordinances and 459 acts were issued. Taking these two units of government together, we find 313 ordinances and 864 acts. Of the total number (1,177) of legislative instruments for those two units of government made effective during that period, 26 per cent were ordinances. The percentage did not vary greatly for the two units of government; in the central government 29 per cent were ordinances, and in the provincial government the ordinance figure was 24 per cent. Numbers alone, of course, cannot reveal a meaningful interpretation of the use to which ordinances might have been put. Final judgment would have to encompass a comparison of subject matter covered by ordinances and acts. It is possible, for example, that ordinances dealt with weighty and crucial policy issues, while acts dealt with less important and less controversial matters. Such a comparative analysis cannot be included in the present study. It would entail careful content analysis of some 1,177 ordinances and acts, and assessment of the significance of the content of each in relation to the total political context at the time of enactment. Until such a study is made, evaluation as to substantive significance lacks validity. Some impressions, however, might be tentatively advanced. It appears that use of the ordinance-making power was a problem of considerable concern during the first decade of Pakistan's existence. One indicator is the incidence of published judgments of the Supreme Court and high courts in the matter of ordinance jurisdiction. There appear to have been approximately fourteen published judgments interpreting the president's and the governor's powers under Articles 69 and 102 of the 1956 Constitution. The cases divide equally between these two levels of jurisdiction. Only two are Supreme Court judgments. One of the judgments is overturned by a subsequent High Court decision; another judgment is overturned by a Supreme Court decision. While the incidence of twelve original cases in a decade may not appear high, it must be kept in mind that during the period from 1947 to 1958, some kind of emergency rule or martial law was proclaimed in all or parts of Pakistan on at least eight occasions. The extent of these periods totals nearly six years, about half the period here under review.[46] During such periods government was entirely by

46. These occasions were (1) in the Punjab from January, 1949, until April, 1951, under Section 92A of the Government of India Act—1935, empowering the

executive action in the area in which emergency was declared; hence, for such periods and areas no assessment can be made of the use of ordinances during normal times. Considering, then, a span of some six years of "normal" government, the incidence of case law is enough to suggest that the use of ordinances was an issue of considerable if not serious dimensions. The case law also reveals instances of abuse of this power, thereby suggesting the possibility of greater abuse were it not for the restraining influence of judicial review. As early as 1949 in East Pakistan (then known as East Bengal) it was held that while the governor cannot make an ordinance continuing the life of an expired ordinance, he can re-enact its provisions if he deems a fresh emergency to exist.[47] Later, this view was interpreted to mean that an ordinance cannot be extended beyond its limits by re-enacting it in "materially identical terms."[48] The question of re-enacting an ordinance, thus usurping legislative powers indefinitely, was a major legal issue. It arose in a Supreme Court case, but the decision was made on other grounds and the issue avoided.[49] The Karachi bench of the High Court subsequently held that re-enactment is valid if a fresh emergency exists but that the courts cannot say whether such an emergency exists or not, for such determination must be political rather than judicial.[50] In a subsequent decision decided by a full bench of the West Pakistan High Court, the Akhlas decision which disallowed re-

provincial governor to assume powers of all provincial bodies, except the High Court; (2) in the Sind from December, 1951, until May, 1953, under Section 92A; (3) in Lahore District from March 6 to May 15, 1953, under Article 193 of the 1956 Constitution; (4) in East Pakistan for two weeks in March, 1954, and again from May, 1954, until June, 1955, under Section 92A, Government of India Act—1935; (5) in all of Pakistan from October 24, 1954, to April 13, 1955, under Article 193, 1956 Constitution; (6) in East Pakistan from May 23 until June 2, 1956, under Article 193; (7) in East Pakistan from August 31 to September 6, 1956, under Article 193; and (8) in West Pakistan from March 21 to July 15, 1957, under Article 193. These instances were in addition to the forty-four months of martial law for all of Pakistan in effect from October 7, 1958, to June 8, 1962, and to the Proclamation of an Emergency of September 6, 1965, under Clause (1), Article 30, of the 1962 Constitution. The latter was the consequence of the outbreak of hostilities between India and Pakistan.

47. *Maulvi Tamiz-ud-Din Ahmed* v. *Province of East Bengal*, PLD 1949 Dacca 1.

48. *Akhlas Ahmad* v. *Noorun Nabi Ahmad*, PLD 1958, Kar. 283.

49. *Begum Zeb-un-Nissa* v. *Pakistan*, PLD 1958 SC 35.

50. *Ihsan Elahi* v. *Custodian, Evacuee Property, Lahore*, PLD 1959 Lah. 924.

enactment was overturned.[51] In that decision the High Court declared that the provisions of an ordinance may be re-enacted, although an ordinance cannot be made by merely continuing the life of an expiring ordinance. A new ordinance must be treated as a fresh piece of legislation, even though it may embody the old ordinance word for word.[52] Three months before the Tirathmal decision, the High Court in what is without question the leading decision on the ordinance-making power struck down an effort to use the ordinance in what the court described as "a case of naked abuse of power."[53] The circumstances of the case show the possibilities of abuse. The governor of West Pakistan had promulgated ordinances on the eve of general elections postponing elections to all local bodies in the province and had put his own nominees in charge of all the local bodies (110 out of 199) which were thus superseded. The High Court declared that no real emergency existed, that the ordinances were promulgated in mala fide for political ends. In coming to this conclusion, the court held that it had the power to inquire into the fides of the use of the ordinance power and that the rule barring inquiry into the fides of the legislature did not apply to the executive using the ordinance power. Finally, it was later made clear by the Supreme Court that the governor's power to legislate by ordinance was of "a transitory, temporary, and contingent nature" and that he could not effect the repeal of a perpetual statute by ordinance.[54]

The use of ordinances to bypass the legislature during the forty-four months of martial law sheds little light on the use of this power. Legislatures were suspended during this period and the President was the sole source of legislation. The incidence of

---

51. *Tirathmal v. The State*, PLD 1959 Kar. 594.
52. *State v. Abdul Muhammad*, PLD 1960 Kar. 733.
53. *Qaseem-ud-Din v. Province of West Pakistan*, PLD 1959 Lah. 76, quotation at 105.
54. *Sargodha-Bhera Bus Service v. Province of West Pakistan*, PLD 1959 SC 127. This decision overturned *Sargodha-Bhera Bus Service v. Province of West Pakistan*, PLD 1958 Lah. 77. A subsequent High Court judgment, *State v. Muhammad Sharif*, PLD 1960 Lah. 236, amplified the Supreme Court's decision in the Sargodha-Bhera Bus Service case. Other judgments on aspects of ordinances not discussed in the text are *Khaliq and Najam Co. v. Sales Tax Officer*, PLD 1959 Lah. 915; *Abdul Aziz v. District Magistrate, Lahore*, PLD 1958 Lah. 104; *Muhammad Waris Shah v. Province of West Pakistan*, PLD 1959 Lah. 898; and *Rajab Ali v. Province of East Pakistan*, PLD 1958 Dacca 552.

ordinances rose sharply during this period, as Tables 2 and 3 reveal, since the ordinance replaced in substance, if not in precise legal equivalence, other forms of statutory enactment.[55] Slightly more than half (241 of 459) of the ordinances issued by the central government from 1947 to September, 1965, were issued during the 1958–1962 martial law period. In West Pakistan, about 42 per cent (177 of 426) of the ordinances during the same period appeared under the 1958–1962 martial law auspices. The subjects dealt with embraced all fields of legislation. Many of the ordinances, particularly those affecting public liberties, were resented by the intelligentsia, many of whom later formed a coalition party against the President in the election of 1965. Yet although the courts had earlier suggested in the Khaliq and Najam Company and Mohammad Afzal cases that ordinances under martial law were subject to the same restrictions as ordinances before martial law, the 1962 Constitution, by grouping all legal instruments under the rubric "existing laws," cloaked ordinances with the same legal effect as regulations and orders, that is, with some exceptions, preserved them as "existing laws."[56] Whether or not martial law ordinances, then, share the transitory quality of pre-martial law ordinances has not yet been decided. That martial law ordinances have been saved by Article 225 of the 1962 Constitution and that they can be questioned is clear.[57] The implication seems to be that they can be questioned in the

55. The legal equivalence of categories of presidential actions under martial law was discussed at some length in *Muhammad Ayub Khuhro* v. *Pakistan,* PLD 1960 SC 237; *Iftikhar-ud-Din* v. *Muhammad Sarfraz,* PLD 1961 SC 585; *Mohammad Afzal* v. *Commissioner, Lahore Division,* PLD 1963 SC 401. Martial law "regulations" were deemed to be at the pinnacle of the hierarchy. Subordinate to them were "orders" meant to implement the general law expressed in "regulations." Both of these instruments derived their validity from the "supra-constitutional" authority assumed by the President in proclaiming martial law. Roughly, they were equivalent to a constitution and to statutes enacted by a legislature. Ordinances made during martial law, however, derived their validity only from the ordinance-making provisions of the 1956 Constitution and were subject to the same restraints. They were, then, "intra-constitutional" rather than "supra-constitutional." This doctrine of the continuity of the ordinance power had been advanced as early as 1959 in the Khaliq and Najam Company case (cited above, n. 54), in which it was held that the non-existence of the legislature did not deprive the president of the power to issue ordinances.
56. Second (1962) Constitution of Pakistan, Article 225(2) through (7).
57. *Mohammad Afzal* v. *Commissioner, Lahore Division,* PLD 1963 SC 401, quotation at 414–415.

same manner as statutory enactments rather than as pre-martial law ordinances. Any other interpretation would render the bulk of martial law enactments "temporary," and each would have to be laid before the appropriate legislature.

Given the history of the use of ordinances in Pakistan, the use to which they have been put after martial law and under the 1962 Constitution is not without interest. Tables 2 and 3 show an increase in the number of ordinances in relation to the total number of legislative instruments. During the period of thirty-eight and a half months from the end of martial law in 1962 to the proclamation of emergency rule in 1965, ordinances account for 52 per cent of the instruments issued by the central government and 63 per cent of instruments issued by West Pakistan. Taking both governments together, ordinances account for 60 per cent of the 263 instruments issued during this period. This is an increase from about 26 per cent before martial law. Again, these statistics must be interpreted with caution. The same caveat earlier made for comparable statistics for the 1947–1958 period are equally applicable for the 1962–1965 period here discussed. Whatever the qualitative nature of these ordinances may be, it is clear that ordinances accounted for about one-quarter of the legislative instruments of the central and West Pakistan governments before martial law, whereas they account for three-fifths of such instruments for the same two units of government after martial law.

The position of the central government on ordinances was given by Khursheed Ahmad, in 1963:

The National Assembly has met during the last eleven months for four times, and the sessions have been very lengthy, and it is the intention of the Government to process most of the legislation in the House. If we thought that the matter was urgent, and if we wanted to short circuit, we could have promulgated an Ordinance. We did not face the National Assembly with a single Ordinance.[58] We have chalked out a programme wherein this Assembly would be considering many measures, including the Constitutional amendments, and we

58. Table 2, above, compiled from data given in the central and provincial statutes volume of *All-Pakistan Legal Decisions* for 1963 and 1964, shows nine ordinances promulgated by the President in 1963. All nine were issued when the National Assembly was not in session, which may be what the law minister meant when he made the observation in this sentence.

would like to place all matters before the House. We are going to
consider the Budget in the first week of June. We are going to consider
two amendments to the Constitution in the month of July. We have
more than seven Bills. Previously when we met in Dacca, three Bills
were referred to the Standing Committees. Unfortunately, those Bills
have still not been reported upon. Democracy is quite a slow process,
and we would like the House to pass all measures. *This should be a
welcome thing to the Opposition that we are processing legislations*
[sic], *and we are minimizing the Ordinances* [italics added] . . . and
you should welcome that we are minimizing Ordinances, and we are
trying to place everything before the House. That is our intention, and
let us see that we enact all laws in this House rather than outside this
House.[59]

Taken at its face value, the law minister's statement suggests a
justifiable frustration with the National Assembly which, conditioned to act in a parliamentary system, has not been able to
adjust to its role in a presidential system nor to focus its energies
on systematic, constructive law-making. Whatever the intent of
the central government may have been in 1963, thirteen ordinances were promulgated the very next year while the National
Assembly passed only nine acts.[60]

Qualitative analysis of legislative acts and executive ordinances
issued during the thirty-four months following martial law does
not indicate either a moribund legislature or an inactive executive. First, the most fundamental, far-reaching enactments on
basic polity of the state have come from legislative enactment
rather than through use of the ordinance. The first amendment to
the Constitution, which restored the term "Islamic" to the name
of Pakistan, enumerated fundamental rights, and restored their
justiciability, was enacted by the National Assembly. The provision which in the name of fundamental rights excluded from
litigation certain martial law-induced changes such as land
reform excited opposition, but the amendment was generally a
reflection of the legislature's will.[61] The restoration of political

59. National Assembly of Pakistan, *Debates*, May 29, 1963, pp. 60–61.
60. See Table 2, above, p. 231.
61. Constitution (First Amendment) Act I of 1964, *Gazette of Pakistan,
Extraordinary*, January 16, 1964. For relevant discussion, see National Assembly of
Pakistan, *Debates*, March 9, 1963, p. 125; March 13, 1963, pp. 344–352; March
14, 1963, pp. 391–394; March 18, 1963, pp. 17–39; March 19, 1963, pp. 520–565;

parties, which had been outlawed under martial law, and which the President thought the nation could do without even after martial law, was an action of the legislature.[62] To be sure, the bill to restore political parties was not the sort of bill universally acclaimed by the National Assembly. The opposition, led by Farid Ahmad, attacked especially the continued prohibition on former politicians disqualified under the Election Bodies Disqualification Order of 1960 (EBDO) from participating in party activity under the new act. Although the bill passed, the opposition, refusing to vote, registered its disapproval by walking out of the National Assembly.[63] When the executive found need to strengthen the Political Parties Act to prevent "EBDO'd" politicians from participating indirectly, it resorted to the ordinance power to amend the act.[64] Other major acts, such as the Referendum Act (providing the machinery for submitting disagreements between the president and the National Assembly to the people) and the Electoral College Act, were initiated by the executive. They implemented existing constitutional provisions and were not necessarily close to the hearts of the legislators.[65]

Another means of judging the use of the ordinance-making power during the post-martial law period is by analysis of legislation which the Combined Opposition party (COP) declared to be objectionable. This party, a coalition of several groups representing orthodox Muslims, eminent lawyers, and politicians, contested against Ayub for the presidency in January,

---

March 20, 1963, pp. 567–623; March 21, 1963, p. 642; March 22, 1963, pp. 714–750; March 27, 1963, pp. 751–821; April 6, 1963, pp. 1418–1425. The law minister's explanation of the amendment is found in *ibid.*, March 18, 1963, pp. 493–499. The Constitution (Second Amendment) Act VI of 1964, *Gazette of Pakistan, Extraordinary,* July 8, 1964, does not involve so fundamental a change in polity as the first amendment.

62. Political Parties Act III of 1962, *Gazette of Pakistan, Extraordinary,* July 16, 1962. For relevant discussion, see National Assembly of Pakistan, *Debates,* July 4, 1962, pp. 1012–1036; July 9, 1962, pp. 1188–1232; July 10, 1962, pp. 1238–1303; July 12, 1962, pp. 1396–1440; July 14, 1962, pp. 1482–1569.

63. See *Debates,* July 14, 1962, p. 1569.

64. Political Parties (Amendment) Ordinance I of 1963. *Gazette of Pakistan, Extraordinary,* January 7, 1963. See discussions in National Assembly of Pakistan, *Debates,* April 12, 1963, pp. 1772–1778; April 16, 1963, pp. 1856–1903.

65. Presidential Election Act VIII of 1964, *Gazette of Pakistan, Extraordinary,* April 18, 1964; Referendum Act IX of 1964, *Gazette of Pakistan, Extraordinary,* September 1, 1964.

1965.[66] The manifesto prepared by the COP called for the repeal of "authoritarian legislation" and named eight such enactments.[67] It is pertinent to ascertain the source of this legislation deemed so unsatisfactory by the opposition. If it originated in ordinances promulgated after martial law, this would suggest the use of ordinances to circumvent the legislature in extremely unpopular matters during that period. But the record sustains no such conclusion. Five of the eight enactments were ordinances promulgated during martial law rather than after it.[68] Two of the most

66. The groups organized into the COP were Council Muslim League, Awami League, National Awami party, Nizam-e-Islami, and the Jamaat-e-Islami. Those associated with this coalition included former Governor General and Prime Minister Khwaja Nazimuddin, former Prime Minister Chaudhri Mohamad Ali (see above, n. 22), former Prime Minister H. S. Suhrawardy, former Governor of East Pakistan Lt. Gen. Azam Khan, the distinguished lawyers A. K. Brohi, Mahmud Ali Qasuri, and Z. H. Lari, and the well-known religious leaders Maulana Bhashani and Maulana Maudoodi.

67. *Nine Point Manifesto and Joint Declaration of the Combined Opposition Party* (Dacca, July 14, 1964), Point 3.

68. These ordinances are the following:

(*a*) East Pakistan Public Safety Ordinance LXXVIII of 1958, as amended by East Pakistan Public Safety (Amendment) Ordinance V of 1964, *Gazette of East Pakistan, Extraordinary*, March 27, 1964. This is a little-known but important enactment which was the subject of a classic case in public liberties, *Mahbub Anam v. Government of East Pakistan*, PLD 1959 Dacca 774.

(*b*) West Pakistan Maintenance of Public Order Ordinance XXX of 1960, *Gazette of West Pakistan, Extraordinary*, December 2, 1960, as amended by West Pakistan Maintenance of Public Order (Amendment) Ordinance XLVII of 1962, *Gazette of West Pakistan, Extraordinary*, September 25, 1962, and West Pakistan Maintenance of Public Order (Amendment) Ordinance IX of 1963, *Gazette of West Pakistan, Extraordinary*, May 13, 1963. It was under this ordinance that Farid Ahmad and Maulana Maudoodi and a group of followers were detained in 1964. The consequent court decisions have become landmarks in the development of public liberties. See *Rahmat Elahi v. Government of West Pakistan*, PLD 1965 Lah. 112; and *Farid Ahmad v. Government of West Pakistan*, PLD 1965 Lah. 135.

(*c*) Press and Publications Ordinance XV of 1960, *Gazette of Pakistan, Extraordinary*, April 26, 1960, as amended by Press and Publications Ordinance LIII of 1960, *Gazette of Pakistan, Extraordinary*, December 24, 1960, and Press and Publications (West Pakistan) (Amendment) Ordinance, 1963, *Gazette of West Pakistan, Extraordinary*, September 3, 1963. Ordinance XV and its amendments were repealed and replaced by West Pakistan Press and Publications Ordinance XXX of 1963, *Gazette of West Pakistan, Extraordinary*, October 10, 1963. Fulfilling an earlier promise made to the press, President Ayub suspended application of the press ordinances for one year with the proviso that a Code of Ethics and a Court of Honor newly adopted by the Council of Pakistan Newspaper Editors would provide adequate self-regulation. The one-year suspension began July 29, 1965. "Press Release No. 22," July 30, 1965 (Washington, D. C.: Embassy of Pakistan).

(*d*) West Pakistan (University of the Punjab) Ordinance XXII of 1961, *Gazette of West Pakistan, Extraordinary*, September 18, 1961, and its ancillary, University of the Punjab Employees (Efficiency and Discipline) University Ordinances 1961, *Gazette of West Pakistan, Extraordinary*, February 2, 1962, and West Pakistan "obnoxious" were acts passed by the Pakistan National Assembly and the West Pakistan Provincial Assembly.[69] Only one enactment, which at first prohibited, later regulated, and then again prohibited the use of loudspeakers, was an ordinance promulgated in the post-martial law period.[70]

It would be inaccurate to conclude from this limited analysis that the use of ordinances has been badly abused during the post-martial law period, even though the relative frequency of their use appears to have increased. This may not necessarily imply any special virtue of restraint on the part of the executive, for as has been pointed out a large number of ordinances on controversial subjects were issued during the last week of martial law, thus cloaking them with the protection of statutes. Notwithstanding this observation, from the point of view of many members of the National Assembly, the ordinance-making power has been abused. Concern for this has been expressed several times. On one

---

(Universities) Removal of Undesirable Servants Ordinance XX of 1962, *Gazette of West Pakistan, Extraordinary,* May 25, 1962. Ordinance XXII of 1961 and the unnumbered Efficiency and Discipline Ordinances have been amended by West Pakistan Universities (Amendment) Ordinance XL of 1962, *Gazette of West Pakistan, Extraordinary,* June 7, 1962.

(e) Frontier Crimes Regulation III of 1901 was invalidated by the High Court of West Pakistan on the ground that a special system of justice established for tribal peoples violated the equal protection of the law guarantee of the 1962 Constitution. See *Malik Muhammad Usman v. The State,* PLD 1965 Lah. 229. Further analysis can be found in *Research on the Bureaucracy of Pakistan,* pp. 187–199.

69. These two enactments are (a) Pakistan Criminal Law (Amendment) Act XL of 1958, *Gazette of Pakistan, Extraordinary,* September 23, 1958. This act authorized the trial of officials accused of corruption before special judges using different judicial procedures and special rules of evidence. (b) West Pakistan Criminal Law (Amendment) Act VII of 1963, *Gazette of West Pakistan, Extraordinary,* April 19, 1963. This act embraces some characteristics of jirga proceedings for certain categories of crimes.

70. The first law against the use of loudspeakers was West Pakistan Use of Loudspeakers (Prohibition) Ordinance XXXI of 1963, *Gazette of West Pakistan, Extraordinary,* October 22, 1963. It included no standards by which to refuse applications for use, nor did it provide for hearings or appeals from decisions. Ordinance XXI was invalidated by the West Pakistan High Court on the ground of violating freedom of speech. See *Mohd. Safdar v. Province of West Pakistan,* PLD 1964 Lah. 718. These omissions were remedied in a new enactment, West Pakistan Regulation of Loudspeakers and Sound Amplifiers Ordinance XIII of 1964, *Gazette of West Pakistan Extraordinary,* September 8, 1964. The 1964 ordinance was repealed and replaced by West Pakistan Regulation and Control of Loudspeakers and Sound Amplifiers Ordinance II of 1965, *Gazette of West Pakistan, Extraordinary,* March 2, 1965, which, invoking the abatement of nuisance doctrine, bans the use of loudspeakers except for religious purposes and does not provide for their use even with permission.

occasion Jalil Ahmad Khan said that he opposed "the idea of governing the people through Ordinances. . . ."[71] S. Zahman warned that the issuance of ordinances was an "infringement on the powers of this House" and that the President be advised not to use "his discretionary powers which will amount to a curtailment of the powers of this House."[72] Abul Quasem was even more pointed in his remarks when he said: "Now today with the promulgation of Ordinances, the President has practically made the National Assembly non-existent. . . . If the Presidential form continues, legislation should be left entirely to the Legislature. . . ."[73]

II. Agents of Executive Power: the Elite Cadre

The bureaucratic system of Pakistan remains divided into discrete, functional entities or cadres between which little permeation of talent has occurred. Structurally, the existing system is not unlike that in effect before independence. Changes which have taken place since then have been largely within the familiar framework.

The prestige of government service continues to be remarkably high; competing elites have not yet risen to positions of sufficient influence to challenge the social and political dominance of government service. Business and engineering elites are gradually emerging, and with the establishment of the Graduate Institute of Business Administration and two engineering and technical universities, these elites may rapidly assume prominent roles in society. The only other powerful elite, the legal community, has been an effective countervailing force to administrative dominance, both in the political and juridical realms.

The magnitude of government employment cannot be precisely determined since there is only one census of government for the three units of government in Pakistan. Table 4 in the concluding

71. National Assembly of Pakistan, *Debates*, March 13, 1963, p. 352.
72. *Ibid.*, p. 353.
73. *Ibid.*, March 19, 1963, p. 562. Similar concern over the governor's use of ordinances in West Pakistan has been expressed in the West Pakistan Assembly. See, for example, the debate of June 14, 1965, as reported in *Pakistan Times*, June 16, 1965, p. 11.

chapter in this volume suggests the pitfalls in estimating magnitude. It is probable that total employment in government is about 995,323, or nearly a million persons, inclusive of police, teachers, railway, postal and telegraph employees, government corporations, and local government employees.[74] This is approximately 1 per cent of the total population of nearly ninety-nine million. We do not know the proportions of employees in various categories of activities for either the central government or for the provincial government of East Pakistan. An excellent census for the provincial government of West Pakistan, however, includes several different analyses of composition of employment totals and affords a clue as to categories for total national government employment.[75] On July 31, 1962, the Government of West Pakistan employed some 376,521 persons, of whom 3,845 were posted in the provincial secretariat and 372,676 in other offices. Of those in the provincial secretariat, only 501 were gazetted employees, or officers in American usage. Monthly salaries earned were distributed as follows for gazetted employees: 54 per cent earned less than Rs. 500; 1 per cent earned between Rs. 2,000 and Rs. 3,000, and .5 per cent received more than Rs. 3,000. The distribution by classes was as follows:

Gazetted Officers	Number	Percentage
Class I (Senior)	1,437	16.3
Class I (Junior)	634	7.2
Class II	5,024	57.0
Others	1,719	19.5
Non-Gazetted Employees		
Class III	203,736	55.4
Class IV	163,921	44.6

Nearly 32 per cent of the total employment is in the railways, 17 per cent in education, and 20 per cent in local government. Of the 8,814 gazetted employees, 879 were women. There were virtually no women among non-gazetted employees. It is not known if this

74. See the author's concluding chapter in this volume, especially pp. 648–649, Table 4, note c.
75. Government of West Pakistan, *Census of West Pakistan Government Employees 1962* (Lahore, 1963).

distribution is nearly the same for East Pakistan, although it is likely to be so. Distribution on a national scale may be somewhat different since a larger percentage of central government employees are in posts, telegraphs, and central secretariat positions.

Public employment is divided into some twenty-six all-Pakistan central services ranging in prestige from the Civil Service of Pakistan (CSP) to the Central Engineering Service, Class II. The total strength of these twenty-six services approximates 1,800. Beneath these superior services are Class III and IV services, the latter comprising menial help. Each of the provinces has a comparable service structure assigned within the province. West Pakistan has fourteen provincial services; East Pakistan has twenty-six. In each province, the provincial service roughly comparable to the CSP is known as the Provincial Civil Service (Executive) for which the designation is PCS. The abbreviated designations, such as CSP, PCS, PFS, are universally used on signboards, calling cards, and in official correspondence. Recruitment to the central services is a function of the Central Public Service Commission.[76] Each of the provinces has a comparable commission for recruitment to the provincial services. Personnel control or establishment matters are divided among the Public Service Commission, the Ministry of Finance, Establishment Division, and the substantive entities and their equivalents in the provinces. There is no unified public service unit in control of all aspects of employment, discipline, salaries, and structure, although as will later be described the establishment division in the central government and comparable units in the provincial governments are rapidly emerging as personnel authorities.

The Elite Cadre and British Influence

Capping the entire public service structure in bureaucratic power and prestige, is the Civil Service of Pakistan (CSP), lineal descendent of the ICS. For reasons alluded to elsewhere,[77] the

---

76. For detailed analysis of public service commissions and service structure, see *Research on the Bureaucracy of Pakistan*, pp. 119–146.
77. See below, pp. 253 ff.

CSP is perhaps unique among the systems inheriting the imperial tradition of the ICS in the respect that its sense of exclusiveness and imperiousness have been only slightly affected since independence. It remains a distinctive, cohesive entity, with a high degree of *élan*. It is the matrix through which pre-independence British values are diffused throughout the bureaucratic system, and at the same time it controls the arena in which highly dynamic reform is taking place.

It is appropriate first to examine the composition of the CSP and to ascertain from that the structural means by which British influence has been diffused. Elsewhere it has been established that in the first five years after independence, British officers who remained in Pakistan's service played a not insignificant role in determining the form of the bureaucratic system and the direction of change, although their role in the substantive policies of government was negligible.[78] Some fifty British officers remained in Pakistan's service, and after independence in 1947 about 28 per cent of the administrative talent available for administrative (as against judicial) work in the higher bureaucracy was that of British officers. The proportion of British officers diminished sharply, however, and by 1954 only thirteen, or about 6 per cent, of the CSP cadre assigned to administrative work remained. Thereafter, there was continued attrition until in 1965 only three British officers remained. One of these, J. Ortcheson, was a High Court judge; another, D. K. Power, some years earlier had become a Muslim; the third, S. B. Hatch-Barnwell, was chairman of the East Pakistan Agricultural Development Corporation. The British officer who remained in the same high office in the central government for the longest period of time, Sir Edward Snelson,[79] left in 1961 after the unhappy circumstance of having been found in contempt of the West Pakistan High Court.[80] But the fact

---

78. See "Public Bureaucracy and Judiciary," esp. pp. 368–376.

79. Sir Edward was joint secretary, Ministry of Law, from 1947 to 1951 and secretary from 1951 until 1961.

80. The Snelson case is treated in considerable detail in relation to the effect of the contempt of court doctrine on legal research in Pakistan in *Research on the Bureaucracy of Pakistan*, pp. 263–272. See *The State v. Sir Edward Snelson*, PLD 1961 Lah. 78; *Sir Edward Snelson v. Judges of High Court of West Pakistan* [1961] 2 PSCR 193.

that British officers served as establishment secretaries (except for an interlude in 1959) from 1947 until 1961 was of significance, for it was this office which formulated basic service policy and perpetuated the ethos of the ICS. It is also worth noting that, from 1951 to 1960, a British officer headed the Civil Service Academy in Lahore, the baronial descendant of Haileybury College. There, nearly two hundred CSP probationers (44 per cent of the total cadre in 1965) in a sustained course of one year came under the direct, daily classroom influence of the best in the ICS tradition. Critics aver that the course of training during this time was archaic and imperial. Be that as it may, the training was rigorous in a sense, and the ancient virtues of promptness, responsibility, dedication, and prudent behavior were inculcated to a moderately successful degree. From 1952 to 1958, organization and methods work was headed by a British officer. British officers were also responsible for four of the eight efforts at administrative reform during the period from 1947 to 1953.[81] It would not be accurate to assign a date to the end of this direct British influence. There was a gradual, almost imperceptible erosion rather than an abrupt termination. But certainly by 1961 the direct influence was gone. The last British establishment secretary, James D. Hardy, resigned to join the overseas staff of the Ford Foundation in Africa. Geoffrey Burgess had left the Civil Service Academy in 1960, succeeded by a venerable ICS officer of great ability, Mian Aminuddin, whom Chief Justice Kayani had characterized as one of "the last of the British."[82] Of

81. These four reports are (1) "Report of the Reorganization Committee" (Sir Victor Turner), September, 1947 (typescript); (2) *Report of Financial Enquiry Regarding Allocation of Revenues* (Sir Jeremy Raisman) (Karachi: Government of Pakistan Press, 1952); (3) *Development of Organisation and Methods Work in the Government: Pakistan, 1952* (K. S. Jeffries) (Karachi, 1952); (4) *Report of Administrative Enquiry Committee* (T. B. Creagh-Coen) (Karachi: Government of Pakistan Press, 1953).

82. This reference by the widely respected chief justice of the West Pakistan High Court to one of the most distinguished and experienced Muslim officers of the ICS (who had served as governor of the Punjab and ambassador to Turkey before becoming director of the Civil Service Academy) has been widely quoted out of context and even more widely misunderstood. Kayani's reference illustrates the high regard which veteran ICS officers (of whom also Kayani was one) had for their British colleagues. Kayani, addressing the annual CSP dinner in 1961, said: "In the future you will talk of solid names in the history of the Civil Service. The Haileys and the Garbetts and the Jenkins, of men lovable like Partab, of Amin-ud Din, the last of the British, men who could bear heavy burdens on their

even greater importance was the fact that the influence of the United States, already quietly strong in the Planning Commission as a consequence of Ford Foundation-supported advisory services since 1953, expanded in scope and increased in visibility in 1960. This expansion was the consequence of an accelerated program by the United States Agency for International Development, involving the establishment of three national institutes of public administration and an expenditure approximating $4 million.[83] In the same year, the Ford Foundation aided in the establishment of an Administrative Staff College, and in 1959 two academies for rural development, both placing emphasis on administration, were also opened under Ford Foundation auspices. Thus, within a two-year period, six completely new institutions were created, some fifty faculty members sent to the United States for training, and approximately the same number of American advisers and consultants were in Pakistan attached to the training institutions. Clearly, from 1961 onward, even after initial dismay with the technical approach of American administrative training, the new allegiance in administrative technology—more perhaps for practical than for intellectual reasons—was to the United States.

With the departure of almost all British officers and a rather massive infusion of American administrative technology starting in the 1960's, leadership in the diffusion of British administrative values rested with a small group of Muslim officers who had been members of the Indian Civil Service (ICS) before independence in 1947. These officers had originally numbered about ninety-six at the time of partition, but as a consequence of normal retirement and attrition, their number was reduced to seventy-five in 1960 and (as shown by Table 4) to some fifty-five in 1965. Within the CSP, these former ICS officers are very much a class apart. This fact derives partly from the important positions they hold.

shoulders, in some cases without shrinking, in other cases without thinking. You will speak of them as Muslims now speak of Tariq and Khalid and Bu Ali Senna, basking in their reflected glory, as though Gibraltar had been conquered by these men here, not by those men there." This quotation comes from the original manuscript of the address which Chief Justice Kayani showed the present author. It is published in substantially the same way in two successive issues of *The Pakistan Times*, April 9, 1961, pp. 6 ff., and April 10, 1961, pp. 6 ff.

83. See below, pp. 329 ff. and esp. n. 178.

Table 5 shows that more than a third of the ICS officers are in secretariat positions in the central government. We know also from Table 7 that they staff 83 per cent of the ministerial and presidential secretaryships in the central government, where their position in the molding of government policy is great. But it is of greater importance to the present study to note that these former

Table 4. *1966 Composition and 1967 Estimate of Composition of CSP by Mode of Recruitment*

A	B	C	D	E
Mode of recruitment	Total number of officers	Percentage of total	Estimated total number in 1967[a]	Estimated percentage of total in 1967
1. Former officers in the ICS who opted for Pakistan in 1947	51	11	47	9.0
2. War service candidates	10	2	10	2.0
3. Promoted from provincial civil services	6	1	3	.6
4. Appointed on results of competitive examinations from 1947 to 1966	400	83	425	85.0
5. Army officers appointed in 1960, 1961, 1962, and 1963	15	3	15	3.0
Totals	482		512	

[a] Data in columns B and C are compiled from sources shown below. Data in columns D and E are extrapolations from data in columns B and C computed on the following basis: Item 1, four officers less by retirement; Item 3, three officers less by retirement; Item 4, twenty-five additional officers are assumed appointed, all by mode 4.

Source: Computed from Government of Pakistan, *Gradation List of the Civil Service of Pakistan* (*corrected up to 1st January, 1966*) (Karachi, 1966), and interviews.

ICS officers are also in an unparalleled position to mold the behavior, attitudes, and bureaucratic style of the entire ministry in their charge. They are, in sum, the chief sources of radiation of their own bureaucratic dispositions, which are essentially British in derivation. The same pattern is found, though with less intensity, in the provincial secretariats, where a much smaller proportion of the secretaryships are held by ICS officers but where they staff the most important posts. The ICS radiation stops with the division commissionerships, where we find only two ICS officers. But division and district officers are British-oriented by virtue of their training abroad and at the Civil Service Academy, as will be shown subsequently. Moreover, division and

Table 5. *Distribution by Position of Sixty Former ICS Officers Remaining in CSP in 1966*

Category of position	Number of officers	Percentage of officers
Central government secretariat and related positions	18[a]	35
Provincial government secretariat and related positions	14[a]	27
Diplomatic assignments abroad	2	4
On leave	4	8
Government corporations	6	7
Advanced training abroad	0	0
Judge, High Court	1	2
Judge, Supreme Court	2	4
Training staff	4	8
Total	51	

[a] These figures are higher than the corresponding figures shown in Table 7 (p. 255) because they include more positions than those included within the formal secretariats described in that table.

Source: Computed from *Gradation List of the Civil Service of Pakistan (corrected up to 1st January, 1966)*, and interviews.

district policy is rather tightly controlled by the chief secretary or additional chief secretary of the provincial government (ICS officers in all instances), who set the tone of local administration. Other factors in setting the ICS group apart are the generally more prestigious nature of their social antecedents[84] and the fact that except for a very few Muslims who were nominated to the

84. No empirical study comparable to Bernard Cohn's analysis of British civil servants recruited from 1600 to 1860 (Chapter 3 in this volume) has been made of the social backgrounds of the remaining ICS officers in the CSP. The observation in the text is based on the present author's association with almost the entire CSP cadre over a period extending from 1958 to 1965. While the author feels confident of the validity of this impression, an empirical survey would be a welcome check.

ICS, these Muslim officers competed with Hindus for admission to the ICS usually against substantial educational odds. The entire ICS group was educated in England for a longer period than the new recruits. Their knowledge of English is often impeccable and usually superior to that of newer officers. Coupled with this linguistic differential is the superior confidence and *élan* resulting from extended residence and travel abroad. Since his initial pre-independence education in England, virtually every former ICS officer has been abroad at least once on government missions or in advanced training programs at such centers as the International Bank for Reconstruction and Development or at Harvard University or the Imperial Defense College. Another powerful influence is the fact that in the entire CSP cadre only the ICS officers received their training in the field as young assistant commissioners apprenticed to experienced British officers. It is difficult to find a former ICS officer who does not regard that training period as the most important part of his career or who does not proudly wax eloquent in a litany of virtues of the British officer who trained him.[85] It is not merely fortuitous that the organization of highest social prestige in contemporary Pakistan is the British Universities Alumni Association. Nor is it without significance that the roster of senior members of the Association, except for the addition of a few barristers and businessmen, is much like the first sixty names of former ICS officers on the Gradation List of the Civil Service of Pakistan.[86]

85. One of the most revealing encomiums of this kind is the delightful account in S. K. Chettur, *The Steel Frame and I: Life in the I.C.S.* (New York, 1962). See also A. D. Gorwala, *The Role of the Administrator: Past, Present and Future* (Poona, 1957), esp. pp. 7–9. Gorwala talks of a "good Collector's house [being] . . . a second home to the young Assistant Collector" . . . [who] "imbibed standards, sometimes without even being told."

86. The two most exclusive social events in Lahore have been the annual CSP dinner and the annual dinner of the British Universities Alumni Association. Governors, Supreme Court and High Court judges, and sometimes the president are in attendance. These two events are usually the occasion of important addresses and sometimes policy speeches by government officials. See, for example, the remarkable address by Chief Justice M. R. Kayani of the West Pakistan High Court at the December 11, 1961, dinner of the British Universities Alumni Association, in which with uncommon grace and wit mixed with satire he explored the ideological roots of the Civil Service which he deemed to lie in the British tradition. Text accessible in *Pakistan Times*, December 12, 1961, pp. 3 ff. The founder of the British Universities Alumni Association and its president for many years was Chief Justice Kayani. In 1965 its president was Justice Anwarul Huq,

Finally, former ICS officers are on a different pay scale than non-ICS CSP officers of comparable rank. Thus, full secretaries who are former ICS officers get Rs. 4,000 a month whereas other full secretaries get Rs. 3,500. This is the rightful consequence of an early agreement not to reduce remuneration of ICS officers so long as they remained in service. The consequent social distance between former ICS officers and newer recruits reinforces the bureaucratic aloofness and detachment of secretaries and commissioners from their associates even though they are members of the same cadre. But this detachment does not separate the values of the entire group. On the contrary, there is strong galvanic attraction to the values and behavior of ICS officers from all those below. The social chasm merely enhances the glamor of the scene on the upper side.

Just as the direct influence of British officers faded after little more than a decade following independence, so the direct impact of British-trained Muslim ICS officers will have faded in about two more decades. This attrition, the consequence of entirely natural causes, is clearly indicated by Table 6. Here we find that given the retirement age of sixty years and an estimated constant strength of 550 officers in the CSP, the proportion of ICS officers, which was 11 per cent in 1966, will drop to about 6 per cent in 1970 and to about 2 per cent in 1975. By 1976 the physical presence of ICS officers in the bureaucracy will be minimal. Without allowing for attrition by means other than normal retirement, there will be fewer than eleven ICS officers left in service in 1976, and probably none by 1979. From 1960 to June, 1965, the compulsory retirement age (superannuation, as it is called in Pakistan) was sixty years. It was announced at the Governors' Conference on June 4, 1965, that retirement age would revert to fifty-five years as it was before 1960. The expectation is that officers needed in service will be re-employed

---

also of the West Pakistan High Court. Membership of the association will probably become increasingly distinct from the roster of government officials as young graduates returning from England enter private commerce rather than government service. Not all of these graduates join the association, as indicated by the plea of its secretary, Dr. Muneer ud Din Chugtai, in a letter to the *Pakistan Times*, May 24, 1965, p. 6. The association for all practical purposes is limited to the Lahore area and is no longer as prestigious an interest group as it once was.

on contract for short terms. If the retirement age continues to be fifty-five, the proportion of ICS officers in service will drop much

Table 6. *Estimated Annual Retirement of Former ICS Officers in the CSP, Projected to 1980*[a]

Year	Estimated projected strength of total CSP cadre[b]	Number of former ICS officers remaining[c]	Percentage of ICS officers in total estimated cadre
1966	482	51	11.0
1967	512	47	9.0
1968	531	41	7.6
1969	550	37	6.7
1970	550	35	6.4
1971	550	34	6.2
1972	550	32	5.8
1973	550	27	4.9
1974	550	18	3.3
1975	550	13	2.4
1976	550	11	2.0
1977	550	6	1.1
1978	550	5	0.9
1979	550	1	0.2
1980	550	0	0.0

[a] Only anticipated retirement upon reaching sixty years of age has been calculated in this table. No attrition due to death or other causes is estimated.

[b] The official estimate of revised strength is 546, although the period of time for which this is forecast is not given. *Report of the Administrative Reorganisation Committee* (Karachi, 1963), pp. 340–341. The actual average net intake of new recruits from 1947 to 1961 has been twenty-two, but from 1961 on, the average intake has been thirty. In the second column, I have arbitrarily increased the strength nineteen each year until reaching 550. This is probably a low estimate of strength which might be from 3 to 5 per cent higher.

[c] This has been determined from the date of birth of officers as shown in the Gradation List (described below under *Source*). Compulsory retirement age is assumed to be sixty years. See *Establishment Manual* (Karachi, 1963), I, 172. From 1960 to June, 1965, compulsory retirement age was sixty years. In June, 1965, the retirement age was changed to fifty-five years, as it had been before 1960. If retirement age remains fifty-five, there will be no ICS officers left in the CSP by 1975. It is likely, however, that some officers will remain in service on a contract basis; hence, this table may be as good an estimate as one based on retirement at fifty-five years.

Source: Compiled from data in *Gradation List of the Civil Service of Pakistan* (*corrected up to 1st January, 1966*), and interviews.

more quickly. By 1975 there would be no ICS officers left in service. Ten or eleven officers are hardly sufficient to staff crucial substantive policy posts and training assignments now held by ICS officers. Table 7 shows the extent to which these positions in the central and provincial governments were held by ICS officers in 1964. Ten ICS officers spread over three units of government would barely be able to staff chief secretaryships and head such crucial ministries as finance, home affairs, and commerce.

This obvious disappearance of the physical presence of British and British-trained officers will not necessarily result in equally definite disappearance of British administrative norms. Erosion and fading will occur, but disappearance will be decelerated by other structural factors of the CSP revealed by Table 4. The cadre composition by mode of entry is especially important as an influence in maintaining a relatively closed arena in which norms are circulated and recirculated. This composition by mode of entry provides one of the most striking points of contrast between the CSP and its counterpart in India, the IAS.[87] Lateral entry by promotion (*ad hoc* recruitment, as it is called in Pakistan) from provincial services never played an important role in the composition of the CSP. Originally, so far as can be determined from records extant, fifteen or seventeen officers entered the CSP from provincial services in 1953 and 1954.[88] Most of these officers were nearly fifty years of age when appointed, and since fifty-five was then retirement age, their services soon ended. In 1965 only five such officers remained in service. Originally, eleven war service candidates were appointed, and since they were in their twenties when appointed, ten remained in service in 1965. But both of these groups constituted less than 3 per cent of the total cadre strength in 1965, hardly enough to challenge the prevailing ideology of the cadre; indeed, the group was small enough to be

---

87. See equivalent analysis of the IAS in Potter's chapter (Chapter 4) in this volume, esp. p. 155 and Table 5, and comparative observations in the author's concluding chapter, esp. p. 650.
88. Typed copy of the gradation list for 1953 clearly designates fifteen officers and mentions that two more were to be appointed and included in the 1954 gradation list. Typed copy of the 1954 gradation list, however, does not identify the two additional officers and it is not known to the present writer if they were, in fact, appointed.

regarded somewhat on the edges of the cadre. The significant factor is that the largest single group, constituting always about 80 per cent of the cadre, has been composed of young men recruited by competitive examination in the traditional mode. This group, combined with the ICS veterans, constitutes more than 90 per cent of the cadre. Allied with this are two other factors of at least equal importance in analyzing the diffusion and persistence of British norms. The first is the affinity in values, even if not in actual social relations, between the ICS officers and the new competition entrants by virtue of common training in England or a Commonwealth country. The 1949 batch and most of the 1948 batch were trained in Australia; subsequent batches until 1960 spent a year at Oxford or Cambridge. While since 1960 there has been no formal, government-sponsored training in England for the CSP as a group, there has been a perceptible increase in the number of recruits who were educated in England prior to entering the service.[89] Thirteen recruits taken in from 1960 to 1964 studied at British universities and one studied at a Canadian university. Two military officers had studied in England, one at Sandhurst. In the context of the 1965 CSP cadre strength of about 457 officers, we find that from 68 to 70 per cent of them have been trained in England and that some twenty of those trained in the last five years hold British degrees. The imprecision of the 68–70 percentage results from absence of data indicating how many war service candidates and provincial service promotees were British-educated. Of course, there will be an annual shrinkage of this proportion as classes of about thirty men enter service each year with no training in England and as veteran ICS officers retire. This shrinkage will be arrested only if the number of recruits who were British-educated before joining service significantly increases or if Pakistan resumes sending all recruits to England for formal training. The former is improbable, and there is now no indication that government policy in the latter will change. But this high proportion of the cadre trained in Britain and respectful of British values makes it easier for recruits to accept the values of senior ICS officers. There is no serious

89. See below, pp. 276–277.

Table 7. Central Government Ministries and Provincial Government Secretariat Departments Showing ICS-CSP Incumbency of Secretaryships, 1964[a]

	Cadre of secretary[b]
Central government	
President's Secretariat[c]	
Secretary to the President	ICS
Cabinet Division	ICS
Establishment Division	ICS
Economic Affairs Division	ICS
Planning Division	CSP
Scientific and Technological Research Division	—
States and Frontier Regions Division	CSP
Ministries	
Agriculture and Works	ICS
Food and Agriculture Division	ICS
Rehabilitation and Works Division	CSP
Commerce	ICS
Communications	ICS
Defence	ICS
Education	ICS
Finance	ICS
Foreign Affairs	ICS
Health, Labour, Social Welfare	ICS
Health Division	—
Labour and Social Welfare Division	—
Home and Kashmir Affairs	ICS
Home Affairs Division	CSP
Kashmir Affairs Division	CSP
Industries and Natural Resources	ICS
Industries Division	CSP
Natural Resources Division	—
Information and Broadcasting	ICS
Law and Parliamentary Affairs	—
Law Division	—
Parliamentary Affairs Division	—
West Pakistan	
Governor's Secretariat[c]	
Personal secretary	—
Chief secretary	ICS
Additional chief secretary	ICS
Planning and Development	ICS
Services and General Administration	CSP

Table 7. (*cont.*)

Departments

Agriculture	—
Auqaf	ICS
Basic Democracies—Local Government	CSP
Communications—Works	—
Cooperatives, Labour, Welfare	CSP
Education	CSP
Finance	CSP
Food	CSP
Health	—
Home Affairs	CSP
Information	CSP
Industries, Commerce	CSP
Irrigation, Power	CSP
Law	—
Revenue, Rehabilitation	CSP
Transport	CSP

East Pakistan

Governor's Secretariat[c]

Personal secretary	CSP
Chief secretary	ICS
Additional chief secretary	ICS
Planning	ICS
Services and General Administration	CSP

Departments

Agriculture	—
Basic Democracies—Local Government	CSP
Communications and Transport	CSP
Education	CSP
Finance	CSP
Food	—
Health, Labour, Social Welfare	CSP
Home Affairs	—
Information	—
Law	—
Revenue	—
Works, Power, Irrigation	—

[a] Assignment of ICS-CSP officers based on analysis of the *Gradation List of the Civil Service of Pakistan* (*corrected up to 1st January, 1964*). Designations of ministries and departments may not be accurate. They are based on comparative analysis of the Gradation List for 1964, cited above, and *Report of the Administrative Reorganisation Committee* (Karachi, 1962), and modifications made by the *Report of the Standing Organisation Committee* (Karachi, April, 1962). For the provincial governments, the *Report of the Provincial Reorganization Committee*

generational chasm based on ideological differences between the ICS group and most of the new recruits. The ease with which British bureaucratic values and social behavior find common acceptance has a strong cohesive effect and tends to separate the entire CSP cadre from the remainder of the bureaucracy. Another factor is the remarkable *élan* created by common residential training at the Civil Service Academy in Lahore, a phenomenon described elsewhere in this chapter.[90]

Recruitment of Elite Cadre

The 83 per cent of the CSP cadre which entered service by open competition was recruited by a system unchanged in its essentials from the pre-partition ICS pattern. From the beginning, recruitment and administration of the examination have been the responsibility of the Central Public Service Commission.[91] Except for the years from 1951 to 1961,[92] one combined examination has

90. See below, pp. 289–298.

91. Throughout the narrative part of this chapter, the term Central Public Service Commission is used to refer to the Public Service Commission of the central government which has been variously designated. The commission was known from 1947 to 1955 as the Pakistan Public Service Commission, from 1955 to 1962 as Federal Public Service Commission, and thereafter by the name which is used in the text.

92. See notes [e] and [d] in Table 8, p. 262, for further explanation.

Part I—West Pakistan (Lahore, December, 1961), and *Part II —East Pakistan* (Dacca, April, 1962), was used. It is not always possible to ascertain if all recommendations have actually been implemented. Nevertheless, possible inaccuracies in the table would be in names of entities and are not likely to affect more than two or three ministries and departments.

[b] In the central government the six units shown in the first column under President's Secretariat are formally organized under that designation, under the general direction of the cabinet secretary. The provincial governments do not have a comparable formally organized governor's secretariat. But since the planning department is headed by an additional chief secretary, and the services and general administration department perform functions equivalent to those of establishments in the central government, there is functional equivalence in showing provincial secretariat groups on a par with the President's Secretariat.

[c] The term ICS used in these columns is no longer an official designation. Ex-ICS officers are members of the CSP, and the old ICS label is never used. It is used in this table as a shorthand means of indicating those officers who, before 1947, were in the ICS.

Source: See note [a] in this table.

been held, usually in October of each year, to recruit for the thirteen Central Superior Services.[93] The examination is held in Karachi, Lahore, and Dacca, as well as in London if enough candidates apply there. Candidates must be at least twenty-one years of age and must not have attained twenty-five years of age by January 1 of the year in which the examination is taken. Kashmiri, Buddhists, scheduled castes, Pathan tribes, and specified tribes in Chittagong, Rajshahi, Dinajpur, and Mymensingh may be up to twenty-eight years of age. Candidates who have served in the armed forces may be up to twenty-seven years of age.[94] Candidates must have at least a bachelor's degree from an approved university and must have passed a qualifying physical examination. Except for tribal and other candidates for whom the age limit was relaxed, each candidate must pay examination fees of Rs. 64. The written examination consists of three compulsory subjects and thirty optional subjects.[95] The compulsory subjects

93. The classification of services changes from time to time. Twenty-six "All Pakistan Central Services" are listed in Government of Pakistan, *Report of the Administrative Reorganisation Committee—1961* (Karachi, 1961) (reprinted in public edition by Efficiency O & M Wing, Establishment Division, President's Secretariat, 1963), p. 348. This report is hereinafter cited as the G. Ahmed Committee Report—1961 after the name of its chairman, in 1965 Pakistan's ambassador to the United States. This list includes some railway services which have been transferred to the provincial governments since provincialization of railways under the 1962 Constitution. Even the twenty or so remaining services in that list are not recruited for by the Central Superior Services' annual examination. That examination in 1964 recruited for the following services: (1) Civil Service of Pakistan, (2) Foreign Service, (3) Police Service, (4) Audit and Accounts Service, (5) Railway Accounts Service, (6) Military Accounts Service, (7) Customs and Excise Service, Class I, (8) Taxation Service, (9) Military Lands and Cantonments Service, Class I, (10) Postal Service, Class I, (11) Section Officers Grade, (12) Postal Superintendents Service, Class II, and (13) Assistant Income Tax Officers Service, Class II. This list is derived from Central Public Service Commission, *Notice No. F.2/1/64-E-II*, dated at Karachi, June 22, 1964, p. 1. This is a seven-page leaflet widely distributed for the information of interested applicants. It is hereinafter cited as *Notice No. F-1964*. The extent to which both India and Pakistan have retained the same general categories of central cadres can be seen by comparing this list with the list for India in Potter's chapter in this volume, p. 144, n. 9.

94. *Notice No. F-1964*, p. 1.

95. The number of points assigned to various subjects has been changed from time to time. The list of subjects and the value of each in 1964 was as follows: A. compulsory subjects (500)—1. essay (100), 2. English (200), 3. general knowledge (200); B. optional subjects (600)—4. pure mathematics (200), 5. applied mathematics (200), 6. statistics (100), 7. accountancy and auditing (200), 8. physics (200), 9. geology (200), 10. geography (200), 11. chemistry (200), 12. botany (200), 13. zoology (200), 14. Islamic history and culture (200), 15. history of Pakistan and India (200), 16. British history (200), 17. European history (200), 18. history of the United States (100), 19. English

total five hundred points. The candidate may choose a group of optional subjects whose aggregate value adds up to six hundred points. Those successful in the written tests must then take viva-voce and psychological tests whose combined value is three hundred points. Thus, the maximum points, or marks as they are officially designated, total 1,400. The written and viva-voce parts of the examination are conducted entirely in English. The viva voce, or interview, is a controversial part of the total examination process. Members of the Central Public Service Commission conduct these examinations personally, grouping themselves into panels of three or four interviewers. Critics of the system point out that favoritism can enter the process at this point, thus vitiating merit "objectively" determined. Others point out that those with very high written marks do not pass the examination because of very low scores in the viva voce. Unfortunately, no analysis has yet been made of the relationship of the viva-voce and written examination scores. Certainly, demeanor, use of English, and general background come into play in the viva voce, and this would tend to give the advantage to those of upper social strata. But it is impossible to distinguish these qualities per se from temperamental characteristics which must be assessed for bureaucratic service. The corporate composition of the interview panels, full public revelation of the marks obtained by all candidates, the quota system, and the fact that part of the three hundred marks assigned are derived from personality tests conducted by psychologists are factors which militate against abuse of the viva voce. For several years, the Central Public Service Commission was concerned that too many candidates chose "soft subjects" such as their native languages from the optional list.[96]

---

literature (200), 20. Urdu, Bengali, Sindhi, Pushto, Punjabi, or Baluchi (100), 21. Arabic, Persian, Turkish, Sanskrit, French, German, Russian, Burmese, Chinese, Japanese, Spanish (200) or Pali (100), 22. philosophy (200), 23. psychology (200), 24. political science (200), 25. economics (200), 26. law (200), 27. constitutional law (100), 28. mercantile law (100), 29. international law (100), 30. international relations (100), 31. agriculture (100), 32. sociology (100), 33. public administration (100); C. viva-voce and psychological tests (300). *Notice No. F-1964*, pp. 3–4.

96. This is analyzed further with relevant documentation in Ralph Braibanti, "The Civil Service of Pakistan: A Theoretical Analysis," *South Atlantic Quarterly*, LVIII (Spring, 1959), 258–304, esp. 279. See also *ibid.*, p. 276, n. 67, for marks assigned examination subjects in 1956.

To safeguard against this, rather rigid rules prohibiting certain groupings of subjects are now in force, and this no longer seems to be a major problem.[97]

Table 8 shows that the annual competitive examination for the thirteen Central Superior Services (CSS) continues to be taken by a steadily shrinking portion of university graduates. In 1950, the first year for which data were available, it appears that 31.5 per cent of the university graduates took the examinations. During that period, the prestige of the services was remarkably high, salary relatively high, and the aura of the pre-independence ICS still prevailed. From 1960 on, the proportion of university graduates taking the examination dropped unevenly, approaching the 1950 figure only once—in 1954 when the proportion rose to 29.3 per cent. From 1960 on, there is a marked drop to less than 10 per cent. Even allowing for some inaccuracy in the data on university degrees granted,[98] it is quite clear that nearly one-third of the graduates of the six major universities in 1950 took the CSS examination in that year and that from 1959 to 1965 less than 10 per cent of graduates of the same universities took them. This proportion appears to have shrunk in 1964 to only 7.5 per cent. The average for fourteen years from 1950 to 1964 is only 8.6 per cent. This finding is rather surprising, for it has been generally assumed that the steady and marked increase in the absolute number of applicants (for example, the increase from 722 in 1950 to 1,708 in 1964 was 264 per cent) has kept pace with the increase in number of university graduates. If the statistics on degrees given in column B of Table 8 are reliable, this assumption is not correct. The proportion of newly graduated men with bachelors' degrees applying for the CSS appears to have significantly dropped, and it is fair to conclude therefrom that the attraction of high-level government service has also diminished.

97. See *Notice No. F-1964* for these rules. Urdu, for example, cannot be offered with Persian or Arabic, and international law cannot be taken with international relations.

98. This is perhaps the most difficult of all statistical data to get in Pakistan. The Inter-University Board's records are not complete. Data in Table 8 were obtained separately from each university, usually by personal visits of the author. Range of error is estimated from 1 to 2 per cent for the years 1960–1965 and from 5 to 10 per cent for the years 1950–1960.

Since data on university degrees for the decade from 1950 to 1960 are not as reliable as those from 1960 to 1965, the shrinkage may not be as pronounced as Table 8 suggests. Whatever the shrinkage, however, it is certain that fewer than 10 per cent of graduates with bachelor's degrees have taken the CSS examination from 1959 on (for which period the reliability of the data is high). This, quite apart from shrinkage, is in itself a significant fact in assessing the role of the higher bureaucracy in Pakistan. Several tentative observations can be drawn from these findings. From 1960 on, some of this shrinkage may be accounted for by the fact that new universities such as Rajshahi, and to some extent old universities as well, enrolled students whose self-images and aspirations did not embrace membership in the higher bureaucracy. The importance of this factor, however, cannot be ascertained. Other possible factors might also be conjectured.

The rather dramatic improvement in the economy of Pakistan has opened up new employment opportunities which are beginning to rival in prestige and surpass in emoluments government employment in the higher bureaucracy. Private industry, particularly foreign firms and engineering, have risen markedly in their attractiveness. The rise of teaching and research positions in institutions connected with foreign technical assistance has also been a factor diminishing the appeal of the CSS examinations. The special appeal of the two academies for rural development, the three institutes of public administration, the administrative staff colleges, the Institute of Development Economics, the two new agricultural universities, and the two new engineering and technical universities is that they are associated with the ideology and technology of modernization. Further, they offer opportunities to study abroad in programs leading to the doctorate and the security of a position in a rapidly expanding activity. A correlative observation is that although the popularity and prestige of the services is still very high in absolute rather than relative terms, it has suffered a jolt. Salaries have not kept pace with the cost of living; martial law and other factors eroded feelings of security; politicians and public alike have steadily attacked the bureaucracy. These observations deduced from the

Table 8. *Number of Candidates Processed in Central Superior Services Exami* nations, *1950–1964*

A	B	C	D	E	F	G	H	I
		Number of	Percentage		Number passing written		Percentage of those writing (E)	
	Number of university degrees	of applicants for	of graduates (B) who are applicants	Number taking written	examination and taking	Number declared	declared successful	Numbe selecte
Year of examination	granted[a]	examination	(C)	examination	interview	successful	(G)	for CSP
1950	2,287	722	31.6	622	229	125	20.1	11
1951	2,867	532	18.6	417	145	68	16.3	17
1952	3,158	645	20.4	486	171	84	17.3	13
1953	3,405	555	16.3	385	126	63	16.4	25
1954, January	—	631	—	422	134	81	19.2	—
1954, December	4,162	598	14.4	382	131	69	18.1	17
1955	4,122	841	20.4	530	164	82	15.5	21
1956	5,076	951	18.7	676	188	102	15.1	20
1957[c]	5,359	806	15.0	630	NA[f]	168	26.7	24
1958[c]	6,159	657	10.7	1,016	236	264	26.0	25
1959[c]	7,328	932	12.7	788	250	187	23.7	25[e]
1960[c]	8,991	571	6.4	1,031	NA[f]	327	31.7	23[e]
1961[d]	10,297	894	8.7	771	256	118	15.3	27[e]
1962[d]	15,455	1,135	7.3	854	406	303	35.5	28[e]
1963[d]	17,944	1,639	9.1	1,242	310	266	21.4	39
1964[d]	22,995	1,708	8.5	1,259	301	253	20.1	NA
Totals	119,605	13,817[h]	12.6[h]	11,511	3,047	2,560	22.2	315[g]

[a] Degrees tabulated are first (bachelor's) degrees: B.A., B.Sc., and B. Com. Data on degrees supplied by registrars of the six Pakistani universities: Panjab, Dacca, Sind, Peshawar, Karachi, and Rajshahi. Peshawar, Karachi, and Rajshahi, created after independence, did not grant degrees, so far as can be determined, until 1955, 1956, and 1959, respectively. Degrees granted by the two new agricultural universities and two new engineering universities are not tabulated since information on them is not available. Range of error in data on degrees is estimated between 1 and 2 per cent for 1960–1964 and between 5 and 10 per cent for 1950–1960.

[b] Only civilians taking the examination and actually selected and appointed to the CSP are included. Other successful applicants (column G) were selected for other Central Superior Services.

[c] From 1957 to 1961 the CSS examination was divided into three examinations: (1) Civil and Foreign Service (combined) examination, (2) Police Service examination, and (3) Finance Services (combined) examination. The figures given for 1957, 1958, 1959, and 1960 relate to the first of these examinations only.

[d] The three examinations were again combined into one common examination in 1961. Figures given for 1961 through 1964 relate to the combined examination.

[e] These figures do not include army officers who did not take the examination but who joined the CSP in these years. There were five such officers in 1960, five in 1961, three in 1962, and one in 1963.

[f] NA: Data not available.

[g] Number selected taken from Gradation List of the Civil Service of Pakistan as of January 1, 1964. The discrepancy between this total of 315 and the total of 432 officers shown in that Gradation List is accounted for in this way: first, 142

evidence presented in Table 8 appear to be supported by another impression: In pre-independence society, it appeared fairly common for sons of ICS officers to enter the same service as their fathers. Yet in contemporary Pakistan a number of former ICS officers have discouraged their sons from entering service and have encouraged them to enter engineering or other "modernizing" professions. Unfortunately, no empirical evidence to corroborate or disprove this impression exists. It would not be incautious, however, to assert that it appears that the attractiveness of the service has diminished among Western-oriented families of some means, who are well-educated and well-connected. Tables 11 and 12 suggest this supposition as well, for while about half of the fathers of new entrants are government servants, only about one-fifth of these fathers have monthly incomes of Rs. 1500 or more. This suggests that somewhat more than half the fathers who are in service have positions below elite cadre status.

Table 8 clearly shows the highly competitive nature of the total examination process. Column H of Table 8 indicates that a remarkably small fraction (22.2 per cent) of those who take the examination ultimately qualify. A much smaller percentage is actually appointed to the CSP (from 1950 to 1964, about 2.7 per cent); and only about 2.2 per cent of those who applied to take the examination were appointed. The Central Public Service Commission has long been concerned about the poor quality of written examinations. In its report for 1963, however, it noted a

---

officers listed in the Gradation List are not included in this table since they entered before 1950; fourteen army officers listed in the Gradation List are not included in this table. These omissions total 156, which added to 315 entries in this table, makes 471. The discrepancy between 471 and 432 results from thirty-nine officers (1963) added to this table but not included in the Gradation List for 1964.

[h] This figure must be qualified. It includes applicants who applied a second or third time after failing the examination once. Records for 1959, 1960, 1961, and 1962 show that these repeaters average 25 per cent of the applicants for those years.

Sources: Data for 1950 through 1957 compiled from annual reports of the Pakistan Public Service Commission. Data for 1958 through 1961, for which reports have not yet been published, were obtained from research by the author in the research branch of the Central Public Service Commission. Data for 1962 and 1963 compiled from the report of the Central Public Service Commission for 1963, p. 118, Table VIII. Data for 1964, were obtained from correspondence with the commission. Source of the data in column B is given in note [a] above.

steady improvement in the quality of applicants.[99] It regarded as significant the progressive increase in the number of candidates for almost the same number of openings each year. The commission's most impressive evidence was the steady improvement in total marks achieved by the applicants. In 1962, for example, twenty candidates scored 60 per cent or more in the written examination, whereas only two candidates attained this score in 1950, 1951, 1952, and 1953, and only three attained it in 1961. While it may not be possible to ascertain with a comfortable degree of reliability whether or not candidates have "improved" over the years, some generalizations can be made about the background and qualifications of applicants who passed the examinations and actually received appointments in the CSP. These observations which follow are based on data compiled in Tables 9 through 19 by the present author.

Background of New Recruits to the Elite Cadre

Data in Tables 9 through 19 have been compiled for 388 CSP officers who entered service by competitive examination from 1948 through 1964. This constitutes the total number of entrants by competitive examination during that period. Except where otherwise indicated in the tables, the analysis includes fourteen armed services officers appointed, but it excludes fifty-five ICS, ten war service candidates, and three officers promoted from the provincial services. Thus, the group here analyzed constitutes 85 per cent of the total cadre strength in 1965 and 100 per cent of the recruits who entered by competitive examination.

Regional and religious representation. From the time of partition in 1947, a marked imbalance existed between East Pakistani (Bengali) and West Pakistani in the higher bureaucracy. Only one East Pakistani had opted for Pakistan. To remedy this imbalance, and at the same time to increase representation of Sindhis, Baluchis, and Pathans, who had never been as heavily represented in the services as the Punjabi, a quota system was put

99. Central Public Service Commission, *Annual Report for the Year 1963* (Karachi, 1964), pp. 6–7.

into effect at least as early as 1950 and possibly earlier.[100] That system provides that 20 per cent of the vacancies in the Central Superior Services shall be filled on merit as a result of the CSS examinations. The remaining 80 per cent of the vacancies are divided among successful candidates as follows: 1. East Pakistan, 40 per cent; 2. areas comprising the former Punjab and Bahawalpur, 23 per cent; 3. Karachi, 2 per cent; and 4. areas comprising former Sind, Khairpur, North-Western Frontier Province and Frontier States and tribal areas, Baluchistan, Azad Kashmir, and Kashmir refugees, 15 per cent. The quota system has not produced the results intended. First, Muslim refugees from India have established legal domicile in areas where candidates are few or poorly trained and have thus entered the service. Secondly, although Bengalis constitute about 54 per cent of the population, the number of Bengalis in the CSP even in 1965 had not exceeded one-third the total strength. This proportion is changing, for as Table 9 shows, Bengalis constitute nearly half of each entering batch since 1962. In its report for 1962, the Central Public Service Commission urged the government to reappraise the quota system to provide greater opportunity for candidates from areas where there are limited educational facilities. However, the commission added that its "repeated advice . . . has not so far received more than a passing attention."[101] Representation of religious groups does not plague the system as it does in countries like Malaysia and Ceylon. Pakistan is overwhelmingly a Muslim country. Neither Christians, Parsis, Buddhists, or Hindus are much interested in government service. While statistics showing the numbers of applicants in each group are not available, it is generally and reliably known that few if any but Muslims apply

100. Printed records available are not adequate to establish whether or not a quota system started with the first examination in 1948 or later in 1950. The earliest reference to the system which the present author has been able to find is in Public Service Commission, *Pamphlet on the Central Superior Services Held . . . in February 1950* (Karachi, 1951), in which a "quota system" is mentioned but not described (p. 14). The first printed description of the system is found in the next year's report, Pakistan Public Service Commission, *Pamphlet of the Combined Competitive Examination . . . Held . . . in . . . 1951* (Karachi, 1951), p. 34. The particulars of the quota system remained exactly the same in 1965 as they were announced in the 1951 report.

101. Central Public Service Commission *Annual Report for the Year 1962* (Karachi, 1962), pp. 12–13.

Table 9. *Distribution of CSP Probationers (1926–1964) According to Domicile*[a]

Year[b]	East Pakistan		West Pakistan		Total entering service
	Number	Percentage	Number	Percentage	
1926	0	0.0	2	100.0	2
1927	0	0.0	1	100.0	1
1928	0	0.0	2	100.0	2
1929[c]	—	—	—	—	—
1930	0	0.0	6	100.0	6
1931	0	0.0	6	100.0	6
1932	0	0.0	3	100.0	3
1933	2[d]	22.2	7	77.8	9
1934	0	0.0	3	100.0	3
1935	0	0.0	1	100.0	1
1936	0	0.0	3	100.0	3
1937	0	0.0	3	100.0	3
1938	0	0.0	10	100.0	10
1939	1[d]	20.0	4	80.0	5
1940	1[d]	14.3	6	85.7	7
1941	1[d]	50.0	1	50.0	2
1942	0	0.0	5	100.0	5
1943	1	16.7	5	83.3	6
1944	1	14.3	6	85.7	7
1945	1[d]	33.3	2	66.7	3
1946	1	25.0	3	75.0	4
1947	0	0.0	8	100.0	8
1948	2	11.1	16	88.9	18
1949	9	45.0	11	55.0	20
1950	6[e]	30.0	14	70.0	20
1951	4	36.4	7	63.6	11
1952	5[e]	29.4	12	70.6	17
1953	3	23.1	10	76.9	13
1954	9[f]	36.0	16	64.0	25
1955	7[g]	41.2	10	58.8	17
1956	11	52.4	10	47.6	21
1957	7	35.0	13	65.0	20
1958	9	39.1	14	60.9	23
1959	13	50.0	13	50.0	26
1960	11	36.7	19	63.3	30
1961	10	34.5	19[h]	65.5	29
1962	13	46.4	15	53.6	28
1963	13	41.9	18	58.1	31
1964	19	48.7	20	51.2	39
Totals	160	33.1	324	66.9	484[i]

[a] Not all entries in the East Pakistan column represent ethnic Bengalis. In some cases, entries represent refugees from India who established official domicile in

for the examination. This is not so much a matter of discrimination as it is a reflection of the social order. The only Buddhists are tribesmen of the Chittagong Hill Tracts. Christians are for the most part a depressed community. Parsis, concentrated largely in Karachi, have traditionally been engaged in commerce. The few Hindus are mostly in East Pakistan and are either relatively wealthy landowners or businessmen or depressed classes. It is perhaps idle to speculate as to the reasons for their non-representation. Suffice it to say that the entire CSP cadre is Muslim, except for one Christian, Chief Justice A. R. Cornelius of the Supreme Court, and two of the three British officers who remain. Unlike the situation in India, women are not eligible for appointment to the CSP. There are, however, representatives of other religions as well as a few women in some of the other Central Superior Services.

Unfortunately, there are no reliable data to show exactly how many CSP recruits migrated to Pakistan from India since partition in 1947, although there is fairly dependable information indicating how many recruits received degrees from universities in India. From the latter we can ascertain how many in the cadre migrated to Pakistan when they were at least twenty years of age. Table 10 shows that approximately 16 per cent of nearly the entire cadre of recruits received their first university degrees from Indian universities (Aligarh, Calcutta, Allahabad, Delhi, Lucknow, Patna, Agra) and migrated to Pakistan. We can assume that other recruits, too young to have received degrees in India, were

---

East Pakistan. Where this is known, notes below so indicate. The distinction between ethnic Bengalis and domiciled Bengalis, however, is not known in all cases. Error in estimate is probably less than 1 per cent.
  [b] Year is date of entry into service, not year of examination.
  [c] Unknown.
  [d] Officers domiciled in East Pakistan.
  [e] One officer domiciled in East Pakistan.
  [f] Two officers domiciled in East Pakistan.
  [g] Three officers domiciled in East Pakistan.
  [h] Two officers of Azad government of Jammu and Kashmir are included in this figure.
  [i] This figure is somewhat larger than the actual strength of the CSP cadre in 1964 due to attrition from date of entrance. Such attrition is not accounted for in this table.
  Sources: Compiled from gradation lists, records of the Central Public Service Commission and of the Establishment Division, President's Secretariat, and interviews.

also refugees. But how many such refugees there are is not known. We can say with certainty only that at least 16 per cent of the recruits entering by examination are refugees from India. It would not be improbable that the actual figure approximates 20 per cent.

Except for Bengali recruits in the CSP, there is no precise information on representation of Pathans, Baluchis, Sindhis, and Punjabis. Fairly reliable estimates, however, can be made by analysis of the source of the bachelor's degree. Here we must assume that Punjabis went to Panjab University, Pathans and Baluchis to Peshawar University, Sindhis to Sind University. This is not an unreasonable assumption, although it cannot result in more than an educated guess. Using Table 10 as a basis, then, we find that 34.6 per cent of the recruits received degrees at the University of the Panjab, 3.2 per cent at Peshawar, and 3.7 per cent at Sind. We already know from Table 9 that Bengalis constitute about one-third of the recruits; this is now corroborated by Table 10 which shows almost the same proportion as having graduated from Dacca University, the only likely university that Bengalis would have attended. It is difficult to place the 5 per cent who attended Karachi University in any ethnic category. Perhaps they were refugees from India; some may have been sons of Punjabis in residence in Karachi. But the likelihood that they were refugees is strong, for Punjabis and other ethnic groups living in Karachi would probably have returned to their established regional universities rather than attend Karachi University, which was established in 1951. We may also assume that a few Sindhis attended Karachi and the Panjab universities. On this assumption, the Sindhi proportion can be increased by 1 per cent. It appears not unreasonable, therefore, to group Karachi graduates with refugees, a group which in any event we safely assume to be larger than the 16 per cent proportion indicated by degrees from Indian universities. Over-all ethnic composition of the examination recruits of the CSP cadre, then, probably approximates this tabulation, which because of its tentativeness is best not included in a formal table:

Punjabi	35%
Bengali	32
Refugees from India	21
Pathans and Baluchi	7
Sindhi	5

It should be reiterated that this analysis of ethnic composition, while probably accurate within a 5 per cent margin, is not based on precise data.

Whatever the merits or disadvantages of the regional quota system, it is not likely to be discontinued in the foreseeable future. The issue of regional representation not only in the CSP but in all government employment continues to be a volatile political issue, raised almost weekly if not daily in one context or another in the National Assembly.[102] Its most crucial aspect is "parity" between the two wings, and it is Bengalis who raise the issue most frequently and with the greatest vehemence. But ethnic groups in West Pakistan as well do not let their representation be forgotten.[103] And the concept of provincial parity already enmeshed in the 1962 Constitution in Articles 14, 16, 17, and 240 has been given additional cognizance by the first amendment which makes it the tenth fundamental right, violations of which are justiciable.[104]

Occupational and income data on recruits' fathers. Table 11 reveals that nearly 60 per cent of the recruits are sons of other government servants and nearly 12 per cent have fathers who are landlords. The fathers of 10 per cent of the recruits are in business, about 6 per cent are teachers, 6 per cent lawyers, and 4 per cent physicians. Thus, it is clear that nearly the entire cadre (98.5 per cent of the 388 officers in the group) come from professional families and have fathers trained in a Western-oriented career. No pronounced trends through these years is

102. For representative comments scattered over a period of several years, see National Assembly of Pakistan, *Debates*, March 21, 1956, pp. 311 ff.; April 5, 1956, pp. 431 ff.; February 15, 1957, pp. 427 ff.; July 3, 1962, pp. 938 ff.; July 18, 1962, pp. 111–113; March 11, 1963, pp. 146–148, 156–157.

103. See, for example, discussion of Sindhi representation in the CSP in National Assembly of Pakistan, *Debates*, June 4, 1963, pp. 449–451.

104. For further analysis, see the author's "Pakistan: Constitutional Issues in 1964," *Asian Survey*, V (1965), 79–87.

Table 10. *Source of Bachelor's Degrees of CSP Probationers, 1948–1964*

Year of entry[a]	Panjab	Dacca	Aligarh (India)	Calcutta (India)	Allahabad (India)	Karachi	Sind	Peshawar	Foreign	Un-classified	Delhi (India)	Lucknow (India)	Patna (India)	Agra (India)	Total
1948	7	1	1	1	4	—	—	—	—	—	1	2	1	—	18
1949	6	4	2	5	—	—	—	—	—	—	—	—	1	2	20
1950	7	1	3	3	1	—	—	—	—	1	1	1	—	2	20
1951	2	2	2	—	2	—	—	—	—	—	2	1	—	—	11
1952	7	3	3	1	2	—	—	—	—	—	—	—	1	—	17
1953	6	1	2	3	1	—	—	—	—	—	—	—	—	—	13
1954	7	6	2	—	2	1	3	2	—	2	—	—	—	—	25
1955	5	3	1	1	1	1	2	—	—	1	—	1	1	—	17
1956	6	10	—	—	—	—	1	1	2	—	1	—	—	—	21
1957	9	8	—	—	—	—	2	2	—	—	—	—	—	—	21[b]
1958	9	9	—	—	—	2	1	—	1	—	—	—	—	1	23
1959	7	12	—	—	—	2	1	2	1	2	—	—	—	—	27[b]
1960[c]	7	11	—	—	—	4	—	2	1	—	—	—	—	—	25
1961[c]	10	10	—	—	—	3	—	—	2	—	—	—	—	—	25[b]
1962	10	12	—	—	—	1	—	2	3	—	—	—	—	—	28
1963	14	12	—	—	—	2	1	1	—	1	—	—	—	—	31
1964	13	15	—	—	—	3	3	—	2	3	—	—	—	—	39
Totals	132	120	16	14	13	19	14	12	12	10	5	5	4	5	381[d]
Percentages	34.6	31.5	4.2	3.7	3.4	5.0	3.7	3.1	3.1	2.6	1.3	1.3	1.0	1.3	100.0

a Year is date of entry into service, not date of examination.
b This figure increased by one because of duplicate counting of one degree.
c Five army officers nominated in 1960 and five in 1961 are not included.
d This figure is not the total strength of the CSP since it excludes army officers and includes three double counts.

Sources: See above, Table 8.

Table 11. *Professions or Occupations of Fathers of CSP Probationers, 1948–1964*

Year of entry[a]	Size of entering class	Government service		Landlord		Business		Teacher		Legal practitioner[b]		Physician		Other	
		No.	Pct.	No.	Pct.	No.	Pct.	No.	Pct.	No.	Pct.	No.	Pct.	No.	Pct.
1948	18	13	72.2	2	11.1	—	—	1	5.6	—	—	2	11.1	—	—
1949	20	15	75.0	4	20.0	1	5.0	—	—	—	—	—	—	—	—
1950	20	11	55.0	5	25.0	1	5.0	—	—	2	10.0	—	—	1[c]	5.0
1951	11	4	36.4	2	18.2	2	18.2	2	18.2	1	9.1	—	—	—	—
1952	17	11	64.7	2	11.8	1	5.9	—	—	1	5.9	2	11.8	—	—
1953	13	6	46.2	2	15.4	4	30.8	—	—	1	7.7	—	—	—	—
1954	25	16	64.0	6	24.0	1	4.0	2	8.0	—	—	—	—	—	—
1955	17	13	76.5	—	—	—	—	—	—	3	17.6	1	5.9	—	—
1956	21	12	57.1	1	4.8	1	4.8	1	4.8	4	19.0	1	4.8	1[d]	4.8
1957	20	13	65.0	1	5.0	1	5.0	2	10.0	1	5.0	2	10.0	—	—
1958	23	13	56.5	2	8.7	7	30.4	—	—	—	—	1	4.3	—	—
1959	26	14	53.8	—	—	2	7.7	7	26.9	1	3.8	2	7.7	—	—
1960	30[e]	18	60.0	5	16.7	5	16.7	—	—	1	3.3	1	3.3	—	—
1961	29[e]	18	62.1	2	6.9	2	6.9	5	17.2	1	3.4	1	3.4	—	—
1962	28[e]	18	64.3	4	14.3	2	7.1	1	3.6	2	7.1	—	—	1	3.6
1963	31[e]	18	58.1	2	6.5	2	6.5	2	6.5	3	9.7	3	9.7	1	3.2
1964	39	18	46.2	6	15.4	7	17.9	2	5.1	4	10.3	—	—	2	5.1
Totals	388	231	59.5	46	11.9	39	10.1	25	6.4	25	6.4	16	4.1	6	1.5

[a] Year is date of entry into service, not date of examination.
[b] Includes pleaders, attorneys, advocates, and barristers in private practice.
[c] Journalist.
[d] Engineer.
[e] Army officers (five in 1960, five in 1961, three in 1962, one in 1963) included.

Sources: Compiled with assistance of Zahid Shariff and S. M. Haider. Information for 1948 through 1958 made available by the Federal Public Service Commission; for 1959 and 1960 by the Establishment Division, President's Secretariat; and for 1961 to 1964 by interview of probationers.

indicated, although a slight decrease in the number of recruits whose fathers are government servants is noted. Fluctuations in other occupational categories do not suggest the identification of other trends. Table 11 does not reveal the background of the fourteen army officers taken into the service. But from unpublished sources it is known that all fourteen are the sons of government servants. Of these, the fathers of four were army officers.

The income data of fathers have been separated into two tables (12 and 13) so that the fourteen army officers may be treated separately. Table 12 shows that approximately half of the group come from families in which the father earns Rs. 800 or less a month. Such income is not characteristic of wealthy, landed classes, or of high-ranking civil servants, or of eminently successful businessmen or lawyers.[105] It represents, rather, the income of what might loosely be called a middle class. About 20 per cent of the group come from families whose father earns Rs. 1,500 or more a month. Some trends are discernible from Table 12. The number of recruits coming from the lowest income families (Rs. 500 and below) appears to have decreased by nearly half. Those coming from families in the highest category (Rs. 1,500 or above) have increased by nearly 40 per cent. The middle categories (Rs. 800 to 1,500) have remained relatively stable. Data available for twelve of the fourteen army officers corroborates that the officers come from families in the highest income bracket. In sum, it can be said that the new CSP recruits represent a broad economic spectrum in their society. They are neither predominantly from

105. To put this income in perspective, a few typical monthly salaries are given below. These are base pay salaries only and do not include various allowances. Except for ministers, legislators, judges, and government secretaries, the salary is average, i.e., the salary made by a person roughly halfway within the range allowed by his bracket. Central government ministers, Rs. 3,000 (plus Rs. 1,250 monthly housing allowance if no official residence is used); member of the National Assembly, Rs. 600 (plus daily allowance of Rs. 50 when in attendance); High Court judge, Rs. 4,000; former ICS officer now full secretary, Rs. 4,000; full secretary (non-ICS), Rs. 3,000; new recruit in the CSP, Rs. 350; senior professor in university, Rs. 1,500; junior lecturer (beginning rank comparable to instructor) in university, Rs. 500; research associate in government, Rs. 600; typist in government, Rs. 150; young executive in private business, Rs. 1,500; eminent barrister, Rs. 12,000. See also Table 7, p. 656, in concluding comparative chapter in this volume, and references to comparable data for the Indian Administrative Service in Potter's chapter in this volume, p. 152.

Table 12. *Monthly Income of Fathers of CSP Probationers (Excluding Army Officers), 1952–1964*

Year of entry[a]	Size of entering class	Rs. 1,501 and above		Rs. 1,001 to Rs. 1,500		Rs. 801 to Rs. 1,000		Rs. 501 to Rs. 800		Below Rs. 500	
		No.	Pct.	No.	Pct.	No.	Pct.	No.	Pct.	No.	Pct.
1952	17[b]	3	18.8	3	18.8	1	6.3	2	12.5	7	43.8
1953	13	2	15.4	2	15.4	3	23.1	1	7.7	5	38.5
1954	25[c]	1	4.2	4	16.7	2	8.3	2	8.3	15	62.5
1955	17	4	23.5	2	11.8	1	5.9	5	29.4	5	29.4
1956	21	2	9.5	3	14.3	2	9.5	2	9.5	12	57.1
1957	20	5	25.0	4	20.0	5	25.0	1	5.0	5	25.0
1958	23	2	8.7	4	17.4	2	8.7	3	13.0	12	52.2
1959	26	5	19.2	6	23.1	1	3.8	2	7.7	12	46.2
1960	25[d]	3	12.0	5	20.0	1	4.0	7	28.0	9	36.0
1961	24[d]	4	16.7	4	16.7	2	8.3	9	37.5	5	20.8
1962	27[e]	8	29.6	6	22.2	2	7.4	4	14.8	7	25.9
1963	31[f]	10	32.3	5	16.1	3	9.7	8	25.8	5	16.1
1964	39	12	30.8	7	17.9	6	15.4	7	17.9	7	17.9
Totals	306[g]	61	19.9	55	18.0	31	10.1	53	17.3	106	34.6

[a] Year is date of entry into service, not date of examination.
[b] Data unavailable for one officer. Percentages based on 16, not 17.
[c] Data unavailable for one officer. Percentages based on 24, not 25.
[d] Data for five army officers not included here. See Table 11.
[e] Data for three army officers not included here. See Table 11.
[f] Data for one army officer not included here. See Table 11.
[g] Since data was unavailable for two officers counted (see notes [b] and [e]), percentages are based on 306, not 308.

Sources: See above Table 9.

Table 13. Monthly Income of Fathers of Army Officers Taken into CSP, 1960–1964

Year of entry[a]	Number of army officers	Rs. 1,501 and above		Rs. 1,001 to Rs. 1,500		Rs. 801 to Rs. 1,000		Rs. 501 to Rs. 800[b]	
		No.	Pct.	No.	Pct.	No.	Pct.	No.	Pct.
1960	5	4	80	—	—	—	—	1	20
1961	5	4	80	1	20	—	—	—	—
1962	3[c]	1	—	—	—	—	—	—	—
1963	1	1	100	—	—	—	—	—	—
1964	—	—	—	—	—	—	—	—	—
Totals	14[c]	10	83.3	1	8.3	—	—	1	8.3

[a] Year is date of entry into service, not date of examination.
[b] No officers earned less that Rs. 500.
[c] Data unavailable for two officers. Percentages based on 12, not 14.
Sources: Compiled from questionnaires completed at the Civil Service Academy.

the traditionally wealthy class nor predominantly from the poorest groups.

Educational qualifications. Even before turning to study the quality of academic training, it should be noted that those who ultimately pass the examinations and are appointed to the CSP are but a small proportion of those who begin the examination process. Table 8 shows that from 1950 to 1964, approximately 11,511 persons took the written examination. About 22 per cent of these persons were declared successful, and about 2 per cent were actually appointed to the CSP.[106] Given a fairly rigid examining and screening process, we can assume that this rather high selectivity does, *ipso facto*, bring into the service men who are well-qualified by training and personality. Moreover, it should be pointed out that the examination process is highly respected. While virtually all other aspects of government are the object of carping criticism and suspicion, the examinations administered by the Central Public Service Commission are regarded as being free from the taint of impropriety.

It is commonly said in Pakistan that the CSP attracts and gets the "best" university graduates. The data arrayed in the five tables numbered from 14 through 18 will help in determining the validity of this statement. We shall avoid determining what "best" means. The evidence permits a judgment *only* in terms of achievement of university distinction by the award of degrees by division. Even this evidence is not conclusive, for the standards for the ranking of a student's performance by division vary by departments within a university and also vary to some extent from one university to another. By and large, a degree awarded in the first division is comparable to achieving an average in the upper 10 per cent of one's class. It must be reiterated, however, that this standard varies greatly. It would be safer to say merely that in the judgment of an academic department, a first-division degree connotes higher academic attainment than degrees in the second and third divisions.

---

106. The number selected in 1964 is not known. I assume it to be thirty for purposes of computing this percentage. See notes b, e, g, and *Totals* line in Column I in Table 8 above, p. 262.

Before coming to an analysis of the "quality" of university degrees obtained, certain objective data relating to educational background are clear. All recruits have at least a bachelor's degree from an approved university. In fact, except for army officers, all members of the CSP, including ICS officers, war-service candidates, and those promoted from the provincial services, meet this requirement.[107] Among the recruits, as Table 10 shows, nearly 6 per cent of the bachelor's degrees came from foreign universities or are not otherwise accounted for. Some 16 per cent came from Indian universities and 78 per cent from Pakistani universities. For the years 1956–1965, only four graduates of Indian universities entered the service. This suggests the virtual termination of significant migration from India of persons more than twenty years of age with educational background and ambition to enter the CSP. It can also be clearly established (Table 16) that nearly 65 per cent of the recruits have a master's degree. The proportion having master's degrees has remained relatively stable during the period considered. Table 17 shows that 15 per cent of the recruits have law degrees and that while the proportion has fluctuated by as much as 27 per cent from year to year, no significant trend in the proportion is indicated. The extent to which the law degrees are held by those who also hold master's degrees is not known. However, additional unpublished data for the 141 recruits who entered from 1960 to 1964 shows that of the twenty-four recruits holding law degrees, twenty also have master's degrees. Whether this proportion is valid for the entire group, however, cannot be determined. Finally, although we do not know the extent of foreign education of the entire group prior to joining service, this information is available (but not published here) for the 141 recruits who entered from 1960 to 1964. Of this group, twenty-five, or 17.7 per cent, studied abroad: seven at Oxford, two at Cambridge, three at London, one at Imperial College of Science (London), one at St. Andrews, one at

107. The fourteen army officers are graduates of the Pakistan Military Academy. One officer, in addition, is a graduate of the Royal Military College (Sandhurst), England. Several others have attended military training establishments in the United States or elsewhere. One officer served as military attaché in the Pakistan High Commission in London.

Lincoln's Inn, one at Manchester, one at Vanderbilt, one at Pennsylvania, one at Iowa, one at Columbia, one at the Massachusetts Institute of Techology, one at American University in Washington, one at American University in Beirut, one at British Columbia, and one at Indiana. Not all of these recruits received their degrees abroad. Many returned to Pakistan in the course of their studies to enter the service, a date for which no deferment is allowed. Of these twenty-five recruits, nineteen received either bachelor's degrees or completed their course of training.[108] Given the available data, it is not known if the proportion of 17.7 per cent holds for those who entered service before 1960. It may be of some significance that ten of the foreign degree holders were in the 1964 batch and that five of these ten earned degrees at Oxford. From the data available it can be said that in terms of formal education the recruits are a remarkably well-educated group. They are certainly not representative of their society in this respect. Their education in terms of formal degrees is derived from multiple sources, although these sources are predominantly Pakistani. Judging from data on recruits who entered service from 1960 to 1964, there may be a trend toward an increase in the number of recruits with foreign degrees, and particularly with British ones. It will be several more years, however, before this can be confirmed as a trend.

The academic standing of the recruits is revealed by a series of tables (14 through 18) which separate bachelor's, master's, and law degrees. About 26 per cent of the recruits obtained a bachelor's degree in the first division. This is a considerably lower proportion than has been commonly assumed, and the proportion has remained fairly stable during the entire period. About 61 per cent of recruits took degrees in the second division, a proportion which also has not fluctuated markedly. The fact that 11 per cent hold only third-division degrees indicates that about one-tenth of the group did little more than pass the course for the bachelor's degree. It can be said, therefore, that about a quarter of the

108. These foreign degrees are not found in any single table. They are bachelor's and master's degrees, certificates, diplomas, or the passing of bar exams; hence, they are concealed and scattered in various categories in Tables 10, 14, 15, and 16.

recruits passed with what are regarded as superior credentials. The proportions change moderately for recruits also holding law degrees. Nearly half of these received a first-division law degree; somewhat more than half, a second-division degree; and only 1.7 per cent finished in the third division. Thus, those who entered with law degrees stood higher academically in relation to their class in law college than did recruits with bachelor's degrees in relation to their university class. The proportions for recruits with master's degrees is somewhat closer to the statistics for bachelor's degrees than those for law degrees. About one-third of these recruits took a first-division, about two-thirds a second-division, and 6 per cent a third-division master's degree.

Perhaps the most revealing way of determining the quality of academic performance is to trace the combinations of degrees

Table 14. *Division of Bachelor's Degrees of CSP Probationers, 1948–1964*

Year of entry[a]	Size of entering class	Bachelor's Degrees					
		Division I	Pct.	Division II	Pct.	Division III	Pct.
1948	18	8	44.4	10	55.6	—	—
1949	20	6	30.0	12	60.0	2	10.0
1950	20	5	25.0	13	65.0	2	10.0
1951	11	4	36.4	7	63.6	—	—
1952	17	7	41.2	10	58.8	—	—
1953	13	8	61.5	5	38.5	—	—
1954	25	8	32.0	15	60.0	2	8.0
1955	17	3	17.6	9	52.9	5	29.4
1956	21	7	33.3	9	42.9	5	23.9
1957	20	5	25.0	11	55.0	4	20.0
1958	23	3	13.0	17	73.9	3	13.0
1959	26	3	11.5	20	76.9	3	11.5
1960	25[b]	4	16.0	19	76.0	2	8.0
1961	24[b]	4	16.7	14	58.3	6	25.0
1962	28[c]	8	28.6	15	53.6	3	10.7
1963	31	7	22.6	22	71.0	2	6.4
1964	39	10	25.6	24	61.5	5	12.9
Totals	378	100	26.5	232	61.4	44	11.6

[a] Year is date of entry into service, not date of examination.
[b] Five army officers not included.
[c] Two army officers not included.
Sources: See above, Table 9.

Table 15. *Division of Bachelor's Degrees for CSP Probationers (1948–1964) Holding Only a Bachelor's Degree*

Year of entry[a]	Size of entering class	Total with only Bachelor's Degree		Division I	Pct.	Totals by division			
		No.	Pct.			Division II	Pct.	Division III	Pct.
1948	18	4	22.2	2	50.0	2	50.0	—	—
1949	20	5	25.0	2	40.0	2	40.0	1	20.0
1950	20	7	35.0	2	28.6	4	57.1	1	14.3
1951	11	3	27.3	2	66.7	1	33.3	—	—
1952	17	4	23.5	1	25.0	3	75.0	—	—
1953	13	4	30.8	2	50.0	2	50.0	—	—
1954	25	8	32.0	2	25.0	6	75.0	—	—
1955	17	10	58.8	—	—	7	70.0	3	30.0
1956	21	12	57.1	4	33.3	5	41.7	3	25.0
1957	20	7	35.0	3	42.9	3	42.9	1	14.2
1958	23	7	30.4	—	—	6	85.7	1	14.2
1959	26	10	38.5	4	40.0	6	60.0	—	—
1960	25[b]	2	8.0	—	—	1	50.0	1	50.0
1961	24[b]	4	16.7	1	25.0	2	50.0	1	25.0
1962	28[c]	2	7.1	—	—	1	50.0	—	50.0
1963	31	2	6.5	—	—	—	—	2	100.0
1964	39	6	15.4	1	16.7	3	50.0	2	33.3
Totals	**378**	**97**	**25.7**	**26**	**26.8**	**54**	**55.7**	**17**	**17.5**

[a] Year is date of entry into service, not date of examination.
[b] Five army officers not included.
[c] Two army officers not included.
Sources: See above, Table 9.

Table 16. Division of Master's Degrees of CSP Probationers, 1948–1964

Year of entry[a]	Size of entering class	Total with Master's Degree		Division I		Totals by division Division II		Division III	
		No.	Pct.		Pct.		Pct.		Pct.
1948	18	14	77.8	4	28.6	10	71.4	—	—
1949	20	15	75.0	7	46.7	8	53.3	—	—
1950	20	13	65.0	6	46.2	7	53.8	—	—
1951	11	8	72.7	2	25.0	5	62.5	1	12.5
1952	17	12	70.6	5	41.7	6	50.0	1	8.3
1953	13	6	46.2	2	33.3	4	66.7	—	—
1954	25	14	56.0	1	7.1	13	92.9	—	—
1955	17	6	35.3	4	66.7	2	33.3	—	—
1956	21	7	33.3	2	28.6	3	42.9	2	28.6
1957	20	10	50.0	2	20.0	7	70.0	1	10.0
1958	23	16	69.6	6	37.5	8	50.0	2	12.5
1959	26	12	46.2	3	25.0	8	66.7	1	8.3
1960	25[b]	20	80.0	12	60.0	8	40.0	—	—
1961	24[b]	15	62.5	2	13.3	12	80.0	1	6.7
1962	28[c]	23	82.1	8	34.8	14	60.9	1	4.3
1963	31	27	87.1	7	25.9	18	66.7	2	7.4
1964	39	27	69.2	5	18.5	19	70.4	3	11.1
Totals	378	245	64.8	78	31.8	152	62.0	15	6.1

[a] Year is date of entry into service, not date of examination.
[b] Five army officers not included.
[c] Two army officers not included.
Sources: See above, Table 9.

Table 17. *Division of Bachelor of Laws Degrees of CSP Probationers, 1948–1964*

Year of entry[a]	Size of entering class	Total with law degrees		Totals by division					
		No.	Pct.	Division I	Pct.	Division II	Pct.	Division III	Pct.
1948	18	4	22.2	3	75.0	1	25.0	—	—
1949	20	4	20.0	4	100.0	—	—	—	—
1950	20	5	25.0	4	80.0	1	20.0	—	—
1951	11	1	9.1	1	100.0	—	—	—	—
1952	17	2	11.8	1	50.0	1	50.0	—	—
1953	13	5	38.5	2	40.0	3	60.0	—	—
1954	25	3	12.0	—	—	3	100.0	—	—
1955	17	1	5.9	—	—	1	100.0	—	—
1956	21	1	4.8	1	100.0	—	—	—	—
1957	20	3	15.0	1	33.3	1	33.3	1	33.3
1958	23	—	—	—	—	—	—	—	—
1959	26	4	15.4	2	50.0	2	50.0	—	—
1960	25[b]	3	12.0	1	33.3	2	66.7	—	—
1961	24[b]	7	29.2	1	14.3	6	85.7	—	—
1962	28[c]	5	17.9	2	40.0	3	60.0	—	—
1963	31	3	9.7	1	33.3	2	66.7	—	—
1964	39	6	15.4	3	50.0	3	50.0	—	—
Totals	378	57	15.1	27	47.4	29	50.9	1	1.7

[a] Year is date of entry into service, not date of examination.
[b] Five army officers not included.
[c] Two army officers not included.
Sources: See above, Table 9.

Table 18. *Academic Standing of Probationers Traced Through Highest Degree,* 1948–1964

Year of entry[a]	Size of entering class	Number with all examinations in first division[b]		Number with first division in all but one examination		All others[c]	
		No.	Pct.	No.	Pct.	No.	Pct.
1948	18	2	11.1	5	27.8	11	61.1
1949	20	6	30.0	5	25.0	9	45.0
1950	20	2	10.0	4	20.0	14	70.0
1951	11	2	18.2	2	18.2	7	63.6
1952	17	4	23.5	3	17.6	10	58.8
1953	13	1	7.7	6	46.2	6	46.5
1954	25	—	—	3	12.0	22	88.0
1955	17	2	11.8	4	23.5	11	64.7
1956	21	5	23.8	3	14.3	13	61.9
1957	20	4	20.0	3	15.0	13	65.0
1958	23	1	4.3	11	47.8	11	47.8
1959	26	1	3.8	8	30.8	17	65.4
1960	25[d]	1	4.0	14	56.0	10	40.0
1961	24[d]	2	8.3	4	16.7	18	75.0
1962	28[e]	1	3.6	5	17.9	22	78.6
1963	31	3	9.7	3	9.7	25	80.6
1964	39	3	7.7	8	20.5	28	71.8
Totals	378	40	10.6	91	24.1	247	65.3

[a] Year is date of entry into service, not date of examination.
[b] The examinations considered are Matriculation (senior Cambridge), Intermediate in Arts (science and commerce), Bachelor of Arts (commerce, science, medicine), Master of Arts (science, commerce, public administration), and Bachelor of Laws.
[c] The possibilities range from all third divisions at one extreme to two second divisions and one first division at the other.
[d] Five army officers not included.
[e] Two army officers not included.

Source: <!-- illegible -->

and their divisions. In so doing, the assumption is made that to pass all pre-collegiate studies and to get all degrees in the first division is truly exceptional academic performance. It would be roughly the equivalent of a straight-A average in junior high, high school, undergraduate school, and graduate school in the American system. Table 18 shows that about 10 per cent of the group achieved such distinction. An additional 24 per cent finished in the first division for at least the pre-collegiate course of study or for the course of study for a degree. The range of possibilities of the remaining 65 per cent of recruits is too wide to allow any conclusion. Table 18 does reveal a finding which has not been generally known, that is, about 10 per cent of the CSP have what by any standard would be considered distinguished and exceptional academic records. To this group can be added another 27 per cent who possess bachelor's degrees earned in the first division. Thus, it can be said that somewhat more than one-third (37 per cent) of the recruits have the best university academic records attainable in the system. Finally, it appears that a remaining 40 per cent have respectable, average academic records, and that somewhat less than one-quarter (23 per cent)[109] have the lowest university academic records attainable.

The next means for assessing the quality of academic attainment is analysis of performance in the CSS competitive examination itself. The only data available (Table 19) have been compiled by the present writer. It is a common assumption in Pakistan that post-independence recruits are not of the "caliber" of ICS veterans. This is attributed to the regional quota system, which allegedly results in the appointment of men who pass the competitive examination but are nevertheless near the bottom of the list of successful candidates. It is difficult to answer this argument with sound empirical data. Table 18 suggests an answer, although it is based on an examination of only 252 recruits, since data for the 126 who entered from 1948 to 1952 and in 1959 and 1962 are not available. Our observations, therefore,

109. This percentage is the sum of the 16.5 per cent of those holding only bachelor's degrees who earned them in the third division and 6.1 per cent and 1.7 per cent of those holding third-division law and master's degrees. See last columns of Tables 15, 16, 17, and 18.

Table 19. Rank in CSS Competitive Examination of CSP Probationers, 1952–1958, 1960–1961, 1963–1964[a]

Rank	1952	1953	1954	1955	1956	1957	1958	1960	1961	1963	1964	Totals	
												No.	Pct.
1–5	3	1	2	3	4	2	2	4	4	5	5	35	13.9
6–10	4	1	1	2	4	4	4	4	1	5	5	35	13.9
11–15	3	1	5	4	4	3	5	3	4	3	5	40	15.9
16–20	2	4	5	2	3	5	3	3	5	5	4	41	16.3
21–25	3	1	1	0	2	2	2	1	2	4	4	22	8.7
26–30	1	3	2	1	1	2	1	2	1	2	2	18	7.1
31–35	1	0	3	1	1	2	0	1	1	2	2	14	5.6
36–40	0	1	1	1	0	0	2	1	1	2	4	13	5.2
41–45	0	0	2	2	1	0	0	2	0	2	1	10	4.0
46–50	0	1	1	1	0	0	2	2	0	0	2	9	3.6
51–55	0	0	1	0	0	0	0	1	1	0	1	4	1.6
56–60	0	0	1	0	0	0	1	0	0	0	2	4	1.6
61–65	0	0	0	0	0	0	1	0	0	0	0	1	0.4
66–80	0	0	0	0	0	0	0	0	0	0	0	0	0.0
81–85	0	0	0	0	0	0	0	0	0	0	2	2	0.8
86–90	0	0	0	0	1	0	0	0	1	0	0	2	0.8
110–115	0	0	0	0	0	0	0	1	0	0	0	1	0.4
130–135	0	0	0	0	0	0	0	0	1	0	0	1	0.4
Totals	17	13	25	17	21	20	23	25	22	30[b]	39	252	100.0

[a] Data unavailable for years prior to 1952 and for 1959 and 1962.
[b] Data unavailable for one officer excluded from this figure.

Sources: Compiled with assistance of Zahid Shariff and S. M. Haider from raw data in unpublished records of Federal Public Service Commission.

derive from a sample of only 66 per cent of the total cadre of recruits. During the years for which data are available, no more than 135 candidates were declared successful. Roughly the first half, or sixty, can fairly be deemed to have performed well. Only 2.8 per cent of the recruits fell below this position. Thus, for this period only about eight recruits performed in the lower half on the competitive examination. If we arbitrarily assume a proportion of roughly 3 per cent for the entire group of 378 recruits, we find there would be eleven or twelve recruits who fall below the sixtieth rank in the examination. Moreover, it should be kept in mind that high academic attainment, the only criterion being analyzed here, is no certain guarantee that the recruit will be outstanding in his subsequent training or that he will make an outstanding officer. Hence, the risk assumed in appointing eleven or twelve recruits below the sixtieth rank may not be great at all. In sum, it would appear that the regional quota system as it has operated during eleven years in a sample of two-thirds of the recruits has not *seriously* lowered the academic quality of the cadre. Moreover, it might be assumed that the same observation is true for the remaining one-third recruited during the other years.

Several miscellaneous observations made by the Central Public Service Commission from its own research, rather than by the present author from his research, are worthy of note.[110] For the decade from 1951 to 1962, 81 per cent of the successful candidates were between the ages of twenty-two and twenty-four. Most of the candidates beyond twenty-four years of age are from tribal or backward areas, hence their low rate of success may be due more to educational disadvantage than to age. The commission suggests keeping the relaxed limits for these classes, but changing the age limits for all others to twenty-one–twenty-four instead of twenty–twenty-five, as is now in effect. Second, the examination may be taken four times, but since 93 per cent of the successes occur during the first two attempts, the commission

110. Central Public Service Commission, *Annual Report for the Year 1963*, p. 4. This report is probably the best of the entire series of annual reports. It reflects the growing sophistication in use of statistics and the maturation of several years' work by the research section organized in 1960.

suggests that a fourth attempt not be allowed. Third, candidates with first-division bachelor's degrees are much more successful in the written tests than those with other bachelor's degrees (68 per cent success as against 43 per cent for second divisioners in 1959, 1960, and 1961). But this lead is not maintained in the oral part. In the over-all examination (written, viva voce, psychological) the rate of success for first and second divisions is about equal, but only 14 per cent of those with third-division degrees pass. Fourth, a large proportion of successful candidates have majored in humanities and social sciences as compared to a smaller group majoring in natural sciences, but there is no significant difference in their rates of success as related to their academic major.

Rowland Egger said in 1953 that "those who are called upon to advise the Government of Pakistan inevitably find themselves operating in very fast intellectual company."[111] Egger had reference to the group of senior ICS officers with whom foreign advisers usually deal. In the present study we have examined in detail the qualifications of the recruits who will gradually assume the places of the ICS officers. Avoiding definition of the term "intellectual," it is difficult to find evidence in the data here arrayed that the recruits of the new period (1947–1965) will be any less able than their ICS mentors. It can be said with certainty that CSP recruitment, within the limits of the quota system and personality qualifications, brings into the service a significant portion of the best-qualified men the nation produces.

Armed forces officers. The fourteen army officers taken into the CSP from 1960 to 1963 have stirred considerable comment in Pakistan, especially among critics of martial law and of President Ayub. Their recruitment is commonly regarded as a martial law effort to militarize the civil bureaucracy by gradual infiltration. The apparent initiation of armed forces officer recruitment in 1960, two years after martial law was promulgated, appears to lend credence to this observation. The facts, however, indicate a somewhat different condition. The first recorded decision to include army officers in the CSP was made by the Cabinet

111. Rowland Egger, *The Improvement of Public Administration in Pakistan* (Karachi, 1953), p. x of letter of transmittal.

Secretariat as early as 1950, three years after independence and eight years before martial law.[112] In coming to this decision, the government may very well have been guided by the inclusion of Indian army officers in the pre-partition Indian Political Service (IPS) which functioned in the princely states. This is suggested by the fact that in the opening paragraph of the 1950 decision reference was made to the composition of the Indian Civil Service and its companion Political Service. Moreover, it must be remembered that after partition Pakistan, much more than India, had retained the services of some twenty-six former officers of the Indian Political Service, of whom twelve were Muslim and fourteen were British. Iskander Mirza who was president from 1955 to 1958 and who in the early 1950's had served as secretary of defense was an officer of this service. IPS officers were, then, part of the everyday scene. Further, the frontier areas of the Pathans and Baluchis presented problems amenable to control by the same kind of government which had been the specialty of the Indian Political Service. Finally, the sense of affinity which Muslims of West Pakistan traditionally had for military ways, and the reservoir of talent in the army drawn from families which had traditionally produced officers, made it not unnatural to think in terms of mixing military and civil talent.

The 1950 policy provided for the selection of suitable officers each year from the armed forces at the rate of 10 per cent of the total annual recruitment into the CSP. Selection was to be made by the Public Service Commission, and selected officers were to be given the same training as "competition" recruits at the Civil Service Academy. The policy of recruitment of military officers was to be re-examined in 1955. In fact, this policy was not implemented. If it had been, the number of military officers in the CSP in 1965 would approximate thirty. In January, 1960, during the period of martial law, the selection of military officers was reconsidered and a revised policy put into effect.[113] Five military

---

112. Cabinet Secretariat (Establishment Branch), *Resolution No. F-25/4/50-Ests. (S.E.I.)*, Karachi, November 8, 1950. Hereinafter cited as *Cabinet Resolution, 1950*.
113. Central Public Service Commission, *Annual Report for the Year 1963*, p. 10.

officers were to be appointed annually. Since the annual total intake of the CSP in the 1960's hovered at thirty, this was somewhat higher than the 10 per cent prescribed in the 1950 policy. Otherwise the selection policy remained much the same. Ultimate selection was to be made by the Central Public Service Commission from a panel of from thirty to fifty officers, not more than twenty-six years of age and preferably with experience on the Frontier. But the Ministry of Defense found it difficult to prepare a panel of suitable candidates. The men likely to be chosen were typically the most promising company-grade officers who were also sorely needed by the armed forces. The five officers selected in 1960 and in 1961 were of uncommon ability and training. They were chosen from a large panel of nominees: one was a graduate of the Royal Military College (Sandhurst), England; two were the sons of army generals. In 1962 the Public Service Commission complained that only sixteen names had been submitted by the Ministry of Defense and that it was able to recommend only three suitable candidates from the armed forces. In 1963 the Ministry of Defense presented a panel of three names, and the commission was able to recommend only one officer. In 1964 no military officers were appointed.

That the government probably thought of the use of army officers in terms of the old Indian Political Service appears to be supported by the assignment subsequently given to former officers. In 1964 ten of the fourteen officers had completed their training and were assigned. Nine of the ten were posted to agencies or districts in the Northwest Frontier. Thus, Pakistan continues a well-established practice begun under British rule. The effect of this assignment of military officers has been to give life to a Frontier List which had been organized as early as 1950 within the CSP. A decision was subsequently taken to invite applications for Frontier service from CSP officers of about three years' service. Such officers would then receive some military training and would be expected to spend their entire careers in Frontier service. Officers so assigned were to pass a special examination on the history of the Pathans and on Frontier problems generally. As it has worked out, most of the army officers in the CSP opted for the Frontier List. This was partly because many of them were Pathans. But probably of greater influence were the qualities of life and administration on the Frontier, which were the same qualities of military life which had attracted these men to an army career in the first place.

Training the Elite Cadre

Upon completion of the competitive examination, the Central Public Service Commission ranks the candidates by marks obtained. Then, using the regional quota formula, the commission declares successful roughly the same number of candidates as there are positions to be filled in the central superior services. The successful candidates then make a choice of service, priority being given by rank of the candidate. From the very beginning in 1948, the CSP was the service preferred by most candidates. The Foreign Service and Audit and Accounts Service ranked next. Statistics compiled by the Central Public Service Commission and published in its report for 1963 show that even among candidates who were simply taking the examination (not those declared successful), the CSP was the first preference of 78 per cent in 1961 and of nearly 80 per cent in 1962. The commission has not compiled comparable data for other years; hence, we cannot say with certainty that this preference has been the same since 1947. But certainly no one who knows the Pakistani bureaucratic system would dispute that from the beginning the CSP has had this preferential position. In this writer's opinion, in fact, the percentage was probably higher for earlier years than it was in the two reported years, 1961 and 1962.

It can be safely asserted that no other service approaches the CSP in desirability. The closest, the Foreign Service, was preferred by only 15 and 14 per cent of the candidates in 1961 and 1962, respectively; the next, the Police Service of Pakistan, was the first choice of somewhat less than 3 per cent each year. The Audit and Accounts Service followed at 1.6 per cent. But the other services were preferred by much less than 1 per cent in every case. There is still another indication of the high order of preference of the CSP. Many candidates who pass the examination with a total score too low to be appointed to the CSP accept appointment in the Audit and Accounts Service, and while still in that service they take the examination a second and third time. Their hope is to achieve a higher mark, leave the Audit and Accounts Service, and accept appointment to the CSP. This approach is so widely practiced that the Central Public Service Commission regarded it as the main reason for the failure of so many Audit and Accounts Service officers in the final "passing-out" examination.[114] That is, these candidates were so busy studying to retake the CCS examination that they neglected their own probationary training in the Finance Services Academy.

Naturally enough, the effects of this order of preference are significant in determining the ethos of the total bureaucracy. The most obvious effect is that except for perhaps fifteen or so recruits[115] chosen because of the quota system, those who entered the CSP for all the years since 1947 were at the very top of the rank list of successful candidates in the examination.[116] A second, less obvious effect is that the paramountcy of prestige of the CSP is thereby reinforced. Those in the "lower" central superior services tend to regard the CSP officers with awe mixed with envy and resentment. It is a service which they did not quite make, but a service which they hold in secret admiration. It is this element of preference, so well validated by the Public Service Commission's 1963 report, that conditions much of the behavior within the upper reaches of Pakistan's bureaucracy.

Since partition in 1947, those candidates selected for the CSP have been sent for a nine-month course to the Civil Service Academy, a baronial estate which was formerly the "Residency" of the political resident to the Punjab states. The very architecture of the building imparts the atmosphere of empire. The academy ranks with the former Punjab Club (now the Adminis-

114. Central Public Service Commission, *Annual Report for the Year 1962*, p. 18.
115. See above, p. 285, for means by which this figure is arrived at. I have added to the figures 11–12 given on p. 285 to compensate for the years not included in the analysis on p. 285, which is based on Table 19, p. 284.
116. Central Public Service Commission, *Annual Report for the Year 1963*, Table 1, p. 105.

trative Staff College), the Lahore Gymkhana, and Government House as one of the finest pre-independence buildings in Pakistan. During this period of training, recruits are officially on "probation" and are not fully confirmed in the service until successful completion of the "passing-out" examination administered by the Central Public Service Commission after training at the academy.

Any just evaluation of training at the academy must be made in terms of the larger context of Pakistani society and particularly of university life. The assumption underlying the course of study at the academy is that at no point in the pre-university and university career of the recruit was he required to adhere to a regular, rigorous schedule over a sustained period of several months. Therefore, a first objective of academy training becomes the molding of the probationer's personal life to fit the new responsibilities of government service. A second assumption is that the irresponsibility of probationers as students has been so deleterious that rigid controls over their conduct in the academy are an essential antidote. A third assumption is that the probationers must be detached from the maelstrom of social and political activity about them in preparation for their assignments as district officers; in the field such detachment is deemed essential in the interests of both effective control and probity.[117] The physical aspects of the schedule were so carefully planned that the probationer had no time to leave the grounds or to think much about any activity except his training. Under the rules set down by some directors, guests could not be invited to the weekly, formal mess night unless approved in advance by the director and unless the guest were a CSP officer or government official of high rank. Much emphasis was placed on Western-style social graces and dress. Formal attire had to be purchased, and probationers were required to be members of the Lahore Gymkhana. The latter was a legacy of British rule when the Gymkhana was the exclusive preserve of British officers. The emphasis on sartorial splendor served to detach if not alienate the probationers from

117. See discussion of the theoretical relationship of this notion to corruption in the author's "Reflections on Bureaucratic Corruption," *Public Administration* (London), XL (1962), 357–372.

the larger society. Moreover, it strained the financial resources of the probationers, most of whom were required to spend about Rs. 1,000 more a year than salary received. Tennis and riding kits, winter and summer formal dress, and business suits cost each probationer well over Rs. 1,000 a year.

A simple aspect of the academy's training affecting the entire course was the daily riding requirement which necessitated arising at 4:30 A.M. This was traditional because the district officer formerly made his tours on horseback, a use of horses which is no longer made. However, government felt strongly about continuing riding for several reasons: it provided vigorous physical exercise, it developed command presence and poise, and it is a unique aspect of Muslim culture of the Punjab and the Frontier. Riding was an expensive luxury, and it certainly connoted identification with feudal aristocracy and the leisured, land-owning classes. East Pakistani tended to be its most persistent critics. Whatever the relative merits of riding, it has certainly been part of the tradition of the area—i.e., of West Pakistan. Probably this is the reason why it has been perpetuated as an institution and has become sustained by a rationale after the fact. One eminent civil servant probably correctly identified the spirit behind the institution when he said that the only reason CSP officers ride horses is because there aren't enough elephants to go around.

Early rising and riding, excellent for physical discipline, produced a physical exhaustion which mitigated against study. The schedule was arranged so that there were lectures every morning without interruption until a late morning tea break. Given this program of activities, research by the probationers and extended study were impossible because of lack of time. Some adjustments were made in this format in 1961 and 1962. Seminars in comparative administration were conducted by an American resident professor, and short research assignments were found to be possible. Judged in terms of a professional school of administration comparable to the École Nationale d'Administration, the Civil Service Academy in Pakistan is likely to be disappointing. There is little likelihood of its becoming a professional school of such high character until the state of higher education so improves that disciplined, responsible graduates with rigorous course training come from the universities. The academy thus fills the weakness in physical rigor of the universities, and in the process it expands somewhat the intellectual and cultural horizons of the probationers.

It must also be kept in mind that the primary, immediate, objective of the academy is the training of district officers, not secretariat executives.[118] The admininstration of districts and divisions is regarded as one of the primary responsibilities of the CSP. Table 21 indicates that in 1964, 51 per cent of the districts were headed by CSP officers. Table 23 shows that from 1951 to 1964, from 22 to 34 per cent of the entire CSP cadre was engaged in district and division administration. This responsibility may diminish in paramountcy in years ahead; but certainly no diminution of this responsibility is now anticipated by the government. After completion of the nine-month course at the Civil Service Academy, all probationers are sent to districts for an additional year as assistant commissioners. After the field training, one or two in each batch may be assigned to secretariat work, but the majority will be in district work for the next decade or so of their lives. This close association with district administration also determines the character of academy training. District work requires somewhat more attention to physical conditioning than to research in intellectual problems. Finally, those who defend the curriculum of the academy point out that research and instruction in professional administration are more appropriate at a later than an early stage in the administrator's career. Such training is provided for by the Administrative Training policy of 1961. Under this policy, senior assistant commissioners about to be given full charge of a district are trained at one of the three national institutes of public administration.

The academy also seeks to weld probationers of divergent social, economic, and ethnic backgrounds into a corporate group

118. See Mirza Rafiq Inayat, "The Civil Service Academy," in Inayatullah (ed.), *Bureaucracy and Development in Pakistan* (Peshawar, 1963), pp. 399–416.

with its own *élan* and sense of tradition. In this regard, some difficulties with respect to Bengalis and probationers from West Pakistan are invariably experienced with each new batch. Residence and common dining, of course, are required. Very few probationers are married. The one or two married men in each batch cannot live outside the academy and can visit with their wives only occasionally. The net result of these physical attributes and curriculum format is a matrix in which corporate *élan* and traditions are diffused with remarkable success. It is, perhaps, a tribute to this success that detractors of academy training claim that probationers after completing the academy course no longer behave like Pakistani.

The directorship of the academy was always held by a former ICS officer of considerable distinction and seniority. The first incumbent was G. Mueenuddin, who later became establishment secretary. He was followed by A. K. Malik, later principal of the Administrative Staff College. From 1951 until 1959 the director was Geoffrey Burgess, a British ICS officer. In 1959 and 1960 Mian Aminuddin, a distinguished retired ICS officer, headed the academy. He was succeeded in 1961 by Agha Abdul Hamid, who held the position until his appointment as chairman of the Central Public Service Commission in 1965. The distinction of the academy has been due in no small measure to the high rank and uncommon ability of the men who have served as director. A deputy director was also on the resident staff, and usually both he and the director carried on much of the instruction. A former public prosecutor served as law lecturer and resided on the premises. Other instruction was carried on by visiting lecturers in economics, public administration, and Islamiat.

Starting in 1960, "development" subjects began to occupy a more significant place in the curriculum. Law, which formerly accounted for nearly 75 per cent of the curriculum, was gradually reduced to about 35 per cent. This change was largely a consequence of a decision of the cabinet made in 1959 as part of a program to "reorientate the civil servants' outlook."[119] The stu-

119. Text of this decision accessible in G. Ahmed Committee Report—1961, p. 348.

dents spent an average of thirty-six hours a week in the classroom attending lectures—about three times the classroom hours of American undergraduate and graduate students. This classroom schedule made it virtually impossible for the students to do research, write papers, or even do much reading. The allocation of time in 1962 was as follows:

Subject	Hours per week
Land Revenue Systems	4
Public Administration	7
(Theory—2)	
(District Administration—3)	
(Management—2)	
Development Economics	3
Law	11
(Penal Code—2)	
(Code of Criminal Procedure—7)	
(Law of Evidence—2)	
Islamiat	2
Debate, Current Affairs, and Special	
Lectures	3
Riding	3
Games	3
	36

Some changes have been made since 1962, but the curriculum is substantially the same. A resident American adviser gave instruction in public administration from 1960 to 1962 and was replaced in 1963 by several members of the staff of the National Institute of Public Administration (Lahore) who gave series of lectures. In 1964 an American Fulbright professor gave instruction in development economics. Also in 1964 the practice of having two batches of probationers in residence simultaneously was started, and a new classroom was added to the academy to accommodate the second batch. The junior batch is the group of new recruits; the senior batch is made up of those who have already completed the nine-month course and have had some training in the districts. They return to the academy for seminars and to relate their district experience to theoretical problems in administration. Except for the two-year interlude when a full-time American adviser was at the academy, the influence of American administrative doctrine and practice was sporadic rather than sustained, since before and after this time there were several different guest lecturers rather than resident faculty members.

Probationers are not actually confirmed in the CSP until they are successful in a final "passing-out" examination administered by the Central Public Service Commission. The proportion of candidates passing this examination cannot be precisely established from the published record. The Central Public Service Commission has published reports for only some years since 1947, and many of the published reports do not indicate the degree of success in the final examination. From the available documents which report this information, we know that ten of nineteen probationers passed in the 1953 batch, eight of fifteen in the 1952 batch, sixteen of twenty-five in the 1960 batch, and that an unspecified number failed the language examinations in the 1949 batch. Since probationers have four chances to pass, the examination has not usually been taken seriously. In its 1962 report, the commission expressed concern about this fact and considered changing the rules to take stringent measures against those "who do not take their . . . examinations seriously and against those who prove incapable of passing their examination in three attempts. [120] In practice, few CSP probationers (none to this writer's knowledge) have ever been released from service during the probationary period. "Grace marks" are added to their scores by the commission, and by stretching the final examination into several instalments, all manage to pass eventually. The prevailing attitude in government is that the initial recruitment procedure is so highly competitive and so fairly administered that the successful candidates must be good men. It is left to the academy to maintain a high level of performance through internal discipline. The final examination is not regarded highly enough to be used as grounds for dismissal. Underlying this rationale, however, is concern for political repercussions consequent to the dismissal of any probationer. Such dismissal would immediately change re-

120. Central Public Service Commission, *Annual Report for the Year 1962*, p. 18.

gional representation in the service and would become a volatile political issue. This is undoubtedly a serious risk, but its consequence is a feeling among all probationers that once they are recruited into the service tenure is permanent without regard to academic performance.

The final determination of seniority on the gradation list is based on three factors: (1) marks achieved on the CSS competitive exam (1,400 maximum), (2) a rating not to exceed 500 marks given by the director of the Civil Service Academy on the basis of performance during the nine-month course, and (3) the marks not exceeding 1,000 obtained on the final "passing-out" examination administered by the Central Public Service Commission. The aggregate of these three sources of marks determines seniority, on the basis of which advancement in the service is made until a person becomes eligible for a selection post, to which assignment is made by a selection board.

A serious effort has been made to change the outlook of the CSP so that the cadre would be less concerned with pomp and circumstance and more concerned with practical problems of a development nature at local levels of government. To this end, as part of their field training, probationers have been sent to the two academies for rural development. The aim was to inculcate in them the spirit of the community development movement. Typically, this assignment has been of a few weeks' duration. The probationers usually look upon the development academies with disdain and get little chance to immerse themselves in the ethos of community development work, which is essentially a shirt-sleeve, rice-roots operation, quite different in nature from the training at the academy. A move was made to have each batch of probationers spend several months at the Pakistan Military Academy at Kakul where they would receive training identical to that of the army cadets. The 1962 batch was sent to Kakul, but they protested so vehemently and exerted such political pressure that the scheme was abandoned. Their objections were that they were older and better-educated than the cadets (who are high school graduates) and that the physical training and military discipline were not pertinent to their careers in the CSP. This incident is important as an index of the immense power and prestige of the CSP. Under a martial law regime, a group of some twenty-five young men, ordered to military training for a few months, succeeded in having this training scheme abandoned. This episode suggests that the forces of elitism are remarkably powerful in the bureaucracy of Pakistan. The CSP has been able to maintain its elitist quality probably more as a result of training at the Civil Service Academy than as a consequence of any other single factor or group of factors.

Assignment of Elite Cadre Officers

The role of a centrally recruited, centrally controlled higher civil service in the power relations of central and provincial governments is crucial. Within wide limits, constitutional allocations of legislative power, discussed earlier in this chapter, can be molded by the role of the CSP officers posted to crucial positions throughout the bureaucratic system. Soon after independence, a decision was made and subsequently confirmed by the Cabinet Resolution of 1950 to maintain the CSP as a central, unified service. This was a departure from the pattern of the pre-partition Indian Civil Service, which was organized into provincial cadres. ICS officers who were allotted to a particular provincial cadre in pre-partition India remained in that one province throughout their careers unless deputed for service with the central government. This provincial deputation was deemed essential in India because of regional and especially linguistic differences among the varied provinces. It remains the system in effect in India today.[121] Until 1955 it would have been possible for Pakistan to adopt the provincial cadre pattern, since there were five provinces—East Pakistan, Sind, Baluchistan, the Punjab, and the North-Western Frontier Province. The unification of the last four in the single province of West Pakistan might have made a provincial cadre system somewhat less convenient.[122] The 1950

121. See Potter's chapter in this volume, p. 145.
122. The Establishment of West Pakistan Act, 1955, *Gazette of Pakistan, Extraordinary*, October 3, 1955.

record of the decision nicely states the objective of unity in administration:

> This decision has been taken in order to create a well-knit Civil Service for the whole of Pakistan, constituted and operated on a centralised basis, thereby increasing association between the various provinces and developing homogeneity in administration. The members of this Service, who shall be liable to be posted to any of the Provinces of the Dominion, will be administratively more useful to the Central as well as the Provincial Governments than if they belonged to Provincial cadres, because of the knowledge and experience they will acquire by serving in the Provinces of West Pakistan as well as in East Pakistan, and uniform standards of administration will also be achieved.[123]

The emergence of Bengali regionalism as a powerful political force, and especially its eruption in anomic form before martial law in 1958, made this policy difficult to implement. East Pakistan disliked having officers from West Pakistan assigned there, and there was particularly strong feeling with respect to officers who did not speak Bengali. Yet in 1959, as Table 9 suggests, there were probably only twenty-five ethnic and domiciled Bengali officers in the CSP with sufficient experience to hold twenty district posts, and fewer than ten officers with experience necessary for the twenty division and secretariat positions. While the central government did post non-Bengali officers to East Pakistan, it was usually cautious in this matter and posted fewer than the number needed. The gap was then closed by the provincial government's use of officers of the provincial civil service (executive), all of whom were Bengali. This accounts for the smaller proportion of CSP officers holding secretariat and division posts in East Pakistan (shown by Tables 7 and 20).

The strong feelings on this matter in East Pakistan were forcefully brought to the central government's attention by Zakir Hussain, a Bengali who was governor of East Pakistan in 1958. Subsequently, as minister of home affairs in the central government, he showed concern for this problem. The matter was considered at a governor's conference in 1959 and later by the

123. *Cabinet Resolution, 1950,* p. 1.

Administrative Reorganisation Committee. The committee recommended to the cabinet a modification of the 1960 policy, which was essentially a compromise between a centralized service and provincialized cadres.[124] It reaffirmed the need for control of the CSP by the central government and for CSP officers to have experience in both wings of Pakistan. It then suggested that all officers should remain in one province for training and service for five years and then serve in the other province for three years; but the central government was to retain the power to assign all CSP officers to the center or to each of the provinces. H. A. Majid, finance secretary, dissented from this view, saying that the Cabinet Resolution of 1950 was better suited to Pakistan's needs.[125] The government did not accept the Administrative Reorganisation Committee's advice nor did it concur in the Majid dissent. At a governors' conference on July 1, 1959, it decided to "provincialize" the CSP.[126] The decision reaffirmed that the central government "should have first claim on the services of CSP officers" but that those recruited after 1959 would be assigned to provinces on the basis of personal choice, domicile, and service requirements. The decision also instructed that an officer is not to be kept in a province other than his home province more than three years, and after thus serving, he will be transferred to his home province unless he requests otherwise. This 1960 "provincialization" accommodates to the needs of Bengalis whose cultural homogeneity is such that residence outside of East Pakistan or marriage with a non-Bengali may involve personal difficulty. Over a period of years, the effect of this policy will be that Bengali CSP officers will probably staff all levels of the East Pakistan government almost exclusively and will serve in the central government for short periods. This may serve to weaken one of the strongest unifying forces in Pakistan, but under the political circumstances of strong Bengali consciousness, it is doubtful if the government can pursue any other acceptable policy.

When posted in the provinces, CSP officers come under the

124. G. Ahmed Committee Report—1961, p. 315.
125. *Ibid.*, p. 316.
126. *Ibid.*, p. 317.

operational control of the provincial governor. Specifically, this means that responsibility is vested in the governor who is appointed by the president. But immediate control is delegated to the chief secretary, who is always a CSP officer. The pattern of assignments to both the central government and provincial secretariats suggests the power of the CSP. According to Composition and Cadre Rules of 1954, as amended, two-thirds of the posts of secretary, joint secretary, and deputy secretary in the central government are to be filled by CSP officers. Table 24 reveals for 1964 (and the pattern has been more or less the same before and since that year) an even more interesting distribution. In the central government, there are now twenty-two divisions in the secretariat, each headed by a full or joint secretary. Some ministries have two divisions; others have none. When a ministry has no divisions, it is officially counted as a division itself, although its designation remains ministry. In addition to these twenty-two divisions, Table 24 includes the cabinet secretary and the principal secretary, both of whom are key presidential assistants.[127] It is not of concern here to determine if the two-thirds quota specified in the Cadre Rules has been exceeded or unfilled. Since the quota is based on two ranks below that of full secretary, this cannot be determined from Table 24. But it is important to note that twenty-two of the twenty-nine (76 per cent) units in the secretariat are headed by CSP officers, of whom sixteen (73 per cent) are ICS officers. We find 71 per cent of the key secretariat posts held by CSP officers in West Pakistan and 61 per cent in East Pakistan. In local government, Tables 20 and 21 show that 75 per cent of the divisions and 51 per cent of the districts are headed by CSP officers. The same data recompiled in different form in Table 22 suggests a concentration of CSP officers in the central government and a progressive diminution of CSP influence as the levels descend in hierarchy.

---

127. In effect, the cabinet secretary is the chief-of-staff for all secretaries, The G. Ahmed Committee felt that he did not have high enough status to carry out this function effectively, and recommended that the post of secretary general be revived to give the cabinet secretary a status clearly higher than that of other secretaries. The government rejected this suggestion and ruled that the cabinet secretary should continue in the same status. *Ibid.*, p. 183.

Thus, in 1964, 89 per cent of central government secretaries were CSP officers, but only 66 per cent of provincial secretaries, 75 per cent of division commissioners, and 51 per cent of the district officers, were members of the CSP. The regularity of the diminution is distorted somewhat by the pattern in East Pakistan, where the greater availability of young Bengali CSP officers has raised the proportion of district officers, and the scarcity of senior Bengali officers has lowered the proportion of secretariat officers. Although Tables 20, 21, and 22 are for assignments in 1964 only, the pattern has been very much the same for earlier years, except that the proportion of CSP officers was somewhat larger.

The pattern of assignments of CSP officers can be analyzed in

Table 20. *Divisions in Provinces Showing Commissionerships Held by CSP Officers, 1964*

Province	Number of divisions	Number of divisions headed by CSP officer[a]	Percentage headed by CSP officer
West Pakistan	12	10 (2)	83.3
East Pakistan	4	2 (0)	50.0
Totals	16	12 (2)	75.0

[a] Figures in parentheses indicate the number of CSP officers who are former ICS officers.

Source: Computed from *Gradation List of the Civil Service of Pakistan* (*corrected up to 1st January, 1964*).

Table 21. *Districts in Provinces Showing District Officers' Positions Held by CSP Officers, 1964*

Province	Number of districts	Number of districts headed by CSP officer[b]	Percentage headed by CSP officer
West Pakistan	54[a]	27	50
East Pakistan	20	11	55
Totals	74	38	51.4

[a] Includes eight political agencies
[b] No officer in charge of a district is a former ICS officer.

Source: Computed from *Gradation List of the Civil Service of Pakistan* (*corrected up to 1st January, 1964*); also interviews and correspondence.

another instructive way. Using the available annual gradation lists for the fifteen years from 1951 to 1966, the proportion of officers placed in different categories of assignments can be determined. These data have been compiled in Table 23 on the following pages. Viewed from the point of view of the CSP cadre as an entity, it is clear that district and division administration at any given time absorbs from one-quarter to nearly one-third of the cadre's strength. This proportion has fluctuated by about 10 per cent during the fifteen years under review. The fluctuations have been irregular, but a steady downward trend seems indicated. The proportion has shrunk steadily by 12 per cent since 1961 and irregularly by nearly 10 per cent since 1954. This may indicate a gradual withdrawal from district administration as the

Table 22. *CSP and ICS Incumbency of Posts by Level of Government, 1964*

Level of government	Percentage posts held by CSP	Percentage CSP posts held by former ICS officers
Central government secretary[a]	89	88
Provincial government secretary	66	27
Division commissioner	75	17
District officer (deputy commissioner)	51	0

[a] Only the President's Secretariat and ministries proper are included.
Source: This table is a summary of data compiled in Tables 20 and 21, above, and 23 below.

primary responsibility of the CSP and a slow transfer of this task to officers of the provincial civil services. But it is still too early to venture a prediction on the basis of this slight trend. The proportion of officers posted to provincial governments has been fairly steady, hovering at about one-fifth of the total strength. The proportion in training is fairly high and has remained steady, about one-fifth of the cadre being so assigned. This is a reflection of the emphasis Pakistan has given to administrative training and also shows that the CSP has clearly assumed the leadership in controlling training programs. The number of CSP officers in training staff posts has risen steadily since 1961 when the national institutes of public administration were opened. Table 23 shows nine officers so engaged in 1966. This is clearly a new activity for the cadre and one which is likely to utilize more of its total strength. The proportion assigned to the central government secretariat has wavered during the period by as much as 6 per cent, and it appears to have shrunk by nearly 5 per cent during the last three years. This trend is somewhat misleading, however, since training responsibilities and assignment to government corporations, both predominantly central government activities, have taken an increasing portion of the cadre strength. In reality, what has occurred is a redistribution of CSP assignments within the central government, with a movement in the direction of positions of more power. This is further indicated by the steady diminution in the number of CSP officers assigned to section officer posts. Originally intended to utilize both CSP and non-CSP personnel, these positions appear to be filled increasingly by non-CSP officers. The CSP has maintained its hold in the judiciary, although there has been a perceptible shift in its level of placement. Its representation on the Supreme Court has been steady, but High Court judgeships have declined from seven in 1952 to one in 1966. The number of lower-level magistrates has increased perceptibly, and this may mean a gradual increase of CSP representation at higher levels as magistrates are gradually promoted within the judicial apparatus. The increase in judicial work for the CSP reflects a decision made at the governors' conference on February 14, 1959, to form a judicial branch of the CSP. The principle is to reserve 10 per cent of the senior judicial posts for the CSP. Transfers to the judicial branch are made at the rate of one or two officers each year until the reserved posts are filled. As this policy is carried out, the intimate organic relationship between the executive and judicial branches which existed under British rule and continued in Pakistan after independence will be further strengthened.[128] A significant finding of Table 23 is

128. There are two aspects of the conjunction of judicial and executive functions as related to the CSP cadre. The first of these is the assignment of judicial powers to district officers and the placing of lower courts under the district officers' control

the gradual increase in the number of officers assigned to government corporations. Like control of training, this represents a new field of activity for the CSP.

To summarize findings of the series of tables on assignments of officers, we find a dynamic exploration of new fields of activity, notably training and corporate management. There is also evidence of a shift upward to the central government, and within the central government another shift toward higher positions. Whether this suggests that the CSP will become increasingly a central government cadre, abandoning provincial and local administration to the provincial civil services, remains to be seen.

Elite Cadre Organization

Since independence and until the very present, the tightly knit corporate nature of the CSP has been attacked from several different sources on several grounds. It is doubtful if any issue in Pakistan's internal affairs has commanded such sustained attention as has the status of the CSP. Intemperate outbursts have been directed against its exclusivity and its alleged arrogance, and debates of the National Assembly are replete with such references against the cadre. As recently as 1962 Maulvi Akhtar Ali, a West Pakistani member of the National Assembly, said that "All the hatred in the hearts of the people against any Government is due mainly to the self-conceited and haughty behaviour of these [CSP] functionaries."[129] When the Pay and Services Commission

rather than under the High Court. This practice has been widely objected to by the legal profession. See *Report of the Law Reform Commission 1958-59* (Karachi, 1959), pp. 25 ff.; *Pakistan Times*, September 13, 1961, p. 4; *Nine Point Manifesto and Joint Declaration of the Combined Opposition Party*, Point 1, (e). Despite this criticism the practice is not likely to be curtailed, especially since separation of judicial and executive functions, included as a principle of state policy in the 1956 Constitution, has been omitted from the 1962 Constitution. The second aspect, the assignment of CSP officers permanently to the judiciary, has not been so widely opposed. The Law Commission approved it in principle with the suggestion that assignment be made before an officers' fifth year of service and that judicial assignment be made more attractive to CSP officers. Enayetur Rahman and Mahmud Ali Qasuri, members of the commission, dissented and proposed the creation of a separate Judicial Service modeled after the CSP. *Report of the Law Reform Commission 1958-59*, pp. 133, 136-139, 141.

129. National Assembly of Pakistan, *Debates*, June 20, 1962, pp. 221-222. An earlier sample of similar criticism can be found in a speech of Maulvi Farid Ahmad of Chittagong in *ibid.*, February 15, 1957, pp. 434-435, part of which is reprinted in Appendix 4 in *Research on the Bureaucracy of Pakistan*.

was holding hearings in 1960 and 1961, the press published a number of letters urging admission of officers of other services into the CSP or the unification of all services. The Provincial Civil Servants Association has spoken out against the failure of the CSP to take in provincial service officers.[130] Ironically, the same sources of bitter criticism have often proposed the creation of other cadres modeled after the CSP. Thus, although many lawyers are against the CSP as an institution, the Law Commission nevertheless proposed a judicial service patterned after the CSP. A scientific service and a medical service have also been proposed. A different kind of criticism has been that the CSP places the generalist executive in positions of power above technical experts, even in agencies in which technical matters are dominant. This aspect of the CSP was criticized by Rowland Egger and Bernard Gladieux, who were among the first of American public administration experts to survey administration in Pakistan.[131]

Some of these criticisms have been met by moderate adjustments in the bureaucratic apparatus, but except for the Cornelius Report's alleged recommendations discussed later in this essay, no agency of the Government of Pakistan has suggested the abolition of the CSP as an elite cadre or its modification by extensive lateral entry. G. Ahmed, who was chairman of the Planning Commission when Gladieux submitted his report to that body, neither then nor subsequently favored abolishing or drastically modifying the elite cadre concept or its important feature of reservation of posts throughout the bureaucratic structure. Questioned on this by the press, "he disagreed with the view that the Civil Service [of] Pakistan was too powerful, or that it needed

130. See, for example, the article, "Snobbery in the Services," by "Profundis" in the *Pakistan Times,* March 11, 1962, p. iv of the magazine section. "Profundis" is reliably said to be a civil servant of high rank. See also letters to the editor, August 1, 1959, p. 4; August 2, 1959, p. 4; September 6, 1961, p. 4; October 1, 1961, p. 6; December 27, 1961, p. 4; January 18, 1962, p. 4; January 25, 1962, p. 4; February 18, 1962, p. 6; July 19, 1962, p. 4.

131. While Egger expressed some admiration for the CSP, he advocated a unified Civil Service, asserting that the "inflated notion of the importance of one service over another . . . is an acquired characteristic which can be disacquired rather readily, especially when it is clearly demonstrated that no one service, or group of services, is the nursery of all the heirs to administrative empires." Egger, *op. cit.,* p. 57. See also Bernard Gladieux, *Reorientation of Pakistan Government for National Development* (Karachi, 1955), pp. 100 ff.

disbandment and substitution. 'What will you substitute it with?'" he asked, and added that "'any new service would also have to carry out the task entrusted to it.'"[132] This attitude of G. Ahmed, now ambassador to the United States, is especially revealing. As a former member of the Indian Police Service and never a member of the CSP, it cannot be said that he was defending his own cadre. Earlier and for a longer period of time than almost any single Pakistani official of high rank, he came in contact as chairman of the Planning Commission with anti-elitist views vigorously presented by American advisers. Yet he did not share the radical revisionist views espoused by many Americans. Subsequently, as chairman of the Administrative Reorganisation Committee, he had ample opportunity to suggest abolition of the cadre but did not. This is indicative of the near unanimity in higher government circles on the issue of maintaining the CSP in essentially the same pattern.

Changes made in the CSP organization relate to monopoly on generalist posts and reorientation of outlook. The question of generalist posts has been approached by creating an Economic Pool whose officers would serve in the ministries of finance, commerce, and industries.[133] This proposal, made by the G. Ahmed Committee, contemplated that approximately 125 positions would be filled by Economic Pool officers. Since 60 per cent of the Economic Pool officers are drawn from the CSP and 40 per cent from other Central Superior Services, this would make possible the appointment of non-CSP officers to posts formerly reserved for the CSP. In 1964 this had not yet occurred, since, as Table 23 shows, the secretary of each of these ministries was a CSP and former ICS officer. The G. Ahmed Committee also recommended that the Ministry of Education and the health division of the Ministry of Health and Social Welfare be manned exclusively by technical officers. As a consequence, said the committee, these ministries would become purely technical organizations. While this may have been done at levels below the secretary, it had not

132. As reported in *Dawn*, January 27, 1961, p. 1.
133. Composition of the Economic Pool and text of relevant cabinet decisions may be found in G. Ahmed Committee Report—1961, pp. 323–337.

affected the secretaryship by 1964. In fact, in 1965, the non-CSP retiring secretary of education was replaced by a CSP officer who had been secretary of the National Assembly. Reorientation of outlook was to be accomplished through training at the Civil Service Academy and through the introduction of development economics courses in the academy curriculum. This has been commented upon elsewhere in this chapter.[134]

Proposals have been advanced in Pakistan to train probationers of all Central Superior Services together in a foundational course comparable to the IAS course in India. The Pakistan Police Commission, which submitted its report to the cabinet in May, 1962, is said to have recommended that recruits taken into the Police Service of Pakistan be trained with CSP probationers at the Civil Service Academy. Some officials in the Ministry of Finance have long wanted the Audit and Accounts Service and other finance service probationers to have common training with the CSP. Since the Police Service recruits fewer than ten officers a year and the Audit and Accounts Service annually recruits about fifteen officers, such common training might have been feasible if the physical facilities of the academy were expanded. However, such proposals for common training have not been accepted. On the other hand, a revealing relationship has been worked out with the Pakistan Foreign Service (PFS), a relatively small cadre with a sanctioned strength of 172 officers and an annual intake of about three officers. A proposal had been made to the Administrative Reorganisation Committee to amalgamate the PFS and the CSP.[135] This proposal was objected to by the Ministry of Foreign Affairs and Commonwealth Relations, which maintained that the special training and "finesse" required for diplomatic service were not necessarily the same qualities as those required for district administration and that a merger would be "a retrogressive step of the extreme type." The Administrative Reorganisation Committee proposed a compromise "merger," which is an interesting clue to the immense prestige of the CSP and its own absorptive

134. See above, pp. 289–298.
135. Text of this proposal and of the committee's recommendation is available in G. Ahmed Committee Report—1961, pp. 318–320.

capacity. The PFS would be a separate wing of the CSP to be known as the Civil Service of Pakistan (Foreign Branch). Officers for both services would be recruited together and would receive common training at the academy for one year, in the field for a second year, and in districts for three years. After these five years of training, CSP officers judged most suitable would be selected for the foreign branch and would then be trained (as PFS officers have been since independence) at the Fletcher School of Law and Diplomacy in the United States. Thereafter, they would be attached for a month to the United States Department of State and the British Foreign Office. The committee also recommended that half the posts of ambassador and a third of the posts of minister be open to senior officers of the CSP not in the foreign branch or to non-career diplomats. The finance secretary, H. A. Majid, filed a dissent to this recommendation, asserting unequivocally that the cadre of the PFS is large enough to conduct its recruitment and training separately. He maintained also that a delay of five years in sending young PFS officers for duty abroad was not wise. The government postponed deciding on the issues raised in the contrary views presented to the Administrative Reorganisation Committee. Subsequently, some of the committee's recommendations were accepted. PFS officers are now appointed from the CSP batch after training at the Civil Service Academy.

Lateral entry in the CSP, or *ad hoc* recruitment as it is officially called, which accounts for nearly 40 per cent of the IAS in India[136] but for .5 per cent of the CSP, was considered at length by the Administrative Reorganisation Committee, but it was virtually rejected. The foreign minister and other members of the cabinet had suggested the possibility of bringing into government qualified persons from business or other non-governmental activities. The committee conceded the right of government to employ any person it deemed suitable but cautioned that *ad hoc* appointments should be temporary and officers thus appointed should be treated as supernumerary officers rather than as integral members of the service. It cautioned also against appointments of business-

136. See Potter's chapter in this volume, esp. Table 5, p. 155.

men who upon leaving service might "make illegitimate use of . . . knowledge of Government policies for the benefit of [the] permanent employer." The committee then surveyed the strength of each of the Central Superior Services and concluded that there would be no deficiency of officers which could not be met by regular recruitment through the competitive examination. It also surveyed the role of the General Administrative Reserve (GAR), a group of officers appointed from other services after independence and posted to assignments usually held by CSP officers. This had been Pakistan's solution to a shortage of officers in the elite cadre, a solution which India met by extensive *ad hoc* recruits in the IAS. But the GAR in Pakistan was never considered part of the CSP, and GAR officers were not appointed to posts above the rank of joint secretary to the central government. The committee noted that no new appointments to the GAR had been made for some years, and that since the strength of the cadre was fast diminishing, its officers should not be appointed to the CSP. The final decision of the government was that there should be no *ad hoc* recruitment to the central services, except for certain engineers and telegraph and wireless service officers, army officers recruited for the Police Service, and retired provincial service officers who might be used in East Pakistan as additional district officers. But none of these *ad hoc* appointments involved integrating such officers into the CSP cadre.[137]

It is probable that the only high-level official effort to change the whole concept of the role of an elite cadre and the rigid exclusiveness of the CSP is found in the recommendations of the second Pay and Service Commission headed by Chief Justice A. R. Cornelius. The terms of reference of this commission authorized it to review the structure, sources and methods of recruitment, and the establishments of all grades of the civilian services under the central government.[138] While these terms of reference are a matter of public knowledge, the three-hundred-page report itself, which was submitted to the President on June 1, 1962, has

137. See G. Ahmed Committee Report—1961, pp. 338–349, for an outline of the main issues and for final decisions of the government.
138. Ministry of Finance Resolution No. 2524—Admn. III/59, published in *Gazette of Pakistan, Extraordinary,* August 31, 1959.

not been released to the public; hence, its contents cannot be discussed. The rather scanty public knowledge of this report is derived entirely from the press or debates in the National Assembly. Press reports indicate that the commission interviewed about four hundred government departments and services and that the commission favored creation of cadres of specialists, technicians, and generalists.[139] The finance minister, M. Shoaib, had reported in 1961 that the recommendations may be "revolutionary in nature."[140] There was considerable stir among officers of the CSP who felt that their position as the dominant generalist cadre would be changed by the commission's proposals. The CSP Association presented a long memorandum to the commission, defending the role of a closed generalist cadre. Another clue to the contents of the commission's report can be found in the official statement of Chief Justice Cornelius upon presentation of the completed report to the President:

They [principles of policy in the 1962 Constitution] have operated as a powerful aid to us in our endeavour to eliminate from the body of the Public Service the ingredients of differentiations and following the dictates of the new Constitution, to replace them by a calculus of integration. In the pursuit of equality, we have attempted to provide a means of eradicating from within the Public Service the remnant of artificial aristocracy left behind by British rule. . . .[141]

In a subsequent address given in Lahore on September 1, 1962, Chief Justice Cornelius had pursued this same theme of infusing the bureaucratic apparatus with the ideology of equality of opportunity found in Islam and in the 1962 Constitution. In the address he stated that "the national test of equality for the determination of the status of two persons engaged in work of the same or equivalent character would appear to turn on the possession of necessary qualifications coupled with the capacity to produce results."[142] This statement was widely interpreted as referring to the reservation of posts for the CSP cadre and for failure to admit provincial service officers performing functions

139. *Pakistan Times*, August 3, 1961, p. 10.
140. As reported in *ibid.*
141. The full text of this statement is reported in *ibid.*, June 2, 1962, p. 1.
142. The full text of this address is available in *Research on the Bureaucracy of Pakistan*, Appendix 12.

identical to those performed by the CSP. In the National Assembly, where persistent questioning tried but failed to get the report released for debate, several comments asserted that the Cornelius Report recommended unification of the services and a basic change in service structure.[143] A final clue which suggests that the commission may have recommended a basic change in structure comes from a statement of President Ayub announcing the decision taken on the commission's report.[144] He stated that the commission had recommended "radical changes" which would have redesigned the existing scheme of services. He felt that such changes should not be made because the nation's development required continuity in functions and organization of the services.

Thus, what we assume to be a formidable effort to revamp the service structure met with even more formidable opposition within the executive branch. The concept of the elite cadre remains stronger than ever in Pakistan. The few lateral entrants have almost all retired. The CSP cadre is more cohesive than ever before, its capacity to absorb new positions of power has apparently been enhanced, and its opponents have been forced to retreat.

III. Institutional Restraints on Bureaucratic Behavior

Legislative Oversight

Theoretically, the legislature has some supervisory control over administrative action derived from its general authority to enact legislation. The enactment of legislation carries with it the power to investigate the need for such enactment and hence the efficacy of implementation of existing legislation bearing on proposed enactment. This is an undisputed power that is well-established in constitutional systems. From it flows the power of legislatures to investigate administrative actions to determine if such actions are in consonance with legislation and to define in such legislation

143. National Assembly of Pakistan, *Debates*, December 5, 1962, p. 413; March 12, 1963, pp. 196–199; April 13, 1963, p. 1807.
144. *President's Speeches and Statements*, VI, 188.

standards of execution. This is the concept of delegated legislation, again well-established in constitutional systems.

The legislatures at both the central and provincial levels in Pakistan have only begun to be concerned with providing that degree of surveillance necessary in a presidential form of government which assumes trifurcation of powers. It has already been shown that the line between central and provincial subjects is by no means fixed.[145] Established procedures for legislative surveillance might easily be vitiated by moving a subject from one ambit to another. The potential use of the executive ordinance-making power to circumvent the legislature also makes hazy the legislative focus on the administrative scene, as was earlier shown.[146] Legislative power is also reduced by Article 27 of the 1962 Constitution which empowers the president to veto any bill of the legislature[147] and by the absence of any provision in the Constitution for the legislatures to confirm either appointment or dismissal of ministers. These actions take place entirely within executive discretion. The Constitution Commission had cautioned against the executive veto and had recommended legislative confirmation of appointment and dismissal of ministers,[148] but these legislative checks did not appear in the Constitution which the President promulgated.

While it is possible in new states for the legislatures to exercise effective control over administration, as do the Estimates Committee and other committees of the Lok Sabha in India,[149] this check has not yet fully emerged in Pakistan.[150] The National

145. See above, pp. 211–220.
146. See above, pp. 230–242.
147. The veto power is not quite absolute. The National Assembly may reconsider a vetoed bill twice, and if still vetoed, a referendum of the Electoral College by majority vote may result in presidential assent.
148. Shahabuddin Report, pp. 55, 59–61.
149. See Potter's chapter in this volume, esp. pp. 163 ff.
150. It is a curiosity worthy of note that nowhere in its report does the Constitution Commission mention the committee system of the United States Congress in which lies much of the genius of executive-legislative balance of power. Yet the commission made copious reference to the government of the United States and devoted fully a third of its excellent report to three issues, (1) parliamentary *vs.* presidential form, (2) unitary *vs.* federal form, and (3) extent of presidential powers, in all of which American experience is rich and the recorded scholarship vast and indispensable. The predicament of the commission was like that of the governmental system subsequently established, i.e., it was drawn by habit and intellectual contact to British experience and doctrine even while

Assembly has created a committee apparatus consisting of both standing and select committees.[151] The standing committees parallel ministries and divisions; except for the committee on public accounts, each consists of six members elected by the National Assembly. A link with the executive branch reminiscent of earlier parliamentary style is maintained by authorizing the secretary of a ministry to attend committee meetings as an expert adviser. A bill cannot be buried in committee, because upon expiration of whatever time limit has been set it may be referred to the

---

subscribing to American practice. The library the commission had at its immediate disposal was that of the West Pakistan Provincial Assembly, in whose building the commission had its headquarters. This library, like other official libraries in Pakistan, had few books dealing with American government. It was symptomatic of the lack of rapport with American scholarship and the low state of respect for it that the commission did not get help from American agencies in evaluating and getting access to standard American source material. Examination of the sources mentioned in the commission's report and consideration of the minimal sources one acquainted with American scholarship would use in drafting a constitution based largely on American principles are revealing. The report mentions thirteen books: Sir Ivor Jennings, *The Approach to Self-Government* (Cambridge, 1956); Arthur B. Keith, *The British Cabinet System* (London, 1939); James Bryce, *Modern Democracies* (New York, 1921); Herbert Morrison, *Government and Parliament* (London, 1954); Joan Coyne MacLean, *President and Congress: The Conflict of Powers* (New York, 1955); C. F. Strong, *Modern Political Constitutions* (New York, 1930); A. V. Dicey, *Introduction to the Study of Law and Constitution* (London, 1927); William Bennett Munro, *The National Government of the United States* (New York, 1937); James W. Garner, *Political Science and Government* (New York, 1935); Albert J. McCulloch, *Suffrage and its Problems* (Baltimore, 1929); Herman Finer, *Theory and Practice of Modern Government* (New York, 1932); and G. A. Campbell, *The Civil Service in Britain* (Middlesex, 1955). Of these only two can be said to be specialized studies of American government; five are comparative studies which include American government but are oriented more to British government; the remaining six deal with British government predominantly or exclusively. Although few political scientists would agree on any single list of books which might be useful, I would venture the following as illustrative of the scope of fundamental, useful works which might have been used by the Constitution Commission in its study of the three issues mentioned at the beginning of this note: Wilfred S. Binkley, *The President and Congress* (New York, 1947); Edward S. Corwin, *The Constitution and What It Means Today* (11th ed.; Princeton, 1964); Edward S. Corwin, *The President: Office and Powers* (New York, 1940); Clinton Rossiter, *The American Presidency* (New York, 1956); Harold Laski, *The American Presidency* (New York, 1940); Clarence Berdahl, *War Powers of the Executive in the United States* (Urbana, Ill., 1921); Max Farrand (ed.), *The Records of the Federal Convention, 1787* (3 vols.; New Haven, 1911); Harold Laski and Don K. Price, "The Parliamentary and Presidential Systems," in *Public Administration Review*, III (Autumn, 1943), 317–335, and IV (Autumn, 1944), 347–359. Papers and memoirs of Grover Cleveland, Theodore Roosevelt, Woodrow Wilson, Abraham Lincoln, Franklin Roosevelt, Harry Truman, and Dwight Eisenhower, and the Federalist Papers should also be included in the list.

151. The committee apparatus is prescribed in National Assembly of Pakistan, *Rules of Procedure* (Rawalpindi, 1963), pp. 26–32. Subjects assigned to standing committees are listed in Schedule III, pp. 47–66.

assembly by any member, minister, or parliamentary secretary. Rule 58(1) of Rules of Procedure requires that a bill be referred to the appropriate standing committee, which then reports to the National Assembly before final action is taken. Rule 58(2) provides that when a bill is submitted by the executive branch, the member-in-charge may move that Rule 58(1) be dispensed with. This is frequently done, presumably as a means of speeding consideration of bills. The motion to dispense with Rule 58(1) has often stirred the opposition, who view such dispensation as a device for circumventing the committee system. Chaudhry Fazal Elahi made an effective analysis of this in 1963, in which he contended that committee deliberation of bills was essential in a presidential system. But government bills, he asserted, are not usually submitted in time to permit committee actions:

if Government wants to follow the presidential system . . . they should not shirk the responsibility of entrusting . . . legislation to the Standing Committees. As many as nineteen Standing Committees have been constituted in this House and out of those nineteen Committee[s] I do not know if a single Committee has been called to deal with such a matter. . . . [The Government has] all the powers of the presidential system but so far as legislation is concerned they revert back to the parliamentary system.[152]

Select committees may be appointed by the assembly whenever a motion is adopted that a bill be referred to such a committee. Membership of select committees includes the minister concerned, the parliamentary secretary, the chairman of the standing committee concerned with the bill, the member-in-charge, and the minister of law. The composition of select committees links them to the executive and enables the executive branch under certain configurations of membership to control the committee. Neither select nor standing committees are provided with office space or clerical and research staff adequate to permit the gradual accretion of expertise. This places them at a disadvantage in relation to the executive branch.

Still another vestige of parliamentary government is the question period which takes place during the first hour of every

152. National Assembly of Pakistan *Debates*, March 9, 1963, pp. 131–132. I have transposed the order of the sentences quoted in the text.

meeting of the assembly. Questions may be both oral and written and may be directed to the minister, the parliamentary secretary, or to another member. Although this can be an effective device of control, unless there is a free press reporting widely on the questions and answers its effectiveness is limited. Further study of the National Assembly *Debates* thus far printed reveals that conflicting interpretations over central-provincial jurisdiction tend to limit the utility of the question period as an institution of control.[153]

Another organic link to a parliamentary system is the institution of parliamentary secretary provided for by Article 35 of the 1962 Constitution. Parliamentary secretaries must be members of the National Assembly and may not exceed the number of divisions in the executive branch. As parliamentary secretaries they are responsible to the president, yet they remain voting members of the National Assembly. There are twenty-two divisions in the central secretariat, but only eighteen parliamentary secretaries were appointed in July, 1965. Several of them were in charge of two divisions. The position of parliamentary secretary is probably not less attractive because it carries with it a salary of Rs. 600 a month in addition to the Rs. 500 a month received by the secretary as a member of the National Assembly. Critics of the pattern of legislative-executive relations evolved under the 1962 Constitution point out that the appointment of parliamentary secretaries can easily be a political act to control the legislature. Appointments can be terminated at any time, and it is said that the president can appoint those who might oppose him or those who influence several other votes in the assembly. With an assembly whose membership is 156, the influence of up to twenty-two parliamentary secretaries can easily be the balance of power. Moreover, since the executive branch has exclusive control over the organization of its own secretariat, the number of divisions— hence, the number of parliamentary secretaries—may be increased without legislative approval. Critics also say that when the total number of parliamentary secretaries allowed are not appointed, the president then has freedom to make subsequent

153. See above, p. 226.

appointments as political exigencies seem to indicate. Whether such criticism of the parliamentary secretary as an institution is justified or not is not known since no careful study of its operation has been made.[154] Parliamentary secretaries deal only with parliamentary affairs rather than secretariat work and are supposed to represent the ministry in a public relations and information sense in the assembly. But the fact that they must submit to questioning on legislative matters relating to their ministries requires that they know a good deal of detail about the ministry's operations. Parliamentary secretaries are organized as a group under the leadership of the chief parliamentary secretary, who serves also as chief whip in the National Assembly and as parliamentary secretary in the Division of Parliamentary Affairs, Ministry of Law and Parliamentary Affairs. The position is an important means of co-ordinating the president's legislative program in the National Assembly.[155]

154. Nor has any comprehensive study yet been made of the legislatures in Pakistan. The intricate maze of relations between legislative, executive, and political functions of the parliamentary secretaries would be an unusually revealing source of insight into the operation of the presidential-parliamentary blend which has emerged in Pakistan. The possible political role of parliamentary secretaries has been regarded with suspicion by the opposition to the government in power. Former Prime Minister H. S. Suhrawardy, in a speech given in Jessore, October 11, 1962, allegedly accused the government of President Ayub Khan of appointing "dozens of parliamentary secretaries" even before legislatures were convened in 1962. The Bengali newspaper *Ittefaq* in its issue of October 12, 1962, as reproduced in the High Court decision cited below in this note, reported part of that speech as follows: "They [parliamentary secretaries] are directed to go from village to village and praise the Constitution and to give speeches and statements maligning Suhrawardy. Official statements manufactured in the Government workshops are being freely issued in their names whereas they themselves might be quite ignorant of those statements." In consequence of publishing Suhrawardy's speech which the provincial governor deemed to be prejudicial to public safety, the publisher of *Ittefaq* was directed to post security of Rs. 10,000 under terms of the East Pakistan Public Safety Ordinance of 1958. The High Court of East Pakistan subsequently voided the government order against the publisher (*Tofazzal Hossain v. Province of East Pakistan*, PLD 1965 Dacca 478). This judgment was supported by the Supreme Court (*Province of East Pakistan v. Tofazzal Hossain*, PLD 1965 SC 520).

155. The chief parliamentary secretary must also be a member of the National Assembly. This post, not provided for in the 1962 Constitution, was created by executive order of the President in 1962. The salary was fixed at Rs. 2,500 a month plus a monthly sumptuary allowance of Rs. 200. The chief parliamentary secretary is also entitled to free furnished residential accommodation and to other perquisites given a minister. When the post was created in 1962 there was no mention of the incumbent receiving the Rs. 500 monthly salary of a member of the National Assembly in addition to the Rs. 2,500 salary. Neither was there a specific prohibition against receiving a member's salary. The precise legal position of this matter remains indeterminate. In fact, however, the chief parliamentary secretary

Judicial Review

Probably in no Asian state inheriting the British bureaucratic tradition do we find the judiciary playing such an important role as in Pakistan. Its close relationship to the bureaucracy has several dimensions which have been developed in considerable detail elsewhere; hence, they will only be summarized here.[156] Before such a summary, however, some analysis of causes may be presented, building on data presented elsewhere but generalizing in a quite different way. It is a fruitful exercise in comparative analysis to speculate as to the causes generating this remarkable judicial activism in the case of Pakistan. India, Pakistan, Ceylon, Malaysia, and Burma all inherited the same traditions of British law, the same almost inviolable position of the civil service in the legal system, and the same uncommonly broad discretion awarded administrators functioning in what was essentially an administrative state. At first glance, it is easy to conclude that this eminence of the judiciary may be the consequence of Muslim civilization with its propensity to classify, codify, record, and accrete cases in the light of cumulative Qur'anic interpretation. Certainly this propensity is present. As Chief Justice S. M. Murshed wrote to the present author about Bengalis, "the generality of the people here are legal-minded." This has been observed by a variety of foreign analysts, including Sir Malcolm Darling who noted in the Punjab as well a "passion for litigation." But this "legal-mindedness" is also found in Burma, which is not predominantly Muslim, and in India among Hindus. And it is much less a conspicuous characteristic of Malaysia, which is

---

in 1965 had not drawn salary as a member of the National Assembly. The post of chief parliamentary secretary, which under the 1956 Constitution was equal to that of minister of state, is equal to that of deputy speaker of the National Assembly under the 1962 Constitution. (The data in this note are derived from letters dated October 4, 1965, and October 27, 1965, to the present author from Abd-Allah Zaheer-ud-Deen [Lal Mian], chief parliamentary secretary and chief whip, Government of Pakistan.)

156. See especially the chapter on legal research (pp. 244–310) and Appendices 10–15 in *Research on the Bureaucracy of Pakistan.* See also "Public Bureaucracy and Judiciary" and the author's "Pakistan: Constitutional Issues in 1964." (Full citation on p. 269, n. 104, above.)

predominantly Muslim. It is doubtful if this condition can be attributed entirely to Islam, although no doubt it is a factor.

It is equally tempting to attribute this condition to the large number of legal practitioners, who in their eagerness for employment seek litigation in every human incident and provoke that which they may not find. No doubt this is also a contributing cause, but hardly a decisive one. For example, in Burma, Guyot suggests ratios of one lawyer for every 10,383 persons and one lawyer for every 108 government employees. In Pakistan these ratios approximate one to 5,500 persons and one to fifty-five government employees.[157] Thus, Burma with about half the proportion of lawyers and with a predominantly Buddhist culture is also said to be a "litigious society." The evidence is sufficiently contradictory to suggest that although the size of the legal community may be operative in explaining this condition, there may be other factors as well.

The present author rather suspects that the principal reason lies in the fortuitous conjunction of three circumstances in the politico-juridical development of Pakistan. The first of these is the severe political instability over a period of several years which prevented the flourishing of institutions capable of infusing order and justice in the bureaucratic system. Legislatures scarcely had time to organize themselves when crisis seized them and dissolution was upon them. The industrial sector was not large enough to have spawned a strong trade-union movement; hence, no redress of internal bureaucratic grievances could be had from employees' unions as in Ceylon. Moreover, in West Pakistan the overarching presence of feudal and tribal values, premised essentially on a master-servant relationship, stood as an ideological deterrent to effective trade unionism. Nor did Whitley Councils develop as they did in Malaysia, probably because that country had an extra decade or so under British rule in which some earlier ideas of modern bureaucracy had a chance to flower. In the haste of

157. See Guyot's chapter (Chapter 6) in this volume, p. 360, n. 12, and *Research on the Bureaucracy of Pakistan*, pp. 249–260, esp. p. 254. These ratios are based on population estimates of 23,200,000 for Burma and 99,000,000 for Pakistan, and on government employment estimates of 242,000 for Burma and 995,000 for Pakistan.

partition, the trauma of its afterglow, and the disorder of its sequel, the bureaucracy of Pakistan could barely maintain itself and even less experiment with new means of employee representation. Hence, a natural vacuum was created into which the power of the juridical order flowed in obedience to the laws of nature. Secondly, the disarticulation caused by partition and especially by the large number of refugees who had to be integrated into the bureaucratic apparatus created the raw materials for litigation. An uncommon amount of distress was to be found, and with it an uncommon amount of injustice. Not only was this true in matters concerning the internal operation of the bureaucracy but in matters of external administrative law as well. For example, the administration of the Evacuee Property Act,[158] which regulated the award of properties of Hindu and Sikhs who had migrated to India in 1947 to Muslim refugees from India, involved the allocation of immense properties to at least a million refugees who had owned property in India. The administrative problems in the face of inadequate or nonexistent records aggravated by bad relations between the governments of India and Pakistan are staggering to the imagination. The potential for inequity and the actual incidence of inequities are equally staggering. Thirdly, the presence of men of intellectual eminence and great courage on the bench of the high courts and the Supreme Court of Pakistan is an important factor. Two of these were officers of the ICS, M. R. Kayani and A. R. Cornelius. Two more, S. M. Murshed and M. Munir, were from the bar. The erudition and courage of these men combined with the persistently and dangerously courageous stands of Shabir Ahmed made the judiciary of Pakistan from 1948 to 1965 an awesome institution. It legitimated martial law juridically, but it did not bow before it. It asserted and reasserted its prerogatives of judicial review against executive efforts to oust its jurisdiction in one area after another. In the end it triumphed, preserving against formidable odds the rule of law as learned from the British. It is doubtful that lesser men could have succeeded in this triumph of

158. Pakistan (Administration of Evacuee Property) Act XII of 1957 and its subsequent amendments.

the juridical order. Fourthly, the courts, which after all could have been abolished at the stroke of a pen under martial law had President Ayub so desired, were supported by a strong legal community of roughly 18,000 persons whose strength lay in its social prestige, in its mastery of Western modernizing values, and in its network of political connections in the hinterland. In sum, it was a formidable political force capable of mustering substantial resistance to any government. Hence, when this community lent its political support to a judiciary which had an ideology of immense appeal, the combination was unassailable.

Prior to the promulgation of the 1962 Constitution, the judiciary accepted jurisdiction of cases in which the citizen sought redress against government for a grievance; redress was sought principally through the use of prerogative writs as extraordinary remedies for violations against fundamental rights. The large number of actions sought against government was an irritant to the executive, which unofficially regarded this an interference in orderly administration. The gentlemanly juridical tug-of-war between the executive and judiciary culminated in the Snelson case, discussed earlier in this chapter and elsewhere at length.[159] The annoyance of the executive branch was exhibited in the failure of the 1962 Constitution to make fundamental rights justiciable. But the National Assembly responded by passing the first amendment early in 1964, about eighteen months after the Constitution was promulgated.[160] Very quickly the judiciary asserted its strength and the supremacy of the rule of law. It made much of Article 2 of the 1962 Constitution. This article declares that it is a person's unalienable right to enjoy the protection of law and to be treated in accordance with law, and that no action detrimental to "life, liberty, body, reputation or property" can be taken except in accordance with law. The fact that this all-embracing provision is included in the Constitution proper meant that the right to seek redress of grievance was not dependent on enumerated fundamental rights, which presumably were not justiciable during the eighteen months before the first amendment was passed. The five

159. See above, p. 245, notes 79, 80.
160. See above, p. 238, n. 61.

classic writs are still available as remedies; indeed, the utility of certiorari seems to have been expanded to include its use as a remedy for ultra vires acts performed by judicial, quasi-judicial, or non-judicial officials.[161]

Since the 1962 Constitution went into effect, several important doctrines affecting the scope and character of administrative discretion have been enunciated. It has already been pointed out that the judiciary in the Fazlul Quader judgment asserted the inherent prerogative of the courts to review legislation for its constitutionality and thereby to interpret the Constitution.[162] Subsequently, in the celebrated case of Maulana Maudoodi,[163] fundamentally a case in public liberties, Chief Justice Cornelius in the leading opinion asserted the general right of the judiciary to review administrative action. The judiciary cannot supervise all administrative acts, he said, for it exists to check them, not to supplant them. Then, referring as much to American as to British doctrine, he asserts that the court must be certain that procedural fairness be observed in reaching a decision. Judicial review will be exercised if (1) a true adversary position has been developed, (2) action within the administration is final, or (3) the statute does not specify the exclusivity of administrative action as a requirement of the public interest.[164]

161. *Mehboob Ali Malik* v. *Province of West Pakistan,* PLD 1963 Lah. 575. See also *Chittagong Engineering and Electrical Supply Co., Ltd.,* v. *Income Tax Officer, Companies Circle IV,* PLD 1965 Dacca 11.

162. *Mr. Fazlul Quader Chowdhury* v. *Mohd. Abdul Hague,* PLD 1963 SC 486.

163. *Abul A'la Maudoodi* v. *Government of West Pakistan,* PLD 1964 SC 673.

164. The propositions relating to judicial review are credited by Chief Justice Cornelius to the *Final Report of the Attorney-General's Committee on Administrative Procedure* (Washington, D. C., 1941), pp. 77–79, 84–92. This reference and others to American case law is worthy of note. Although Pakistani administrative law has cited American precedent somewhat more than other types of law, British precedent has predominated. This case marks a growing acquaintance with relevant American experience. It is probably the consequence of more extensive accession of American legal materials in court libraries and a rising awareness that American experience in presidential government, federal relations, and public liberties has a special relevance to recent developments in Pakistan. This new probing into juridical precedent represents an expansion of bibliographic and intellectual horizons in the four years since the deliberations of the Shahabuddin Commission in 1960, which were almost exclusively oriented toward British scholarship. See above, p. 313, n. 150. See also Sardar Mohammad Iqbal's judgment in *Farid Ahmad* v. *Government of West Pakistan,* PLD 1965 Lah. 135, which relies almost exclusively on American precedent, and Chief Justice S. M. Murshed's judgment in *Ghulam Zamin* v. *A. B. Khondkar,* 16 D.L.R. (1964) 486, discussed below, pp. 324–326.

Then—and this is a point of great significance—Cornelius edges away from a previous line of reasoning which held that the American concept of due process of law is not applicable to Pakistan law in precisely the same way that it has been interpreted in the United States.[165] Citing W. W. Willoughby and law derived from cases decided by courts in the United States,[166] Cornelius affirms the right to strike down not only the statute but also executive action taken under the statute if due process has not been observed. Due process embraces notice in advance and an opportunity to be heard when deprivation of private rights is threatened. These elements of due process are part of British common law and to that extent are applicable to Pakistan. Chief Justice Cornelius was "clearly of the opinion that it is within the power of the Courts of Pakistan, relying on the principles declared and the practice followed by the British courts for well over a century, to subject an executive order, which is in derogation of a private right deriving from the Constitution, to judicial review."[167] The importance of this decision lies in four characteristics. It bases the power to review executive action on a broader pedestal than that provided by alleged violation of fundamental rights. (There would, of course, be an allegation of such a violation in every grievance complained of, but the assumption of an inherent right based on the common law doctrine of due process frees this action from dependence on the justiciability of fundamental rights or from such issues as their existence or abrogation.) Secondly, it allows for judicial review of almost any executive action regardless of whether or not it is quasi-judicial. Thirdly, it transfuses into Pakistani jurisprudence the same formularies for valid administrative action regnant in the United States. Lastly, it gives renewed emphasis to procedural niceties as a means of achieving justice.

The Maudoodi decision is somewhat expansionist in its concept

165. This view had been expressed in several cases, among them *Jibendra Kishore Achharyya* v. *Province of East Pakistan* [1957] 1 P.S.C.R. 1, cited by Chief Justice Cornelius in the Maudoodi opinion.

166. W. W. Willoughby, *Constitutional Law of the United States* (2nd ed.; New York, 1929), III, 1681; *Chicago, Milwaukee and St. Paul Railway Corporation* v. *Minnesota*, 134 US 418; *Smyth* v. *Ames* 169 US 466.

167. *Abul A'la Maudoodi* v. *Government of West Pakistan*, PLD 1964 SC 673, quotation at 718.

of judicial review. One of the earliest major decisions regarding administrative behavior held that the courts could not review a finding of fact, even when erroneous, unless the mode of ascertaining the fact is outside the spirit and intent of the statute.[168] A subsequent leading case held prior exhaustion of administrative remedies to be an essential condition of judicial review, and it went on to find that the appeal must be against an action of a judicial, not an executive, nature. Scrutiny of the process by which the executive is empowered to arrive at the decision was to be the determinant of whether the action is judicial.[169] A subsequent case[170] illustrates the different role of the judiciary in Pakistan from that suggested by the very fountainhead of British juridical norms, the Privy Council. In Faridsons case the court held that it had the power to prescribe that a hearing process should precede withdrawal of a license, even if such process was not statutorily prescribed. This departs from a Privy Council judgment for Ceylon which held that the court will not compel an administrator to act judicially unless the statute so prescribes.[171] This, said the Pakistan Supreme Court, speaking of the Nakhuda Ali doctrine, "goes too far in restricting the power of the superior courts to control actions of the executive under statutes which plainly import the performance of a quasi-judicial act."

The issue of delegated legislation has been particularly vexing in Pakistan. Legislatures have functioned only intermittently, and forty-four months of martial law without legislatures once again elevated the executive to a position of dominance controlled by no agency except the courts. This condition of near executive paramountcy of administration resulted in excessive, unregulated discretion exercised by administrators. Such a condition is neatly illustrated by the historic decision in the "Pan case," written by

168. *Muhammad Saeed* v. *Election Petitions Tribunal* [1957] 1 P.S.C.R. 109.
169. *Tariq Transport Company* v. *Sargodha Bhera Bus Service* [1958] 2 P.S.C.R. 71.
170. *Messrs. Faridsons Ltd.* v. *Government of Pakistan* [1962] 1 P.S.C.R. 1.
171. *Nakkuda Ali* v. *M. F. De S. Jayaratne* (1950) Privy Council 102. See also Kearney's chapter (Chapter 8) in this volume, p. 500, n. 40. Ceylon continues to accept the jurisdiction of the Privy Council; Pakistan abolished its jurisdiction in 1950. While Privy Council decisions prior to 1950 are no longer binding on the Pakistan courts, "those decisions are entitled to the greatest respect." *Noor-ul-Hassan* v. *Federation of Pakistan* [1956] 1 P.S.C.R. 128.

Chief Justice S. M. Murshed of the East Pakistan High Court.[172] The executive branch of the central government issued a notice on January 12, 1964, claiming that since regulation of inter-provincial trade was a central power, trade in pan would now be handled by the Ministry of Commerce. The notice established a committee to devise procedures for allocating quotas to "deserving parties" for air shipment via Pakistan International Airlines. The committee invited traders to submit applications for quotas. The President then promulgated an ordinance[173] with retrospective effect empowering the central government to delegate its powers to any subordinate authority of either the central or provincial governments or to an authority subordinate to a provincial government. The High Court voided the January 12 notice on the ground that traders were compelled to apply for quotas merely by an administrative order when there was no law empowering the issuance of that order. The government admitted this but argued that the ordinance passed in June constituted the necessary legal authority and that it retrospectively validated the January 12 order. To this the court answered that the plaintiff, compelled to apply when no law existed, was being deprived of the protection of Article 2 of the 1962 Constitution which

172. *Ghulam Zamin v. A. B. Khondkhar* 16 D.L.R. (1964) 486. In the present writer's view, this decision is one of the ten most significant judgments in the development of Pakistan's jurisprudence. Unfortunately, it is not widely known, simply because judgments of the East Pakistan High Court are not as widely or as quickly disseminated as those of the West Pakistan High Court. The official reporter for East Pakistan, *Dacca Law Reports*, in which this case appears, is virtually unobtainable in West Pakistan, not to mention other countries. Although it had been decided as early as August 18, 1964, and appeared in the October, 1964, issue of *Dacca Law Reports*, this judgment did not appear in the 1964 issue of PLD. Subsequently, it appeared in the March, 1965, issue (PLD 1965 Dacca 156). It should be noted that the East Pakistan High Court plays a major role in the evolution of juridical policy in Pakistan. This case and the Fazlul Quader case (see above, pp. 218–220, esp. n. 15), which defined presidential government and asserted the right of judicial review, were East Pakistan High Court decisions written by Chief Justice Murshed.

I have used the shorthand designation "Pan case" in the text because pan is the word for betel leaves, the regulation of which is the subject of the case. Betel leaf, as commonly used in Pakistan as tobacco is in other countries, is grown exclusively in East Pakistan but is consumed in both provinces. Since the leaves must be fresh when chewed, transportation between the two provinces has long been an important function (and problem) of government which has always used Pakistan International Airlines for this purpose.

173. Inter-Provincial Trade Ordinance IV of 1964. *Gazette of Pakistan, Extraordinary,* July 1, 1964.

prohibits action detrimental to, *inter alia,* life, liberty, and property of any citizen except in accordance with law. Forced to apply, he risked not getting a quota; this was detrimental to property. Since there was no law, he was not treated in accordance with law. "The guarantee that has been given by the Constitution cannot be washed away by an ingenuous legislative device which can wipe out an illegal invasion of today by an artful enactment of tomorrow, pretending to act retrospectively, without any constitutional change to that effect," wrote Chief Justice Murshed.[174] The ordinance could not retrospectively make law since the ordinance itself was *ultra vires.* It was *ultra vires* because only the legislature can make law, and when it delegates to the executive it must prescribe limits and standards for the scope of administrative discretion. Chief Justice Murshed relied on Indian, British, and American precedent, especially on the Schechter Poultry Company and Panama Refining Company cases.[175] The legislature (in this instance the President exercising the ordinance-making power derived from the legislature) gave to the executive untrammeled power to regulate any commodity.

What policy has it laid down? [asks Chief Justice Murshed] What standard has it formulated? What yardstick has it given? What principles has it formulated? What limitations has it imposed? What guidance has it given? None whatsoever. . . . An effective and efficient legislation could easily be passed to meet the exigencies of the situation within the framework of the Constitution. The Constitution is not unworkable in this behalf. If a valid law had been passed, it could have started functioning from the date on which such law had come into existence. We should not be understood to hold that we do not consider such a legislation to be desirable or expedient, but the essential condition of a valid law is that it must be confined within the limits set by the Constitution. It should not be allowed to "burst the banks" and the protective barrage set up by our Fundamental Law, namely, the Constitution. There can be selection of commodities for regulation of transport. There may be a specification of means of transport sought to be regulated. Frontiers of regulation may be defined. Standards and norms can be laid down for such regulation of movement. The objects and purposes of regulation can be set out. It

174. *Ghulam Zamin* v. *A. B. Khondkhar,* quotation at 513.
175. *A. L. A. Schechter Poultry Corp.* v. *United States,* 295 US 495; *Panama Refining Co.* v. *Ryan,* 293 US 388.

would be a salutary provision to require orders in this behalf to be made under public notification. The Constitution requires, and it is possible to do so, that reasonable direction and guidance should be given in various ways under which the Executive may be vested with substantial discretionary powers to work out the details of legislative policies and norms.[176]

IV. Administrative Reform

Modernization of Training

Reform activity in Pakistan has been vigorous from its beginning in 1947, but the effect of reform has been in evidence largely since 1960. In sheer quantitative terms, Pakistani surveys of administrative reform have been impressive. As is shown in Table 8 in the concluding chapter of this volume, some seventeen reports totaling nearly 2,500 pages and dealing only with the central government have been issued by the government on administrative problems. If we include all reports including those issued by the provincial governments (as we should for this purpose), we count twenty-eight reports of about 3,621 pages issued in Pakistan from 1947 through 1962.[177] While modernization has been facilitated by extensive foreign assistance, the operating design and implementation of reform have been under the direction of government officials. Moreover, government officers have headed and staffed virtually all positions on administrative reform bodies. It is commonly said that the elite cadre, oriented toward a literary-generalist tradition and steeped in the ethos of British colonial administration, cannot be an effective instrument for modernization. Whatever validity this generalization may have cannot be substantiated by the Pakistan case. It was, in fact, the elite cadre which carried the initiative in administrative reform. To be sure, the issues for reform were

176. *Ghulam Zamin* v. *A. B. Khondkhar*, quotation at 502, 514.
177. The figures given in Table 8 in the concluding chapter of this volume are different from those given in the text above. Table 8 omits reports concerned exclusively with provincial government problems so as to increase comparability with reports of other countries in that table. Complete tabulation, description, and bibliographic data on all twenty-eight reports for Pakistan can be found in *Research on the Bureaucracy of Pakistan*, Table 2 and pp. 213–243.

defined, identified, and framed by external foreign sources who infused the indigenous system with a modern administrative ideology from which Pakistan had been cut off since 1940 by war, imperial rule, partition, and political trauma. It is also true that the initial sternness of a martial law regime in 1958 pushed the elite cadre into reform activity which they might have resisted or even scuttled. But we cannot be certain that such scuttling would have occurred, since the excessive secretiveness and reluctance to change so obviously manifested by the higher bureaucracy from 1947 until 1958 was the consequence of many factors. Not the least of these was severe political instability. Once martial law restored a sense of certainty and an uneasy liaison developed between the military and civil bureaucratic elites, the pace of change became rapid.

The extent of elite cadre participation in reform efforts and the rather surprising absence of other groups is shown by analysis of the personnel of administrative reform efforts. Taking the twenty-eight reports of 3,621 pages issued in Pakistan from 1947 through 1962, we find that some 147 persons staffed the various committees and commissions which prepared these reports. Of this group, nearly 80 per cent were government officials. Some 53 per cent were CSP officers, all of whom were veterans of the ICS; about 7 per cent were members of the Audit and Accounts Service; 21 per cent came from various other services; 2 per cent were judges, and 1 per cent were from the Police Service. Only four foreigners participated. It is particularly significant that no military officers served on these groups, although since fully sixty-five of the appointments were made after the 1958 declaration of martial law there would have been ample opportunity to have used military personnel. This latter statistical evidence is symptomatic of the relationship between the military and civil bureaucracies under martial law, a relationship marked by ultimate military paramountcy but total reliance on the civil component for all administration through regular, unrevolutionary procedures. In the light of earlier discussion in this chapter on the dominant role of the ICS veterans as an inner elite of the CSP elite, it must be noted that it was the ICS veterans who for the

most part directed the reform efforts. The significant exception is
G. Ahmed, an officer in the Police Service of Pakistan, who
headed the three most important reform entities, the Planning
Commission, the Federal Reorganisation Committee, and the
Administrative Reorganisation Committee.

The dominant role in technical assistance in administrative
reform has been shared by the United States Agency for International Development and the Ford Foundation. The support of
these two agencies was complementary rather than overlapping.
The United Nations Technical Assistance Programme, ascertaining that the area had already been pre-empted, concentrated its
help in other fields. The Ford Foundation was first in the field,
providing as early as 1953 substantial advisory services to the
Planning Commission through Harvard University. The long
chapter on public administration in the First Five Year Plan, a
tempered revision of a report earlier prepared by Bernard
Gladieux, is an excellent comprehensive survey of the direction to
be taken in administrative modernization. Subsequently, the Ford
Foundation helped in the community development program by
assisting in training a faculty and creating academies for rural
development at Peshawar and Comilla. In 1961 the Ford Foundation assisted in establishing the Administrative Staff College in
Lahore. The complementary thrust of Ford Foundation activity
embraced both programmatic and training functions.

The United States Agency for International Development, on
the other hand, concentrated almost exclusively on training
activities. Advisory activities were limited almost entirely to
statistical work and the preparation of a census of government
employment. The first USAID-sponsored training activity was the
establishment of the Institute of Public and Business Administration in Karachi in 1955 under contract with the University of
Pennsylvania. The institute graduated several persons with
master's degrees who by 1965 held important research positions
in government. Its main contribution was establishing a bridge-
head for further administrative training in a rather hostile environment. This institute was subsequently disbanded and in 1961
was replaced by an enlarged network of training institutions

initially operated and subsequently advised by the University of Southern California.[178] Advisory services were gradually diminished, according to plan, and by 1965 the training institutions were staffed entirely by Pakistani. The national institutes of public administration at Karachi, Lahore, and Dacca have trained nearly one thousand officers through a series of management training programs of varying lengths. In addition, eighty-eight officers (of whom thirty-three were members of the CSP) were sent to the United States to participate in an executive development program of at least six months' duration at the University of Southern California. Forty-five Pakistani have been sent to the United States for advanced training through the doctor of public administration degree, and eight more were scheduled to begin doctoral studies in 1965 and 1966. If we add to this number some twenty government officials sent to the United States or England for public administration training under other auspices and some sixty trained annually at the Administrative Staff College, we find that somewhat more than 1,200 officers have had direct contact with American public administration technology. Of these, nearly two hundred have studied abroad, mostly in the United States; the remainder have studied in Pakistan. This is a significant proportion of the total bureaucracy, as suggested by several comparisons. It is a little more than twice the size of the CSP cadre alone. The 1,200 thus trained almost equal the number of senior Class I gazetted officers (1,437 in 1962) in the provincial government of West Pakistan. Comparable figures are not available for East Pakistan or the central government, but if we assume a total of 3,600 Class I gazetted officers in the three units of

178. This program was carried on primarily under terms of United States Agency for International Development Contract ICA-c 1690, March 24, 1961, with the University of Southern California. It is further described in Ralph Braibanti, "Transnational Inducement of Administrative Reform: A Survey of Scope and Critique of Issues," in John D. Montgomery and William D. Siffin (eds.), *Approaches to Development: Politics, Administration and Change* (New York, 1966), pp. 133–185. See also the comprehensive semiannual reports on Contract ICA-c 1690 submitted by the University of Southern California in mimeographed form. The latest of these is University of Southern California, "Eighth Semi-Annual Report, Public Administration Program in Pakistan," April–September, 1964 (Los Angeles, 1965). Data on the number of officers trained are derived from a letter to the author from International Programs, University of Southern California, August 22, 1965. Figures are exact except for estimates of those trained in Pakistan.

government, the number trained would be about one third of that group. Still another gauge is the number of officers in the central superior services—about 1,500. These figures, while lacking precision, give a rough comparative dimension to the number trained in these various programs. It would probably be correct to say that approximately 10 per cent of gazetted (both senior and junior) Class I officers in Pakistan have been trained in public administration under American auspices. Whether this proportion will increase cannot be predicted. Current plans call for the training of about two hundred officers annually at the national institutes of public administration, but whether the proportion thus trained will continue to increase depends on the rate of increase in the number of officers eligible for such training. By any measurement, however, the figure of 10 per cent (probably an underestimate) is impressive. It is doubtful if any other Asian state inheriting the British imperial tradition has trained so large a number of officers since independence. I have omitted from this estimate persons trained at the two rural development academies, whose foreign-trained faculties number about forty. The academies have trained probably close to a thousand officers in community development concepts. While this is not public administration at the secretariat or management level, it is an important kind of administrative ideology which may eventually affect administration as much as or more than training at a higher level.

Perhaps the most noteworthy characteristic of American-induced administrative training in Pakistan is the manner in which it has become accepted at the highest level of government, attracted some of the best talent, and been absorbed by the elite cadre as an important part of its function. In Table 23 we have seen the large proportion of CSP officers engaged in training, a proportion which Table 6 in the concluding chapter of this volume shows us to be larger by at least 11 per cent than that of any other country considered in this volume. Rigidly centralized control of all training as well as reform is vested in the establishment division of the President's Secretariat, in which a joint secretary in charge of training now serves. The entire training program, embracing eight institutions, is co-ordinated by the Training Policy of 1961,[179] which attempts to establish the doctrine that training is a continuous process which must be given the necessary prestige to enlist the interests of everyone in government. To accomplish this, the policy links training courses with the prospects of promotion. No officer will ordinarily be eligible for appointment as secretary to the central government unless he has attended the Administrative Staff College. Similarly, promotion to joint secretary is to be made only after attendance at one of the national institutes of public administration. Junior officers to be advanced to the rank of deputy commissioner are to be sent to the Rural Development Academies. At the pinnacle of prestige are appointments to the Imperial Defense College and to Eisenhower Exchange Fellowships for study at Harvard University. Such appointees will be those "earmarked" for secretaryship to the central government. The training policy then sets quotas for various units of government for officers to be sent to each of the schools. Several characteristics of this training policy should be noted. First, in the course of time, senior officers will have attended at least three different institutions, each with a distinctive method and point of view. Thus, at the rural development academies, the young assistant commissioner will come in contact with a sociological approach, and with rural administration taught by a faculty trained primarily, though not exclusively, at Michigan State University. After five years, the same officer will be trained at one of the national institutes of public administration in scientific management oriented toward secretariat work and taught by staff members trained predominantly at the University of Southern California. Finally, at the Administrative Staff College he will encounter some British influence, and a staff of whom some are trained in Britain but most are from Syracuse University. The few secretaries sent to Harvard and the Imperial Defense College will be agents for the continued infusion of British administrative norms

179. President's Secretariat, Establishment Division, Letter No. 2/17/61-A-IV, "Public Administration Training Policy" (Rawalpindi, October 31, 1961). Permission to quote from this memorandum was given by the Establishment Division in a letter to the author dated November 14, 1964.

at the highest level. Thus, the influence now emanating from ICS officers at the top will not fade completely with retirement of ICS officers. On the contrary, it will be buttressed, though certainly on a lesser scale, by about one graduate of the Imperial Defense College each year. The second observation to be made is that the training is for various officer ranks from all cadres of the Central Superior Services. Thus, for the first time in these courses officers of different cadres study together and compete in a limited way. While this may not appear unusual when compared to other systems, in the context of bureaucratic compartmentalization in Pakistan it is a departure from past experience.

Modernization of Organization

Most of the twenty-eight reports on administrative reform paved the way for renovation of administration by identifying deficiencies and injecting into imperial bureaucratic values canons of administrative ideology from which these values had been insulated. But the contemporary bureaucratic organization is derived primarily from a group of five reports, the last two of which were brief adaptations to the 1962 Constitution of the principles of the first three.[180] The most comprehensive and valuable of these is the 1961 report of the G. Ahmed Committee which gives summaries of opinions presented by witnesses and the text of government decisions on the committee's recommendations.

Central-provincial administrative relations. The new organizational structure of Pakistan is based on the need for maximum delegation of administrative or operational aspects of government to the provinces. The complex and shifting contours of power

180. These five reports are those of the Administrative Reorganisation Committee, 1961 (G. Ahmed); Provincial Administration Commission, 1960 (Akhter Husain); Provincial Reorganization Committee (N. A. Faruqui), Part I, West Pakistan, 1961, Part II, East Pakistan, 1962; Committee on Decentralization of Institutions, 1962 (N. A. Faruqui); Standing Organisation Committee on the Reorganisation of the Functions and Structures of the Central Government in the Light of the New Constitution, 1962 (M. Shoaib). The report of the Pay and Services Commission—1962 (A. R. Cornelius) is necessarily omitted from this discussion because it has not been released for public use.

described in detail earlier in this chapter[181] are reflected in an organizational pattern which permits the central government to have a hand in all activities, whether central or provincial. Because of the various possibilities of "necessary" central government intervention by ordinance, proclamation of emergency, invocation of Article 131, or by issuance of directions to the governors under Article 66(2), the central government is organized to discharge such responsibilities. Regnant doctrine assumes that the central government deals with international aspects of subjects even when they are residual provincial subjects. This is especially so in the case of education, health, and welfare, for which much foreign assistance is received. It must also reserve for itself the national planning function, and to co-ordinate such planning it must keep in touch with the provincial discharge of duties involving provincial subjects. Only by maintaining such scrutiny of provincial matters can the central government assess the need for central legislation or intervention by the president. For these reasons—although these are thought of as provincial subjects—there continue to be central ministries dealing with education, health, food and agriculture, labor, social welfare, industries, communications, and fuel and power. The doctrine is that a strong central government should control only broad, national policy, but operational aspects should reside with the provinces. Theoretically, this should mean an eventual progressive increase in the provincial bureaucracies and a corresponding decrease in the size of the central apparatus. Whether this has yet occurred or will occur in the near future remains to be seen.

Secretariat organization. The generic term "secretariat" embraces ministries and divisions in the central government and includes both ministers and secretaries assigned to them. Within this larger secretariat is a smaller President's Secretariat consisting of six divisions: economic affairs, planning, scientific and technological research, states and Frontier regions, cabinet, and establishment. The grouping of these divisions, some of which were formerly ministries, directly under the president removed

181. See above, pp. 211–241.

them from political, ministerial control and placed them exclusively within bureaucratic channels. Each of the divisions is headed by a secretary who may report directly to the president. The cabinet secretary is regarded as co-ordinator of all secretaries of ministries and comparable units in the central government. Attached to the president's office is a personal secretariat, consisting of about thirty-five persons under the direction of the president's personal secretary.

The establishment division has gradually evolved into a central personnel agency of considerable power. It controls administrative training through eight institutions and controls administrative reform through a very effective efficiency, organization, and management wing, whose power has been increased. The Central Public Service Commission is in a sense subordinate to the establishment division. Thus, the division embraces functions of the Bureau of the Budget, office of the President, Civil Service Commission as organized in the United States, and extensive training functions not found in the American system.

Secretaries to ministries traditionally had status rivalling if not exceeding that of ministers to whom they were nominally subordinate. This was a consequence of the fact that in imperial days secretaries were British ICS officers and ministers were Indian politicians. This relationship has not been completely changed, although the ethnic and imperial differentials have been supplanted by other factors. The special position of secretaries is indicated by the suggestion of the G. Ahmed Committee that they continue to have direct access to the president and governors.[182] The theoretical division of responsibility is not hierarchically divided, for the secretary is deemed to be responsible for execution of policy; but whether he is responsible for such execution to the minister or to the president or governor through the cabinet secretary is not clear. Financial responsibility, for example, is assigned to the secretary of a ministry. If the minister disagrees with the secretary on a financial issue, it is not the minister's view which is

---

182. G. Ahmed Committee Report—1961, p. 293. This diffusion of responsibility has not yet been tested in Pakistan as it was in India in the "Mundhra Affair," described in Potter's chapter in this volume, pp. 172–176.

controlling; rather, the issue is submitted to the president for orders.

After a period of forty-four months of martial law, during which there were no ministers heading departments in the provinces and only a few ministers (frequently changed) in the central government, the apparatus must now accommodate itself to the re-emergence of ministers. It was shown earlier in this chapter that the president and governor *may* appoint a Council of Ministers; this is not mandatory, although there is a strong obiter dictum suggesting that the constitutional provisions are mandatory rather than permissive.[183] The Constitution clearly does not prescribe that members of the Council of Ministers shall head ministries or departments; it merely states that they shall "assist him [president and governors] in the performance of his [their] functions."[184] The practice is for ministers to head ministries and departments, although rarely have there been as many ministers as units of administration at either the center or the provinces. Table 24 shows that ten ministers had been appointed in the central government as of September, 1965, although there were twelve officially designated ministries and five more divisions, which are as important as ministries, in the President's Secretariat. In East Pakistan there were nine ministers but thirteen departments; in West Pakistan there were sixteen departments and only eight ministers appointed. Grouping all three units of government together, we find about two-thirds of the possible number of ministers were appointed.

The administrative implications of so large a proportion of ministerial vacancies are worth considering. The first is that a ministerial vacancy throws the policy and administrative direction of the ministry or department to the secretary, who is then responsible only to the cabinet secretary and the president. Thus, a ministerial vacancy eliminates political interference and assures professional bureaucratic domination of both policy and execution. This has happened to a remarkable degree in the central secretariat. It has also occurred by reducing former ministries or

183. See above, pp. 218–220, and pp. 224–225, n. 28.
184. Second (1962) Constitution of Pakistan, Articles 33, 82.

equivalents to divisions and grouping them directly under the president. No ministers are needed for such divisions, which report only through bureaucratic channels to the president. By this means and through ministerial vacancies, Table 24 shows that eight important ministries or equivalents are removed from political control. This same pattern is found in the provincial secretariats. In West Pakistan where there are eight ministers for sixteen departments, four of the eight ministers hold two portfolios each; in East Pakistan, no minister holds two portfolios, and about 30 per cent of the ministerial posts are vacant. In both cases, much of the policy control is thereby thrust into exclusively bureaucratic channels. This situation may be temporary; it was valid as of September, 1965, only seven months after election. But even the fact that this situation prevailed for seven months is not without interest. There is another element to be added here, namely, the parliamentary secretaries, an institution described earlier in this chapter.[185] Table 24 shows that nearly all the central parliamentary secretaryships are filled. Since there are only six ministers but eighteen parliamentary secretaries, there are at least fifteen situations (counting double portfolios) in which the parliamentary secretary works with the secretary rather than with the minister. This projects the secretary into the political maelstrom, even though it is the parliamentary secretary (not the secretary) who must bear the brunt of questioning on the floor of the National Assembly. Another effect of this situation is likely to be the subordination of the parliamentary secretary to the secretary when a ministerial vacancy exists. Ordinarily, the parliamentary secretary would be responsible to the minister. All of these factors contribute to a situation wherein political influence may be sedated and controlled by professional bureaucracy without being eliminated entirely.

Another important aspect of the secretariat has been the continued separation of policy-making and executive functions. The secretary of the ministry confines his function to policy-making, planning, direction and control; he leaves technical considerations and implementation to attached departments and

185. See above, pp. 316 ff.

Table 24. *Ministerial-Secretariat Organization in the Central Government, August, 1965*

Ministry or equivalent	Minister	Secretary	Parliamentary secretary
President's Secretariat			
Cabinet Secretary	—	ICS	M. M. Kasim[a]
Principal Secretary	—	ICS	—
Economic Affairs Division	—	ICS	J. S. Ali[a]
Establishment Division	—	ICS	Shaheedullah
Planning Division	—	CSP	J. S. Ali[a]
Scientific and Technological Research Division	—	non-CSP	Raisuddin Ahmad
States and Frontier Regions Division	—	CSP	Abdul Awal[a]
Ministries			
Agriculture and Works	—	ICS	—
Food and Agriculture	—	ICS	Ataur Rahman
Rehabilitation and Works	—	CSP	A. A. Talpur
Commerce	Ghulam Faruq	ICS	Nurul Haq
Communications	Khan A. Sabur	ICS	M. R. Saigol
Defence	—	ICS	M. M. Kasim[a]
Education	K. A. Huque[a]	ICS	Maulana A. Haye
Finance	M. Shoaib	ICS	M. H. Khan
Foreign Affairs	Z. A. Bhutto	ICS	M. A. Awal
Health, Labour, Social Welfare	K. A. Huque[a]	ICS	F. K. Khan
Health	—	non-CSP	—
Labour, Social Welfare	—	non-CSP	—
Home and Kashmir Affairs	—	ICS	—
Home Affairs	—	CSP	H. R. Gilani
Kashmir Affairs	—	CSP	Abdul Awal[a]
Industries and Natural Resources	—	ICS	S. Kizer Hayat Khan
Industries	—	CSP	—
Natural Resources	—	non-CSP	—
Information and Broadcasting	—	ICS	Malik Allahyar Khan
Law and Parliamentary Affairs	—	non-CSP	Fakhruddin Ahmad
Law	—	non-CSP	—
Parliamentary Affairs	—	non-CSP	Alhaj Z. Lal Mia
22 ministerial divisions			
17 ministries and president's divisions	6 ministers[b]	29 secretaries	18 parliamentary secretaries

[a] Indicates double portfolio held by same person.
[b] By September, 1965, ten ministers had been appointed, but their portfolios were not announced.

other subordinate offices. This system has been roundly criticized by technically oriented officials. They feel that technical considerations are not given due emphasis and are not only demeaned in prestige but subordinated at every turn to ICS-CSP secretaries who are not equipped to deal with technical matters. Fundamentally, this problem is behavioral rather than structural; it can be solved only when technical experts enjoy parity of esteem with generalists in the larger society. A change is slowly taking place, but in the meantime some slight institutional adjustments have occurred. The Economic Pool, described elsewhere in this essay, makes it possible for technical financial officers to head financial departments, although this has not occurred. By dividing such technical ministries as Health, Labour, and Social Welfare, Industries and Natural Resources, and Agriculture and Works into divisions, it is possible to appoint as division head a joint secretary who is a technical officer. This has happened in the two divisions of the Ministry of Health, Labour, and Social Welfare and in one division in the Ministry of Industries and Natural Resources. Since 1961, this has also been the pattern in both divisions of the Ministry of Law and Parliamentary Affairs. The admission of technical executives in a few positions may appear inconsequential, but in actuality it is very important because it admits such technical incumbents to the inner circle of the secretariat for the first time. Beyond that it is not much of a concession to the opponents of generalism, for division heads are still responsible to the secretary of the ministry, who in every case except that of the Ministry of Law and Parliamentary Affairs is a generalist CSP officer. Another adjustment has been the delegation of some authority over personnel and finances to heads of attached departments, and the vesting of responsibility for the technical soundness of proposals in the directors of departments. Technical aspects of such proposals will not ordinarily be examined by the ministry. Such were the excesses of generalism in the past that department heads had to submit proposals to CSP generalist officers far junior to them. Secretariat procedure now requires that papers bearing the signature of department heads be dealt with by the secretary or joint secretary, or in smaller departments by a generalist officer of status comparable to that of the department head. The generalist officer is required to act in the matter "straight-away," and if additional information is needed, he is to give instructions in "language . . . invariably . . . polite." Department heads may be allowed direct access to ministers in the event of disagreement with the secretary. But this is not as significant a privilege as it may seem, for with so many ministerial vacancies the department head can go only to the cabinet secretary or to the president—both improbable visitations.

In the provincial secretariats the same pattern has been maintained, i.e., ministerial vacancies and enlargement of the chief secretary's staff have removed important sectors of activity from the political arena. Here administrative domination is even stronger than in the center. Since department secretaries have been of varying seniority and have come from various cadres, there has been a tradition of somewhat more direct control and co-ordination by the provincial chief secretary. The role of the chief secretary has been further strengthened by the assignment of additional chief secretaries for planning and development and for establishment. The regnant doctrine is that the status of all provincial secretaries should be elevated and should never be below that of a deputy secretary in the central government. It is anticipated that there will be increased interchange of provincial and central government secretaries, which will not be possible unless officers of greater seniority are assigned to the provincial secretariats. The role of provincial secretaries has expanded as the provinces have become responsible for the execution of a larger sphere of the governmental program. Likewise, the responsibilities of provincial secretaries in local government have increased, as they must now supervise division commissioners in their substantive spheres. The existing administrative tiers—i.e., secretariat, directorates (equivalent to attached departments in the central government), divisions, districts, and subdivisions—have been retained, and divisions especially have been strengthened. There is an effort to allocate more "functional authority" to lower levels of government while retaining policy authority in the provincial secretariat. These adjustments are characteristic of administrative modernization in Pakistan: positive response to pressure has been made, but without sacrifice of ultimate generalist and bureaucratic control and without revolutionary departure from pre-partition structure.

A change recommended by the G. Ahmed Report and approved by the government is the introduction of the Section Officers' Scheme.[186] This plan was first introduced experimentally in the Ministry of Finance in 1954; by 1957 it had been introduced in the West Pakistan secretariat. It is one of the more drastic changes made in bureaucratic structure in Pakistan. By routing all action papers to a section officer with high enough status, clerical help, and files necessary to make a decision, the scheme eliminates at least three tiers in the processing of programs. One of the characteristics of secretariat organization in the past was distended physical separation of various echelons. The secretary and other officers rarely entered their file rooms and were dependent on a series of lower officials for the acquisition of proper information. But since knowledge of English and general efficiency dropped sharply at those levels below officer status, the secretary in reality depended upon nonexistent or uninformed staff advice. The new Section Officers' Scheme creates small cells capable of staff assistance and decision-making. Earlier conditions are suggested by the Government of West Pakistan's instruction, "the section officer must either sit in the same room with his assistant, clerk, and steno-typist, or in adjoining rooms readily accessible. The record must also be kept in the section in *almirahs* [cabinets] under lock and key."[187] The Section Officers' Scheme has also made possible a reduction in the number of Class IV employees who serve as messengers and office attendants. The G. Ahmed Committee reported that these employees approximated 1,900 in the central secretariat, constituting nearly 30 per cent of the total strength of the secretariat. A minister had one jamadar, with elaborate livery and gold sash and three peons; a

186. For a description of this scheme, see G. Ahmed Committee Report—1961, pp. 255–264. A description of its operation can be found in *Abdul Latif Sethi and others* v. *Pakistan*, PLD 1961 Kar. 457.

187. Government of West Pakistan, Services and General Administration Department, "DO No. 11–1 (O & M)," May 15, 1957, as reproduced by the National Institute of Public Administration, Karachi.

secretary had one jamadar and two peons. This, said the G. Ahmed Committee, "is a legacy of the pre-Independence days when ceremony and pomp was an essential feature of administration."[188] Now, a secretary is allowed only one jamadar, and the number of Class IV employees in the central secretariat has been reduced by about five hundred. The same proportionate reduction has occurred in the provincial secretariats.

The planning function. Probably the principal source for the introduction of reform in administration, and undoubtedly the most successful, has been the Planning Commission, the predecessor to which, the Planning Board, received assistance from the Ford Foundation as early as 1951. In 1954 an agreement was concluded under which Harvard University was to provide advisers to assist the Planning Board, as it was then called, in drafting a long-range development plan and training planning personnel. This assistance extended through 1965 and involved grants of about $4,175,000 and the services of some fifty-six advisers and twenty-six consultants. The official Ford Foundation report on its planning activities in Pakistan[189] stresses activation of planning, by which is meant translating "an inert document into an active process" by "creating new institutions, systems, and attitudes." In this respect, the foundation asserts, "Pakistan has made more progress than most emergent countries in establishing the planning process as an effective instrument of policy and action."[190] The advisers and consultants came from several countries, about half from the United States and the remainder from Great Britain, Canada, Australia, the Netherlands, Norway, Sweden, Greece, and Burma. The international character of the advisory group had several advantages. The mission was not associated with the vagaries of diplomatic relations between Pakistan and the United States, and it made possible a wider base for recruiting talent. But it also facilitated the introduction of experience and point of view from countries where central

188. G. Ahmed Committee Report—1961, p. 355.
189. An analytical survey of the role of the Ford Foundation in the planning function of Pakistan can be found in the Foundation's *Design for Pakistan, A Report on Assistance to the Pakistan Planning Commission by the Ford Foundation and Harvard University* (New York, 1965).
190. *Ibid.*, p. 3.

planning was a well-established activity of government. It is significant also that the foreign advisers did not function as a group but were assigned to sections of the commission and reported directly to the executive head of the commission. The need to train competent Pakistani staff was recognized early in the activity, and the Ford Foundation financed several fellowships for training, first through the M.A. and later through the Ph.D. level in development economics. It also financed the establishment of the Institute of Development Economics, which in 1961 started two-year work-study courses for staff members of the Planning Commission and other economic agencies in the government. Responsibilities assumed by Pakistani increased gradually. The Second Five Year Plan for 1960–1965 was prepared largely by Pakistani staff. One of the first graduates of the Ph.D. fellowship program, Nurul Islam, of East Pakistan, became in 1965 the director of the Institute of Development Economics.[191]

Although the planning function received strong government support from the outset, its position in the structure of government was improved as a consequence of recommendations of the G. Ahmed Committee accepted by the government in July, 1961. The committee had access to a working paper presented by Dean Edward Mason of Harvard University, which had been associated with the planning function in Pakistan since 1954.[192] Mason called attention to the belief in the Western world that India's capacity to use aid effectively is greater than Pakistan's. This, he said, was a misconception arising largely from the superior Indian planning organization and machinery for negotiating with aid-giving nations. He suggested that the status of the planning apparatus be raised to a ministry, that it be enlarged, and that it evaluate programs and prepare materials necessary for negotiating aid. The committee approached the problem somewhat differently. The final government decision elevated the status of

191. An example of the high level of competence resulting from this training and reflected in the work of the institute can be found in the chapter by Nurul Islam, "The Economic System of Pakistan," in Calvin B. Hoover (ed.), *Economic Systems of the Commonwealth* (Durham, N. C., 1962), pp. 401–462.
192. Texts of the Mason paper, the committee's analysis, and consequent government decisions are accessible in G. Ahmed Committee Report—1961, pp. 223–237.

the Planning Commission by placing it in the President's Secretariat and making the president chairman. In June, 1965, the deputy chairman was given the rank of cabinet minister and was elevated in the Warrant of Precedence to Rank 5, where he is listed last among members of the cabinet. Prior to this he had been listed in Rank 11 as a minister without cabinet status. In addition to the deputy chairman, who in 1965 was Said Hasan, the Planning Commission also includes two members, one from East Pakistan and one from West Pakistan. Either the chief secretaries of each of the provinces, or in their absence the additional chief secretaries in charge of planning, are ex officio members of the commission. Against the advice of several government agencies, the committee recommended and the government approved the integration of the projects division (now called the progressing wing), an agency supervising execution of plans, as a unit of the Planning Commission. In 1962 this unit was taken out of the Planning Commission, and the function of checking on plan implementation was delegated to the provincial government under an additional chief secretary for planning. The unit negotiating foreign aid, the Economic Affairs Division of the Ministry of Finance, was not integrated into the Planning Commission as Mason had suggested. It was taken out of the Ministry of Finance and placed directly under the president in his secretariat. Since both planning and foreign aid negotiations come under the president, almost the same result as that envisaged in the Mason memorandum is achieved. Approval was given to increase the number of economists, and in 1965 the commission had about 115 professionally trained staff members and a sanctioned strength of 130 professional and administrative officers. The commission itself had requested a staff of 119, and the Harvard advisory group had recommended 141. The commission is now moving in the direction of associating the genesis of planning more closely with operating agencies of government. Planning cells have been established in each ministry and division in the central secretariat, except those dealing with subjects "wholly provincial in nature," in which instances the ministry or division has a coordinating rather than an initiating function. Each cell consists of a professional economist and two officers with professional training in the field administered by the ministry or division. The planning cells have not been established as quickly as was hoped simply because there are not enough qualified economists to staff both the commission and cells. The function of the cells is to collect data, prepare annual and five-year development plans, formulate projects, and make progress reports. The G. Ahmed Committee stressed that the programs of the planning cells had to be sophisticated, integrated, "genuine sector planning," and that cell staff therefore had to be highly trained.

When the 1962 Constitution was put into effect, the possibility of decentralizing the organization and functions of the Planning Commission was explored. The decision was that central planning, by its very nature, cannot be decentralized. No branch of the commission has been established in Dacca, nor is one contemplated. It was decided that the commission should meet in Dacca at least four times a year, staying there for two or three weeks at a time, and that closer liaison should be maintained with the provincial planning organizations. Nevertheless, each of the provincial governments now has the principal responsibility for initiating plan projects and for supervising implementation of the plans. This increased responsibility was reflected in the assignment of seven out of a total of thirteen Harvard advisers to the provincial planning and development departments.

There is little doubt that the planning apparatus in Pakistan is now one of the most effective of those found in developing states. It has been the primary institution for the introduction and diffusion of the ideology and technology of modern administration. It has already been pointed out that the thirty-two-page seventh chapter of the First Five Year Plan was a comprehensive blueprint for administrative reform, almost all provisions of which have been put into effect. The commission's concern for the activation of planning led it inevitably to vigorously push the apparatus by which plans are implemented. Finally, the fact that G. Ahmed was the first chairman of the Planning Commission and subsequently became chairman of the Administrative Reorganisation Committee which pushed through the implementation of the administrative reform elements of the five-year plans suggests the diffusion of administrative reform doctrine in the entire system. It appears clear that the single most important source of administrative reform in Pakistan has been the radiating influence of the planning function.

Government corporations.[193] One of the significant facets of administrative modernization has been the rapid growth of government corporations, which in 1965 numbered some thirty-six—both central and provincial. Very little is known of the corporate device in Pakistan because not much research on corporations has been done. Government corporations were suggested in the First Five Year Plan for implementing programs with a "commercial . . . or multi-purpose approach," were praised in the Second Five Year Plan, which also warned against too many corporations, and were suggested by several commissions almost as a panacea for a variety of bureaucratic evils.[194] The rationale for the use of corporations is that enterprises conducting essentially commercial activities must have greater flexibility in financial and personnel controls than "line" agencies possess. Critics of the corporate device are quick to point out that if line organizations were given equivalent discretion, they would perform as effectively. But this criticism overlooks the heavy encrustation of a colonial ethos and the stasis inherent in any bureaucracy. It is often easier to build anew than to reform an established organization. This is particularly true when the new activity requires an attitude of risk-taking and leadership by a technical rather than by a generalist elite. Government corporations have become huge sub-bureaucracies, nominally submitting annual reports to ministries and nominally answerable to the National Assembly, but actually functioning quite independently of either of these agencies of government. The legislatures appear to be

193. This brief survey of government corporations and Table 25 are adaptations of pp. 236–243 and Table 4, *Research on the Bureaucracy of Pakistan.*
194. Government of Pakistan, *First Five Year Plan—1955–60* (Karachi, 1958), pp. 100–101; *Second Five Year Plan, 1960–65* (Karachi, 1960), p. 118; *Report of the Jute Enquiry Commission* (Karachi, 1960), p. 172; *Report of the Credit Enquiry Commission* (Karachi, 1959), p. 187; *Report of the Food and Agriculture Commission* (Karachi, 1960), pp. 212–248.

vaguely aware that some degree of legislative oversight of corporations is their responsibility, but except for occasional outbursts against them[195] and complaints that various regional groups are not fairly represented on their staffs, they have taken no positive steps to achieve this control. The fault may not be entirely that of the National Assembly, as the frequent use of Rule 58(2) suggests.[196] The ambiguity in the status of corporations and the absence of acute awareness of legislative control as a legitimate legislative function is suggested by the omission of all corporations from the list of named subjects and entities assigned to standing committees.[197]

One complaint of legislators is not that corporations need to be controlled but that they are being controlled excessively by the executive branch. The allegation is that corporate autonomy has been destroyed by the posting of government officials to serve in ex officio capacities on boards of directors or to serve full-time as managing directors or chairmen.[198] The validity of this allegation is difficult to establish simply because the composition of the thirty-six boards embracing some thirty-six full-time managerial posts and about 236 directorships changes almost from month to month. Analysis of composition of the boards in February, 1964, reveals that nearly half (114) of the directorships were held by government officials, of whom twenty-two were retired officials. Nearly one-third were held by businessmen, about 6 per cent by engineers, and 6 per cent by army officers. The objective of infusing fresh non-bureaucratic outlooks and skills into the corporations seems hardly to have been fulfilled by so large a proportion of government officials. On the other hand, the acute scarcity of entrepreneurial talent may justify this circumstance to some extent. Closely related to the composition of boards of directors is

195. See, for example, Provincial Assembly of West Pakistan, *Debates,* June 22, 1962, p. 22; National Assembly of Pakistan, *Debates,* March 9, 1963, pp. 130–131; April 1, 1963, pp. 1095–1099; April 2, 1963, pp. 1154–1170.
196. See above, p. 315, n. 75.
197. National Assembly of Pakistan, *Rules of Procedure,* Schedule III, pp. 47–66. The executive branch appears to have taken the initiative in co-ordinating and regulating the activities of government corporations. In May, 1965, the National Economic Council decided to "examine the workings of various autonomous bodies." As reported in *Pakistan Times,* May 24, 1965, p. 1.
198. National Assembly of Pakistan, *Debates,* April 2, 1963, pp. 1158–1159.

Table 25. *Central and Provincial Government Corporations, 1965*

Name of corporation	Date established
Central Government	
1. Pakistan Refugees Rehabilitation Finance Corporation	1948
2. Pakistan Industrial Development Bank	1949
3. Security Printing Corporation	1949
4. National Bank of Pakistan	1949
5. House Building Finance Corporation	1952
6. Pakistan Insurance Corporation	1952
7. Pakistan International Airlines Corporation	1955
8. Agricultural Development Bank	1957
9. Pakistan Industrial Credit and Investment Corporation	1957
10. Atomic Energy Commission	1959
11. Capital Development Authority	1960
12. Oil and Gas Development Corporation	1961
13. National Shipping Corporation	1963
East Pakistan	
14. Dacca Improvement Trust	1956
15. East Pakistan Jute Marketing Corporation	1957
16. Film Development Corporation	1957
17. East Pakistan Small and Cottage Industries Corporation	1957
18. Inland Water Transport Authority	1958
19. East Pakistan Water and Power Development Authority	1959
20. East Pakistan Forest Industries Corporation	1959
21. Chittagong Development Authority	1959
22. East Pakistan Road Transport Corporation	1961
23. Khulna Development Authority	1961
24. East Pakistan Agricultural Development Corporation	1961
25. East Pakistan Industrial Development Corporation	1962
26. East Pakistan Shipping Corporation	1964
27. East Pakistan Fisheries Development Corporation	1964
West Pakistan	
28. Karachi Port Trust	1886
29. Karachi Electric Supply Corporation	1952
30. Karachi Development Authority	1957
31. West Pakistan Water and Power Development Authority	1958
32. Karachi Road Transport Corporation	1959
33. West Pakistan Agricultural Development Corporation	1961
34. West Pakistan Small Industries Corporation	1962
35. West Pakistan Industrial Development Corporation	1962
36. West Pakistan Road Transport Corporation	1963

the issue of managing directorships or chairmanships. It has already been shown by Table 23 that in 1964, 4.4 per cent of the CSP cadre held management positions in government corporations. This proportion has not fluctuated markedly except in 1961 when it rose to nearly 10 per cent. From this finding it appears that the CSP cadre has not moved into corporate management to any significant extent. Nevertheless, analysis of the quality of the assignments reveals a somewhat different dimension. The two agricultural development corporations, which are perhaps the most potentially powerful of all thirty-six entities, had four CSP officers in key positions in 1964: the chairman of the East Pakistan Agricultural Development Corporation, the secretary of the West Pakistan Agricultural Development Corporation, and the full-time managing directors of two of the project areas of the West Pakistan Agricultural Development Corporation. CSP officers also served as chairmen of the West Pakistan Water and Power Development Authority (WAPDA) and finance director of the National Shipping Corporation. While it cannot be said that the elite cadre dominates the new government corporations, it is clear that three of the four most important corporations have CSP officers in strategic places. It would be somewhat less than cautious to conclude from this evidence that the autonomy of corporations has been destroyed and that they have been absorbed into the orthodox bureaucracy. The real question is whether or not comparable talent from the private sector is being passed over in favor of placing government officials on boards of directors. Careful entrepreneurial and business leadership studies are needed before such a question can be answered.

Financial controls. Perhaps the most vexing procedural problem in Pakistani government has been the transaction of financial affairs. This has been the consequence in part of loss of personnel records and other files at partition, and in part because of highly centralized decision-making and an elaborate maze of checks and counterchecks designed to assure probity. The changes made in financial procedures are among the most far-reaching of all administrative reform measures. These changes focus largely on the use of the budget as an instrument of control and planning, decentralization of financial responsibility, and simplification of the process of authorization (sanction) of expenditures from funds already appropriated. The new system, which has gradually been put into effect since February, 1960, places financial responsibility within a ministry upon the secretary, who for this purpose is designated the ministry's principal accounting officer. In this capacity he is assisted by a financial adviser who is an officer of the Ministry of Finance and is appointed to the other ministries by the ministry concerned. The annual confidential (efficiency) report is written by the secretary of the ministry to which the financial adviser is assigned, although the secretary of the Ministry of Finance may also record remarks on his performance as a financial officer. Disagreements between the secretary and the financial adviser are resolved by the minister, and disagreements between the minister and his secretary are resolved by the president. The financial adviser is concerned with preparation of the budget as well as with approval of expenditure. The financial procedures of the provincial secretariats have been reorganized into the same system. Final scrutiny of accounts to insure that expenditure has been made in accordance with allocation rests with the comptroller and auditor general, whose former subordinate position in the Ministry of Finance has been raised to a position higher than that of secretary to government.

V. Summary

Pakistan appears to be distinctive among the systems considered in this volume by the fact that its governmental polity remains essentially that of an administrative state. The political process was in abeyance during the forty-four months of martial law extending from October 7, 1958 to June 8, 1962. Even after the restoration of constitutional government in 1962, followed by the re-emergence of political parties and a vigorous presidential election in 1965, politicization has been sedated so that its interference with administrative and economic modernization is minimal. This sedation is accomplished by an indirect electoral system, the retention of elements of the classic unitary state (namely, appointment of governors and local officials), ambiguity of legislative and executive powers, the near paramountcy of the administrative process, and the partial curtailment of public liberties. Whether or not this contrived asymmetrical development of political and administrative sectors has contributed to the noteworthy stability of the past half-decade and to the remarkable rate of economic growth, it is too early to say. If such a causal relationship exists, the experience of Pakistan offers a *via media* in political development models, namely, the achievement of a high economic growth rate by means of administrative dominance without mass party support and within a constitutional framework with limited popular participation. This is neither the tutelary democracy nor the communist system of some Asian states, nor is it the dominant mass party or multi-party system of others. It also is not, as is sometimes assumed, a military dictatorship of the type commonly found in some Middle Eastern states with which Pakistan, because of Islam, is inevitably associated. It is in essence a juridical-administrative state of indirect popular participation, embodying unitary and federal, parliamentary and presidential attributes. Although it is a mixture which defies categorization and facile analysis, its apparent operating success has confounded its most vigorous critics.

Certain other characteristics of Pakistan's total political evolution stand out clearly. There has been no sharp ideological break with the past. The apparatus of government remains essentially the same, although adjustments to modernization have been made. Nevertheless, a British officer experienced in imperial administration would still find himself in a familiar system; whereas an American or French bureaucrat would not feel quite as much at home. The principal reliance for modernization has been on attitudinal reorientation coupled with institutional adjustment rather than on attitudinal revolution and radical institutional innovation. This modernization is to be accomplished within a highly original and sophisticated legal order which blends both the presidential and parliamentary forms of government. This aspect of Pakistan's polity is of special note, since it is the first major state within the Commonwealth which after deliberation of alternative polities abandoned the parliamentary system as it was known before independence. It is also clear that the judiciary looms large as a powerful force in the political process and as a source both of significant ideology and of major structural and procedural innovation. Finally, the episode of martial law was not revolutionary. There was no break with the past, juridically, administratively, or ideologically. Except for President Ayub and two or three military men in the cabinet for part of the period, there was no overt supercession of civil authority by the military. On the contrary, the civil bureaucracy, rid of political harassment, became stronger than ever. The martial law period was a mood, a quickening of pulse, a stability contrived by the imminence of an alternative military apparatus of administration and of a monopoly of physical force poised in readiness to act. The transition to constitutional government was nearly as smooth as the abrogation of constitutional government had been nearly four years earlier. Connections with British traditions remain strong and are carried on largely by the elite cadre, some 70 per cent of whom have been British-trained. These values remain vigorous but have been jostled by certain administrative reforms which have emanated from the United States. These reforms, generated largely by the planning function and subsequently by training in administration, have been incorporated into the bureaucratic apparatus which has gained in power as a consequence. While thus far the principal inspiration for training has come from the United States, it is not at all certain that this relationship will necessarily continue. It is noteworthy that one of the first projects planned in the Regional Cooperation Development organization formed by Iran, Pakistan, and Turkey in 1964 deals with collaboration in public administration and management. A regional training institute which will sponsor training, research, and other professional administrative activity was planned at a meeting of the RCD Ad Hoc Working Group in Rawalpindi in May, 1965. Both Turkey and Iran have received substantial technical assistance in public administration from the

United States and as a consequence are in a position to collaborate with Pakistan at a common level. It is not unlikely that this activity will supplant direct American aid and that public administration reform will thus be generated one step removed from its ideological wellsprings in older Western states.

The principal controls over bureaucratic behavior are those of the judiciary and a slowly emerging political process manifest in the Basic Democracies Scheme. This has been strengthened somewhat by the rise of the Combined Opposition party which contested so effectively, though unsuccessfully, against President Ayub in 1965. In sum, we find here a system in which the pace of politicization is controlled to minimize interference in administration. The point at which politicization is permitted to mobilize its demands and try to put them into effect by direct elections has not yet been reached. This encounter is the crucial test for any administrative system which permits partial popular participation and seeks to regulate the pace of its development.

· 6 ·

Bureaucratic Transformation
in Burma*

James F. Guyot

In Burma, as in India before, the British developed a "steel
frame" of administration animated by a guardian class of civil
servants. In time these guardians met their antithesis in an
indigenous political elite, which brought independence for
Burma out of the turmoil of World War II and then harassed the
Civil Service until both elites were displaced by the Burmese
army. This new class of guardians operated as a synthesis of both
political and administrative institutions. This chapter will analyze
the transformation of the bureaucracy as Burma moved from
British rule to independence under parliamentary democracy,
and then to revolutionary army rule in terms of changes in (1)
the purposes of government, (2) the structure of administration,
and (3) the character of the guardian class at each stage.

I. The Steel Frame

The bureaucratic system developed by the British in Burma[1]
fulfilled the functions of government prescribed by nineteenth-
century liberalism—the maintenance of law and order, the ad-

* The field work upon which much of this analysis is based took place from
July, 1961, to November, 1962, with support from the United States Educational
Foundation in Burma (Fulbright Program) and the Human Ecology Fund. The
analysis itself was carried out with support from the Faculty Senate Research
Committee and a Summer Faculty Fellowship at the University of California at
Los Angeles.

1. Materials on prewar British administration of Burma are well-assembled and
diversely interpreted by four former members of the Indian Civil Service in
Burma. Particularly relevant are John S. Furnivall, *An Introduction to the Political*

ministration of justice, and the collection of revenue. With the new century, a concern for welfare and an increase in government's role in economic development fostered an elaboration of organization, while constitutional changes added complexities to the pattern of authority. Yet the basic structure and well-established practices prevailed, hindering the advance of welfare programs and imparting an air of unreality to institutions of self-government.

The rationale for establishing and maintaining the British imperial connection was largely commercial, as it was in India. Trade and the exploitation of Burma's great agricultural and natural resources required a settled civil condition. To provide

Economy of Burma (3rd ed.; Rangoon, 1957); John S. Furnivall, *Colonial Policy and Practice: A Comparative Study of Burma and Netherlands India* (Cambridge, 1948); F.S.V. Donnison, *Public Administration in Burma: A Study of Development during the British Connexion* (London, 1953); G. E. Harvey, *British Rule in Burma: 1824–1942* (London, 1946); and F. Burton Leach, *The Future of Burma* (Rangoon, 1936). A documentary source of uncommon value is Volume XI, "Memorandum Submitted by the Government of Burma," one of the twenty-seven volumes constituting the *Report of the Indian Statutory Commission*, May, 1930, Cmd. 3568 (1930). Hereinafter cited as Simon Commission Report, Vol. XI.

A broader list of the major works relating to administrative developments in Burma would include James Russell Andrus, *Burmese Economic Life* (Stanford, 1947); U Ba U, *My Burma: The Autobiography of a President* (New York, 1959); John F. Cady, *A History of Modern Burma* (Ithaca, N. Y., 1958); John F. Cady, *Southeast Asia: Its Historical Development* (New York, 1964); John L. Christian, *Modern Burma: A Survey of Political and Economic Development* (Berkeley and Los Angeles, 1942); E.C.V. Foucar, *I Lived in Burma* (London, 1956); John S. Furnivall, *The Governance of Modern Burma* (2nd ed.; New York, 1960); Everett E. Hagen, *On the Theory of Social Change: How Economic Growth Begins* (Homewood, Ill., 1962); D.G.E. Hall, *A History of South-East Asia* (2nd ed.; London, 1964); Dr. Maung Maung (ed.), *Aung San of Burma* (The Hague, 1962); Khin Maung Kyi, *Patterns of Accommodation to Bureaucratic Authority in a Transitional Culture: A Sociological Analysis of Burmese Bureaucrats with Respect to their Orientations Towards Authority.* Unpublished Ph.D. dissertation, Cornell University, 1966; Dr. Maung Maung, *Burma in the Family of Nations* (2nd ed.; Amsterdam, 1957); Dr. Maung Maung, *Burma's Constitution* (2nd ed.; The Hague, 1961); Daw Mya Sein, *Administration of Burma: Sir Charles Crosthwaite and the Consolidation of Burma* (Rangoon, 1938); Manning Nash, *The Golden Road to Modernity: Village Life in Contemporary Burma* (New York, 1965); Lucian W. Pye, *Politics, Personality, and Nation Building: Burma's Search for Identity* (New Haven and London, 1962); U Sein Win, *The Split Story* (Rangoon, 1959); Hugh Tinker, *Foundations of Local Self Government in India, Pakistan, and Burma* (London, 1954); Hugh Tinker, *The Union of Burma: A Study of the First Years of Independence* (3rd ed.; London, 1961); Frank N. Trager, *Building a Welfare State in Burma, 1948–1956* (New York, 1958); Louis J. Walinsky, *Economic Development in Burma, 1951–1960* (New York, 1962). A broad-ranging bibliography is Frank N. Trager, *Annotated Bibliography of Burma* (New Haven: Human Relations Area File, 1956). More recent bibliographies are Cecil Hobbs (comp.), *Southeast Asia: An Annotated Bibliography of Selected Reference Sources in Western Languages* (Washington, D. C., 1964), and Stephen N. Hay and Margaret H. Case (eds.), *Southeast Asian History: A Bibliographic Guide* (New York, 1962).

this the British found it necessary to annex successive portions of Burmese territory beginning with the maritime provinces of Arakan and Tenasserim in 1824–1826 and ending with the capture of Mandalay in 1885. This extension of British rule met with less popular support than was expected, and a period of pacification was required after each of the three Anglo-Burmese wars. Many of the early civil officers were men seconded over from the army. Following the final pacification, Burma knew only one major rebellion (Saya San in 1931) before the Japanese occupation. Yet the continuing concern with problems of law and order is symbolized in the maintenance as late as the 1930's of nine battalions of military police distributed throughout the country in addition to the regular police forces.[2]

The administration of justice meant, on the criminal side, the substitution of Anglo-Saxon legal proceedings for the caprice of an ineffective despotism; on the civil side, it meant the continuation of customary law in matters of family, inheritance, and religion, and the introduction of the law of contract in commerce. Government economic policy brought into play extensive capital investments by British firms in the extraction of teak, oil, and other minerals, and opened the province to Chettyar moneylenders who financed the expansion of cultivation in the rich delta lands. However, the government showed little aggressive concern for distribution of wealth, refusing, for instance, to interfere with the activities of the Bullinger Pool which lowered the prices received by cultivators for their paddy during the 1920's[3] when world prices were high.

As in India and Ceylon, the collection of revenue was the most important governmental function. The pacification of Upper Burma required five years of intensive effort. As a result, Burma was long a deficit province within the Indian Empire.[4] Following the Indian pattern and not too far out of line with traditional Burmese practice, revenue was collected largely as a tax on the productivity of the land. Much of the work of district adminis-

2. Leach, *op. cit.*, p. 107.
3. Furnivall, *Colonial Policy and Practice*, p. 198.
4. But by the time of separation in 1937 Burma had paid in more to the Government of India than that government spent in Burma. Leach, *op. cit.*, pp. 31–32, 69; Furnivall, *Colonial Policy and Practice*, p. 71.

tration in the early days involved producing maps, settling rates, and effecting collections. Of the three cardinal functions of government, revenue collection was the one which established governmental contact with the whole population, as was true also in India where today in some districts the general district officer is still known as the collector.

The administrative apparatus that came to be known as the "steel frame" was a highly centralized hierarchy of offices, descending from the governor general in India and deployed over the districts of Burma down to the village level. The design came almost intact from India, as did many of the men sent into Burma to staff the structure.[5] The impress of India-based institutions was fortified by the tight system of central control.[6] Gradually the requirements of administrative efficiency and demands for political autonomy reduced the dependence of the chief civil officer in Burma on instructions from India. The chief commissioner in charge of the local government became a lieutenant governor in charge of a province with his own legislative council in 1897, and with separation from India in 1937, a governor responsible only to London and his local legislature.

The steel frame had both vertical and horizontal dimensions. In its most advanced form, the main line of communication and command flowed down from the governor and his secretariat (with occasional advice or intervention from elected ministers) and out through eight divisional commissioners to deputy commissioners (or district officers)[7] in the thirty-five districts of Burma proper.[8] The district officer was the key member of the structure, bearing the Burmese title *ayebain*, which means "plenipotentiary." He was the first line of that heaven-born class, the

5. See Tinker's chapter (Chapter 2) in this volume, pp. 66 ff. After the first annexation Tenasserim, which lay on the other side of the Andaman Sea, drew its personnel from Penang, and attempts were made to accommodate indigenous practices. Ten years later, under commissioners appointed from India, the system was remodeled in the Indian image. Donnison, *Public Administration in Burma*, pp. 17, 18; Furnivall, *Colonial Policy and Practice*, pp. 35–36.

6. The commissioner of Pegu received detailed supervision from the viceroy even in such matters as the transfer of junior officers. Leach, *op. cit.*, p. 38.

7. The generic term "district officer" is used in this chapter, as it is in the chapters on India and Pakistan, although "deputy commissioner (D.C.)" is the usual designation used in Burma.

8. The Shan States and other "Frontier Areas" were administered separately under a system of indirect rule until they were merged at independence into the Union of Burma.

Indian Civil Service. A district was divided into two or three subdivisions, each under a subdivisional officer (SDO), who was a member of the Provincial Civil Service; below them were the townships headed by myooks, or township officers, members of the Subordinate Civil Service.[9]

At the end of the chain came the thugyi, or headman of a village tract, of which there were approximately 12,000 at the 1931 census. The thugyi stood at the point of contact between the indigenous system of local authority and the imposed system of district administration. Although an agent of the central government, he usually inherited his office, even when elected, and was not subject to transfer as were other officers of the general administration.

In the early, unsettled stages of British administration the district officer (then called an assistant commissioner) could indeed act as plenipotentiary—preserving law and order, dispensing justice, collecting revenue—all with the help of only a few assistants. As the volume of work and the complexity of tasks increased, a division of labor along functional lines appeared with the establishment of specialist departments and specialist services first at the center and later in the districts. From the beginning the district officer, who may well have previously held military rank,[10] had various police forces at his disposal. The uneasy aftermath of the Second Anglo-Burmese War (1852) called for more specialized attention, and an inspector general of police was appointed in 1861. The district officer remained generally responsible for the maintenance of law and order. As district magistrate he was head of the police, but he was assisted by a district superintendent of police, who was directly responsible to the inspector general of police for the discipline and the professional character of the force.[11]

9. With separation from India, the rank equivalent to the Indian Civil Service became the Burma Civil Service, Class I, while the Provincial Civil Service became Burma Civil Service, Class II. See below, Chart 1, p. 370.

10. More than one in five of the members of the executive branch of the Burma Commission in 1920 was seconded from the Indian army. See *Quarterly Civil List for Burma, No. 201* (July, 1920).

11. Furnivall, *Colonial Policy and Practice*, pp. 40–41; Leach, *op. cit.*, pp. 122–123.

This pattern of "dual supervision" of specialists by both a generalist and a specialist superior was followed when revenue collection in the district was divided between a superintendent of land records and a superintendent of excise, each responsible to his own specialist commissioner in Rangoon. Only part of the judicial function (civil and a few criminal cases) was parceled out to a district and sessions judge, but in this he was responsible solely to the High Court. Other specialist departments, most of which were concerned with economic development (e.g., agriculture, fisheries, veterinary) or promoting welfare (e.g., public health, co-operative credit, public instruction), established district-level officers outside of the direct control of the district officer. Some of these, such as the executive engineer of the public works department or the deputy conservator of forests, often controlled jurisdictions of a different size or shape from that of the district officer's district.

It was the responsibility of the district officer to co-ordinate the activities of this increasing number of technical specialists. The authority to transfer and promote personnel resided in the specialist department, although the district officer wrote an annual confidential report on the performance of technical specialists assigned to his district. Any control the district officer might wish to exercise, especially if it involved some innovation, required approval by higher levels in Rangoon in the appropriate department or departments. The proliferation of specialist departments required co-ordination at the center no less than in the districts. To achieve this the office of the chief commissioner was expanded into a multi-headed secretariat, which by the end of the 1930's had become a policy-oriented generalist superstructure of secretaries, additional secretaries, deputy secretaries, and assistant secretaries, dominating and in some ways duplicating the functional directorship of the various executive departments.

The deployment of officials who were generalists in administration but specialists in their geographical responsibilities was probably a more suitable structure for the early administration of British Burma than would have been a division of the tasks of government among a number of specialist services. At that time there were few functions to perform and they were grounded in geography—the collection of land revenue, the suppression of banditry, and the adjudication of disputes in a sparsely settled territory with limited communication facilities.

By the time government policy encompassed positive action toward economic and welfare goals and specialist structures had been developed, the steel frame of general administration was firmly established. It clearly dominated the specialist services both in the districts and in Rangoon. This domination was based not only on the seniority of the service and its position astraddle the formal lines of communication but also on the elitist corporate character of the ICS, whose guardianship will be discussed in a later section.

Incompatibility of Structure and Function

The administrative structure so rationally designed in terms of the purposes of government showed little compatibility with the social structure of the province it governed. To begin with, Western concepts of the rule of law, abstract justice, and impersonal authority which undergirded British guardianship in Burma ran counter to traditional habits of accommodation and compromise in the arbitration of disputes and deprived the exercise of power of its personal, and hence intelligible, qualities. A. D. Maingy, the first commissioner of Tenasserim, made a noble attempt at continuity with the previous system of law and administration. Since most of the indigenous officials had fled or were hostile, he had to rely on available records of particular cases to discover the principles of the system. The traditional flexibility of principle and variety of practice seldom survived the translation. The code Maingy drew up provided a precise procedure for arriving at determinate decisions. As the system of courts came into full swing, the old practices of co-operation and compromise, which had been carried over to some extent by Burmese judges, declined while controversy increased and litigation became a paying practice for a rising lawyer elite.[12]

12. See Furnivall, *Colonial Policy and Practice*, pp. 30–33, for analysis of the development of the judicial system, and pp. 131–137, for the distortion of Burmese

Impartial and impersonal administration was a new and scarcely credible experience for the Burmese. Many appeared not to believe it, and today some still doubt that it ever came to pass. If an official denied a seemingly reasonable petition because to his mind it conflicted with some abstract rule or policy, the Burmese petitioner, expecting omnipotence in all officials, took his defeat as a sign that he stood in disfavor with that official. Over the years the Burmese came to understand what the British meant by impartial administration, but total conviction was never attained. The special protections granted European business and the racial barriers erected in Rangoon society were too much in evidence.

At the village level the demands of rational organization and rule book procedure redrew the map of local allegiances and shattered the integrity of the village community. On arrival the British found scattered over the Burmese countryside an untidy assortment of headmen (thugyi) with varying degrees of personal authority over territories of different sizes and in some cases over particular people regardless of location. Settling on the myo or taik, a "circle" which might encompass several villages, as the most stable unit for administration, territorial jurisdictions were sorted out in appropriate sizes for administrative convenience. When Sir Charles Crosthwaite returned from India as chief commissioner, following the annexation of Upper Burma, he effected a plan conforming to the pattern of the other provinces in India which abolished the circle and strengthened the village

---

practice and the growth of litigation. The 1931 census identifies 2,334 practicing lawyers in contrast to 1,320 registered medical practitioners and 466 dentists. If we may characterize law as a "contentious" profession and medicine as a "constructive" one, which seems roughly to have been their roles in Burma, this overbalance of lawyers represents a misallocation of educational resources. By contrast, in a developed society such as the United States, there are now about 213,058 lawyers and judges against 310,899 doctors and dentists, a ratio that has held for the last fifty years. J. J. Benison, *Census of India, 1931* (Rangoon: Government Printing and Stationery, 1933), Vol. XI, Part II, pp. 110–111. United States Bureau of the Census, *U. S. Census of Population, 1960* (Washington, D. C., 1964), Vol. I, Part 1, Table 205. Dr. Maung Maung discusses the growth and prestige of the lawyer elite in *Burma's Constitution*, pp. 9–10; and *Law and Custom in Burma and the Burmese Family* (The Hague, 1963), chap. viii. For a different view of the utility of a large legally trained elite in a developing society, see the chapter on legal research in Ralph Braibanti, *Research on the Bureaucracy of Pakistan* (Durham, N. C., 1966), pp. 248–261, esp. p. 254.

headman as the unit of administration. Crosthwaite's Village Act[13] destroyed the largest unit of self-government and the basis for inter-village co-operation while converting the village from an organic society into a largely administrative entity. The size and shape of the village was determined by the application of two principles: (1) it must not be so large as to exceed the headman's span of control; (2) it must be large enough to bring in revenue sufficient to support a headman of quality. Emphasis on the first principle led to a subdivision of existing villages, but by the turn of the century concern for the second principle fostered a policy of amalgamation. This creation and re-creation of artificial units headed by a taxing and policing instrument of the distant central government left the village population with little interest in positive action for the common good.[14]

The lack of public support was the primary problem confronting welfare programs attempted by the government. Furnivall diagnosed this as a distinction between needs and wants. The cultivators need capital to invest in improved agricultural practices, but they want money to spend on traditional religious practices, such as the shinbyu, a ceremony in which every son briefly re-enacts the princely life of Gautama Buddha before entering his novitiate in the Buddhist priesthood. Consequently, co-operative agricultural credit societies collapsed as members failed to repay loans. Similarly, villagers need a supply of uncontaminated water such as could be provided by a system of tanks and tube wells, but they want water that is convenient.

To translate public needs into the language of private wants requires imagination, understanding, and perhaps some missionary zeal. Unfortunately, government officials were perceived by the population and generally did behave more as coercive than as

13. Sir Charles Crosthwaite, *The Pacification of Burma* (London, 1912), p. 23.
14. The view from the top in an annual report on administration found the village headman "efficient as a petty judicial officer and revenue collector, apathetic in matters of excise [opium and liquor] and sanitation, willing as an assistant to police and district officers. . . ." Metaphorically, this description of village administration fell under the section of the report devoted to police, where it was sandwiched between subsections on the "Rangoon Town Police" and "Wild Animals and Snakes." *Report on the Administration of Burma for the Year 1924–25* (Rangoon: Government Printing and Stationery, 1926), pp. 21–22.

persuasive agents. The civil surgeon, for instance, was also superintendent of the district jail, and some public health practices such as vaccination of people and inoculation of cattle were sufficiently resented that officers were commonly bribed not to carry them out.

Frequently, technical specialists went to Burma with little knowledge of the territory and inaugurated inappropriate programs. At one time agricultural officers trained in England promoted deep plowing to bring up new soil, with the consequence that the moisture accumulated during annual monsoon rains was not retained until the end of the crop cycle. In addition, a number of the specialist services were staffed largely by Indians at the lower ranks. While they could communicate with their superiors in English, effective contact with the local population often required the mediation of Burmese occupying the lowest rungs of the steel frame.

The responsibility for making a success of welfare programs fell ultimately to the district officer and his subordinates in the general administration, but there was such rapid circulation of posts that few officers had time to develop a concern with or understanding of the problems of their district. Even when a sympathetic officer had formulated a program, the chances were that he would be transferred before seeing it through to completion.[15]

The Development of Self-Government

The purely administrative character of government in prewar Burma was diluted by two tendencies toward self-government: the establishment at the local level of municipal and district councils which included elected members; and at the national

15. Maurice Collis, one of the twentieth-century ICS officers with an expressed sympathy for the Burmese, during his twenty-two-year career was posted to twelve different charges as subdivisional officer or district officer in the ten and one-half years that he spent in the districts. See his *The Journey Outward* (London, 1952); *Into Hidden Burma* (London, 1953). Furnivall spent most of his twenty-year career in the districts and was posted to fourteen different locations. He strongly advised a system which would commit the district officer and his career prospects to performance within one district. See his "Planning for Welfare in Burma," mimeographed (Rangoon: Ministry of National Planning, 1948).

level, dyarchy, the transfer of certain subjects to the control of two ministers who were selected from a partially elected legislative council. To the members of the steel frame both experiments were bothersome obstacles to the efficient prosecution of the business of government.

As the economic development of Lower Burma drew an increasing population into cities and towns, urban problems such as sanitation grew to proportions that could not be managed by the regular district administration. Municipalities were set up and run by committees of nominated, official members. Later, elected members were added, but they had little connection with their constituencies since the public at large was not interested in the services the municipal committee was supposed to provide and desired only relief from tax burdens. In response to rising expenditures and declining efficiency, most committees had reverted to the nominated members by the time that dyarchy brought a new impetus to self-government in 1923. Then the official members were withdrawn and given the responsibility for supervising the work of the newly elected committees, and the level of efficiency declined further. Self-government in district councils fared no better. The experiment seems to have been an alien form transferred from Britain through India to Burma too early in the latter's political and social development.[16]

Under dyarchy, what were then called the "nation-building" functions of government (education, public health, agriculture, forests, excise, public works, and local government) were administered by the governor with the advice of two elected ministers, while officials nominated as a home member and a finance member of his executive council advised him on finance and revenue, law and order, justice, and police. Later, with separation from India the governor was confronted by a prime minister and cabinet coagulated out of the tangle of personal politics in an expanded legislature and commanding the very important ministries of home affairs, judicial affairs, and finance in addition to the nation-building ministries.

16. See Tinker, *Foundations of Local Self-Government in India, Pakistan and Burma*, pp. 214–244. See also Furnivall, *Colonial Policy and Practice*, pp. 144–156.

The steel frame held firm during dyarchy. The two elected ministers were dependent on the favor of the government for their princely salaries, and their influence on departmental policy was negligible. When as home member he became acting governor, even so high an official member of the council as Sir Joseph Maung Gyi felt he could take no action contrary to the sentiments of his European "subordinates"—the acting home member, the chief secretary, and the commissioner of Pegu (the most important division, which included the capital).[17] The main impact of dyarchy on administration was the multiplication of reports and other tasks.

With separation from India in 1937 more ministries came under political direction, the governor's reserve powers over the administration were severely taxed, and political pressure was felt by officials on down the line. U Saw, minister for forests and agriculture as well as prime minister in the last cabinet before the Japanese invasion, loved to tour the countryside with all the district officers in tow "to show the people that the Burmese were on top now." When campaigning for a supporter of his Myochit (Patriot) party during an election in Myitkyina, his attention was drawn by the sayadaw of a large monastery to the deterioration of the monastery's buildings. U Saw calculated that reconstruction would require about one hundred tons of teak, then turned to the deputy conservator of forests and ordered that amount contributed from the government forest reserves. The support of the sayadaw and the subordinate priesthood (sangha) proved so successful that U Saw applied the same technique in helping to build his Myochit party in other districts.[18] Even if corruption of impartial administration in order to build political support may be justified as facilitating the smooth functioning of a polity, a different justification must be sought for a more banal corruption —the sale of favors by the subordinate administrative staff in order to increase their personal income. The latter was endemic in Burma from the British annexation onward. A Bribery and

17. Collis, *Into Hidden Burma*, p. 185.
18. Interview by Dorothy H. Guyot with U Ba Maung, member of the House of Representatives from Myitkyina and staunch supporter of U Saw, September 29, 1962, Rangoon.

Corruption Enquiry Committee, headed by Bernard Swithinbank, ICS, and including several Burmese politicians, made a
broad investigation and issued its report in 1940.[19] The published
report omits references to ministerial involvement (the text is
riddled with elipsis marks) and finds no evidence of taint in the
superior services (ICS and BCS[I]) and other Class I services.
But among provincial and Class II officers and their subordinates
(township officers, sub-inspectors of excise, veterinary assistants,
police, cadastral surveyors, clerks of all kinds), the officials in
closest contact with the population, conventional and ingenious
examples of bribery and extortion were found aplenty. Of less
immediate consequence for the public but highly significant for
the efficiency of the service was the evidence of internal corruption, such as payments for appointment and promotion and to
prevent undesired transfers. Any statistics on corrupt behavior
are highly unreliable; still, the committee could agree that the
excise department, which dealt with liquor and opium, was the
most corrupt. The committee noted that a number of writers have
related corruption in the services to the traditional Burmese
system in which officials received no salary, but the committee
pointed out that the fees collected in those circumstances were
regulated by custom. The startling aspect of corruption during
British rule is that the superior officers were so little aware of it
and scant effort was made to control what went on between their
subordinates and the public.[20]

Barriers to communication and effective co-operation which
separated superior and subordinate become more understandable
when we look at the ethnic and class composition of the membership of the services.

Character of the Services

In Burma, as in India, the steel frame was supported by the
members of a guardian class, who were distinguished from the
ruled population and from a number of other government serv-

19. *Report of the Bribery and Corruption Enquiry Committee, 1940* (Rangoon:
Superintendent, Government Printing and Stationery, 1941).
20. *Ibid.,* pp. 8–9.

ices by race and by passing an extremely difficult entrance examination. The development of the Indian Civil Service and its extension to Burma have been described in Tinker's chapter (Chapter 2) in this volume. In the concluding chapter Braibanti points up the significance of the adaptations made by the ICS and its variants in other countries at the coming of independence. Here we deal with the salient characteristics of the development in Burma of a Civil Service of its own.

The competitive examination stood as the central symbol of the ICS. The candidate followed this exercise by a year as probationer at a British university studying the history, law, and language of the Indian subcontinent, followed by another examination, then a year's service under training, after which a departmental examination had to be passed. This accumulated evidence of merit provided a store of confidence for the new ICS officer sent into the swamps of the delta or the jungles of central Burma. It evoked trust on the part of his superiors and backing for initiative he might take to solve the problems of his district.[21]

Since merit so rigorously proved needed no continuing confirmation, the ICS officer was granted security of tenure with promotion assured in due time. The stability of the seniority system is attested by the fact that only two of the twenty-one members of the ICS serving as district officers in Burma in 1941 were senior to the junior-most of the eight divisional commissioners. Such a system, stressing achievement at entrance and ascription in operation, developed internal strength in the steel frame, which as Braibanti points out[22] enabled it to carry on the tasks of

21. See Tinker's chapter (Chapter 2) in this volume. About one-third of the early members of the Burma Commission of the ICS entered from outside the regular channels. The expanded cadre necessary to rule the newly acquired territory in Upper Burma drew on the ranks of the Indian army and a range of non-officials. G. E. Harvey, "The Conquest of Upper Burma," chap. XXIV in H. H. Dodwell (ed.), *The Cambridge History of India* (Cambridge, 1932),VI, 422. These were not necessarily inferior men. One, a former journalist, James George Scott, proved himself one of the most colorful and competent Englishmen in Burma. See the account in Philip Woodruff, *The Guardians* (London, 1953), pp. 130–137. Scott is best known for his pioneering anthropological study, *The Burman* (London, 1888; reprinted, New York, 1963), and several historical works.

22. Ralph Braibanti, "Elite Cadres in the Bureaucracies of India, Pakistan, Ceylon and Malaya Since Independence," in W. B. Hamilton, K. Robinson, and C. D. W. Goodwin (eds.), *A Decade of the Commonwealth, 1955–1964* (Durham, N. C., 1966), pp. 274–299.

governance in the midst of political turmoil in India, Pakistan, Ceylon, and Malaya. The failure of an ascriptive bureaucracy to achieve similar success in independent Burma helps us identify some of the flaws in an otherwise nicely articulated machine.

The education and training of the young guardians was in the best of the generalist tradition. The common knowledge and the community of values shared by each class of entrants created an administrative machine of almost completely interchangeable parts. If a deputy secretary in the department of health were going home on leave, his post might be filled by the additional deputy commissioner of Mandalay, whose charge in turn may have been taken by an assistant collector of customs.

In such a well-designed and neatly run machine small allowance was made for indigenous influences. The normal bureaucratic pressure to conform was reinforced by isolation from the mainstream of life back home and by awareness of the superiority of the institutions the guardians sought to establish in a less civilized land.[23] Nevertheless a few individuals did venture across the boundary between the ICS ethos and village Burma, bringing back with them non-regulation sentiments and projects for reform. Maurice Collis, an Irishman, has recorded the internal conflict felt by himself and others who were "highly sympathetic to Burmese aspirations . . . [yet] loyal, obedient and extremely capable servants of the government which held the people in political subjection."[24] Better known is John S. Furnivall, who resigned from the ICS in 1923 so that he could be free to assist rather than direct the Burmese in reconstructing their own society. In 1948 he was retained as adviser on national planning by the government of independent Burma.[25]

23. A grotesque yet insightful picture of these forces appears in George Orwell's *Burmese Days* (New York, 1958).

24. The quotation is from Collis, *Into Hidden Burma*, p. 35, and refers to Bernard Swithinbank. Burmese respect and affection for Swithinbank appears in Maung Maung, *Burma's Constitution*, p. 5. The personal conflict is particularly noted in Maurice Collis, *Trials in Burma* (London, 1945).

25. Furnivall's work in Burma is briefly described and his writings fully noted in Frank N. Trager (ed.), *Furnivall of Burma: An Annotated Bibliography of the Works of John S. Furnivall*, Bibliography Series No. 8, Yale University Southeast Asia Studies (New Haven, 1963). Voluntary resignations from the ICS were so uncommon that such a move usually increased the prestige of the official who resigned. Furnivall, the "grand old man" of Burma, died in 1960.

The more usual attitude of those guardians sympathetic to Burma and Burmese ways was expressed by Fielding-Hall. He found the Burmese a charming people and district administration interesting and exciting, but he felt there could be no bridges between the English officer and the life of his district. He tells the story of a district officer departing on transfer who hears a crowd of villagers compare him to a predecessor who involved himself too much in agriculture, education, and other village matters.

"Your Honour?" they all said in chorus. "We never saw your Honour except in court, or in business which was finished very quickly. For the most of the time your Honour might never have been here at all. That is indeed the officer we respect. . . ."[26]

Mediating between the English guardians and their Burmese charges were the Anglo-Burmese and Burmese members of the Provincial Civil Service, which by 1923 was 79 per cent Burmese. In the early years each district had relied on a "head native" (gaung-gyo or sitke) as a link between the European and native branches of the administration. As British fears declined that Burmese appointed as higher-level officials might "revert to the days when bribery and corruption held unlimited sway," the head natives were promoted to magistrates and judges.[27] Officials of the former Burmese government became headquarters assistants, treasury officers, and subdivisional officers in the higher grade of the Provincial Civil Service, while a Subordinate Civil Service of myooks (township officers) spread out to represent the British district officer in the townships. The structure of the three services and their promotion paths are illustrated in Chart 1 on the following page.

The Provincial Civil Service, as its exemplar, the ICS, had done in its infancy, selected its early officers by nomination, 30 per cent of them being promoted from the Subordinate Civil Service. The members of the Subordinate Civil Service in turn had often been originally appointed as clerks by the district officer. With the development of higher education, competitive examinations were

26. H. Fielding-Hall, *A People at School* (London, 1906), p. 168. See also Foucar, *op. cit.*, p. 209.
27. Furnivall, *Colonial Policy and Practice*, p. 38.

Chart 1. *Shifts in Service Structure in the Executive Branch of the General Administration*

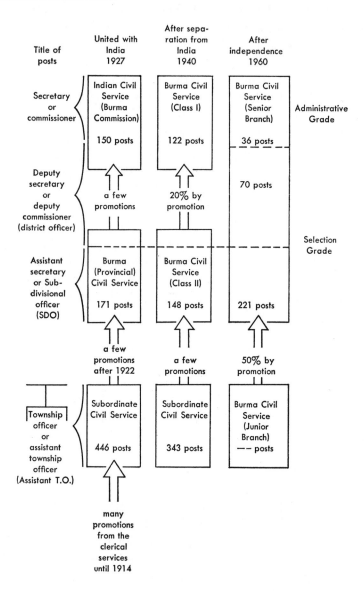

Sources: Column 1, Simon Commission Report, II, 232–233; column 2, *Quarterly Civil List for Burma,* No. 284 (*corrected up to 1 October, 1940*) (Rangoon: Government Printing and Stationery, January, 1941); column 3, Union of Burma, *Civil List,* No. 10 (*corrected up to 31 December, 1959*) (translated by Burma Research Center, Bethesda, Md.).

introduced for direct recruitment, first to the Subordinate Civil Service, then in 1921 to the Provincial Civil Service. These competitive appointments of young Burmans holding university degrees created some jealousy among older officers in lower services who had anticipated due promotion to the Provincial Civil Service. The examination also gave the new officers a stamp of superiority and a basis for identification with the ICS. It was not surprising that his colleagues said of U Than Tin, O.B.E., who stood first in the 1921 provincial examination, that he "spoke just like an Englishman." This identification was nurtured by the hope that after sufficient years of loyal service in the Provincial Civil Service one might officiate as a district officer or in some other post reserved for the ICS and perhaps eventually gain promotion to the ICS itself. By 1941, fourteen out of thirty-six districts were under the charge of officiating district officers, as were four other posts ordinarily reserved for the ICS. Eighteen of the 147 members of the ICS serving in Burma were men promoted from the Provincial Civil Service.[28]

An example is the career of U San Pe. With an honors degree in English from the University of Calcutta (Rangoon College did not yet grant its own B.A.), he received a direct appointment as myook in the Subordinate Civil Service in 1914 at the age of twenty-one. After a succession of district and secretariat posts, he passed the Burma Civil Service competitive examination on his second try in 1922 and was appointed EAC. (District officers were originally titled assistant commissioner; hence, the rank of the inferior service was extra assistant commissioner.) U San Pe then went through a cycle of posts, including akunwun (treasury officer), subdivisional officer, personal assistant to the private secretary to the governor, and government translator, before becoming secretary to the Public Service Commission which had been established in Burma following separation from India. In 1939 he was given charge of a district, having reached the top of the Burma Civil Service (Class II)—the title given to the Provincial Civil Service when the Burma Commission of the Indian

28. *Quarterly Civil List for Burma*, No. 284 (*corrected up to 1 October, 1940*) (Rangoon: Government Printing and Stationery, January, 1941).

Civil Service became Burma Civil Service (Class I). With the British return U San Pe was confirmed at the rank of deputy commissioner and thus promoted to the BCS(I). However, the war had taught him how little the people now respected the position of district officer, so he asked not to be given another district but to be returned to his post as secretary to the Public Service Commission.[29]

Those Burmese who entered the ICS as equals (by nomination or examination rather than promotion) were drawn from the most Anglicized sections of Burmese society. Often they were the sons of officers in the Provincial Civil Service. The first four to be selected were barristers, and a number of the others also had been educated in England before selection and their year as a probationer at an English university. U Kyaw Min, the only Burmese to pass the open competitive examination for the ICS before it became the BCS(I), came from an Arakanese family in Akyab and held B.A. and LL.B. degrees from Cambridge.[30] There were five other Arakanese among the thirty-two Burmese appointed to the BCS(I) cadre by October, 1941,[31] and a number of the early appointees came also from Tenasserim, the other of the maritime provinces first to come under British control.

The revenue secretary in recommending one such fortunate young Burman for admission to an English university noted:

His father Po Thu Daw, A.T.M.—a decoration which he received for the prominent part which he took in making the experiment of recruiting Burmans for the Indian Army a success—and for good service rendered in many capacities—is a very capable member of the Provincial Civil Service of Burma who recently acted as Deputy Commissioner of the Shwebo district. His mother was a daughter of U Shwe late Extra Assistant Commissioner—a very well known and

---

29. Author's interview with U San Pe, October, 1961, in Rangoon. See also "Who's Who in Burma," the *Guardian: Burma's National Magazine,* VI (November, 1959), 53.

30. See Tinker's chapter in this volume, p. 69. See also Simon Commission Report, XI, 23.

31. This figure excludes Eurasians and also those Burmese promoted from the BCS(II). It is compiled from *The Quarterly List for Burma,* No. 287 (October, 1941).

respected officer in his day. Both Po Thu Daw and his wife are well connected and have many relatives in government service. . . .[32]

The revenue secretary might have added that the paternal grandfather as well held the rank of extra assistant commissioner, and a later commentator would have noted that this well-born guardian married a woman who counted a district officer for a father, extra assistant commissioners for grandfathers, and could name two preceding generations of officers in the courts of Mindon and Pagan Min. Throughout his career he drew encouragement from the Burmese proverb that only the royal stars go straight.

Traditional Burma has been described as a society with considerable social mobility. A novice from whatever class could rise by merit through the ranks of the sangha (Buddhist priesthood), and since the sangha was celibate there was always room at the top. A government officer of whatever rank could fall when his patron fell, a frequent occurrence since a new king usually insured his legitimacy by eliminating all near relatives.[33] The coming of British rule seems to have stabilized the circulation of elites. The importance of the sangha declined, and the Burmese court was replaced by a merit bureaucracy in which rank at entry depended upon one's level of formal education. British education was preferred, and such education was expensive. Consequently, the Burmese recruits to the "heaven-born" ranks of the ICS did not constitute so much a new class as an old class transformed.

While the transfer of British values to the adopted elite was impressive in scope and duration, it was by no means complete. The young guardian's primary and secondary education took place most likely in an "English school," often one maintained by

32. This letter is from the personal files of one of the early entrants. The names used are pseudonyms. See also the royal origins of U Ba U, a chief judge in British times who became the second president of independent Burma. See Tinker's chapter in this volume, p. 68, n. 76; and U Ba U, *op. cit.*, pp. 1–5.

33. Contrasting Burma with Siam, Riggs has calculated that the Alaungpaya dynasty averaged twelve years per king, while the Chakri kings in Siam during a comparable period averaged twenty-five and one-half years. Fred Riggs, *Thailand: The Modernization of a Bureaucratic Polity* (Honolulu, 1966), pp. 50–51.

missionaries. He attended University College or Judson College
in Rangoon where the professors were largely British and American, or he may have gone to India or perhaps to England. On
entering the service he went out to the field for training in a close
relationship with an experienced British officer, who often played
the combined role of parent and teacher. All these Westernizing
influences had a profound effect on standards of bureaucratic
behavior as well as on habits of dress and social style.[34] Yet there
were two barriers to complete Westernization. First, the Burman
was not the equal of an Englishman in his own country and he
felt it strongly. Burmese members of the ICS could not join the
Pegu or Gymkhana clubs, where many of the important administrative decisions, particularly those affecting the big British firms,
were made in an environment free from the restraints of formal
bureaucratic routine.[35] Second, the Burmese member of the ICS
retained Buddhism as his religion.[36] Theravada Buddhism and
the personal ethic which it enjoins have frequently been blamed
for inducing a low level of entrepreneurship. Obviously, those
who have attained the ranks of the ICS were not deficient in
achievement motivation. Yet certain principles of interpersonal
relations derived from their religion—such as the injunction
never to "break another man's rice pot"—run counter to the firm
fixing of responsibility and other rational bureaucratic norms.

The pace of Burmanization in the superior services lagged

34. Even today senior Burmese who were civil servants during British rule
remember with pride and some sentimentality the commissioners who trained
them in their first district assignments. An imaginative analysis of the acculturation
of Burmese elites to British norms and the psychological crisis many experienced
following independence is displayed by Pye, *Politics, Personality and Nation
Building.* The same phenomenon is reported by Braibanti in his chapter on
Pakistan (Chapter 5) in this volume, p. 250, n. 85.

35. See U Ba U, *op. cit.,* p. 114; and Collis, *Trials in Burma.* Foucar, a lawyer
connected with one of the British firms, explains in *I Lived in Burma,* p. 207, that
the Burmese picture of a monolithic "Pegu Club Government" was much
overdrawn.

36. For most Burmese, to say "Burmese" means to say "Buddhist." Since the
beginning of the British connection Christianity made converts among the animist
hill people (Karens, Kachins, Chins) but few among the Burmese majority. For an
explanation see J. S. Furnivall, *Christianity and Buddhism in Burma: An Address
to the Rangoon Diocesan Council, August, 1929* (Rangoon, reprint *ca.* 1959). The
Anglo-Burmese, on the other hand, were almost totally Christian. John Clement
Koop, *The Eurasian Population in Burma,* Cultural Report Series No. 6 (New
Haven, 1960), p. 2.

behind Indianization just as Burma lagged behind India in the development of educational resources and political maturity. Burma had no university of her own until the unorthodox promotional activities of Sir Harcourt Butler changed Rangoon College to University College in 1920. When the General Council of Burmese Associations was founded that same year, the Indian National Congress had been in operation for thirty-six years. Recognizing the rejection by Burmese political opinion of the differential stages of constitutional advancement proposed for Burma and India in the Montagu-Chelmsford Reforms, the Lee Commission in 1924 recommended—with regret—that the same rate of indigenization be applied in Burma as in India.[37] The first Burmese was elevated to the post of district officer in 1908 and he stood alone until 1916.[38] In 1921 U Tin Tut became the first Burmese appointed to the ICS. Four more Burmese were appointed during 1922 and 1923, by which time thirteen were holding posts in the executive and judicial branches of the ICS, either officiating or by appointment or promotion. By 1928 the number had risen to twenty-one, and by October, 1941, it reached sixty-seven out of a total of 163.[39] By this time also, having attained separation from India, the legislature set up a committee (on which U Tin Tut served as adviser) which recommended the end of further recruitment of Europeans to the

37. *Report of the Royal Commission on the Superior Civil Services in India,* Cmd. 2128 (1924), p. 55. Hereinafter cited as Lee Commission Report.
38. Harvey, "Conquest of Upper Burma," p. 447; and U Ba U, *op. cit.,* p. 61.
39. The year 1941 is taken as the last normal year of British rule in Burma. The political and military elites of the postwar period came to power during the Japanese occupation, and the three years of the British "reoccupation" were acknowledged as transitional by both British and Burmese. *The Quarterly Civil List for Burma,* No. 287, shows a cadre of 145 members for the executive and judicial branches of the ICS and BCS(I). Harvey, *British Rule in Burma,* p. 31, calculates that eighty-one of the 145 were English, ten Eurasians, and the remainder (fifty-four) Burmese. An additional eighteen persons were officiating in posts reserved for the BCS(I). If these are added in, the total comes to 163, of which ninety-six are English and Eurasian and sixty-seven are Burmese and other Asians, according to the calculations of Saya Tha Hto in *Kayin Myar Hnint Lutlatye [Karens and Independence]* (Rangoon, 1948), p. 10. These figures do not include eight Burmese and two Englishmen appointed to the BCS(I) in April, 1942, during the British retreat, such as U Maung Maung, who is now permanent secretary in the Ministry of Defense, and U Ba Nyein, who became a leader of the above-ground Communists during the 1950's and is financial adviser to the current army government. *Quarterly Civil List for Burma,* No. IV (1947). Figures for 1923 and 1928 are from the Simon Commission Report, XI, 23.

Class I services, as European officers were "in the process of becoming an anachronism under the present Constitution and in the present conditions of Burma."[40] The pace of Burmanization is summarized by decades in Table 1 below.

Table 1. *Ethnic Composition of the Higher Civil Service in Burma, 1910–1960*[a]

Period	British	Eurasian[b]	Burmese and other Asian[c]	Totals	Percentage British
1910	120	0	2	122	98.4
1920	154	0	6	160	96.3
1930	124	0	26	150	82.7
1941	81	10	54	145	55.9
1948	0	5	48	53	0
1960	0	8	98	106	0

[a] By "Higher Civil Service" is meant the executive and judicial branches of the Burma Commission of the ICS, the Burma Civil Service (Class I), and after independence the Administrative Grade and the Selection Grade of the Burma Civil Service. See above, p. 370, Chart I. The figures for 1960 are those for the executive branch alone.

[b] Determination of whether or not a person was a Eurasian depended on judgments of his associates, such as those made by G. E. Harvey, *British Rule in Burma: 1824–1942* (London, 1946), p. 31, for the 1941 cadre and by Burmese civil servants for the 1948 and 1960 cadres. Hence, no figures are available for the first three decades.

[c] In 1910 both members of this category were Indians. In 1920 the category included two Indians; in 1930, one Indian and one Indo-Burman; in 1941, one Indian, one Indo-Burman, and one Sino-Burman; in 1948, one Indo-Burman and one Sino-Burman; and in 1960, one Sikh, three Indo-Burmans, and three Sino-Burmans.

Sources: The Quarterly Civil List for Burma, No. 162 (*corrected up to 1 October, 1910*), No. 201 (*corrected up to 1 July, 1920*), No. 242 (*corrected up to 1 October, 1930*), No. 287 (*corrected up to 1 October, 1941*); Union of Burma, *Civil List,* No. 5 (*corrected up to 1 April, 1948*), No. 10 (*corrected up to 31 December, 1959*).

As Burmanization progressed, fears were expressed that a concentration of European officers in the choice secretariat posts (which presumably required a higher level of training and deeper perspective, and did provide higher pay and opportunities for living in Western style) while Burmese officers were concentrated in the districts would impart a racial complexion to the

40. Government of Burma, *Report of the Committee on Expenditure in the Public Services, 1939–40* (Rangoon: Superintendent Government Printing and Stationery, 1940), Part I, pp. 6–8; quotation at p. 7.

headquarters-field cleavage. In fact, by 1941 more than half of the district officers (eighteen out of thirty-three) were Burmese. This was accounted for largely by the number of officiating district officers drawn from the Provincial Civil Service.[41] Curiously, in Ceylon the indigenous members of the CCS were under-represented in the districts on the assumption that these were critical posts which should be held by Europeans.[42]

Just as the district officer stood closer to the Burmese masses than did the officials walled up in the secretariat, so the judiciary dealt more directly with the people than could the executive branch. In India the closeness of the courts to the people found consonance in a more rapid pace of Indianization than took place in the executive branch. In Burma the pace was roughly the same for both branches. By 1941, 40 per cent of the judicial branch and 36.6 per cent of the executive branch of the BCS(I) were staffed by Burmese.[43] Within the judicial branch the ethnic distinction between Rangoon and the districts paralleled that on the executive side. Registrars and the "civilian" (ICS) judges of the High Court were English or Anglo-Burman, while eleven of the district and sessions judges were Burmese, one was Indian, three Anglo-Burman, and seven English.

Perhaps the judiciary made no more rapid an advance in Burmanization because the British feared that the courts might become too close to the people. The lower courts were notoriously corrupt, and a European lawyer practicing in Rangoon at the time noted the grave misgivings when Burmese judges were first appointed to the High Court in the 1920's. In time, the Burmese on the High Court proved as able and honest as their English,

41. This problem is analyzed by Donnison, *Public Administration in Burma*, pp. 65–66. If, however, the comparison includes BCS(I) officers in the field at higher and lower ranks as well (commissioner, headquarters assistant, and subdivisional officers), the disproportion becomes much less significant.

42. See Kearney's chapter (Chapter 8) on Ceylon in this volume, p. 491, n. 15.

43. The comparison with India is derived from Ralph Braibanti, "Public Bureaucracy and Judiciary in Pakistan," in Joseph LaPalombara (ed.), *Bureaucracy and Political Development* (Princeton, N. J., 1963), pp. 410–411. The Burmese figures are from Harvey, *British Rule in Burma*, p. 33, and the *Quarterly Civil List for Burma* for January, 1941. This rough balance between executive and judicial in Burma had continued for some time. In 1928, when the Provincial Civil Service stood at 87 per cent Burmese, the Provincial Judicial Service was only slightly higher at 94 per cent. Simon Commission Report, XI, 23.

Indian, and Anglo-Burman brothers.[44] While the English judges
were above corruption and would dispense justice fairly in a case
between Asians, there is some question whether they were fair in
disputes between Europeans and Asians. A similar question of
partiality arose regarding the executive branch as a supporter of
British firms in conflict with indigenous interests.[45]

The High Court served as a testing ground also for the claims of
ICS omnicompetence. Several of the High Court judges were
drawn from the ICS while others came from the bar in Burma,
India, or Great Britain. U Ba U, a Burmese barrister who served
on the court, found that the "civilian" judges exhibited an
executive bias, favoring conviction. Harvey, an ICS member with
judicial experience, considered the rate of appeals allowed from
lower courts appalling. Both agreed that the least competent
High Court judges were the barristers who came out from Great
Britain and had no understanding of the country.[46]

The Specialist Services

The general administration was the senior service at both the
Class I and provincial levels and it maintained its superiority to
the end of the British connection. Their examinations were stiffer,
and those who stood low on the list were often selected for one of
the specialist services. The generalist skills were considered the
more difficult ones; hence, top posts in a number of specialist
departments were reserved to the ICS. The general administration played the central role, directing and co-ordinating the
activity of the government at each level of the hierarchy.

Competition for power and status between the general administration and the specialist services, and among the specialist
services themselves, reflected differentials in education, pay,
strategic position, and seniority. It was also colored by variations
in the ethnic composition of the various services. The particular

44. Foucar, *op. cit.*, p. 210; and Harvey, *British Rule in Burma*, pp. 36–37. For
the general level of corruption, see Foucar's delightful stories and U Ba U, *op. cit.*,
passim.

45. U Ba U, *op. cit.*, pp. 89–90, 130. See also Collis, *Trials in Burma*, pp. 34,
57–82, 187–213.

46. Harvey, *British Rule in Burma*, pp. 33–37; U Ba U, *op. cit.*, p. 115 and
passim.

role each of the minority communities played in the public services is therefore of special significance.[47]

Indians, the most significant Asian minority in Burma before the war, had first come to Burma in small numbers as traders, ponnas (astrologers), and pagoda slaves. With the annexation of Lower Burma thousands were brought in as higher- and lower-level public servants, as clerks in private firms, and as coolies. By the time of the 1931 census, Indians, accounting for less than one-tenth of the total population, occupied almost one-third of the jobs in public administration; Rangoon, the capital of Burma, had become in effect an Indian city.[48] Indians held an initial advantage over Burmese in the public service through their greater knowledge of English, acquaintance with British administrative procedures, and adaptability to the British working style. In addition, the British were accustomed to working with Indians and felt they were more reliable. The early police subalterns were Indians because the Indian army officers who commanded them could not speak Burmese. Later, this force was divided into the civil police, who were largely Burmese, and the military police, who were Indian.[49] Within the civil police, the top posts were almost exclusively held by Europeans or Anglo-Indians.[50] By the turn of the century Indians had been displaced in the general administration, but they still bulked large in the engineering and medical staffs until World War II. The Class I Indian Service of Engineers was almost exclusively British, while the Burma Engineering Service had an Indian majority and only a few Burmese were found in both. Indians were also strongly repre-

47. For analysis of the distribution between British, Burmese, and Indian members in each service and a discussion of the problem of Indians in the civil services of Burma, see the minute of Sir Reginald Craddock in Lee Commission Report, pp. 139–146.

48. B. R. Pearn, *The Indian in Burma*, Racial Relations Studies in Conflict and Cooperation, No. 4 (Ledbery, 1946), pp. 1–11. James Baxter, *Report on Indian Immigration* (Rangoon: Superintendent, Government Printing and Stationery, 1941), p. 25. See also Usha Mahajani, *The Role of Indian Minorities in Burma and Malaya* (Bombay, 1960).

49. Harvey, "Conquest of Upper Burma," p. 443.

50. Up to 1928 no Burman had risen above the post of district superintendent of police. Among the assistant superintendents of police, the lowest rank in the Class I service, were twenty-six Europeans, eight Anglo-Indians, and three Burmese. Even by 1941 only one of the seven deputy inspectors general was Burmese, and he was officiating. Simon Commission Report, XV, 457, 464; *Quarterly Civil List for Burma*, October, 1941.

sented in posts and telecommunications and composed three-quarters of the subordinate staff of the Railway Service.[51] Much the same picture appears in the Medical Department for the earlier period; by 1941 only three out of thirty-eight members of the Class I Indian Medical Service, two out of eighteen civil surgeons, and seventeen out of sixty-four assistant civil surgeons were Burmese. In fact, the medical profession at large was dominated by Indians, who made up almost three-fifths of the registered medical practitioners; less than one-quarter were Burmese, and the rest were equally distributed between Europeans, Anglo-Indians, and Karens.[52] In jobs dealing with the counting of money, particularly in customs and the accounts department, Indians held a virtual monopoly—perhaps, as Craddock explained, because the Burmese were not overly fond of routine. Indian clerks dominated the secretariat and other central offices, although clerks in the districts were mainly Burmese. The relations between areas of those services dominated by Indians and other services were naturally influenced by the fear and contempt Burmese felt for Indians elsewhere in society—the big and small businessmen, the Chettyar moneylenders, the seasonal immigrant laborers and carters of night soil.

Burma was the one country in Southeast Asia where the Chinese played a lesser role than the Indians before the war. Since independence, the Chinese and Sino-Burmese have been displacing the Indians. Already akin in religion and related by race, the Chinese readily adopted Burmese dress and language, and intermarriage between the two groups was common. Most of the Chinese engaged in trade, and although they enjoyed a near monopoly in certain areas—opium and liquor licenses, carpentry, petroleum distribution—they were not found concentrated in any particular government service.[53]

---

51. Harvey, "Conquest of Upper Burma," p. 447; Craddock's Minute in the Lee Commission Report, p. 142; Andrus, *op. cit.*, p. 243.

52. The 1924 figures are in Craddock's Minute, Lee Commission Report, p. 142; the 1941 figures come from Saya Tha Hto, *op. cit.*, p. 12; and the breakdown of the medical profession is found in the Baxter Report, p. 34, and the *Census of India, 1931*, Part II.

53. Christian, *op. cit.*, pp. 269–274. See also Victor Purcell, *The Chinese in Southeast Asia* (Oxford, 1951), pp. 55–101.

Karens were an indigenous minority, which, like the Kachins, accepted Christianity in great numbers and provided the armed forces with Burma's counterpart to the martial races of India. Following missionary guidance, many became teachers and medical personnel (particularly nurses), but few entered the Civil Service. The only services with significant Karen representation are education, where twelve out of the seventy-three indigenous deputy inspectors of schools serving in 1941 were Karen, and forests, where again they composed one-sixth of the indigenous members of the lowest gazetted rank.[54]

Eurasians, who were mostly Anglo-Indians and Anglo-Burmans, came from a variety of sources and found their common bonds in the Christian religion, the English language, and identification with the European elements in Burma. They constituted the backbone of the Railway service and Posts and Telegraphs Department. They played a significant role as subordinate officers in a number of other services, notably the Rangoon town police, in which the English monopolized the top and the Burmese the bottom ranks.[55] Their status in the public services was supported by claims on the conscience as well as by cultural affinity with British officers and a unique royal sanction in the Government of Burma Act.[56] When these supports were withdrawn and their numbers reduced by wartime and postwar emigration, many of the Eurasian community changed their names and their style of dress to maintain for themselves a place in the new society.[57]

---

54. Saya Tha Hto, *op. cit.*, pp. 10–12, has classified the gazetted ranks of most of the services in the 1941 Civil List into Burmese, Karen, and others to show that the Karens have been grossly underrepresented.

55. Koop, *op. cit.*, pp. 19–20; Christian, *op. cit.*, p. 161; and the *Quarterly Civil List for Burma*, October, 1941. Where the testimony of personal acquaintances is not available, Eurasians in the Civil List can be roughly identified as those with European names who do not draw overseas pay.

56. The *Draft Instrument of Instructions* to the governor of Burma requires him "to secure that the members of the several communities are afforded full opportunity to obtain the appointments in Our Service to which their qualifications and attainments entitle them," and if any community appears unfairly prejudiced in this regard "to reserve a due proportion of appointments for . . . each community . . . [having] due regard to the past association of the Anglo-Burman community with the customs, postal and telegraph services and the various branches of the Railway Service." *Government of Burma Act, 1935, Draft Instrument of Instructions* (London, 1936), p. 4.

57. Koop, *op. cit.*, pp. 31–36.

Conditions of Service

The ICS officer in Burma was a man from another world, and he brought the living standard of that world along with him in the shape of a pay scale that was remarkably high by local standards. The gap between the standards of these two worlds is illustrated by the pre-dyarchy budget for the secretariat, in which thirteen officers (from chief secretary down to registrar) cost an average of Rs. 1,785 per month, while the rest of the secretariat staff (almost three hundred employees) cost an average of Rs. 139 per month.[58] Burmese who bridged this gap must certainly have been transformed; they may well have faced some of the same psychological problems as the nascent nationalist politicians who accepted posts as ministers in the dyarchy government at Rs. 5,000 per month and were accused by their brother politicians of sacrificing principles for pay.

After several years of the great depression there were complaints in the Burmese Parliament that a Ford country could not support a Rolls-Royce administration.[59] A fiscal committee and a committee of the Burmese Parliament recommended downward revision of pay scales as an economy measure.[60] Throughout the provincial or Class II services, where the largest number were employed, pay scales were cut at top and bottom by about 20 per cent. One exception is the police Class II, where the maximum was cut but the minimum raised in hopes this action might reduce the temptations of bribery and extortion.[61]

The Class I services (except for the engineers, whose scale was raised) were relatively untouched. The superior position of the general administrative service remained. Entrants to the

---

58. Simon Commission Report, XI, 35.
59. Harvey, *British Rule in Burma*, p. 32.
60. *Report of the Committee on Expenditure on the Public Services, 1939–1940* (Rangoon: Government Printing and Stationery, 1940), pp. i, ii, 2–4.
61. The Bribery and Corruption Enquiry Committee noted that the lowest ranks of the police, constables and head constables, could not reasonably be expected to resist temptation on pay which was no better than that of an urban coolie. They recommended a starting pay of at least Rs. 25 per month. Others on the lowest rungs of their particular ladders whose pay was not commensurate with their powers over the money of others were the deputy myooks, revenue surveyors, and apprentice clerks. *Report of the Bribery and Corruption Enquiry Committee, 1940*, pp. 39–42.

BCS(I) began at Rs. 450 on the inferior scale, rising by stages to Rs. 2,500 on the superior scale at twenty-four years of service. The maximum pay for Class I members of the police, forest, engineers, education, and agricultural services stood near Rs. 1,350, which was the maximum for the inferior scale in the BCS(I).[62]

High salaries set the indigenous public servants apart from their countrymen but were not a sure insulation from the temptation to accumulate wealth on the side. In fact, some observers suggest that the steep scale promoted unrealistic aspirations for those in the lower ranks, opening them to the inducements of corruption. Further insulation from public pressures or the need to accumulate personal wealth came in the form of the pension system set up to accommodate expatriate public servants. In those prewar years a member of the ICS with twenty-five years of service (of which four years were leaves of various kinds) received a pension of £1,000 annually. Since the age limit at entry was twenty-three, this left the Indian civilian rather well off before the end of his first half century.[63]

The most important institution protecting the public service from public pressure was supposed to be a Public Service Commission, which was set up in Burma after the Indian model on the recommendation of the Simon Commission. The chairman, a British member of the ICS with extensive experience in Burma, and his two Burmese colleagues were appointed by the governor; their independence was further buttressed by a disqualification from serving in any other office under the Crown in Burma. The commission was to advise the government on appointments, postings, promotions, and transfers of public servants in all

---

62. The rates quoted are base pay. Super-scale pay was available in certain top posts in all services. In addition to base pay, the Class I services received a Burma allowance of Rs. 90–165 to offset the difference in cost of living between Burma and India, a Rangoon compensatory allowance of up to Rs. 120 for those stationed in the capital, and overseas pay of from Rs. 150 to Rs. 250 for those not domiciled in Burma. Government housing rented for 10 per cent of salary, and medical services were free. Lee Commission Report, pp. 51–54, and Appendix III; *Quarterly Civil List for Burma*, October, 1941.

63. Lee Commission Report, pp. 38–39. By the 1930's the government of Burma was paying out more in pensions than in salaries. *Financial and Economic Annual of Burma* (Rangoon: Bureau of State Printing Office, July, 1943).

services with the exception of the subordinate ranks of the police. However, patronage was something the elected ministers could not abjure, and the common practice of posting unco-operative officers to the Upper Chindwin or some other inhospitable post worked a demoralizing effect on the guardians, Burmese and British alike.[64]

The constitutional reforms of the inter-war period had been intended as preparation for eventual "home rule." Some of the problems that arose in the public services during this period foreshadowed difficulties that were to overwhelm Burma after independence in 1948.

II. Cutting the British Connection

On January 4, 1948, Sir Hubert Rance, the last of the British governors of Burma, handed over his charge to the ministers of the Union of Burma. He thus ratified a transfer of power that had begun on December 15, 1941, at Victoria Point on the southern tip of Tenasserim when Japanese troops crossed the Isthmus of Kra to capture their first town in Burma. The speed of the conquest—in fact, the very conquest itself—came as a surprise and a shock to British and Burmese alike. To the British civil servant, humiliated by the collapse of civil government in advance of the fighting line, this defeat meant betrayal by Britain of a whole people who had placed trust in them. Their earnest hope was for an early opportunity to redeem that trust.[65] To the Burmese civil servant the British retreat meant the eclipse of his known world. The eclipse was temporary: the British were expected to return. But doubts about their divinity had been raised, and these doubts reflected on those Burmese individuals and Burmese institutions closely identified with the British.

The war brought about a number of fundamental changes in

---

64. Donnison, *Public Administration in Burma*, pp. 77–80; Harvey, *British Rule in Burma*, pp. 89–90.

65. See in particular the sentiments of Sir Reginald Dorman-Smith, the then governor, in Maurice Collis, *Last and First in Burma: 1941–1948* (London, 1955), pp. 179–183.

Burmese politics,[66] which in turn had their impact on administration then and in the future. First, the course of political development was redirected and accelerated. The British model was rejected as Britain had lost the mandate of might. Dr. Ba Maw, defense attorney for the magical rebel leader, Saya San, and first prime minister under the 1937 Constitution, was brought out from a British jail and established as head of the government by the Japanese. No democratic institutions survived. In fact, democracy as such was disparaged by public figures, while traditional Burmese symbols were glorified. In 1943 the Japanese granted nominal independence to Burma, which made things even more difficult for the returning British when they tried to set the clock back even beyond the 1937 Constitution. A second change was the emergence of a new institution, a victorious Burma Independence Army, when Aung San and others of the "Thirty Comrades" trained by Japan on Hainan Island were introduced into Burma as a political-military arm of the invading Japanese forces. When Japan went down in defeat, the Burmese army was again victorious, this time in combination with British and American forces. After the war the Burmese army experienced its splits and defections, various elements going underground in a time of political turmoil. Throughout, there remained a core loyal to General Ne Win which was sufficiently motivated and disciplined to assume the reins of government from 1958 to 1960 as a legitimate caretaker regime and again in 1962 in a coup that has since evolved into a full-scale revolution. Thirdly, a new political class arose, based on the Thakins, a prewar party of radical students and other urban nationalists, which during the war drew many rural nationalists into the fold. When a resistance movement against the Japanese developed late in the war, all relevant political movements merged under Aung San's leadership into an Anti-Facist People's Freedom League, or AFPFL, a

66. For a full account, see Dorothy H. Guyot, "The Political Impact of the Japanese Occupation of Burma," a doctoral dissertation submitted to the Department of International Relations, Yale University, May, 1966. See also her "The Burma Independence Army: A Political Movement in Military Garb," in Josef Silverstein (ed.), *Southeast Asia in World War II* (New Haven: Yale University Southeast Asia Studies, in press).

party which through all its splits and defections and one care-taker army government ruled the country until the second army takeover. Symbolic of the irrelevance of the prewar political elite was the futile attempt of U Saw to gain the premiership by the assassination of Aung San and the AFPFL cabinet in the last months of British guardianship. A fourth influence was expansion of the politically mobilized public and the rise of mass organizations which bridged the gap between town and country, a function previously performed only by the steel frame of administration. The Wunthanu Athins of the 1920's, mutual benefit associations that adopted a political role, had no urban contacts. The Rangoon-centered elite political parties of the 1930's did not integrate rural elements into national politics. The havoc of the British retreat and later the dangers of Allied bombing drove townspeople into the villages where they established ties of obligation and identity with village folk and introduced modern ideas and organizations to the countryside. Finally, the habit of violence, legitimated in war, perfected in the numerous organizations which sprang up in the disarray of civil society, and fed by the large supply of arms deposited in Burma for various purposes, guaranteed that any postwar government would have to give priority to problems of law and order.

Considering the drastically altered political conditions and the variety of purposes toward which it was directed, the administration of Burma in the interim between the British defeat and the final grant of independence shows a striking degree of continuity in structures, practices, and personnel. The Japanese army was interested primarily in labor and supplies to support their war efforts. Dr. Ba Maw wanted to stage a social revolution, executing his New Order Plan by means of the administration in conjunction with his mass organizations. The returning British set their central task as the rehabilitation of a war-torn country.

The Japanese themselves ran the railroad, the port of Rangoon, telecommunications, the oil fields, in fact all businesses formerly owned by the British and any other activities crucial to the prosecution of the war, leaving law and order, justice, and revenue functions to the Ba Maw government. What little the civil administration did followed the earlier pattern of the strong area generalist. Representative institutions in the cities and the countryside were abolished, the specialist services atrophied, and the communications system broke down, leaving the responsibility for decisions in the districts. In fact, the only significant officers in the districts were the district officer and the district superintendent of police, whose main functions were to moderate the demands the Japanese made on the population.

The British and most of the Eurasian members of the Burma Civil Service had followed their army out of Burma. Almost all Burmese stayed behind with their families. A few retired to the villages, but most returned to administrative appointments with the Ba Maw government. All in all, less than one-third of the districts were headed by political appointees. At the secretariat political appointees settled largely in the newly created departments, such as labor, war co-operation, and religion. A notable nationalist innovation was the valiant effort to introduce Burmese as the language of administration. Still, day-to-day practices followed the prewar office manuals as closely as possible given the disruptions of a major war, Japanese occupation, and political intervention.

As the Allied armies recaptured portions of Burma, civil functions were turned over to a Civil Affairs Service (Burma), known as CAS(B), which drew for its officers and most of its subordinate staff on the British and Eurasian civil servants, businessmen, and clerks who had evacuated to India.[67] Those civil servants who had served during the Japanese occupation were classified as "black," "gray," or "white" by screening boards set up under CAS(B). The classifications decreased in severity as the Allied armies advanced and more resident Burmese were added to the boards. In the end, almost all the "collaborators"

67. Of the fifty-four ICS officers in the CAS(B), only one was Burmese. The ethnic classification of the total officer staff as of the end of 1944 was British, 42 per cent; Anglo-Indian and Anglo-Burmese, 27 per cent; Burmese, 10 per cent; Indian, 21 per cent. Burma (Simla), *British Military Administration, Burma, 1944* (Calcutta: Government of India Press, 1945), p. 81. The natural conflicts that developed between CAS(B) and the resident Burmese population are enumerated in F. S. V. Donnison, *British Military Administration in the Far East* (London, 1956), p. 127.

were cleared and granted back pay for their services during the war.

The corps of civil servants which had been divided by the war was reunited in a semblance of the old pattern of administration during a tumultuous two years of British civilian government between the demise of the military administration in 1945 and the granting of final independence. Ninety-three of the 145 Class I BCS officers serving in 1941 returned to serve during this period. This represented about 70 per cent of the Burmese officers and 60 per cent of the British and Eurasian officers.[68] A number of demobilized British servicemen were added to the Class I service as probationers, but they were shortly replaced by Burmese promoted from the ranks.[69] Coming changes were also evident in other aspects of the administration. The general structure of the steel frame remained, but special-purpose agencies such as the Civil Supplies Board arose in response to urgent problems of reconstruction. Many of these problems and their attendant organizations continued on into the independence period. Although the offices were largely the same as before, the style of administration reflected the uncertainty of the times. Symptomatic of this uncertainty was the high rate of turnover. Between liberation from the Japanese and independence, one lower Burma district passed through the charge of seven different district officers, averaging four months of tenure each. To the British civil servant on the way out, the road ahead for Burma seemed truly ominous.

III. Programs and Problems of Independence

Pyidawtha is the slogan under which U Nu sought for ten years to inspire the government and people of Burma to expend the energies released by their newly found independence in building

68. These figures are compiled from the Record of Service in *The India Office and Burma Office List, 1947* (London, 1947). This disparity in rate of return remains, even when length of service with the likelihood of retirement for age is accounted for.

69. *Quarterly Civil List for Burma* (*corrected up to October 1, 1947*), No. IV (Rangoon: Government Printing and Stationery, 1948).

a better, happier life out of the disruptions of war, foreign occupation, and home-grown insurrection.[70] The new tasks of government set out in the Pyidawtha plans called forth new organizations and provoked a tangle of relationships between the older services, the new services, the politicians, and the people. As the high hopes and welfare schemes of the early 1950's receded into factional strife and administrative malaise, the Burmese public, following the traditional magic formula for transposing vowels, switched the slogan Pyidawtha (A Royal Happy Land) to the stigma Pyadawthi (A Pile of Royal Ashes).

The war had deprived Burma of a greater proportion of her physical wealth than any other country in the world, with the exception of Greece; even by 1946–1947, the second full year of postwar reconstruction, total output was still 40 per cent below the 1938–1939 level.[71] While the postwar British administration set about rehabilitating the economy, the new Burmese political leaders sought independence as their primary goal, with the expectation that the solution of most economic problems would follow suit. The new Constitution was presented by U Nu as a decidedly "leftist" path to carry the nation to justice, liberty, and equality. The first Two-Year Plan of Economic Development and U Nu's Leftist Unity Program outlined steps to achieve the goals of the Constitution through a system of state socialism. Programs were established for eliminating landlordism, protecting the cultivator from fluctuations in the market while guaranteeing him a decent standard of living, and regaining prewar levels of rice production. The main emphasis, however, lay on industrialization and economic self-sufficiency, for which a series of projects in industrial development, communications, and resource exploitation were spelled out. Socialist principles were to be applied in conformance with the Burmese situation. This required the

70. The long-range plan implicit in Pyidawtha is described in the format of a quasi-popular report to the people, Economic and Social Board, Government of the Union of Burma, *Pyidawtha—The New Burma* (London, 1954). See also Union of Burma, Ministry of Information, *The Pyidawtha Conference, August 4–17, 1952: Resolutions and Speeches* (Rangoon, 1952). Hereinafter cited as *Pyidawtha Conference*. See also Knappen, Tippetts, Abbett Engineering Co. (with Pierce Management, Inc., and Robert R. Nathan Associates, Inc.), *Economic and Engineering Development of Burma* (2 vols.; New York, 1953).

71. Walinsky, *op. cit.*, pp. 57, 59.

Burmanization of the government services and most of the economy, yet it permitted certain forms of private enterprise and the acceptance of foreign capital and technical assistance under conditions that would not compromise Burmese independence. This Two-Year Plan set the general trend and specified a number of the projects found in later plans.

External Assistance

Burma has accepted consultants, equipment, and funds from a variety of sources, eschewing dependence on any one nation or bloc. In the military field, where independence was a concrete concern, the last tie with Britain was severed a few years after independence. The British Military Mission, which had advised on training and procured equipment, was displaced by reliance on Israel for advice and on Yugoslavia for equipment. In recent years military equipment has been procured from the United States under a series of agreements not publicized in Burma.[72]

The largest donor of economic aid has been Japan. The Burmese have no fear of compromising their independence in accepting this aid since they regard it as reparations due from World War II damage.[73] Goods delivered under the reparations agreements provided a basis for expanding trade between Burma

72. See, for instance, the delivery of F–86 jet fighters in mid-1964. *Christian Science Monitor*, July 11, 1964, p. 4.

73. Walinksy, *op. cit.*, p. 511, calculated Japanese reparations deliveries at $99,330,000, or 37.8 per cent of total foreign aid delivered to Burma by 1960. Japan accounted for over half of the foreign aid contributions to the 1964–1965 government budget. *Far Eastern Economic Review: 1965 Yearbook* (Hong Kong, 1965). An additional reparations agreement for $140 million in goods and services, to be supplied over a twelve-year period starting in 1965, was concluded by the second army government. The same agreement included a $30 million commercial loan. *Forward* (Rangoon: Directorate of Information), February 7, 1963, pp. 2, 3.

Since *Forward* is cited for the first time in this note and is referred to frequently in subsequent notes, an evaluation of its utility as a scholarly source seems justified here. *Forward* (*Shei-tho'*), a bi-weekly, and *The Working People's Daily* (*Loketha Pyithu Nezin*) were established by the Revolutionary Government in 1962 and 1963 and have become the major source of both official and day-to-day news in Burma, particularly since the nationalization of privately managed newspapers in the fall of 1964. Each issue of *Forward* contains short topics presented in straightforward, unanalytical fashion and often including extensive extracts from speeches. Descriptive and exhortatory articles and a cryptic chronology of events are also included in each issue. The Burmese and the English editions vary slightly in the topics covered, in emphasis, and in tone, with a more anti-Western flavor evident in the former.

and Japan. Early in the second army period many schemes were announced for joint ventures between Burma and private Japanese companies to assemble and eventually manufacture small cars, light bulbs, refrigerators, and other consumer goods in Burma.

During the Pyidawtha period the major role in economic planning was played by advisers from the United States. A British group known as the "Oxford economists" had made several general suggestions and ratified in 1951 the Two-Year Plan's decision to industrialize. The next year a preliminary report drawn up by private American consulting firms—Knappen, Tippetts, Abbett Engineering Company, Pierce Management, Inc., and Robert R. Nathan Associates, Inc.,—provided the base for an Eight-Year Development Plan which was expounded and approved at a massive Pyidawtha Conference of members of Parliament, secretaries and other government officers, and representatives of the AFPFL and the All-Burma Peasants Organization. Following completion of the comprehensive report, Burma rejected further official aid from the United States government as a sign of displeasure over America's indirect support of Chinese Nationalist guerrillas along the Burma-China border. The Robert Nathan team was continued at Burmese government expense until 1959 when the caretaker army government terminated their contract. The Robert Nathan consultants advised the government on a broad range of planning and development problems at large and also on specific projects, such as negotiations for aid from the United States and other governments. They made numerous studies, organized systems of reporting, and helped train and organize their successors as the Central Statistics and Economics Department in the Ministry of National Planning.

In 1961 the Central Statistics and Economics Department drew up a four-year plan which set modest objectives and recommended strengthening the private sector of the economy.[74] With the military coup of March, 1962, the national policy-making

74. Ministry of National Planning, *Second Four-Year Plan for the Union of Burma* (*1961–62 to 1964–65*) (Rangoon: Government Printing and Stationery, 1961).

machinery was drastically reorganized and economic planning became much less open to outside advice.

Following Burmese termination of United States government grants in 1953, United States aid took the form of several agreements for sales of surplus agricultural commodities under Public Law 480,[75] a development loan, a special police loan, and the sale of military equipment at bargain prices. The first army government showed less fear of compromising Burmese neutrality and sent an emissary direct to President Eisenhower asking for an outright grant of $37 million to construct a new trunk road from Rangoon to Mandalay. Negotiations over both the procurement and the implementation of United States aid for a variety of projects have been complex and tedious. Some restrictions imposed by the United States rasped Burmese pride, and others such as the Battle Act were viewed as threats to her neutrality.[76] A number of significant projects, such as the rehabilitation of Rangoon port facilities and the reclamation of waste land, were quite successful. Still others, such as the on-and-off Rangoon-Mandalay highway project, conclusively cancelled by the second army government five years after its inception,[77] left in the Burmese mind uneasiness about American intentions and uncertainty about Burma's potential for progress.

By contrast, Soviet aid, the magnitude of which did not approximate the volume of United States contributions,[78] was

75. Public Law 480 (68 Stat. 454) is the Agricultural Trade Development and Assistance Act of 1954 and its subsequent amendments. For general description and analysis, see Lawrence J. White, "Public Law 480: Something for Everyone," *Public Policy*, XIII (1964), 152–169. The latest such agreement with Burma was signed by the Revolutionary Government in November, 1962. Revolutionary Government of the Union of Burma, Ministry of National Planning, *Economic Survey of Burma—1963* (Rangoon: Government Printing and Stationery, 1963), p. 142.

76. Public Law 213 (65 Stat. 644), popularly known as the Battle Act, is the Mutual Defense Assistance Control Act of 1951. The Battle Act attempts to control trade in strategic materials with the Soviet Union, or any nation "threatening the security of the United States," both by American firms and by any nation receiving military, economic, or financial assistance from the United States. The particular political difficulties of United States aid programs in Burma are explored in John D. Montgomery, *The Politics of Foreign Aid: American Experience in Southeast Asia* (New York, 1962), pp. 31–35, 40–43, 140–146.

77. *Forward*, May 22, 1964, p. 23.

78. By 1960 Soviet contributions stood at 8.8 per cent of the total and United States contributions at 26.3 per cent. Walinsky, *op. cit.*, p. 511. See also D. Vasilyev and K. Lvov, *Soviet Trade with South-East Asia* (Moscow: Foreign Languages Publishing House, 1959), pp. 63–65 and Appendix.

conceived and carried out in what appeared to be a successful style. During their 1955 visit to Burma, Khrushchev and Bulganin offered a number of major gift projects and at the same time proposed to purchase Burmese rice which was then difficult to move on the world market. U Nu accepted the rice sale proposal and offered a gift of additional rice in return for the Soviet gift projects. The terms of the gift exchange were hazy and were arrived at amicably. Concern by the Robert Nathan consultants and by the caretaker army government about Burma's capacity to absorb the gifts within her total development plan, reduced the projects to three—a technical institute, a hospital in Shan States, and a tourist hotel in Rangoon. Although the projects were completed and began operation in 1961–1962, they had been paid for in rice shipped in 1956 so that for a period of years Burma was a lender rather than a receiver of aid from the Soviet Union.[79] Nevertheless, the spirit of the exchange carried the day and the "gift" label stuck.

Early in the period India, too, was a major source of financial aid to Burma with a $42 million loan in 1955. But perhaps the greatest impact of Indian assistance on Burmese development was the large number of medical personnel contracted on a temporary basis to fill Civil Service vacancies created by the Burmanization policy and by the new development plans.

On his independence day visit to sign the Burma-China border agreement on January 4, 1961, Chou En-Lai offered U Nu an $84 million loan without interest. In subsequent years a large number of Chinese technical study missions have dispersed over the countryside investigating an array of potential projects, ranging from small irrigation dams to a diesel pump factory and a mill for processing paper from bamboo.

Multilateral aid from United Nations agencies and the Colombo Plan was primarily advisory, although there were a few direct action projects, such as the World Health Organization's malaria eradication program. The Ford Foundation supported programs of research, advice, and training, which along with the Fulbright Program helped the educational system adjust to the

79. Walinsky, *op. cit.*, pp. 539–540. On United States and Soviet competitive giving, see Montgomery, *op. cit.*, pp. 40–43.

strains of nation-building. The Asia Foundation contributed less money but did it more decisively and over a wider range of projects. Within a few months of coming to power, the second army government ordered the personnel of all private foundations to leave the country. The motive seems to have been a desire to reduce the number of foreigners in the countryside since the World Health Organization's malaria control teams were removed at the same time. The realigned neutralism of the government gradually reduced the amount of technical assistance accepted from "Western" countries, including Israel, while encouraging aid from the "Socialist Bloc."[80] State scholars are still sent out to England and Commonwealth countries but no longer to the United States. An increasing number are sent to the Soviet Union and Eastern Europe but few to China.[81] Typical of this shift was the nationalization of the Burma Oil Company, Ltd., which had been a joint venture between the government and British investors with a mixed management. It was reorganized as a government corporation operated with the help of Rumanian advisers.

Program of Administrative Reform

Just as foreign aid supported and helped shape many of the programs undertaken by the government of independent Burma, so, too, external advice played a role in reappraising the machinery of administration. During the war a reconstruction department of the government in exile at Simla prepared a series of reports including an extensive examination of problems of district administration. This series served as an intermediate step from the pre-invasion structures and practices to the wide-ranging

80. John S. Everton, who directed the Ford Foundation's work in Burma in the late 1950's and was United States ambassador there until 1963, comments on the Revolutionary Government's reactions to Western aid in "The Ne Win Regime in Burma," *Asia: A Journal Published by the Asia Society, New York,* II (1964), 1–17. See esp. pp. 9–13.

81. Of the students sent abroad on foreign scholarships in the fall of 1965, forty-five were announced as going to the Soviet Union; thirty-five to Eastern Europe, primarily East Germany; twenty-seven to Great Britain, Australia, and Canada; six to West Germany; six to China; and six to India, Pakistan, Japan, and Malaysia. *Working People's Daily,* II (September 3, 1965), 1.

reforms recommended by an Administration Reorganization Committee, appointed on the morning of independence and composed of Burmese civil servants and John S. Furnivall, whose influence is obvious throughout the report.[82]

Probably the greatest foreign impact on the organization and operation of public administration in Burma came from eight years of continuous contact between the top levels of government and the Robert R. Nathan consultants. Another avenue of influence was opened in the fall of 1952–1953 when George T. Jackson, a United Nations expert on leave from the Canadian Civil Service Commission, came to make a six-month survey of public administration and drew up a forthright and comprehensive analysis of the overcentralization, overstaffing, underpayment, and outmoded procedures which plagued the system. Other United Nations advisers from Commonwealth countries followed over the years, and the process of analysis and recommendation was institutionalized in an indigenous Directorate of Public Administration set up within the Home Ministry.[83]

82. The first report of the Administration Reorganization Committee laid the basis for a sweeping reform of local government, which was only partially carried out (see below, pp. 397 ff.). In 1957 a survey report by the Public Administration Service of Chicago urged a more thoroughgoing application of the reforms to effect representative government on the American model, but these recommendations ran against the trend of events. The ten major reports on administrative reform are listed in Table 8 in Braibanti's concluding chapter in this volume. More detailed citations are given in this note and in notes 83 and 85 below. This note also lists a report issued in 1944, somewhat before the period included in Braibanti's comparative Table 8. The name of the chairman or author is given with each report. Some of these reports will hereinafter be cited by the name of the chairman or author, when they are thus commonly known. Government of Burma, *Report of the District Administration (Reconstruction) Committee* (Simla: Government of India Press, 1944); Government of the Union of Burma, *The First Interim Report of the Administration Reorganization Committee* (Rangoon: Government Printing and Stationery, 1948) (U Lun Baw); Government of the Union of Burma, *The Final Report of the Administration Reorganization Committee* (Rangoon: Government Printing and Stationery, 1951) (U Lun Baw); Public Administration Service, *The Local Government Democratization Program of the Government of the Union of Burma* (Chicago, 1957) (Wendell G. Schaeffer). Spirited rejoinders to Schaeffer's report are J. S. Furnivall, "The Plan of the Administrative Reorganization Committee: An Explanation and Summary," mimeographed (Rangoon: Ministry of National Planning, December 28, 1957), and Furnivall, "The Reports of Dr. W. G. Schaeffer on Local Government in Burma," mimeographed (Rangoon: Ministry of National Planning, January 16, 1958).

83. Jackson, as a Canadian, perhaps had better access to Burmese officials than did the British, who represented the former occupying power, or Americans, who by that time seemed too much in evidence. His *Report of a Survey on Public Administration in Burma,* presented to the Government of Burma in 1954, was

The major role played by the United Nations Technical Assistance Programme distinguished Burma from India, where administrative reform was generated by the Ford Foundation, and Pakistan, where the United States Agency for International Development and the Ford Foundation played complementary roles.[84] Burma differed also in this respect from Ceylon and Malaya, where virtually no systematic technical assistance for administrative reform was given. On the other hand, so far as the United Nations Technical Assistance Programme's influence on administration is concerned, Burma was similar to Nepal.

In a last, major reform effort before the second army takeover, a Public Services Enquiry Commission composed of senior civil servants traveled to a number of Western European and Commonwealth countries seeking information and advice on the status and organization of public services. The commission's report draws on comparisons with practices in India, England, Sweden, Thailand, and a range of other countries in arriving at recommendations for promoting the independence, efficiency, and honesty of the public services in Burma. Many of the recommendations echo earlier reports—the amalgamation of departments into their parent ministries, a reduction of control by the Ministry of Finance, delegation and decentralization of functions, competitive recruitment for all positions by the Public Service Commission. The most notable recommendation and one that was to have repercussions for the role of the Civil Service under the second army government was that a guarantee of

confidential, although portions are found in Walinsky, *op. cit.*, pp. 477–490. The present author read an earlier version of this report and discussed some of the problems of administration with Mr. Jackson. Other reports by United Nations advisers are F. J. Tickner, "Report on Public Administration in Burma," mimeographed (United Nations Technical Assistance Administration, March–April, 1954); S. T. Divers, *Public Administration in Burma: Progress 1953–1956* (New York: United Nations Technical Assistance Programme TAA/BUR/17, August, 1956); A. S. Pankhurst, *Public Administration in Burma: 1956–58* (New York: United Nations Technical Assistance Programme TAO/BUR/28, August, 1959).

84. For a description of United Nations, United States Agency for International Development, and Ford Foundation activities in administrative reform generally, see Ralph Braibanti, "Transnational Inducement of Administrative Reform: A Survey of Scope and Critique of Issues," in John D. Montgomery and William D. Siffin (eds.), *Approaches to Development: Politics, Administration and Change* (New York, 1966), pp. 133–185.

tenure for civil servants similar to the one provided in the Indian Constitution be written into the Burmese Constitution.[85] However, the significant changes in the practices of public administration were brought about not by design but by the force of circumstances—the expansion of government responsibilities and the pressure of political events.

Implementation of Reform

Before the war the steel frame of administration had been built around ten ministries (then called departments), each headed by a Burmese minister under whom a member of the ICS served as secretary. An exception was the Ministry of Defence, which remained under direct British control. Table 2 below reveals that during the British occupation the number of ministries was kept to eleven, but the expanded responsibilities of the regular administration forced an increase in staff of over one-third.[86] During the push toward Pyidawtha the number of ministries multiplied, at one time reaching a peak of thirty-one and standing at twenty-six just before the second assumption of control by the army. Although in the twenty-year span from 1940 to 1960 the administrative staff doubled, the mere expansion and elaboration of existing forms of machinery was inadequate for the new tasks of government. Outside of the regular services, there were created economic organizations known loosely as "boards and corporations," whose employees brought the government rolls close to a quarter of a million.[87]

85. Government of the Union of Burma, *Report of the Public Services Enquiry Commission, 1961* (Rangoon: Government Printing and Stationery, 1961). The chairman of this commission was U Chan Tun Aung.

86. The cost of the increased staff was actually less than before the war in terms of constant kyats, since salaries of the higher ranks had been reduced, and more importantly, inflation had cut real wages to about one-third. The burden on the country was greater, however, because of the great decline in production. While administrative staff costs were 82 per cent of the prewar level, gross domestic product was 72 per cent of the prewar level in 1947–1948 and dropped to 61 per cent by 1949–1950. *Final Report of the Administration Reorganization Committee*, pp. 77–78; Walinsky, *op. cit.*, Appendix VIII.

87. By November, 1963, the Revolutionary Government estimated that more than 300,000 nationals were serving in government departments, boards and corporations, commissions and committees, state and local bodies, and state banks. With the nationalization of retail trade and most other economic activities in the spring of 1964, the number has probably grown considerably. *Forward*, November 22, 1963, p. 3; *ibid.*, March 22, 1964, p. 2.

The reluctance of British and Indian firms to invest new capital to replace their wartime losses and the urgent needs of rehabilitation compelled the postwar British administration to establish semi-state organizations for distributing essential commodities and for marketing rice and timber in the export trade. When the

Table 2. *Growth of Administrative Establishment*

	Prewar	Postwar	Early Pyidawtha	Late Pyidawtha
Number of ministries[a]	10	11	22	26
Size of administrative staff[b]	56,400	77,800	93,495	118,000 (242,650)[b]
Cost of administrative staff[c] (in millions of kyats at constant prices)	Ks. 179.7	Ks. 147.5	—	Ks. 360.0 (Ks. 466.0)[b]

[a] Excluded from the count in the early and late Pyidawtha periods are the ministries for the five states incorporated in the Union of Burma.

[b] Figures in parentheses are adjusted to include government boards and corporations.

[c] Costs are calculated on the basis of a consumer price index presented in Appendix VIII of Louis J. Walinsky, *Economic Development in Burma, 1951–1960* (New York, 1962). The kyat is the Burmese equivalent of the pre-independence rupee.

Sources: Figures for the number of ministers are drawn from *The Quarterly Civil List for Burma, 1941; The India Office and Burma Office List, 1947,* p. 51; United Nations Economic Commission for Asia and the Far East, "Seminar on Organization and Administration of Public Enterprises in the Industrial Field–Papers," mimeographed (Rangoon: March, 1954), paper No. 35; *Report of the Public Services Enquiry Commission, 1961,* p. 131. The figures for the size and cost of the administrative staff covering 1939–1940, 1946–1947, and 1950–1951 are taken from *The Final Report of the Administration Reorganization Committee,* p. 77. Figures for 1959–1960 come from the *Report of the Public Services Enquiry Commission, 1961,* p. 65.

AFPFL government took over at independence these were continued as the Civil Supplies Management Board, the State Agricultural Marketing Board, and the State Timber Board. In some cases pre-existing private firms were taken over whole. Thus, the Irrawaddy Flotilla Company, Ltd., came under the Inland Waterways Transport Board, and the Rangoon Electric Tramway and Supply Company, Ltd., became the Rangoon Electricity Supply Board. In other cases the government went into a "joint-venture" with a prewar capitalist firm, such as the Burmah Oil Company, in which the government subsequently obtained a controlling share of the stock and eventually national-ized the firm outright.

U Shwe Mra, an Arakanese member of the ICS, headed up a study mission in 1952 which observed the workings of the TVA, the nationalized industries in England, Turkish industrial banks, and development corporations in Latin America. Their report stressed the importance of freedom from standard governmental procedures for such public economic enterprises and suggested the establishment of a Mineral Resources Development Corpora-tion and an Industrial Development Corporation to finance and direct a series of projects proposed in the Two-Year Plan, in the preliminary report of the Knappen, Tippetts, Abbett Engineering Company, and at the Pyidawtha Conference.[88] Projects included a steel rolling mill, two sugar mills, a jute mill, the development of coal fields, and several other industries. An Agricultural Research and Development Corporation took the initiative in land reclama-tion to boost paddy production, introduced jute production, and reinvigorated a number of projects which were faltering because of inadequate leadership and staffing in the agriculture, irriga-tion, and veterinary departments.

By 1962 the government was operating four corporations and twenty-seven boards, ranging from the Burma Railways Board and the Agricultural and Rural Development Corporation to the National Housing, Town and Country Development Board and the Dock Labour Board.[89] The directing board of each public enterprise was composed of secretaries and other officials from the relevant government departments, while the chief executive officer was most likely a transferred civil servant with no indus-trial or technical experience. Up to 1961 a minister was desig-nated the chairman of the board "to expedite the snapping of red

88. "Brief Report of the Planning, Observation and Study Mission," mimeo-graphed (Rangoon, August 18, 1952).

89. *Report of the Public Services Enquiry Commission, 1961*, p. 143. Descriptions of various boards and corporations appear in the Directorate of Information's annual, *Burma: the Fourteenth Anniversary*, Vol. XI, January, 1962. A classification of those operating prior to the first army administration may be found in Furnivall, *Governance of Modern Burma*, pp. 70–76.

tape," and members of Parliament were included as members to represent the consumer interest.[90] These practices were compelled by the scarcity of managerial talent and the necessities of politics. As a consequence, the anticipated autonomy and freedom from regular governmental procedures never materialized. Nor was co-ordination between the boards and the regular departments of the government achieved. Membership on multiple boards diffused the attention of high-level officials and cut seriously into their regular departmental work. Even though the minister for finance and the financial commissioner for commerce were members of the board of the Industrial Development Corporation, the usual delays in granting financial sanction held up a good number of Industrial Development Corporation projects.

As the first government of independent Burma had fashioned new administrative forms to assume many of its new responsibilities, so too the first army government displayed much of its energy and inventiveness in a new general-purpose organ for economic development. The Defense Services Institute, which had begun as a commissary for defense services personnel, expanded into a variety of business ventures such as ocean shipping, a department store, and building construction. Successes were so great that the operation was continued and expanded as the Burma Economic Development Company (BEDC) when U Nu's civilian government returned to power in 1961. The BEDC operated as a private holding company under a special law on funds borrowed largely from the government and managed by active or retired military personnel. Its successes rested primarily on its ability to hire capable managers and to some extent on preferential treatment in import licenses and monopoly sales.[91] The quality of management was a large factor also in distinguishing those other governmental enterprises that turned a profit during the army period. Under the second army

90. *Report of the Public Services Enquiry Commission, 1961*, pp. 148–149. See also United Nations Technical Assistance Programme, "Development of Public Industrial Enterprise in Burma," in *Public Industrial Management in Asia and the Far East*, SI/TAO/M/65 (1960), pp. 45–61.

91. Walinsky, *op. cit.*, pp. 576–577.

government, in which Brigadier Aung Gyi, long the head of BEDC, was the "number two" man, the BEDC began to consume such profit-making government enterprises as the Mandalay Brewery and a number of successful private firms, and took monopoly control of pawn shops and liquor stores. A few months after Aung Gyi's fall from grace, the thirty-nine subsidiary firms of the Burma Economic Development Corporation were parceled out among the relevant boards and departments of the government.[92]

Despite the manifestos and new machinery, the advance to Pyidawtha on the economic front turned out to be a slow march. By the end of the first army government, per capita gross domestic consumption was only 87 per cent of what it had been twenty years earlier.[93] Modernization was evident in many aspects of the economy from caterpillar tractors in place of elephants to the bright synthetic fabrics which brought both durability and color to the clothing of the poor. Yet there had been no improvement in the fundamental structure of the economy. A relatively diversified export economy had become more concentrated on one product—rice, which had accounted for 47 per cent of the total value of exports before the war and 70 per cent in 1959–1960. The pattern of occupations showed little improvement from the 1931 census, in which agriculture claimed 70 per cent of the labor force, to the 1953–1954 census, in which the share of agriculture was 63 per cent while industry, trade, service, and the other categories retained their earlier positions.[94] The real change in the economy was a political one. Ownership and control of land, industry, trade, and finance were now largely in the hands of the Burmese government or Burmese citizens rather than foreign or resident British, Indian, and Chinese institutions.

92. *Forward*, September 22, 1963, p. 4.
93. Paddy production was 93 per cent of the prewar level, while rice exports were down to 64 per cent. Electric power generation stood at five times the prewar levels and railroad passenger traffic at twice the levels before the war, but freight traffic and almost all other economic indicators were down while population was up. *Second Four-Year Plan*, pp. 17–20. See also Walinsky, *op. cit.*, pp. 352–368; and Douglas Paauw, "Economic Progress in Southeast Asia," *The Journal of Asian Studies*, XXIII (1963), 69–92. For an assessment of changes under the Revolutionary Government, see below, pp. 408 ff.
94. *Second Four-Year Plan*, pp. 18–19.

Groundwork for a Social Revolution:
Education and Health

Pyidawtha meant more than economic development and the level of living. Pyidawtha Conference Resolutions called for reform and expansion of government efforts in education and public health. The challenges set and the responses made in these two areas are fairly typical of the behavior of the Burmese bureaucracy throughout the welfare field. In traditional Burma, education had centered on the local monastery where every male child was taught morals and the ability to read. When British troops first marched into lower Burma they were conquering a nation with a higher rate of literacy than their own.[95] During the British times the Buddhist monkhood decayed and the standards of monastic education declined. The motivation for education was no longer moral but careerist. A bright lad who learned English well might get a clerkship in the government or in a British firm. One of the chosen few who could follow an arts curriculum to higher levels, where the competition from Indians, Chinese, and Anglo-Burmans was fierce, might aspire to become a government official. Most schools were private, and those aided by government funds were divided by language into Vernacular, Anglo-Vernacular, and English. Graduates of the English schools had the brightest prospects, while those passing out of the Vernacular system could hope at best to become a teacher in a Vernacular school, a vaccinator, or a revenue surveyor.[96] This was the system that nationalist politicians came to call "slave education," a scapegoat still blamed for many of the current problems of independent Burma. Reforms pursued three goals: Burmanization of the English system, expansion of enrolments at all levels, and greater emphasis on vocational, technical, and scientific training.

The first step in reform was taken by the British military

95. Furnivall, *Political Economy,* preface to 3rd ed., p. x.
96. Union of Burma, Ministry of Education, *Octennial Report on Education in Burma* (1947–48 to 1954–55) (Rangoon: Government Printing and Stationery, 1956), p. 4.

government when it abolished the distinction between Vernacular, Anglo-Vernacular, and English schools following the recommendations of a prewar government committee.[97] In both private and government schools the Burmese government set the standards for the curriculum. All would teach English from the fifth standard up: none could teach it below the fifth standard. Before the war Judson College, operated by the American Baptist Mission, and University College, which was modeled after Oxford and Cambridge and had an outstanding and predominantly British faculty, were largely foreign or at least non-Burmese institutions. About two-thirds of the students at University College were Burmese. At Judson College Indians outnumbered Burmese four to one. Following independence the two colleges were amalgamated to form Rangoon University, in which the ratio of Burmese students increased from a little over half in 1939–1940 to about four out of five in the postwar period.[98] Burmese became the only acceptable language for the matriculation examination, but a test paper in English was still included. Intermediate (Freshman and Sophomore) courses were offered in either English or Burmese, and a succession of deadlines were set for complete conversion to Burmese instruction. Although Burmese had become the official language of government and the administration on independence day, English ranked first among the subjects which graduates of the University in 1959 felt were helpful to them in securing a job.[99]

The expanded scale of the educational system transformed the

97. Burma, Education Department, *Report of the Vernacular Education and Vocational Reorganizational Committee, 1936* (A. Campbell) (Rangoon: Government Printing and Stationery, 1936).

98. The figures for University College and Judson College appear in Burma, Education Department, *Report on Public Instruction, 1939–1940* (Rangoon: Government Printing and Stationery, 1941), p. 12. Ethnic classifications of the postwar student body for 1947–1948, 1955–1956, and 1959–1960 are found in Joseph Fischer, *Universities in Southeast Asia: An Essay on Comparison and Development,* International Education Monographs, No. 6 (Columbus, Ohio, 1964), p. 118, Table 14.

99. From a survey of those who obtained degrees in all programs that year reported in *The University Teacher's Review* (Rangoon: Rangoon University Press), Vol. 2, No. 1 (Monsoon, 1961–1962), pp. 23–27. An English vocabulary test developed for high school students by the University Counseling Service proved to be a better predictor of academic success than the regular matriculation examination. It is small wonder that a large number of private schools focusing on the English language flourished in Rangoon.

elite, English-style colleges and technical schools, which had produced slightly more than six thousand holders of bachelor's degrees by 1953, into a countrywide university system with almost seven thousand registered students in that same year and double that number by the end of the decade. The impetus for this increase came not only from political resentment of the previous system and its association with a foreign ruling elite, but also from the general social mobilization brought about by the war and by the influx of population to the cities during the insurrections. In addition, the Pyidawtha plans created a great need for trained personnel. To meet the demand for higher-level training, the program for sending state scholars abroad was expanded with particular emphasis on training in the United States.[100] At lower levels the multiplication of enrolments during the Pyidawtha period was even greater, necessitating an expansion of enrolments in teacher-training colleges.[101]

Discipline in the public schools deteriorated as the greatly expanded and pitifully staffed educational system was wracked by an onslaught of student politics, in which the young men of the 1950's acted out the legendary roles that the current political elite had played in the 1930's. Civil servants and other middle-class families sent their children to mission schools for the discipline they could not get elsewhere. Under the Revolutionary Government's program of stamping out foreign influences the missionary schools were nationalized outright in the spring of 1965 and the process of nationalizing other private schools was initiated.

A major component of the "slave education" indictment was the relative neglect shown scientific and technical education during British times. Furthermore, what scientific and technical

100. Before the war six to twelve state scholars were selected annually for training primarily in the United Kingdom; a few were sent elsewhere in Europe or to the United States or Japan. By 1956, 379 state scholars were abroad with over two hundred of them in the United States. Burma, Education Department, *Rules Relating to the Award of Burma State Scholarships, 31 August, 1939* (Rangoon: Government Printing and Stationery, 1941), pp. 2, 6. *Octennial Report on Education in Burma*, p. 42.

101. Walinsky, *op. cit.*, p. 366.

education was available attracted primarily the non-Burmese.[102] The Pyidawtha plans called for correction of both these failings, and during the 1950's bipolar foreign assistance was accepted with enthusiasm. The United States built the Technical High School in Rangoon and helped rehabilitate and staff the Technical Institute at Insein and the Agricultural School at Pyinmana. The Soviet Union built the sumptuous Burma Institute of Technology and helped to staff it with eight to ten professors during the first years. Sixteen years after independence the Revolutionary Government made new promises to "completely demolish a system of education formulated by the colonialists" and turn the emphasis to science and the training of needed specialists.[103]

When university and post-graduate faculties opened for the fall term of 1964 they had been renamed and restructured, and a number of rectors had been replaced by military men. The students were eager enough to study such needed specialties as medicine, engineering, education, and agriculture, but the limitations of staff and equipment kept the proportions in each field of study much the same as they were before for the first two years of the reform, as is shown in Table 3 below. The new enthusiasm for agriculture may have come directly from Army urging. Career interests in medicine or engineering, however, were of longer standing. The proportions of university matriculates giving their first choices to medicine (31%) and engineering (15%) in 1965 are about the same as the vocational preferences of a sample of high school seniors in 1962 where 30 per cent chose "doctor" and eighteen per cent chose "engineer." Perhaps the more significant reform was the diversion of a large proportion of the student body to intermediate colleges in their home areas,

102. In 1937 only twenty-six of the 138 graduates of the university obtained degrees in science and only nine of these were Burmese. In that same year Burmese nationals comprised only four of the fourteen graduates of the medical college, thirty-nine of the 128 licentiates of the medical school, two of the four engineering graduates and four of the twenty graduates of the Government Technical Institute. *Pyidawtha Conference*, p. 96.

103. Col. Hla Han, minister of education, addressing the faculty of the university during a suspension of instruction due to student political disturbances. *Forward*, April 22, 1964, pp. 4–5. See also his speech at the first convocation of the reformed university. *Forward*, February 1, 1966, p. 3.

Table 3. *Distribution of University Students in Major Fields of Study Before and After Army Reforms*[a]

Field of Study	Enrolment 1961–62		Admissions 1964		Admissions 1965		Preference Ratio[b]
	Num-ber	Per-cent	Num-ber	Per-cent	Num-ber	Per-cent	1965
Arts and Science[c]	10,633	69.3	2,927	50.9	4,688	60.1	0.29
Economics	—	—	359	6.2	449	5.8	1.49
Worker's College[d]	—	—	1,124	19.5	894	11.5	0.96
Engineering	2.095	13.7	505	8.8	555	7.1	2.08
Medicine	1,430	9.3	438	7.6	540	6.9	4.53
Dentistry and Veterinary	—	—	40	0.7	121	1.5	0.67
Agriculture	105	0.7	52	0.9	200	2.6	1.72
Education	1,074	7.0	306	5.3	350	4.5	2.64
Total	15,337		5,751		7,797		

[a] In comparing distributions, enrolments (for 1961–62) are roughly comparable with admissions (for 1964 and 1965) since the course of study in most fields is about the same length, four years, except for those in medicine taking the MBBS, which requires seven years.

[b] This is the ratio of the number of first preference applications to the number of admissions.

[c] Unfortunately this category obscures any shift in the ratio of science students to arts students within the Faculty of Arts and Science. In 1961–62 Economics was included in this faculty. The 1961–62 figures are for Rangoon University, Mandalay University, and two of the five intermediate colleges. Inclusion of the other three intermediate colleges might raise the figure by 500–600.

[d] Before the reforms this was a non-degree granting, part-time Adult Education University. Its curriculum is primarily Arts and Science.

Sources: For enrolments in 1961–62, Joseph Fischer, *op. cit.,* Table No. 13, p. 117 and Director of Information, *Burma: the Fourteenth Anniversary,* (Rangoon: Government Printing and Stationery, 1962), p. 105.

For admissions in 1964, *Forward,* November 1, 1964, pp. 2, 3.

For admissions and preferences in 1965, *Forward,* November 1, 1965, p. 2, and *The Working People's Daily,* October 3, 1965, pp. 1, 8.

See also James F. Guyot, *The Clerk Mentality in Burmese Education,* a paper prepared for a conference on "The Social Sciences and the Comparative Study of Educational Systems," School of Education and Institute of International Studies, University of California, Berkeley, March, 1966.

thereby reducing the concentration of undergraduates on the Rangoon campus where they had rioted sporadically throughout the first two years of Army rule. Significant changes also took place at the secondary level where vocational and technical schools burgeoned and a Luyechun (Pioneer Youth) program identified, glorified, and provided special training and privileges for outstanding high school students.

Policy reforms and external pressures on the educational

system created or intensified a great number of administrative problems. For instance, the scarcity of qualified teachers led to widespread hiring on a temporary basis. A deputy inspector of schools found his charge so expanded that he had to forego inquiries into the qualifications of the staff. Instead he concentrated on checking on the correctness of columnar totals in the school records. A vast corps of township-level workers in community development and mass education was trained and deployed —and eventually discharged. While these problems in the administration of education are typical of difficulties besetting other Pyidawtha programs, they are additionally significant for their influence on the quality and the character of the personnel subsequently recruited into the bureaucracy.

Burma is a land of sunshine, adequate rainfall, and an exportable rice surplus. Burma also has the highest death rate in the world, according to the Pyidawtha Resolution on Medical and Public Health Plans.[104] If true, this is in part a result of the traditional Burmese aversion to Western medicine and public health practices. Nursing and the collection of night soil were occupations beneath the Burman's dignity and fell to the lot of ethnic minorities. Public health discipline was a tiresome bridle on the Burman's free spirit and became at times the symbol of repressive government: the British health officer who separated the leper from his family; the Japanese authorities who seized and forcibly inoculated all travelers; the first army government which cleared the squatters from the downtown streets of Rangoon and poisoned the pariah dogs.

In spite of this tradition, or perhaps precisely because of it, the major thrust of the Pyidawtha health plan was toward preventive medicine and the establishment of rural health centers. United Nations agencies gave extensive help to fairly successful malaria control and tuberculosis testing campaigns and assisted in organizing a system of maternal and child health clinics. A corps of

---

104. *Pyidawtha Conference*, pp. 102–114. This claim should be taken with some caution since public health statistics in underdeveloped countries are notably unreliable.

health assistants who took a two-year training course in Rangoon headed up rural health centers which operated as substations of the township hospitals.

As in the field of education, private hospitals and private practice co-existed with public agencies in providing health services. In fact, the majority of doctors and nurses working in Burma were in private practice.[105] Often the private hospitals were foreign missionary endeavors and provided a higher standard of service for a price, although some were free.[106] Again as with teachers, government doctors usually carried on a private practice after hours, sometimes to the detriment of their public performance.

Health standards in general rose during the Pyidawtha period, but two problems common to other welfare programs remained. One was the poor distribution of benefits; doctors were concentrated in the major cities, where a profitable private practice could be carried on.[107] The other was a performance gap between input and output. The Rangoon-trained Lady Health Visitor, young, shy, perhaps Christian, went out into the villages; but once there she could not communicate with the village mothers across the barriers of age, race, and education. Malaria control teams did an enthusiastic job of spraying swamps to keep down mosquitoes, but the anti-malaria tablets, the vitamin pills produced by the Burma Pharmaceutical Industry, and other preventive health measures were accepted by the village population only during the presence of officials.

IV. The Steel Frame Under Stress

How did the expansion of functions and proliferation of governmental machinery affect the steel frame of administration? It may be well to look separately at the two levels—the secretariat

105. Walinsky, *op. cit.,* p. 365.
106. Shortly after the death of Dr. Gordon S. Seagrave, the "Burma Surgeon," on March 28, 1965, his hospital in the Shan States was nationalized along with the three remaining missionary hospitals. *New York Times,* July 6, 1965, p. 2.
107. One of the first moves of the Revolutionary Government was to drastically reverse the proportions of government and private doctors by forbidding foreign nationals to carry on private practice and by drafting private doctors to serve in government hospitals out in the districts. *Far Eastern Economic Review,* 1965 *Yearbook,* p. 96.

and the districts. Any increase in the number of tasks, the number of organizations, or simply the number of people at work in a bureaucracy naturally calls for greater efforts at co-ordination. This is especially true of social and economic development, which requires special planning, scheduling, and interlocking of projects. The secretariat had been developed explicitly as a tool of co-ordination during the British times. Its fundamental organization carried over into independent Burma. But the secretariat structure bore within itself the seeds of confusion. A ministry encompassed a number of related departments or directorates, each with its own field service. Thus, in the Ministry of Forests and Agriculture were found departments of agriculture, veterinary affairs, forestry, irrigation, and salt, supported in the field by such entities as the agricultural service and the forest service. Unfortunately, the relation of the ministry to its departments was not strictly hierarchical, but rather that of overlapping yet separate organizations. The secretary, deputy secretary, and assistant secretary of a ministry were officers in the general administrative branch of the Burma Civil Service and frequently rotated between ministries and out into the districts. Their role was to consider questions of policy and to co-ordinate the work of departments within the ministry and with outside organizations. The director of a department and his headquarters officers were usually specialists drawn from the departmental service whose task was conceived as the execution of policy. Although this enshrined distinction between policy and execution was unreal, communications between a ministry and its departments had to bridge a gap in values and training between the specialist and generalist services. Furthermore, these communications had to pass through the clerical barrier surrounding each ministry and each department, a difficult and time-consuming operation. When the nine to ten ministries of the prewar period expanded to between twenty-five and thirty ministries, not to speak of the boards and corporations, the ancient machinery of co-ordination broke down.[108]

108. The Japanese had not understood this peculiar secretariat organization and tried to revamp it, yet the system persisted. Japan, *Rikugun, Biruma Homengun*

The traditional superiority of ICS generalists over members of the specialist services, an integral part of the secretariat system, also continued, but there was less certainty of its appropriateness. In 1938 there was official acceptance of the doctrine that men of broad training and high administrative skill could best head up most ministries and departments and relate the work of one to the whole. But doubts were expressed about the direction of certain specialized functions being assigned to secretaries who were not specially trained.[109] After independence a number of senior posts formerly reserved to members of the ICS or BCS(I)—auditor general, commissioner of income tax, commissioner of land records and surveys, commissioner of excise, and commissioner of land nationalization—were in time filled by men from the specialist services. In selecting chief executive officers and other management personnel for the industrial and commercial boards and corporations, the question of whether civil service generalists were suitable was again raised. The issue was resolved by appointing generalists on the ground that they were the only trained administrators available and acceptable.[110] The Burmanization policy excluded from consideration most managers of private enterprises, who were Indians.

Even during the first and second army governments the generalist tradition, or some form of it, survived. Army officers taking command as minister, secretary, chief executive officer, or merely officer on special duty were generalists in that they were men appointed primarily on the basis of their proven general qualities, even though some assignments seemed to capitalize on

(Army, Burma Area Army), *Biruma Gunseishi.* (*History of Military Administration in Burma*), (Tokyo: *Gunmu-kyoku*, September, 1943), pp. 37, 318. Since independence several commissions and a number of foreign experts urged the merging of ministries with departments, but with no obvious success. *Final Report of the Administration Reorganization Committee*, pp. 10–11; *Report of the Public Services Enquiry Commission, 1961*, pp. 132–134; Divers, *op. cit.*, pp. 10–11.

109. *Final Report of the Administration Reorganization Committee*, p. 96. The specialist-generalist controversy has a long tradition in American as well as British doctrines of public administration. For a recent analysis of the issues and a forceful attack on generalist competence, see Victor A. Thompson, *Modern Organization: A General Theory* (New York, 1961). Thompson applies this critique to American advice to developing nations in "Administrative Objectives for Development Administration," *Administrative Science Quarterly*, IX (1964), 91–108.

110. *Report of the Public Services Enquiry Commission, 1961*, pp. 146–147.

special training or experience. Only five of the fourteen members of the enlarged Revolutionary Government of September, 1964, headed civilian ministries related in some way to their previous army experience. Brigadier Tin Pe, who was minister of supply and cooperatives and of trade development, had been quartermaster general. Colonel Kyaw Soe, who had been military secretary (the War Office equivalent of home secretary), held several portfolios including those of home affairs and judicial affairs. Colonel Hla Han, who became minister of education and of health, was a graduate physician who had headed the Burma Army's medical branch. Colonel Ba Ni, who had been director of army signals, became minister of transport and communications. Colonel Maung Lwin, a trained army physician, became minister of relief, resettlement and national solidarity. A few, such as U Thi Han, the foreign minister, whose military specialty was as director of military procurement, occupied the same or similar posts as they had in the first army government. Most of the others, however, had played no prior role in civil affairs.[111] These army generalists differed from the civil service generalists in fundamental ways—social background, education, career patterns, expectations, and motivation. These points of contrast will be analyzed in subsequent discussion of the special character of the personnel of the post-independence Civil Service.[112]

As the old forms of co-ordination—the secretariat, the *élan* of ICS generalists, the financial controls of the Ministry of Finance —seemed inadequate to the enlarged tasks, new specialized structures were devised. For one, there was a new ministry, the Ministry of National Planning, which was charged with the integration of economic activities. There was also the Economic and Social Board, a super-cabinet agency with an attached committee of experts, which bore responsibility for the supervision and co-ordination of the whole development program. A former member of its committee of experts has detailed the

111. This information on army officers is derived from *Forward,* October 1, 1964, p. 2; Director of Information, *Is Trust Vindicated?* (Rangoon, 1960), Appendix 9, "List of Defence Services Officers Attached to or Serving on a Part-Time Basis in Civil Departments," pp. 561–567.
112. See discussion below, pp. 423 ff.

confusion of responsibility between the board and other organizations as well as the failure of this very important board to take up
important matters, to come to firm decisions, to implement these
decisions, and to check on performance.[113] During the first army
government such co-ordination was the responsibility of an
economic advisory committee. With the second army government
a series of crash programs operating under general orders (for
instance, to reclaim wastelands in the delta) was launched
under the direction of committees incorporating various combinations of the membership of the ruling Revolutionary Council.
Presumably co-ordination of these and other programs was
accomplished by way of overlapping membership of the committees or within the Revolutionary Council itself.

The structure of the steel frame had a real, and in many ways
baneful, influence on the style of administration. Those officers of
the ICS and other Class I services who spent the war in Simla,
where they could reflect on what they had been doing during all
those busy days at the secretariat and out in the districts, agreed
that their procedures for handling routine work had become
costly and time-consuming rituals. They hoped that a reduction
in formal correspondence, a cutback in the excess noting of files
passed up through the levels of the hierarchy, and an extension of
the telephone system would speed work considerably.[114] United
Nations specialists brought in to survey the administration during
the 1950's found the movement of paper very slow indeed. The
Manual of Secretariat Procedure had been drawn up in the days
before dyarchy when decisions could with reason be drastically
centralized. It was revised in response to criticisms by the Fiscal
Committee in 1937, but throughout the postwar period many
dysfunctional practices prevailed.[115] This general style of administration may have been appropriate for the execution of repetitive
acts and the handling of cases where consistency and correct
procedure were prime concerns; it was not the appropriate style
for the accomplishment of concrete goals such as the construction
and operation of a tile factory or the development of new

113. Walinsky, *op. cit.*, pp. 465–476.
114. *Report of the District Administration* (*Reconstruction*) *Committee*, p. 123.
115. Furnivall, *Governance of Modern Burma*, p. 64.

cropping and marketing practices. In recent years a public administration division set up in the Home Ministry, then moved to the prime minister's office for greater effect, has attempted to reform administrative practices through training programs and attention to organization and management work. But practices were shaped strongly by the character of the personnel and the climate of the political environment, neither of which have been conducive to effective management of a development program.

During British times the centralization of decision and routinization of procedure served as a guarantee of British control of activities carried out by Burmese. In independent Burma it functioned as a protection for civil servants operating in an uncertain political environment. Imaginative administrators who exercised initiative and made decisions were bound to create enemies among the ranks of the politicians. Several outstanding men of this sort were sacrificed by the Prime Minister.[116] Not all attacks came from outside. In his zeal to create and breathe life into a new enterprise, an energetic civil servant might violate a minor regulation and suffer suspension or imprisonment as a result of investigation by the Bureau of Special Investigation (BSI). In 1951 U Nu had set up the BSI, headed by a trusted civil servant, U Chan Tha, ICS, responsible only to himself and to the prime minister. Its task was to arrest the moral decay brought on by (1) civil servants who misappropriated government goods, (2) magistrates who took bribes, (3) members of the armed forces who traded with insurgents and trafficked in opium, (4) politicians who took their cut of agricultural loans, and (5) traders who played the black market and avoided their income tax.[117] The BSI made its greatest showing against civil servants. In a short time many an honest civil servant learned to avoid innovation and cover every act with correct procedures.

In consequence, decisions were rarely made at an appropri-

116. See the case of U Hla Maung in Walinsky, *op. cit.*, p. 473 and *passim*.
117. U Nu, "Arresting Moral Decay" and "Bribery and Corruption" in *Burma Looks Ahead* (*Translation of Selected Speeches by the Honorable U Nu, Prime Minister of the Union of Burma, Delivered on Various Occasions from 19 July, 1951 to 4 August, 1952*) (Rangoon: Ministry of Information, 1953), pp. 7–12, 23–24. While both the BSI and its predecessor, the Public Property Protection Police, were initially headed by former ICS men, subsequent leadership came from the police.

ately low level, where the relevant information and the tools of execution were at hand, but were bucked up to a level where sufficient courage could be found to make a commitment. This meant that the cabinet was swamped with a mass of minor matters whose elevation to such a general forum had broadened the opportunities for objection to them. In addition to these psychological incentives to centralization, perhaps the major restraint on initiative and the exercise of discretion at lower levels was the requirement of detailed sanction by the Ministry of Finance—in other words, the remaking of decisions by an agency alien to many of the issues at stake.[118]

Out in the districts Pyidawtha was a call for two complementary programs—the organization of self-help schemes and the democratization of local administration.[119] Self-help during the late 1930's appeared in the form of a rural reconstruction movement led by volunteers from Judson College under the encouragement of Professor J. Russell Andrus. During the war some of the constructive enthusiasms of the new nation were channeled into the East Asia Youth League and the Wundan Aphwe (National Service Organization). In the Union of Burma planning and execution of welfare and development work in the countryside became the responsibility of Pyidawtha committees organized at township, district, and divisional levels. These committees were fundamentally a collection of the significant officials at each level, to which had been added political representatives from the AFPFL and a budget. In addition to the budget for approved projects, each township committee was given a discretionary grant of Ks. 50,000. In the best cases this discretionary grant was used for the construction of schools, water storage tanks, village roads, and like projects to which voluntary labor and materials were also contributed by the citizenry. In other instances the Pyidawtha Committee became just another committee consuming the time of the official members, and the discretionary grant a payment to the political

118. *Report of the Public Services Enquiry Commission, 1961*, pp. 92, 126–127.
119. The first two resolutions of the *Pyidawtha Conference*, pp. 1–22.

faithful. After the first army interval U Nu reorganized the scheme to avoid extensive corruption by elevating decisions on the use of the discretionary fund to the level of the divisional commissioner.

The Democratization of Local Administration Act was an attempt to redress the political and administrative wrongs of the British tenancy of Burma. It planned to do this by abolishing the steel frame of administration and transforming the district officer and other members of the steel frame from agents of the central government exacting obedience and revenue into leaders of local bodies reconstructing the social and economic life of the countryside. If local self-government were to command the respect and constructive participation of the people, it must work to satisfy the wants of the people rather than to carry out alien welfare schemes. This had been the failing of the district councils and municipalities in the 1920's and 1930's. The people did not want what was needed to bring about social and economic progress. Converting objective needs into felt wants was to be the task of the new district officer. He would be an executive officer carrying out the commands of the new district council; at the same time, as an experienced administrator devoted to the welfare of his district, he would provide sound advice for his elected associates.[120] This plan of reform was reflected below the district at the village level in an attempt to restore a sense of community to the village, which had become merely a tax-collecting and law-enforcing unit of administration during British times. An elected village council was to replace the headman, who in many cases would become chairman of the council. The village would still be responsible to higher authorities for revenue and minimum standards of law and order, but it would also have a broad range of rights and powers of its own.

In practice a few village councils were successful in collecting taxes or carrying out co-operative economic activities, such as the farming of common land. But by and large those councils which

120. *First Interim Report of the Administration Reorganization Committee.* A more extensive argument is made in John S. Furnivall, "Planning for Welfare in Burma," mimeographed (Rangoon: Ministry of National Planning, 1948). It was serialized in the *Guardian,* January, 1961.

did exist were either paper organizations or became arenas for factional conflict. In the independence period, factional politics spread from Rangoon down into the villages. Competition for political support, waged with favors and fire, foredoomed attempts to reintegrate the small community.[121]

At the district level the consequences of democratization were different but no more successful. The law was first put into effect in three relatively secure districts in 1954; later it was extended to seven others, most of them lying in the central Pegu division. After a year and a half of operation, an American specialist in public administration observed that no real change had come about in district administration. The district officer was still the man responsible for everything, and he, like his colleagues heading up the specialist departments in the district, took his commands from Rangoon.[122]

It is true that the district council did not control the district officer. He treated it as another bothersome committee, much like the District Pyidawtha Committee. However, the district officer did not control his district, even in those districts not yet democratized under the act. In contrast to British times, the district officer in independent Burma had to share leadership or contest for it with one or more members of Parliament, a nearby military commander, and in a number of districts the insurgents. And what leadership he was able to claim for the administrative arm of the government was eroded by the newly found independence of an increased number of specialist services carrying out a myriad of projects which had not been co-ordinated back in Rangoon. Co-ordination in the district was by committee, and the resulting paper work in the district officer's office was calculated

121. See editorial comment on the suspension of the Democratization of Local Administration Act in the *Guardian*, September 21, 1961, p. 5. Examining one of two up-country villages, an anthropologist noted: "A village such as this was held together peacefully only under the twin constraints of administration and military force. With the introduction of a political process soliciting people for adherence to national parties, the village fissured along the cleavages inherent in it." Manning Nash, "Party Building in Upper Burma," *Asian Survey*, III (1963), 200.

122. The Schaeffer Report had recommended in 1957 that local councils be given more power. The present author's interviews with district officers in 1961 and 1962 suggest that such devolution of authority had not occurred. See also above, p. 395, n. 82.

at six to seven times the prewar volume. This tied the district officer down to his desk with little time for touring. As a result, his understanding of the district was limited, and his authority in the villages declined.[123]

An example of the three-cornered leadership game played between the district officer, the army, and a local strongman took place in a central Burma district which was a center of insurgent activity. One of the original "Thirty Comrades," a Bo, who had settled in the district during the war and became its representative in Parliament, joined up with an exceptionally courageous district officer and the army to dislodge the Communist insurgents.[124] It was a time of general confusion, with many opportunities for the display of individual initiative and skill; the district officer took the opportunities, earning himself a reputation that stood him well in subsequent posts. However, when a home minister who supported him was succeeded by one more yielding to army pressure, the district officer was transferred to another district. The Bo's success in cleaning up the district and the private army with which he accomplished it established him as the king of half the district, a potentate whom the district officer must handle with great diplomacy. He was chairman of the land distribution committee under the land nationalization law and was able not only to protect the extensive holdings of a rice-miller friend and supporter, but also to accumulate some very good lands for himself. A number of villages which became virtually his fiefs prospered when he arranged for a large processing plant to be located among them, where it was far from the railroad, in the line of spring floods, and plagued with overemployment. His methods were harsh. Several political and personal opponents

123. Some attempts were made to strengthen the role of the general administration in the districts when civilian rule returned in 1960. Decisions made by the district co-ordinating committee, for instance, were no longer by majority vote but lay with the district officer as chairman; at the township level the functions of the mass education, social welfare, peace, and other organizations were merged into the office of an assistant township officer for community development. This reform barely had a chance to take hold before the army took control again.

124. U Law Yone, editor of the *Nation*, has described the general role of such local strongmen in "Burma's Socialist Democracy: Some Problems of Practical Politics," *Perspective of Burma: An Atlantic Monthly Supplement* (New York: Intercultural Publications, Inc., 1958), pp. 61–66.

were murdered. When the insurgent danger declined, a second district officer, who was protected by a brother in the army, disarmed the Bo and his private army. (The first district officer had collected the Bo's arms prior to an election campaign. The army returned them afterward.) Although reduced in power, the Bo was not abandoned by his former colleagues. In the parliamentary elections of 1954 and 1960 it was the vote of the local garrison that carried him into office. The third district officer, who came from and returned to a successful career in the Agricultural Research and Development Corporation, found it useful to get along with the Bo and was able to accomplish a series of fairly important agricultural development projects.

These three district officers were exceptionally capable. The first two took charge of this, their first, district before the age of thirty and later attained senior rank (secretary or commissioner) by their middle thirties. All three were able to keep the post for a period of three or four years.[125] A survey of district officers serving during the same time in a number of other districts found few who would tangle actively with politicians or the army, or who would take the initiative in the areas of economic development and social welfare. Threats from politicians and the expectation of failure and corruption in Pyidawtha projects left most district officers defining their role in restrictive prewar terms—the maintenance of law and order, administration of justice, and collection of revenue. They played out that role in ritual fashion.

The generalists of the steel frame found serious challenges in the commitment to build a road to Pyidawtha and the consequent flowering of government services, the devotion to democracy and rule by elected politicians, and the continuing insurrection which created special problems of law and order and guaranteed the prominence of the army in national and district life. In the face of these challenges, the generalists retreated from responsibility. Decisions were neglected or left to higher levels, while officers who should have been making them immersed themselves in a

125. Over the same period, Amherst, a similarly disturbed district, had seven different district officers.

flood of procedures carried over from British times and multiplied by the expansion of the scope of government activity.

The Changing Guardians

Who were the generalists of the steel frame in independent Burma and how did they compare to the guardians of the golden age before the war? How did they compare to the other elites operating in the new nation? A look at the social profiles, career patterns, and self-images of these competing elites may go a long way toward explaining why both the politicians and the military were shooting at the civil servants and why the civil servants retreated under fire.[126]

Before the war, more than half of the 145 Class I officers in the executive and judicial branches of the Burma Civil Service were British. None of the British officers who returned after the war was invited to remain after independence. Burma, in contrast to Pakistan and India, was making a clean break with the personal embodiment of one element in her colonial past.[127] Table 4 suggests that the vacuum left at the top levels of the BCS and of the specialist services was enormous. Well over half of the senior generalist officers serving during the interim between war and

126. This is generally the approach adopted by Morris Janowitz in *The Military in the Political Development of New Nations: An Essay in Comparative Analysis* (Chicago, 1964). See particularly the methodological rationale in the Appendix. Two approaches seeking more sophisticated and psychologically deeper explanations are Pye's *Politics, Personality, and Nation Building* and Hagen's *On the Theory of Social Change*. In a case study of Burma, Hagen focuses on the Burmese reaction of rage to years of cultural disparagement by the British resulting in (*a*) a refusal to identify with the rational administrative style of life, and (*b*) ritualistic identification with the most inappropriate aspects of British culture, i.e., an anti-business bias and a disinclination to engage in manual, technical, or other demeaning work. To Pye the central problem is the "crisis of identity" of the politician or civil servant who finds himself caught between the conflicting elements of Burmese and British (or world) culture and consequently is unable to engage in responsible, rational decision-making. While the insights suggested by these two analyses are fascinating, the evidence upon which they rest is not altogether secure; hence, we will rely in this section mainly on sociological variables and their more obvious psychological implications.

127. See above, pp. 384 ff., and Tables 1 and 2 in Braibanti's final chapter in this volume. While the other British officers left the service, John S. Furnivall, who had retired from the ICS in 1923, was retained as adviser on national planning up until the first army government.

independence were gone, and a number of those remaining were actually on leave preparatory to retirement. In the specialist services where the proportion of indigenous officers had been even lower, the rate of depletion was generally higher.

Table 4. *Depletion of Senior Personnel at Independence*

	Officers serving in October, 1947	Officers remaining in April, 1948	Percentage depletion
BCS Class I (Executive Branch)	99	42[a]	57.6
Police Service (DSP and above)	37	6	83.8
Civil Medical Service (Civil surgeon and above)	36	18	50.0
Public Works Department (Executive engineer and above)	23	5	78.3

[a] A number of the 42 BCS(I) "officers remaining" were actually on leave preparatory to retirement, bringing the total depletion up from 57 per cent to 61 or 62 per cent. Furnivall's figure is 71 per cent, but this may be a typographical error since it appears to be incompatible with other figures he reports from the same table in the Civil List.

Sources: Quarterly Civil List for Burma, No. IV (*corrected up to 1 October, 1947*) and No. V (*corrected up to 1 April, 1948*). John S. Furnivall, *The Governance of Modern Burma* (2nd ed.; New York, 1960), p. 28.

The ethnic dimension of this depletion is described by Foucar:

Upon the transfer there were 20 major departmental heads. Only those in charge of Civil Hospitals and Education were Burmans. Of 7 Divisional Commissioners, the most senior Civil Servants in the country, two were Burmans. Three Burmese officers were amongst the 50 or so holding senior posts in the Civil Police. The Medical service were grossly understaffed, many senior appointments being vacant; of those that were filled eight were held by Burmans, 22 by British officers. In the Public Works Department Burmans held four of forty senior posts; in the Forest Department they had fifteen of eighty-eight appointments. . . .[128]

Yet this exodus was not solely on ethnic grounds. Departure from

128. Foucar, *op. cit.*, pp. 212–213.

the service reflected as well the expectations of individual civil servants that they would find it difficult serving new masters. At least six or eight of the indigenous members of the BCS(I) departed along with the English, and a similar number retired shortly afterward.[129] At the same time a number of Eurasians in the superior services remained. Exceptional individuals such as James Barrington, long permanent secretary in the Ministry of Foreign Affairs and now Burma's representative at the United Nations, continued into the second army period.

The general shortage of trained managerial and technical personnel, aggravated by the expansion of government operations, posed a major administrative problem for the new nation. This problem was attacked in several ways. The government sought great infusions of technical assistance from abroad. Middle-level civil servants moved into higher-level posts, while lower-level civil servants filled in the middle-level posts. At the same time, a new generation of officers was brought into existence with the reinstitution of a reformed BCS examination and examinations for the other services. The first method of attack produced mixed results; the last two methods had a direct impact on the character of the new Civil Service.

The Rise of the Rankers

Considerable personnel resources were available to the new government at the BCS(II) and lower levels where almost all officers were indigenous. Less than one in five of the BCS(II) officers retired over the independence weekend. These persons were replaced by promotions from the ranks of the Subordinate Civil Service.[130] This rapid promotion of scarce talent is evident in the appointment of district officers, the key members of the steel frame. Before the war the majority of district officers were ICS

129. Some, such as U Kyaw Min, Myanaung U Tin, and U Chan Tha, translated their old roles into the new setting by going into politics. U Paing and several others practiced law. Still others retired to minor business interests and meditation. *Who's Who in Burma* (Rangoon: People's Literature Committee and House, 1961); "Who's Who in Burma," the *Guardian*, Vols. VI–X (1959–1963).

130. Of the 131 members of the BCS(II) in October, 1947, only twenty-five retired or went on leave preparatory to retirement, while four were promoted directly to senior administrative posts, the top of the old BCS(I).

men, confirmed at district rank after an apprenticeship as township officers and subdivisional officers. A minority of fourteen were officiating district officers drawn from the senior members of the Class II service. In the spring of the independence year, thirty-three of the thirty-five districts were headed up by district officers drawn from the BCS(II), over half of them recently promoted to that post. In time, with the democratization of the service structure, some of these district posts came to be occupied by men promoted step by step all the way up from the subordinate service. The three-class structure of BCS(I), BCS(II), and Subordinate Civil Service (SCS), with entrance at each class level by examination, was transformed into a two-class structure by merging the top two classes (see Chart 1, p. 370). Entrance into this new senior branch was half by examination and half by promotion from the junior branch.[131] Within the senior branch, movement up to the selection grade and then on to the administrative grade was by regular promotion based primarily on seniority. This democratization of the grade structure eroded the overlord confidence of the senior service. Positions of responsibility and discretion were held by men, many of whom had not been trained and had never expected to rule. Moreover, they brought along with them habits of routine, and petty corruption developed in the lower levels of the bureaucracy.[132] These guardians were no longer "heaven-born."

131. Formerly, one or two officers a year were promoted from the SCS to BCS(II) in order to allow them after fifteen or twenty years of service to retire on a higher pension.

132. Corruption seems to have grown enormously, although comparative statistics on this would be difficult to find and would be highly unreliable. Outstanding among the causes for corruption are (a) an increased inclination toward corrupt practices on the part of civil servants resulting from the growing gap between their real incomes (see below, p. 426) and their image of the civil servant's style of life in the golden age before the war, and (b) the increasing opportunity for corruption provided by the expansion of governmental welfare and economic development activities. Thus, the focus of corruption shifted from extortion of the victims of the police powers and revenue collection to bribery by the beneficiaries of welfare and economic development projects. Significantly, an official of the Bureau of Special Investigation ranking departments in order of corruption placed forests first, followed by income tax, then customs. For an analysis of many causes, see Ralph Braibanti, "Reflections on Bureaucratic Corruption," *Public Administration*, XL (Winter, 1962), 357–372. The inducements on the political side are outlined in Edward Shils's *Political Development in the New States* ('s-Gravenhage, 1962), p. 40, and rather thoroughly examined in Ronald Wraith and Edgar Simpkins, *Corruption in Developing Countries* (London, 1963), esp. pp. 196–207.

The New Men

By the time of the second assumption of control by the army, members of the prewar Class I services had either advanced to the topmost posts or retired from government service. At the selection-grade level, where the district officers, deputy secretaries, executive engineers, directors of departments, and administrative officers of government corporations are to be found, two distinct generations are discernible in a sample of government servants drawn from a variety of services: (1) those who matured during the prewar years, many of whom entered government service at subordinate levels, and (2) a larger group who came of age during, but mostly after, the war. The gap between these generations represents a period when the Burma Independence Army and the other new nationalist organizations held greater attractions for a young man than did the standard Civil Service career (see Table 5).

From a comparison of social profiles the postwar generation seem more appropriate inheritors of the guardian role than the prewar rankers promoted beyond their expectations.[133] Almost all of the new men but less than half of the prewar generation operating at the selection-grade level in 1962 had completed a university education. The majority of the new recruits were sons of civil servants, almost half of whom had been gazetted officers.[134] Over one-third of them had a grandfather who had been a civil servant. The prewar generation was predominantly made up of sons of merchants or traders; a smaller proportion came from the non-Civil Service professions of teacher, lawyer, and manager (see Table 6).

133. Pye provides an analysis of psychological differences between administrators with prewar experience and those with only postwar experience. Unfortunately, he makes no distinction in terms of the degree to which individuals in either of these generations were among the elect of their generation. *Politics, Personality and Nation Building*, pp. 227–229.

134. "Gazetted" ranks begin just below the selection grade. The lowest gazetted posts in a sample of services are subdivisional officer or assistant secretary in the general administration; second lieutenant in the army; assistant lecturer in the university; deputy superintendent in the police; assistant engineer in irrigation or public works; and assistant civil surgeon in the medical department.

Table 5. *Age Distribution of Sample of Selection Grade Civil Servants in 1962.*

Age group in 1962	Percentage of sample in each age group
Postwar generation	
28–30	3.75
31–33	15.00
34–36	16.25
37–39	12.50
40–42	11.25
	58.75
Prewar generation	
43–45	15.00
46–48	10.00
49–51	7.50
52–54	8.75
	41.25

Source: This is a sample of eighty officers attending the nineteenth, twentieth, and twenty-first Selection Grade Orientation Seminars in Rangoon in the summer and fall of 1962. These eighty officers appear to be fairly representative of the some seven hundred Selection Grade officers in service, since each of the three classes drew from a variety of services and attendance was compulsory for Selection Grade officers at some stage in their careers. While reliability of the sample cannot be certain, this writer believes it to be high.

The new men themselves were of varying levels of ability depending on circumstances of the year of recruitment. This was particularly evident in the senior branch of the Burma Civil Service. The year of the first postwar BCS examination, 1947, was a good one. The age limits for taking the examination were lifted, and the backlog from the war years provided over seven hundred competitors for fifteen positions. Several of the winners of this competition became outstanding commissioners and secretaries ten or twelve years later. Over the next seven years the prospects for the general administration service appeared dim in contrast to opportunities opening up in other areas such as the burgeoning boards and corporations. Competition was meager. One year only thirty persons turned out to seek fifteen positions. Quality im-

Table 6. *Social Background of a Sample of Selection Grade Civil Servants in 1962*

	Postwar generation (Percentages)[a]	Prewar generation (Percentages)[a]
University graduate	95.8	48.5
Civil Service tie		
Father in Civil Service	51.0	33.3
Father identified as a gazetted officer	23.4	9.1
Grandfather in Civil Service	36.2	24.2
Occupations of non-Civil Service fathers		
Professional	21.3	18.4
Trader, merchant	21.3	36.8
Agricultural	6.4	12.5

[a] Totals are more than 100 per cent since many individuals fall into more than one category.

Source: See above, Table 3. Those aged twenty-two and younger in 1942 are counted as members of the postwar generation. All others are of the prewar generation.

proved somewhat when the swelling tide of college graduates and a number of junior officers from specialist departments seeking to improve their position increased the competition for the BCS. Over three hundred candidates appeared for twenty-four posts in 1954 and 248 for twenty posts four years later. Still, the new men harbored doubts that they were meeting the standards of their ICS predecessors. The quality of education was generally felt to be below the prewar standards. The examination itself had been reduced to three general sections—Burmese, English, and current affairs—and an interview. Training on entry had also been simplified, in part because the work load on senior officers provided so little time for attention to their successors.

Hand in hand with the decline in power and prestige sustained by the Civil Service in independent Burma went a reduction in money wages for the higher ranks and in real wages for all ranks. The pay scales were telescoped by the Fiscal Committee of 1947 in line with the prewar nationalist prescription. Over a period of time the earning level of the lower ranks was raised even more by increases in the cost of living allowance.[135] The impact of a rising cost of living on civil servants forced both civilian and army governments to place moratoria on debts owed by government staff to private moneylenders.

In the midst of these democratizing trends, some distinctions were maintained by the civilian governments. Generalists of the BCS still drew higher pay than comparable ranks in the specialist services. Members of the various services at the officer grade were recruited and presumably protected by the Public Service Commission; they enjoyed a security of tenure, pensions rights, and greater housing and health benefits than did employees of the boards and corporations. The spirit of generalist separation was symbolized and supported by a Burma Civil Service Association which exercised considerably more influence over government employment policy (for instance, in the seminar discussions of the report of the Public Services Enquiry Commission) than did other employee organizations.[136]

As the Revolutionary Government incorporated more elements of the Burmese economy and society into the governmental structure, it took several steps toward consolidation, further dissolving the distinctions that had formerly characterized the steel frame. Up to October, 1963, one-third of the roughly 300,000 government employees had been on temporary appointments (particularly in the boards and corporations). These appointments were made permanent and provided with the same leave, promotion, and pension benefits due permanent employees. At the same time the distinction between superior employees and

135. In 1960 the base pay for a district officer stood at the prewar level of Ks. 1,000 (the Burmese kyat had replaced the Indian rupee at par), while the base pay of a commissioner had been cut from Rs. 3,000 down to Ks. 1,600 and the entering pay for a subdivisional officer had been raised from Rs. 300 to Ks. 350. Meanwhile, the cost of living for an urban family had risen by 238 per cent from 1939 to 1960. Thus, the commissioner's salary, including a cost-of-living allowance of Ks. 540, had been reduced by 78.8 per cent, while the subdivisional officer's salary plus CLA of Ks. 450 had been reduced by only 21 per cent. *Report of the Committee on Expenditure on the Public Services, 1939–40,* Part II, see esp. chap. xix, "Emoluments of the two Secretary of State's Services"; *Burma Civil List No. 10 (corrected up to December 31, 1959)* (translation by Burma Research Center, Bethesda, Md.); Walinsky, *op. cit.,* Appendix VIII.
136. *Burma Weekly Bulletin,* X (July 27, 1961), 97–104; *ibid.,* X (August 3, 1961), 111.

inferior employees (drivers, cooks, peons) was abolished and similar employment benefits followed. A revised Public Service Commission handled appointments to all positions above the Ks. 200 per month level, and a system of People's Worker Councils took the place of all previous employee's organizations. As a final rectification of previous contradictions between the requirements of politics and those of bureaucratic recruitment, political influence in selection was recognized and formalized with a provision for clearance by the Burma Socialist Programme party.[137]

V. Competing Elites: Political, Military, and Civil

The second-in-command of a Burma regiment in one district town, proud to display the wisdom he had accumulated in attaining the Bachelor of Laws as well as the Bachelor of Arts degree, commented that "in Burma we have our own separation of powers just as you do in the U. S. There is the civil power, the political power, and the military power. . . ." Although this is not the description set forth in Burma's Constitution, it does approximate the pattern of elite rule in independent Burma. These three elites have remained fairly distinct since the war, although there have been a few exchanges of personnel. Brigadier Aung Gyi at one time left the army to help organize the Socialist party within the AFPFL, but he soon returned. Brigadier Kyaw Zaw and several other army purgees took up political careers, but there has been no reverse flow of politicians into the formal structure of the army. U Tin Tut, the first Burman appointed to the ICS, became adjutant general for a brief period immediately after the war, then went into politics and was assassinated, with no official report ever made of the crime. Several others, U Chan Tha, U Kyaw Min, Myanaung U Tin, U Chit Pe and U Hla Gyaw, achieved a measure of success in politics, but there was never a significant Civil Service faction. There was no flood of politicians into strictly Civil Service positions, the only exceptions to

137. *Forward,* July 7, 1963, p. 22; *ibid.,* November 7, 1963, pp. 3, 4; *ibid.,* November 22, 1963, p. 3; United States Department of Labor, *Labor Law and Practice in the Union of Burma,* Bureau of Labor Statistics, Report No. 264 (Washington, D. C., 1964).

regular appointment being U Thant, U Vum Ko Hau, and U Maung Maung Soe in the Foreign Office. A goodly number of politicians did luxuriate in powerful appointments to various government boards and corporations. Prior to the second assumption of control by the army, the only army appointments to Civil Service positions were to ambassadorships, which were used as a form of exile, and to posts in the semi-governmental Burma Economic Development Corporation. The one "civilian" member of the Revolutionary Council, U Thi Han, was no outsider to army affairs, having long served as director of procurement in the Ministry of Defence, and before that he was a member of the BIA.

In British times the Civil Service was in effect the government. After the war it had to compete with the new political and military elites. The character of that competition was shaped in large part by differences in social profiles, career patterns, and particularly elite identifications. These differences have in turn raised questions about which elite represents the more modernized segment of society.[138] For all its changes, the social profile of the Civil Service bore a closer resemblance to its prewar counterpart than did the political and military elites which had developed out of the same wartime revolutionary movement.[139]

138. A common judgment has been that the military are the more effective modernizers. Pye states this as a general principle in his essay on "Armies in the Process of Political Modernization," in John J. Johnson (ed.), *The Role of the Military in Underdeveloped Countries* (Princeton, N. J., 1962), pp. 69–89, giving reasons that seem to fit the Burmese case (see pp. 74–77). See also Janowitz, *op. cit.*, and Trevor N. Dupuy, "Burma and Its Army: A Contrast in Motivations and Characteristics," *Antioch Review*, XX (Winter, 1960–1961), 428–440. Yet Pye also finds that the Burmese Civil Service "represents the most modernized, the best educated, and the most skilled people in the entire society." *Politics, Personality and Nation Building*, p. 213. Much confusion stems from the diffuse meanings of the term "modern," which makes it difficult to establish comparable empirical referents among the various elites. Even if the term is restricted to Eisenstadt's definition as the ability to absorb change, or Pye's definition as the creation of effective organizations which are "more adaptive, more complex, and more rationalized," we are not helped much, since then the concept has become an abstract evaluation depending on judgments of the long-run consequences of acts rather than the classification of currently observable characteristics. S. N. Eisenstadt, "Bureaucracy and Political Development," in LaPalombara (ed.), *Bureaucracy and Political Development*, pp. 96–119. Pye, *Politics, Personality and Nation Building*, pp. 38–42. Still, the concepts "modern" and "modernization" are important and perhaps fruitful concepts. Hence, an attempt will be made to point out criteria for their application to comparisons of the three elites.

139. By contrast, note the homogeneity of the military, political, and Civil

The prewar army was composed of Karens and hill people with a scattering of Indian units and British officers. At the end of the war the remnants of this army were amalgamated with the descendants of the politically motivated Burma Independence Army, trained by the Japanese. With independence the British and most of the Indians and Anglo-Burmans departed, and shortly afterward those Karen officers who did not join the Karen insurrection were retired. This left the army ethnically Burmese and drawn largely from district towns and the countryside. There was a significant Sino-Burmese element, including General Ne Win, Brigadier Aung Gyi (the former vice-chief of staff for the army), Brigadier San Yu (the current vice-chief of staff for the army), Brigadier Tin Pe, and Col. Tan Yu Saing, but this presents no particular communal complexion since Sino-Burmese are fairly well integrated into Burmese society. The sprinkling of Anglo-Burmese officers was confined largely to the lesser branches, the navy and air force. Kachin troops compose some of the best fighting units but rarely rise to the officer ranks.

The politicians, too, were a new class and bore a non-metropolitan stamp. Only nine of the 132 members of the prewar House of Representatives were returned to the Constituent Assembly in 1947. Released from the system of communal representation, the postwar political class gave much greater weight to the ethnic Burmese majority, particularly as the Karens and several other ethnic communities compromised their standing in the nation through insurrection. Yet some communal influences remained, since individual politicians ultimately based their power on particular constituencies. The army as a relatively autonomous bureaucratic organization faced no need to represent or resemble the complexion of the whole population; hence, their greater nationalist orientation.[140] To the limited extent that the civil

Service elites in post-independence Malaya. See Robert O. Tilman, "Policy Formulation, Policy Execution and the Political Elite Structure of Contemporary Malaya," in Wang Gungwu (ed.), *Malaysia: A Survey* (New York, 1964), pp. 346–355.

140. Here "nationalist" means ethnic Burmese to the exclusion of other races. For an argument that armies should be relatively "nationalist" in an inclusive sense, see Janowitz, *op. cit.*, pp. 43, 54. It is noteworthy that the immediate justification given for the second army coup was the threat of dismemberment of the Union of Burma by politicians representing minority ethnic communities.

bureaucracy was autonomous, however, the reverse effect occurred. Disproportionate numbers of particularly well-qualified minorities, such as Anglo-Burmans and Arakanese, were recruited.

Education of Civil Servants

The most obvious and probably the most important background characteristic distinguishing civil servants from soldiers and politicians was education. In traditional Burma every male child went through at least a minimal monastic education. In British times formal education became the sure road to success, particularly in the Civil Service. The post-independence civil servants as the major custodians of prewar values and practices readily perceived the difference between themselves and the politicians in terms of education. Although the prewar political scene boasted such foreign-trained leaders as Dr. Ba Maw, and the coming generation of Aung San and U Nu began their political careers as student leaders, war and the independence movement brought into the political fold many with less formal qualifications. A tabulation of the eighty-two currently active politicians listed in *Who's Who in Burma in 1961* shows 30.5 per cent with a bachelor's degree, 28.0 per cent with some university education, and 41.5 per cent with at most a high school education. By contrast, fifty-nine of the sixty-three civil servants in the listing, or 93.6 per cent, have a B.A., and for most of them it is an honors degree. There is little systematic information available on the educational background of members of the Burma army, including its top leaders. General Ne Win attended the university, but he did not graduate. So did a number of the other members of the top army leadership. It is also generally known that most of the senior army officers are not university graduates.

The educational differential established at the senior level during the period of war and the independence struggle persisted in subsequent generations of recruits to the political, military, and civilian elites. At the university, students have long been divided between those who pursue their studies and those who pursue politics. Student leaders may stay on at the university for years, taking a few courses and failing their exams. In fact, much student political activity was mobilized by high-school organizations, whose leaders may never complete a college education.[141] Recruits to the army's officer corps also ran generally outside the main stream of the educational system. Prior to the graduation of the first class from the Defense Services Academy in 1960, new officers either came up from the ranks through the nine-month Officer Training School or followed the typical course of two years of university education and four months of summer training with the Young Officer's Corps.[142] Few university graduates who had been members of the University Training Corps (UTC) went on into a military career during the 1950's. Membership in the UTC seems to have been motivated largely by the joys of camping and hiking and perhaps also the immunity from the universal conscription law (which has never yet been applied). However, a trend toward an increasing proportion of graduates going into the army began as the army came to play a more significant role in national life and the number of desirable jobs elsewhere failed to keep pace with the supply of college graduates.

The comparative attractiveness to university students of Civil Service and military careers is difficult to measure and varies over time. Prior to the second Army takeover, pay and prestige were generally higher for comparable ranks in the BCS; for instance, a district officer compared to a regimental commander (major) and a divisional commissioner compared to an army area commander (colonel). On the other hand, the army provided more incidental benefits, such as housing on or off the base and family allowances for officers in training overseas. A military career also offered greater opportunities for transfer to or retirement into a lucrative

141. Josef Silverstein and Julian Wohl, "University Students and Politics in Burma," *Pacific Affairs*, XXXVII (1964), 50–65.

142. The changeover in army officer ranks from the "old bolsheviks" of the resistance movement to the new college-educated officers is described in Richard Butwell, "Civilians and Soldiers in Burma," in Robert K. Sakai (ed.), *Studies on Asia, 1961* (Lincoln, Neb., 1961), pp. 74–85.

business and the gratification of playing an increasingly important political role. A negative factor militating more against military than Civil Service careers was the rather pervasive Burmese indifference to discipline and resentment of it.[143]

As the current army government continues to reshape Burmese society, incentives toward a military career will no doubt grow. Evidence for such a change can be discovered in a preliminary analysis of vocational choice questionnaires given to students in one of Rangoon's elite private high schools half a year after the 1962 coup. Although only fifteen of the 383 students were sons of army officers, three times that number listed a military career as their first choice, and almost all of these gave patriotic rather than personal reasons for that choice. It may also be significant that by and large students choosing a military career stood below the median scores for their class both on tests of verbal and of non-verbal abilities.

Since the civil servants were more educated and came from more urbanized and more Westernized backgrounds than the military and the politicians, a prima-facie argument could be made that the civil servants were the most modern segment of Burmese society. Yet a number of observers consider the military to be the greater modernizing force.[144] The question may turn on a distinction between *being modern*, i.e., highly educated and aware of Western values, and *acting to modernize*, or perhaps simply to change one's society. The propensity to change probably depends more on the character of one's education than on its quality or quantity. Here we need more (and more systematic)

143. Working from a different balance of incentives, Moshe Lissak came to the conclusion that the military attracted the most qualified personnel in the country. This difference in the evaluation of incentives results largely from (1) a different estimate of the prestige of the military profession (this judgment varies depending on whether one talks to soldiers, civil servants, or students), and (2) a not quite appropriate matching of civil and military ranks to determine the ratio of pay scales. For instance, Lissak matches brigadier with cabinet secretary and divisional commissioner, yet the army has never had more than four brigadiers at one time compared to twenty-seven senior administrative posts in the BCS; in the current Revolutionary Government cabinet, secretaryships are held by colonels and lieutenant colonels. Moshe Lissak, "Social Change, Mobilization, and Exchange of Services between the Military Establishment and the Civil Society: The Burmese Case," *Economic Development and Cultural Change,* XIII (1964), 1–19, esp. pp. 8, 9. See also n. 135, above.

144. See above, p. 428, n. 138.

information on the kinds of education received by the military and the civil servants. The propensity to change would also seem closely related to the pattern of one's own career development.

Career Patterns

Differences in social profiles which distinguished the civil servants from both their military and civilian counterparts were reflected in the pattern of careers within each elite. With minor variations dictated by the idiosyncracies of political pressure, the career lines of civil servants in independent Burma followed much the same pattern as they had in British times. Objective achievement criteria—formal education and a Civil Service examination—controlled entry into a Civil Service career, after which ascriptive criteria—seniority and the specific service in which one started out—determined fairly closely the course of the subsequent career.

By contrast, both military and political careers developed within a system of continuous competition. Membership in the Burma Independence Army or the comradeship of early agitational work granted admission to the arena but provided no guarantee of preferred position. In a system of perpetual splits and defections, loyalty was subject to continuous testing.[145] If the question is again raised—Which of the elites appears the most modern in terms of career patterns?—the answer must again be indeterminate. The Civil Service with its achievement-ascriptive career stages seems a less obvious instrument for promoting change, yet in other circumstances a civil service operating on such lines may provide the stable foundation needed to absorb change.[146] Whether the continuous competition within the politi-

145. A historian of splits in the ruling AFPFL up to and including the big split that brought the army in for the first time is U Sein Win; see his *The Split Story* (Rangoon, 1959). The army, too, has suffered defections and purges, but no concise history of them exists. The tendency is indicated in Pye, "The Army in Burmese Politics," in Johnson (ed.), *op. cit.*, pp. 231–251. The saving factor for the army, in contrast to the political elite, is that since the inception of insurrections in the immediate postwar period, no defector or purgee has been able to establish a significant base of independent support.

146. See the case of the CSP in Braibanti, "Public Bureaucracy and Judiciary in Pakistan," in LaPalombara (ed.), *op. cit.*, pp. 360–440.

cal arena and within the army represents elements of rationality and adaptability or of chaos and court politics depends upon the relative importance of competence or loyalty as criteria for promotion in each elite. From this perspective the military elite seems more modern than the political elite, but a comparison with the Civil Service would be inconclusive.[147] As the army widened its political role, questions of personal loyalty became crucial. Seven of the seventeen members of the Revolutionary Council that took power in 1962 had been removed by the spring of 1965. One, Brigadier T. Clift, an Anglo-Burman who had been air chief of staff, later emigrated to the United Kingdom.[148] Another, Colonel Saw Myint, the minister of information, was convicted along with several other officers of violating a currency demonetization order.[149] Four others, Brigadier Aung Gyi, Colonels Chit Myaing, Kyi Maung, and Khin Nyo, had been outstanding economic modernizers during the first army government.

Elite Identifications

Linked with these characteristic social profiles and career patterns were distinctive self-images and images of each other which helped shape the pattern of competition among the three elites. The civil servants distinguished themselves from the politicians and the military through identification with predecessors of a golden age when administrators alone ran the country. This was particularly true of the generalist officers of the BCS and even more so of those who were promoted rankers. The career pattern of lifelong validation by early academic criteria reinforced this "traditionalist" orientation. On the other hand, there were many new men whose ideals and aspirations were wrapped up in the new Burma. Unfortunately, the services scarcely had a chance to establish new traditions before the attacks of politicians and the failures of Pyidawtha programs

147. The anti-modern fashion in which issues of predictability and trust are handled within the Burmese culture is explored by Pye in *Politics, Personality and Nation Building*, esp. pp. 121–174.

148. *Working People's Daily*, II (August 8, 1965), 1.

149. *Forward*, September 1, 1965, pp. 3, 23.

eroded their confidence and forced most of them back under the protective covering of ritual and routine.[150]

Politicians in Burma have traditionally distrusted each other as well as outsiders. The glory and intrigue of court politics from the time of the Burmese kings appeared again in the new political roles that developed under dyarchy and in the elected House of Representatives. The Japanese occupation and the resistance movement produced a unified mass political organization, the AFPFL, which began to splinter on ideological and personal grounds once ultimate independence came into sight. What common identifications the post-independence politicians did share added up to an undefined anti-British nationalism. This set them quite naturally against the civil servants who were perceived as handmaidens of the previous occupying power. This ideological antagonism was intensified by a certain jealousy of the prewar status and educational superiority of the civil servants; also displayed was an underlying fear of those "clever chaps," such as U Kyaw Min of the ICS, who did enter politics themselves. In addition to a nationalist identification, most members of the political elite shared a true devotion to the development of a new Burma along both economic and social dimensions. Unfortunately, they held no corresponding devotion to rational decision-making procedures or the disciplined avoidance of opportunities for self-aggrandizement. As a consequence, there were few inhibitions on using and abusing the Civil Service.[151]

Both the army and the AFPFL claimed the mantle of the wartime and postwar liberation movement. The growing diver-

150. Evidence about the character and identifications of postwar civil servants is scanty and uneven. The BCS has not produced the self-analytical writings of a Fielding-Hall, a Furnivall, or a Collis, although several perceptive articles have appeared in the *Guardian:* U Win Pe, "The District Officer," December, 1955, pp. 27, 28; Theippan Soe Yin, "Portrait of a Civil Servant," March, 1957, pp. 16, 17; U May Aung, "Experts and Experts," December, 1957, pp. 21, 22; U Moe Nyunt, "Reorganizing the BCS," July, 1963, pp. 32–33. Extensive contacts of American and other technical assistance specialists with Burmese civil servants produced within the foreign community a fairly consistent folklore about the outlook and motivations of civil servants, some elements of which have been confirmed by systematic interviewing. See especially the "Profiles of Administrators," in Pye, *Politics, Personality, and Nation Building,* pp. 231–243.

151. This problem was publicly recognized by U Nu in addressing Parliament on his return to power following the first army government. Part of the speech appears in Walinsky, *op. cit.,* p. 405.

gence between these two elites in both outlook and styles of action must be understood in terms of fundamental differences in their experiences after independence.[152] The Burma army grew from birth through maturity with its self-confidence relatively unimpaired. At birth the Burma Independence Army joined with the Japanese army in driving the British out of Burma. Later the Burmese army repeated this success by driving the Japanese out of Burma with the help of British and American forces. After independence the Burma army successfully turned back the tide of insurrections which threatened to extinguish what was then called by some the "Rangoon government" since it controlled little of the countryside. It is true that in seventeen years the army has not yet succeeded in extinguishing the insurrections, which are today more numerous in kind though less threatening in size. Yet much of the blame could be placed on the shoulders of politicians, at least up until the Revolutionary Government abolished all independent political organizations in March, 1964.

The army developed a set of reverse images vis-à-vis politicians. Politicians conspired with insurgents and betrayed the union to separatist forces: the army fought insurrection to preserve the union. Politicians, guided by self-interest and corrupted by power, lived on the people: the army, constrained by its professionalism, served the people both as a constabulary force and, when needed, as a caretaker government and eventually as the cadre for a new ruling political organization. Politicians talked of great programs but accomplished little: the army set itself firm goals and produced results. When the army took over the reins of government for good in 1962 these points of compari-

152. By and large only those who had served in the BIA and its successors found any success in the post-independence army. Members of the political elite were drawn from both the BIA and other mass organizations which sprang up during the occupation. The qualitative distinction in Brigadier Maung Maung's remark in 1960 that "the cream of the resistance movement stayed with the Burma army, and most of the rest became politicans" cannot apply to U Nu, U Kyaw Nyein, and U Ba Swe, who were both leaders in the resistance movement and able politicians, as was for a time Maung Maung's chief competitor, Brigadier Aung Gyi. This statement and the further remark that "It was irksome to find that those who could not hold their own in the Army came in time to be our political superiors" present a concise illustration of military perceptions of their political masters. Both statements by Brigadier Maung Maung are from an interview with Richard Butwell quoted in Sakai (ed.), *op. cit.*, p. 74, and in Lissak, *op. cit.*, pp. 7, 9.

son became the base-line assumptions for most statements of policy.[153]

The army image of the Civil Service was conditioned in the first instance by resentment of the superior education and status the Civil Service inherited from British times. Along with this resentment went a certain respect for the Civil Service as an appropriately trained instrument of government. Thus, in the caretaker government civil servants took the place of politicians as ministers, and the Civil Service itself, relieved of pressure from politicians, purged of several thousand corrupt or incompetent members, and coached or cajoled by a scattering of officers on special duty, became the active partner of an action-oriented government. But on the second time around the military viewed the Civil Service in a less comradely light. General Ne Win gave an assembly of senior civil servants a severe tongue-lashing for having desired in the past to seize power from the less competent politicians, and the Revolutionary Council announced that:

In our road to socialism the existing bureaucratic administration is a big stumbling block. To achieve our socialist aims with this effete machinery is impossible. Steps will have to be taken to remove this bureaucratic machinery and lay firm foundations for a socialist democratic one.[154]

This time all the ministers but one, U Thi Han, long an associate of the army, were military men; within a few years, after a number of senior civil servants had been forced to retire, most of the secretaries and a good number of the directors of departments were men in uniform.

153. A sincere but not altogether balanced self-portrait of the army is U Ba Than, *The Roots of the Revolution: A Brief History of the Defence Services of the Union of Burma and the Ideals for Which They Stand* (Rangoon: Director of Information, 1962), reproduced from the *Guardian* of March 27, 1962. Dhammika U Ba Than is a retired colonel who was director of defence services, education, and psychological warfare in the caretaker government. The official documentation of the successes of the first army government are a preliminary report, Ministry of Information, *The Nine Months after the Ten Years* (Rangoon, 1959), and *Is Trust Vindicated?*, a concluding report, which, significantly, is introduced with a recounting of the fable of Hercules cleaning the Augean Stables. The basic policy declaration of the Revolutionary Government is *The Burmese Way to Socialism* (*Myanma Soshalit Lanzin*), (Rangoon: Information Department, 1962).
154. *Burmese Way to Socialism*, p. 5.

There is no doubt that the military elite in Burma perceived itself as—or at least claimed to be—more modern than the politicians or the civil servants. This belief does not mean that in reality the army's outlook or actions were more modern, nor did it prevent the army from making full use of traditional symbols to establish its legitimacy and motivate the population.[155] It did, however, provide a degree of self-assurance which the Civil Service lacked. This hallmark of the ICS was one of the more important elements of the bureaucratic tradition that did not survive the transition to independence.

VI. The Army Synthesis

The army coup of March, 1962, has since worked itself into a full-blown revolution, with the army now cast in both political and administrative roles. The Revolutionary Government blends elements of the purpose, structure, and character of the previous political and administrative elites. In its political role the Revolutionary Council has rededicated the government to the socialist principles of Burma's independence which the politicians once espoused. It has developed a cadre party, the Burma Socialist Programme party, by building down from top army leadership, and it has abolished all other political organizations after jailing both government and opposition leaders of the preceding regime.

Elements of the steel frame style of administration have reappeared in the districts and at the center. Power over local

155. See in particular the Revolutionary Government's attempt to develop philosophical underpinnings by amalgamating Buddhist cosmology and Marxist dialectics in *The System of Correlation of Man and His Environment: The Philosophy of the Burma Socialist Programme Party* (Rangoon: The Burma Socialist Programme Party, 1963). While the separate observation of the Buddhist sabbath and several other measures promulgated by U Nu to bind the state to Buddhism have been abolished by the Revolutionary Government, such other ties with tradition have been developed as the discovery of white elephants (one during the first army regime and another shortly after the second came to power), correcting the calculation of traditional holidays, and re-emphasizing the significance of Burma's own history. Especially notable is the prominence given at the 1965 Peasant Seminar to the Saya San revolt of 1930, the "Burmese Revolution of 1292 B.E. [Burmese Era]," which was interpreted as the first stage of the current army-led revolution. See the *Working People's Daily*, Vol. II, February 24–March 5, 1965.

officials and the local population which had slipped from the hands of the district officer has been reconcentrated in a Security and Administrative Council (SAC) composed of the district officer, the district superintendent of police, and the local military commander. A central SAC at Rangoon and SAC's at divisional, subdivisional, and township levels complete the old pattern of administration by geographically based plenipotentiaries. At the capital, administration is again controlled by an elite cadre of generalists, this time members of the Burma army rather than the ICS. Senior officers can be given discretion and responsibility for carrying out programs, since they are trusted members of a guild, or rather, a brotherhood. Co-ordination can be accomplished through uniformity of outlook and ideology rather than by reverting to negotiation between separate organizational entities. The atmosphere is one of aggressive confidence, committed competence, and quick action. This is less true at lower levels, among the generation that did not participate in the brotherhood of the BIA. As the army stretches its supply of top-level talent with the expansion of governmental activities and the increase of army control over government operations, an increasing number of captains and majors finding themselves charged with major responsibilities pass minor decisions up to the top for confirmation.

The announced accomplishments of the first army regime had suggested to a number of foreign observers and many highly educated Burmese that Burma's future as a stable, developing nation might lie with the army, although there hovered some doubts about the army's long-run political capabilities.[156] Now that Burma has experienced four years of Revolutionary Government, some further questions about the army's effectiveness may be raised.

156. The most sanguine of these is perhaps I. R. Sinai's *The Challenge of Modernisation: The West's Impact on the Non-Western World* (London, 1964). Several Western observers also seem to have been impressed by the army's accomplishments. See Butwell, in Sakai (ed.), *op. cit.;* Dupuy, *op. cit.;* Lissak, *op. cit.* Doubts are expressed by Pye, who otherwise acclaims the accomplishments of the first army regime. See his "The Army in Burmese Politics," in Johnson (ed.), *op. cit.* Pye's view of the second army regime is decidedly less favorable. See his "Burma: Opening on the Left in a Military Manner," mimeographed

Changes took place in all areas of governmental concern. District administration was strengthened. Law enforcement became stricter and justice quicker. The educational system passed through the fire of student revolt and emerged reorganized and focused on new goals. Private doctors were registered and distributed throughout the countryside. These changes were usually initiated without consultation with, and often against the wishes of, the district officers, lawyers, teachers, doctors, or other groups concerned. The long-run success of these and other social and administrative reforms is not altogether certain, although on the face of it some of their effects seem to be beneficial.

The target of most intensive reform was the economy. The goals were to socialize, to Burmanize, and to raise the level of development of the productive forces of the nation. The resulting structural transformation of the economy is similar in form but much more thoroughgoing than that which took place with independence, some fifteen years before. Foreign economic institutions such as banks and joint-venture corporations have been nationalized. Foreign nationals, Indian and Pakistani businessmen in particular, have been driven from the country. Private domestic industries have been nationalized or placed under the direction of Supervisory Committees. Wholesale and most retail trade was brought under a People's Stores Corporation (later reformed as a Trade Council with subordinate functional corporations). The short-run consequences have been erratic rates of industrial production, a per capita decline in agricultural production, rising unemployment, and a collapse of commodity distribution. General Ne Win conceded at a December, 1965 Party Seminar that the army's inexperience in economics had been costly and that nationalization of distribution had been, "as if we had caught hold of a tiger's tail," but pledged to hold on until they had learned to build socialism.[157]

(Boston: Center for International Studies, Massachusetts Institute of Technology, June, 1963). A more optimistic forecast for the army is John H. Badgley, "The Source of Burma's Revolution: Intermediary Leaders," (mimeographed; Oxford, Ohio: Department of Political Science, Miami University, 1965). A general critique of the political competence of military regimes appears in Janowitz, *op. cit.*, pp. 75–106.

157. *The Working People's Daily*, II (December 12, 1965), 1, 5, 8. During

Two characteristics of the army regime to which much of its past success has been attributed were its pragmatic orientation and the energies both within the army and outside that it could mobilize to accomplish public tasks. How pragmatic has the army been after all, and is its pragmatism always appropriate? The army prides itself on pursuing the main goal, unencumbered by procedural considerations. Often this pragmatic orientation has supported energetic but oversimplified solutions to complex problems. On the other hand, much of the strength of the Burma army as an institution derived precisely from the high degree of formalism that characterizes any military organization.[158] In some circumstances this formalistic spirit has led to doctrinaire policies. The conjunction of the unfortunate sides of both the pragmatic and the formalistic orientations in the Revolutionary Government's approach to the business community resulted in the breakdown of certain sectors of industry and commerce and the denial to the nation of scarce managerial and organizational talents.[159]

Of the army's enthusiam for action there can be no doubt. The army elite has set a fast pace, both by example and by command.

---

the first full year of the Revolutionary Government (1962–1963) the productivity of certain elements of the public sector increased dramatically, while production in the private sector remained more or less constant. But the following year the budget report noted that "obstructive tactics on the part of the private industrial sector had inevitably led to a significant decrease in industrial production." In fact, the private sector declined to 86.4 per cent of the 1962–1963 level, while the public sector stood at 99.0 per cent of the previous year. *Economic Survey of Burma—1963*, pp. ix, x. *Forward*, October 1, 1964, p. 4; *Far Eastern Economic Review: 1965 Yearbook*, p. 96. By 1964–1965 total industrial production was seven per cent above the 1962–1963 level. *The Working People's Daily*, II (October 3, 1965), 1, 8. However, from 1962 through 1965 rice exports, Burma's main earner of foreign exchange and the government's main source of revenue, have been declining. *Far Eastern Economic Review*, LI (February 24, 1966), p. 384. Aggregate agricultural output, which stood at 102 per cent of the prewar level in 1959–1960, the last year of the first army government, had risen to 112 per cent of the prewar level by 1962–1963, the first full year of the Revolutionary Government, but dropped to 109 per cent the following year due to adverse weather and admitted administrative difficulties. Thus, the volume of agricultural production of twenty-five years ago was supporting a population larger by 40 to 50 per cent. *Second Four-Year Plan*, p. 17; *The Working People's Daily*, II (February 19, 1965), 5; United Nations, *Economic Survey of Asia and the Far East, 1963* (New York, 1964), pp. 184, 191.

158. Pye, "Armies in the Process of Political Modernization," in Johnson (ed.), *op. cit.*, p. 79.

159. This was an exacerbation of one of the main policy failures of the previous political regimes. See Walinsky, *op. cit.*, p. 604, and Hagen, *op. cit.*, pp. 467–470.

New assistant township officers with hair cropped short and wearing blue uniforms with military boots and caps attend the Central Services Training School for a year of basic military training, agriculture, economics, and the ideology of the "Burmese Way to Socialism." In the secretariat at Rangoon civil servants now work long into the night on numerous occasions. Volunteers from the Burma Socialist Programme party, government offices, schools, and nationalized industries are mobilized to handle the immediate administrative chores involved in nationalizing retail trade, demonetizing large currency notes, or taking the census. The state spinning and weaving industry, long plagued by absenteeism and mechanical breakdowns, now runs on three shifts with a disciplined labor force. Here and in other industries regular unpaid over-time work is organized for evenings or weekends. The enthusiasm the army has elicited is hardly total and rarely voluntary. In the agricultural sector there have been mass peasant seminars and tractor demonstrations. But the leadership and organizational skills developed in a military setting have not yet proved effective in stimulating peasant cultivators to higher productivity. The cultivators are the ultimate pragmatists and continue to behave in terms of cautious self-interest. As a major positive incentive General Ne Win announced the abolition of agricultural tenancy rents on Peasant's Day, 1965. Subsequent policy statements and several pilot projects have hinted that the next solution to problems of agricultural production may be some form of collectivization.[160]

Economic and administrative development cannot escape politics. The steel frame of administration was bent by the pull of politics during the later days of British rule. In independent Burma the primacy of politics all but collapsed the structure. The Revolutionary Government set out to solve the problem of politics

160. The Peasant's Day announcement is reported in *The Working People's Daily*, II (March 4, 1965). The government estimated that as of June, 1963, some 1,100,000 tenant families were paying rent to 350,000 landlords. *Forward*, May 1, 1965, p. 2. An additional 1,806,000 families were classified as owner cultivators. *Working People's Daily* (October 9, 1965), p. 1. Thus, abolition of these rents may be calculated to benefit directly over one-third of the agricultural labor force or about one-fourth of the total population. On the choice between positive incentives and structural reorganization, see the conflicting editorials in *The Working People's Daily* on August 23 and September 7, 1965.

by casting out parliamentary democracy and attempting to establish a totalitarian system with a disciplined party which could facilitate the administration of the country. It has not yet mobilized sufficient support for its programs and its methods among all segments of the population to elicit both the sacrifice of self-interest and the creative imagination needed to make these programs work. Neither respected politicians nor rebellious students nor major segments of the insurgents have yet been induced to work within the framework set out by the Revolutionary Government. Ironically, some of the same cultural conditions that made administrative and economic development so difficult in the past seem to be impeding the development of the totalitarian system intended to make such progress possible in the future.

The governance of Burma is once more in the hands of a single guardian class. This time, however, the task is more complex, the pace faster, and the outcome less certain.

7

Ceylon: The Imperial Heritage

Sir Charles Collins

This chapter considers how far the administrative machine established by the British during the colonial period in Ceylon contributed toward the peaceful transition to independence, and to what extent it exhibited a capacity to adjust to new administrative needs during the pre-independence period of partial self-government and after the attainment of independence. Gradual reformation of the administration to meet modern needs during these periods will also be considered.

As in India, Malaya, and most other countries of the Commonwealth, the mainstay of administration during the British period was the Civil Service. Other services—most notably the technical services, public works, irrigation, the railway, the police, and education and health services—played important roles in the social and economic growth of the country, but this chapter will concern itself mainly with the Ceylon Civil Service (CCS), the elite cadre whose members, approximately two hundred in the 1950's, held the main administrative posts of government.

The Ceylon Civil Service had much in common with its larger fellow service, the Indian Civil Service. The type of officer entering the service and the mode of recruitment were by and large the same in both instances. Ceylon made some use of Haileybury while it was available, and for many years recruitment was accomplished by means of the same examination as for the Indian Civil Service, the first division of the Home Civil Service, and Eastern Cadets. This examination was based generally on the honors schools of Oxford and Cambridge, and it generally assured the entrance to the service of university graduates with good degrees. As in India, the average entrant to the service was what has become known technically as a "generalist" (i.e., non-specialist), whose value in the service was based largely on the theory (whether held consciously or subconsciously) that a thorough grounding in the humanities was the best and safest basis for the evolution of the administrator. Many members of the service retained this predilection for humanistic studies and have been responsible, as in India, for significant research on the customs, history, archeology and languages of the country.[1]

1. One of the first civil servants to attain high proficiency in Sinhalese was Sir John D'Oyly (see below, p. 450). His *Diary . . . with an Introduction and Notes by H. W. Codrington* (Colombo, 1917), and his *Constitution of the Kandyan Kingdom* (Colombo, 1832), are standard works. Several civil servants made contributions to the study of Pali texts and literature. The Hon. George Turnour and William Tolfrey were among the first Europeans to study the language. The former translated thirty-eight chapters of the *Mahavamsa*, the great Ceylon chronicle, while Tolfrey, an authority also in Sanskrit, made scholarly translations of parts of the Bible into Sinhalese. R. C. Childers in 1873 became professor of Pali and Buddhist literature in University College, London, and produced the first Pali-English dictionary (*Dictionary of the Pali Language* [London, 1875]). T. W. Rhys Davids, after a short stay in the Civil Service where he studied Pali and Buddhist philosophy, was later appointed to the same chair. Rhys Davids founded the Pali Text Society, under whose auspices most of the Pali texts which have been published have appeared. From 1882 to 1928, the Pali Text Society published 106 volumes. Rhys Davids also published *Milinda* (2 vols.; Oxford, 1890–1894), a classical Pali text of the first and second century A.D., which survived from the literature of northwest India. In collaboration with H. Oldenberg, he edited *Vinaya Texts* (3 vols.; Oxford, 1881–1885) and in collaboration with W. Stede produced the *Pali Dictionary* (London, 1921). In a subsequent work, *American Lectures* (3rd ed.; London, 1908), Rhys Davids describes the contents of major Pali texts. Mrs. Rhys Davids was also a translator of Pali and with F. L. Woodward wrote *Psalms of the Early Buddhists* (London, 1900) and several other books. W. T. Stace, a civil servant from 1910 to 1932, successively private secretary to the governor, mayor of Colombo, and controller of revenue, left the service to teach at Princeton University, retiring in 1955 as Stewart Professor of Philosophy. Stace wrote some twelve books on philosophical subjects, including *Critical History of Greek Philosophy* (London, 1920), *Religion and the Modern Mind* (Philadelphia, 1960), and *Mysticism and Philosophy* (Philadelphia, 1960).

A number of civil servants became interested in natural history. Prominent among these in the middle of the nineteenth century were Joseph Joinville, who was a member of the first group of civil servants, and Edgar Layard. W. E. Wait, a senior civil servant of recent times, became Ceylon's foremost ornithologist, and his *Birds of Ceylon* (London and Colombo, 1925) is a standard work. Sir J. Emerson Tennent's *Ceylon: An Account of the Island, Physical, Historical and Topographical* (2 vols.; London, 1859) is still regarded as one of the best descriptive works on the island. Tennent was colonial secretary from 1845 to 1850.

Sir Paul E. Pieris, a distinguished Ceylonese officer of the CCS, wrote several

What distinguishes Ceylon from India and other Commonwealth countries in their progress toward independence is the
fact that for some sixteen years during the last part of the British
period the country was administered under a special constitution,
peculiar to itself. The Donoughmore Constitution, as it was
called, provided a large measure of self-government and supplied opportunities for civic education, not only for ministers and
members of the legislature and public servants, but by the
operation of universal adult suffrage for the ordinary citizen as
well. Thus, the transition from British imperial rule to independence was somewhat more deliberate and planned than in many
ex-colonial states.

I. Cultural and Physical Setting

A short description of Ceylon may be useful here as a background to a study of its problems of administration.[2] The island,

important volumes of Ceylonese history, among them: *Ceylon: The Portuguese
Era* (2 vols.; Colombo, 1913–1914), *Ceylon and the Hollanders, 1658–1799*
(Tellippalai, 1918), *Ceylon and the Portuguese* (Tellippalai, 1920), *Tri Sinhala:
The Last Phase, 1796–1815* (Colombo, 1939), and *Sinhale and the Patriots,
1815–1818* (Colombo, 1950). Another civil servant who was a productive scholar
was Simon Casie Chitty, who compiled the first gazetteer, *The Ceylon Gazetteer:
Containing an Accurate Account of the Districts, Provinces . . . Cities . . . etc.
of the Island of Ceylon, etc.* (Colombo, 1834). Chitty also wrote *The Castes,
Customs, Manners and Literature of the Tamils* (Colombo, 1934). H. W.
Codrington, who wrote the notes to D'Oyly's diary mentioned above, also wrote *A
Short History of Ceylon* (rev. ed.; London, 1947) and several works on land law
and customs. Another outstanding scholar was H. C. P. Bell, who was appointed
archeological commissioner in 1890 and who was instrumental in discovering and
restoring archeological sites in Ceylon. See H. C. P. Bell (ed.), *The Ceylon
Antiquary and Literary Register* (Colombo, 1915), and H. C. P. Bell (ed.),
Wilhelm Geiger, *Maldivian Linguistic Studies*, Vol. 27 (extra number), *Journal of
the Ceylon Branch of the Royal Asiatic Society* (Colombo, 1919). L. J. B. Turner
and John P. Lewis were two other historians, both of whom specialized in the
earlier years of British rule. Turner wrote *Collected Papers on the History of the
Maritime Provinces of Ceylon, 1795–1803* (Colombo, 1923), and Lewis contributed studies on customs relating to agriculture and on the Tamil and Sinhalese
languages to the *Journal of the Ceylon Branch of the Royal Asiatic Society*. He
also wrote *Ceylon in Early British Times* (Colombo, 1914). Finally, Leonard
Woolf, who became a literary figure in England and who wrote a novel, *The
Village in the Jungle*, based on Ceylonese experience, served in the CCS from
1904 to 1911. Woolf also extensively discusses his Ceylon experience in the first
volume of his autobiography, *Growing: An Autobiography of the Years 1904 to
1911* (London, 1961). Woolf's wife was the well-known author, Virginia Woolf.

2. Following is a short list of general works on Ceylon with particular reference
to the British and post-independence periods: S. D. Bailey, *Ceylon* (London,
1952); H. W. Codrington, *A Short History of Ceylon* (rev. ed.; London, 1947);

lying off the southeast coast of India, is tropical and has an area of just over 25,000 square miles (about half the size of England). The 1963 preliminary census estimated the population as 10,644,-809. Almost seven in every ten of its inhabitants are Sinhalese, either Kandyan in the island's central districts or low-country Sinhalese in the western and southern coastal areas. The north and east form the home of the Tamil part of the population. They are a Dravidian people, speaking Tamil, and mainly Hindu in religion. The Sinhalese, whose language is in the Indo-Aryan group, are mainly Buddhist. About three-quarters of a million of the population are Christian, and over half a million are Muslims. Much of the western, southwestern, and central parts of the island have plentiful rainfall and luxuriant vegetation, and it is in these areas that the principal crops—tea, rubber, and coconut—are mainly grown: tea in the higher parts and rubber and coconut at the lower elevations. The remainder of the island forms a dry zone, getting its rain mostly from one monsoon, the northeastern, while the wet zone benefits also from the southwest monsoon. Coconuts are grown in the wet zone and near the coast in the dry zone, but rubber and tea grow only in the wet zone. Rice, the staple food, is grown in most parts, although not in sufficient quantity to meet the whole demand; in the dry zone especially irrigation on an elaborate scale is necessary for a successful crop.

An important feature of modern Ceylon is the large and

Colvin R. de Silva, *Ceylon under the British Occupation, 1795–1832* (Colombo, 1942); Sir Charles Jeffries, *Ceylon: The Path to Independence* (London, 1962); Sir W. Ivor Jennings, *The Constitution of Ceylon* (London, 1949); Sir W. Ivor Jennings and H. W. Tambiah, *The Dominion of Ceylon: The Development of Its Laws and Constitution* (London, 1952); E. F. C. Ludowyk, *The Story of Ceylon* (London, 1962); G. C. Mendis, *Ceylon under the British* (Colombo, 1948) and *Ceylon Today and Yesterday* (Colombo, 1957); Lennox A. Mills, *Ceylon under British Rule, 1795–1932* (London, 1933); Sagarajasingham Namasivayam, *The Legislatures of Ceylon, 1928–1948* (London, 1951) and *Parliamentary Government in Ceylon 1948–1958* (Colombo, 1959); S. A. Pakeman, *Ceylon* (London, 1964); S. G. Perera, S.J., *A History of Ceylon for Schools*, Vol. II, *The British Period* (Colombo, 1946); Marshall Singer, *The Emerging Elite: A Study in Political Leadership in Ceylon* (Cambridge, 1964); J. R. Toussaint, *Annals of the Ceylon Civil Service* (Colombo, 1935); I. D. S. Weerawardana, *Government and Politics in Ceylon, 1931–1946* (Colombo, 1951); W. Howard Wriggins, *Ceylon: Dilemmas of a New Nation* (Princeton, N. J., 1960). A recent bibliography is Jean J. Hediger (comp.), "Some Books on Ceylon: A Selected and Partially Annotated Bibliography, Including a Short Section on the Maldive Islands," mimeographed (Ithaca, N. Y.: Cornell University, 1964).

continuous rise in the numbers of its population. No really reliable estimate of the population of the island when the British took over the administration exists, but it seems unlikely that its total population, including the autonomous kingdom of Kandy, much exceeded one million. As stated above, it is now well over ten times that number and is still increasing rapidly. Ceylon is not, of course, singular among South Asian or Asian countries generally in having to face the problem of a rapidly growing population, but the present rate of increase in Ceylon is claimed to be one of the highest in the world and causes many difficulties and problems in administration.

It was against this general background that during the century and a half of British rule an administrative system was evolved and developed, autocratic in its early stages, then throughout the greater part of its history almost purely bureaucratic, and finally much leavened with democratic theory and practice.

II. Development of the Bureaucracy

In the early days of British rule, after an unpopular attempt to introduce an Indian system of administration with Indian officers to administer rural areas and collect taxes, Ceylon was divorced from control by the Government of India. It became a Crown Colony in 1802 with its own government directly subordinate to the secretary of state in England. The first governor of Ceylon to be appointed by the Crown was Frederick North, who arrived in October, 1798. It was during his governorship that the authority of the governor general of India and of the British East India Company ceased. The new constitution creating Ceylon as a Crown Colony was introduced on January 1, 1802, and since that time the island has had its own administration, which for many years developed on the generally accepted Crown Colony lines.

When Governor North arrived to assume his office he was accompanied by eight British officers, some well-experienced in administration, others young men just starting their official life.

He also made some local appointments and obtained a few experienced men from India. From these he formed a complete central office of government, under a secretary to the government, or chief secretary, as he was then known. His office became the central co-ordinating secretariat and core of the whole bureaucratic system and remained so at least until 1931. All administrative and technical departments communicated with it, and from it were issued all central government orders and instructions.

Subject to the overriding authority of the secretary of state in England, the governor held the executive power. On the advice of the secretary of state[3] a local council was established for consultation on executive and legislative acts and for the promulgation of these acts and measures. Members of the council were all senior government officials, and though members could record a dissent, the council had no statutory authority. It became an important part of the government machinery, however, and was the forerunner of the Executive Council of later days. It seems correct to say that at this period the government was autocratic, and the governor was the autocrat, the main check on his actions being the secretary of state, to whom he had to report and who kept a watchful eye on developments in the colony. There was no official institution for the articulation of representative Ceylonese opinion. One of the main tasks falling to the earlier governors was the establishment of an administrative system suitable for the needs of the country.

The staff of eight which accompanied North when he assumed his duties on October 12, 1798, may for all practical purposes be considered to be the first members of the Ceylon Civil Service. Twenty-four more officers, recruited by the secretary of state in England, arrived in Ceylon in September, 1801. Thus, the nucleus of a covenanted Civil Service was formed. Placement and promotion of officers was a matter for the governor, but the secretary of

3. Dundas to North, Despatch, dated March 21, 1801, Public Record Office, London, C.O. 55, Vol. 61. This was the first of a long series of dispatches between the secretary of state and the governor.

state kept recruitment in his own hands and did not agree to appointments being made by the governor. The new officers manned the headquarters offices in Colombo and were posted to outstations to represent the government in the rural areas. There, after the attempt to introduce an Indian system collapsed, the government decided to revive arrangements for using the services of native chiefs and headmen, who again became part of the administrative machine. This pattern of local government had been inherited from native rule and had survived the Portuguese and Dutch eras. The chief headmen, bearing their old titles which varied in different parts of the country (mudaliyar in the low country of the southwest, ratemahatmaya in the central Kandyan provinces, maniagar in the far north, district adigar in Mannar in the northwest, and vanniyar in Batticaloa on the east coast), had charge of divisions and worked under the officer in charge of the district, called variously "collector" (the Indian title) or "agent of government." Intermediate and village headmen functioned below the chief headmen. The system was understood and liked by the villagers, who had been accustomed to going to their headmen in case of need. In the conditions which prevailed in the country at the time, this was probably as good an arrangement as any that could have been devised.

The authority of the Portuguese, Dutch, and (during roughly the first two decades of their rule) the British extended only to the coastal areas, while the central part of the island formed the independent Sinhalese kingdom of Kandy. In 1815 Kandy was ceded to the British, and the whole island was united under the British Crown. The newly acquired districts were at first administered separately from the remainder of the island, the governor being represented there by a resident and soon after by a Board of Commissioners. The first resident and first commissioner of the board was John (afterward Sir John) D'Oyly, a member of the second batch of civil servants. Besides being one of the best scholars of Sinhalese the CCS has produced, he was an able administrator who carried on the negotiations with the Kandyan chiefs which led to the cession of the Kandyan kingdom. He was said to have changed from "a Cambridge boy into a Cingalese [*sic*] hermit."[4] The administrative system for the Kandyan provinces was established by proclamation, dated November 21, 1818. For the next fifteen years or so the administration remained divorced from that of the maritime provinces. The Board of Commissioners remained in direct charge under the governor, with agents of government in charge of districts where the headman system was retained working much as in the maritime provinces.

Meanwhile, the British government for various reasons decided to send out a royal commission to investigate conditions in certain eastern colonies, and Ceylon was included, ostensibly because its finances, part of which were supplied by the British treasury, were not at the time very satisfactory. The commission's terms of reference were very wide; it was empowered to survey and report on the whole field of administration, including the judicial.[5] In Ceylon the main task fell to Major (later Colonel Sir) William Colebrooke, who arrived in the island in April, 1829. He was joined a year later by Charles Hay Cameron, a barrister, whose task was to prepare reports on the judiciary. As a consequence of the commissioners' very thorough and exhaustive inquiry and the ensuing recommendations, the form of government underwent an almost complete change.[6] Probably the most valuable and lasting of the Colebrooke recommendations were those relating to constitutional development. One of the most important of these was that the separate administration of the Kandyan provinces should now cease, and that all parts of the island should have a unified and

---

4. R. J. Mackintosh (ed.), *The Memoirs of the Life of the Rt. Hon. Sir James Mackintosh* (2nd ed.; London, 1836), II, 6. This description of D'Oyly is taken from the journal of Sir James who met D'Oyly in Colombo in 1810.

5. Secretary of State to the First Commissioners, January 18, 1823, Public Record Office, London, C.O. 49.8.

6. See Colebrooke's Report on Administration, December 24, 1831, Public Record Office, London, C.O. 54, Vol. 122; and Parliamentary Paper 274 of 1832. C.O. 416 also contains interesting information relating to the work of the commission. Probably the fullest and best account of the commission generally is given in *The Colebrooke-Cameron Papers*, G. C. Mendis (ed.) (2 vols., London, 1956). The text of the various reports of the commission are in Vol. 1, Part 1; Colebrooke's in sections iii, iv, vi and vii (pp. 9, 77, 189 and 212) and Cameron's in section v (p. 121). Summaries are given in de Silva, *op. cit.*, II, pp. 569 ff., and in Collins, *Public Administration in Ceylon* (London, New York, 1951), pp. 57–70.

uniform government centrally administered. For provincial administration there were to be five provinces (eventually increased to nine) under government agents. In regard to the central government, Colebrooke was particularly concerned with the position of the governor. During the early days of the colony it was probably inevitable that the governor should be an autocrat, and it was probably with something of this sort in mind that after North the next four governors were military men. The last of these, Lt. Gen. Sir Edward Barnes, was governor when Colebrooke arrived. Autocracy was an idea foreign to the school of thought to which Colebrooke owed allegiance, and although it was clear that ultimate authority had to remain with the governor and the secretary of state, he considered that the time had come when there should at least be open discussion of proposed measures and an opportunity given for expression of public opinion. Accordingly, he proposed the establishment of executive and legislative councils to assist the governor. The Executive Council would consist entirely of officials. Though it would have an official majority, the Legislative Council would at his suggestion include nominated members; they would be local residents, whether European or native, who would be able to state their views and advise on any proposals the governor might bring forward.

The ideals of Adam Smith and Jeremy Bentham and their followers undoubtedly also influenced both Colebrooke and Cameron in their other proposals. Some of these recommendations were in advance of the time as regards Ceylon but were implemented later. For example, Colebrooke mooted the idea of village councils, thus giving impetus to local government responsibility. Again he was in advance of the time in his proposal to open the public service to local people much more rapidly than was taking place, even though it might mean lowering the standards. A number of other recommendations can only be mentioned here in passing. For example, he suggested a more liberal land policy which would enable Europeans to open up land; abolition of government monopolies (e.g., in cinnamon); changed taxation, especially by placing more reliance on indirect taxation; the abolition of compulsory service on public works such as roads, paths, and bridges (rajakariya); and better educational facilities, particularly to enable Ceylonese to qualify for higher appointments.

Much more doubtful were some of the financial proposals, intended to meet the objective of a balanced budget, the attainment of which was one of the main purposes for which the commission came to the island. One of the main methods of retrenchment proposed was to reduce salaries of public servants, abolish pensions, and cut the number of higher posts, thus making promotion difficult. A further recommendation was that there should be tighter control over Ceylon affairs from England, particularly regarding financial matters.

Cameron's report[7] had for its object a reformed judicial system, based largely on the British pattern. The existing system, which originated in the Royal Charter of April 18, 1801, had outgrown its usefulness. It included practices which were no longer suited to the developing colony. For instance, there had been a marked civilian element in the courts, particularly in the appeal courts. Cameron recommended that this should cease and that there should in future be no interference by the executive government in the work of the judiciary. All distinctions between courts, e.g., between those of the Kandyan and of the maritime provinces, were to cease, and there was to be a unified system for the island. The apex of the new system was the Supreme Court, with a chief justice and two puisne justices, and with original criminal and appellate civil jurisdiction. The island was to be divided into circuits, and district judges and magistrates were provided for. The jury system which had been introduced earlier was retained, and provision was made for appeal in certain instances to the Privy Council in England. A new Royal Charter to give effect to these proposals was promulgated on February 18, 1832.

The implementation of so many of the recommendations of the

---

7. This is the Report on Judicial Establishments and Procedure written in conjunction with the Colebrooke report described above, p. 451, n. 6. The text of Cameron's report is accessible in Mendis (ed.), *Colebrook-Cameron Papers*, I, 121–188. It is included with Colebrooke's reports in C.O. 54, Vol. 122, and printed with them in Parliamentary Paper 274 of 1832.

commission, which was of fundamental importance in the political and economic growth of the country, resulted in the consolidation of a bureaucratic system, though it is doubtful if this was in anyone's mind at the time or even later. It might even be said that the opposite may have been intended, for Colebrooke criticized the exclusive nature of the services and gave the new Legislative Council at least the right of criticism.

The establishment of the new Executive Council presented no special difficulty, as its members were all official, and it was practically a continuation of the old council, though with more influence and importance. Its deliberations were private and did not come into the public eye. The Legislative Council was different. It had an official majority but included six unofficial members, all nominated, three being Europeans, to represent special interests, and three Ceylonese, who were selected by the governor to represent local interests and were chosen mainly on a racial basis. The secretary of state at first retained full financial control and was responsible for the annual budget, but from 1848 the legislature was responsible for passing the budget as an annual enactment, and while the secretary of state had the ultimate authority, the Legislative Council was able to scrutinize every item of expenditure and taxation.

Thus, a more or less typical Crown Colony form of government was established in the island, with the secretary of state and the governor ultimately responsible but with a legislature which could be and was both critical and advisory. The governor presided and could get his way because there was an official majority, but the power and influence of the legislature was considerable and grew with the years. With these developments the administration became less autocratic but undoubtedly more bureaucratic. The colonial secretary's office developed further toward being the effective center of the administration and toward assuming responsibility for the dissemination and co-ordination of government policy.

The next few years, however, were not very happy ones for the public service. This is generally considered to be a result of what is probably the weakest and least satisfactory part of the Cole-brooke recommendations. There was a general reduction in salaries of about 33 per cent on the average, and more in some cases; merit gave way to seniority as a criterion for promotion. Many government servants found their remuneration and pros-pects unsatisfactory and began to turn to agriculture—such as the opening up of new lands in coffee, which was then permissible— as a means of augmenting their income. Dispatches of the period show evidence of a deterioration in the quality and standard of the services. It took about ten years for matters to come to a head, but in 1845 the secretary of state agreed that the Colebrooke innovations regarding the services should be scrapped, and on his instructions new rules were issued for the future organization of the services.[8] These provided for adequate salaries, pensions based on the British Superannuation Act, and promotion by merit. It also laid down that no civil servant should in future be permitted to engage in any agricultural or commercial pursuit for the sake of profit, and officers had to remain in service until they were fifty-five years of age (or retired on medical grounds) before they could receive a pension, thus abolishing an old rule by which officers could retire after twelve years' service. The result of these changes was soon felt; the general standard of the services greatly improved, and they quickly reached and main-tained a high level of efficiency.

At this time the Civil Service was almost exclusively British. Colebrooke's recommendation that the selection should be on a wider basis to include Ceylonese, although accepted in principle, was not acted upon to any great extent. The first Ceylonese to receive an actual appointment to a post graded in the CCS is stated to be Mr. F. de Livera, who was appointed assistant agent and district judge in 1838 and was absorbed into the Civil Service in 1844.[9] A few more Ceylonese were admitted into the CCS during succeeding years; they were generally employed on the

8. Governor's Minute of February 14, 1845, accompanying Despatch No. 37, February 15, 1845, from Governor Sir Colin Campbell. Public Record Office, London, C.O. 54, Vol. 222.

9. Toussaint, *op. cit.*, p. 106.

judicial side as magistrates or judges, but for a considerable time these appointments were casual and no scheme for regular recruitment of Ceylonese was introduced at the time.

The period which followed may be considered the hey-day of bureaucracy in Ceylon. The Executive Council and Legislative Council, though entities with important functions of their own, were not much involved in the daily business of administration. There were no ministers in charge of departments; heads of departments were responsible to the governor and communicated with and received instructions from the colonial secretary's office. The main safeguard to civil rights and liberties was a strong and independent judiciary. This goes back to the earliest days of British rule, to the Royal Charter dated April 18, 1801. The new charter issued on February 18, 1832, established a more advanced judicial system based on the British pattern, as recommended by Cameron.[10] The Supreme Court had final jurisdiction throughout the island, and there was no civilian element as there had been before in the appeal courts. The Supreme Court judges were always members of the legal profession. In Ceylon, unlike India, it was not the practice to promote members of the Civil Service to the Supreme Court bench. The minor judiciary, however, was usually provided by civil servants. The Legislative Council provided another safeguard to civil liberties. Unofficial members could and did on occasion criticize the government, and their advice, opinion, and criticism was of great value in helping to shape public policy.

The backbone of the civil government of the period was undoubtedly the system of provincial administration. After the reforms of 1832–1833 the island was divided into five provinces and the larger or more advanced provinces were subdivided into districts. The government agent had general supervision of the whole of his province and particular responsibility for his district, while the other district or districts in the province were in the immediate charge of an assistant government agent. Under the government agent or assistant government agent were the chief headmen with intermediate and minor headmen below them.

10. See above, p. 453, n. 7.

Thus, a line of authority was established from the governor and colonial secretary to the provincial and district officers, and through them to the chief and minor headmen. As technical departments in the central government were established, they generally used the provincial and district system, with local officers working apart from but in close harmony with the government agents. Thus, there were provincial surgeons and district medical officers, provincial engineers and district engineers, superintendents and assistant superintendents of police, all of them co-ordinated above through the heads of their departments and the secretariat, and co-ordinated below by the system of provincial administration.

This pattern of government lasted with few important changes for some eighty years, and its main features lasted even longer. The system was suited to the way of life of the great body of the inhabitants, and generally it worked smoothly. There were few disturbances, probably the only serious one being in 1848 in part of the Kandyan provinces. This was caused largely by attempts to introduce financial innovations, including taxes on carts, guns, and dogs, mainly with the idea of controlling and regulating their use. The villagers did not like innovations, particularly if they affected their pocketbooks or interfered with their usual routine. In general, it can be said that relations between the government agent and the headmen and villagers were happy; provincial officers generally identified themselves with the interests of their people and were able to represent and press their views when matters arose affecting those interests.

The position of the provincial officer vis-à-vis the government, on the one hand, and the people of their areas, on the other, varied a great deal at different times and different places. The government agent of Colombo, in particular, and also the government agents of Kandy and Galle were in closer touch with the central government than those further away. The government agent of Colombo was generally a member of the executive and legislative councils, and the other two government agents were frequently members of one or both of these bodies. These three officers thus had considerable influence in shaping central government policy. In these sophisticated areas the government agent's office (kachcheri) was not so dominantly the center of authority as it was in the outstations. Again, in early days in particular, before the introduction of the telephone, the railway, and the motor car, when transport was by horse or bullock vehicle, the local government agent had to act much more on his own and could not consult the central government quickly in an emergency. The system produced a number of able administrators from the CCS, who did much useful work in their provinces and districts. Two outstanding examples may be quoted, both government agents of the Northern Province with headquarters at Jaffna. The first, P. A. Dyke, served for forty-five years (1822–1867) in the Civil Service, some thirty-seven of which he spent at Jaffna. The *Ceylon Observer* on the occasion of his death characterized him thus,

> Mr. Dyke was in every sense a Rajah in Jaffna, and the people invariably treated him as such. They knew they were safe in his hands and they liked him, but his disciplinarian habits astounded them, and we doubt if there is or has ever been a Government Agent so thoroughly feared. . . . Notwithstanding his austerity, however, the natives always felt that Mr. Dyke was a friend because he took such an absorbing interest in native affairs, and because he defended their claims against all other classes.[11]

The other, Sir William Twynam, was a quite different type of official who held office as government agent of the Northern Province from 1869 to 1896 and lived on in Jaffna until his death at the age of ninety-four in March, 1922. Toussaint wrote of him:

> It is said that "to his ability as an administrator he joined rare sympathy with the needs and aspirations of the people. His sympathy was felt, not only by the educated classes, but by the poorest and most ignorant section of the people. He knew the whole of Jaffna in a way in which very few Jaffnese know it."[12]

Many other examples could be given, but one more will suffice —that of Mr. H. R. Freeman, who as government agent of the

11. *Ceylon Observer*, October 14, 1867.
12. Toussaint, *op. cit.*, p. 113.

North-Central Province frequently supported his people against the central government. He did so particularly on the issue of chena cultivation, a form of cultivation which the government considered extremely wasteful and desired to discourage, but which he thought suited to the genius of the people. It can be said that he gained not only the admiration of the villagers but their affection, so much so that after he retired he continued to live in the province and was elected by popular vote to represent the province in the Legislative Council and afterward the State Council.[13]

This era of more or less pure bureaucratic administration coincides with a period of very considerable material progress, to which the prosperous planting industry largely contributed. Developments included the building of railways and new roads, restoration of ancient irrigation works and construction of new ones, development of medical services, and the spread of vernacular and English education, both by government and by the missionary societies.

While it appeared that many were quite satisfied with the existing administrative arrangements, others regarded as desirable more pronounced changes toward a more democratic system. Indeed, the advances already implemented made further modernization inevitable. Most of the professional and many of the landed classes were now educated in English and regarded themselves with some justification as quite capable of a reasonable share in the government and administration of the country. Europeans who were engaged in planting and commerce also pressed for greater participation in public affairs; they were particularly anxious to see a more democratic control over finance and a strengthened legislative procedure.

It was in the realm of local government that the policy of associating the people of the country more with the administration was first introduced. In 1865 an ordinance was passed which established municipal councils, in the main on British lines, with majorities of elected members in the major towns of

13. See Navasivayam, *Legislatures of Ceylon, 1928–1948*, p. 95.

Colombo, Kandy, and Galle. The governor of the time, Sir Hercules Robinson, explained the purpose of the bill in a speech to the Legislative Council on September 27, 1865:

[The bill] is one calculated, I think, to exercise an important influence on the future political and social conditions of the colony. If ever the bulk of the population can be fitted for the right use of a larger measure of political power, it can only be effected through the training which the exercise of municipal functions affords. They can thus establish a claim to further concessions by proving that they are prepared to make personal sacrifices for the public good. . . .[14]

These councils, however, had official chairmen, the government agents in the case of Kandy and Galle, and a special officer who was chosen from Class I of the Civil Service in the case of Colombo. To this extent it may be considered that the establishment of the councils was at the time an extension of the bureaucratic system, though the official now had not only to administer the ordinance but had to work with and advise an elected body.

Bodies with rather similar power were established in 1876 for the smaller towns. Known as "local boards of health and improvement," they each had three elected and three nominated members, again with the government agent or his assistant as chairman. In 1892 an act was passed[15] providing for the management of the larger villages and bazaars. It established a nominated board, the sanitary board, for each district, again under the chairmanship of the government agent or his assistant. Still earlier, in 1856, another important step had been taken in the development of local self-government. This was the Irrigation Ordinance, designed to control cultivation and the use of water.[16] This ordinance provided for the revival of the village council (gam sabhava) with power to make rules for these purposes, and in 1871 it was extended to cover other aspects of village life. The

---

14. Addresses delivered in the Legislative Council of Ceylon by Governors of the Colony (Colombo, 1877), Vol. II, document no. 9.

15. The Local Sanitary Rates Ordinance, 1892. Text accessible in *Legislative Enactments of Ceylon* (Colombo, 1923), II, 207.

16. The original Irrigation Ordinance was enacted in 1856. As amended, the act appears as Irrigation Ordinance, No. 45 of 1917. The text is accessible in *ibid.*, III, 544.

village committees, as they were called, which were intended to revive a supposed ancient system of village government,[17] consisted of members chosen from among the principal landowners of the area. They were presided over by the chief headmen under the supervision of the government agent and had power to make rules for the regulation of village facilities. The same ordinance also provided for the establishment of village tribunals—local courts which not only tried breaches of village rules but had jurisdiction in minor criminal and in certain civil cases. The courts were presided over at first by the chief headmen, but later special presidents of village tribunals were appointed. Appeals went to the government agent or assistant government agent, and from him to the governor. A good deal of the revenue officer's time was taken up by deciding appeals and in inspecting and supervising these local institutions, but there is no doubt as to the value of the institutions both immediately and in the long term.

Though the establishment of local government bodies did not at first mean any diminution of bureaucratic control, they were certainly an advance toward a more liberal administration, and before long further steps were taken. One of the first changes was that chief headmen ceased to be chairmen of village committees, which were now allowed to elect their own chairmen. Later, municipalities and towns elected their own chairmen. A further and later step was to change village tribunals into minor courts and to appoint lawyers instead of chief headmen to preside, with appeal to the district courts and the Supreme Court instead of to the government agent and governor. In all these cases there was a transfer of authority from the bureaucracy when the various bodies concerned were considered ready to assume such responsibility. Toward the end of the British period, a headman's commission, appointed under the chairmanship of a senior civil servant at the instance of the State Council, expressed the view that the existing system had become antiquated and needed changing to meet modern conditions. In accordance with their recommendations, divisional revenue officers selected by open competition were substituted for chief headmen in charge of

17. This parallels the revival of the panchayat in India.

divisions.[18] The officers did not need to have property and influence in their divisions and were liable to be moved anywhere within the specified areas (low-country, Kandyan, or Tamil) to which they were appointed. "This brought to an end what has been called a local 'feudal system'—a system which had persisted from ancient times, and made a definite and decisive break with old traditions."[19] The new officers carried on the same duties as were performed by the chief headmen, and the change made no practical difference as regards the government agent, but it was one further step in the gradual transition to modern conditions.

New constitutions for the country were proclaimed in 1912, 1920, and 1924. The Constitution of 1912 introduced the elective principle into the selection of members of the Legislative Council, but left an official majority. The next change reconstituted the Legislative Council, the new council consisting of fourteen official and twenty-three unofficial members, of whom eleven were elected on a territorial basis. It also amended the constitution of the Executive Council by authorizing the governor to appoint three unofficial members to it. The public servants in this council now for the first time had unofficial colleagues, an innovation which proved valuable. This Constitution, however, did not work very well in practice and was followed by a still more liberal Constitution in 1924. The latter provided for thirty-seven unofficial and twelve official members of the Legislative Council and added two more members to the Executive Council, chosen from the elected members of the Legislative Council.[20]

The new constitutions were thus on advanced Crown Colony lines. Though there was an unofficial majority in the Legislative

18. In 1959 there were 126 divisional revenue officers in service and only a handful of chief headmen. *Civil List of Ceylon, 1960* (Colombo, 1960).

19. This is developed further in Collins, *op. cit.*, p. 106.

20. The earlier constitutions were usually based on Letters Patent, an order-in-council constituting the councils, and Royal Instructions given to the governor. The Constitution of 1924 was brought into operation by a proclamation by the governor published in *Government Gazette*, 7373 (February 16, 1924), and by the Ceylon (Legislative Council) Order-in-Council, 1923, printed in the same issue of the *Government Gazette*. The previous constitutions were brought into operation in the same way. The semi-official *Ceylon Manual of 1912–13* (Colombo, 1913) gives on p. 47 a full text of the Letters Patent of November 24, 1910, constituting the office of governor and commander in chief of the island of Ceylon and its dependencies. On p. 51 of the same source, a copy of the Royal Instructions of the same date may be found.

Council, the governor and the secretary of state still exercised the final authority, and the administration still centered in the secretariat to which departments were responsible. The 1924 Constitution also proved unsatisfactory, largely because the members of the legislature had more power but no responsibility for administration and could criticize and harass the government to their hearts' content. The Finance Committee of the council, which included all the unofficial members along with the colonial secretary, the treasurer, and the controller of revenue, proved especially difficult to work. This committee met in private for the discussion of any matter which had financial implications. Senior government officers and heads of departments called before it were often treated as hostile witnesses and had a rough passage. The effect was felt mainly in the higher branches of the administration, but it filtered down through the whole public service. Administration was carried on, but the atmosphere was wrong.[21]

It was obvious that the 1924 Constitution was becoming increasingly unsatisfactory both to the government and to the Legislative Council. It was never intended that this should be a final constitution, but rather a further transitional phase toward self-government, at least at the local level. On the advice of the governor, therefore, a special commission was sent from England under the chairmanship of the Earl of Donoughmore, and on its recommendation a completely new Constitution was established in Ceylon.[22]

Before discussing the main features of the new form of government and their effects on the administration and the services, however, it would appear desirable to review developments in the Civil Service up to 1924.

21. Probably the best account of the situation is that given in *Ceylon: Report of the Special Commission on the Constitution*, Cmd. 3131 (London, 1928), chaps. iii and viii. This is the report of the commission headed by the Earl of Donoughmore and will hereinafter be cited as Donoughmore Report. As a corrective to the views expressed in the Donoughmore Report, see Governor Sir H. J. Stanley's dispatch of June 2, 1929, to the secretary of state, printed in *Despatches Relating to the Ceylon Constitution*, Ceylon Sessional Paper XXXIV (1929). See also Ludowyk, *op. cit.*, p. 241. For a short account, see Collins, *op. cit.*, pp. 119 ff.

22. One of the best accounts of the Donoughmore Constitution is found in Navasivayam, *Legislatures of Ceylon, 1928–1948*, pp. 29–128. See also Weerawardana, *op. cit.*

The method of recruitment to the Civil Service by competitive examination in London began in 1856, and since then this method, designed to attract mainly university graduates, had been the only method used for obtaining British entrants. Examination had also been a main method for the recruitment of Ceylonese. A few Ceylonese had been appointed to the service before 1856. In 1844 two men already holding judicial posts were so appointed, and three more were appointed in 1845 and 1846— one, for the first time, from the clerical service, one through the public works department, and one from a district judgeship. Up to 1863 the few local candidates who were admitted were not selected by this examination and, in fact, were appointed on the nomination of the governor without examination. From 1863 on, however, candidates were subjected to a non-competitive examination to test their general "attainments." In 1870 it was arranged for the entrance examination to be held in Ceylon as well as in London, with identical papers. As these were based on British university courses, few Ceylonese were able to compete. However, at least one Ceylonese, Mr. (later Sir) P. Arunachalam, who afterward had a brilliant career in the service and in public life, obtained his appointment in this way. From 1880 the examination was held only in London, but few Ceylonese had acquired the necessary qualifications to be able to take advantage of the examination. In fact, though the intention was to recruit more Ceylonese, the number was decreasing. Governor Sir Arthur Gordon, in a despatch dated May 7, 1890, wrote:

Fifteen or twenty years ago there were ten or twelve natives in the regular civil service. In 1880 their number had sunk to five. There are now in 1890 but three who regularly entered the service as cadets. There are three others . . . who have been appointed from those who have already served the government long and well outside the ranks of the Civil Service proper.[23]

As a consequence of that despatch a "lower" or, as it was called later, a "local division" was created to be filled by British subjects born in Ceylon whose families were permanently resident in the

23. *Papers Relating to the Re-classification of the Ceylon Civil Service* (Sessional Paper XXVII, 1897), p. 3.

island. (This definition covered Ceylonese and a few British.) Nominations were made by the governor but were limited to persons who had passed the Cambridge senior local examination or the London matriculation or some other examination deemed to be of equally high standard. The nominees' merits were further tested by a competitive examination. Members of this local division were eligible for appointment to six cadetships and to eighteen ordinary appointments in the CCS, including one in Class I, and were graded for purposes of promotion in one list with the higher division. It was specified, however, that they were not to be promoted unless special fitness for work in an upper class was shown. The local division remained in being until 1920, when its members were integrated into the higher division.

It is tempting to liken the lower division of the Civil Service to the provincial services in India. There is some similarity in regard to recruitment, but there the likeness ends, as the Ceylon local division officers performed (within limits) the same duties as the other members of the Civil Service and were liable to be sent to any part of the island.

The endeavors to increase the proportion of Ceylonese in the service were not at first very successful. In 1896, out of a total strength of seventy-nine officers, the number of "Ceylonese" in the CCS was thirteen, of whom four were Sinhalese and three Tamil. The remainder were other British subjects including Europeans born in Ceylon. The governor at the time, Sir J. West Ridgeway, wished to make some alterations mainly in classification which would improve the position of the Ceylonese in the service and satisfy their "legitimate aspirations."[24] The secretary of state, however, preferred to give existing schemes further trial. The rate of recruitment improved slightly, and some competent Ceylonese entered the service via the local division, but it never proved a really satisfactory method of recruitment.

Later, a new class, Class V (later Class III), of the CCS was created to enable the occasional appointment without examination of "members of the Government service possessing aptitude

---

24. Despatch No. 316 of October 31, 1896, to the secretary of state, in *Papers Relating to the Re-classification of the Ceylon Civil Service*, p. 1.

for public business." In making these appointments it was prescribed that "regard will be had to [their] ability, social standing, high reputation and long experience."[25] There was provision for promotion to higher classes of specially qualified officers in this class.

The London examination continued to be the main means of entry into the service. To facilitate entrance of Ceylonese, provision was made that a proportion of the new entrants, to be fixed from time to time, should be Ceylonese. If the London examination did not produce the required number of Ceylonese, a local examination to fill the vacancies was to be held. More Ceylonese were attending British universities; hence, more were qualified to sit for the examination. The establishment of a University College in Colombo in 1921 and arrangements for holding examinations locally for the external degrees of the London University made it possible again to hold entrance examinations in the island, simultaneously with those held in London. In 1932, in order to insure that the educational standard of recruits remained high, only graduates of London University or holders of degrees of equivalent standard were nominated to sit for the local examination.

Notwithstanding the efforts made to bring more Ceylonese into the CCS, the number remained disproportionately small up to 1920 at least. The proportion was much higher in such technical departments as public works and medicine. Ceylonese members of these departments had proved efficient and able, and there seemed small justification for a lower proportion of Ceylonese in the Civil Service. In 1919 a committee which was appointed to advise on "Ceylonization" in the higher ranks of the public service recommended that one-third of the CCS should be Ceylonese and that this proportion should be raised gradually to one-half.[26] In April, 1920, the secretary of state approved the recruitment of one Ceylonese to every two British, and by

25. Civil Service Minute of January 13, 1932. Text accessible in *Ceylon Civil List, 1932* (Colombo, 1932), p. 178.
26. *Report of the Committee on the Further Employment of Ceylonese in the Public Service* (Sessional Paper I, 1919). See also *Recruitment of Cadets for the Civil Service* (Sessional Paper XVII, 1920).

1927 the desired proportion of one-third was realized. For a year or two before 1935 no recruitment of British was made, owing to uncertainties about salaries and conditions of service, but when in 1935 recruitment of British was resumed, one-third of the vacancies only were filled from this source. In 1938 the secretary of state agreed that there should be no further British recruitment, but he added a proviso, which he never needed to use, that his approval was subject to there being no apparent deterioration of the service in quality or efficiency. The last British cadets were appointed in 1937, and since then all new entrants to the CCS have been Ceylonese.

The following table gives the approximate total number of Civil Service appointments made during various periods up to 1937, each period being subdivided for convenience into approximately two decades. The first period, up to 1801, covers the time

Table 1. *Ethnic Composition of Appointees to the Ceylon Civil Service, 1798 to 1937*

| | Number of appointments made | | | | Percentage |
Period	British	Ceylonese	Indian	Total	British
Before 1801	21	—	—	21	100.0
1801 to 1824	77	2	—	79	97.5
1825 to 1844	55	1	—	56	98.2
1845 to 1864	67	15	—	82	81.7
1865 to 1884	79	5	—	84	94.0
1885 to 1919	123	43	5	171	71.9
1920 to 1937	41	59	—	100	41.0
Totals	463	125	5	593	78.1

Sources: Figures were compiled from a list of Civil Servants in *Ceylon, Its History, People, Commerce, Industries and Resources,* compiled and published by Plate, Ltd. (Colombo, 1924); and from official Civil Lists of Ceylon.

when Ceylon was governed from India. The second period, from 1801 to 1844, covers the time between the date when Ceylon became a Crown Colony to the reform of the service in the latter years. During the third period, 1845 to 1919, Ceylonese were recruited, but not on any definite numerical basis. In the last period, 1919 to 1937, definite proportions of Ceylonese were recruited.

Table 1 indicates the intake of British and Ceylonese into the CCS until European recruitment ceased. Thereafter, the intake was entirely Ceylonese. From this time the number of British in the service decreased, mainly by retirements. The reductions were very gradual and no pressure was put on British officers to retire. Table 2 shows this gradual reduction in the number of

Table 2. *Ethnic Composition of the Ceylon Civil Service, 1920–1950*

Year	British	Ceylonese and Indians (if any)	Local division	Class V (later Class III)	Percentage of British	Percentage of British, less Class V (III)
1920	79	11	26	—	68.1	68.1
1930	83	55	—	15	54.2	60.1
1940	49	81	—	13	34.3	37.7
1947	32	116	—	20	19.0	21.6
1950	10	124	—	15ᵃ	6.7	7.5

ᵃ Plus ten temporary posts.

Source: Table with modifications derived from Sir Charles Collins, *Public Administration in Ceylon* (London, New York, 1951).

British officers, and the buildup of Ceylonese, at ten-year intervals from 1920 to 1950, by which time Ceylon had acquired independence and new conditions had come into play. Figures are also given for 1947, this being the last full year of colonial government.

While it was not laid down that any particular posts in the CCS were to be filled by British officers, in practice the senior posts in the secretariat and treasury, the senior customs posts, and the government agencies were usually held by Europeans until a fairly late date. From about 1930, Ceylonese were appointed government agents occasionally, and other higher posts gradually opened to them during the later years of the British period. Up to 1932 there was not very much change in the nature of the posts filled by civil servants. The senior posts in the secretariat and treasury and in customs, the positions as government agents and assistant government agents, registrar general, land commissioner and several land settlement officers, and the controller of labor were generally filled from the CCS, but CCS officers were often used for other special purposes, and the practice had begun of using some as administrative officers in technical departments.

The distribution of Ceylonese members of the CCS among the island's major ethnic communities is of considerable interest. A study by S. J. Tambiah indicated that until about 1935 most of the Ceylonese officers in the Civil Service and other higher services were either members of the Burgher or Tamil communities and that a disproportionately small number of Sinhalese, who compose the majority community, belonged to these services. With the spread of education and other altered conditions, however, a change took place from about 1935, with larger numbers of Sinhalese entering the higher services, until in Tambiah's words: "By 1946 the Sinhalese dominance in the Administrative service is complete."[27] The policy of the British administration was not to recruit local officers from any particular community but to recruit men well educated in English, capable of performing important administrative duties, and with sufficient standing to command respect from the populace. The figures, however, do seem to support Tambiah's contention. Prior to 1870, the year when some sort of examination was first introduced, eleven Burghers, two Tamils, and seven Sinhalese were given places in the Civil Service (approximate figures). Between 1870 and 1907, five Burghers and five Sinhalese were recruited. According to Tambiah, in 1907 there were four Sinhalese, two Tamils, and six Burghers in the CCS. The corresponding numbers in 1925 were seventeen Sinhalese, eight Tamils, and fourteen Burghers (in addition, the CCS contained four Indians). In 1946 the figures were sixty-nine Sinhalese, thirty-one Tamils, and sixteen Burghers.

III. The Transition to Self-Government

The new Constitution for Ceylon, generally known in the island as the Donoughmore Constitution, was brought into opera-

27. See S. J. Tambiah, "Ethnic Representation in Ceylon's Higher Administrative Services, 1870–1946," *University of Ceylon Review*, XIII (April–July, 1955), 113–134.

tion by the Ceylon (State Council) Order-in-Council, 1931. The Constitution has many very interesting features, among which, from the point of view of the present study, one of the most important undoubtedly is the manner in which it was intended to supervise and control administration. The Donoughmore Commission recognized that the old Legislative Council had "displayed a predominating interest in administration," which

rather than legislation has loomed large in the eyes of the politician . . . and to a great extent this will always remain the case . . . it would seem wise to make a virtue of necessity and to render it more easy for the Legislative Council to participate in the administrative functions of Government with knowledge and intelligence.[28]

Under the new arrangements the Executive Council and Legislative Council disappeared, and in their place a single-chamber legislature, the State Council, was created with both legislative and executive functions. Universal suffrage was introduced, and fifty of the sixty-one members of the State Council were elected for territorial constituencies. There were eight nominated members to represent special interests and three officers of state—the chief, legal, and financial secretaries who had no vote in the council. The Donoughmore Report lists forty departments of government, which were arranged into ten groups. The members of the State Council, after they had been elected, were divided into seven groups, each of which formed an executive committee.[29] Each of these committees had charge of a group of departments, while the remaining three groups came under the control of officers of state. The chief secretary had charge of the public service administration, external affairs, and defense. Each executive committee elected its chairman from among its members, and these were appointed ministers for their subjects and collectively with the three officers of state formed the Board of Ministers. The chief secretary was chairman of the board, though neither he nor the other two officers of state had a vote at board meetings. The Board of Ministers had responsibility for the

28. Donoughmore Report, p. 44.
29. See Wriggins, *op. cit.*, p. 88, for comparison with committee structure in the Congress of the United States.

annual budget and for financial matters generally. It was not intended to be a cabinet or to formulate policy, which was the function of the executive committees and of the State Council. In practice, however, the board tended to become more and more like a cabinet and to concern itself increasingly with matters of policy.

A Public Service Commission was established, but it was an official body, with the chief secretary as chairman. As there was an appeal to the secretary of state, the position of the services in relation to such matters as appointments, transfers, and discipline was not very different from what it had been, except that the executive committees had a right and a duty to make recommendations through the Public Service Commission in the case of senior appointments in their departments.

Public servants, both British and Ceylonese, whose appointments had been made by the secretary of state and who were in office when the new Constitution came into operation were given a continuous and unlimited (or in certain cases a limited) right to retire with proportionate pension and compensation for loss of career. A considerable number of officers took advantage of these provisions for retirement. The Soulbury Commission reported that by July, 1945, some 347 officers had opted for retirement, 247 officers possessing the unlimited option were still in service, while five officers had taken advantage of the limited option open to them.[30] In the CCS, however, the number of early retirements was small. Between 1930 and 1932, when the new Constitution came into full operation, only about twelve CCS members retired. No statistics are available to show how many of these retired under the special provisions, but the number did include a few senior and experienced officers. Of 137 members of the CCS in 1932, all the sixty-nine British and three Indians were appointed by the secretary of state and had the right to early retirement. Thirty-one of sixty-five Ceylonese in the CCS in 1932 were appointed by the secretary of state and had the same right to retire as the British. The other Ceylonese civil servants,

30. *Ceylon: Report of the Royal Commission on Constitutional Reform,* Cmd. 6677 (1945), par. 364. Hereinafter referred to as Soulbury Report.

including twelve in Class III, were appointed by the governor and did not have the right to early retirement. Twelve British and eighteen Ceylonese who obtained the right to retire under the special provisions had not exercised their option and were still in office in 1947.[31]

Officers who opted for retirement were not asked to give reasons for this action; hence, it is not possible to analyze precisely the motives which activated them in making their choice. It may be conjectured that some left on being offered transfers to other posts under the Colonial Office, and it is certain that some left because they feared that the possibilities for promotion would be fewer than in the past and thought it desirable to get away while still young enough to obtain other employment. Others left because the whole nature of the service appeared to have changed.

This, of course, was the case. The coming of the new administrative system saw the beginning of the end of the old bureaucratic order. The colonial secretary's office, the central office of a bureaucratic administration, ceased to exist. The new chief secretary was, it is true, his lineal successor in a number of respects, particularly in regard to his function of being in charge of the public service. He was the senior civil servant, and his name appeared first among the "staff" appointments in that service, but his office ceased to be the main office of record, and his function as the governor's mouthpiece was taken over (save in the State Council) by a new officer, the secretary to the governor. Decentralization of control from the secretariat was one of the main recommendations of the Donoughmore Commission, which felt "compelled to recommend the simultaneous adoption of measures of administrative devolution as well as of constitutional reform."[32]

One of the most interesting and important features of the new Constitution was the creation of the three officers of state and the functions and duties assigned to them. The following extracts from

31. These figures were extracted from the *Ceylon Civil List* for the various years and are approximate.
32. Donoughmore Report, p. 67.

the report of the Donoughmore Commission show what they had in mind:

In framing this scheme for a new constitution we have aimed throughout our task at devolving on to the shoulders of the Ceylonese themselves as great a degree of responsibility for the management of the affairs of the Island as is compatible with a system which must inevitably fall somewhat short of full responsible government. The responsibility thus granted to them will, we have no doubt, be fully justified, but in order that it may exercise its full effect it is essential that it should be realised by the Council and appreciated by public opinion that the Government will in no sense be run by the Chief Secretary and his official colleagues, but that on the contrary the burden will be now shifted to Ceylonese shoulders, the Officers of State being present in the deliberations of the Board of Ministers and of the Council, for the main purpose of giving that expert advice and assistance with which no new Government can dispense. It is true that the Officers of State will be responsible in a Ministerial capacity for administering the special Departments which we have recommended should be retained in their charge, and in this sense will be executive officers, but they will administer these Departments with the primary object of assisting and not of hampering their Ceylonese colleagues, of whose policy their activities will be largely implementary. In pursuance therefore of our intention that the Officers of State should be regarded as advisory rather than as executive officers we would propose that . . . he [the chief secretary] should not be the Leader of the Council. Just as at the Board it would be his duty to give his fellow Ministers the benefit of his expert advice and administrative experience, while leaving to them the responsibility for decision, so in Council it would be primarily his duty to advise and point out dangers and difficulties rather than to assume any personal responsibility for the proposals under discussion.[33]

It is noteworthy that the commission envisaged a crucial role for the officers of state as guardian advisers during a transition to complete self-rule. This institutionalization of transitional help was not adopted elsewhere in the same form, but the principles underlying it were of general application.

The position of the governor was also greatly changed. He no longer had an Executive Council to consult and to work with, and gubernatorial orders no longer took the form of being issued by

33. *Ibid.*

"The Governor-in-Council." He had a number of reserve powers, but most of his powers of initiating policy devolved on the new executive. The following extract from the Royal Instructions to the governor, dated April 22, 1931, sets out the position:

I. In the exercise of the powers conferred on him by the Ceylon [State Council] Order in Council, 1931, the Governor shall have regard to our desire to promote by that Order the devolution upon the inhabitants of Ceylon of responsibility for the management of the internal affairs of the Island.

In all matters in which powers and functions are by that Order assigned either to the State Council, or to the Board of Ministers, or to Executive Committees, the Governor, in the exercise of that authority which is reserved to him in relation to those matters, shall give the most favourable consideration to the views expressed and to the advice tendered to him by the body in which those powers and functions reside. In all such matters he shall exercise his authority according to his own deliberate judgment, but in such manner that it shall be supervisory rather than executive, and he will not act contrary to the views or to the advice aforesaid unless he shall consider that the principles of Our said Order, or his own responsibility under it, shall so require.

II. The Governor shall consult freely with his Ministers and shall keep himself fully informed of their wishes and opinions and those of the people of the Island.[34]

The new scheme marked a complete departure from much of the old tradition. It meant an end to the bureaucracy as previously understood and to centralization in one office. Policy was determined in executive committees, and ministers worked with their own heads of departments, who were generally called to meetings of the committees when matters affecting their departments were under consideration. Ministers became responsible in council for the conduct of their departments, although heads of departments and all other government servants continued to look to the chief secretary, who was head of the public service establishment and chairman of the Public Service Commission, to safeguard the interests of the services.

Each executive committee had a small office presided over by a

34. Text of these instructions accessible in *Ceylon Government Manual of Procedure* (Colombo, 1931), pp. 97–103.

secretary to the minister, who was graded in Class II of the CCS. Such secretaries need not necessarily have been civil servants and frequently were not. Under this arrangement, secretaries did not function as heads of departments and were not intended to occupy a position such as those of permanent secretaries in a British ministry, or of permanent secretaries under the later independence Constitution in Ceylon. Their function was to see that the machinery of the ministry worked smoothly, and they were actually forbidden to write minutes on official papers passing between ministers and heads of departments.

It is clear that such a system would be very difficult to work without the assistance of some form of co-ordinating authority. It was intended that this should be provided by the State Council sitting in executive sessions when reports from the committees would come before it. In practice, however, this provision became a dead letter, and co-ordination was effected mainly by the Board of Ministers. The board as such had no policy-making powers over the executive committees, but it had control of the purse through the annual budget and through supplementary votes. In fact, as time progressed the board gradually became more like a conventional "cabinet," though it never quite attained this position. The Constitution was so formulated that there were no political parties and so no question of "government" and "opposition" arose. This did not imply that there could be no conflict of ideologies among members, but this did not prevent men of quite different political views from working together in the same committees.

With such a drastic and radical change in the central government, the nature of the public service changed also, especially at the higher levels. Senior government agents and other senior officers who had in the past been members of the executive and legislative councils and had had a share in policy-making no longer acted in this way. Government agents became heads of departments working under the home ministry and helping various other ministries and departments. Theoretically, the executive committees and the ministers, their chairmen, had between them the full control of the everyday running of their departments—though they could only spend money within the limits of the sanctioned estimates, and these were controlled by the Board of Ministers and the State Council. There were also treasury control, legal sanctions, and a strong and incorruptible judiciary to see that they were applied, and in the background were the governor's reserve powers which were used as infrequently as possible.

Heads of departments had the right to attend committee meetings when matters concerning their departments were under consideration, and some heads of departments undoubtedly had considerable influence with the committees in settling what was to be done. Moreover, the chief secretary and the deputy chief secretary had the right to attend and speak at meetings, but not to vote. This right, which often proved useful, was exercised more in the early days of the Constitution than in the later days. However, it was never given up. The committees, then, were not without advice and assistance, and the relationship between them and departments was generally though not invariably very good.

Nevertheless, the arrangement by which three or four very senior public servants were charged with the special duty of being "councillors and Friends-in-need" did not prove altogether happy. Personal relationships were generally though not always good throughout. Nonetheless, the system was never really liked. As might have been expected, the three officers of state soon acquired the sobriquet of "the three policemen," and their presence at meetings was often regarded with a certain amount of suspicion. There was little difficulty when it came to running their own departments like other ministries, but it was with regard to their functions as general advisers that irritation and misunderstanding sometimes arose. These problems never became really serious, but the feeling was there; so that however helpful the arrangement was intended to be, it was not one that proved to be very effective. One reason for this probably was that on the few occasions when it was found necessary to exercise the governor's reserve powers, it was an officer of state who had to propose and defend the motion in the State Council and see to its formal adoption.

It is interesting that during the last few years of the Constitution the financial secretary was Sir Oliver Goonetilleke, a Ceylonese who later served as governor general of Ceylon from 1954 to 1962. Sir Oliver had long been a member of the public service of Ceylon, though not of the Ceylon Civil Service, and he had rendered able assistance during the war as civil defense commissioner and in other capacities. As financial secretary he was able not only to carry out the functions and duties appertaining to an officer of state, but also was greatly concerned with the Ceylonese ministers in preparing the way for a new Constitution and independence. The other officers of state were also concerned with this question, but perhaps their interest stemmed less from a political and more from a practical and administrative point of view.

The officer-of-state system may not have been the happiest means that could have been adopted for assisting a developing country toward a maturity which would fit it for evolution into a fully self-governing dominion, but it was not entirely unsuccessful. The State Council period saw the birth or early development of a number of the changes and new tendencies in the political, economic, and social life of Ceylon, which have been a feature in the development of the country since the attainment of independence. As the official *Ceylon Year Book* for 1950 puts it: "In retrospect it is seen that the State Council period (1931–46) was the seed-time of the new nation. It was during this time that many of the nation-building activities that contribute to the well-being of Ceylon were initiated. . . ."[35] Much of the credit for the new or renewed activity in these fields must go to the new ministers and executive committees responsible for initiating many of the new schemes, and in this they received support from

35. *Ceylon Year Book, 1950* (Colombo: Department of Census and Statistics, 1951). See also Soulbury Report, par. 118. The *Ceylon Year Book* has been published annually by the Ceylon Department of Census and Statistics since 1948. It replaced the *Annual General Report*, which was published between 1928 and 1940, and contains a considerable amount of descriptive and statistical information on government, economics, education, and social conditions in Ceylon compiled from official sources. *Ceylon Year Book, 1948* contains what is probably the best account of developments during the latter part of the Donoughmore period. Due to wartime conditions, no annual report had been issued for some years before 1948 and the yearbook publication of that year covered the period from 1938 to 1947.

members of the Civil Service and other services, British and Ceylonese, both in the initiation and in the carrying out of the schemes.

Ceylon was and still is essentially an agricultural country, and some of the more important developments were in this field. Mr. D. S. Senanayake, later Ceylon's first prime minister, was the minister of agriculture and lands for much of the period. (Among other things he was a competent farmer.) Under his direction much was done to further local agriculture. Many of the great irrigation works of old Ceylon which were derelict when the British came to the country had already been restored, but a number of others were still in unusable condition. Restoration was started on several of the old irrigation works and new projects were started, with the result that much cultivable land, particularly for food crops, became available. Colonization schemes were started to place peasant and "middle-class" families on dry-zone lands which were irrigable but had not previously been included in the schemes. In 1935 a Land Development Ordinance[36] was passed which provided for the "mapping out" of Crown land mainly for village purposes, and villagers were settled on the lands reserved for this purpose under conditions intended to insure good cultivation. Much of the very considerable work entailed fell to the government agents and their assistants.

In the industrial field attempts were made to establish some factories for the supply of articles in local demand. A coir (coconut yarn) factory was started in 1940 and a plywood factory in the following year—the latter supplying many of the tea chests used in the tea industry. Other small "pilot" and "state model" factories were opened, and though a number of these did not prove very successful, they indicated a trend toward industrialization. The first really large-scale factory which had its origin during the period was a cement plant at Kankesanturai in the Northern province, intended ultimately to supply the cement

36. The Land Development Ordinance, No. 19 of 1935. Text constitutes chapter 320 of *Legislative Enactments of Ceylon* (Colombo, 1938), Vol. VI.

needs of the whole island. A British civil servant, D. H. Balfour, was a pioneer in the field of industrial development.

Considerable strides were made also in the field of rural co-operatives. The movement had its origin as early as 1913, and the first societies were mainly in the country districts, generally among peasants. The enthusiasm of another civil servant, W. K. H. Campbell, was responsible for much of the development, modeled after Scandinavian practice. Later, many consumer societies were founded, in urban as well as rural areas, and as in England a co-operative wholesale society was started to supply the needs of the retail societies. In 1945 a department of co-operative development was formed to plan and guide the movement. In the following year there were 6,500 societies of which over four thousand were consumer societies, with a membership of over one million and sales amounting to Rs. 165 million. The first phase of a hydroelectric scheme for the island, utilizing water power from rivers in the hilly districts of the interior, was begun in 1942. Another step to aid the development of the country was the foundation of the state-sponsored Bank of Ceylon in 1939.

Of perhaps greater interest to the bulk of the population were the developments in health, education, and social services. Many small rural hospitals (usually of about twenty beds) were provided to supplement the provincial and district hospitals. By the end of 1945, forty-five rural hospitals were functioning, and there were plans for building more—up to a total of 250. Important advances were also taking place in preventive medicine. Two of the worst and most insidious diseases that had been common in early years in the rural areas, parangi (yaws) and anchylostomiasis, had been practically eliminated by modern methods, but malaria so far had defeated all attempts at complete elimination. Spraying of pyrethrum was begun in 1939, and the yet more effective DDT spraying was started in 1945; by these methods a real start was made toward the elimination of the disease.

In education the most spectacular event of the period was probably the conversion on July 1, 1942, of the University College into a full University of Ceylon. But what contributed perhaps more than anything else to development toward greater political maturity was the emphasis placed on vernacular and Anglo-vernacular education in the life of the country. This derives from the advances which had been made in education from about the middle of the nineteenth century. Education in English was encouraged in order to provide a class of professional men and public servants for whom English was a necessity and to give opportunities locally for a liberal education on Western lines for those who desired it. The development of vernacular education, on the other hand, was intended to spread literacy and culture among the general public, including the peasantry. Government and mission schools throughout the country provided the means. Some of the schools, especially in the urban areas, were Anglo-vernacular—English as well as Sinhalese or Tamil was taught. These schools were a boon to traders, craftsmen, and town dwellers generally, for whom some knowledge of English was of great importance. Literacy grew until the population of the island was, apart from Japan, the most literate in Asia. In 1945 there were 2,391 government schools and 3,335 state-assisted (mainly mission) schools, and education was available to every child save in the most remote parts. In 1946, 62 per cent of the men and 38 per cent of the women were literate.[37] In consequence, the effect on administration was considerable and was growing. Interest in affairs not purely parochial began to be aroused, vernacular newspapers circulated, and the radio was widely listened to. Villagers began to take more interest in local government, and as they now had the right to vote in national affairs, interest in politics was spreading beyond the ranks of the "English educated." The full effects, not so obvious at the time, became apparent later on with the growth of a party system in the new Ceylon. Another result which had already begun to show itself was a tendency among constituents of members of the State Council to turn to them for advice and assistance, instead of going to their headmen—a tendency which became an important feature of the parliamentary system after independence.

The effect of these developments on the public service was

37. Soulbury Report, pp. 33–35. See also the *Ceylon Year Book, 1948,* chap. vii.

considerable. The technical services expanded. The Ceylon Civil Service, rather curiously, did not. The total number of members of the service in 1947 was 148, plus twenty in Class III, a figure which showed little change from previous years. Even a decade later (1958) the total was about the same (147), plus fifty-six in Class III. Though its numbers remained more or less static, the nature of the service and much of the work it was called upon to undertake was altering rapidly, and civil servants found their time more and more occupied with social service tasks, land work, and local government. Since they were now working for and with Ceylonese ministers and executive committees, their task became more that of implementing policy than of initiating it.

While there were many criticisms of the Donoughmore Constitution, it achieved one of the objects of its authors, which was to provide, while the country was still under British rule, a transition from a colonial form of government to a democratic one, destined to prepare the way for complete local self-government.

The Donoughmore Constitution came to an end in October, 1947, after protracted negotiations with the Ceylon ministers, who wanted a more orthodox form of government, and after the Commission on Constitutional Reform, led by Lord Soulbury, had made its report. The Constitution which followed (known locally as the "Soulbury" Constitution) lasted only about four months, but it was useful because it enabled the administrative changes required by a cabinet form of government to be made before the final step to independence was taken. Elections to the new House of Representatives were held, for the first time on party lines, and Mr. D. S. Senanayake's United National party won with a large majority. The executive committees' functions were taken over by responsible ministers. Much of the work of the public service continued as before, but one very important change was made: a permanent secretary with a small secretariat was appointed to each ministry to administer the affairs of departments coming under the ministry. The permanent secretaries were generally but not invariably chosen from the senior ranks of the CCS; in a few cases selections were made from among departmental officers, who besides having a good knowledge of the technical side of their departments had shown themselves good administrative officers. The idea was based on British practice, where each ministry has a permanent secretary in charge of administrative matters while the minister looks after the political aspects of the ministry. In practice, however, the British system was not followed in its entirety. In Britain all the functions of the ministry were welded together into one whole department, with sections or divisions under deputy or assistant secretaries. It was felt that this arrangement might not be suitable to the circumstances of Ceylon; the ministers might prefer to retain separate heads of departments within their ministries as in the days of the State Council, with perhaps more direct access to the minister than might be usual if the full British system were introduced. Accordingly, the functions of the permanent secretaries were not too closely defined. Though this has been regarded as a fault by some, it has advantages in that it provided for a grade of trained and experienced administrative officers whose functions could be defined as the ministers wished.

Meanwhile, negotiations had been going on with the British government for full independence; February 4, 1948, was set as the date for this event. On that day Ceylon ceased to be a Crown Colony and became of its own choice a fully self-governing and independent dominion within the British Commonwealth of Nations. The transfer of power passed smoothly, and the new era started well. This may be ascribed partly to the experience gained during the Donoughmore and Soulbury regimes, but there were other reasons, not the least of these being the existence of the CCS, with its long record of efficiency and integrity, and a judiciary free from political or other extraneous control, which had firmly established the concept of rule of law.[38]

The CCS was predominantly Ceylonese at the time of independence, but there were still British in the service. As previously stated, British recruitment ceased in 1937, but ten years later, just before independence, there were still thirty-two British officers out of a total of 169. The independence Constitution, like its predecessors, contained special provisions

38. For further discussion, see Jeffries, *op. cit.*, p. 130.

for retirement on advantageous terms, but no compulsion was brought to bear or other special inducement given to hasten retirement, and a number of officers who had the right to retire stayed on. The CCS in 1947 consisted of three staff or super-grade officers; twenty-five Class I officers (eight in Grade I and seventeen in Grade II) who held the most senior and important posts, such as those of government agents; ninety-five officers in Class II, composed of heads of smaller departments and assistants in larger departments; twenty-six cadets (all Ceylonese); and twenty officers in Class III—i.e., officers with good records promoted from other services. Of the staff-grade officers, two, the chief and deputy chief secretaries, were British, and the third, the financial secretary, was Ceylonese. Two of the eight Grade I and nine of the seventeen Grade II of Class I officers were British. In Class II, nineteen of the ninety-five officers were British.

In the following year, 1948, after the declaration of independence, though the number of British members of the service decreased sharply, an appreciable number remained. Most of the retirements at this time were among the more junior of the British members. Of those remaining in the service, four were appointed permanent secretaries and one became secretary to the governor general. Two were in Class I, Grade I, out of a total strength of eight. Five remained in Grade II out of a nominal strength of thirteen but an actual strength of seven. Only seven British remained in Class II. The permanent secretaries and the secretary to the governor general had important parts to play, but the remaining officers had no special role except to work with their Ceylonese colleagues in the ordinary tasks of government. The senior remaining member of the service was Sir Charles Jones, an able and efficient officer with secretariat and treasury experience. He was appointed to the most senior post in the public service, that of secretary to the treasury, in which post he was able to help in the transition stages. He was, however, nearing retirement, and when he left the service the office was given to a senior Ceylonese officer.

By 1950 the number of British permanent secretaries had

been reduced to two. Four of the five members of Class I, Grade I, were British, as were three of the ten in Grade II; but nearly all the junior British members had retired, and only two remained in Class II. In 1954 there were still two British permanent secretaries, and the secretary to the governor general was also British. No British remained in the service below Class I, Grade I, in which grade three of five officers were British. Two years later only three British officers remained in the service, and by 1958 the number had fallen to two, one being the last British permanent secretary, while the other was in Class I, Grade I. By 1959 all British members of the CCS had retired, and all permanent secretaries and all civil servants were Ceylonese.

The CCS had changed materially during the century and a half of its existence. It had begun by being an all-British service and ended by being all-Ceylonese. The bureaucracy of early days had been leavened by democratic ideologies, but there can be no doubt that the Civil Service and other public services (created and developed in British days) and the traditions of these services materially assisted in carrying the country over the hurdle of independence and were the mainstay of the administration during the early and peaceful years of the new era. The services felt the strain during the period of rapid development and the admittedly difficult period which followed, but they stood up to it and showed a remarkable degree of flexibility in accepting innovations and new conditions. A recent Salaries and Cadre Commission wrote:

The question that really arises is to what extent has the Public Service found it possible to adapt itself? The answer to this is, we think, that despite the many problems and situations that have arisen since 1948 when we were left to govern ourselves, the Public Service has, by and large, survived, and can hardly be said to have failed the people it serves.[39]

39. *Report of the Salaries and Cadre Commission, 1961*, Part I (Sessional Paper III, 1961), p. 11. This report is dealt with more extensively in Kearney's accompanying study (Chapter 8), pp. 486 ff., esp. n. 3.

8

Ceylon: The Contemporary Bureaucracy

Robert N. Kearney

The bureaucracy Ceylon inherited at independence in 1948 appeared to be one of the principal assets of the new state. It had evolved in a century and a half into a well-developed and effective public service engaged in a wide variety of public functions. Ceylonization was nearly complete, and a trained and experienced Ceylonese staff existed at all levels. While the welfare functions of the Ceylonese government had expanded considerably, particularly in the period of internal self-rule from 1931 to 1947, the bureaucracy at independence nevertheless retained much of the tradition, ethos, and to some extent the organization associated with upholding the majesty of the government, preserving the peace, and gathering taxes.[1] After independence, and especially since emerging nationalist and egalitarian sentiments led to a marked political re-orientation in the mid-1950's, a heavy responsibility for economic and social development has been thrust upon the public service. Neither selected, trained, nor organized for development activities, the public

1. Although specialized departments had taken over many government functions, including police duties, the government agent held ultimate responsibility for the preservation of law and order and tended to be regarded as the center and symbol of governmental authority within his area, a position his predecessors in earlier days had in fact held. For discussion of the earlier development of the bureaucracy, see the study in this volume by Sir Charles Collins (Chapter 7). Also see S. D. Saparamadu, Introduction to Leonard Woolf, *Diaries in Ceylon, 1908–1911,* published as *Ceylon Historical Journal,* IX (July, 1959–April, 1960), vii–xlvii; and A. J. Wilson, "The Public Services in Ceylon," in C. R. Hensman (ed.), *The Public Services and the People,* Community Pamphlet No. 3 (Colombo, 1963), pp. 9–37.

service has been faced with a difficult challenge.[2] At the same time, the bureaucracy was subjected to growing criticism and demands for reform intended to eliminate alleged vestiges of colonialism. This study will examine major characteristics and problems of the contemporary bureaucracy of Ceylon amid the strains of attempted rapid development and the political changes and desires for reform following in the wake of independence.

I. Structure and Salaries

The Salaries and Cadre Commission which completed an extensive study of the Ceylonese public service in 1961 observed in its report: "Looking back to the time of our Independence in 1948, one can hardly recognize in the vast network of Governmental organisation that now obtains in Ceylon the simple and almost primitive administrative set up we inherited from colonial times."[3] The commission was impressed by the rapid growth in size of the public service and the proliferation of new agencies and activities since independence. In the first decade of independence the bureaucracy doubled in size, and the costs of salaries and allowances increased three-fold.[4] The public service expanded in its traditional roles of maintaining law and order, collecting taxes, and providing basic utilities and social services,

2. The economic development role of the bureaucracy was emphasized by the minister of finance in 1961. See Felix R. Dias Bandaranaike, *The Budget and Economic Development* (Colombo: Government Press, 1961), pp. 67–68. On the performance of the public service in rural development activities, see D. Ghosh, Christopher Sower, and C. F. Ware, *Report of a Rural Development Evaluation Mission in Ceylon* (New York: United Nations Technical Assistance Programme, October 18, 1962); G. V. P. Samarasinghe, "Rural Development in Ceylon," in *Public Administration Aspects of Community Development Programmes* (New York: United Nations Technical Assistance Programme, 1959), pp. 83–92; and Murray A. Straus, "Cultural Factors in the Functioning of Agricultural Extension in Ceylon," *Rural Sociology*, XVIII (September, 1953), 249–256. A discussion by a public servant emphasizing the administrative and social problems faced by the administrator in attempting to carry out development activities appears in V. A. J. Senaratne, "Some Aspects of Provincial Administration in Ceylon," in Hensman (ed.), *op. cit.*, pp. 91–96.

3. *Report of the Salaries and Cadre Commission, 1961*, Part I (Ceylon Sessional Paper III, 1961), p. 10. Part II of this very informative report was published as Sessional Paper IV, 1961. The 1961 Salaries and Cadre Commission, under the chairmanship of Wilmot A. Perera, will hereinafter be referred to as the Perera Commission and the commission's report will be cited as Perera Report.

4. *Ibid.*, Part I, pp. 12–13.

but a far greater expansion occurred in areas of the government's considerably enlarged welfare and economic activities.[5] The distribution of public servants by type of activity a decade after independence is presented in Table 1. Since this tabulation, the

Table 1. *Distribution of Public Servants by Type of Governmental Activity, 1958–1959*

Type of activity[a]	Number employed	Percentage of total public service
General administration	38,923	17.5
Public utilities	62,411	28.0
Economic activities	44,510	20.0
Social and cultural activities	77,096	34.5
Totals	222,940	100.0

[a] The Perera Commission explained that in arriving at this classification "we have included under General Administration departments concerned with revenue collection, the preservation of law and order, defence, overseas representation, etc.; Public Utilities include Posts, Public Works, Railway, Electrical Department, Broadcasting and so on; Economic Activities cover the whole range of departments engaged in the utilization and development of resources; while Social and Cultural Activities include Education, Health, Labour and allied departments." The commission, however, noted considerable difficulties in determining the exact size of the public service and stressed the need for an accurate census of public employment. As of 1965 no such census had been made.

Source: Perera Report, Part I, pp. 14–16.

government has taken over formerly private, state-assisted schools with more than 25,000 employees, nationalized several commercial undertakings, and extended its economic activities, swelling both the total number of public employees and the proportion engaged in economic and social activities.

Despite the commission's impression of tremendous change in the public service, except for employees of public corporations,[6]

5. The Perera Commission judged that the scope of the government's role in Ceylon surpassed that of most governments in Asia or Europe. *Ibid.*, Part I, pp. 10–14.

6. Workers in public corporations are employees of the corporations rather than direct employees of the government and are not commonly considered a part of the public service. Public corporations are treated separately in this chapter, pp. 529–540. Elsewhere in this study the discussion will be limited to public servants organized in the traditional departments and subject to public service regulations unless otherwise indicated.

the basic structure of the bureaucracy has not changed fundamentally since the colonial period. There are three major groups of public servants, arranged hierarchically and separated from each other by wide gaps of status and pay.[7] At the top are the staff grades, followed by the clerical and technical grades, and at the bottom the group of public servants suggestively termed "minor employees." The staff officers, holding administrative and professional positions, with few exceptions are graduates of the University of Ceylon or foreign universities. Administrative officers comprise less than 1 per cent of the entire central government bureaucracy, while professional officers form slightly more than 1 per cent. Clerical and technical officers generally are graduates of secondary schools, until recently English-language schools, or technical training schools.[8] The middle level of the public service includes slightly more than one-third of all central government employees. The public servants classified as minor employees form nearly two-thirds of all employees of the central government.[9] Literacy is not required for recruitment into the minor grades.

Administrative officers serving in ministries are commonly titled assistant secretaries, additional assistant secretaries, or office assistants. Heads of departments usually are commissioners or controllers, or less frequently, directors. A few bear descriptive titles, such as government printer, public trustee, or conservator of forests. The second-ranking departmental officer has the title of deputy, most commonly deputy commissioner or deputy controller. Other departmental administrative officers are generally styled assistant commissioners or controllers, or by some other

7. The stratification of the bureaucratic hierarchy is discussed in greater detail in Robert N. Kearney and Richard L. Harris, "Bureaucracy and Environment in Ceylon," *Journal of Commonwealth Political Studies,* II (November, 1964), 253–266.

8. Qualifications in the clerical grades vary tremendously, particularly in what is known as the quasi-clerical service, created by the absorption into the permanent ranks of the bureaucracy of large numbers of temporary clerical employees. See Perera Report, Part I, p. 103.

9. The proportions of employees in each level were computed from *Statistical Abstract of Ceylon, 1962* (Colombo: Government Press, 1963), pp. 167–168. The figures are for September 30, 1961. Nearly 47,000 teachers employed by the Education Department are excluded. Miscellaneous employees of intermediate rank such as policemen, headmen, and storekeepers, as well as clerical and technical workers, have been included in the middle level.

designation consistent with the title of the department head. The typical departmental administrative officer is recruited from the university as an assistant commissioner or an assistant controller and is likely to spend all or a major part of his career with this rank. Some departments have other titles, such as land officer or assistant settlement officer. Professional officers, heavily concentrated in specialized departments, are chiefly physicians, engineers, legal officers, and accountants. As could be expected, a large number of physicians are employed in the huge Department of Health, and many engineers serve in the Public Works Department and Irrigation Department. The most numerous and important of the middle-level employees are the clerical officers. Each ministry or department has a chief clerk, a post carrying considerable prestige and almost always held by an officer with long years of government clerical experience. Clerks are found on the small ministry staffs and in all the offices throughout the rambling departmental organizations. Among the minor employees are peons, orderlies, attendants, messengers, watchers, and semi-skilled and unskilled laborers.

The bureaucracy bears the imprint of a highly compartmentalized and poorly integrated administrative system. Prior to 1931 the colonial administrative structure was headed by a colonial secretary, a colonial treasurer, and an auditor and accountant general, under the authority of the colonial governor.[10] With the introduction in 1931 of a large measure of self-rule, the growing number of government departments were grouped under executive committees of the legislature with the committee chairmen styled as ministers.[11] Such co-ordination of departmental activities as occurred took place at the political level, and no major attempt was made to achieve an administrative integration of the depart-

10. Lennox A. Mills, *Ceylon Under British Rule, 1795–1932* (London, 1933), p. 95.
11. The experimental and unique executive committee system was inspired by the London County Council and was intended to make internal self-government possible despite the absence of political parties, which were considered essential to the operation of a cabinet system. See *Ceylon: Report of the Special Commission on the Constitution*, Cmd. 3131 (London, 1928); *Ceylon: Report of the Commission on Constitutional Reform*, Cmd. 6677 (London, 1945); and Sagarajasingham Navasivayam, *The Legislatures of Ceylon, 1928–1948* (London, 1950).

ments. With the adoption of cabinet government in anticipation of independence, departments were collected into ministries, which were expected to co-ordinate and integrate departmental activities. However, despite the appointment of ministry permanent secretaries and staffs, the expected integration never took place. The approximately 150 departments in the Ceylonese administrative system have continued to be the basic units of administration, and control and co-ordination by the ministries is tenuous or in some cases virtually nonexistent.[12]

The weakly integrated administrative system has produced considerable organizational confusion and inconsistency of personnel policy within the bureaucracy. As departments were created to perform new functions, they tended to establish their own departmental "services."[13] Some services, notably the recently abolished Ceylon Civil Service and the General Clerical Service, were interdepartmental and their members were subject to transfer from department to department. However, until the creation in 1963 of a Unified Administrative Service, the numerous staff officers who were not members of the CCS were recruited by individual departments and served under somewhat different terms and conditions established by the departments. A number of departments, including customs, railway, post office, irrigation, and public works, have maintained their own clerical services. Minor employees apparently invariably belong to separate departmental services. As a result of this departmentalization of the public service, there is wide variation in salaries, duties, terms of service, and standards for recruitment and promotion within the bureaucracy.[14]

The field officers of the public service, once the backbone of the bureaucracy, have tended in recent years to be overshadowed by

12. The Perera Commission severely condemned extreme departmentalization and lack of ministerial control, and appealed for administrative reform to effectively integrate the departments within a ministry. For a discussion of the existing system and the commission's recommendations, see Perera Report, Part I, pp. 19–26. Many other criticisms of excessive departmentalization in the Ceylonese administrative system have been made, e.g., Ghosh, Sower and Ware, *op. cit.,* pp. 33, 76; Senaratne, *op. cit.,* p. 93. This rigid departmentalization is discussed by Richard L. Harris and Robert N. Kearney in "A Comparative Analysis of the Administrative Systems of Canada and Ceylon," *Administrative Science Quarterly,* VIII (December, 1963), 356–357. See also Collins' study in this volume, p. 474.
13. Saparamadu, *op. cit.,* p. ix; Perera Report, Part I, p. 74.
14. See an elaboration of these variations in Perera Report, Part I, pp. 55–70.

the growing numbers of government planning and development officers, clerks, peons, and industrial workers in and around Colombo. Through much of the British colonial period, the bureaucracy consisted of a small secretariat in Colombo and provincial hierarchies of officials. A government agent directly responsible to the colonial secretary was in charge of each province. Under the government agent were several assistant government agents in charge of districts. Below these officers, who were European members of the Ceylon Civil Service,[15] was a quasi-feudal hierarchy of Ceylonese officials extending down to the village headman in charge of a village or group of villages. Since 1954 the district has been the principal unit of field administration, and the officers in charge of districts have been titled government agents. There are now twenty-two such districts in Ceylon. The office of the government agent, known as a kachcheri, was once the focus of all governmental activities in the territory. Although specialized departments began to establish their own field staffs, and units of local government were created to perform limited local functions, the government agents, now under the Ministry of Home Affairs, still hold a wide range of governmental responsibilities, including responsibility for the co-ordination of the activities of field officers not under their direct control and for many of the expanding number of development activities undertaken by the government.[16]

The Perera Commission in 1961 discovered more than four hundred different salary scales in existence in the public service.[17] The remuneration public servants receive consists of (1) a basic salary, (2) a cost-of-living allowance, (3) a special living allowance, and (4) a rent allowance. At the lower levels, the total remuneration received may be more than double the basic salary

15. After Ceylonese had entered the CCS at the end of the nineteenth century they tended to be shunted off into judicial or staff functions and were not entrusted with these critical provincial and district posts. The first Ceylonese was named assistant government agent in charge of a district as late as 1928. Saparamadu, *op. cit.*, p. xviii. See also S. J. Tambiah, "Ethnic Representation in Ceylon's Higher Administrative Services, 1870–1946," *University of Ceylon Review*, XIII (April–July, 1955), 120–123.

16. See W. Hoven and A. van den Elshout, *Local Government in Selected Countries: Ceylon, Israel, Japan* (New York: United Nations Technical Assistance Programme, 1963), esp. pp. 6–8.

17. Perera Report, Part I, p. 54. The information on salaries and allowances in this paragraph is from pp. 48–60.

while the allowances are of considerably less significance at the higher levels. Consequently, the total of salary and allowances is much more meaningful than the basic salary, and the pay referred to hereinafter will be the total of basic salary and allowances. The pay received by minor employees ranges from Rs. 126 to Rs. 300 (about $26 to $63) a month—with a basic salary range of Rs. 40 to Rs. 166. Clerical and technical employees receive a minimum of Rs. 181 and a maximum of Rs. 803 ($38 to $169) per month. Administrative and professional officers receive between Rs. 579 and Rs. 2,042 ($122 and $429) per month. The maximum pay within this last group is that of the highest-paid department head, of which there were only twenty-nine at the time of the Perera Commission study. A handful of officers, including permanent secretaries and Supreme Court judges, receive a monthly pay in excess of Rs. 2,200.

The distribution of total salary and allowance levels within the public service (Table 2) indicates a considerable concentration of public employees at the lower pay levels. Some 75 per cent of all public servants receive Rs. 300 ($63) per month or less. Only about 5 per cent draw more than Rs. 600 ($126) monthly, and

Table 2. *Distribution of Salaries and Allowances in the Public Service,* ca. 1960[a]

Monthly salary and allowances (rupees)	Percentage of public servants
150 and under	28.5
151–200	23.2
201–300	23.7
301–600	19.3
601–1,000	4.2
1,001–1,400	0.8
1,401–1,800	0.2
1,801 and over	[b]

[a] The Perera Report gives no indication of the date of the data. The report was submitted to the printer in March, 1961; hence, it is assumed the data were compiled in 1958 or 1959 and are valid through 1960.
[b] Less than 0.04 per cent.
Source: Computed from Perera Report, Part I, p. 51.

only about 1 per cent receive more than Rs. 1,000 ($210) per month. Ninety-nine per cent of all members of the public service are paid less than half the highest pay level in the public service.

The Perera Commission indicated the existence of considerable sentiment to reduce the wide spread between top and bottom salaries in the public service. The commission, however, noted that a considerable reduction of the gap between higher and lower pay levels had occurred in the preceding two decades, during which the real wages of an unskilled laborer had doubled while the real wages of a staff officer had shrunk to about half of their value twenty years earlier. The commission further claimed that public servants' salaries at the upper levels were not particularly high in relation to salaries for comparable private employment in Ceylon.[18]

Little dependable or conclusive information on income and wealth in Ceylon is available. Nonetheless, it seems likely that while the top incomes from business, the professions, planting, and land ownership are considerably in excess of the highest public service salary, the significance of the differential is somewhat reduced by the outside incomes and family wealth of many higher public servants. Although education has been an avenue of social mobility, until quite recently most persons with university educations have been from affluent families. For the most part, only the moderately wealthy have been able to obtain the advanced English-language educations necessary for appointment to the staff grades. Often members of a single family are found in the bureaucracy, planting, and the professions. The custom of giving dowries and the ability of the public servant to command a large dowry has added to the private wealth and income of higher public servants and transformed many staff officers into absentee owners of agricultural land. It is not unreasonable to speculate that most public servants in the administrative and professional grades have some outside income, chiefly from land ownership, and a number may have substantial incomes above their public service salaries.

18. *Ibid.*, Part I, pp. 48–52.

II. Recruitment and Control

The Ceylon Constitution vests authority over the appointment, transfer, dismissal, and disciplinary control of public servants in an independent three-member Public Service Commission appointed by the governor general (acting on ministerial advice). The Constitution allows the commission to delegate its powers to any public officer, with the stipulation that appeal from a decision by an officer to whom such delegation is made may be taken to the commission.[19] Under this provision, the commission has delegated to department heads authority over appointments and promotions to posts in their departments with annual basic salaries of less than Rs. 4,080, and disciplinary authority over officers with annual salaries of less than Rs. 2,700.[20] Consequently, the direct control of the commission extends only to the upper levels of the bureaucracy. Since salaries (exclusive of allowances) of the staff officers begin at Rs. 4,080 annually, by this provision the Public Service Commission has retained authority over the recruitment and control of all members of the important administrative and professional grades.

Outside the purview of the Public Service Commission are a small number of public officials in addition to political officeholders. Permanent secretaries enjoy the unusual distinction of constitutional authorization for their office. The Constitution establishes the post of permanent secretary for each ministry, provides for appointment of permanent secretaries by the governor general, and outlines their responsibilities.[21] They are considered to be outside the regular public service ranks and receive a salary above the highest regular public service salary. Although they may be selected from outside the public service, permanent secretaries in practice have been chosen from among senior

19. Ceylon (Constitution and Independence) Orders in Council, 1946 and 1947. Sections 58–61 deal with the Public Service Commission. Hereinafter, these orders-in-council will be cited as Constitution of Ceylon.

20. *Annual Report of the Public Service Commission, 1962* (Ceylon Sessional Paper XII, 1963), pp. 1–3.

21. Constitution of Ceylon, section 51.

administrative officers, predominantly from the Ceylon Civil Service. Special constitutional provisions are similarly made for the appointment of judicial officers. A separate Judicial Service dividing judicial from administrative officers has existed since the late 1930's. The Constitution created a Judicial Service Commission vested with authority to appoint, transfer, dismiss, and discipline judicial officers excluding Supreme Court judges and commissioners of assize. The Judicial Service Commission consists of the chief justice of the Supreme Court who serves as chairman, a judge of the Supreme Court, and a third member who is or has been a judge of the Supreme Court. The latter two members are named by the governor general. The commission is authorized to delegate to the secretary of the commission power over transfers and acting appointments.[22]

A Local Government Service Commission was established by statute in 1945 with authority over appointments, promotions, transfers, salaries and other terms of service, and discipline of employees of local government bodies, following numerous complaints of nepotism and favoritism in the recruitment and promotion of these employees. The commission consists of the commissioner of local government as chairman and eight members named by the minister of local government, four of whom represent local government bodies. A Local Government Service consisting of employees of local bodies was established under the control of the commission in 1946, but later daily-paid workers and salaried employees at the lower end of the salary scale were removed from the service and the control of the Local Government Service Commission. The Local Government Service presently consists of about 8,000 employees, who are transferable from one local government body to another. About 7,000 other employees are outside the Local Government Service Commission's jurisdiction and subject to the control of individual local bodies.[23]

22. *Ibid.*, sections 53–55.
23. *Report of the Commission on Local Government* (Ceylon Sessional Paper XXXIII, 1955) pp. 75–76; Hoven and van den Elshout, *op. cit.*, pp. 38–40.

Although recruitment to the central government bureaucracy in principle is the responsibility of the Public Service Commission, it is in fact largely a function of individual departments, and there appears to be little standardization of qualifications or procedures.[24] Some public servants are chosen by competitive written examination and others by departmental oral interview.[25] Qualifications are often formed in vague and ambiguous terms, and charges have been made that requirements are changed to benefit favored applicants. The lack of clearly fixed qualifications and the use of oral interviews in recruitment have led to numerous accusations of religious or caste favoritism, political influence, and nepotism.[26]

At various times large numbers of temporary recruits have been taken into the public service with little regard to qualifications, and eventually they have established a claim to permanent posts in the bureaucracy. Since 1957, public servants recruited as temporary employees automatically acquire permanent status with the passage of fixed periods of time, even if they lack the qualifications established for their positions. The recruitment and retention of temporary employees was blamed by the Perera Commission for overstaffing in the bureaucracy, resulting in the existence of large numbers of employees in some departments for whom no work exists.[27]

Promotions involve many of the same problems as recruitment. Practices vary from department to department. Some departments have established promotion boards to advise the department head but others have not.[28] The general principle of promotion on the basis of merit appears to be subject to the same uncertainty as recruitment on the basis of merit, and belief that political influence, caste, religion, ethnic community, and family connections play a role in promotion is not uncommon. The Perera Commission's conclusion was that promotions made osten-

24. E.g., Perera Report, Part II, pp. 3–5.
25. *Ibid.*, Part I, p. 161.
26. *Ibid.*, Part II, pp. 3–4, 101–102.
27. *Ibid.*, Part II, pp. 7–11; also Part I, p. 103.
28. *Ibid.*, Part II, p. 18.

sibly on the basis of merit were usually in fact made on the basis of seniority and age.[29]

Some groups of public servants are subject to transfer from one locality to another. Others remain in a single office or district throughout their careers. The frequency with which transfers of officers are made from one field assignment to another or from Colombo to the field has been criticized repeatedly as detrimental to the performance of the public service.[30] As a result of marked geographical differences in the availability and quality of schools, housing, shops, and recreational facilities, many public servants display a strong preference for assignment in Colombo and vigorously resist transfers to field posts outside Colombo, Kandy, Galle, and Jaffna, the major urban centers of the island. In commenting on the reluctance of officers to accept assignments to less favorable posts, the Perera Commission conceded: "There is no doubt that there are still in the Public Service several stations at which communications are bad and amenities practically nonexistent, and an officer posted to such a station is virtually cut off from civilization."[31] Transfers seem particularly susceptible to political influence, and probably more complaints of political interference relate to transfers than any other bureaucratic matter. The Perera Commission attributed much of the disruption of the orderly arrangement of transfers which has occurred to the frequent intervention of politicians on behalf of individual public servants.[32]

Disciplinary procedures in the public service are extremely complicated, time-consuming, and difficult, with many delays and opportunities for appeal. Consequently, superior officers frequently avoid instituting formal disciplinary action in the face of indiscipline.[33] The protracted and cumbersome nature of

29. *Ibid.*, Part I, p. 76. The same conclusion was reached by a similar commission a dozen years earlier. See *Report of the Commission on the Organisation, Staffing and Operative Methods of Government Departments* (Ceylon Sessional Paper V, 1948), p. 21.

30. E.g., see Perera Report, Part II, p. 21; Ghosh, Sower, and Ware, *op. cit.*, p. 74; and Straus, *op. cit.*, p. 254.

31. Perera Report, Part II, p. 20.

32. *Ibid.*, Part II, p. 19.

33. *Ibid.*, Part II, p. 102.

disciplinary procedures, however, is not the only and perhaps not the primary obstacle to strict enforcement of discipline in the Ceylonese public service. A former minister of finance, explaining why certain undesirable public servants had not been dismissed, cited a disposition which seems deeply embedded in Ceylonese culture and has implications for the bureaucracy as well as for other social institutions. He explained:

At every stage we are stuck with the position that you cannot prove a charge against an officer, however much you know him to be an undesirable sort of person, without beginning to think of the other side of the coin: how does it affect this man's life, his prospects, his wife and children? On considerations like that, one begins to see the picture completely differently and then one begins to hesitate and vacillate and takes no decision whatsoever, when, indeed, what is necessary in the interests of the country is the taking of positive action to eliminate elements whom the administration considers should be eliminated.[34]

Because of the difficulties involved in formal disciplinary action or reticence to instigate such action, the common practice in the Ceylonese public service has become to transfer the alleged offender rather than to bring charges against him. Disciplinary transfers seem to take place almost constantly for a wide range of offenses. In one reported instance, government schoolteachers were transferred for engaging in prostitution.[35] Because a transfer is not viewed as seriously as dismissal or other formal action, and the prescribed procedures for disciplinary action do not have to be followed, transfers tend to be used rather indiscriminately, with little effort made to evaluate the validity of charges and in some cases without attempting to fix individual guilt. Thus, accusations of wiretapping by Posts and Telecommunications Department employees resulted in the mass transfer of about one hundred officers of the department.[36] Disciplinary action has been as subject to charges of political interference as most other bureaucratic activities. The general secretary of the large Public Service Workers Trade Union Federation once singled out politi-

34. Ceylon House of Representatives, *Parliamentary Debates* (*Hansard*), Vol. 48, col. 1916.
35. *Ceylon News,* January 10, 1963.
36. *Ceylon Observer,* October 21, 1961.

cal interference with discipline in the public service as "the most sordid of all interference," claiming that "no action is taken against rogues and scoundrels when they are detected owing to the interference by politicians."[37]

III. Judicial Supervision of Bureaucratic Behavior

The courts of Ceylon have been relatively restrained in the exercise of judicial supervision over bureaucratic actions. This appears to apply in general both to administrative processes affecting private persons and action relating to internal bureaucratic matters. The scope of judicial review of administrative processes affecting the general public has not been extremely wide. A 1947 Supreme Court decision appeared to open the way for substantial examination of bureaucratic behavior by the courts. The decision asserted the courts' power to review by use of the writ of certiorari administrators' acts performed in a judicial or quasi-judicial manner, and held that the controller of textiles was necessarily acting judicially in cancelling a license under a regulation authorizing him to cancel the licenses of textile dealers when he had "reasonable grounds" to believe the dealers unfit.[38] This finding, however, was reversed by a Privy Council decision in *Nakkuda Ali* v. *Jayaratne*,[39] which narrowed the definition of judicial or quasi-judicial actions by administrative officers and, hence, the scope for judicial intervention. As in the earlier case, the question was whether the action of the controller of textiles in cancelling the license of a dealer he deemed unfit was subject to examination by the courts. The Privy Council affirmed the power of the Ceylon courts to intervene by issuance of writs when administrative bodies function in a judicial or quasi-judicial manner. However, it concluded that the regulation

---

37. *Ceylon News*, January 3, 1963.
38. *Abdul Thassim* v. *Edmund Rodrigo* [1947] 48 N.L.R. 121. On the use of prerogative writs in Ceylon, see Sir W. Ivor Jennings and H. W. Tambiah, *The Dominion of Ceylon: The Development of Its Laws and Constitution* (London, 1952), pp. 85–87, 125–126.
39. [1950] 51 N.L.R. 457.

under which the controller acted contained no indication of a judicial process, as it did not prescribe a procedure or provide for an inquiry or appeal. The requirement of "reasonable grounds" did not compel the controller to act judicially. Consequently, the controller was simply performing an executive act which was not subject to judicial inquiry.

The Nakkuda Ali decision seems to have produced some restraint by the Ceylon courts in reviewing administrative action, and the discretion allowed the bureaucracy in the exercise of licensing powers appears to be somewhat broader than in some other Commonwealth countries.[40] Judicial hesitation to intervene was reflected in *Gunapala* v. *Kannangara*,[41] where the action of the minister of local government in removing a village committee chairman under a statute authorizing removal if the minister "is satisfied" that there is sufficient proof of certain undesirable behavior was held to be exclusively executive and beyond the competence of the courts to review.

While not questioning the Nakkuda Ali decision, the courts in a group of subsequent cases have displayed indications of greater readiness to impute judicial qualities to acts by administrators in certain areas. A Supreme Court decision in *Leo* v. *The Land Commissioner*[42] immediately after the Privy Council ruling cited the Nakkuda Ali precedent but proceeded to find judicial qualities in the administrative act under consideration. The case involved the compulsory acquisition of land by the land commissioner under a statutory authorization to acquire certain categories of agricultural land. The court interpreted the commissioner's action as involving three decisions. The first decision was that the land in question was agricultural land within the meaning of the statute; the second involved determining that the land fell within the

40. In Pakistan, for example, the Supreme Court ruled that the Privy Council in the Nakkuda Ali case "goes too far in restricting the power of the superior Courts to control actions of the executive under statutes which plainly import the performance of a quasi-judicial act." *Messrs. Faridsons Ltd. and another* v. *Government of Pakistan* [1962] 1 P.S.C.R. 1. Thus, the Pakistan court held that the statutory omission of prescribed judicial process was insufficient to deny that process. A hearing was deemed essential if judicial considerations are implied in the administrative action.
41. [1955] 57 N.L.R. 69.
42. [1955] 57 N.L.R. 178.

categories of agricultural land that the commissioner was authorized to acquire; and the third was the commissioner's decision whether or not to acquire the land once he was satisfied that it was land he was authorized to acquire. The court held the last decision to be an administrative act guided by policy, expediency, and individual judgment and not subject to review. However, in the two prior decisions the commissioner must decide solely on the basis of facts before him without reference to policy or expediency. Consequently, these two decisions are judicial in nature and subject to examination by the courts. A later Privy Council decision involving an identical action followed similar reasoning. In *The Land Commissioner* v. *Ladamuttu Pillai*,[43] the Privy Council held that a provision in the statute declaring the land commissioner's decision to be "final" meant only that his decision was final on whether or not to acquire land which came under the statute. "The antecedant question as to whether any particular land is land which the Land Commissioner is authorized to acquire . . . is not one for his final decision but is one which, if necessary, must be decided by the courts of law." This ruling, although not overturning the Nakkuda Ali decision, seems to have reduced the rather marked judicial self-restraint of the earlier Privy Council decision.

Several other cases indicate a willingness by the Ceylon courts to review bureaucratic acts. An officer directed by statute to forward to the minister an application for citizenship if certain circumstances obtain was held to be performing a quasi-judicial function in deciding whether or not to act.[44] In *Tennekoon* v. *The Principal Collector of Customs*,[45] the court declared that customs officials deciding a certain matter on the basis of evidence before them rather than on policy grounds were acting judicially and therefore were required to conform to the rules of "natural justice" which necessitate granting to a person adversely affected an opportunity to present his case and refute allegations detrimental to his case. Judicial intervention was approved in *Buddha-*

---

43. [1960] 62 N.L.R. 169.
44. *Manickam* v. *The Permanent Secretary, Ministry of Defence and External Affairs* [1960] 62 N.L.R. 204.
45. [1959] 61 N.L.R. 232.

dasa v. *Nadaraja*[46] to prevent a public servant from performing a wrongful act which he claimed to be within his statutory powers but, as determined by the courts, in fact was not.

With respect to internal matters within the bureaucracy, the courts generally have upheld the authority of the Public Service Commission. The Supreme Court in *Wijesundera* v. *The Public Service Commission*[47] refused to examine alleged irregularities in an investigation by the commission which led to the dismissal of a public servant, stressing the constitutional conferral of authority over the public service on the commission. The court subsequently distinguished between "mere rules" made by the Public Service Commission and statutory enactments which would be a term of contract. The rules were held not to have the force of law, and consequently a violation of these rules was not grounds for judicial intervention.[48] However, the court declared invalid a dismissal of a public servant by the Public Service Commission in *Silva* v. *The Attorney-General*[49] on grounds that the commission had delegated the power of dismissal in this instance and could not resume this power without formally retracting the delegation. The court added that the person to whom powers of appointment, dismissal, and control are delegated must exercise these powers himself and cannot re-delegate them.

A decision of the Colombo district court in April, 1964, in a case which attracted much public attention, impeded government efforts to complete the transition from English to Sinhalese as the language of administration. The court ruled that a Tamil public servant was entitled to a scheduled salary increment, although a Treasury circular directed that increments were to be stopped for public servants who did not pass a proficiency examination in Sinhalese. The court questioned the authority of the secretary to the Treasury to alter conditions of service of a public servant appointed by the Public Service Commission without action by the commission.[50] A government appeal is pending.

46. [1955] 56 N.L.R. 537.
47. [1953] 55 N.L.R. 94.
48. *De Zoysa* v. *The Public Service Commission* [1960] 62 N.L.R. 492.
49. [1958] 60 N.L.R. 145.
50. *Ceylon News*, April 30, 1964.

IV. Environment and Attitudes

Ceylonese society is undergoing transition from a traditional social order in which the individual was totally enmeshed in hierarchically arranged particularistic kin and caste groups toward a modern society in which universalistic and egalitarian values and achievement criteria are operative.[51] The bureaucracy, possibly the most modern (or Westernized) institution in the society, bestows official recognition on universalistic and impersonal values and norms, but public servants as individuals commonly retain strong attachment to particularistic social groups. In traditional Ceylonese society, as in many other village peasant societies, the family was the center of the individual's concern and was crucial to his status and security. The Kandayan Peasantry Commission, describing traditional village life, explained that "because one's own level was so intimately connected with that of every other member of one's family, the care and maintenance of the entire family unit to which one belonged became a social obligation."[52] Despite considerable social and cultural change, the Ceylonese typically still feels a first and most imperative sense of duty to his family. Influences of family

51. On traditional Ceylonese society, see M. B. Ariyapala, *Society in Mediaeval Ceylon* (Colombo, 1956); Wilhelm Geiger, *The Culture of Ceylon in Mediaeval Times* (ed. Heinz Bechert; Wiesbaden, 1960); Robert Knox, *An Historial Relation of Ceylon* (first published in 1681; Glasgow, 1911); G. C. Mendis, *The Early History of Ceylon* (Calcutta, 1947); C. W. Nicholas and S. Paranavitana, *A Concise History of Ceylon* (Colombo, 1961); and Ralph Pieris, *Sinhalese Social Organization: The Kandyan Period* (Colombo, 1956). The impact of British economic and social values and policies on Ceylonese society and culture in the first half of the nineteenth century is described in Ralph Pieris, "Society and Ideology in Ceylon during a 'Time of Troubles,' 1795–1850," *University of Ceylon Review*, IX (July, 1951), 171–185; IX (October, 1951), 266–279; and X (January, 1952), 79–102. For discussion of the changes occurring in contemporary Ceylon, see Bryce Ryan, L. D. Jayasena, and D. C. R. Wickremesinghe, "Secularization Processes in a Ceylon Village," *Eastern Anthropologist*, XI (March–August, 1958), 155–161; and the studies by Bryce Ryan and S. J. Tambiah cited below, n. 52, 54, 55, 61, and 62.

52. *Report of the Kandyan Peasantry Commission* (Ceylon Sessional Paper XVIII, 1951), pp. 85–86. See also Bryce Ryan, "The Sinhalese Family System," *Eastern Anthropologist*, VI (March–August, 1953), 143–163; and S. J. Tambiah and Bryce Ryan, "Secularization of Family Values in Ceylon," *American Sociological Review*, XXIII (June, 1957), 292–299.

loyalties in contemporary Ceylon are suggested by the regular accusations of nepotism in local government and recently in public corporations, usually involving the appointment to public posts of the kinsmen of politicians.

In the regular central government public service, the effects of family loyalties are much more difficult to detect and describe. Recruitment policies are entirely impersonal and achievement-oriented. So long as Europeans controlled recruitment there was probably little opportunity for extending preferential treatment to kinsmen, and through habit and example the universalistic and achievement values of the colonial bureaucracy seemingly became quite firmly established, at least at the higher levels. Belief that nepotism has grown in recent years in the regular public service as well as in the new public corporations is frequently encountered among public servants and others. However, few public charges have been made and seldom are specific instances cited. The strength of family loyalty can easily be seen only in the presumably innocuous behavior of public servants in hurriedly calling to the attention of their kinsmen any openings existing in their offices and in accompanying cousins in need of employment to various offices in which they have former classmates or friends from previous assignments. The kinsman in search of public employment must find an opening, satisfy the qualifications established for the position, and pass the examination or interview. The fact that many members of a single family are often found in the public service can be attributed to the family's capacity to afford the educations necessary to meet the achievement criteria of selection, rather than to preference one public servant has secured for his kinsmen. The lingering influences of family loyalty on attitudes regarding public service recruitment appeared in a proposal to the Perera Commission that the children of public servants be accorded preference in recruitment, and the strength of universalistic and egalitarian attitudes was displayed in the commission's summary rejection of the proposal.[53]

The effects on the public service of caste discrimination and

53. Perera Report, Part II, p. 7.

solidarity can be detected somewhat more readily. This is not because caste loyalties are stronger than or even as strong as family loyalties, but it is presumably because the caste is a much wider group. While an officer considering appointments or promotions is unlikely to have any attitude toward the families of applicants, he may frequently have personal attitudes toward the caste groups to which applicants belong. Governmental policy for more than a century has been to disregard caste, except in the assignment of officers to certain posts involving intimate contact with the public. Contemporary values among the urban upper and middle classes frequently condemn caste distinctions in matters other than marriage and the family.[54] There are indications that even the more traditional villagers often are willing to countenance the appointment of qualified low-caste persons to the public service.[55] Nonetheless, it is a commonly held belief that caste occasionally continues to exercise some covert influence in recruitment and promotion. Low-caste applicants allege that interview boards seek by indirect means to discover their castes and public servants of low caste often claim that caste bias reduces their prospects for promotion.[56] Accusations of discrimination against low-caste individuals periodically are made, usually privately but occasionally publicly. Thus, one member of Parliament, charging discrimination against the low-status Padu caste, claimed "the feeling among the people of that caste [is] that they will not get any public office, that they are not being treated equally in a matter like appointments of even police constables."[57]

Probably more important than discrimination against persons of low caste is preferential consideration in appointment or promotion accorded persons of the same caste as the responsible officer. Caste solidarity, like family obligation, depends on the belief that one's own status is closely related to the status of the

54. Bryce Ryan, *Caste in Modern Ceylon* (New Brunswick, N. J., 1953), pp. 308–321.

55. Bryce Ryan, *Sinhalese Village* (Coral Gables, Fla., 1958), pp. 165–168; Bryce Ryan, "The Ceylonese Village and the New Value System," *Rural Sociology,* XVII (March, 1952), 18–20.

56. E.g., Ryan, *Caste in Modern Ceylon,* pp. 323–326.

57. House, *Debates,* Vol. 48, col. 1809.

entire group. The persistence of caste endogamy and the intimate relationship between the family and caste systems help to produce a sense of caste loyalty that is roughly similar to the sense of family obligation. Caste solidarity makes common caste membership a strong basis for appeal for favoritism. Indeed, it has been argued that castes, which have largely lost their traditional functional characteristics, have tended to transform themselves into communal associations for mutual protection and support.[58]

Charges of caste or family favoritism probably grossly exaggerate the real significance of these influences in bureaucratic recruitment and promotion. However, the frequent lack of precision in fixing qualifications for posts and practice of using oral interviews in examining applicants make possible the unauthorized application of such particularistic standards and strongly encourage the suspicion that these factors operate.[59]

The public service has little competition in attracting educated Ceylonese. According to a recent estimate, 68 per cent of all graduates of the University of Ceylon had taken government jobs.[60] The strong desire for bureaucratic employment is in part a product of the great prestige and high social status enjoyed by the public servant. The prestige of the government official may be traced to lingering attitudes originating in the fusion of social position and political office in traditional Sinhalese feudalism.[61] Although ascriptive criteria in bureaucratic appointment were abandoned during the colonial period, it can be argued that traditional Sinhalese status values emphasizing rank, office, and title were reinforced by the experience of bureaucratic colonial rule.[62]

In addition to cultural factors which enhance the attractiveness

---

58. Such a development was suggested by G. C. Mendis, *Ceylon Today and Yesterday* (Colombo, 1957), pp. 105–107.
59. See Perera Report, Part II, pp. 3–4.
60. Joseph Fischer, "Universities and the Political Process in Southeast Asia," *Pacific Affairs*, XXXVI (Spring, 1963), 7.
61. S. J. Tambiah, "Ceylon," in Richard D. Lambert and Bert F. Hoselitz (eds.), *The Role of Savings and Wealth in Southern Asia and the West* (Paris, 1963) pp. 64–65.
62. This is persuasively argued by Bryce Ryan, "Status, Achievement, and Education in Ceylon," *Journal of Asian Studies*, XX (August, 1961), 463–466.

of the bureaucratic career, the demand for public employment is undoubtedly a product of the severely limited alternative sources of employment.[63] Opportunities for educated Ceylonese outside the public service are generally few in number or uninviting. Planting and the urban professions emerged in the latter part of the nineteenth century as possible alternative careers and became avenues of social mobility for a narrow but important segment of Ceylonese society. However, planting requires few educated persons, and with the rapid population growth and consequent pressure on the land the possibilities of expansion of estate agriculture are limited. The most popular of the urban professions, law, is manifestly overcrowded, and many persons with legal training seek public service posts. Other professions do not attract large numbers of Ceylonese, and a major proportion of the engineers, doctors, and accountants are found in the public service. Business management, another potential competitor for talent, similarly has failed to offer attractive employment opportunities to many educated Ceylonese. Commercial and industrial enterprise in Ceylon has remained too small to absorb large numbers of managerial personnel. The larger business firms are often foreign-owned, and until recently the higher management positions frequently have been staffed by aliens. The businesses owned by Ceylonese and Indians commonly keep the more desirable posts within the family, narrowing the opportunities for a person without family connections. In recent years the government has assumed a major role in many formerly private economic activities, including transportation, insurance, petroleum distribution, banking, and the export-import trade, which collectively represent a relatively substantial source of managerial employment. Most new industrial activity is undertaken by public corporations. Consequently, the modest number of careers in private business management is shrinking. Although planting, business, and the professions attract some talent that might

63. The Perera Commission noted the dominant position of the government in employment in explaining the impracticality of determining government salaries on the basis of salaries paid employees of private concerns. In contrast to Western countries, private wages and salaries in Ceylon tend to follow those in the public service. Perera Report, Part I, p. 30.

otherwise be available to the public service, the demand for bureaucratic appointments consistently exceeds the supply. With an expanding output of university graduates in the arts and humanities, an increasingly serious problem of educated unemployed may be in prospect. During 1963 the Public Service Commission received 2,698 applications for eighty-nine posts in the staff grades of the public service.[64] The dearth of opportunities outside the public service was illustrated by a report of a Ceylonese scholar in Pali, Sanskrit, and Indian philosophy, returning to the island with M.A. and Ph.D. degrees from Cambridge, who after a futile six-month search for appropriate employment took a position as an assistant commissioner of local government.[65]

Entrance into the bureaucracy is on the basis of merit, determined more or less competitively. However, once a recruit has entered the public service, usually in his early twenties, status and position are little related to achievement. For many Ceylonese, it appears that the pinnacle of life's attainment comes with his initial appointment to a government job, which will assure him of highly valued security and an attractive dowry. There seems to be little expectation of further striving or keen desire for accomplishment. Salary increases come almost automatically each year until an officer reaches an "efficiency bar," which is to test his suitability for further advancement. However, the Perera Commission found that seldom was any specific examination to determine competence required and concluded that the efficiency bar was little more than a formality. The commission further maintained that seniority and age were more often determinants of promotions than merit.[66]

In a society with serious unemployment and underemployment, some tendency to view the public service as a scheme for unemployment relief is almost unavoidable. The continuation in the public service of temporary employees with questionable qualifications long after they are needed is an example of the

64. *Annual Report of the Public Service Commission, 1963* (Ceylon Sessional Paper V, 1964), p. 2.
65. *Ceylon News,* January 16, 1964.
66. Perera Report, Part I, pp. 74–76.

hesitancy on both humanitarian and political grounds to discharge any employees once they are on the public service rolls. The government has attempted to absorb into the bureaucracy workers who lost their jobs when the British naval base at Trincomalee was dismantled. A recent decision was made to absorb into the public service former employees of British and American petroleum companies who became unemployed as a result of the nationalization of petroleum distribution facilities. Department heads were ordered to disregard educational and age qualifications and in some cases to dispense with examinations or interviews in recruiting the former oil workers.[67] The demand for public employment far exceeds the availability of government posts. Once, 14,000 applications were received for five hundred openings as police constables.[68] The cabinet was reported to be considering a proposal by a member of Parliament that priority in public employment be given to applicants from poor families suffering from unemployment.[69] The "superfluity" of employees at the lower levels of the public service observed by the Perera Commission[70] is probably almost inevitable in a society with few economic opportunities and considerable unemployment.

There has been considerable criticism of the hours worked by staffs of government offices. A thirty-six-hour week is usual for government office workers. Public employees are given thirteen holidays annually, compared to seven to nine received by employees of private firms. While annual leave provisions vary considerably, in grades above those of minor employees public servants usually receive twenty-one days' casual leave and twenty-seven days' vacation leave annually.[71] In addition, a practice has developed of taking what is termed "short leave"— that is, absence from work for periods of an hour or so. "Short leave," the Perera Commission contended, "has now come to be regarded as an alternative to ordinary leave and in many cases, it

67. *Ceylon News*, April 23, 1964.
68. *Ceylon Observer*, September 22, 1961.
69. *Ceylon News*, February 27, 1964.
70. Perera Report, Part II, pp. 10–11.
71. *Ibid.*, Part II, pp. 27–33.

is taken so regularly that it adds up to an appreciable number of days."[72] Morning and afternoon tea breaks and arrival at the office a few minutes late and departure a few minutes early are deeply entrenched habits among government office workers. A commentator in a Department of Information periodical wrote: "Today public servants stroll in long after the appointed hour, . . . take several tea breaks and a prolonged lunch interval, go through non-official work at their desks, . . . [and] leave office before the appointed hour. . . ."[73] It was the Perera Commission's judgment that the net annual hours worked by government office employees in Ceylon "are perhaps the lowest in the world."[74]

Political interference in the bureaucracy, manifest since the establishment of representative government in the early 1930's, seems to have risen sharply in the past decade. The Perera Commission in 1961 detected in the bureaucracy a "feeling of frustration and helplessness created by the creeping growth of political interference and intervention in the Public Service."[75] The commission conceded that appointments, promotions, transfers, and other public service matters were often subject to political influence, and it fixed partial responsibility for this condition on the public servants who sought political intercession for their personal benefit and who allowed political considerations or politicians to influence their decisions.[76] To a major extent, the growth of political involvement in administration and the bureaucracy is a response to changing political conditions and growing popular political awareness and demands. In an attempt to win the support of the increasingly restive masses, many politicians have sought bureaucratic action to construct village schools and roads, obtain pensions and permits, and arrange public service appointments or transfers for constituents or supporters.[77] Bribery and corruption, however, have played a role of more than nominal significance in the spread of political interference. For example, a special commission appointed to investigate

72. *Ibid.*, Part II, p. 38.
73. "Lanka Diary," *Sri Lanka*, June 27, 1964.
74. Perera Report, Part II, p. 26.
75. *Ibid.*, Part I, p. 3.
76. *Ibid.*, Part II, pp. 101–102.
77. This trend is discussed more fully in Kearney and Harris, "Bureaucracy and Environment in Ceylon."

allegations of bribery against members of Parliament concluded that many of the 642 sub-postmasters' jobs created between 1956 and 1960 were sold, reportedly at a price of Rs. 2,500 each. The commission also commented on the heavy pressure by politicians for the appointment of their supporters to these positions.[78] The Public Service Commission was proposed largely to shelter the bureaucracy from political interference in appointments and promotions after independence.[79] How successful it has been, however, is subject to question. The commission itself has not escaped accusations of susceptibility to political manipulation. One M.P. recently charged, "all that the P.S.C. is today is a glorified and expensive rubber stamp for the decisions of politicians."[80] Another claimed: "We have heard that every Minister is interfering with the Public Service Commission" and asserted that "favouritism and nepotism are the order of the day."[81] A former prime minister, Dudley Senanayake, acknowledged the existence of a "convention" that the chairman of the Public Service Commission consults the prime minister before making appointments of heads of departments.[82]

V. The Official Language Problem

Ceylon progressed to independence without political upheaval under the guidance of a national independence movement which was strikingly moderate and co-operative.[83] The usually affluent,

78. *Reports of the Parliamentary Bribery Commission, 1959–60*, Parliamentary Series No. 1, Fifth Parliament (Colombo, 1961), pp. 65–66. The commission was empowered to inquire into charges against members of Parliament only, and consequently did not explore bribery and corruption by public servants.

79. See *Ceylon: Report of the Commission on Constitutional Reform*, pp. 97–101.

80. House, *Debates*, Vol. 48, col. 418.

81. *Ibid.*, Vol. 48, col. 393.

82. *Ibid.*, Vol. 48, col. 407. Jennings raised a question as to the desirability of depriving ministers in a parliamentary system of control over the public service. Sir W. Ivor Jennings, *The Constitution of Ceylon* (3rd ed.; London, 1953), pp. 133–134.

83. For a recent study, see Sir Charles Jeffries, *Ceylon: The Path to Independence* (New York, 1963). On the Ceylon National Congress and the independence movement, see S. W. R. D. Bandaranaike (ed.), *The Handbook of the Ceylon National Congress, 1919–1928* (Colombo, 1928); Sir W. Ivor Jennings, "Nationalism and Political Development in Ceylon," *Ceylon Historical Journal*, III (July, 1953–April, 1954), 62–84, 99–114, 197–206; and I. D. S. Weerawardana, *Government and Politics in Ceylon, 1931–1946* (Colombo, 1951).

English-educated political leaders of the State Council and the Ceylon National Congress who formed the United National party and came to power at independence supported few radical ideas or goals. Ceylonese politics in the first years of independence, as in the preceding period, was generally placid. The comparative calm, however, was shattered in the 1950's by the eruption of a cluster of interrelated demands and discontents involving revolt against felt discrimination and inferiority by the Buddhist majority, social protest over the privileges of the small Ceylonese elite educated in English, nationalist attacks on the elite's Westernization and alienation from indigenous culture, and rivalry between the Sinhalese ethnic majority and the Tamil minority. The various streams of discontent, fed by a growing political awareness among the rural villagers, tended to converge in the explosive official language controversy. In 1944, the State Council had resolved gradually to substitute Sinhalese and Tamil, the two indigenous languages, for English as the language of government. However, implementation lagged, and after independence pressure from opposition politicians mounted for a swift transition to swabhasha. In the early 1950's the demand among the Sinhalese shifted to the immediate replacement of English by Sinhalese only. Despite a last-minute UNP switch to the Sinhalese-only camp, an election in 1956 swept the UNP from office and brought to power a coalition headed by S. W. R. D. Bandaranaike which quickly enacted legislation declaring Sinhalese to be the sole official language of Ceylon.[84]

84. A detailed examination of the language problem is not attempted here. For more extended analyses, see W. Howard Wriggins, *Ceylon: Dilemmas of a New Nation* (Princeton, N. J., 1960), pp. 228–270; I. D. S. Weerawardana, *Ceylon General Election, 1956* (Colombo, 1960), pp. 1–15, 98–109; and Robert N. Kearney, "Ceylon: A Study in Political Change" (unpublished Ph.D. dissertation, University of California, Los Angeles, 1963), chaps. i and vi. A historical sketch of Sinhalese-Tamil relations is contained in B. H. Farmer, *Ceylon: A Divided Nation* (London, 1963). On educational developments, which are fundamental to bureaucratic employment and the language problem, see H. A. Wyndham, *Native Education* (London, 1933), pp. 33–66. For a perceptive discussion of British colonial policy regarding the language of administration and education, see Hugh Tinker, "People and Government in Southern Asia," in *Transactions of the Royal Historical Society*, 5th Series, IX (London, 1959), 141–167. A discussion of communal tensions as an outgrowth of competition for public service employment appears in Mendis, *Ceylon Today and Yesterday*, pp. 97–107. On ethnic representation in the bureaucracy, see Tambiah, "Ethnic Representation in

Among the conflicting emotions and interests which generated the force of the language controversy was competition for employment in the public service. After the establishment of British rule at the beginning of the nineteenth century, English became the language in which government was conducted in Ceylon. Knowledge of English was essential for employment in the clerical and administrative posts of the public service, which increasingly were sought by Ceylonese.[85] From the late nineteenth century and particularly after the constitutional changes of 1931, vernacular education expanded rapidly, producing by 1953 a literacy rate of 65 per cent. However, few vocational opportunities awaited the vernacular-educated graduate. In the agricultural economy of Ceylon, the type of white-collar employment eagerly sought by the educated youth was almost a monopoly of the government. Resentment against the hold of the small English-educated elite on government employment contributed to the strength of the official language agitation. Bandaranaike spoke for this resentment when he demanded the swift abandonment of English, declaring "over ninety per cent. of the [government] jobs of this country are restricted to ten per cent. of the people who know English. In this land of ours, those ignorant of English are capable of obtaining much less than 10 per cent. of Government jobs!"[86] Some years later his widow, who had become prime minister, asked: "Was not the whole idea of independence incomplete so long as an exclusive knowledge of the English language was more or less the only passport to the Public Service?"[87]

In multilingual Ceylon the official language question almost

Ceylon's Higher Administrative Services, 1870–1946," pp. 113–134. On the more recent developments, see Robert N. Kearney, "The New Political Crises of Ceylon," *Asian Survey*, II (June, 1962), 19–27; and the same author's "Sinhalese Nationalism and Social Conflict in Ceylon," *Pacific Affairs*, XXXVII (Summer, 1964), 125–136.

85. In 1868, Ceylonese held more than 80 per cent of all public service posts, including all of the lower positions and about one-third of the posts of higher rank (the top 25 per cent of public service posts). They formed a small minority in the CCS, however. Mills, *op. cit.*, pp. 91–92.

86. S. W. R. D. Bandaranaike, *Towards a New Era* (Colombo: Information Department, 1961), p. 927. This work is a collection of Bandaranaike's speeches in the State Council and Parliament between 1931 and 1959.

87. *Sunday Times of Ceylon*, December 3, 1961.

inexorably came to involve not only a contest between the English-educated and the vernacular-educated, but also a contest between those educated in Sinhalese and those educated in Tamil. The Sinhalese comprise approximately 70 per cent of the island's population. The Ceylon Tamils, who have lived in the north and east of the island for many centuries, form about 11 per cent of the total population. Another group of Tamil-speaking people called Indian Tamils, who comprise about 12 per cent of the population, were brought to Ceylon during the nineteenth and twentieth centuries to work on the tea estates of the interior hill country. After independence, most of the Indian Tamils were denied Ceylonese citizenship. The rivalry for public service positions has been between the Sinhalese and the Ceylon Tamils. The Ceylon Tamils had early acquired English educations and turned to the public service in relatively large numbers. Among the Sinhalese, disproportionate Tamil representation in the public service often was seen as limiting the opportunities for Sinhalese aspirants and, after independence, maintaining an advantage obtained under colonial rule. Competition for government employment became an element in the entangled considerations of ethnic group status and solidarity and ancient communal suspicions which boiled up into tensions and violence after 1956.

The 1956 enactment declaring Sinhalese to be the sole official language of the island[88] immediately produced profound political repercussions. The impact on the bureaucracy was somewhat slower to be felt. The act directed that the transition was to be completed by 1961. Political instability and lack of a clear definition of the relationship among Sinhalese, Tamil, and English complicated the serious administrative and personnel problems encountered and prevented many major steps prior to 1960. Typically, an annual administration report for 1960 complained:

One of the chief difficulties in the way of the more intensive use of the Official Language was that sufficient officers with a knowledge of Sinhala [Sinhalese] had not been made available to the department.

88. Official Language Act, No. 33 of 1956. This act was followed by the Tamil Language (Special Provision) Act, No. 28 of 1958. Both are reproduced in *The Official Language and the Reasonable Use of Tamil* (Colombo: Information Department, n.d.), pp. 39–44.

The position has not still [*sic*] improved very much and it is only when the staff asked for is allowed that the implementation of the Official Language can be effected on a better scale.[89]

Public servants were encouraged to learn Sinhalese by the use of incentive bonuses and threats to suspend periodic pay increases until proficiency in Sinhalese was attained. Government reports and publications began to appear in Sinhalese, often after considerable delay and confusion.[90] Nearly five years after passage of the Sinhalese-only act not more than half the public servants were estimated to be able to perform their duties in Sinhalese.[91] Public servants who entered the bureaucracy prior to 1956 were allowed to retire on grounds that they could not work in the new official language, and by mid-1964 more than three thousand public servants had chosen to retire under these provisions.[92] After elections in 1960, the cabinet declared that the changeover was to be made by 1961, as provided in the original act. Later, with mounting delays and difficulties, a "final" completion of the transition was announced for January 1, 1964.

Leaders of the Tamil-speaking people expressed grave concern both for the public employment opportunities of Tamils and for the language in which governmental administration would be conducted in the traditional Tamil-speaking areas in the Northern and Eastern Provinces. In the 1956 election the Federal party emerged as the principal political spokesman of the Ceylon Tamils. The party is devoted to the attainment of Tamil political and cultural autonomy in the north and east and has been more concerned with the language of government in these areas than with the fate of Tamil public servants in the south. After the adoption of Sinhalese as the language of government in 1956 the Federal party president declared, "it has become necessary for us to eschew Government Service and find other avenues of employ-

89. *Administration Report of the Commissioner and Chairman, Colombo Port Commission, for 1960* (Colombo: Government Press, 1961), p. 38.
90. For example, in 1959 the minister of finance blamed delays created by the language changeover for the fact that only two of seventy-three administration reports of the preceding year had been published on schedule and many were still to be published months later. House, *Debates*, Vol. 37, cols. 830–831.
91. Perera Report, Part II, p. 11.
92. *Ceylon News*, August 13, 1964.

ment in the near future."[93] The Federal party repeatedly urged Tamil public servants to refuse to learn Sinhalese.[94] Unable to reach agreement with the government on the use of Tamil in the administration of the north and east, the Federal party early in 1961 launched a satyagraha campaign which brought civil administration to a virtual standstill for more than two months and led to the declaration of an emergency and the imposition of military rule in the Tamil-speaking areas. In order to carry out its policy of requiring Sinhalese to be used in government offices in the Tamil-speaking areas, the government has assigned increasing numbers of Sinhalese public servants to the kachcheris in the north and east.[95]

In January, 1964, the Ministry of Finance was authorized to dismiss any public servant who was not proficient in the official language. At the beginning of March, 1964, the first compulsory retirements on language grounds were ordered. Within a short time the government relented and decided to retire only those who had made no effort to study Sinhalese. Public servants who were not able to pass the proficiency examination in Sinhalese were given two additional years to develop the necessary language skill. A number of Tamil public servants who had not attempted to learn Sinhalese were served with notices of their compulsory separation from the Public Service.[96] A challenge in the courts, however, has caused a suspension of the notices.[97]

Considerable administrative dislocation and a significant amount of bureaucratic demoralization have accompanied the change. Public servants trained in English must work in a

93. C. Vanniasingam, *Presidential Address, Ilankai Tamil Arasu Kadchi Annual Convention,* 1956 (Jaffna, 1956), p. 18. Ilankai Tamil Arasu Kadchi (literally, Ceylon Tamil State party) is the Tamil name of the Federal party.

94. E.g., *ibid.,* p. 16; S. M. Rasamanickam, *Presidential Address at the National Convention of the Ilankai Tamil Arasu Kadchi,* 1962 (Colombo, 1962), pp. 7–8, and a statement by S. J. V. Chelvanayakam, appearing in *Ceylon Daily News,* May 12, 1962.

95. E.g., *Times of Ceylon,* December 11, 1963. Ironically, the task of implementing the change to Sinhalese fell to a Tamil public servant, a deputy secretary to the Treasury. He eventually resigned, claiming that he felt someone else (i.e., a Sinhalese) would be more acceptable to the public in discharging this responsibility. See *Ceylon News,* January 2, 1964.

96. House, *Debates,* Vol. 56, cols. 248–249.

97. Subsequently, the notices of compulsory retirement were withdrawn by a new government which came to power after an election in March, 1965.

medium in which few are fluent.[98] Many problems of printing and typewriting have appeared. Presumably, most of these problems are of a temporary nature, although all are not likely to be overcome in a few years. Considerable development of the Sinhalese language must occur if it is to acquire the vocabulary and precision necessary for effective administrative use after exclusion to the village and the temple for more than a century. Education in Sinhalese is only gradually progressing beyond the secondary level,[99] and primary and secondary education in Sinhalese frequently is of uncertain quality. For many years most public servants and particularly those in the higher grades will be English-trained. Tensions produced by bureaucrats educated in English but required to work in Sinhalese are likely to plague the bureaucracy for a considerable period of time. The ethnic composition of the public service may be altered permanently in favor of the Sinhalese, although the ease with which Tamils mastered English has caused some speculation over their ability similarly to master Sinhalese and compete successfully against Sinhalese aspirants.

If the transitional problems can be overcome and a generation of Sinhalese-educated public servants moves up the bureaucratic hierarchy, the character of the bureaucracy may be fundamentally altered. For more than a century the public service has been an elite clearly set apart from the mass of Ceylonese society. With their esoteric command of English, public servants, particularly at the higher levels, commonly adopted Western or quasi-Western values and modes of living, generally abandoning traditional Ceylonese culture. The severing of the connection between scarce educations in an alien language and the bureaucracy, probably accompanied by a reduction of the cultural gap between the public service officers and the rest of the society, may profoundly

98. English-educated members of the Sinhalese ethnic group often are unable or scarcely able to read Sinhalese and use the spoken language chiefly in addressing servants and tradesmen. See *First Interim Report of the Official Languages Commission* (Ceylon Sessional Paper XXI, 1951); H. A. Passé, "The English Language in Ceylon," *University of Ceylon Review*, I (November, 1943), 50–65.

99. On the problems of language and education at the University of Ceylon, see Fischer, *op. cit.*, pp. 3–15; and Ralph Pieris, "Universities, Politics, and Public Opinion in Ceylon," *Minerva*, II (Summer, 1964), 435–454.

affect the elitist character of the bureaucracy. The disappearance of this elitist conception within the bureaucracy could lead to a closer identification between the public servants and the people. At the same time it might dissipate the ethos of impartial and incorruptible guardianship which has been one of the most outstanding bureaucratic legacies of colonial rule.

VI. The Elite Cadre

The Ceylon Civil Service, founded with the commencement of British Crown Colony rule at the beginning of the nineteenth century, was the powerful superior cadre of the colonial bureaucracy from its inception until more than a dozen years after independence. It is slight exaggeration to claim that the CCS was the virtual ruler of Ceylon until the constitutional changes of 1931.[100] The CCS remained both small in size and elite in position throughout its existence. As the bureaucracy expanded rapidly before the conclusion of colonial rule, the need for administrative personnel was met by the recruitment of departmental administrative officers, creating two sets of public servants at the administrative level. The civil servants, however, generally retained the top posts in the bureaucracy. The commanding position of the CCS did not change significantly with the coming of independence. Permanent secretaries placed at the apex of the bureaucratic hierarchy after independence were not a part of the Civil Service, but they were almost invariably drawn from the ranks of the senior Civil Service officers. The first appointment of a non-CCS administrative officer as a permanent secretary did not occur until 1957.[101]

The assignments of CCS officers at the end of 1959, a dozen years after independence, revealed the concentration of civil servants in the coveted posts of district administration and in the higher ministry and departmental positions (see Table 3). Dis-

100. This claim is made by Saparamadu, *op. cit.*, p. x.
101. The same individual was reported to have become the first non-civil servant appointed as an assistant commissioner of local government in 1938 and the first non-civil servant named commissioner of local government in 1947. See *Ceylon News*, April 23, 1964. Permanent secretaries to the Ministry of Justice have been chosen from the Judicial Service rather than the Civil Service.

Table 3. *Assignments of Ceylon Civil Service Officers as of December 31, 1959*

Assignment	Number	Percentage
I. District administration		
Government agent	21	
Assistant government agent	16	
Office assistant and attached to kachcheri	25	
	62	30.5
II. Central government		
A. Department—non-development activities		
Department head	22	
Deputy department head	5	
Other departmental	38	
	65	32.0
B. Ministry		
Acting permanent secretary[a]	4	
Assistant secretary	27	
Attached to ministry	5	
Office assistant and other	9	
	45	22.2
C. Department—development activities[b]		
Department head	5	
Deputy department head	5	
Other departmental	8	
	18	8.9
D. Training	—	—
E. Planning Commission	—	—
III. Government corporations		
General manager	2	
Unit manager	4	
Assistant unit manager	1	
	7	3.4
IV. Public Service Commission		
Secretary	1	
Assistant secretary	1	
	2	1.0
V. Miscellaneous		
Secretary to special commissions	2	
Attached to special commissions	1	
Member, United Nations delegation	1	
	4	2.0
Total	203	

[a] Thirteen of seventeen permanent secretaries were former CCS members, but as required by regulations they left the service on appointment as permanent secretaries.

[b] The following departments were selected as being specifically charged with and substantially engaged in social or economic development activities: Commissioner of Co-operative Development, Rural Development and Cottage Industries, Land Commissioner, Land Settlement, Irrigation, Land Development, Agriculture, Agrarian Services, Town and Country Planning, National Housing, Education, Fisheries, and Social Services. A number of other departments are incidentally concerned with development activities.

Source: Compiled from data in *Ceylon Civil List, 1959* (Colombo: Government Press, n.d.).

trict administration had been the stronghold of the CCS since early colonial times, and historically CCS preparation and experience were largely directed toward eventual assignment as a government agent or assistant government agent. The monopoly of the Civil Service over these positions was unaffected by independence and was not broken as long as the CCS existed. Many civil servants were also assigned to ministry and departmental duties, and their numbers in top positions such as assistant secretaries and department heads is particularly noteworthy. The distribution of assignments suggests that agencies in the expanding fields of development activities, economic undertakings, and planning did not depend extensively on CCS members. Officers in district administration, however, have assumed increasing developmental responsibilities in addition to their revenue and order-preserving functions.

The Civil Service throughout its long history was firmly under the influence of the "generalist" concept of education and training for administration. Entrance examinations were oriented toward language and literary skills and general knowledge. Educational backgrounds in the arts and humanities predominated among civil servants. Of sixty-seven recruits to the Ceylon Civil Service between 1951 and 1961, only two offered science and six mathematics as examination subjects. Thirteen offered Sinhalese; ten, history; nine, English; six, classics; five, economics; four each, Sanskrit and law; two each, Pali, Tamil and geography; and one each, philosophy and sociology.[102] With increasing realization of the technical and scientific needs of the bureaucracy, this educational bias in the top level of the public service has been subjected to frequent criticism. One M.P. remarked: "It is not that I want to say anything against the Civil Servants. There are some who are fit to be professors of Pali, Sanskrit, or Sinhalese in universities but who are absolutely unfit to be in charge of administration. They have selected the wrong profession. . . ."[103]

After independence challenges to alleged vestiges of colonial privilege within the bureaucracy gradually began to mount.

102. *Annual Report of the Public Service Commission, 1962*, p. 13.
103. House, *Debates,* Vol. 48, col. 2623.

These attacks were frequently directed against the small and exclusive CCS, eventually producing the abolition of the venerable elite service and its absorption into a much larger administrative service. The CCS was closely identified with alien colonial rule. Although in 1875 Sir Ponnambalam Arunachalam, later to play a leading role in the independence movement, became the first Ceylonese to enter the service by competitive examination, extensive Ceylonization of the CCS did not occur until near the end of the colonial period. In 1925, one-third of the Civil Service was Ceylonese, and by 1940 the proportion of Ceylonese stood at about two-thirds.[104] Many of the privileges of the colonial CCS survived after independence. Although non-CCS administrative officers frequently staffed identical posts and performed the same duties, members of the CCS continued to enjoy greater status, higher salary levels, and superior promotional prospects. They could be transferred among departments as opportunities for advancement appeared, while other administrative officers normally were restricted to a single department throughout their careers.[105] A number of top administrative posts were reserved exclusively for CCS officers.

The Perera Commission reporting in 1961 condemned the special position of the CCS as creating a "caste" system deleterious to the public service. Commenting that "the need for unifying all administrative grades in the Public Service has long been recognized as a reform that was urgently necessary," the commission recommended the abolition of the CCS and the absorption of its members into a single administrative service.[106] Under a plan developed to create a unified administrative service, all staff officers, including CCS officers, were to be

104. Navasivayam, *op. cit.*, p. 94. Nationalization of the public service came relatively earlier and more smoothly in Ceylon than did the comparable process in many, perhaps most, other colonies. However, nationalist spokesmen in Ceylon frequently are less impressed by this than by the long identification of the public service with colonialism.

105. Perera Report, Part I, pp. 161–162.

106. *Ibid.*, Part I, pp. 161–163. A unified administrative service had been urged by the minister of finance in 1951, and the Poulier Commission in 1953 recommended such a scheme, but no action was taken on the proposals. See *Scheme for an Administrative Service* (Ceylon Sessional Paper XXIX, 1951); and *Report of the Salaries and Cadres Commission, 1953*, Part II (Ceylon Sessional Paper XVII, 1953), pp. 540–552.

absorbed into a service composed of five classes. All future recruits to the new service were to enter at the lowest class. Recruitment was to be chiefly from among university graduates between twenty-two and twenty-six years of age by competitive examination, although provision was also made for recruitment of members of the lower levels of the public service by limited competition.[107] As envisaged by the Perera Commission, the lowest class consisting of about three-fourths of all administrative officers would be roughly equivalent to the executive class, and the higher grades to the administrative class of the British civil service. The commission, however, recommended officers be selected for the more responsible classes by promotion from the lowest class of the unified service rather than by separate recruitment for the two levels of responsibility.[108] The proposed reform went into effect and the 160-year-old Ceylon Civil Service passed out of existence on May 1, 1963. The 209 members of the CCS were absorbed into a Ceylon Administrative Service of 1,030 officers, 795 of whom were in the lowest class and the remainder in the four higher classes.[109]

VII. Continued Agitation for Change

Pressure for reform of the bureaucracy was notably absent in Ceylon immediately after independence. Ceylonization of the bureaucracy was virtually complete at independence,[110] so that demands for the rapid replacement of expatriate officers with indigenous officers, which vexed many newly independent countries, did not arise. English-language educations, cultural Westernization, and not infrequently ties of kinship tended to unite the political leaders of the first years of independence and the higher

107. *Ceylon Observer*, May 13, 1962.
108. Perera Report, Part I, pp. 12–166. The commission recommended six classes with approximately seven hundred officers in the lowest and 220 in the five higher classes. The commission used the term "grades" for the levels within the service, but subsequently they have generally been referred to as "classes."
109. *Ceylon News*, May 9, 1963.
110. See Collins' accompanying study (Chapter 7) in this volume.

public servants.[111] Despite some early realization that the role and position of the bureaucracy would change with independence,[112] little inclination to alter the character of the public service was displayed until after a change of political leadership in 1956.

With the 1956 election, a political leadership came to power possessing a much more critical attitude toward the continuation of what were believed to be colonial features and practices in the bureaucracy. S. W. R. D. Bandaranaike, who became prime minister in 1956, had charged a few years earlier: "The entire structure of the Public Service still continues to be that of a colonial administration."[113] In 1958 he declared: "You think that public servants [in the colonial period] looked upon themselves as servants of the people? The people seldom entered into their minds . . . and all that was necessary for them was to conduct themselves in a way to please the British heads of departments and carry out rules and regulations." Moreover, he contended, independence produced "no change in spirit in the public service. . . ."[114]

A strong tide of discontent with the bureaucracy, generally identifying bureaucratic practices and characteristics with the needs of colonial rule, developed and continued after the death of Bandaranaike. The leader of the opposition in the Ceylon Senate in 1962 voiced a sentiment common among political leaders:

In that [1946] constitution we have a system of parliamentary democracy which has been rather unsuitably developed on top of a bureaucratic administrative structure which we have inherited from colonial days, which has not been changed. The two do not match. One system of government by a hierarchy of officials was developed in

111. E.g., Saparamadu, *op. cit.*, p. xxii. The top political leaders of subsequent years were of similar social backgrounds, but they came to power espousing Sinhalese nationalist and populist causes with strong support from village traders, vernacular schoolteachers, ayurvedic physicians, and bhikkhus.

112. Thus, D. S. Senanayake, Ceylon's first prime minister, once lectured graduating students of the University of Ceylon on their need to overcome their urban, English-speaking, middle-class backgrounds if they were to be useful public servants. D. S. Senanayake, "The Qualities Required of Public Servants," reprinted in *The D. S. Senanayake Memorial Number,* special issue of *Ceylon Historical Journal,* V (July, 1955–April, 1956), 107–110.

113. Bandaranaike, *Towards a New Era,* p. 719.

114. S. W. R. D. Bandaranaike, *The Government and the People* (Colombo: Information Department, 1959), pp. 65–66.

colonial times to run this country, and somewhat patched up on this we have a system of parliamentary democracy. There are bound to be points of conflict. . . .[115]

Insistence on bureaucratic reform appeared repeatedly in the 1960 election campaign. The Lanka Sama Samaja party's 1960 election manifesto demanded: "Radical reorganization of the obsolete administrative system, starting with the Treasury. Abolition of the headman system and the kachcheri system. . . . A unified administrative service."[116] Almost identical demands appeared in the manifestos of the Communist party and the Mahajana Eksath Peramuna.[117] The manifesto of the Sri Lanka Freedom party, which under the leadership of Bandaranaike's widow won the election in July, 1960, promised study of the forthcoming report of the Perera Commission with a view to reorganizing and reforming the public service.[118] The Speech from the Throne following the election promised an "overhaul" of the public service, Treasury, field administration, and headman system, and a review of relations between the central government and local government bodies.[119] The dissatisfactions, distrust, and determination to change the bureaucracy evident among the political leaders led to the abolition of the Ceylon Civil Service and produced attempts at further reform and demands for continued change.

At the same time that the CCS disappeared another even more venerable bureaucratic institution was abolished. Throughout the colonial era field administration in the rural areas had rested on the broad base of village headmen, chosen from among the eminent local landowning families of high caste and status.[120] The

115. Ceylon Senate, *Parliamentary Debates* (*Hansard*), Vol. 17, col. 2676.

116. *Election Manifesto of the Lanka Sama Samaja Party* (Colombo, 1960), p. 4.

117. *Manifesto of the Communist Party* (Colombo, 1960), p. 4; *Anduren Eliyata: Mahajana Eksath Peramunē Māthivarana Prakāsanaya* [*From Darkness to Light: The Mahajana Eksath Peramuna's Election Manifesto*] (Colombo, 1960), unpaged.

118. *Sri Lankā Nidahas Pakshayē Māthivarana Prakāsanaya, 1960* [*Sri Lanka Freedom Party's Election Manifesto, 1960*] (Colombo, 1960), p. 18. Only the United National party showed no great enthusiasm for bureaucratic reform. See *Progress Through Stability: United National Party Manifesto* (Colombo, 1958).

119. *Ceylon Today*, IX (August, 1960), 9.

120. See Wilson, *op. cit.*, pp. 15–16.

hierarchy of headmen, superior headmen, and chief headmen inherited by the British colonial rulers from their Dutch predecessors at the beginning of the nineteenth century was not basically modified at the lower levels until well into the present century.[121] Slowly in recent decades, reforms led to the replacement of semi-feudal officials by career public servants. The former were chosen on the basis of status and caste; the latter, on the basis of merit. Beginning in 1938 the chief headmen were gradually retired and replaced by divisional revenue officers. After a similar process of gradual retirement, in 1961 the post of superior headman was abolished.[122] The village headman system, the sole remaining survival of a feudal administrative structure, began to come under increasing attack with the growth of nationalist and democratic values. Headmen, once wielding tremendous local power, were denounced as undemocratic, arbitrary, incompetent, corrupt, and tainted by long collaboration with the colonial regime.[123] The headmen, as agents of the central government, frequently came into conflict with elective local government bodies, the members of which were assuming increasing political significance. In the same stroke which ended the CCS, the centuries-old headman system was abolished. The headman was replaced at the base of the field administration by a grama sevaka (village servant), selected by competitive examination and transferable from one locality to another.[124]

Another frequent target of the political leaders intent on bureaucratic reform has been the kachcheri system of field administration. Kachcheri, a term of Indian origin introduced

121. While the structure at the levels below the government agent and assistant government agent changed little, the powers and functions of the lower officials underwent greater change. The structure of colonial field administration bore a basic similarity to the traditional Sinhalese feudal administration, the government agent being roughly equivalent in position in the hierarchy to the traditional disawa who administered a territory for the monarch. See Saparamadu, *op. cit.*, p. xxiv.

122. *Ibid.*, p. xxvi. See also Collins' accompanying study in this volume, p. 461.

123. A discussion of changing attitudes toward authority in the village and consequent changes in the position of the headman is contained in Arthur L. Wood, *Crime and Aggression in Changing Ceylon* (Philadelphia, 1961), pp. 39–42. For a view of the former position of power held by the village headman, see Wriggins, *op. cit.*, pp. 41–42.

124. *Ceylon News*, May 9, 1963.

into Ceylon during the brief period of East India Company rule, is the name given to the office of the government agent, who administered a province until 1954 and thereafter a district. The kachcheri came to symbolize highly centralized, paternalistic rule from Colombo, not infrequently accompanied by disdain for the opinions or preferences of the public upon which government was imposed.[125] A Commission on Local Government in 1955 reported a widespread belief that "whilst the Kachcheri system may have been appropriate in the days of a Colonial regime, it was completely out of place in the democratic set-up of modern times."[126] Local self-government, originally limited to the major cities, gradually was extended to the rural areas. Local government bodies, however, possess sharply circumscribed powers and are under the close scrutiny of the Local Government Department in Colombo. Despite this growth of completely separate local bodies, the kachcheris retained and in some respects increased the importance of their role and position as the functions performed by the state expanded at a much more rapid rate than the powers conferred on local government bodies. Tensions often developed between the kachcheris or the kachcheri-sponsored rural development societies and the organs of local self-government.[127]

S. W. R. D. Bandaranaike, who had served as minister of local government from 1936 to 1951, was long interested in decentralization and democratization of the administrative structure in the field. He once urged the creation of locally elected regional councils to replace the kachcheris, but the scheme became entangled in the controversy over the official language and the Federal party's demand for Tamil political autonomy, and it was not carried out. The idea reappeared in modified form, however, with a cabinet proposal in 1963 that locally elected district councils be created to replace the kachcheris.[128] A committee

125. Indications of this tendency for public servants to impose the directives of the department without regard for local attitudes or conditions are numerous. E.g., see Straus, *op. cit.*, pp. 249–256; Samarasinghe, *op. cit.*, p. 83; B. H. Farmer, *Pioneer Peasant Colonization in Ceylon* (London, 1957), p. 285.
126. *Report of the Commission on Local Government*, p. 35.
127. *Ibid.*, pp. 50, 70–74.
128. *Ceylon Today*, XII (July, 1963), 2.

subsequently appointed to work out details of the reform recommended that authority relating to the politically sensitive problems of language, education, and allocation of land in state-sponsored colonization schemes be withheld from the district councils.[129] Despite reservations in these matters on which the Sinhalese and Tamil communities are sharply divided, the implementation of the district council proposals will produce a marked change in the highly centralized and Colombo-oriented administrative environment of the public service in the field and is likely to contribute further to the erosion of the bureaucracy's distant and elitist image.

Insistent demands that Buddhists secure a more equitable share of posts in the public service have accompanied a new Buddhist political militancy, arising in close association with the Sinhalese-only official language movement.[130] Spokesmen for the growing Buddhist demands have claimed that Buddhists, who constitute nearly two-thirds of the island's population, have been denied equal access to the public service because of Christian educational advantages and favoritism in recruitment extended to Christians by Christian superior officers and by the colonial regime.[131] From late in the nineteenth century, Christian denominational schools dominated the field of English-language education, to which public service entrance requirements were geared. As the Christian schools were largely supported by grants of public funds, Buddhists came to feel that they were required to support an educational system run by Christians to serve the needs of the Christian community, a situation which perpetuated Christian advantages in preparing for public service appointment.[132] As a result of rising demands for equality of opportunity in education and employment, the state-assisted religious and

129. *Ceylon News*, March 26, 1964.
130. Discussions of this growth in Buddhist self-consciousness and political activism are contained in Wriggins, *op. cit.*, pp. 169–210; and Mendis, *Ceylon Today and Yesterday*, pp. 108–116.
131. Buddhist grievances are set out in detail and with considerable passion in a report authorized by the powerful All-Ceylon Buddhist Congress, Buddhist Committee of Inquiry, *The Betrayal of Buddhism* (Balangoda, 1956).
132. Christian educational advantages, as reflected in enrolments in the University of Ceylon, are examined in Sir W. Ivor Jennings, "Race, Religion and Economic Opportunity in the University of Ceylon," *University of Ceylon Review*, II (October, 1944), 1–13.

other private schools were taken over by the government in 1960.[133] The takeover of the schools, however, did not end Buddhist desires for an alteration of bureaucratic recruitment practices to nullify previous Christian advantages and compensate Buddhists for past discrimination. The All-Ceylon Buddhist Congress in 1962 urged that in recruitment to the public service each religious group should receive a share of posts proportionate to its size.[134] Simultaneously, the National Education Commission, claiming that the educational disadvantages of Buddhists would exist for some time, recommended the establishment of religious quotas, based on relative size of religious groups among Ceylonese citizens, to control entrance into the public service.[135] The government has given no indication that the proposals for recruitment on the basis of religion would be accepted.[136] Such an action might be held to conflict with a constitutional provision which forbids conferring a privilege or advantage or imposing a disability on persons of one religious group or community.[137]

In June, 1964, a coalition government was formed by the Sri Lanka Freedom party and the Lanka Sama Samaja party, an affiliate of the Trotskyist Fourth International. A program worked out as the basis for the coalition promised the adoption of regulations to secure the "compulsory retirement of Government servants who obstruct Government work, who are inefficient or who are not co-operative." The program also pledged to establish labor advisory boards in all government agencies—including public corporations —to investigate waste, inefficiency, and obstruction, and to advise on administrative matters.[138] These proposals were incorporated in a subsequent Speech from the Throne.[139] However, before major

133. The schools issue is treated in more detail in Kearney, "Sinhalese Nationalism and Social Conflict in Ceylon."
134. *Ceylon Daily News*, May 28, 1962.
135. *Final Report of the National Education Commission, 1961* (Ceylon Sessional Paper XVII, 1962), pp. 152–153.
136. The pledge of the 1960 Sri Lanka Freedom party election manifesto to recognize Buddhism as the religion of the majority without abridging religious freedom or discriminating against other religions has been repeated periodically, most recently in an agreement which formed the basis for a coalition government in 1964. The 1960 pledge is contained in *Srī Lankā Nidahas Pakshayē Māthivarana Prakāsanaya*, 1960, p. 11; and the recent reaffirmation in *Sri Lanka*, June 20, 1964.
137. Constitution of Ceylon, section 29.
138. The program is contained in *Sri Lanka*, June 20, 1964.
139. *Ceylon Today*, XIII (July, 1964), 1–7.

action was taken, the SLFP-LSSP coalition was defeated in an election in March, 1965. A government formed by the United National party and several smaller parties came to power, and the prospect of fundamental bureaucratic changes appeared to recede.

VIII. Public Corporations

The public corporation is becoming increasingly important in Ceylon as a device to secure greater flexibility in the operation of government economic undertakings than can be obtained through customary bureaucratic organization. With the commitment of the political leadership since 1956 to the introduction of socialism and the achievement of economic development through public initiative,[140] public corporations have appeared in growing numbers. Utility services, long provided by the government, are administered through conventional departments such as the departments of electrical undertakings, railway, posts and telecommunications, and broadcasting. In recent years, however, the creation of special public corporations has been the preferred method of organizing governmental economic activities (see Table 4). As explained recently by the minister of finance, the corporate device has been adopted "with the objective of providing the industrial and commercial undertakings of Government

140. The United National party in power before 1956 was committed to a certain amount of public economic initiative. See *Economic and Social Development of Ceylon (a Survey), 1926–1954* (Colombo: Ministry of Finance, July 1, 1955), pp. 40–55; and Henry M. Oliver, *Economic Opinion and Policy in Ceylon* (Durham, N. C., 1957), pp. 50–55. However, since the coming to power in 1956 of the Mahajana Eksath Peramuna coalition dominated by S. W. R. D. Bandaranaike's Sri Lanka Freedom party and the election victory in 1960 of the SLFP led by Bandaranaike's widow, Sirimavo, the emphasis on socialism and public initiative has increased substantially. E.g., *Joint Programme of the Mahajana Eksath Peramuna* (Colombo, 1956); National Planning Council, *The Ten-Year Plan* (Colombo: Planning Secretariat, 1959); and Felix R. Dias Bandaranaike, "The Democratic Middle Path to Economic Recovery," *Ceylon Today*, XI (May, 1962), 1–4, 7. Recently a cabinet minister and leading figure in the SLFP told the London Chamber of Commerce: "Economically we have abandoned the policy of *laissez faire*, which was the policy of the previous capitalist [UNP] Government—and have made to some extent the Government into the principal instrument of economic development. . . . We also realized that the socialisation of some key sectors in the economy was necessary to achieve quickly the objective of a free society." Maithripala Senanayake, "Foreign Investment," *Ceylon Today*, XII (October, 1963), 2.

Table 4. *Public Corporations in Ceylon, 1964*

Corporation	Year established[a]
I. Corporations created by statute	
Ceylon State Mortgage Bank	1931
Agricultural and Industrial Credit Corporation	1943
Central Bank of Ceylon	1949
Co-operative Wholesale Establishment	1949
Gal Oya Development Board	1949
Air Ceylon Limited	1951
Milk Board	1954
Development Finance Corporation	1955
Ceylon Transport Board[b]	1957
Ceylon State Plantations Corporation	1958
Port Cargo Corporation[b]	1958
Bank of Ceylon[b]	1961
Ceylon Petroleum Corporation[b]	1961
Insurance Corporation of Ceylon[b]	1961
People's Bank	1961
II. State industrial corporations[c]	
Ceylon Ceramics Corporation	1957[d]
Gintota Plywood Corporation	1957[d]
Leather Products Corporation	1957[d]
Ceylon Mineral Sands Corporation	1957
Kantalai Sugar Corporation	1957
National Salt Corporation	1957
Paranthan Chemicals Corporation	1957
Ceylon Oils and Fats Corporation	1958[e]
Eastern Paper Mills Corporation	1958[e]
National Small Industries Corporation	1958
National Textile Corporation	1958
Ceylon Cement Corporation	1959
Ceylon Hardboard Corporation	1959
Industrial Estates Corporation	1960
Ceylon Steel Corporation	1961
Engineering Corporation	1961
Ceylon Tyre Corporation	1962
Ceylon Fertiliser Corporation	1963
Ceylon Hardware Corporation	1963
Ceylon State Flour Milling Corporation	1964

[a] For corporations established by statute, the year of the enactment is given. For state industrial corporations, the year the corporation was authorized by ministerial order is given. In many cases, operations did not begin for a year or more after establishment.

[b] Corporation created to operate existing enterprises which were nationalized.

with the flexibility required for their efficient operation, thus freeing them from the financial and administrative regulations of Government which apply to normal departments."[141] The public corporations are under the administrative control of boards of directors, and their employees are not subject to public service regulations and wage scales and are not considered to be a part of the public service.

The government corporation is not a new device in Ceylon. However, whereas a decade ago most public corporations were financial institutions largely independent of cabinet control and intended to influence the economy indirectly through the provision of capital to private entrepreneurs or fiscal operations,[142] the last decade has seen a marked trend toward the creation of public corporations subject to close ministerial supervision in the fields of industry, commerce, and transportation. The Ceylon State Mortgage Bank, founded in 1931, and the Agricultural and Industrial Credit Corporation, founded in 1943 to provide credit for private economic development, are the oldest public corporations. In 1949, shortly after independence, the Central Bank of Ceylon was created to perform the usual central banking functions. A Development Finance Corporation under joint government and private ownership and control was incorporated in 1955 to meet capital

141. N. M. Perera, *Budget Speech, 1964–65* (Colombo: Government Press, 1964), p. 30.
142. See *Economic and Social Development of Ceylon*, p. 40.

---

c State industrial corporations are incorporated by an order of the minister of industries under provisions of the State Industrial Corporations Act, No. 49 of 1957. To the author's knowledge, no complete or authoritative list of these corporations including the dates of establishment has been published by the government. Widely scattered sources, including a variety of government reports, newspaper articles, and conversations with public servants and political officeholders, were used in compiling the list presented here. This list agrees with one included in the 1964–1965 budget speech and appears to be complete as of mid-1964, although some error as to the dates of establishment of state industrial corporations is possible.

d Corporation previously established under the Government-Sponsored Corporations Act, No. 19 of 1955, and reconstituted under the State Industrial Corporations Act, No. 49 of 1957.

e Year reorganized.

Sources: Principally, the statutes establishing the corporations; the *Ceylon Year Book* for 1948–1961; N. M. Perera, *Budget Speech, 1964–65* (Colombo: Government Press, 1964), and the Colombo newspapers. See also note c above.

needs for private industrial expansion. In 1961 the tendency for direct government provision of goods and services was reflected in the addition to the public sector of two banks serving the general public. A People's Bank was established principally for small rural savings and loans, and ownership of the Bank of Ceylon, the only private Ceylonese-owned commercial bank in operation, was assumed by the government.

The growing tendency to use the government for economic development and to rely on the public corporation can be traced more readily in the establishment of non-financial corporations. In 1949 the Co-operative Wholesale Establishment was incorporated to supply consumer goods to retail co-operative societies, an activity which was begun in 1943 by a government department. In subsequent years the Co-operative Wholesale Establishment has expanded its functions considerably in wholesale and retail trade. The Gal Oya Development Board, also formed in 1949, is a multipurpose development scheme modeled on the Tennessee Valley Authority. Air Ceylon Limited was established in 1951 to provide internal air service and contract for international flights. The Milk Board was created in 1954 to handle the supply and retail distribution of milk. In 1958 the Ceylon State Plantations Corporation was formed to develop agricultural production on public lands. It operates eight plantations and two processing plants.

Some of the largest and most important public corporations have been created to operate nationalized enterprises. Following the nationalization of private bus companies, the Ceylon Transport Board undertook operation of the island's bus services in 1958. The same year, cargo handling activities in the port of Colombo were nationalized and placed under control of a Port Cargo Corporation. Both corporations originally functioned under the direction of the minister of labor and nationalized services, a cabinet post created for the purpose;[143] responsibility for them was recently transferred to the minister of communications. These two public corporations are among the island's principal employers of non-agricultural labor. The Ceylon Trans-

143. *Sri Lanka Annual: Progress Report, 1958* (Colombo: Information Department, 1959), p. 59.

port Board employs 26,000 workers,[144] and the Port Cargo Corporation has nearly 14,000 employees.[145] Another series of nationalizations occurred in 1961. The nationalization of the Bank of Ceylon in that year was mentioned earlier. Insurance business, eventually extended to include nearly all categories, was taken over by the Insurance Corporation of Ceylon. The Ceylon Petroleum Corporation was formed to import, store, and distribute petroleum products. Originally, it compulsorily acquired about one-fourth of the distribution facilities of three British and American petroleum companies operating in Ceylon. However, after protracted disagreement with the companies and the withdrawal of American economic aid as a result of the seizure, the corporation at the beginning of 1964 took over the remaining facilities of the companies and assumed virtually complete responsibility for the importation and distribution of petroleum.[146]

The development of new industrial activity in recent years has largely been through state industrial corporations, incorporated under ministerial order authorized by the State Industrial Corporations Act.[147] A few previously existing government enterprises were reconstituted under this act, and subsequently more than a dozen others have been formed. By 1964, twenty industrial corporations had been established and a number of others were planned. Generally, these corporations are relatively small organizations, often consisting of a single shop, mill, or factory employing in most cases no more than a few hundred workers. A total of five thousand workers were employed by the state industrial corporations in 1962. However, an expansion was anticipated which would more than double the size of this labor force by 1968.[148] The state indus-

144. *Nationalised Bus Service,* Information Brochure No. 4 (Colombo: Department of Broadcasting and Information [1964]), p. 4.
145. *May Day, 1962* (Colombo: Ministry of Labour, 1962), p. 21.
146. The new government formed in 1965 by the United National party, which had previously displayed slight enthusiasm for nationalization, promised that all nationalized undertakings would remain in the hands of the state. *Ceylon Today,* XIV, 3–4 (March–April, 1965), 13.
147. No. 49 of 1957. The text of this and other acts referred to can be obtained in *The Acts of Ceylon* (Colombo: Government Press, 1948–   ) for the year of the act.
148. "Prospects for Industrialisation," *Ceylon Today,* XI (September, 1962), 1.

trial corporations are under the control of the Ministry of Industries (renamed the Ministry of Rural and Industrial Development in 1964). Since 1961 a Development Division in the ministry has undertaken planning, co-ordination, and policy supervision of these corporations.[149] If the hopes for substantial industrial development by public initiative are fulfilled, the state industrial corporations can be expected to grow considerably in number and importance in the next decade.

The public corporations involved in industrial, transport, or commercial activities are under close and direct ministerial control and appear to have little autonomy. Responsibility for the day-to-day operations of the corporations is vested in boards of directors consisting of between five and nine members. However, the responsible minister has wide discretionary powers to appoint and remove directors. In a number of cases, the statute authorizing the corporation provides for removal of directors by the minister "without assigning a reason."[150] Directors of state industrial corporations may be removed if the minister "thinks it expedient to do so."[151] The minister is empowered to issue binding directives to the board on specific as well as general policy questions,[152] and it appears that close ministerial supervision including involvement in minor administrative matters and frequent inspections of corporation activities is a common practice, particularly regarding the larger and more prominent corporations.

The recruitment, discipline, and terms of service of public corporation employees are determined by the corporation without reference to public service regulations. Commonly, the corpo-

149. See "Development Programme of Ceylon," *Ceylon Today*, XI (April, 1962), 19–28.

150. See the Motor Transport Act, No. 48 of 1957; the Milk Board Act, No. 12 of 1954; the Ceylon State Plantations Corporation Act, No. 4 of 1958; and the Port (Cargo) Corporation Act, No. 13 of 1958. The latter act adds that the minister's action in removing a director "shall not be called in question in any court."

151. State Industrial Corporations Act, No. 49 of 1957. Similar provision was made by the Co-operative Wholesale Establishment (Amendment) Act, No. 36 of 1955.

152. A typical provision is: "The Minister may, from time to time, give the Board of Directors general directions, and, after consultation with such Board, give such Board special directions, as to the exercise of the powers and the discharge of the duties of such Board, and such directions shall be carried out by such Board." State Industrial Corporations Act, No. 49 of 1957.

rations are given a blanket authorization to employ staff. For example, the Ceylon State Plantations Corporation "may employ on such terms and conditions as may be determined by the Corporation, such persons as the Corporation considers necessary for performing the work of the Corporation."[153] Workers in the nationalized enterprises, who form the vast bulk of public corporation employees, are mostly former employees of the private firms which were nationalized. The act establishing the Ceylon Transport Board provided in some detail the procedures and conditions under which former employees of the private bus companies would be absorbed into the staff of the board.[154] Nepotism or political favoritism seem to have played a significant role in recruitment to several public corporations. Public disclosure has been made of flagrant nepotism in one corporation,[155] and allegations concerning other corporations appear regularly in Parliament and the press. Defeated parliamentary candidates and party officeholders of the governing party can be identified on the boards and staffs of many corporations. A minister once announced that he would appoint only supporters of his political party to corporations under his ministry.[156]

A severe shortage of administrative and managerial talent in Ceylon has created problems of staffing at the higher levels in the public corporations. An attempt has been made to solve this problem by turning to the administrative grades of the public service. As one minister recently observed: "Lacking a strong industrial and commercial history and tradition, we must perforce rely on our public service to provide the personnel for the management of nationalized and state ventures."[157] The statutes establishing public corporations often contain provisions for the assignment of public servants to the staffs of the corporations. Although it is stated explicitly in some cases that public servants

153. *Ceylon State Plantations Corporation Act*, No. 4 of 1958.
154. *Motor Transport Act*, No. 48 of 1957. Some of the problems involved in absorbing former employees of a large number of private firms which had followed varying practices and procedures are discussed in M. Rafeek, "The Insurance Corporation of Ceylon," *Ceylon Today*, XI (September, 1962), 8–13.
155. See *Report of the Commission on the Salt Corporation* (Ceylon Sessional Paper IX, 1963), pp. 20–34, 86–88.
156. *Times of Ceylon*, November 21, 1961.
157. House, *Debates*, Vol. 43, col. 904.

accepting permanent corporation appointments "shall be deemed to have left the public service,"[158] temporary appointments (on "secondment") can be accepted without jeopardizing public service status and benefits. Public service officers serving with the corporations receive higher salaries than officers of the same rank and seniority in departmental posts. The Perera Commission contended that this pay differential created an excessive demand for such assignments and caused considerable discontent within the public service. The commission also criticized a practice of appointing officers to corporation boards in addition to their regular duties.[159] Heavy reliance on public servants appears to have continued, however. During 1962, 132 officers were released from regular public service duties for service in the corporations.[160] In 1963 and 1964 a department head was selected as chairman of the Ceylon Transport Board, a former government agent became general manager of the Insurance Corporation of Ceylon, and a former member of the Ceylon Civil Service was named chairman of the Port Cargo Corporation. In the same period, thirteen of sixteen state industrial corporations were headed by public servants or former public servants. In several instances, one public servant was serving as the head of more than one corporation.[161]

While flexibility in personnel policy has been claimed as an advantage of the public corporate device, some difficulties have resulted from the differing personnel policies of the conventional bureaucracy and the public corporations. Mention has already been made of the dissatisfaction resulting from the higher pay at the administrative levels in the corporations. Since the nationalization of harbor facilities in 1958, a merging of the Port Cargo Corporation and the Colombo Port Commission into a single administrative unit has been planned. However, a serious obstacle to the merger has resulted from the different status and condi-

158. Motor Transport Act, No. 48 of 1957; State Industrial Corporations Act, No. 49 of 1957.
159. Perera Report, Part II, pp. 23–24.
160. *Annual Report of the Public Service Commission*, 1962, p. 4.
161. See *Ceylon News*, November 14, 1963.

tions of employment of the commission's employees, who are public servants, and the corporation's employees, who are outside the public service.[162]

Despite the continued growth in number of public corporations, the performance of the corporations has been disappointing to many. In the course of the 1962 budget speech, the minister of finance spoke of the need for profits from the operation of the corporations to provide investment funds for development and added: "I regret to inform Hon. Members of the House [of] a matter I suppose which they already well know, that most public Corporations do not show profits."[163] Inexperience, inadequately trained staffs, shortages of critical skills, and poor administrative practices have all been blamed for the losses regularly suffered by many of the corporations.[164]

Recurring labor problems have constituted one of the principal sources of difficulty for public corporations. Labor disputes were cited by a Ministry of Industries report as a major cause of unsatisfactory performance by the state industrial corporations.[165] After repeated requests by trade unions, plans were announced to provide for the representation of workers on the boards of these corporations.[166] Labor unrest aggravated by trade-union rivalry has been blamed for seriously interfering with other government enterprises.[167] Particularly serious have been the strikes and disputes which periodically have disrupted the large nationalized enterprises. The Ceylon Transport Board has experienced a number of major labor disputes, and strikes in 1961 and 1963 halted bus service through much of the island. A committee inquiring into the operation of the Ceylon Transport Board recommended that or-

162. *Ibid.*, February 6, 1964.
163. Felix R. Dias Bandaranaike, *Budget Speech, 1962–1963* (Colombo: Government Press, 1962), p. 15.
164. E.g., the delays in reporting, inadequacies of record-keeping, and faulty managerial practices of the corporations are sharply condemned in *Report of the Auditor General on the Accounts of the Government of Ceylon for the Financial Year 1960–61*, Part I, Parliamentary Series No. 11, Fifth Parliament (Colombo: 1962).
165. "Prospects for Industrialisation," p. 1.
166. *Ceylon News*, April 16, 1964.
167. E.g., House, *Debates*, Vol. 48, cols. 3146–47.

ganized labor be represented on the board to alleviate the organization's severe labor problems.[168] Labor tensions and strikes have been endemic in the port of Colombo. A bitter port strike that lasted fifty-one days, ending in February, 1962, and a strike of more than two months' duration, ending in January, 1964, created considerable economic dislocation on the island and led to the use of military personnel to maintain essential port operations. The 1963–1964 strike involved union protest against the retention of public service officers in the Port Cargo Corporation.[169] The proliferation of trade unions in a single enterprise, which is characteristic of labor organization in Ceylon, extends to the public corporations. Seventeen trade unions represented Port Cargo Corporation employees in 1961.[170] Rivalry among competing trade unions in the harbor has been severe, and it has been blamed for much of the labor unrest that has plagued the port since before its nationalization.[171]

The nationalization of port facilities and transport has been followed by considerable pressure for wage increases by employees of the newly formed public corporations. In the first two years of governmental operation, five wage increases were granted Ceylon Transport Board employees, and the average monthly wage of the board rose from Rs. 2.7 million in 1958 to Rs. 4.1 million in 1961.[172] A similar but less steep rise occurred in the wage bill of the Port Cargo Corporation in its first years.[173]

The growing resort to organizations outside the customary public service has had many ramifications for public employment in Ceylon. Perhaps the most immediate and obvious effect is a rapid growth in public employment, both in absolute numbers and as a proportion of the total work force, as state initiative in produc-

168. *Report of the Committee of Inquiry into the Ceylon Transport Board* (Ceylon Sessional Paper IX, 1962), p. 20.
169. House, *Debates*, Vol. 55, cols. 233–234.
170. *May Day, 1962*, p. 21.
171. See *Report of the Commission of Inquiry on the Working of the Commercial Sector of the Port of Colombo* (Ceylon Sessional Paper II, 1957), p. 8.
172. *May Day, 1962*, p. 25. See also the testimony of the corporation's former chairman, *Ceylon Observer*, February 1, 1962.
173. See *Ceylon Daily News*, April 6, 1962.

tive activity increases. Consequently, the availability and conditions of employment in Ceylon are likely to become still more subject to political decision-making than at present. Nationalization and the creation of public industrial corporations have already complicated the relations between the government and organized labor and have increased the importance of public policy on personnel and wage questions. With the expansion of employment by public corporations, the proportion of public employees involved in activities related to economic production is growing, and the proportion occupied with the traditional law and order and service functions of the state is declining. If the present determination to use the state for economic development continues, the number of public employees involved in economic activities and the governmental attention devoted to economic matters may completely overshadow the old regulatory activities of government. This may have far-reaching consequences for public policy on the recruitment, training, and conditions of service of public employees.

The tendency for public corporations to fill administrative posts from the ranks of the public service threatens to thin the none too abundant administrative talent available to the bureaucracy, and in time it could weaken the competence and effectiveness with which the basic law and order functions of the state are performed. The availability of staff officers with administrative experience, who are attracted to the public corporations by higher pay, presumably has contributed to the lack of interest shown by the state industrial enterprises in developing recruitment and training procedures fitted to their particular needs. However, the suitability of bureaucratic officers for major posts in these organizations is subject to question. Recruits to the staff levels of the public service display a strong bias toward educational backgrounds in the arts and humanities and entrance examinations tend to stress literary skills, whereas state industrial ventures commonly require business and technical skills. Bureaucratic experience tends to emphasize the careful following of prescribed procedures hedged by many checks and reviews, practices which are desirable in activities affecting the rights and liberties of individuals but less relevant to the management of enterprises where innovation and swift decision are often necessary. With the heavy reliance placed on officers experienced in the methods of the government departments, the new organizations often seem to have absorbed the traditional practices and customs of the bureaucracy at the expense of the flexibility and adaptability they were created to achieve.

IX. Trade Unionism among Public Servants

Few characteristics of the contemporary Ceylonese bureaucracy are as prominent or noteworthy as the high level of trade unionism, including a marked readiness to engage in strikes against the government.[174] Trade-union militancy has been as pronounced among clerks and other office workers as among laborers and semi-industrial employees. The number of union-organized public servants has been increasing at a remarkable rate in recent years (see Table 5). In 1963, at least 208,456 central government employees—almost three-fourths of the entire central government bureaucracy—belonged to trade unions.

The issue of government employees' trade-union rights first arose just before independence. At the time, trade-union membership in the public service was restricted to casual laborers who were paid on a daily basis. Nonetheless, six unions representing other categories of public servants were organized and registered with the commissioner of labor.[175] Demands for full trade-union rights for public servants were major issues in two general strikes in 1946 and 1947, which involved a large number of public servants, particularly in the clerical grades. The strikes were punctuated by sporadic violence and clashes between strikers and police. A few strike leaders were dismissed from the public

174. The following discussion does not include trade unionism among employees of the public corporations, but is limited to trade unionism among members of the conventional public service.

175. *Memorandum by the Chief Secretary on Trade Unionism among Public Servants in Ceylon* (Ceylon Sessional Paper VI, 1947), p. 4.

service, and milder disciplinary action was taken against many of the strikers.[176]

Table 5. *Central Government Employees Belonging to Trade Unions*[a]

Year	Number of employees
1952	41,510
1953	48,841
1954	51,943
1955	57,360
1956	48,242
1957	79,994
1958	76,953
1959	115,291
1960	144,379
1961	158,579
1962	193,292
1963	208,456

[a] Does not include membership of unions failing to submit a compulsory annual report to the commissioner of labor.

Source: *Administration Report of the Commissioner of Labour* for 1952 through 1962–1963 (Colombo: Government Press, 1953–1964).

Following the strikes, in 1948 the law relating to trade unions was amended to allow organization of public servants—with some restrictions. The principal restrictions were provisions that public service trade unions (1) must be limited to public servants in a single department or service, or to a single category of public servants; (2) must not affiliate or federate with other trade unions either of public servants or of workers outside the public service; (3) must not have any political objectives or maintain a political fund; and (4) must not engage in any strike for political objectives or in support of any labor dispute outside the public service.[177] After the passage of this act, the trade-union movement

176. See *First and Second Interim Reports of the Strike Committee* (Ceylon Sessional Paper XIV, 1947); V. Sarvaloganayagam, "Trade Unionism in Ceylon," *Ceylon Today*, VII (June, 1958), 16–17.
177. Trade Unions (Amendment) Act, No. 15 of 1948.

among public servants grew rapidly in size and importance. A further impetus to trade-union organization was provided by the 1956 election. The victorious Mahajana Eksath Peramuna coalition had promised full trade-union rights for public servants and the repeal of "undemocratic" public service regulations and limitations on association.[178] The inauguration of a government sympathetic to trade unionism encouraged organization of both public and private employees.[179] Public servants who had been dismissed for leading the 1946–1947 general strikes were reinstated and in some cases later offered compensation for their dismissal.[180]

As is common throughout the labor movement in Ceylon, public service trade unionism is marked by a proliferation of unions. In 1963, 622 public servants' trade unions were registered with the commissioner of labor.[181] Often, a very large number of trade unions attempt to represent the same body of employees. In addition, many organizations recruit members from a single restricted category of public servants. The fragmentation of trade unionism within the public service is probably encouraged by the legal requirement that a union be limited to one department or service, or to one category of employees. A change in government policy toward public service trade unions in 1958 contributed to an abrupt rise in the number of unions in existence. Previously, a trade union had been required to include within its membership at least 40 per cent of eligible public servants to obtain Treasury recognition, which was necessary for the organization's representatives to speak for its members before official bodies. In 1958

178. *Joint Programme of the Mahajana Eksath Peramuna,* pp. 4–5.
179. A recent government publication claimed: "Until the victory of the late Mr. S. W. R. D. Bandaranaike, the aspirations of the working class to emancipate itself from exploitation and servitude had been thwarted, and workers and trade unions were regarded as a nuisance. . . . The two Bandaranaike Governments have since 1956 given workers and their unions an honoured place in Society and have taken several steps to protect their interests and improve their conditions." As evidence, the publication cited the growth of trade-union strength from 352 unions with 262,249 members in 1956 to 973 unions with 789,349 members in 1961. *Labour Policy Since 1956,* Information Brochure No. 3 (Colombo: Department of Broadcasting and Information [1964]), p. 1.
180. Leslie Goonewardene, *A Short History of the Lanka Sama Samaja Party* (Colombo, 1960), p. 56; *Ceylon Observer,* October 20 and November 27, 1961.
181. *Administration Report of the Commissioner of Labour for 1962–63,* p. 150. Registration of trade unions is compulsory in Ceylon.

the requirement of Treasury recognition was abolished and any organization which was registered as a trade union, regardless of size, became eligible to represent its members.[182] The number of public servants' trade unions climbed from 182 in 1955 to 479 in 1959.[183] The impact of social cleavages is also a likely cause of the proliferation of unions. Strong consciousness of status has made difficult the development of a sense of identity and solidarity between workers at different levels—as between minor employees and clerks—resulting in the appearance of separate organizations to represent each level of employees. Furthermore, within any one level workers tend to divide on caste or communal lines, and often duplicating organizations appear which obtain their members from particular caste or communal groups among a single category of workers. The result is a large number of very small unions.

Apparently the largest and probably the best organized of the public service unions is the Government Clerical Service Union with a claimed membership of more than 8,500 in 1961. Among other major unions are the Government Health Service Workers Union with more than 7,600, the Government Minor Employees Union with nearly 6,000, and the Land Development Department Workers Union with 5,100 claimed members in 1961.[184] Although there is an explicit statutory prohibition against federation of public service trade unions, two large and powerful federations exist and smaller ones occasionally appear. The Public Service Workers Trade Union Federation is reputed to include affiliated organizations with a total membership of 100,000 public servants. The other major federation is the Government Workers Trade Union Federation allied with the Lanka Sama Samaja party.[185]

182. Perera Report, Part II, p. 103; *Administration Report of the Commissioner of Labour for 1958*, p. 181.

183. *Ceylon Year Book, 1960* (Colombo: Department of Census and Statistics, 1961), p. 172.

184. Figures on union membership are from United States Department of Labor, *Directory of Labor Organizations: Asia and Australasia* (rev. ed.; Washington, D. C.: GPO, March, 1963), Vol. I, chap. x.

185. Both federations are cited in *ibid.* as claiming a 1961 membership of 100,000. While neither claim is necessarily accurate and exact membership is usually difficult to determine, as dues payment is often irregular and seldom rigorously enforced in Ceylon, the PSWTUF is commonly credited with a considerably larger membership than the GWTUF.

The federations are not officially recognized, but in practice they are allowed to appear before official bodies and present their members' claims.[186] In deference to the restrictions on political objectives and federation with unions of non-government workers, the public service unions sympathetic to the LSSP are not included in the federation of non-government workers affiliated with the party; instead, they are grouped in the GWTUF without formal ties to the party. However, the unofficial connection of the GWTUF with the LSSP is common knowledge.

More significant than the growth of trade unionism or the multiplicity of trade-union organizations within the bureaucracy is the absence of restraints on strikes by public servants. As the Perera Commission remarked, strikes are neither illegal nor considered a breach of discipline, and indeed "public servants who have resorted to strike action have demanded and even received pay for the days on which they were on strike."[187] The 1948 statute allowing the organizing of public servants forbade only strikes "wholly or partly for the purpose of influencing or overawing the Government on any political issue not affecting public servants in their capacity as such, or wholly or mainly for the purpose of supporting workmen, other than public servants, in any strike or trade dispute."[188] Except under emergency regulations,[189] strikes by public servants over wage demands or workers' grievances are not prohibited by law and have not led to administrative disciplinary action. Such strikes have occurred repeatedly in many different sectors of the public service. More remarkable are a number of strikes by public servants, including some of the largest and most disruptive labor disputes on the island, for political and other purposes unrelated to the bureaucracy. Government employees in large numbers participated in a violent hartal in 1953, protesting a cabinet decision to increase the

186. Perera Report, Part II, p. 103. Both major federations were listed among the groups presenting evidence to the Perera Commission.
187. *Ibid.*, Part II, p. 104.
188. Trade Unions (Amendment) Act, No. 15 of 1948.
189. Under the Public Security (Amendment) Act, No. 8 of 1959, the government can designate "essential industries" within which strikes are illegal during a declared state of emergency.

price of subsidized rice.[190] In 1959, public servants joined in an avowedly political strike as a demonstration against a measure which was being debated in Parliament.[191] The major public service trade unions and federations took part in a general strike in January, 1962, which was intended to force the government to withdraw troops from the strike-bound Colombo harbor.[192] Although these strikes appeared to be in contravention of the statutory prohibition against strikes with political objectives or in support of strikers outside the public service, no disciplinary action has been taken against the public servants or trade unions involved.

The frequency and seriousness of labor disputes in the public service is with little question related to the economic problems, social and political tensions, and general unsettled conditions of the island in recent years. Labor disputes outside the public service have become increasingly serious in the same period. The tendency for public service trade unions to resort to strikes and demonstrations may be in part a product of the highly politicized character of the trade-union movement in Ceylon.[193] The lack of effective machinery for settling disputes has been blamed for the frequency with which dissatisfactions culminate in work stoppages. Attempts have been made to establish machinery for resolving disputes on the model of British Whitley Councils, but they have not proved to be successful.[194] Public servants' trade unions have frequently demanded representation on departmental promotion and transfer boards, and the cabinet recently agreed to the demand in respect to transfer boards.[195] The Perera Commission took the position that "in an institution like the Public Service, which has obligations to the community at large . . . the ethics and traditions of the service should be

---

190. See Wriggins, *op. cit.*, p. 134; Goonewardene, *op. cit.*, pp. 42–46.
191. Goonewardene, *op. cit.*, p. 60.
192. See *Ceylon Observer*, January 5, 1962.
193. This was cited as a cause of labor troubles in the public service by a former minister of finance. See Felix R. Dias Bandaranaike, *Budget Speech, 1960–1961* (Colombo: Information Department, 1960), p. 20. More pointed observations were made by an earlier minister of finance, in House, *Debates*, Vol. 31, col. 1161.
194. Perera Report, Part II, pp. 105, 108–109.
195. E.g., *Ceylon News*, August 22, 1963, and January 9, 1964.

sufficient to prevent officers from even asserting the right to strike."[196] The public service in recent years has been subjected to tensions arising from social conflict and political instability and the pressure of a steadily rising cost of living. It has also undergone a period of great expansion and has suffered the confusion and dislocation accompanying the change in the official language and other reforms. Given the stresses of the external environment and internal problems, it is perhaps not surprising that tradition and ethics of the service have been insufficient to prevent militant trade-union action, including strikes, to win the demands of public servants.[197]

Closely associated with discussions of trade-union rights has been the question of political rights of public servants. Present regulations prohibit membership in a political organization or an organization associated with a political party, dissemination of political propaganda or participation in a political meeting, activity in support of a candidate for parliamentary or local government office, and candidacy for elective office.[198] Public service trade unions have agitated insistently for the removal of restrictions on the political activity of public servants. The Perera Commission recommended against extending the political rights of government employees, including industrial workers in the public service, arguing that Ceylon lacked the political maturity that made possible the granting of political rights to certain categories of public servants in Great Britain.[199] The demand for full political rights for public servants has received the enthusiastic backing of the Marxist parties, including the Lanka Sama Samaja party,[200] and recently other parties have acceded to the demand. The Sri Lanka Freedom party government had shown no

196. Perera Report, Part II, p. 104.
197. The role of trade-union activity and strikes in expressing public service discontents in Ceylon appears to be comparable to the role of writ petitions and appeals for judicial intervention in Pakistan. See Ralph Braibanti, "Public Bureaucracy and Judiciary in Pakistan," in Joseph LaPalombara (ed.), *Bureaucracy and Political Development* (Princeton, N. J., 1963), pp. 360–440.
198. Perera Report, Part II, p. 105.
199. *Ibid.*, Part II, p. 107.
200. E.g., *Election Manifesto of the Lanka Sama Samaja Party*, p. 4; Lanka Sama Samaja Party, "May Day 1962 Resolutions," mimeographed (Colombo, 1962), p. 2.

inclination to remove restrictions on public servants' political activity until it joined the LSSP in a coalition government. The coalition was preparing to ease the restrictions at the time of the 1965 election. Although the coalition fell from power, the government formed after the election promised to extend political rights to some categories of public servants.[201]

X. Conclusion

Independent Ceylon inherited from its colonial past a modern, well-trained, and competent bureaucracy. Like most states emerging from colonial rule, the administrative structure of government in Ceylon was developed, experienced, and confident, while political parties, politicians, and legislatures functioned with much less self-assurance and carefully cultivated expertness. Disregarding the largely indirect rule of the Portuguese and Dutch for three centuries, the bureaucracy had behind it nearly 150 years of experience at the time of independence. Whether the development of modern and relatively sophisticated political activity is dated from the founding of the United National party in 1946, or from the formation of the Lanka Sama Samaja party in 1935, or, with less justification, from the organization of the Ceylon National Congress in 1919, the development of a system of politics was far behind the development of the administrative system at independence. Although after the 1931–1947 Donoughmore period Ceylon reached independence with more experience in self-government and political decision-making than most colonial areas, it was not until the language and religious ferment of the 1950's stirred the Sinhalese villager that political awareness seeped down to the broad masses of Ceylonese society.

The period of political development and change which has followed independence has had a considerable impact on the bureaucracy. Many features of the bureaucracy have been attacked as relics of colonialism. The elite position of the bureauc-

201. *Ceylon Today*, XIV, 3–4 (March–April, 1965), 10.

racy in the society and elitism within the bureaucracy have been weakened by reforms and altered attitudes. Public servants, particularly the upper levels of English-speaking, university-educated staff officers, have come under severe criticism. It has become commonplace to hear denunciations such as that of a former prime minister, who spoke of "the Treasury officials who form the last bastion of reactionary bureaucracy,"[202] or the accusation by an M.P. that the public service is "disloyal, inefficient, unenterprising and lethargic."[203] The middle and lower levels, too, appear to have experienced a sense of frustration and futility as they have been exposed to economic stresses, a steep rise in political interference within the bureaucracy, and the political and communal tensions which have appeared. The journal of the Government Clerical Service Union responded to a government appeal by retorting: "We are asked to sacrifice. We ask frankly, 'What for?' "[204] The values, sense of duty, and certainty of status and position which helped to steady the bureaucracy under colonial tutelage have become uncertain in the present political environment.

As the public service has adjusted to independence and to the frequently chaotic and bewildering politics of the past decade, signs have begun to appear of a decline in the standards of integrity, effectiveness, and discipline which generally typified the colonial public service. The perceptive Perera Commission observed in 1961:

We also have some evidence to support the feeling that there has been a general deterioration in the output and efficiency of the Public Service, and that public servants today, like others, are more concerned with obtaining for themselves maximum benefits and privileges, while giving as little as possible in return. Absenteeism and unpunctuality, lack of interest, and indifference toward work, coupled with an excessive sense of self interest and self importance, inevitably affect the usefulness of a public servant to the general detriment of the community at large.[205]

202. Wijayananda Dahanayake, in House, *Debates*, Vol. 48, cols. 390–391.
203. *Ceylon Observer*, November 5, 1961.
204. Quoted in *ibid.*, October 7, 1961.
205. Perera Report, Part II, p. 100.

The deterioration, if indeed a deterioration has set in, has not yet destroyed the potential usefulness of the public service as an instrument of social purpose. The public service still contains a remarkable proportion of the talent, skill, and inspiration on the island. In the chaos of the 1958 communal riots, many public servants conducted themselves with considerable credit and in a few cases responded with acts of heroism.[206] A transformation of roles from that of a law-and-order bureaucracy to an engine of social and economic change is being demanded of the public service. At the same time the bureaucracy is required to navigate the difficult passage from a colonial administration standing above the people and acting in their interest to a publicly controlled administration responding to popular aspirations. The transition is bound to be difficult and involve some cost. The question is whether the sense of distant and impersonal guardianship can be replaced by a sense of identification with the people and responsiveness to their desires without sacrificing the qualities of duty, integrity, efficiency, and impartiality which were a part of the heritage of the public service.

206. See Tarzie Vittachi, *Emergency '58* (London, 1958).

9

Bureaucratic Development in Malaya*

Robert O. Tilman

Prior to World War II the Malayan Peninsula was a heterogeneous association of seven separate, but in varying degrees interrelated, political and administrative systems. British control over the affairs of Malaya radiated inland from three peripheral settlements—Penang, Singapore, and Malacca—which after 1826 were collectively known as the Straits Settlements.[1] Politically, Britain's first formal inroads into the Malay Peninsula were made in the tin-rich but strife-ridden state of Perak by the Treaty of

---

* Material in this essay has been derived in part from the author's *Bureaucratic Transition in Malaya* (Durham, N. C., 1964). Due to the difference in focus, such material has sometimes been summarized, sometimes elaborated, and occasionally utilized almost verbatim. Although Malaya is now the major part of the larger Federation of Malaysia, the term Malaya is used in the title and throughout this chapter, since it refers to the period before 1963. For the period prior to independence in 1957, the term may sometimes include the island of Singapore, a Crown Colony administered separately after 1946. For the period after 1957, the term includes only the eleven states on the peninsula, including the island of Penang. Malaysia was formed in 1963 by the union of Singapore, Sabah (North Borneo), Sarawak, and the old Federation of Malaya. In matters of bureaucracy, the old Federation on the peninsula remains the most important entity and provides the bureaucratic model for all of Malaysia.

1. On the complicated maneuvering that preceded the incorporation of the settlements into an administrative unit, which was motivated primarily by economic considerations, see *Straits Settlements Records*, Vol. B1, *Penang: Letters to London, 1805–1806*, letter dated November 12 (possibly 19), 1805, paras. 11–13, pp. 5–6; *ibid.*, Vol. A3, *Penang: Consultations, 1807*, council meeting of November 17, 1807, pp. 23–24; *ibid.*, council minute of November 20, 1807, p. 36; *ibid.*, Vol. H11, *Penang: Letters and Orders in Council, 1824*, letter from Fort William dated October 14, 1824, pp. 591–660; *ibid.*, Vol. C2, *Penang: Letters from London, 1815–1816*, dated February 7, 1816, pp. 354–358, 386–387; *ibid.*, letter dated February 7, 1816; *ibid.*, Vol. A26, *Penang Consultations, 1826*, council meeting of July 31, 1826, pp. 968–970; *ibid.*, Vol. I28, *Penang: Miscellaneous Letters (Out), 1825–26*, p. 33. Citations to the *Straits Settlements Records* (hereinafter cited as SSR) are made to the cataloguing system and pagination employed by the National Archives, Singapore.

Pangkor of 1874. Although the residency system, which was introduced by this treaty, had an inauspicious beginning when the first resident to Perak was murdered, Britain had begun what was to be a continuing move into the interior, and only once was it necessary to call upon military force against the established government to achieve this penetration.[2] One by one, residents (termed advisers in five of the states) were accepted by each of the nine native states of the Peninsula, the last being Johore, which agreed in 1914 to receive a British officer.

British control was most apparent and most direct in the Straits Settlements, which prior to 1867 was ruled as an appendage of India, at times subordinate to the Bengal Presidency but during the period 1805–1830 itself a Presidency equal in administrative status to the other Indian Presidencies.[3] In 1867, primarily at the insistence of commercial interests in Singapore, administration of

2. The single military expedition was occasioned by the death of Perak's first resident, J. W. W. Birch, who was probably one of the most inappropriate choices for the post. The attitude characteristic of Birch, who came from the Ceylon service to become the colonial secretary of the Straits Settlements, can best be summarized in his own words: "It concerns us little what were the old customs of the country nor do I think they are worthy of our consideration." Quoted in G. P. Dartford, *A Short History of Malaya* (London, 1957), p. 131. The second resident, probably more suitable but still not the ideal choice, fortunately resigned almost immediately to return to his Singapore law practice, thus avoiding further incidents. The third appointee, Sir Hugh Low, who inherited a task by then doubly difficult, was one of the most competent colonial servants ever sent to Malaya.

3. From the beginning there was considerable optimism about the economic worth of Penang and, later, of Malacca and Singapore. It is ironic that the company, discovering that its faith in the value of Penang had been ill-founded, exhibited considerable restraint in welcoming the addition of Singapore to the list of possessions. Until Singapore emerged as an entrepôt center in the mid-nineteenth century, the Straits Settlements was a constant drain on the company's treasury. On the economic plight of each of the Straits Settlements, see the material cited above, n. 1. Thomas S. (later Sir Stamford) Raffles is remembered as the founder of Singapore in 1819, but it is seldom mentioned that he was also the person singularly most responsible for rescuing Malacca from destruction. Raffles, then secretary to government at Penang, was at sea for his health in 1807, when, calling at Malacca, he was appalled to find that the British officer-in-charge was destroying the facilities of the city on instructions from Penang for fear that when returned to Dutch hands the port would provide serious competition for Penang. In a lengthy dispatch to Lord Minto, the Governor General of India, he set out in detail the advantages of retaining Malacca intact. The Governor General, recognizing the ability of the author as well as the worth of the argument, ordered that the destruction cease, and, while the settlement reverted temporarily to the Dutch in 1818, it was returned to Britain by the Anglo-Dutch Treaty of 1824. See SSR, Vol. A3, *Penang: Consultations, 1807,* council meetings of November 17, 1807, and November 20, 1807; and *ibid.,* Vol. H11, *Penang: Letters and Orders in Council, 1824,* letter dated October 14, 1824, from Fort William.

the Straits Settlements was transferred from the India Office to the Colonial Office, thus placing it in the hands of the Crown directly and severing the tie to the subcontinent that had lasted for almost three-quarters of a century.[4]

While British direction in the Federated Malay States (FMS) may have been somewhat less apparent, it was certainly no less real.[5] British residents in each of the four states were responsible to a resident general[6] at Kuala Lumpur, who was in turn responsible to the governor of the Straits Settlements in his concomitant role of high commissioner of the FMS. The terms of federation theoretically vested sovereignty in the hands of the native rulers, and after the creation of a Federal Council in 1909 supreme authority resided legally in the Rulers-in-Council. In fact, however, the centripetal movement of political power was focused on British officials in Kuala Lumpur, except for brief periods of attempted decentralization. The Unfederated Malay States, or UMS[7], were subjected to varying degrees of British direction, though compared with the Straits Settlements and the FMS, all five were less affected by the direct participation of European officers in the affairs of government.

I. The Historical Roots of Malayan Bureaucracy

The term "civil service" was apparently first used by the English East India Company to distinguish its non-military

4. On the agitation of the merchants for the administrative transfer, see Great Britain, *Sessional Papers, 1862*, XL, 583, 594–595. For a discussion of the actual act, see *ibid., 1866*, V, 327–330.

5. In 1895 the states of Pahang, Perak, Selangor, and Negri Sembilan united to create the Federated Malay States (FMS). The official exchange of letters leading to federation has been retained in the now very scarce publication, Federated Malay States, *Correspondence Respecting the Federation of the Protected Malay States* (Taiping, Perak, 1896). The actual treaty is also reproduced in this document (p. 9). In terms of practical politics there was less difference between the FMS and the UMS than the use of the two terms might suggest. Sir George Maxwell in fact wrote only half jestingly of "the act of federation" and "the act of unfederation." (Later correspondence of Sir George Maxwell, British Association of Malaya, London.)

6. The title and the duties changed several times throughout the period. The office was in turn resident general, chief secretary, federal secretary, and, for the second time, chief secretary.

7. Perlis, Kedah, Kelantan, Trengganu, and Johore.

civilians from those of the military, maritime, and ecclesiastical establishments.[8] The term seems to have been well-established by 1765 and is employed in the Charter Act of 1793. Within this general category of civil servants the company made a further distinction between the "covenanted" and the "uncovenanted." The term "covenanted" indicated that the servant had posted a bond of £500 and had signed an oath promising to execute the duties of his post honestly and faithfully; it was the covenanted posts that were financially the most rewarding and thus the most sought after. Uncovenanted posts were usually filled by Europeans who had originally gone to the possessions for reasons other than company business and were thereafter recruited locally.

Unlike the other Presidencies of India, covenanted civil servants sent to the Eastern Presidency were not members of an Eastern civil service. The Charter Act of 1793, by restricting promotions to servants located in the Presidency where the vacancy occurred, practically trifurcated the company Civil Service into a Bengal service, a Madras service, and a Bombay service. Most civil officers serving in the Straits Settlements were attached to the Bengal civil service, and military officers were usually drawn from the Madras establishment.[9] There was the suggestion on several occasions that the company should turn toward China as a source of civil servants, but no serious effort was ever made to carry out this idea.[10]

8. Sir Edward Blunt, *The I.C.S.: The Indian Civil Service* (London, 1937), pp. 1–2. See also, Tinker's chapter (Chapter 2) in this volume, p. 26, n. 5.

9. Memorandum from the Governor General of India in council to Lord Stanley, dated November 7, 1859, in Great Britain, House of Lords, *Parliamentary Papers, 1862*, XL (1862), 592.

10. Colonel Orfeur Cavenagh, governor of the Straits Settlements in 1860, recommended this change and the suggestions received a favorable reply from the Government of India, with the stipulation added by Bengal that the scheme must not involve any additional expenditure of funds. See *SSR*, Vol. S28, *Governor, Letters from India, 1860*, dated December 21, 1860, p. 264. As a result of this final condition, the governor of the Straits Settlements confessed that he was "not very sanguine as to the result" of his request for servants to quit Hong Kong voluntarily for service in the Straits Settlements. As the governor pointed out, unless the positions could be made considerably more attractive so as to compete with opportunities in Hong Kong, it seemed unlikely that any servant would transfer, and to increase the attractiveness of the posts would undoubtedly involve additional expenses. See *SSR*, Vol. R38, *Governor's Letters to Bengal, 1860–1861*, dated January 19, 1861, pp. 201–204. It appears that Cavenagh was correct in this assumption, for nothing more was heard of the plan after this date.

At first, selection of potential civil servants for the East India Company service was exclusively by patronage to all ranks. However, by the provisions of the Charter Act of 1793, the recruitment to higher positions through the patronage of members of the Court of Directors was proscribed, but the practice was permitted to continue in the selection of young men for the lowest covenanted grades.[11] The company took considerable precautions to eliminate the most blatant forms of corruption in the recruitment of young civil servants, but questionable practices were not eliminated completely until late in the history of the company.

Wages of civil servants, both in India and in the Straits Settlements, were considerably below the responsibilities of the posts. Initially, the East India Company had encouraged private trading on the part of company servants as a means of supplementing their meager income; however, it soon became apparent that this practice caused a greater loss in revenues than the amount saved. The company then reversed its policies and proscribed all private trading, but the proscription was ineffective since it had to be enforced through senior servants located almost half-way around the world—servants who stood to lose the most through complete enforcement of the company's edicts. Company servants in the Straits area, however, were not so fortunate as their Indian colleagues. Although they were removed a considerably greater distance from London and thus the possibility of private trading might have been greater, they suffered the misfortune of an assignment to an area that at the time produced far less of value to Europe than did the subcontinent of India.

In matters of retirement from the service of the company, as in salaries, the position of servants in Malaya was considerably inferior to that of their Indian colleagues. By 1826 Penang was the only Presidency not participating in some form of an annuity

11. The company took considerable precautions to eliminate the most blatant forms of improper transactions between the appointee and his patron, and the most frequent method of controlling this was the questionnaire and affidavit required of all young covenanted servants before they were permitted to assume their duties. Briefly, it required the applicant to state under oath and bond that to his knowledge no person could be expected to receive monetary gain by his appointment to the company service.

fund from which pensions could be paid after retirement from company service. An annuity plan apparently was considered at the time of the elevation of Penang to the status of a Presidency, and at various times there was the suggestion that the island should unite with Bengal to establish such a fund; however, neither of these developed, and Penang was left the only establishment without retirement provisions.[12]

Home leave in England was provided by the company for servants after 1826, though under the provisions of the scheme it was unlikely that a company officer serving in the Straits Settlements could expect to enjoy this privilege more than once during his career of service. A covenanted civil servant with more than ten years' service could return to England for three years at a salary of £400 per annum, but the granting of this leave was surrounded by numerous qualifications. Only one servant could leave the Presidency each year, and no more than a maximum of three officers could be absent from the Settlements at any one time. Preference for leave went to those who were forced to return to Europe for reasons of health, but if there were none in possession of these medical certificates, preference was then based on length of service in the Straits area. If a civil servant with service of less than ten years found it necessary to return to England to restore his health, he was permitted to do so (but under the restrictions regarding the number of absences from Penang mentioned above) on the reduced salary of £200 a year for a period not to exceed three years. Moreover, a servant who had once taken advantage of this provision was not eligible later for the regular home leave unless he could again secure a medical certificate, and on this second leave the company servant would be permitted to draw a salary equivalent only to the difference between the amount already received on the first leave and the usual annual salary (£400) multiplied by the maximum length of leave permitted (three years). Although by comparison with the home-leave regulations later adopted by the British government these provisions may not appear unduly liberal, the plan did

12. SSR, Vol. A26, council meeting of June 29, 1826, p. 682.

indeed represent a marked departure from the company's earlier attitude toward its civil servants and may be considered the predecessor of the leave regulations of the present-day Malaysian public services.

In recruitment of civil servants to the Straits Settlements, patronage played a major, though diminishing, role under the administration of the East India Company, and to a lesser extent the practice continued during the decade of direct control by the India Office (1858–1867). In the seven years following the administrative transfer of 1867, several appointments to "Straits Cadetships" were made by the secretary of state for the colonies, and in these appointments it is probable that an increasing emphasis was placed on securing youths most competent to fill these posts.[13] However, it was not until 1869 that a system of competitive examinations for potential cadets was introduced into the service of the Straits Settlements. Even this plan did not follow the open competition of the ICS, for following the schemes of Ceylon (after 1855) and Hong Kong (after 1861) examinations were not thrown open to all applicants. The privilege of sitting for these examinations was limited to those applicants nominated by the secretary of state for the colonies.[14] This system of prior selection of candidates for the prescribed examination continued until 1882 when the Colonial Office, following the existing practice of the ICS, opened the competitive entrance examination to all qualified applicants. Although the procedures of recruitment were similar after 1882, the content of the examinations and the conditions of employment differed between the Eastern Cadetships (Ceylon, the Straits Settlements, and Hong Kong), on the one hand, and the Indian Civil Service and Home Civil Service, on the other. It was not until 1896 that the syllabi of

13. This is the position taken in Tan Kok Fong, "The Development of the Straits Settlements Civil Service, 1867–1896" (unpublished B.A. Honours thesis, University of Malaya, Singapore, 1957), pp. 13 ff.

14. Except where otherwise noted, this section dealing with the development of the services from 1867 to 1919 derives chiefly from Straits Settlements and Federated Malay States, Commission Appointed by His Excellency the Governor of the Straits Settlements and the High Commissioner of the Federated Malay States (Sir John A. S. Bucknill, chairman), *Report* (London, 1919). Hereinafter cited as Bucknill Report.

examination and the terms of recruitment were standardized for the three major branches of the civil services: the Indian Civil Service, the Home Civil Service, and the Eastern Service (which after 1896 also included the services of the Federated Malay States).

According to the scheme of open competition adopted after 1896, which was administered by the Civil Service commissioners in London, applicants were judged on total marks achieved in various fields of examination, and successful applicants were given their choices of services on the basis of first choice to those most successful in the examinations. Commenting on the system as it was operating in 1919, the Bucknill Commission Report[15] stated that among those applicants for whom a choice was possible, youths with adequate private financial resources as a rule elected to join the Home Service. If without private income, those with the privilege of choosing usually selected the more profitable Indian Civil Service, while the Eastern Service was generally left to those so low on the examination lists as to be without a choice. Moreover, according to the Bucknill Report: "as between Malaya, Hong Kong and Ceylon it is a striking commentary on the unpopularity of the service of the first named that those who have any choice almost invariably choose Ceylon first, Hong Kong next and Malaya last."[16]

When the Eastern Cadetships were instituted, it was anticipated that there would be considerable interchange of officers between the areas; however, as the English East India Company had found a half-century earlier, the great variations between the needs of the three areas, the varieties of languages spoken, the inconsistent classification of posts, and the highly dissimilar salaries made such projected homogeneity unrealistic. While several transfers between areas were made, the association was more nominal than real; by 1919, though continuing in theory, unification of the three areas within the Eastern Service had ceased in practice. However, the fiction of a unified Eastern Service continued until the service was absorbed into the greater

15. *Ibid.*, p. 35.
16. *Ibid.*

but almost equally fictitious entity, the Colonial Administrative Service.

Created in 1932, the Colonial Administrative Service attempted to play a unifying role, and as such this reorganization was part of a much more general unification program intended to combine all similar services—administrative, technical, and professional—throughout the colonies. This amalgamation of the many diverse services grew out of the report of the Warren Fisher Committee of 1930,[17] the provisions of which were introduced in stages beginning in 1932 by the secretary of state for the colonies after approval in principle by the Colonial Office conference in June, 1830.[18] The Colonial Administrative Service was the first unified service, followed by the Colonial Legal Service (1933), Colonial Medical Service (1934), Colonial Agricultural Service, Colonial Veterinary Service, and Colonial Forest Service (1935), Colonial Police Service (1937), Colonial Survey Service, Colonial Mines Service, Colonial Geological Survey Service, and Colonial Postal Service (1938), Colonial Engineering Service (1945), and Colonial Civil Aviation Service (1947).[19]

All of these services combined to form what is loosely termed the "Colonial Service," but to define Colonial Service presents a difficult undertaking. Although, in theory, all officers of the Colonial Service were liable to transfer among the various colonies, in practice transfer was infrequent since languages, salaries, and conditions of service varied greatly throughout the colonial empire. Moreover, even methods of recruitment varied considerably. Although administrative officers (personnel known after 1932 as officers of the Colonial Administrative Service) had been recruited throughout by the Colonial Office, technical (and some professional) personnel were usually recruited by the

17. See Great Britain, *Sessional Papers, 1929–30*, Vol. VIII, Cmd. 3629, "Report of a Committee on the System of Appointment in the Colonial Office and the Colonial Services." Hereinafter cited as Warren Fisher Report.

18. *Ibid.*, Vol. IX, Cmd. 3628, "Summary of Proceedings of the Colonial Office Conference, 1930;" and *ibid.*, Cmd. 3629, "Appendices to the Summary of Proceedings."

19. For a sanguine account of unification by a member of the Colonial Office, and later deputy under-secretary of state for the colonies, see Sir Charles Jeffries, *The Colonial Empire and Its Civil Service* (Cambridge, 1938), chaps. v–vii.

individual colonies or protected states through the Crown agents for the colonies, a centralized organization located in London. For personnel recruited through the Crown agents, salaries, responsibilities, and conditions of service varied so greatly that "unification" was even less meaningful than it was for officers of the Colonial Administrative Service, and for administrative officers it meant very little.

When the Warren Fisher Committee recommended the unification of the colonial administrative services in 1930, members recognized that one of the major obstacles was the varying and inconsistent methods of recruitment. From 1869 onward the Eastern Service had based recruitment on a prescribed examination, and after 1896 this examination had been standardized for the three major services (the Home, Indian, and Eastern). Although the services of the other colonies did not require an examination as part of the recruitment procedure, the Warren Fisher Report argued that the two methods of recruitment could stand side-by-side in a unified service, for the committee could not recommend the abolition of the examination for the Eastern Cadetships:

There is nothing in the experience of appointments under this system to the Eastern Cadet Services which would justify us in recommending that the present system of appointment by competitive examination under the control of the Civil Service Commissioners should not be maintained for those branches of the Service to which it at present applies.[20]

However, the examination system that was suited to the needs of the Eastern Service could not satisfy the demands of the African colonies:

For a variety of reasons we find ourselves unable to recommend the system of open competitive written examination. . . . So far as the African Administrative Services are concerned, we are satisfied that it would be inexpedient, at any rate under existing conditions, to rely on the test of written examination.[21]

20. Warren Fisher Report, p. 12.
21. *Ibid.*, p. 20.

When the recommendations of the Warren Fisher Committee were submitted to a special subcommittee of the Colonial Office conference, the principle of unification of the administrative services was accepted; but the committee could not agree that some officers should enter through the medium of competitive examination while others should be recruited solely by selection.

In our view this state of affairs must, so long as it persists, retard the realization of the full benefits of unification. We are aware of no sound reason why uniform method of entry should not be prescribed for the "Colonial Administrative Service;" and we tentatively suggest that the lines on which the future method should be based might be . . . provisional selection followed by a University course with serious and stringent qualifying examinations at the end, the results of which would determine seniority in the unified service. In any case we deprecate any extension of the system of entrance by examination without selection.[22]

The recommendations of this committee were accepted by the Colonial Office in 1932 in regard to the administrative services, and the Eastern Service was severed from its last tie with the Indian Civil Service when the competitive recruitment examination was abolished. Examinations were never re-established, and recruitment procedures of today are similar to those established for the unified Colonial Administrative Service almost three decades ago.[23]

In 1954, in recognition of the changing political status of dependencies and former dependencies, the title Colonial Service was dropped. Thereafter, the various unified services, which by 1954 numbered twenty, were grouped together into an amorphous body labeled Her Majesty's Overseas Civil Service. Although the number of such officers serving in Malaysia today has

22. Cmd. 3628, pp. 87–88.
23. There is one major exception to this generalization. Although for a time the examination conducted at the close of the colonial administrative course at Oxford and Cambridge served much the same purpose as the entrance examination, this practice was disrupted by World War II, and at the present time there is neither a competitive recruitment examination nor a rigid post-entry administrative course. Only the routine confirmation examination remains as a reminder of the system established in 1869. For an excellent and engaging analysis of recruitment to the Colonial Administrative Service during the period between world wars, see Robert Heussler, *Yesterday's Rulers: The Making of the British Colonial Service* (Syracuse, N. Y., 1963).

been considerably diminished, the present-day bureaucracy of the Federation is a direct outgrowth of the British experience in the Peninsula, the roots of which can be traced to the Civil Service of the English East India Company.

II. The Formal Bureaucratic Legacy

Structure, Salaries, and Perquisites

Structurally, the public services of the Federation of Malaya were those derived from British colonial administration, and this bureaucracy itself was a complicated machine that had grown around and within the seven diverse but interrelated political entities in the archipelago. Some colonial servants were assigned directly to the Straits Settlements; some were posted to the Federated Malay States; each of the Unfederated Malay States recruited British officers individually; and all seven of the units borrowed or lent colonial servants among themselves. Such confused posting as this led to a proliferation of public services that is still in evidence today. Each of the five formerly Unfederated Malay States has both a state civil service and state clerical services; the four formerly Federated Malay States each has its own state clerical service but no state civil services;[24] and the two present-day states that at one time were part of the Crown Colony of the Straits Settlements have state civil services and distinct clerical establishments, which unlike the other nine states utilize no personnel drawn from the federal clerical services.

Even if discussion is confined to the federal public services,[25] the influence of the historical fragmentation of government is

24. The posts usually filled by the state civil services in the formerly Unfederated Malay States generally devolve upon personnel of the Malay Administrative Service in the states of the former FMS. The MAS was a creation of the FMS, and a half-century later its officers are still posted only to the four states that composed the FMS. On the development and the role of the MAS, see the author's "The Malay Administrative Service, 1910–1960," *Indian Journal of Public Administration*, VII (April–June, 1961), 145–157.

25. Since federal officers in Malaya may be assigned to posts that are under the direction of the states, a confusion arises in the term "federal officer" or "federal public servant." By this term I mean public servants who are recruited by, and whose terms and conditions of service are governed by, the federal government, even though many of these officers may be responsible to the individual states in the execution of their duties.

everywhere evident. Except for the "general user services" (the administrative and clerical services), which are not themselves nearly as "general" as the description implies, the public services are structurally fragmented throughout.[26] While the public services are not unduly large by international comparison,[27] this fragmentation leads to a complex array of diverse schemes of service and obscure titles of services that may at first confuse and confound even the most experienced student of administration.[28] In fact, though it is seldom recognized by members of the bureaucracy, the whole complex web of federal-state public services is legally held together by a quasi-treaty between the federal government, on the one hand, and each of the states individually, on the other.[29]

26. The public services are structured vertically around the various functional departments, which represents an accidental and pragmatic historical development, and horizontally by design. The horizontal stratification of Divisions I–IV grew out of the recommendations of the Trusted Commission Report. See Malayan Union and Singapore, Public Service Salary Commission of Malaya, 1947 (Sir Harry Trusted, chairman), *Report* (Kuala Lumpur, 1947), pp. 6–7. Hereinafter cited as Trusted Commission Report.

27. The precise size of the bureaucracy is difficult to estimate. Table 4, note °, in Braibanti's concluding chapter in the present volume sets forth the difficulties and the formula by which an estimate of magnitude has been made. The total of 93,932 employees is about 1.27 per cent of the total population of Malaya. While the size of the bureaucracy is viewed with alarm by many Malayans, this percentage compares not unfavorably with equivalent percentages for India, Pakistan, Ceylon, and Burma, as data shown in Table 4 reveal. The ratio for Malaya, in fact, is below the average of 1.85 per cent for all five countries compared in Table 4. It also compares favorably to what is reported as 1 to 2 per cent for Latin American countries, 2.2 per cent for Egypt, and 6 per cent for the United Kingdom. See Joseph J. Spengler, "Public Bureaucracy, Resource Structure, and Economic Development: A Note," *Kyklos*, XI (1958), 479.

28. In the proliferation and fragmentation of services, the clerical services now suffer the most chaotic situation. In the Federation and the eleven states there were fifty-five different schemes of service for clerical personnel in 1960; in mid-1962, after repeated attempts to reorganize, there were fifty-three. Several are severely dated and have only one or two members. (The most outstanding example of this is the Chandu—opium—Monopoly Service, which in early 1960 still had several officers, even though the monopoly was abolished during World War II.) The problem arises because the scheme of service under which an officer enters into employment is regarded as a contract that binds the government as well as the individual. Thus, unless an officer opts voluntarily to convert to a new scheme, he will remain under his original scheme until he leaves the service.

29. The original Malayan Establishment Agreement was negotiated in 1934 to facilitate the transfer of personnel among the various political units. See Federated Malay States and Singapore, *Malayan Establishment: Agreement, Conditions of Service and Salary Schemes* (Kuala Lumpur, n.d.). The last published agreement appeared almost one year before independence. See Federation of Malaya, *Agreement for the Constitution of a Federation Establishment* (Kuala Lumpur, 1956). Meeting several weeks before independence, the Conference of Rulers approved certain necessary amendments to the agreement that included the deletion of certain colonial titles and other such changes. (The amendments were

While the preceding comments indicate considerable confusion in the structuring of the public services as a result of the divergent colonial experience of the constituent units of the present Federation, nevertheless there emerges a remarkable order in the over-all structure. To a large degree this has been accomplished by standardizing salary scales and conditions of service and by attempting to persuade many officers in the more obscure services to opt for these revised schemes.[30]

The salaries of present-day bureaucrats also reflect the colonial past. On the whole, the salaries of senior bureaucrats are considerably higher than those of supervisors and managers with comparable responsibility, education, and experience in private industry, while at the lower echelons government salaries are about equal or perhaps slightly inferior to those on a comparable level of private industry.[31] Salaries of senior posts were designed to attract competent colonial officers to Malaya, while it was expected that junior posts would almost invariably be filled by local recruitment. Thus, in a sense, senior-level salaries have been pegged to a very comfortable British standard of living, while local conditions largely determined the salary structure of the more junior posts. Similarly, perquisites accompanying government service were designed primarily to serve the needs and comforts of expatriates[32] serving in a tropical country where

---

not published, though the author was given access to them in FEO Conference Series 1180 of the Federation Establishment Office.) It was provided in these amendments that the appended schedule of posts of the Federation Establishment could thereafter be amended on the initiative of the government concerned, with the approval of the Yang di-Pertuan Agong. The last major revision seen by the author was issued on July 1, 1958, and is contained in the unpublished FEO Series 4910; however, many minor changes have been made since that time.

30. The trend toward standardization began under colonial auspices in 1954, and although it has been pursued diligently by all officials since that time, it will be some time before complete uniformity is achieved. See the recommendations of the Trusted Commission Report, which were followed by implementing regulations contained in *FEO Circular No. 5 of 1955* (Kuala Lumpur, 1955).

31. The lowest salary of Division IV is M$53.50 per month; the highest post of Division I draws M$2,270 per month. As is mentioned below, a cost of living allowance is added to all salaries on a sliding scale. (At the present time M$1 is approximately U. S. $0.33.)

32. The use of the term "expatriate" to describe a European serving abroad is common in most countries once under the administrative direction of the Colonial Office. Curiously, it did not seem to penetrate the walls of the India Office despite the geographic proximity of the two. It is now a part of the working vocabulary of every English-speaking Malayan and has been expanded to include "commercial" as well as "colonial-service" expatriates.

normal living conditions might have fallen considerably below those of England. As a result, the government assumed responsibility for providing adequate Western-style housing at a fraction of the economic rent; it granted liberal leave provisions that would permit frequent visits to hill stations and occasional home leaves; and in numerous other ways the government granted liberal concessions to officers willing to serve in Malaya. As the composition of the senior services changed, these concessions were passed on almost intact to the incoming indigenous officers, and most of them remain in force today, thus adding to the disproportionate attractiveness of a career in senior government service.[33]

Public Service Commissions

During the period of colonial administration in Malaya, the responsibilities usually assumed by service commissions, such as

33. To list in detail all the perquisites of government service would be a tedious undertaking that would serve no useful purpose; mention will therefore be made only of the major benefits. In addition to the cost of living allowance, expatriate officers only receive a pensionable expatriation allowance. Housing is provided by the government at low rents, or the officer is provided a housing allowance in the absence of quarters. (The government is just now, however, attempting to alter these regulations.) Officers receive medical treatment at a small fraction of its cost. Leave provisions are extremely liberal, including as they do such categories as vacation leave, medical leave, pilgrimage leave, and study leave. Government employees may qualify for interest-free loans to purchase a means of transportation, and the amount of the loan is determined by the salary of the employee. Finally, though by many considered to be the most important, the Federation provides a retirement plan for all government employees, which is particularly attractive for members of the senior bureaucracy. Cost of living allowance rates are set out in *FEO Circular No. 8 of 1955* (Kuala Lumpur, 1955) and *FEO Circular No. 4 of 1956* (Kuala Lumpur, 1956). Housing regulations are presently under review, but policies in the past have been governed by "Federal Secretariat Circular No. 3 of 1949," mimeographed (Kuala Lumpur, 1949); and *General Orders*, Cap. E. Presumably, future policies will be based on the recommendations contained in G. A. Atkinson, *Report on the Housing for Division I Government Officers in the Federation of Malaya* (Kuala Lumpur, 1952); and G. A. Atkinson, *Report on Housing for Government Officers in Divisions II and Lower Divisions, the Federation of Malaya* (Kuala Lumpur, 1953). On the medical plan for government servants, see *General Orders*, Cap. F. On leave regulations in general, see "Service Circular No. 9 of 1960," mimeographed (Kuala Lumpur, 1960); and *Service Circular No. 10 of 1959* (Kuala Lumpur, 1959). Regulations concerning interest-free loans to purchase transportation vehicles are outlined in *Financial General Orders*, Nos. 282–290 (Kuala Lumpur: Government Press, 1951), and *Treasury Circular No. 8 of 1957* (Kuala Lumpur, 1957). The government pension plan is detailed in *The Pensions Ordinance, 1951* (Kuala Lumpur, 1951) and amplified in *Service Circular No. 2 of 1960* (Kuala Lumpur, 1960), *Service Circular No. 4 of 1959* (Kuala Lumpur, 1959), *Service Circular No. 8 of 1959* (Kuala Lumpur, 1959), and *Service Circular No. 9 of 1959* (Kuala Lumpur, 1959).

matters dealing with recruitment, promotion, and discipline of members of the public services, were either delegated to various local department heads or, in the case of overseas recruitment, left in the hands of the Colonial Office or Crown agents. Recruitment of local personnel was undertaken either by the chief secretary, by department heads in the name of the chief secretary, or by departmental selection boards composed of senior government officers who conducted interviews and advised the department head in making selections. For overseas recruitment, from which came most of the higher administrative and professional personnel, machinery was set up in the United Kingdom by the secretary of state for the colonies. The promotion of lower grade servants, as in local recruitment, was generally left to the discretion of the department heads, usually acting on the advice of departmental boards composed of senior officers. In the case of senior officers, after 1934 recommendations for promotion emanated from a special board constituted within the Malayan Establishment Office. Disciplinary measures also were generally within the purview of the departments, except in the case of senior public servants, and for this latter group such matters were the concern of the secretary of state for the colonies.

The Colonial Office White Paper No. 197 of 1946 introduced a new era in the internal administration of the colonial services, for according to this pronouncement of official policy Great Britain, recognizing that "the future of each Colony rests ultimately in the hands of its own people," proposed to establish in each of the colonies conditions that would foster the development of local responsibility. One of the means of producing conditions conducive to the development of responsible self-government was the establishment of local public service commissions:

Public Service Commissions should be established in the Colonies. Subject to the general overriding powers of the Secretary of State, the selection and appointment of candidates in the Colonies to posts in the local service will lie with the Governor of the Colony. It is desirable that the Governor should be advised in these matters by a Public Service Commission appointed by him and so composed as to command the confidence of the Service and the public.[34]

34. Great Britain, Colonial Office, *Organization of the Colonial Service* (London, 1946), p. 9.

Following this White Paper, which was concerned with all colonies, the Trusted Commission Report of 1947[35] recommended the establishment of a public service commission—composed of one carefully selected permanent officer and at least one other senior officer—which could have the advantage of the advice of a puisne judge[36] and direct access to the governor. It must be so constituted, the commission pointed out, as to gain the confidence of the services, for as it was sagely concluded, "it is essential not only that justice should be done, but also that it should appear to be done."[37]

Shortly after the publication of the recommendations of the Trusted Commission, a member of the federal Legislative Council introduced a motion recommending that the government should "create a Public Services Commission for the Federation of Malaya," but upon the urging of the government the motion was "deleted for further consideration" in order to permit time to study all aspects of the subject more closely, although the government conceded that it felt sympathetic toward the point of view expressed by the member.[38] It was almost immediately following this expression of interest in the establishment of a Public Service Commission that the Emergency was declared, and for five years the subject was not officially reopened.

In 1953 a committee was established to investigate further the creation of a Public Service Commission, and on March 31, 1954, the committee's report was placed before the Legislative Council.[39] This report, recognizing the desire of the Colonial Office as

35. See above, p. 562, n. 26.
36. "Puisne judge" is used technically by the Judicial and Legal Service to describe the posts of High Court judges in the Federation, of which there are nine appointments at the present time. It refers to judges other than the chief justice.
37. Trusted Commission Report, p. 13.
38. The motion was introduced in March, 1948. See Federation of Malaya, Legislative Council (First Session), *Proceedings* (Kuala Lumpur, 1951), pp. B74–B78.
39. Federation of Malaya, Legislative Council (Seventh Session), *Minutes and Council Papers*, Paper No. 9 of 1954, "Establishment of a Public Service Commission" (Kuala Lumpur, 1954). The future role of a Public Service Commission in connection with recommended Whitley Councils was discussed briefly in another report of the period; however, the chief topic was Whitleyism and little attention was devoted to service commissions. See W. J. Haimes, "Report to His Excellency the Officer Administering the Government, Sir Donald MacGillivray," dated May 29, 1953, mimeographed (Kuala Lumpur, 1953), paras. 74–77. Hereinafter cited as Haimes Report.

expressed in 1946—that public service commissions should be established in colonial territories—recommended the creation of such a body, advisory in nature, in order that the head of administration might have the benefit of its experience and that there might be secured "a satisfactory system of recruitment and promotion in the Government Service which will have the confidence of the public." The report continued by pointing out that the changing composition of the more senior public services of Malaya had made some form of local control imperative:

So long as the majority of the higher appointments to the Public Services were the concern of the Secretary of State for the Colonies, expert advice concerning the examination and selection of candidates for service in Malaya was available through machinery long established in the United Kingdom, but with the steadily increasing number of local officers entering Division I of the Public Service, there is now a pressing need to provide suitable local machinery for regulating the selection of candidates to new appointments. The present . . . Departmental Selection Boards . . . were not designed for the task which has now to be undertaken. . . . It would be more appropriate that these important functions should be undertaken by a permanent body . . . above the level of a Departmental Committee.[40]

Specifically, the report recommended that there should be created, by legislation to be introduced in the Legislative Council in "due course," a Public Service Commission, which would include within its jurisdiction all matters dealing with (1) appointments to the public services, including methods of recruitment, conditions and qualifications governing entry into the public services, and the recommendation of specific applicants for particular posts; (2) all questions of promotion, including the making of recommendations in individual cases, and (3) "such other matters as the High Commissioner may specifically refer to the Commission for advice." Until such a statutory commission could be established, it was announced that an interim body would be created almost immediately thereafter, functioning "on the same lines as the Commission" in order that there might be the

40. *Ibid.*, para. 5.

opportunity "to test the machinery . . . as well as the range of functions" to be assigned to the statutory commission.[41]

The jurisdiction of the Public Service Appointments and Promotions Board, as the interim body was known, was not intended to extend so broadly as would the statutory commission but was limited to advising the high commissioner on the selection of candidates for first appointment (other than temporary agreements) to posts in Divisions I, II, and III and on the promotion and transfer of serving government officers in these posts. Excluded from the jurisdiction of the board were six classes of officers.[42]

Consisting of a chairman and six members, the Public Service Appointments and Promotions Board, which began functioning in May, 1954, made no final decisions in the selection and promotion of personnel since the board was purely advisory in nature. In offering its advice, however, the board's record appears outstanding, for in its more than two and one-half years of existence there was not a single case in which the advice of the board was rejected outright,[43] although in several relatively minor cases the board had been requested to reconsider its decisions.[44]

Since, as it has been pointed out, it was intended that the life of the temporary board should be brief, the Public Services Commission Bill was introduced by the government in June, 1955.[45]

41. *Ibid.*, para. 7.
42. (*a*) The chief justice of the Federation, the attorney-general, a judge of the Supreme Court, and the solicitor-general;
  (*b*) any office of which the holder is ex officio a member of the Executive Council for the Federation or a member of the Government of the Federation of Malaya;
  (*c*) appointments in the staff grades A and B of the Malayan Civil Service;
  (*d*) first appointments to the Malayan Civil Service whether by promotion or recruitment;
  (*e*) any office or rank (other than a civilian office) in any naval, military, or air force constituted by or raised under any written law;
  (*f*) any office or rank of a member of any police force constituted or raised under any written law.
43. See Federation of Malaya, *Report of the Public Services Commission for the Years 1957 and 1958* (Kuala Lumpur, 1960), p. 16. The Constitution (Article 146 I) requires that the service commissions shall lay annual reports before both houses of Parliament.
44. Public Service Appointments and Promotions Board, "Report for the Year Ending 31st December 1956," mimeographed (Kuala Lumpur, 1957), pp. 9–10.
45. Federation of Malaya, Legislative Council (Eighth Session), *Proceedings* (Kuala Lumpur, 1956), pp. B573, B680–690.

This bill encountered immediate opposition on the floor of the Legislative Council, and its merits were never rationally debated. In the main, criticism centered around the posts to be excluded from the jurisdiction of the proposed commission, which several members of the council regarded as certain evidence that the British intended to delay the Malayanization of senior appointments as long as possible. To the chief critic of this bill:

the intention behind the proposed creation of the Public Service Commission—at least my own intention—is solely and primarily for the purpose of establishing and accelerating the Malayanization of the Government service in the country . . . , and all of us are in favor of Malayanization in the shortest possible time.[46]

The same speaker urged the rejection of the bill in order that "we ourselves [may] decide and fix the functions of the Public Service Commission in such a manner as to attain complete Malayanization to suit our own aspirations." Facing such strong opposition, the second reading of the bill was promptly deferred, and the temporary Public Service Appointments and Promotions Board gained several added years of life.

From January 18 to February 6, 1956, British and Malayan representatives met in London to work out a basic scheme to secure "the early establishment of a fully self-governing and independent Federation of Malaya within the Commonwealth on the basis of parliamentary institutions." Recognizing that "an efficient and contented public service . . . is of particular importance during time of rapid political change," and that this can be achieved only when there is "a reasonable security of tenure and absolute freedom from the arbitrary application of disciplinary provisions," the report recommended including in the Federation Agreement a Public Service Commission, a Judicial Service Commission, and a Police Service Commission.[47] It was agreed that details for the

46. *Ibid.*, p. B684 (speech by Inche Mohamed Rashid). The motives of the member might be questioned, but in view of British thinking at the time—as expressed in the first Malayanization report—there was a sound basis for his belief that Britain did not wish to rush the process of Malayanization.

47. Federation of Malaya, Second Legislative Council (First Session), *Minutes and Council Papers* (Kuala Lumpur, 1957), Paper No. 6 of 1956, "Report of the Federation of Malaya Constitutional Conference Held in London in January and February 1956," pp. 3–10.

operation of these commissions must necessarily be left to the Federation government, but the report set forth five principles it considered essential to any such machinery, suggestions that were followed closely in constituting the present-day service commissions:[48]

(a) it is of vital importance that the Public Service Commission should be independent and free from political influence;

(b) the members of the Public Service Commission should be appointed by the High Commissioner, in his discretion, after consultation with the Chief Minister;

(c) taking advantage of experience elsewhere, care should be taken in delineating the respective functions of the Public Service Commission and those of Government in relation to the public service, the broad principle being that the government and legislation are necessarily responsible for fixing establishments and terms of employment while the Public Service Commission is charged with the internal administration of the service as a professional body and with the responsibility for public service matters, including appointments, promotions, and the application, when necessary, of disciplinary provisions in respect of members of the public service;

(d) members should be carefully chosen to be widely representative but should be men capable of working as a team and speaking not merely for sectional interests.

(e) the Chairman should be a person who will command the respect both of government and the Service and should be given the authority and standing necessary to establish the Commission as an important and respected national institution.

The report acknowledged that to create the necessary statutory basis for these commissions would unquestionably take considerable time, but a goal of not later than July 1, 1957, should be set for its establishment. During the interim period of approximately eighteen months the report recommended that commission members should be designated and that this new group should take over in an advisory capacity the responsibilities of the Public Service Appointments and Promotions Board "with terms of reference extended as necessary to cover the subjects which will be dealt with by the Public Service Commission." Following the recommendations of the London Conference Report, the three

48. *Ibid.,* p. 10.

commissions (designate), as they were officially known, began functioning on January 1, 1957. The delay was occasioned by the necessity of awaiting the outcome of the deliberations of the Reid Constitutional Commission, which had completed its work in the closing months of 1956.[49]

The Reid Commission, composed of a distinguished group of jurists, statesmen, and scholars from Great Britain, Australia, India, and Pakistan,[50] met in Malaya beginning in June, 1956. Proceeding beyond the suggestions of the London Conference of early 1956, the Reid Commission chose to place the service commissions on a constitutional basis rather than establish them on legislative statutes passed pursuant to the amended Federation Agreement.

The Constitution of the Federation of Malaya originally provided for an Armed Forces Council and four service commissions. Three of the four commissions—the Judicial and Legal Service Commission, the Public Services Commission, and the Police Service Commission—had been recommended by the Reid Commission Report, while the fourth, the Railway Service Commission, made its initial appearance in the Constitution of 1957.[51] By amendments to the Constitution of April, 1960, the number of service commissions was reduced from four to three by eliminating the Judicial and Legal Service Commission and transferring most of its functions to the Public Services Commission.[52]

With certain exceptions, jurisdiction of the specialized commis-

49. Although the commission completed its deliberations late in 1956 and communicated pertinent decisions regarding the service commissions to authorities of the Federation, the report was not published until February, 1957. See Great Britain, Colonial Office, *Report of the Federation of Malaya Constitutional Commission 1957* (London, 1957), esp. chap. viii.

50. The chairman and one member (Sir W. Ivor Jennings) were appointed by the United Kingdom. Australia selected a former Governor General, Sir William McKell; India sent a former chief justice of the Allahabad High Court, B. Malik; and Pakistan nominated Sheikh Abdul Hamid, a justice of the West Pakistan High Court. (The Canadian appointee was forced to withdraw at the last moment due to illness.) The high quality of their collective effort reflects the individual competence of the commission members.

51. Although members of the Railway Service were recognized at the time as public servants, it was decided that a separate commission should be established. See Federation of Malaya, *Constitutional Proposals* (Kuala Lumpur, 1957), p. 15.

52. At the same time the Police Service Commission was reconstituted similar to the Armed Forces Council and was renamed the Police Force Commission.

sions extends over the services from which their titles are derived. However, to delineate the jurisdiction of the Public Services Commission requires a more detailed investigation. All members of the "general public service of the Federation" and the "joint public services" fall within the jurisdiction of this general commission.[53] In addition, the state public services of both Penang and Malacca are included within the constitutional jurisdiction of the Public Services Commission, and it is provided that other states, by law of the appropriate state legislature, may invite the commission to extend its jurisdiction to that state.[54] Moreover, after any state has incorporated certain stipulated provisions[55] into its constitution, such a state must either establish its own public service commission, or failing to do this, the jurisdiction of the Public Services Commission may be extended to the public services of this state by federal law. To prevent the abrogation of this provision through state inaction, the Constitution provided that any state which had no public service commission and had failed to incorporate the provisions of the Eighth Schedule by December 31, 1962, would thereafter be liable to the jurisdiction of the Public Services Commission should Parliament by federal law so provide.

Prior to the 1960 constitutional amendments, there was interlocking membership among the four service commissions that was centered on the Public Services Commission, and at the present time this practice continues in the case of the Public Services Commission and the Railway Service Commission. The Public Services Commission consists of a chairman and a deputy chairman, one or both of whom shall have been members of a public service within five years prior to their first appointments, and four

53. Constitution, Article 139(1). "Joint public services" is defined by the Constitution (Article 133 I) as services "common to the Federation and one or more of the States . . . or to two or more States. . . ." As yet no "joint public services" have been formed, and the Federation Establishment Agreement continues to serve as a "temporary" substitute. See above, p. 562, n. 29.

54. *Ibid.*, Article 139(2).

55. These provisions are contained in the Eighth Schedule, Part I. The states have been requested, although they are not required, to incorporate these provisions into their state constitutions with a view to standardizing state constitutional law throughout the Federation.

to eight members, all of whom are appointed for five-year terms (and are eligible for reappointment) by the Yang di-Pertuan Agong acting on the advice of his prime minister. The Railway Service Commission is composed of a chairman and a deputy chairman, one or both of whom must have been public servants within the five-year period preceding their first appointments, and two to six other members, one of whom shall be a member of the Public Services Commission and two of whom (if such persons are available) should have had experience in railway service or railway administration. All appointed members of the service commissions serve five-year terms and can be removed from office only through the elaborate procedures established by the Constitution for the removal of a judge of the Supreme Court.[56]

The Constitution provides that, "it should be the duty of a Commission . . . to appoint, confirm, emplace on the permanent or pensionable establishment, promote, transfer and exercise disciplinary control over members of the service or services to which its jurisdiction extends."[57] In addition to these duties, commissions may be assigned such other duties as federal law may provide. Thus, it may be seen that the basic duties of the service commissions fall into the broad categories of appointment, promotion, and discipline, and in the case of the Public Services Commission there has been added the task of selecting officers for study leave and training courses and selecting candidates for the award of federal and Colombo Plan scholarships and bursaries.[58]

56. To remove a judge of the Supreme Court, the Yang di-Pertuan Agong must receive the recommendation for such removal from a special *ad hoc* tribunal presided over by the chief justice and composed of at least five judges or former judges of the Supreme Court (or persons who have held equivalent offices in any Commonwealth country). See Article 125(3), (4).

57. Article 144(1).

58. These additional duties, which have greatly increased the work of the commission, were assigned to the Public Service Appointments and Promotions Board in 1956 (see "Report for the Year Ending 31st December 1956," p. 6) and apparently devolved automatically upon the board's successor, the Public Services Commission. Strictly speaking, these duties are extra-constitutional since they were not assigned by federal law, the rationale for them being that—in the case of training awards—officers will return qualified for higher posts, and, in the case of scholarships and bursaries, most of these recipients will eventually enter government service. Added to this is the simple fact that the machinery necessary for handling a large task was ready at hand.

The procedures adopted by the service commissions[59] for selecting appointees to the public service are those outlined for the commissions (designate) on the eve of their establishment in January, 1957.[60] After an advertisement of a vacant post in the government *Gazette* (or in the public press, or in both), applications are screened by a single member of the service commission working in conjunction with the head of the department in which the vacancy occurred. As a result of this screening process, it is recommended that several (usually four or five) applicants be requested to appear for interview before a preliminary board, which is composed of two or three members of the commission and, in an advisory capacity, the department head concerned. The report of this interview board is then forwarded to the full commission, which in most cases ratifies the recommendations of the preliminary board, but which may request the re-appearance of any applicant before the full board. Similar procedures are followed in matters of promotion, with the difference, of course, that applications emanate from within rather than without the government service. Moreover, if the appropriate Scheme of Service limits promotion to members of a particular service, advertising in the *Gazette* is unnecessary. In such cases, the Federation Establishment Office forwards to the service commission a list of the officers within the promotion zone, together with their service records and the specific recommendation of the department head concerned. From this point, the screening and interview procedures are almost identical to those used in the case of first applications.

Little can be said at this time of the work of the Public Services Commission in the field of disciplinary matters, since recently published reports have touched only lightly on the subject.

59. See *Report of the Public Services Commission for the Years 1957 and 1958*, pp. 4–6; Federation of Malaya, *Report of the Police Service Commission for the Years Ending 31st December 1957 and 1958* (Kuala Lumpur, 1960), p. 5; and Federation of Malaya, *Report of the Activities of the Judicial and Legal Service Commission for the Years Ending 31st December 1957 and 1958* (Kuala Lumpur, 1960), p. 5.

60. For these procedures in detail, see Federation of Malaya, *General Circular No. 2 of 1956*, "The Public Services Commission, the Judicial and Legal Service Commission and the Police Service Commission" (Kuala Lumpur, 1956), pp. 1–8.

Moreover, the Constitution of the Federation outlines no avenue of appeal beyond the service commissions, and there has been little attempt to induce the courts to assume responsibility for overseeing the rulings of the organs of internal administration of the bureaucracy. In fact, there have been only two cases appealed from the Public Services Commission to the judiciary, and the substance of each of these is not directly relevant to questions of judicial overseeing, though of course they are important from the point of view of setting precedents for appeal.

The first case grew out of a writ of mandamus to compel the Public Services Commission to reinstate an employee to the position of assistant passport officer, Federation Overseas Service, from which he had been removed after it became known that he did not in fact possess the requisite qualifications for the post. The case was complicated by several legal technicalities and by an earlier criminal suit brought against him by the government, a charge on which the appellant was acquitted, but again on legal technicalities.[61] Although the actions of the commission were upheld in this case, obiter dicta of the court clearly indicated that it felt itself competent to review the manner by which the commission arrived at its decisions. Pointing out that certain procedures in disciplinary matters are detailed in the Constitution (Article 135[2]), the court commented that "any action by the Commission in contravention of the Article must be constitutionally invalid. . . . In such cases, *certiorari* can and must issue to quash the order, because it is the right and the duty of the Court to maintain the rule of law and declare invalid any transgression of the limits of the constitution."[62]

The second case, now of lessened importance in view of the constitutional amendments of 1960, involved a police inspector who was dismissed from his post in July, 1958, by the commissioner of the police under the authority not of the Police Service

61. *Public Prosecutor* v. *Rasiah Munusamy,* Kuala Lumpur Summons Case No. 1 of 1958; and *Public Prosecutor* v. *Rasiah Munusamy,* Supreme Court of the Federation of Malaya in the High Court at Kuala Lumpur, Criminal Appeal No. 11 of 1958.

62. *Rasiah Munusamy* v. *The Public Services Commission,* Supreme Court of the Federation of Malaya in the High Court of Kuala Lumpur, Originating Motions 2/59 and 3/59.

Commission but by the provisions of the Police Ordinance, 1952. In a decision of March 24, 1960, Mr. Justice Rigby, admitting that "it is with the greatest possible regret that I have arrived at my conclusion," agreed with the applicant that regardless of the transitional provisions of the Constitution "the whole purpose and effect of Part X of the Constitution [the legal basis for the bureaucracy and service commissions] is to entrench within its provisions the security of tenure of persons in the public services and to place the control thereof . . . in the various commissions specifically appointed and entrusted with such functions." Thus, he concluded, those "sections of the *Police Ordinance* conferring these powers [appointment, promotion, and dismissal] upon the Commissioner of Police must be regarded as modified—that is to say, repealed."[63] This decision was then overturned by the Supreme Court of the Federation, where the chief justice argued that the lower court had failed to consider Part X of the Constitution within the total context of the document, and thus a statutory limitation on the functions of a service commission were not automatically repealed at the time of independence.[64] Chief Justice Thompson was then overruled by the Privy Council, which in essence agreed with the reasoning of the Penang High Court.[65] The important point of this case is the expressed willingness of the judiciary to consider appeals from administrative organs, a practice that has not been eagerly undertaken even in the more mature judicial system of Singapore. In *Alkaff and Co. v. Governor in Council*[66] the judge argued that courts should be hesitant to interfere in the work of administrative tribunals, requiring in such cases considerably weightier reasons for intervening than they would for overseeing the work of lesser courts. This is the view that has generally prevailed throughout Malaya.[67]

63. *B. Surinder Singh Kanda v. the Government of the Federation of Malaya,* High Court of Penang, Civil Suit No. 232 of 1959.
64. *The Government of the Federation of Malaya v. B. Surinder Singh Kanda,* Supreme Court of the Federation of Malaya in the Court of Appeal of Kuala Lumpur, Civil Appeal No. 30 of 1960.
65. *B. Surinder Singh Kanda v. Government of the Federation of Malaya,* Privy Council Appeal No. 9 of 1961 (1962), 2 M.L.R. 1153.
66. *Malayan Law Journal,* 6 (1936), 28.
67. See L. A. Sheridan (ed.), *Malaya and Singapore; The Borneo Territories,* "The British Commonwealth: The Development of Its Laws and Constitutions"

Whitley Councils

The first suggestion of Whitley[68] machinery in Malaya appeared during the period of the Malayan Union, when the Interim Joint Council was established with the power to make recommendations and issue reports.[69] It was intended that the council should attempt to improve employer-employee relations in the public service by recommending to government areas in which agreement might be possible; however, due primarily to the disorganized state of public service staff associations, accompanied by (and in part because of) a lack of understanding of the principles of Whitleyism, the council did not live up to early expectations.[70]

By the time that W. J. Haimes arrived in Malaya in 1953 a few seeds of Whitleyism had already been scattered about, but it remained his appointed task to attempt to create the requisite machinery and to impart the idea of Whitleyism.[71] Haimes

(London, 1961), IX, 168–170. Mention might be made here of the reporting of law cases in Malaya, since it seems indicative of the relative importance attached to the judiciary in the Federation. At the present time the Federation government does not publish any law reports. *Federated Malay States Law Reports* were published between 1906 and 1941; the *Law Reports of the Malayan Union* were issued in 1946–1947, and this series was replaced by *Malayan Law Reports* during the period 1950–1954 (there were apparently no cases reported officially in 1948–1950). There have been no official reports for the past decade, and the *Malayan Law Journal*, published privately in Singapore, is the only source for cases. Unfortunately, the journal often publishes only summaries or extracts, and in the case of minor decisions it only notes their existence. See Bashir A. Mallal, "Law and Law Reporting in Malaya," *University of Malaya Law Review*, I (1959), 71. Also see Sheridan, *op. cit.*, pp. xxii, 27.

68. Whitleyism in Britain grew out of the report of a committee (under the chairmanship of J. H. Whitley) appointed to investigate means of improving employer-employee relations in industry. See Great Britain, *Accounts and Papers, 1917–1918*, Vol. XVIII, Cmd. 8606, "Interim Report on Joint Standing Industrial Councils." In 1919, under pressure from staff associations, Whitleyism was adopted by the public services, with "labor" and "management" becoming the "staff side" and the "official side."

69. Malayan Union, Advisory Council, *Proceedings, 1946* (Kuala Lumpur, 1948), pp. C69–71, Paper No. 36, "Memorandum on Interim Joint Council."

70. The composition of the council placed the staff side at a distinct disadvantage from the beginning, for it was chosen on an *ad hoc* basis for the discussion of each question. The official side, on the other hand, was made up primarily of ex officio members and was thus of a much more permanent nature. Moreover, staff associations were highly disorganized at the time. It is estimated that in 1951 there were no less than 130 registered staff unions, many having only the minimum number of seven members to qualify for registration.

71. Even today the Haimes Report remains the handbook that guides Malayan Whitleyism. See above, p. 566, n. 39.

proceeded forcefully, and by the time he left Malaya most of the necessary machinery had been created and most of the rules for the operation of this machinery had been spelled out. He had sponsored the creation of a National Whitley Council (Divisions I–IV), a National Whitley Council (daily rated), and a number of departmental Whitley Councils. Since that time the number of departmental councils has increased, and there has also emerged a Police Council and National Joint Council of Teachers. However, of these the National Whitley Council (Divisions I–IV) is by far the most important since its jurisdiction encompasses most of the senior and junior bureaucracy. Moreover, the procedures employed by the council and the problems that it faces are typical of the other groups, and thus it will be sufficient to limit our discussions here to this single body.

The National Whitley Council representing the monthly-salaried public servants of the Federation of Malaya is composed of forty-one members, including a chairman, a vice-chairman, and two secretaries. Of this total membership, nineteen are appointed by the Yang di-Pertuan Agong (the official side) and twenty-two are selected by groups of staff associations and unions (the staff side).[72] The official side must be government servants and must include seven representatives of the state governments and at least four department heads, including the principal establishment officer.[73] The twenty-two members appointed for the staff side may be either public servants or full-time officers of government unions or associations and must be constituted of the following groups:

(1) Congress of Unions of Employees in the Public and Civil Services, twelve members;
(2) The European Civil Servants Association of Malaya, three members;
(3) Malayan Civil Service Association, two members;
(4) Senior Government Officers Association, two members; and

72. Federation of Malaya, Federation Establishment Office, "Constitution of the Whitley Council for Divisions I–IV of the Public Services in the Federation of Malaya (As Amended June 1959)," mimeographed (Kuala Lumpur, n.d.), para. 1. Amendment of the Constitution is by unanimous agreement of the two sides reached in the joint council. *Ibid.*, para. 25.
73. *Ibid.*, para. 2.

(5) The Malay Administrative Service Association, one member.[74]

Officers of the council are distributed evenly between the two sides, the chairman and one secretary being appointed from among the membership of the official side and the vice-chairman and the staff-side secretary being selected by the staff side.[75]

According to the constitution of the council,[76] it is the object of the council to secure maximum co-operation between employer and employee, to deal with grievances, and generally to provide a forum where opposing points of view can be voiced and discussed. Specifically, the functions of the council may be summarized as follows: (1) to permit government to utilize the experience of staff members; (2) to give public servants a greater voice in determining conditions under which their duties are executed; (3) to determine the general principles (but not individual cases) governing terms and conditions of service, including recruitment, hours of duty, promotion, discipline, tenure, remuneration, and superannuation; (4) to encourage further education and training after entry into government service; (5) to consider improvement of office procedures and to assure that staff suggestions on such matters do not go unheard; and (6) to consider proposed legislation so far as it affects the employment position of officers of Divisions I through IV.

To carry out the duties outlined in the council's constitution, the council has established two committees, one designated for general purposes and one for combined grades,[77] which actually

74. *Ibid.*, para. 3. To this total of twenty must be added the elected chairman of the staff side and the secretary, thus increasing the total to twenty-two.

75. *Ibid.*, paras. 7, 8. In practice, the chairman of the council has always been the permanent secretary, prime minister's department (the administrative head of the public services), and the vice-chairman of the council has been the chairman of the staff side.

76. *Ibid.*, paras. 9, 10.

77. Originally, as recommended in the Haimes Report (para. 5), in addition to the general purposes committee, there were four grade committees, each dealing with a specific division of officers. These committees, however, were abolished in 1956 and there was established the Combined Grades Committee. See Federation of Malaya, National Whitley Council (Divisions I–IV), Staff Side, *Third Annual Report* (Kuala Lumpur, 1956), section 5 and Appendix E. Moreover, the work of the Combined Grades Committee was suspended during the period of the government-imposed wage freeze. See Federation of Malaya, National Whitley Council (Divisions I–IV), Staff Side, *Sixth Annual Report* (Kuala Lumpur, 1959), p. 3.

assume most of the work of the council. The joint council—that is, the full membership of forty-one—meets only once each year to ratify the recommendations of the two committees.[78] In addition to these standing committees, the constitution[79] provides that in the event of disagreement between the two sides (decisions must be unanimous) the question will be referred to an informal meeting of the chairman, vice-chairman, and the two secretaries, frequently referred to as the "deadlock committee." Here, where no minutes are kept and all discussion is off the record, the decision reached by an informal understanding of both sides will then become the decision of the council.

The general-purposes committee, composed of twelve staff-side members and an equal number representing the official side, considers only policy matters affecting the public services as a whole—that is to say, questions transcending divisional demarcations. The eighteen staff-side members and six official-side members of the combined-grades committee discuss specific questions, such as the revision of examination syllabi, claims for revision of salary scales in a particular range, and other matters that affect a particular grade or group of employees.

Although in itself not conclusive, a preliminary suggestion of the magnitude of the undertakings of the National Whitley Council can be gained from examining Table 1 on the following page. However, statistics alone provide little information about the nature of the work undertaken. The following summary of selected cases, when considered together with the statistics above, should give a clearer picture of the work of the council.

(1) *Atkinson housing proposals.* The Atkinson housing proposals,[80] which represent the broadest topic considered by the

78. The constitution of the council (para. 13) originally provided for two meetings each year, but it has now been reduced to a single meeting. See Staff Side, *Sixth Annual Report,* p. 2; and Federation of Malaya, Federation Establishment Office, Whitley Council (Divisions I–IV), *Sixth Bulletin* (Alor Star, 1959), p. 1.
79. Paras. 20, 21.
80. See above, p. 564, n. 33. The proposals would provide government-guaranteed loans at attractive interest rates to permit government employees to own their own homes rather than rent government quarters at highly subsidized rates.

council, have also been the most troublesome. Considered by the joint council originally in 1953, the subject has appeared on the agenda in every successive year. Debate has been heated and emotionally charged. For some a vested economic interest is at stake, while others seem more motivated by a middle-class

Table 1. *Summary of Deliberations of the National Whitley Council, 1954–1961*

Year	Subjects considered	Agreements	Disagreements	Other[a]
1954–1955	82	24	5	53
1955–1956	108	33	4	71
1956–1957	110	36	2	72
1957–1958	135	75	1	59
1958–1959	97	42	1	54
1959–1960	115	66	1	48
1960–1961	107	49	0	58

[a] This category includes items withdrawn, items submitted to arbitration, items held in suspense, and items outstanding at the time of publication.

Source: Eight annual reports of the staff side. The first report (1954–1955) was not published but is available in mimeograph in Kuala Lumpur. The remainder of the reports were published privately in Kuala Lumpur but have not been widely circulated.

conservatism that prefers the benefits already in hand to any new ones offered by the government. Even the deadlock committee has remained deadlocked throughout the discussions, and it has become apparent from these experiences that the Whitley machinery cannot generate consensus where some agreement does not already exist.

(2) *Changes of office hours.* The staff side pressed for a five-day work week for public employees, and the official side countered with a proposal that the hours be changed to 8 A.M. to 4 P.M. Monday through Friday and 8 A.M. to 12:30 P.M. on Saturday. The staff side rejected this schedule, and the official side thereupon requested that it be deleted from the agenda since the question of weekends and holidays was not a matter for discussion in Whitley Council. The staff side rejected this latter

contention, and it was agreed to place the matter on the suspense list.

(3) *Publication of a new* General Order. The staff side agreed to the publication, as a temporary measure, of Appendix C3 to Chapter C of the General Orders, which concerned the payment of subsistence allowance to officers granted study leave in the United Kingdom.

(4) *Political interference in the Civil Service.* After the Batu Gajah branch of the United Malays National Organization had resolved that the district officer of Kinta should be removed from his post on the grounds of public dissatisfaction arising from his administration, the staff side requested reassurances from the official side that government would not be influenced by such resolutions and that there was no change in the position of government regarding non-interference by political groups. The staff side was satisfied with the assurance of the official side that political interference would not be permitted.

(5) *Claim for upward revision of salary scales for revenue officers.* Originally introduced in 1957, this claim continued under discussion, with each side putting forth proposals and counter-proposals, until agreement on an increase was reached in 1958.

(6) *Point of entry to the salary scale of officers promoted to Division I.* The staff side accepted an improved plan whereby Division II officers promoted to Division I should enter at an increment higher than the lowest pay grade, and the staff side approved Service Circular Letter No. 12 of 1959 implementing this change.

(7) *Claim for revision of salaries in the Government Printing Service.* This claim, put forward by the staff side, was rejected by the official side. It was subsequently deleted from the agenda in order that the union might seek direct negotiations with government.

Although the constitution of the National Whitley Council very

81. Para. 11 (iii).

specifically prohibits the discussion of individual cases,[81] it is apparent that such cases can be considered so long as they involve questions that can be regarded as dealing with general principles. For example, the staff side presented the case of an individual (unnamed in the joint council *Bulletin*) serving at the Institute for Medical Research. Assigned additional responsibilities, this officer was granted a non-pensionable increase in salary of $50 per month (Malayan currency) without promotion, since at the time there was no appointment to which he could be promoted. Two years thereafter a new super-scale post was created, and immediately afterward the officer was promoted. The staff side argued that the creation of the post should be made retroactive to the date the officer began drawing the extra allowance, a contention the official side would not accept. The outcome of the claim is unimportant in the present context, but it is noteworthy that this was obviously a discussion of an individual, and seldom was the point made that it was the principle that was under consideration and not the particular officer. It would appear that the interpretation of what constitutes a principle is very liberal, and that the chief requirement is a willingness by the staff side to espouse the claim and acquiescence on the part of the official side.

A second observation of Whitleyism at the national level regards the emphasis placed on personal contacts and informal relations. Decisions are made by the two committees, and it remains for the joint council only to ratify these decisions. Moreover, even at the committee level most of the work is carried out by informal conversations between members of the two sides, and it is not unusual when more minor decisions are reached by agreement between the two secretaries, which are then ratified by the committee, and these in turn are ratified by the National Council. It is frequently only the most difficult questions that are aired in formal committee sessions. This attitude of informality and emphasis on personal contacts in resolving potential disagreements was urged throughout the Haimes Report, and there is considerable evidence that this document is still referred to for guidance in procedural matters.

III. The Departure of European Officers

"Malayanization" is the term used in the Federation of Malaya to describe the modern nationalization program enunciated in 1956 whereby expatriate officers (usually British colonial servants) serving in the Malayan public services were to be replaced by native officers on payments of variable sums of compensation according to a fixed scale drawn up by the British and accepted by the Federation of Malaya. The process of replacing expatriate officers with natives is not new, however, for it is possible to trace the origin of such schemes to the creation of the Malay Administrative Service in 1910.[82] An even earlier date might be suggested. It was in 1896 that the first suggestion of local recruitment was put forward, and in this case too it was done for the express purpose of relieving better-qualified European servants for duty in more responsible posts.[83]

While "Malayanization" might be equally well applied in a number of historical circumstances, in present usage the term carries a considerably more narrow connotation. It is only this modern scheme that will be examined in the present section. Specifically, it will be my purpose here to examine the broad policies governing Malayanization, to analyze the specific provisions of compensation, to review the cost of the program to the Federation government, and to present the statistical results of Malayanization.

Malayanization: The Scheme and the Costs

The present Malayanization scheme was first considered in detail at the London Constitutional Conference of 1956;[84] how-

82. The MAS was (and still is) limited exclusively to Malays. Its purpose was to provide a group of native administrators to staff the lower echelons of the bureaucracy. In later years the senior administrative service, the Malayan Civil Service, was opened to Malays through promotion from the MAS. On the development of the MAS, see this author's "The Malay Administrative Service, 1910–1960."

83. See *Correspondence Respecting the Federation of the Protected Malay States*, p. 9.

84. See Federation of Malaya, Second Legislative Council (First Session), *Minutes and Council Papers* (Kuala Lumpur, 1957), No. 6 of 1956, "Report of the Federation of Malaya Constitutional Conference Held in London in January and February 1956," Part V, esp. paras. 49–58.

ever, two years previously the general outlines for all colonial nationalization programs had been sketched by *Colonial No. 306 of 1954.* In summary, the Colonial Office proposed that the following guide should be utilized when nationalization policies were formulated in each of the colonial territories:

(1) terms and conditions of service for expatriate officers should not be made less favorable than those enjoyed prior to independence;
(2) pensions should be safeguarded;
(3) Her Majesty's Government should continue to regard the expatriate officers as Her Majesty's servants even after the officers had become the employees of an independent state;
(4) the employing government should agree: (a) to respect a reasonable request for transfer, (b) to consider expatriates on equal terms with local officers in matters of promotion, and (c) in the event of transfer, to guarantee earned pensions;
(5) expatriate officers should be given reasonable notice of the termination of their services, and Her Majesty's Government should attempt to find alternative employment; and,
(6) in the event of the premature retirement of public servants by the employing government, arrangements should be made for payment of adequate compensation.[85]

At the London Conference, before detailed plans for the Malayanization program could be drawn up, a basic policy decision was necessary concerning the rate at which Malayanization should proceed. Reduced to simplest terms, the conference had to choose between nationalization through normal attrition and a program based on the accelerated retirement of expatriate officers. According to the Malayanization Committee Report of 1954, accelerated Malayanization would result in the following disadvantages:

Firstly, the prospects for promotion of local officers of the professional departments in Division II must for the future be safeguarded. Secondly, an uneven rate of recruitment will produce periods of stagnation in later years; it is on the whole to the Service's advantage to maintain recruitment at a steady level even though this rate of annual recruitment may be less than the numbers required to fill the vacancies occurring in a particular year. Thirdly, there is the danger

85. Great Britain, Colonial Office, *Reorganization of the Colonial Service,* Colonial No. 306, (London, 1954), p. 4.

that through overanxiety to fill all possible vacancies with Malayans now, there will be no places left for better candidates who become available in succeeding years.[86]

Viewing these disadvantages, the committee concluded that "Malayanization should not, as a general policy, proceed faster than the normal occurrence of vacancies."

From a purely rational point of view, there can be little argument that the disadvantages posited by the committee were valid objections to accelerated Malayanization. It would be equally impossible to dispute the contention, however, that the emerging nations of Asia and Africa are seldom in positions to formulate policies in a vacuum of rationality. The proposals of the first Malayanization Committee were not well received, and by the time of the London Conference it was apparent that some concessions would have to be made to public demands that were probably based more on emotion than on reason. The London Conference suggested that some form of premature retirement might be both possible and desirable, but following the policies of *Colonial No. 306 of 1954* the conference also agreed that certain guarantees and compensations must be made to those colonial servants departing from Malaya prior to the time of normal retirement.

Thus, following the meeting of the London Conference, the Malayanization Committee of 1956[87] faced three possibilities: first, it could recommend the immediate Malayanization of all government services as soon as independence was achieved; second, it might adhere to the report of the first Malayanization Committee, suggesting the nationalization of the services through normal attrition; or, third, the second committee might follow the lead of the London Conference and choose a middle course between the two extremes. The committee, arguing that a public

---

86. Federation of Malaya, *Report of the Committee on the Malayanization of the Government Services* (Kuala Lumpur, 1954), p. 6.

87. Two reports were issued by this committee. See Federation of Malaya, *Malayanization of the Public Service: A Statement of Policy* (Kuala Lumpur, 1956), and, Federation of Malaya, *Report of the Committee on the Malayanization of the Public Service* (Kuala Lumpur, 1956). Hereinafter, citations to these documents will be made in abbreviated form.

service "is more than a rapidly assembled aggregate of competent individuals,"[88] chose the last course of action and adhered to the suggested pace of nationalization put forward by the London Conference. While it was both necessary and desirable that general goals should be defined, the committee agreed that the exact rate of Malayanization should be determined primarily by the availability of competent and experienced manpower. The policy of the government "should be to Malayanize as fast as the availability of suitable and qualified Malayans permits."[89]

Within this broad policy of accelerated but controlled Malayanization, certain time limitations were suggested. Complete Malayanization was to take place in three phases, and the public services were then catalogued according to the rate at which Malayanization could reasonably be expected to proceed. The first category included twenty-three departmental services, or particular cadres within departments, which were scheduled for complete Malayanization by July 1, 1960. Category II, seventeen services, should be Malayanized over a period of time not to extend beyond January 1, 1962. Category III consisted of professional and technical personnel whose replacements would have to undergo extensive training and on-the-job experience, a process that would delay complete Malayanization until 1965. In addition to these three categories, the committee also recognized a small group of miscellaneous services that were assigned no definite target date for Malayanization. In most cases these services were at the time predominantly Malayan, or held promise of becoming predominantly Malayan in the very near future. Thus, for this group, Malayanization could be almost immediate, and in several services nationalization was accomplished even prior to independence.[90]

In 1954, realizing that locally recruited officers would necessarily assume increasing responsibilities in the public services, the government initiated a concentrated program whereby Malayan officers were sent to the University of Malaya and abroad to

88. *Statement of Policy,* p. 1.
89. *Second Malayanization Report,* p. 6.
90. *Statement of Policy,* pp. 6–8, and *Second Malayanization Report,* pp. 20–22.

receive the necessary training to equip them to replace European officers. Although it was possible to secure some assistance through the Colombo Plan, the financial burden for this program was borne chiefly by the Federation government. Between 1959 and 1961 the cost of training averaged $750,000 per year (United States currency), though the peak has now been passed and future expenditures can be expected to diminish progressively as the close of the Malayanization program approaches.

In dealing with the specific provisions of Malayanization, two related but dissimilar aspects must be considered: first, it is necessary to examine the terms under which expatriate officers remained in the service of the Federation prior to their Malayanization; and, second, at least cursory attention must be given to the nature and the amount of the compensation these officers receive upon leaving the Malayan public services.

According to the provisions of the Tenth Schedule of the *Federation of Malaya Agreement*,[91] all "entitled officers"[92] were required to state in writing prior to the beginning of the Malayanization scheme (July 1, 1957) their desire either to retire immediately or to remain in the service of independent Malaya. Those choosing to remain in Malaya were then informed by the Federation government within two months whether their continued service was desired (as it was in almost every case), and, if so, officers at the same time were offered periods of guaranteed employment. Officers were assured that as a general rule they should not expect involuntary retirement prior to the expiration of these proffered periods of service. After this information was received by each expatriate officer, he was given an additional month to indicate his acceptance or rejection of the government's offer. Officers who accepted the Federation's commitment continued to serve in Malaya on the same terms and conditions of service under which they were recruited, and at least from an

91. The Tenth Schedule was appended by law in 1956 to the Federation of Malaya Agreement, 1948. See Federation of Malaya, *The Federation of Malaya Agreement (Amendment No. 4) Ordinance, 1956,* No. 59 of 1956 (Kuala Lumpur, 1958).

92. The term "entitled officer" is the official abbreviation for an "officer entitled to loss-of-career compensation"—that is, an expatriate officer on the pensionable establishment who was serving on or after July 1, 1957.

official point of view they enjoyed promotion opportunities during this final period of service equal to those of their Asian colleagues.[93] Whether retiring immediately after the beginning of the program or departing voluntarily or involuntarily at a later date, all entitled officers leaving the service of Malaya after July 1, 1957, upon six months prior notice, are entitled to financial compensation not received by their expatriate colleagues retiring prior to the implementation of the Malayanization program.

The amount of "loss-of-career compensation" received by expatriate officers is based on their pensionable salary and allowances multiplied by a table of factors appended to the Tenth Schedule of the *Federation of Malaya Agreement*. In general, these factors were computed by taking into account the combination of age and length of service, with the added stipulation that no loss-of-career compensation could exceed £11,000. The maximum factor, 4.96, is applicable in the case of officers thirty-nine years of age with eight or more years of pensionable service in the Federation. The rationale is that such officers suffer the most severe disruption of their careers; they are too young to retire and too old to seek a new profession. It is difficult to generalize about the amounts of compensation that individual officers receive, since they may vary greatly according to individual circumstances. Although not rare, cases of officers receiving the maximum are the exceptions rather than the rule, and while no statistical studies have been made, it seems probable that the mean compensation falls considerably below the optimum figure of £11,000. However, even if the average fell as low as one-half the maximum (which seems an unlikely supposition), each retiring officer would have received an average of more than $15,000 (U. S. currency).

As these figures will suggest, the cost of the Malayanization program to the Federation government has indeed been great. With slightly more than 80 per cent of the expatriate officers retired as of January 1, 1962, the cost to the government in the

93. Promotion opportunities were equal in theory but not in fact, according to the comments of both European and Asian officers. The necessity of promoting Asians to the senior posts over the heads of expatriates seems to have been recognized and accepted by most European colonial servants.

payment of loss-of-career compensation alone has been more than $15 million (U. S. currency).[94] It is impossible to estimate the total cost of the program by the close of the operative period, but it has been suggested that it may exceed $23 million. No one could deny that Malayanization with compensation has indeed been expensive, but most Federation officials seem in agreement that in tangible and intangible benefits the program has been worth the investment.

Malayanization: Statistical Results

The following summary of expatriate officers serving in Malaya illustrates well the departure of European colonial servants from the Federation.

Table 2. *Malayanization of the Senior Bureaucracy*

Date	Entitled officers remaining
May, 1956	2,060
July, 1957	1,564
January, 1958	936
January, 1959	736
January, 1960	555
January, 1961	382
July, 1962	200[a]

[a] Estimated.
Source: This table has been tabulated by the author from unpublished statistics provided by the Federation Establishment Office.

In the senior administrative service, the Malayan Civil Service, the change in composition has been the most dramatic of all the services. At the beginning of the operative period of the Malayanization program, expatriate officers held 67 per cent of the posts of the service, while the remaining 33 per cent were staffed by Asians. As of January 1, 1962, Malayans accounted for 90.8 per

94. This figure is derived from a tabulation of the *Federal Estimates* for 1958–1961 inclusive.

cent of the total posts, while the European segment had shrunk to 9.2 per cent. European officers throughout all the public services have been reduced to less than one-tenth their original numbers in the period between May, 1956, and January, 1962. Table 3 below details the departure of expatriate officers for the three-year period following independence on August 31, 1957.

It should also be pointed out that unlike the public service staffs of many of the emerging nations of Africa and Asia, the number of pensionable officers is not augmented by a large group of contract officers. In fact, the total number of European officers employed on a contract basis is negligible, and there is no indication that a substantial increase may be expected.[95] Figures for the total bureaucracy cannot be tallied with nearly the accuracy expected of the MCS computations, but there is ample evidence to prove that the departing expatriates have been replaced by Malayans of all communal groups. It has often been contended that the senior governmental services of Malaya are the preserved domain of the Malays, but statistics do not support this assertion. To be sure, in those services in which quotas are maintained (and it should be pointed out that these are the most influential of the services),[96] Malays are to be found in vastly disproportionate numbers. However, in the total senior bureaucracy of the Federation, the Chinese and the Malays are represented in almost equal numbers, and non-Malay Asians actually outnumber Malays by a considerable margin.[97]

In the schedule of Malayanization, July 1, 1960, was set as the target date for the first part of the program, and thus it provides a useful segment for analysis. However, even within this single category only eleven of the twenty-three services lend themselves to statistical examination, since only these represent complete

95. Unlike Nigeria, for example, nationalized officers are barred by law from re-employment on contract. In fact, it is becoming increasingly difficult for Malayanized officers to re-enter Malaya even for commercial employment.

96. By administrative directive, sanctioned by the Constitution, the Malayan Civil Service must recruit at a ratio of four Malays to each non-Malay. In the External Affairs Service the ratio imposed is three to one. This ratio applies only to recruitment, not to promotions within the services.

97. Detailed statistical analyses of the communal composition of Malayan bureaucracy is contained in the author's *Bureaucratic Transition in Malaya,* Tables 17–28.

services. (The remaining twelve, being particular groups within larger services, are therefore not tallied separately in quarterly Malayanization statistics.) Viewing these eleven services alone, it is possible to gain several impressions of the degree of success of the Malayanization program.

As of January 1, 1961, six of the eleven services had met the target date for complete Malayanization; three services each had but a single expatriate officer remaining; and two services had delayed the Malayanization of a small group of officers when it became apparent that qualified replacements were not yet available through local recruitment. Thus, of 416 officers scheduled for Malayanization by mid-1960, only sixty-one remained in the

Table 3. *Malayanization of the Senior Bureaucracy, by Component Services, 1957–1960*

Service	Entitled officers	1957 September	1957 December	1958 December	1959 December	1960 June
MCS	202	130	122	86	54	43
Accountants	11	5	5	5	4	4
Agriculture	45	32	27	21	17	11
Broadcasting	8	6	6	4	4	3
Chemistry	8	6	6	6	5	4
Civil Aviation	5	4	4	4	3	3
Civil Defense	1	—	—	—	—	—
Cooperatives	1	—	—	—	—	—
Commerce	2	—	—	—	—	—
Customs	61	38	35	28	18	16
Drainage	31	20	19	14	14	11
Education	94	65	57	44	37	31
Federation Military	6	4	4	3	2	2
Fisheries	6	2	2	2	2	—
Forestry	31	23	22	20	15	9
Game	4	4	4	3	3	1
Geological Survey	18	14	14	13	12	11
Immigration	3	2	2	1	1	1
Income Tax	2	1	1	1	2	2
Information	1	1	1	—	—	—
Legal	35	27	25	18	16	15
Machinery	11	7	5	3	3	3
Marine	8	6	5	4	4	4
Marine Survey	1	1	—	—	—	—

Table 3 (*cont.*)

Service	Entitled officers	1957 Septem-ber	Decem-ber	1958 Decem-ber	1959 Decem-ber	1960 June
Medical	163	97	93	76	55	46
Mines	18	12	12	12	10	7
Museums and Aborigines	2	2	2	2	2	2
Police	333	197	117	117	81	60
Postal	19	11	10	7	4	1
Printing	5	5	4	3	2	2
Prisons	39	18	17	16	7	4
Public Works	168	121	119	104	86	77
Railways	68	45	38	33	26	19
Registration	2	1	1	1	—	—
Road Transport	17	9	8	6	4	1
Social Welfare	8	4	5	4	2	—
Staff Training	1	—	—	—	—	—
Statistics	1	1	1	1	—	—
Survey	26	20	20	17	15	13
Telecommunications	59	40	39	34	28	22
Town Planning	5	4	4	3	3	3
Trade Unions	2	1	1	1	1	1
Treasury	2	2	1	1	—	—
Veterinary	8	1	1	1	—	—
Miscellaneous	25	15	17	16	13	11

Source: This table has been prepared by the author from unpublished statistics supplied by the Federation Establishment Office.

service of the Federation by the end of that year. Although the first target date did not find the complete Malayanization of all the scheduled services, the results at least demonstrated that the present government intends to pursue the program with determination tempered by rationality. The schedules set out in the Malayanization reports were necessarily formulated with considerable haste, and it was almost inevitable that many complicating factors could not be taken into account, or even dimly foreseen, at the time. It is not surprising that considerable revision was necessitated as Malayanization progressed, and it seems most fitting that the deadline of each phase was approached with flexibility. However, in view of the progress of the scheme at the time of writing, it seems probable that the bureaucracy will be of virtually indigenous composition by 1967.[98]

IV. Bureaucracy and the Political Process

The Role of the Administrative Services

During the colonial period in Malaya the administrative services—and primarily the Malayan Civil Service—constituted the predominant voice in the day-to-day control of the affairs of government. The decisions of MCS officers, particularly those in the field, were likely to be highly discretionary, and MCS personnel had a hand in policy formulation on the federal level.[99] Thus, the senior administrative service was often involved in decision-making of a nature that affected the structure of Malayan society and altered the distribution of power within this society. In this sense, the MCS was often as political as it was administrative, and this dominant position of the MCS in the political process elevated the service and its members to a unique status, a status comparable (and perhaps superior) to that of the ICS in India.

As the MCS shaped and administered policy under the colonial regime, so today it continues to influence the course of Malayan politics. However, the MCS of today has both a "first-" and a "second-generation" legacy. Senior officers now holding important posts have derived much of the MCS tradition by lengthy association with the junior administrative service (the Malay Administrative Service) under the watchful eyes of their senior expatriate colleagues of the MCS, while the younger officers are

98. The coming of Malaysia may arrest some of the progress of the Malayanization scheme, but with less than two hundred European officers remaining this is not likely to become a political issue.

99. MCS officers constituted a large and important part of the federal Legislative Council, where, in 1937 for example, they accounted for almost one-half the total membership. This included, among other MCS members, the four residents, the federal secretary, legal adviser, financial adviser, adviser on education, commissioner of customs and excise, controller of labor, and secretary for Chinese affairs. See Federated Malay States, *Proceedings of the Federal Council, 1937* (Kuala Lumpur, 1938).

increasingly being recruited directly into the MCS upon graduation from a recognized university.[100] Thus, a bifurcation of the
modern MCS can be detected, and a certain amount of tension is
evident between the two groups. For the present time at least, it
is the senior group that molds the character of the MCS, and it
was largely through the MAS that the traditions of the MCS have
been passed on and communicated, primarily to the older officers,
but to a lesser extent to the younger group as well.

It would, in fact, be difficult to overestimate the continuing,
though perhaps unapparent, influence of the MAS on the present-
day MCS, for as the MCS was Malayanized it became thoroughly
permeated with officers whose background and experience had
been gained from service in the MAS. In January, 1962, of fifty-
nine of the most senior posts held by Malayan officers of the MCS,
forty-two were filled by Malays formerly of the MAS. These forty-
two appointments included secretaries or permanent secretaries
to ministries, deputy secretaries, state secretaries, commissioners
of lands and mines, and the private secretary to the Yang di-
Pertuan Agong. Moreover, these tabulations take into account
neither retired MCS officers serving as appointed heads of public
corporations and other public bodies[101] nor subordinate former
MAS officers who hold MCS field posts throughout the Federation. There can be little doubt that the MAS, although in its own
right of diminished importance today, still exerts considerable
influence on the composition of the MCS, and perhaps more
important, it continues to shape the outlook of the senior bureaucrats.

Created in 1910, the MAS originally drew potential officers
only from Malay College at Kuala Kangsar[102] with the intention of

100. As of January 1, 1962, more than 40 per cent of the 204 Malayan officers
holding time-scale posts had been recruited directly into the MCS from
universities. For details of recruitment into this group, see the author's
Bureaucratic Transition in Malaya, chap. v., n. 18. For statistical analysis of
recruitment into the superscale posts, see the author's "Policy Formulation, Policy
Execution, and the Elite Structure of Contemporary Malaya," in Wang Gungwu,
(ed.), *Malaysia: A Survey* (London, 1964), p. 352, Table 55.
101. Such bodies as the Public Services Commission and the Central Electricity
Board are headed by former MCS officers.
102. The influence of Malay College on the development of Malaya should not
be underestimated. Shortly after its establishment, the report of the adviser on

utilizing these to staff subordinate administrative posts, particularly those in district and sub-district offices. Although the first Malay officer of the MAS was not promoted to the MCS until 1921,[103] the original Scheme of Service more than a decade earlier had foreseen the possibility that exceptional officers might expect to receive such promotions. Until the MCS was opened to direct local recruitment in 1953, the MAS remained the only avenue open to Malays interested in pursuing an administrative career.[104]

There is a sense of tradition and an *esprit de corps* that surrounds the MCS and is particularly evident among the older officers. Although there is now complete parity of salary scales among the various services,[105] no appointment carries with it prestige comparable to entry into the MCS. Moreover, following the lead of the prewar expatriate elite of the MCS, older Malay officers of the Malay College–MAS tradition often attempt to communicate to younger officers something of the aura that has surrounded the old MCS. While these attempts have not been completely successful, the younger officers have absorbed enough

education commented that "from this school Government have great hopes that the sons of Malays of the Raja and higher classes will be educated and trained on the lines of an English public school and be fitted to take a share in the Government of their country." Straits Settlements, *Report for 1910 on the Federated Malay States,* p. 23, in Great Britain, *Accounts and Papers, 1911,* Vol. LIII, Cmd. 5902. For the next fifty years the normal course of an aspiring Malay's career was from Malay College, to Raffles College (after 1929), to the MAS, to the MCS.

103. The present chairman of the Public Services Commission, Dato' Hamzah bin Abdullah, was promoted from the MAS to the MCS in 1921, but he was not the first Malay to be accepted in the senior service. The Raja Chulan bin Ex-Sultan Abdullah entered the MCS in 1903 from the Perak service, and thirteen years later this was duplicated by the Raja Chulan's younger brother, the Raja Kechil Tengah Said Tauphy. These two appointments, however, were exceptional, and no other Malays joined the MCS until 1921.

104. It should also be pointed out that British policies in the creation of Malay College and its policies governing the relationship of the MAS and the MCS meant that there was no avenue of recruitment open to non-Malay Asians until 1953.

105. The salary scales of technical and professional personnel are now equal to those of the administrative services. However, the struggle for equality was a lengthy and sometimes bitter one. Parity was achieved as a result of the Himsworth Report of 1954. Federation of Malaya and Singapore, *Report of the Committee on the Examination of Superscale Salaries of Division I of the Public Services of the Federation of Malaya and the Colony of Singapore* (Kuala Lumpur, 1954). This was only the close of a struggle that reached its climax in 1950. See Federation of Malaya, Special Committee on Salaries in the Federation of Malaya (F. C. Benham, chairman), *Report* (Kuala Lumpur, 1950); and Federation of Malaya, Professional Officers' Committee (Harold Willan, chairman), *Report* (Kuala Lumpur, 1950).

of the proud tradition to maintain the prestige of the service.[106]

Viewing the posts held by MCS officers throughout government, it is easy to support a claim to bureaucratic superiority. With the exception of the Ministry of External Affairs, which itself has a large number of former MCS officers, personnel of the MCS are to be found in some of the most senior posts in each of the ministries.[107] In addition, an analysis of the grade structure of various components of the bureaucracy reveals that by far the most advantageous position is held by the MCS in that personnel of that service can expect the greatest opportunity for promotion to senior posts.[108] There is little doubt that the MCS is the senior service and that this seniority is recognized, though perhaps somewhat grudgingly, by the remainder of the bureaucracy.

Several characteristics of the MCS itself need to be pointed out. First, in composition the MCS is primarily Malay and not Malayan. By administrative order, sanctioned by the Constitution,[109] recruitment into the MCS must be maintained at a ratio of four Malays to each non-Malay.

106. In mannerisms, speech, and habits some of the older MCS officers of the Malay College–MAS tradition seem much more akin to the prewar expatriates than they do to the new breed of MCS officers that arrived after the Japanese occupation. This Japanese interregnum, in fact, provides much more of a hiatus in Malayan administrative history than does the coming of independence. A careful comparison of the staff lists of 1940 (the last reliable list before the war) and 1947 (the first list published after the Japanese surrender) reveals some significant changes. Of 238 MCS officers in 1947, 107 (44.9 per cent) had not seen previous service in Malaya. Of forty-nine officers holding senior posts on the 1940 list, only fourteen appeared on the 1947 list. In the junior MCS posts, where the day-to-day contacts with Malay subordinates took place, the average length of service among expatriate officers dropped from 12.6 years in 1940 to 5.4 years in 1947, and in this latter group 55 per cent had seen no previous service in the Malay Peninsula. This, together with the hardships connected with the occupation and reconstruction, probably go far to account for the marked decline in the attitude of elitism between the prewar and the postwar MCS.

107. The administrative head of each ministry is, of course, an MCS officer, and—except in rare cases—the administrative head is usually the senior-most officer in terms of grade and salary.

108. In the MCS, 37.3 per cent of the total service falls into the category of senior (superscale) posts. The comparable figures for other components are: police, 10.7; professional, 16.0; and non-professional, 10.1 per cent. These figures were tabulated by the author from the annual staff lists of the Federation Establishment Office. For a graphic representation of this structuring, see the author's *Bureaucratic Transition in Malaya*, p. 103, Graph 2.

109. Article 153 provides that the Yang di-Pertuan Agong, whose responsibility it is "to safeguard the special position of the Malays and the legitimate interests of other communities," in order to "ensure the reservation for Malays of such proportion as he may deem reasonable of positions in the public services," may therefore "give such general directions as may be required for that purpose to any Commission," and the commission "shall duly comply with the directions."

The reluctance to admit non-Malay Malayans to the administrative services,[110] and later to encourage the recruitment of
Malays, could be regarded as a direct continuation of the historic
British policy of attempting to bring some Malays out of the
kampongs to introduce them to the realities of modern life, all the
while insulating this indigenous community from possible interference by the more vigorous communities of immigrants.[111] It
was not, in fact, until 1953 that any non-Malay Asians were
admitted to the MCS. It was at that time that the high commissioner, Sir Gerald Templer, with the consent of the Malay rulers
and the advice of the Executive Council, proposed the admission
of non-Malays; however, according to the high commissioner, in
view of the necessity "that the special position of the Malays
should be retained in the Civil Service and improved in the whole
economic field," it was intended that recruitment of non-Malays
should "be limited to one for every four Malays admitted . . . in
the future."[112] It was this policy that was adopted by the
government at the time of independence. Thus, while the total
bureaucracy of the Federation has achieved a remarkable cosmo-
politan quality, the administrative services have remained almost
a Malay preserve, and it is the MCS that predominates in the
bureaucracy and plays a vital role in the conduct of government.

Dynamics of the Bureaucratic Machine

(1) *The integrity of the bureaucracy.* There have been no
official reports on the occurrence of corruption in the bureaucracy
of sufficiently current nature to merit any conclusions on a subject
as delicate as this. The most recent study, which itself was highly

110. Non-Malays are admitted to the Executive Service, which was created in
1957 primarily to relieve senior administrative officers of some of the time-
consuming but important tasks of a more routine nature. It must be candidly
admitted that the Executive Service has not lived up to its expectations, due to a
number of reasons too lengthy to consider here.

111. Today there are quotas established for Malays in industry, transportation,
educational bursaries and scholarships, police, the External Affairs Service, and in
numerous other fields.

112. Speech by the high commissioner before the Federal Legislative Council,
in Federation of Malaya, Federal Legislative Council, *Proceedings* (Fifth Session)
(Kuala Lumpur, 1953), pp. 473–474 at 473.

controversial since it considerably exceeded the commission's terms of reference, was published in 1955, and today we are dealing with an almost entirely different bureaucracy.[113] However, some of the commission's more general observations may still prove valid when the next investigation is made, for they concern some of the major problems that Malayan bureaucracy could logically expect to face. The commission concluded that

we believe that bribery and other forms of corruption are practiced in all vulnerable departments but there is no evidence from which either the actual or the comparative incidence can be estimated. . . . The most vulnerable departments are those . . . which necessarily have large numbers of the lower ranks in direct contact with the public in circumstances where both are tempted and supervision is difficult and remote.[114]

The "vulnerable" areas of the bureaucracy seem most likely to be the departments employing large numbers of junior officers having daily face-to-face contacts with the general public for whom they perform a service not available through any other organization. Most of the public with which they deal may be illiterate in English and thus are largely unaware of the intricacies of government and are generally awed by the magnitude and complexity of the whole operation. The public servants, on the other hand, would probably have no more—and often considerably less—than a secondary school education; moreover, they would probably represent some of the less qualified, since the demands of Malayanization decimated Division II and caused widespread promotions from Division III to fill these vacancies.[115] Added to this is the cultural fact that the servant and the receiver of the services operate within a mental frame of reference where "tea money" is an accepted way of getting something done.

113. See Federation of Malaya, Commission to Enquire into Matters Affecting the Integrity of the Public Services, 1955, *Report* (Kuala Lumpur, 1955). The government, while agreeing with the general conclusions of the commission, took exception to some of their specific criticisms of individual bureaucrats and took the unusual step of including this rebuttal as an insert in the official report.

114. *Ibid.*, p. 59.

115. The group of public servants described here would largely fall into Division III, described by the Trusted Commission Report as being composed, among others, of technical assistants, land administration personnel, and personnel of most of the clerical services. Such officers as immigration and customs clerks and rank and file police would also be in Division III.

Personal observation—which of course is a highly unreliable gauge where such a subject is concerned—suggests that corruption in Malayan bureaucracy is not widespread, at least at the levels of government where it might constitute a pernicious force subversive of the bureaucratic structure. It seems most likely that where it occurs it probably involves "tea money" accepted by a servant to perform a legal and expected service somewhat more expeditiously than he might otherwise have done. Or, perhaps it involves encouraging a client to engage some outside private service, which in fact he really did not need. This, of course, is corruption, but it is the same sort of corruption that mature bureaucracies throughout the world have had to be watchful of for centuries.

(2) *Rural and community development.*[116] Under British administration rural development existed only in the sense that commercial development took place on or around the estates, plantations, or mining concessions, which are located in the countryside and are thus "rural." It was only in the political climate of the postwar period, as internal self-government was approaching, that the first mentions of "rural" or "community development" were to be heard. The first bureaucratic organization that emerged to carry out some of these goals was the Rural and Industrial Development Authority. RIDA, which was created in 1950 under the direction of the founder of the United Malays National Organization, Dato Onn bin Ja'afar, was originally intended to provide physical amenities for rural areas, to change the structure of the rural economy through the elimination of the middle man, and to foster a spirit of self-reliance in the rural people. RIDA early became involved in the political struggles between its director (who resigned from the United Malay National Organization, UMNO, to create Party Negara, a group that commanded very little following) and the newly emerging Alliance party, which incorporated as one of its major units the party

116. Except where otherwise noted, this section is drawn chiefly from the forthcoming monograph on rural development in Malaya by Gayl D. Ness of the University of Michigan. The author is indebted to Mr. Ness for permission to read and to utilize material from his excellent manuscript, which for the first time will provide a detailed account of the internal dynamics of one important sector of Malayan government.

that Dato Onn had originally created. Though RIDA was reconstituted as a governmental corporation in 1954, its budgets have always been small and its projects more accidentally than rationally planned; its services have been tinged with racial exclusiveness, and its accomplishments have been no more outstanding than might have been expected under the political and economic circumstance within which it operated. In fact, were RIDA not still a political issue, it is possible that the most rational approach might be to scrap the organization and hand its limited functions over to one of the other more effective bureaucratic organizations concerned with rural development. Although RIDA—as the first organization concerned with rural development—represents a milestone, the most effective bureaucratic structures within this field emerged after the first elective government assumed office in 1955.

The *Report of the Land Administration Commission* of 1958 pointed out that at the time of writing 116,000 applications for land were awaiting decision, 37,000 titles were awaiting registration, and 50,000 titles were awaiting issue.[117] In part this backlog could be attributed to the Emergency, which had caused all other responsibilities in the rural areas to be relegated to a very low priority in the interest of defeating the communist revolutionaries. In part, however, it was a manifestation of a much larger problem involving a continuation of the British practice of letting land administration operate under the initiative of local direction without the benefit of more comprehensive planning above the state level.[118] Begun in 1956 just prior to independence, the Federal Land Development Authority was created originally to provide land for those who were seeking it, but the approach represented a distinct break with policies of the past. Though in the original plans there was some emphasis on local initiative to guide the program, FLDA soon began to lay out development areas, clear the jungle, build the houses and other amenities, and

117. Federation of Malaya, *Report of the Land Administration Commission* (Kuala Lumpur, 1958), para. 119.
118. In part, this was occasioned by the demands of indirect rule. Land was purely a matter of state concern, a position that it retained under the federal Constitution of independent Malaya.

then to turn the projects over to landless peasants who in theory had been screened beforehand to select those most likely to benefit from the scheme.[119]

The most dynamic force in rural development has been the Ministry of Rural Development, which was created at the center of political power under the direct control of the deputy prime minister in 1959. Though it became involved in the crosscurrents of political exchanges between the deputy prime minister and the minister for agriculture, with the dismissal of the latter from the cabinet in mid-1962 the ministry has been the real driving force for development in the Malayan countryside. In fact, despite political differences, it has been a highly effective bureaucratic organization since 1960, and the extent of the construction of roads, schools, wells, water systems, and other amenities in the rural areas provides striking evidence of this effectiveness. Rural poverty is still the major problem that Malaya must solve, for political as well as economic reasons, and it is probable that funds allocated for such development must continue to capture a large share of the annual budget.[120]

(3) *Public corporations, statutory bodies, and the bureaucracy.* It is always a hazy line that separates public and private bureaucracy when one enters the field of public corporations. Employees of Malayan railways, for example, were considered public servants at the time of the creation of the service commissions, yet government officials were so unsure of the future status of railway employees that they found it desirable to create a separate Railway Service Commission to make it less cumbersome to reclassify these employees if necessary.[121] Table 4 below, which is based on the careful work of a former Colombo Plan adviser, attempts to demonstrate in a summary manner the extent to which public corporations and statutory bodies are to be found in

119. In addition to Ness, *op. cit., passim,* see D. E. M. Fiennes, "The Malayan FLDA," *Journal of Local Administration Overseas,* I (July, 1962), 156–163.

120. For a detailed analysis of the allocation of financial resources for development purposes over the period 1950–1965, see Ness, *op. cit.,* chap. iii, Table 3. Ness provides in this chapter a fascinating and well-documented account of the shift from custodial to developmental goals in Malaya.

121. See above, p. 571, n. 49.

the Federation of Malaya. The list is perhaps not comprehensive, though it is probably the most complete collection now available, for much work remains to be done in Malaya on the nature and role of these public bodies. Moreover, the brief notations appearing in the extreme right-hand column should be taken only as a general guide to the extent of governmental control. Reference should be made to the authorizing statutes for more specific details.

(*4*) *The bureaucracy and the decision-making process.* Malaya is not an "administered" state, as some observers are quick to describe the politics of the new states of Africa and Asia, for there are elected and appointed politicians who guide the government just as much as does the bureaucracy. Yet the bureaucracy is not perfectly neutral in the sense of being a lifeless instrument silently carrying out the directives of the elected representatives of the Malayan people. An attempt has been made in another essay[122] to suggest that decision-making in Malaya cannot correctly be viewed at the present time as a struggle among the various elite groups for the acceptance of differing basic policies or approaches to government. Statistics suggest that most of the political, bureaucratic, royal, and perhaps military elite have come through approximately the same process of political socialization; they all speak the same political language (in form as well as in meaning); they have all accepted the same political game; they are all willing to abide by roughly the same rules of the game. There are of course dissenters, but these are presently outside, not inside, the government. Recruitment procedures at the present time assure the continuance of a bureaucracy drawn from this socialization process, and political realities seem to indicate that the general character of the political, military, and royal elite is not likely to change in the foreseeable future. Thus, it is only within this general elite consensus that one can speak of the neutrality of Malayan bureaucracy. This may or may not constitute a genuine neutrality; it simply means that this neutrality has not yet been tested.

122. See the author's "Policy Formulation, Policy Execution, and the Political Elite Structure of Contemporary Malaya," in Wang (ed.), *op. cit., passim.*

Table 4. Public Corporations and Statutory Bodies, Federation of Malaya, 1962

Public corporation or statutory body	Authorizing or controlling statute	Extent of governmental control or responsibility
Board of the Rubber Research Institute of Malaya	Rubber Research Institute of Malaya Enactment (FMS Cap. 108)	acde
Malayan Railway Administration	Railway Ordinance, 1948	bcfgh
Central Electricity Board	Electricity Ordinance 1949	acdfgi
Social and Welfare Services Lotteries Board	Social and Welfare Service Lotteries Board, 1950	cdejk
Housing Trust of the Federation of Malaya	Housing Trust Ordinance, 1950	cdf
Employees Provident Fund Board	Employees Provident Fund Ordinance, 1951	cgi
Rubber Industry (Replanting) Board	Rubber Industry (Replanting) Fund Ordinance, 1952	ci
Rural and Industrial Development Authority	Rural and Industrial Development Authority Ordinance, 1953	acfg
Tin Industry (Research and Development) Board	Tin Industry (Research and Development) Ordinance, 1953	cl
Penang Port Commission	Penang Port Commission Ordinance, 1955	acfghijk
Federal Land Development Authority	Land Development Ordinance, 1956	cdfgi
Malayan Pineapple Industry Board	Pineapple Industry Ordinance, 1957	cgi
Central Bank of Malaya	Central Bank of Malaya Ordinance, 1958	acfg
Malayan Rubber Fund Board	Malayan Rubber Fund (Research and Development) Ordinance, 1958	cf
Board of Trustees of the National Art Gallery	National Art Gallery Ordinance, 1959	cf
Board of Control of the Dewan Bahasa dan Pustaka	Dewan Bahasa dan Pustaka Ordinance, 1959	cf
Commissioner of the Federal Capital of Kuala Lumpur	Federal Capital Act, 1960	acf

a. Appointment of director.
b. Appointment of director as concurrent power shared with another constitutional or statutory body.
c. Appointment of some or all members of directorate.
d. Determination of remuneration and/or expenses and allowances of members of the directorate.
e. Power to formulate general policies concerning operation of the body.
f. Power of direction more specific than formulation of general policies.
g. Power of approving or making regulations, policy directions, permits, schedules, bylaws, or contracts.
h. Power to make or approve rates or fares.
i. Power to approve stock issues, investments, borrowing, or loans.
j. Power to inspect, or to authorize the inspection of, accounts other than in the annual budget review.
k. Power to disallow specific expenditures or expenses.
l. Power to recommend, approve, or impose tax on exports.

Source: Federation of Malaya, *Malayan Constitutional Documents* (2nd ed.; Kuala Lumpur, 1962), II, 287–292. The author is also indebted to the compiler of this volume, R. H. Hickling, for several helpful suggestions in regard to the above information.

10

Administrative Change in Nepal

Merrill R. Goodall

No assessment of Nepal's administrative system can be made without some knowledge of those elements of history and tradition which have shaped and continue to influence the conduct of public administration in Nepal. Because Nepal has only recently come to the attention of the Western world, it seems appropriate to describe the ecological factors of significance.[1]

1. Since so little is known of Nepal, a general bibliography is included at this point. Much of the literature is difficult to find, hence citations follow a more complete form than that used in most other notes throughout this volume.

Leonhard Adam, *Buddhastatuen, Ursprung und Formen der Buddhagestalt* (Stuttgart: Strecker und Schroder, 1925); Leonhard Adam, *Hochasiatische Kunst* (Stuttgart: Strecker und Schroder, 1923); C. U. Aitchison, "Nipal," in *A Collection of Treaties, Engagements, and Sunnuds Relating to India and Neighboring Countries* (Calcutta: G. A. Saviele and P. M. Cranenburgh, 1893), II, Part 1, 187–225; C. U. Aitchison, "Treaties and Engagements Relating to Nepal," in *A Collection of Treaties, Engagements, and Sunnuds Relating to India and Neighboring Countries* (Calcutta: Government of India, 1929), XIV, Part III, 35–69; Jagdish Man Singh Amatya, *Picturesque Nepal; a Handbook for Tourists* (Kathmandu: Commercial Company, 1956); Kaiser Bahadur, *Assessment of the Judicial Customs of Nepal Through Inscriptions and Authentic Documents from the Buddhistic Period to the 6th Century*, A.D. (Kathmandu: the author, 1958); Poorna Bahadur, *Nepal Behind the Screen* (Kathmandu: Nepal Youth League, 1957); Henry Ballantine, *On India's Frontier; or Nepal, the Gurkhas' Mysterious Land* (New York: J. Selwin Tait and Son, 1895); Radhagovinda Basak, "The Kingdom of Nepal," in *The History of North-Eastern India: Extending from the Foundation of the Gupta Empire to the Rise of the Pala Dynasty of Bengal* (320–760 A.D.) (Calcutta: The Book Company, 1934), chap. xi, pp. 239–302; R. N. W. Bishop, *Unknown Nepal* (London: Luzac and Co., 1952); Jennifer Bourdillon, *Visit to the Sherpas* (London: Collins, 1956); Percy Brown, *Picturesque Nepal* (London: Adam and Charles Black, 1952); Orfeur Cavenagh, *Rough Notes on the State of Nepal: Its Government, Army, and Resources* (Calcutta: W. Palmer, 1851); *Census of Population, Nepal, 1952–54* A.D. (Kathmandu: Department of Statistics, 1958); Herbert B. Edwardes and Herman Merivale, "Some Account of the Kingdom of Nepaul . . . ," in *Life of Sir Henry Lawrence* (London: Smith, Elder, and Co., 1873), chaps. xi–xiii, pp. 316–379; Francis Egerton, *Journal of a Winter's Tour in India; with a Visit to the Court of*

Nepal was isolated from the modern world until the 1950's.
Reliable historical records do not appear until the later decades of

Nepaul (2 vols.; London: J. Murray, 1852); James Baillie Fraser, "Historical Sketches of Nepal," in *Journal of a Tour Through Part of the Snowy Range of the Himala Mountains and to the Sources of the Rivers Jumna and Ganges* (London: Rodwell and Martin, 1820), Part 1, pp. 1–48, 507–544; G. H. D. Gimlette, *Nepal and the Nepalese* (London: H. F. and G. Witherby, 1928); Anirudha Gupta, *Politics in Nepal* (Bombay: Allied, 1964); Toni Hagen, *Nepal* (Berne: Kummerly and Frey, 1961); Toni Hagen, *Observations on Certain Aspects of Economics and Social Development Problems in Nepal*, Report No. TAO/NEP/1 (New York: United Nations, 1959); Francis (Buchanan) Hamilton, *An Account of the Kingdom of Nepal, and of the Territories Annexed to This Dominion by House of Gurkha* (Edinburgh: Archibold Constable and Co., 1918); Norman Hardie, *In Highest Nepal; Our Life Among the Sherpas* (London: George Allen and Unwin, Ltd., 1957); William Wilson Hunter, *Life of Brian Houghton Hodgson; British Resident at the Court of Nepal* (London: John Murray, 1896); William Wilson Hunter, "Nepal," in *The Imperial Gazetteer of India* (London: Trubner and Co., 1881), VII, 103–117; Pradyumna P. Karan, *Nepal* (Lexington: University of Kentucky Press, 1960); W. Kirkpatrick, *An Account of the Kingdom of Nepaul. Being the Substance of Observations Made During a Mission to that Country in the Year 1793* (London: Miller, 1811); Percival Landon, *Nepal* (2 vols.; London: Constable, 1928); Sylvain Levi, *Le Nepal; Étude Historique d'un Royaume Indou*, Annales du Musée Guimet; Bibliothèque d'études, tomes XVII, XVIII, XIX (3 vols.; Paris: Ernest Leroux, 1905, 1905, 1908); Ella Maillart, *The Land of the Sherpas* (London: Hodder and Stoughton, 1955); Isabelle Massieu, *Nepal et pays Himalayens* (Paris: Librarie Felix Alcan, 1914); C. J. Morris, *The Gurkhas. A Handbook for the Indian Army* (Delhi: Manager of Publications, 1933); Henry Ambrose Oldfield, *Sketches from Nipal. Historical and Descriptive, with Anecdotes of the Court Life and Wild Sports of the Country in the Time of Maharaja Jang Bahadur, G.C.B., to Which is Added an Essay on Nepalese Buddhism, and Illustrations of Religious Monuments, Architecture, and Scenery from the Author's Own Drawings* (2 vols.; London: W. H. Allen and Co., 1880); Laurence Oliphant. *A Journey to Kathmandu (The Capital of Nepaul) with the Camp of Jung Bahadur; Including a Sketch of the Nepaulese Ambassador at Home* (London: John Murray, 1852); Dilli R. Regmi, *Ancient and Medieval Nepal* (Kathmandu: the author, 1952); Dilli R. Regmi, *A Century of Family Autocracy in Nepal* (Banaras: Commercial Printing Works, 1950); Dilli R. Regmi, *The Nepali Democratic Struggle; Its Aim and Character* (Banaras: Nepali National Congress, 1948); Mahesh C. Regmi, *The Land Grant System: Birta Tenure* (Berkeley: Institute of International Studies, University of California, 1964); Thomas Smith, *Narrative of a Five Years' Residence at Nepaul from 1841 to 1845* (2 vols.; London: Colburn, 1852); Richard Temple, "Remarks on a Tour Through Nepal in May, 1876," in *Journals Kept in Hyderabad, Kashmir, Sikkim and Nepal* (2 vols.; London: W. H. Allen, 1887), II, 221–262; W. Tilman, *Nepal Himalaya* (Cambridge: Cambridge University Press, 1952); Giuseppe Tucci, *Preliminary Report on Two Scientific Expeditions in Nepal*, Serie Orientale Roma, X, Materials for the Study of Nepalese History and Culture (Rome: Instituto Italiano per il Medio ed Estremo Oriente, 1956); Francis Tuker, *Gorkha, the Story of the Gurkhas of Nepal* (London: Constable and Co., 1957); Eden Vansittart (revised by B. U. Nicolay), *Gurkhas; Handbook for the Indian Army* (Calcutta: Superintendent Government Printing, 1915); Christoph von Furer-Haimendorf, *The Sherpas of Nepal: Buddhist Highlanders* (Berkeley: Institute of International Studies, University of California, 1964); James Talboys Wheeler, *Diary of Events in Nipal 1841 to 1846* (Calcutta: Foreign Office Press, 1878); Daniel Wright (ed.), *History of Nepal with an Introductory Sketch of the Country and People of Nepal* (Cambridge: Cambridge University Press, 1877).

the nineteenth century, and these records relate almost entirely to the Kathmandu Valley. The word "Nepal" is still commonly applied to the Kathmandu Valley alone; outside the valley there is only a slight sense of national unity and little identification of the population with the Nepalese state. It is not easy for the national government to develop effective bonds of loyalty stronger than the many particularistic ties which abound beyond the Kathmandu Valley.

Communication within the country is not easily achieved in Nepal's physical and cultural setting; there are many obstacles to the development of a national consciousness and a national administration. Not the least of the barriers to administrative development is the country's geography, which presents an extraordinary diversity of landscape. Nepal's northern frontier is with China; the southern border, of equal length, is with India. Three strikingly dissimilar physical zones, each reaching east-west across the 550-mile extent of the country, divide the Nepal nation. East-west travel is not easy; many district headquarters are as much as four weeks' walk from the central government's offices in the Kathmandu Valley. The first of the physical zones, a northern zone, consists of the high Himalaya; the second, a central belt, known as the "hill districts," is rugged terrain difficult to traverse and includes a number of well-populated but isolated valleys, the most notable being the Kathmandu Valley; the third zone, on the southern border, the terai, is not greater than twenty miles wide and is culturally linked to India. Three great river systems, the Kosi, the Gandaki, and the Karnali, move down the southern slopes of the Himalaya and empty into the Indian plains. The Karnali, in particular, acts as a hindrance to communication and commerce; its current is too rapid for the available dugout canoes and the local bridge builders are unable to span its deep canyons. This river, among others, is a divisive force.

The country's population, 9,756,390 according to the preliminary census report of 1961, is heterogeneous. Many different ethnic groups are concentrated in isolated valleys, where population densities are high; the extraordinary ethnic variety found in the small, heavily populated river valley settlements does not contribute to the development of political community. Two religions—Hinduism and Buddhism—have met in Nepal. The nearly ten million Nepalese speak a variety of languages and dialects; moreover, they represent two major human physical types, the Indo-Nepalese and the Tibeto-Nepalese. The Indo-Nepalese type totals more than seven millions and includes the Pahari, the Indians of the terai, the Tharu, and the Newar; the Tibeto-Nepalese group includes the Tamang, Magar, and Rai. The official national language is Nepali (also known as Gurkhali, Khaskura, and Parbatiya). The Indo-European languages found in the country include Nepali and the various languages spoken in the terai; the Tibeto-Burman languages include Magar, Gurung, Rai, and the Bhoto dialects of Sherpa and Thakali. Newari is usually classified as a Tibeto-Burman language. Competence in Nepali is spreading slowly and it is gradually becoming a lingua franca. English is spoken by at least 10,000 as a principal secondary language. Few foreign technicians are skilled in Nepali; the proposals and documents which they present to His Majesty's Government are invariably in English.

Unlike its southern neighbor, Nepal did not experience colonial rule. Though some sections of what is known today as Nepal have fallen to external control, foreign domination of internal affairs has never been complete and has never touched the core of the administrative system. Separatist geographical factors tended to be reinforced by policies of cultural isolation imposed by the Rana regime. The task of organizing that administrative system and of unifying a remarkably heterogeneous society is today the responsibility not of colonial rule but of the king, who alone controls all principal instruments of power.

Beginning in the sixteenth century the Gurkha kings sought to edge the country toward a degree of national unification; their control reached the Kathmandu Valley in 1767 when Prithvi Narayan Shah conquered the four principalities of the valley. The Shah dynasty withstood effective challenge until 1846. In that year, Jang Bahadur Rana killed the king's advisers and took for himself the title of maharaja, or prime minister. He was thereby given the powers of life and death and punishment, of appointing and dismissing all Government servants, of declaring war, concluding peace and signing treaties with all foreign powers including the British, the Tibetans and the Chinese; and finally, he was given the authority to make new laws and repeal any old ones, whether civil, criminal or military.[2]

The activities of successive kings were restricted; they were virtual prisoners, without freedom of movement and with only carefully controlled access to public funds and to educational opportunities. The prime ministership was hereditary in the Rana family and their rule survived until 1951.

No clear distinction between state revenue and the prime minister's personal income was drawn during the Rana regime. At the end of each year the surplus of revenue over expenditure for that year became the personal property of the ruler. The prime minister, therefore, had a personal interest in limiting public expenditure. Administration had two primary goals: the maintenance of order and the collection of revenue. Land tax was the almost exclusive source of revenue. Members of the Rana family, however, received grants of land, known as birta, which were frequently though not always tax-free.[3] The political effects of birta persist to this day. The number of public employees was limited; they were poorly paid, and their financial accounts were supervised in close detail by the rightly feared Department of Audit, kumarichowk.[4]

The kumarichowk acted as auditor and maintained the nominal accounting records which were thought necessary. Although each item of expenditure was carefully scrutinized, the system of accounting made it impossible to identify types of classes of expenditure and revenue. If the object of the system was to conceal the amount of surplus for any year, it can be judged an ideally functioning system. All public officials were subject to

2. Landon, *op. cit.*, I, 147.
3. For a careful description of the varying tax status of birta land, see Mahesh C. Regmi, *op. cit.*, II, 47–59.
4. The Department of Audit was separately organized and housed, and it was especially sensitive to the ruling Rana's attention. Activities of the department are considered by J. F. Luba, *Survey of the Organization of Government Accounting and Auditing in Nepal* (Kathmandu: United Nations, 1960).

dismissal at any time, and a formal review of all appointments, pajani, was conducted once a year. Moreover, an office known as haziri goswari undertook surprise inspections of public offices in the Kathmandu Valley. Attendance and performance were presumably checked daily; unexplained absences and work regarded by the inspectors as faulty were subject to fine. Although the work force was small, it was highly stratified, there being fifteen grades in the administrative and clerical services. There were no in-grade salary increments, and promotion was based wholly on chakari and seniority. Chakari was a distinctive, highly developed practice of Rana administration whereby civil servants paid formal obeisance to their seniors; today, not much more than a decade after the end of Rana rule, marvelous subtlety and refinement have become incorporated in chakari.[5]

Rana traditions are hardly a spent force in financial administration. Until 1959 no budget was determined in advance of the financial year. Expenditures are still approved on an *ad hoc* basis, as and when required, except for salaries and for certain recurrent commitments. Payments are made to individuals, not to departments, with the consequence that those who receive public funds are reluctant to handle them since they are personally responsible for them. Though understandable, such reluctance does not contribute to administrative effectiveness. The system of audit does not yield the sort of financial data the administrative system requires. But above all, the type of restraints which served well the purposes of Rana rule, act now to still initiative and capacity for decision.[6]

Administrative activities under the Ranas were most noticeable within the Kathmandu Valley; few services of government extended beyond that valley. The structure of administration con-

5. During the Rana regime, government servants gathered at the residence of their chief after a day's work to pay their respects and often waited hours for their senior to appear. Promotion was determined both by seniority and chakari. Today loyalty to one's superiors is expressed through unassigned, personal services, only nominally voluntary, and include such errands and domestic service as runs for kerosene permits and the guidance of shipments through customs.

6. See the summary of Eric Himsworth in "Public Finance," in Harry B. Price (ed.), *Economic Survey of Nepal*, Report No. TAO/NEP/3 (New York: United Nations, 1961), pp. 12–20. A more complete statement of this issue is found in Himsworth's *Report on the Fiscal System of Nepal* (Kathmandu: United Nations, 1959), pp. 2–5.

sisted of a dozen departments, each under the authority of a director general who, with very few exceptions, was a member of the Rana family and an officer in the army of at least the rank of colonel. Directors general were paid according to their military rank. Departments were established for such purposes as the conduct of the small Kathmandu telephone service, the care of public buildings in the capital, the maintenance of the some forty miles of roads, and for the construction of a projected road link to India. Serving under each director general was a hakim, who reported daily to the director general, as did many other government employees, whose time and energy were otherwise consumed in the preparation of remarkably detailed written accounts for submission through the hakim to the director general and to the kumarichowk.

Administration outside Kathmandu Valley was in the hands of centrally appointed bada hakims, or governors. Hardly any governmental authority was given anyone beyond the Rana family, and this principle extended, wherever practicable, to bada hakim appointments. The bada hakim raised what land revenue he could with the help of a revenue office, the mal adda, though the actual task of collection was then as today in the control of private agents. The bada hakim, through rackams, or *corvée,* found the labor to keep the trails open and the fields of the Ranas cultivated. Conscriptees were similarly secured for military service. The locally recruited militia helped the bada hakim fulfil his responsibility for law and order. District courts—amini in the hills and adalat in the terai—were established independently, formally, from the bada hakim. Few central departments functioned in any sense outside Kathmandu; where they could be said to exist at all, they operated inside the office of the bada hakim and that officer handled their communications to the center. The rules governing the work of the bada hakim differed according to the location of the office and differed, also, depending on whether a member of the Rana family headed the office. While the volume of administrative work in the districts is somewhat greater today than during the old regime, the formal structure of local administration has yet to see substantial change. It can be said, and often is said, that the present sovereign exercises *de jure,* but not *de facto,* rule over his kingdom.

Rana rule withdrew Kathmandu Valley from the world beyond; no more than a few hundred foreigners reached the capital by the early 1950's, and only limited numbers of Nepalese were permitted to travel abroad. But political traditions were susceptible to change to the south, in India, and the prohibition of travel to India was easily breached in the third and fourth decades of the twentieth century. Pilgrims, traders, and students entered India and returned with ideas new to Nepal. In 1950–1951 the Rana regime was challenged, and Mohan Shamsheer, the last of the hereditary maharajas, was forced to resign; in 1951 the monarchy, in the person of King Tribhuban, was restored as effective head of the state. The challenge was engendered by a dissident Rana faction which allied with the royal, Shah, family; Nepali Congress "popular" forces, mainly from the terai, were also a factor in the change. The "revolution" was a shift from Rana rule to Shah rule, with some Ranas partisans of the king.

From 1951 to 1959, government was conducted in accordance with the Interim Government of Nepal Act, promulgated by the King on February 18, 1951.[7] This act endowed the "King and his Council of Ministers" with executive and legislative authority. An auditor general and a Public Service Commission, among other agencies, were provided for by the act. During this eight-year interval, six different cabinets were appointed by the King; there were, as well, several periods in which King Tribhuban and then his successor, the present King Mahendra, assumed direct rule. In the absence of elections, no clear index of party strength was available to guide the King as prime ministers were named. During the periods of direct rule, the Palace Secretariat grew in

7. The Interim Government of Nepal Act was commonly described as the Interim Constitution of Nepal. An English translation is found in Narendar Goyal, *The King and His Constitution* (New Delhi: Nepal Trading Corporation, 1959), pp. 103–112. Drafts of the act had been submitted by officers of the Indian Embassy in Kathmandu, and certain sections of the approved version were drawn from the Indian Constitution. The sections on directive principles of state policy and fundamental rights (Part II) are notable examples. The act transferred the powers of the Ranas to the king and held that the "aim of the Interim Government shall be to create conditions, as early as possible, for holding elections for the Constituent Assembly which will frame a Constitution for Nepal" (clause 41, Part VI).

strength, in some areas duplicated the work of the ministries, and developed links of its own to the secretaries of government. During direct rule, those issues normally dealt with by a cabinet ministry were presented directly to the palace for decision. No well-established, permanent cabinet secretariat was encouraged. The links thus forged by the palace were not readily ended when governmental operations next passed to the guidance of a prime minister and his party colleagues. Singha Durbar—the government secretariat—and the palace secretariat became rivals; the competitive relationship persisted after the 1959 election and finally ended only in the months after the assumption of control in December, 1960, by the monarch.

The Act of 1951 was not supplanted until February, 1959, when King Mahendra assented to a Constitution which provided for a cabinet ministry responsible to an elected Parliament.[8] General elections were begun in February, 1959, and Parliament, organized by the Nepali Congress party, which earned two-thirds of the seats, met in June, 1959. Article 56 of the 1959 Constitution provided for the suspension of parliamentary government if the king, after consulting the Council of State, determines that representative, parliamentary government is unworkable. Among other objectives, the governing Nepali Congress party sought to alter landlord-tenant relations and impose new taxes on land. On December 15, 1960, the King invoked Article 56 and dissolved the Parliament. The prime minister was deposed and placed in jail, where he remains today. Political parties were then, and are today, prohibited; the King embarked on direct rule, initially as chairman of a self-appointed Council of Ministers. The months following December 15, 1960, witnessed successive political screenings of the Civil Service, without reference to the Public Service Commission, and the unquestioned ascendancy of the

8. The 1959 Constitution was drafted by a four-man Draft Constitution Committee appointed by the King on March 6, 1958. Two members of the Committee were affiliated with the Nepali Congress party and the Constitution they helped draft reflects the strength of their party. For a brief period the committee was advised by Sir W. Ivor Jennings. King Mahendra announced the new Constitution on February 12, 1959; an English version is found in Goyal, *op. cit.*, pp. 1–102; a perceptive analysis of the Constitution was made by Kul Shekhar Sharma, *The Constitution of Nepal* (Kathmandu: Ministry of Home Affairs, 1959).

rapidly expanding Palace Secretariat over the Singha Durbar, the Civil Service Secretariat.

That ascendancy was confirmed by terms of the Constitution given the country on December 16, 1962.[9] The new Constitution provides for directly elected village (gaun) panchayats and town (nagar) panchayats, and for indirectly elected and nominated higher-level panchayats at the district, zonal, and national levels (jilla, anchal, and rastriya panchayats). The national panchayat, substantially an advisory body, is given no control over the Council of Ministers. That body is appointed by the monarch and is responsible to him. A second series of institutions, six class organizations, again with a four-tier structure, were designed to represent peasants, labor, women, students, youth, and children. These class organizations, however, cannot yet be said to function; their sponsor, the National Guidance Ministry, was dissolved in April, 1963. Functions of the National Guidance Ministry were passed to the Panchayat Ministry. By early 1966 there was little evidence that the class organizations had begun to play a vital political role.

Administration After the Overthrow of the Ranas

The revolution of 1950–1951 carried forward more from the past than it changed. At the same time, new elements of administration were introduced alongside the old. The forms and façade of the modern state were introduced. A central secretariat was established in the Singha Durbar, the residence of the former hereditary Rana prime ministers. Ministries were established, and in them departments responsible for executive action were installed. The country's first budgets were prepared, cabinets appointed, Civil Service rules promulgated, and economic devel-

9. According to the 1962 Constitution, "The Sovereignty of Nepal is vested in His Majesty and the executive, legislative and judicial powers emanate from him. Keeping in view the highest traditions of the Shah dynasty and the welfare and desires of the people His Majesty shall exercise these powers through bodies provided by this Constitution and the other laws for the time being in force" (Part V). The king is thus the sole source of power. A principal contributor to the document was Kulshekhar Sharma, at the time a secretary in the Education Ministry. An English translation was published by the Government; see *The Constitution of Nepal* (Kathmandu: Ministry of Law and Justice, 1963).

opment plans announced. But the new elements did not supplant the older systems of running the government of the country, and to those who had inherited the power and prestige of the Ranas there were good reasons why it should not be allowed to do so.

A multiple system of government persists, though the more potent and older part is usually unknown to foreigners, including the technical personnel of foreign aid missions. Three major administrative entities may be identified: the most visible of these is Singha Durbar—the formally constituted civil administration; a second is the foreign aid community; and a third is the Royal Palace and its secretariat. Though interrelated, these entities are also competitive; but each is itself segmented and faction-ridden. The first of these—the formally constituted ministries, departments, and agencies of central and local administration—employ (as of January, 1964) 1,081 gazetted officers and 23,664 non-gazetted servants, including in that number 13,379 peons. The combined services spent in 1965 about 29 crores Nepali rupees. But that sum was split nearly evenly between the regular and the development budgets. At least 96 per cent of the development budget was contributed to His Majesty's Government of Nepal by foreign aid missions. The predominantly foreign-financed development-budget activities in such areas as education, irrigation, mines, health, and forests conduct operations which often parallel the work of the rival regular-budget activities in identical fields. In each of these fields, among others, two departments which are only nominally unified and each with separate leadership carry on operations with their own allies and clients.

The substantial role of the second of the major administrative entities—the foreign aid missions—as financier has already been indicated. No important sector of Nepalese life is untouched by the external assistance agencies, and a description of administration in Nepal would be incomplete without notice of their activity. Nepal receives aid from the United States, India, the People's Republic of China, the Soviet Union, Israel, West Germany, and the United Nations, among others. Foreign aid personnel in Nepal in January, 1964, numbered about 290; there is nearly one foreign technician for every three Nepalese gazetted officers. The leading missions, measured by number of personnel, are India and the United States, each with eighty-seven officers. The Indian total includes ten military mission advisers but does not include 204 teachers and professors; the United States total includes nine cableway and telecommunication project personnel who are private contractors to the United States Agency for International Development but does not include Peace Corps volunteers. The external assistance teams offer advice but also contribute grants and loans, training, factories (sugar and tobacco from the USSR, brick and ceramics from China), roads (the United States, India, China), assistance to agriculture and community development (the United States, India)—to list a few subjects of aid only. Where advice is proffered, it may be drawn not from a single but rather from several and contrasting models of development. Moreover, conflicting advice may be pressed upon His Majesty's Government by several advisers, each of them working from common developmental premises but each expressing the varying internal needs of separate aid organizations. Such situations are not easily resolved by a perplexed host government whose own administrative resources are slim. Bizarre solutions are sometimes found. In an effort to accommodate both Indian and American assistance in community development, the country was at one time divided in half with one part assigned to the Indian aid mission and the other given over to the United States. Whatever final assessment can be given the work of the foreign assistance missions, one effect—the most evident in the competitive relationship of regular budget and development budget agencies—has been to segment the administrative structure. By any standard, however, the foreign aid community must be counted among those administrative entities now active in the country.

The Royal Palace, third of the entities, is the summit from which influence for administrative and economic development might emanate. The sovereign power of the country resides at this summit, and the inspiration of the public service could start from this source. In most circles in Nepal the king is held as an equal of Vishnu, and while many would not openly admit this, most permit it to influence their actions. Since the fall of the Ranas and again after the King's assumption of direct rule in 1960, the Royal Palace has grown in strength. Several indices of its strength and purpose may be cited. The Royal Palace now receives about one-sixth of the total revenue; an additional one-third of the total revenue is received by the army and the police, on whose support the royal power rests. The size of the Palace Secretariat has multiplied, though personnel statistics for the force are inexact. The Royal Palace directly employs more than three hundred officers and subordinates. Its Principal Secretariat, which governs relations with Singha Durbar, employs about sixty persons. Relations with the army and the police are supervised by the Principal Military Secretariat, numbering about fifty employees. A Principal Personal Secretariat, perhaps the advisory and task force closest to the king, employs some ninety persons. There are offices as well for the king's private secretary, a press secretariat, a public relations group, and a comptroller. Finally, a Special Department on the Reporting of Grievances, headed by a former assistant minister, invites civil servants to express privately their complaints.

The prohibition placed upon political parties after the assumption of royal control has not meant that the king, either through the Palace Secretariat or by other means, is assured of disinterested and qualified advice. While the conflict of party opinion has been avoided, divergent views do not now reach the summit of authority in the kingdom. The chief executive of the nation, no longer a maharaja but now a king, is supported by a Council of Ministers who are themselves nominees of the king and are trusted not to defect to the Congress and other parliamentary remnants. Singha Durbar—and all the formally constituted agents of administration—are now clearly subordinate to the Royal Palace.

Efforts at Administrative Reform

The initial impulse toward administrative reform came from external sources. As early as 1948 the Indian prime minister,

Nehru, sought to convince the fading Rana regime of the necessity of reform. After the Ranas fell, the Nepali Congress leadership, which had been given much of its political education in India, received the assistance of Indian advisers in administration. Nepal has since experienced a continuing flow of foreign advisers. The first advisers were almost exclusively Indian, and Indian influence in this sensitive field was dominant until the mid-1950's. Greatest reliance was next placed—from about 1957 to 1964—on United Nations experts. Today the United Nations' presence in this field is shared by technicians from the United States Agency for International Development; about 70 per cent of Nepal's development budget is contributed by the United States. The national composition of foreign advisers can be expected to vary in the years ahead, depending on such factors as the seriousness of Nepalese interest in administrative reform, the relative strength of the foreign aid missions and the extent of their stake in improved administrative performance, and political need as seen by the host government.

Two Indian advisers served from April, 1951, to February, 1952; two others were added for short periods during that interval; and still another, a Punjab police officer, used his holiday to study police and security affairs in Nepal. These officers, two of them senior ICS men, thus constituted India's first technical assistance group in public administration. Though they had the interest of a generally pro-Indian cabinet ministry, they owed their assignment to India's concern with its northern neighbor's stability and not primarily because Nepal itself was conscious of deficiencies in its administrative capacity. The Indian advisers circulated materials drawn from the Government of India's central secretariat; these materials were written in English and consequently reached only a very limited audience in Singha Durbar. A Nepalese civil servant, in a perceptive unpublished note written not long after the departure of the Indian advisers, described their work as

a failure to understand the temperament and past training of the employees for whom the reforms were being suggested, and also a failure to understand the old system, a knowledge of which would have not only given a better idea of the kind of approach to be made to the whole question of reorganization, but would have also, to a great degree, sobered down the rather facetious attempt to directly copy methods and practices prevalent in the Indian Government and simply applying them to the conditions found in Nepal. Whereas the old personnel would have done better in the old imperfect structure with which they were familiar, the new conglomeration of both the old and the new practices was not comprehensible in its entirety to anyone.

The advisers acted not as a team but as individuals, though occasional study sessions which the advisers chaired brought together many of the secretaries. These meetings, however, were discontinuous and rarely included Nepalese civil servants below the level of secretary. No agency of Nepal government was established with management-improvement responsibilities, and the papers distributed by the group are not now to be found in Singha Durbar. The Indian advisers pioneered in an unusually difficult environment. Few if any channels of communication were open to the advisers with the older civil servants of government whose experience was acquired under the regime of the Ranas. They did have contact with officers at the secretary level; but most of these men were new to administration, were unacquainted with traditional Nepalese administrative methods, and were beginning to experience the first of many successive political screenings. Even architecture made difficult the work of the advisers. Singha Durbar was designed as a private residence at a time when a maximum of privacy, isolation, security, and protection was sought for the occupants, including concubines, of its hundreds of rooms. The new administration found obsolete and restrictive the many blocked corridors and dead-end landings; simple communication inside the structure was, and is now, a time-consuming process. Finally, the political security of the new administration was far from assured; Singha Durbar itself was occupied by rebel forces for a few days in January, 1952.

Conversations in New Delhi in December, 1951, between a party led by the Nepalese prime minister and Indian officials produced a proposal for large-scale Indian assistance in administration. Tentative plans were made for an Indian team consisting of more than one hundred officials, including officers of under-secretary and deputy secretary rank, commissioners, deputy inspectors general of police, district officers, and superintendents of police. Some among the Nepalese feared that the presence of so large a mission would stimulate anti-Indian sentiment in Kathmandu. The two governments decided finally that no more than three Indian experts, led by N. M. Buch, ICS, should be dispatched. Yet another, and independent, assessment was wanted, and this writer, upon invitation of the Government of Nepal, served as adviser in administration to the prime minister, Matrika Prasad Koirala, during April and May, 1952, prior to the arrival of the Indian experts. Recommendations were made for the terms of administrative survey and for the foundation of the more extensive effort that was to follow.[10] The Indian advisers arrived in late May and were in Nepal one month. Their terms of reference were (1) to study the existing organization of the civil administration in Nepal in the various departments both at the center and the districts and make recommendations for its reorganization, and (2) to assess the needs of the Nepal government for Indian officers to give assistance, the qualifications of the officers required, and the period for which their services would be needed. The practice of mixing the nationality of advisers persists to this day; dependence on a single country for assistance in any field of activity has been avoided where possible. Some of the foreign advisers have actually focused their attention on similar issues at an identical time but in ignorance of each other's presence and purpose. Two officers of the Government of Nepal, one of whom had had service as a bada hakim, were deputed to assist the Indians. The Indian experts necessarily worked from their own experience; their proposals for ministerial and departmental organization and for revenue and district administration reflect Indian models. A major recommendation urged the deputation to Nepal of more than one hundred Indian officers for varying periods; the posts to be filled by these officers included that of chief secretary and undersecretary in each of the major ministries and the Public Service Commission, chief engineer of

10. Merrill R. Goodall, *Report on Administration in Nepal to the Prime Minister* (Kathmandu: Government of Nepal, 1952).

the Public Works Department, and a number of bada hakims. Other Indian experts were to be employed as advisers, and a training team of forty-five men was to work in police administration. Considerable descriptive material on Nepalese administration was included in the committee's report.[11] That report, however, was marked "confidential" when published by the Ministry of External Affairs of the Government of India, and no more than one or two copies were made available to the Government of Nepal. The foreign community in Kathmandu was more amply supplied.

The Buch Committee proposals for Indian assistance did not bear fruit, and little systematic attention to administrative reform could be given between 1952 and 1956 by either foreign aid missions or Nepalese civil servants. These were years of discontinuous political leadership and included periods of direct rule by King Tribhuban, intervals of both single-party and coalition cabinet rule headed by a prime minister, and after Tribhuban's death a return to direct rule by King Mahendra, the successor to Tribhuban. Not until Tanka Prasad Acharya's prime ministership, which extended a record eighteen months from January, 1956, to July, 1957, was it possible to re-examine administrative issues. The Tanka Prasad Acharya cabinet prepared a draft five-year plan; this document, essentially an estimate of economic resources and needs and of government expenditure for the 1956–1961 period, considered the importance of administration to planning.

Successful conduct of the Five-Year Plan is inconceivable without substantial modifications in our governmental organization and the creation, as needed, of new mechanisms. For the administrative machinery which we have inherited from the past is coated with rusty procedures, laws, regulations, and practices that slow down and obstruct even routine operations. To carry out a many-sided programme of national development calling for daily decisions and extending across the country until it ultimately reaches every village, we require an efficient, smoothly running executive organization.[12]

11. Nepal Administrative Reorganization Committee, *Report* (New Delhi: Ministry of External Affairs, 1952).
12. *Draft Five Year Plan: A Synopsis* (Kathmandu: Government of Nepal), p. 6.

Until 1956 efforts toward the improvement of administration were
undertaken by *ad hoc* committees which were staffed primarily
and sometimes exclusively by foreign advisers. But in July, 1956,
the prime minister appointed an Administrative Reorganization
Planning Commission which consisted substantially of senior civil
servants; the prime minister chaired the commission, which
drafted the country's first Civil Service act.[13] The commission
recommended that an organization and methods office be established; this was done at once, in July, 1956, and located in the
Ministry of Finance.

The Acharya government also sought the support of an international team of administrative experts and accordingly invited the
United Nations Technical Assistance Division to supply advisers.
For half a dozen years thereafter the United Nations participated
in Nepalese government under its OPEX program,[14] whereby
experts secured appointment to such posts inside the Nepalese
Civil Service as chief conservator of forests, legal officer of
government, and manager of the Nepal Bank. The efforts of the
advisers were at first committed almost wholly to data collection.
Thus, the personnel administration adviser assembled the first
personnel statistics;[15] and in 1961 the economic planning adviser edited an *Economic Survey of Nepal,* the work of nine advisers and still a basic reference.[16]

The Administrative Reorganization Planning Commission's indigenous support at a high level did not last long, though during
its existence it was able to submit recommendations concerning

13. *Nepal Gazette,* 22 Bhadra 2013 (September 6, 1956). The Civil Service Act
includes provisions for the constitution of the civil service, appointments, tenure
of service, protection of civil servants against arbitrary removal or reduction in
rank, recruitment and conditions of service, and principles regulating transfers and
promotions.

14. For a description of this program generally, see Ralph Braibanti,
"Transnational Inducement of Administrative Reform: A Survey of Scope and
Critique of Issues," in William D. Siffin and John D. Montgomery (eds.), *Approaches to Development: Politics, Administration and Change* (New York, 1966),
pp. 133–185. An assessment of United Nations' programs in public administration
is found in Edward W. Weidner, *Technical Assistance in Public Administration
Overseas: The Case for Development Administration* (Chicago, 1964), pp. 12–15,
24–30, 74–77, 122–123, 146–148.

15. Walter Fischer, "Personnel Administration in Nepal," typescript (Kathmandu, 1958).

16. Price, *op. cit.;* pp. 7–12, prepared by Hartvig Nissen, deal with public
administration.

the duties of the district officer, the bada hakim, and the revision of the boundaries of districts.[17] As early as March, 1957, a special seven-man committee consisting of six foreign advisers and a Nepalese chairman was appointed to advise on the founding of an institute of public administration. The Organization and Methods Office itself experienced a series of interruptions, sometimes encouraged by the country's leadership and sometimes neglected by that leadership. Initially located in the Finance Ministry, this office was moved to the Home Ministry in September, 1958, then made an independent entity outside the jurisdiction of any ministry, and subsequently returned to the Home Ministry, again sent to the Finance Ministry, and most recently (in July, 1962) attached to the vice-chairman and then to the chairman of the Council of Ministers. These frequent shifts did not reflect the intrinsic attractiveness of the agency. The office's utility was unexplored and other agencies made frequent and successful raids on its staff.

High hopes for its successful functioning were often expressed, and these were as often shattered. The office was not unaffected by the political screenings which followed the King's assumption of direct rule in December, 1960; nearly all secretaries of government were released from service in the months following December, 1960. Again, on January 20, 1962, when the office (then known as the Public Administration Department) was transferred to the Finance Ministry, the then United Nations senior adviser in public administration, in an unpublished note, declared: "A most hopeful stage has now been reached. Public Administration is now accepted fully as the keystone to progress. The Public Administration Department is in being and anxious to start active work. . . ." Less than a month later, on February 21, 1962, in a final and unpublished report, this retiring senior adviser had to write that because of transfers of personnel

the Department has been destroyed for all practical purposes. There is now but one Under-Secretary and one Section Officer left serving; all

17. Subcommittee of the Administrative Reorganization Planning Commission, "Report on Reorganization of District Administration in Nepal," mimeographed (Kathmandu, 1957).

the remaining gazetted officers have been posted away or are on leave. . . . The organization through which the public services of Nepal might become more efficient has been destroyed.

The 1956 Administrative Reorganization Planning Commission recommended as well that an Institute of Public Administration, essentially an in-service training institute for all levels of government employees, be established. This was done by the King on February 18, 1959. In the first year of its existence, the institute organized lectures and short courses which were attended by well over five hundred civil servants. In 1961 the institute's separate identity was dropped and it was combined with the Organization and Methods Office (then known formally as the Public Administration Board). By March, 1962, the institute was defunct. It had no staff, no budget, and could not be said to exist. The rooms in Singha Durba which were allocated to the institute were literally ankle-deep in rubble, and its office equipment, gift of a foreign aid mission, covered with dust. The institute's library of some three hundred volumes was unavailable to prospective users.

The Report of the 1962 Committee on Administration

Expanded governmental services had been proposed by the governments of Tanka Prasad Acharya and his successor, Bisheshwar Prasad Koirala; their proposals led to concern in some quarters, though primarily in the foreign aid community, over the capability of the country's administrative system. In particular, broadened demand for increased governmental services was made by the first elected Parliament, which convened June 30, 1959. The 1959 Constitution defined Parliament as composed of the king, a House of Representatives of 109 directly elected members, and a Senate of thirty-six members. Half of the Senate's membership was elected by the House, and half nominated by the king. To become law, bills needed the approval of both houses and the assent of the king. The Nepali Congress party won seventy-four of the 109 seats in the popularly elected House. Behavior of the elected representatives conformed to the practices of legislators elsewhere; they asked for schools, roads, and bridges, among other utilities, for their districts. When that Parliament was dissolved on December 15, 1960, and its prime minister jailed, interest in quickening administrative effectiveness lessened. Turnover in the senior-most Civil Service grades approximated 100 per cent in the next few months. The Palace Secretariat and the groups around the king gained prestige and power at the expense of the civil servants housed in Singha Durbar. While the stake, financial and other, of the foreign aid groups in the economy and administration did not diminish in the months following the royal takeover, the significance of their encounter with their Singha Durbar counterparts declined sharply. Foreign assistance groups, moreover, were unable to relate themselves readily with the Royal Palace, in whose hands decision-making now lay—defining decision-making here as the capacity to veto proposals originating in Singha Durbar and the foreign community. Thereafter, the foreign donors' prime concern with the country's administration became defensive and self-protective, stimulated very largely by their own reporting and accounting requirements. Similarly, the Royal Palace's interest in public administration turned toward the values of order, stability, and qualities of neatness at the expense of any risk-taking commitment to the sort of development activities which had been voiced in Parliament.

In May, 1962, however, and only after considerable discussion, His Majesty's Government assented to a fresh review of its administrative resources, and a Committee on Administration was appointed.[18] Impulse for the new survey came from the United Nations advisory group in public administration. In the delicate area of administration, and confronted by a contentious foreign aid community, local leadership was relatively more receptive to the observations of an international, not a bilateral, agency. The

18. The committee was appointed May 15, 1962, and consisted of Premnarsingh Pradhan, secretary, Public Administration Department; Kulsekhar Sharma, secretary, Education Ministry; Yadunath Khanal, secretary, Foreign Affairs Ministry; and Merrill R. Goodall, senior adviser in public administration, United Nations Technical Assistance Board, who drafted the report. The committee's final report was submitted on July 6, 1962.

committee's terms of reference were deliberately not overly ambitious. The report held that:

part-time, short-term survey committees, which have usually acted without the benefit of explicitly written terms of reference, cannot meet the urgent and pressing needs of management-improvement in Nepal. Administrative study and administrative reorganization are continuing responsibilities and require a high order of technical and professional competence. They require, as well, the support of strong and interested top-most leadership.[19]

The committee added, "An organization already exists inside His Majesty's Government to promote the quality of administrative operations. This organization is the public administration department." Strengths and weaknesses of the department were described, and the report proposed new responsibilities for a reconstituted department. Relatively modest goals were set by the committee for the Public Administration Department. According to its report:

It is not unfair to say that this department has yet to realize its potential. It needs assurance of greater continuity than it has hitherto enjoyed. Its junior staff members need relief from the assignment of duty outside the jurisdiction of the department; and they need as well the sort of professional training that comes only from day-to-day practical work. The mission of the department is such that young Nepalese, trained in administrative studies, should be given responsible assignment in the department.

But above all, the department needs to complete successfully the initial urgent tasks on its agenda. The department should be enabled to move from one success, even though it be a modest one, to yet another success; and then find it possible to go ahead to the larger tasks which await its attention.[20]

Three initial areas of action were specified: studies in organization were given priority, an expansion of the department's responsibilities in training was recommended, and it was contended that foreign assistance activities in public administration should follow a better-planned, less competitive pattern.

In the sphere of organization studies, it was noted that the

19. His Majesty's Government of Nepal, Committee on Administration, *Report* (Kathmandu, 1962), p. 1.
20. *Ibid.*, p. 2.

government lacked valid data, or in some cases data of any kind, on the current allocation of functions and operations carried on by the ministries, the manner in which subordinate units were actually grouped within the ministries, what functions such groups undertake, what goals they pursue, and what resources they use. Basic informational needs had to be met and the committee urged that the department prepare at the earliest a descriptive manual of Nepal government. At this time no written summary of governmental structure and function was available. The top-most levels of the Civil Service in Nepal were, and are, unusually fluid, and the committee attached special significance to the circulation of a manual which would describe in simple terms the existing structural arrangements. The committee felt that consultation throughout Singha Durbar was a prerequisite to any description of structure and function and that such consultation, in itself, was a goal to be sought. Survey teams, the report recommended, would move beyond Singha Durbar and extend their study to the work of administration in the districts. The committee expected that as the Public Administration Department gained experience and as the initial general survey neared completion, several more specialized surveys would be carried on. These included an assessment of development administration, a study of the role of public participation in development activities, and an evaluation of personnel administration.

An effort was made by the committee to relate the work that was to be done in organization to the conduct of training programs. The report urged that the Public Administration Department develop its training section, which at the time consisted of one officer then on overseas study leave, and accept new responsibilities. Proposals for pre-service and post-entry training were made:

The public administration department has already laid the foundation for the initial training of all gazetted officers. Pre-service training will consist of an orientation to the government services; a period of academic work which should be common to all gazetted officers regardless of their likely field of specialization; a term of special training closely related to the officer's special service; and an interval of varying length in which the incoming officer is given a planned series of rotating assignments, under guidance, in a variety of departments and ministries.

Training is continuous throughout a civil servant's career. Plans must be made for the development of a senior officer's training program that will move beyond the mere instruction of specialized procedures and instead generate a service-wide perspective and a capacity for vigorous decision-making and action. Training of a specialized sort must continue and expand; specialized training programs will encompass accounting, personnel administration, and organization and methods, among other subjects.[21]

Teaching responsibilities were to be given to an institute of public administration, which was to be re-established as a subordinate wing of the department and financed by funds provided by Public Law 480, which the United States Agency for International Development had agreed to make available. Although the committee's report identified a number of functions for such an institute, it urged that plans should not be excessively rigid and should be subject to continuing experimentation. The committee also concluded that the Government of Nepal, through the Public Administration Department, should take the lead in planning for the development of the institute; an indigenous, Nepalese agency was sought as the vehicle for administrative improvement.

Foreign assistance groups and their relationship to administrative improvement were also considered by the committee:

The ground must be prepared carefully for the arrival and productive employment of foreign consultants. The financial and personnel obligations such programs impose on the Government of Nepal, both during the presence of the consultants and after they leave, require thorough mutual consideration.[22]

The committee, which was interested in the content of public assistance programs proposed for Nepal, wanted for the host country a hand in shaping that content. The committee also expressed concern regarding the administrative and other effects of such foreign aid programs. It was remembered that as late as 1957, when two reports on the advisability of creating an institute

21. *Ibid.*, pp. 5–6.
22. *Ibid.*, p. 8.

of public administration were received, a majority of the committee members were foreigners.[23]

The committee, therefore, proposed new activities for an expanded Public Administration Department. The draft report, dated June 26, 1962, which was given wide distribution, and the final report, which followed on July 23, 1962, urged that the department be organized independent of any one ministry and that it be located at a high executive level. On July 8, 1962, following circulation of the draft report, the department was given a new location in the governmental structure; it was attached to the vice-chairman of the Council of Ministers. The chairman of the council at the time was the King; when subsequently His Majesty vacated that office, the department was assigned to the chairman of the Council of Ministers. For the first time, an agency vested with responsibility for the improvement of the country's administrative system was situated close to the fount of executive authority.

Activities of the Public Administration Department, 1962–1964

Over the succeeding twelve months, the department's staff grew very substantially. By July, 1963, it had gained a body of adequately trained, enthusiastic officers. As recently as March, 1962, it will be remembered, it had been deprived almost completely of any staff whatever. But in the year following acceptance by government of the committee's report, four young men completed overseas public administration programs under United Nations fellowships. One of these men, who was given opportunities for on-the-job training in the United Kingdom, the United States, Canada, and Burma, returned to assume responsibility for the conduct of training programs and for general administrative analysis. A second, who earned a master's degree at a leading American graduate school, took charge of the

23. Ad Hoc Advisory Committee Regarding an Institute of Public Administration in Nepal, *Report* (Kathmandu, 1957); and Committee on the Institute of Public Administration in Nepal, *Report* (Kathmandu, 1957).

department's organization studies. A third United Nations fellow studied at the Institute of Social Studies, the Hague; his work there was supplemented by practical activity in Israel. This man was drawn into the training activities of the department. A fourth United Nations fellow was sent to Australia for general administrative studies; his responsibility in the department now lies in the fields of periodical reporting and assessment work. Still another member received a United States Agency for International Development grant for study in an American university; he returned to supervise the department's interests in personnel administration.

It would be wrong to give undue attention to those members of the department who were given opportunity for study outside Asia. Other of their colleagues who shared in the growing responsibility of the department had benefited from training programs in India as well as from the training work of the department itself. One of them, who was this writer's assistant in an intensive study of district administration, had slight academic training but had talent and a relentless appetite for constructive endeavor.

For the first time, then, Nepal in 1964 possessed a reasonably well-manned Public Administration Department, an agency endowed officially with responsibilities for improvement of the country's administrative system. By 1964 it had demonstrated some survival power, it had remained intact for well over a year, and it retained its location relatively close to the center of affairs in Singha Durbar.[24]

The committee's report of July, 1962, chose targets for the department which it considered feasible, within reach, and appropriate to the opportunities for useful change. Not all of the limited goals which had been identified for the department were in fact attained; it would have been surprising if they were. The department did produce an organization manual which described the functions and responsibilities of all public agencies.[25] The

24. This summary of the staffing and activities of the department are drawn from the author's *Development of Public Administration in Nepal, Final Report to the Government of Nepal* (United Nations: Kathmandu, 1963), pp. 24–32.

25. Department of Public Administration, *Organization of His Majesty's Government of Nepal* (Kathmandu, 1963).

manual included excerpts from the agencies' organizing statutes and incorporated detailed charts of the official structure for each of the thirteen ministries and major independent establishments. The manual was accompanied by a single large chart which offered for the first time a comprehensive overview of the country's administration. While the ninety neat squares on that chart offered an improbable view of actual social groupings, they did attract unusual attention to formal ties and relationships. The department was also able to conduct an intensive survey of district administration. An effort was made to measure the impact of administration in a district two hundred miles west of the Kathmandu Valley. The appearance of competitive models of administration in that district, the first stemming from the security and revenue activities of the Finance Ministry and the Home Affairs Ministry and the second drawn from the development works financed by the foreign aid community, had led to strongly confusing lines of authority from Kathmandu to the district level. In other respects the department worked toward establishing itself as a central staff resource in administration; weekly meetings of all ministerial secretaries were held on the department's premises. The department was also given information on the roles of prospective United Nations and United States Agency for International Development public administration advisers, a new departure in governmental practice. Job descriptions of the prospective advisers were submitted, though decisions concerning their fields were made elsewhere. The department attempted to lay plans for an effective institute of public administration, though plans for the institute are still in the offing. The department sought, within its own resources, to develop an in-service training program. Although no training premises whatever were available in March, 1962, suitable quarters were soon found, and by July, 1963, about four hundred civil servants had taken a variety of training courses, mainly in clerical activities.

The department did not, however, earn the active, interested support of the country's leadership; that leadership rests elsewhere than in Singha Durbar, the government secretariat. While a beginning toward management-improvement goals was made, the major characteristics of the country's administrative system were untouched by the Public Administration Department.

Major Characteristics of the Administrative System

(a) *The purposes and scale of operations.* Administration in Nepal, as evidenced by such key indicators as the expenditures of government and the assignment of public employees, reflects primary concern with national security and the control processes of law and order. The largest single class of expenditure in the Nepal budget is for the military; the second largest consumer of revenue in the country is the police. Security expenditures have risen rapidly in the past three years, as is shown by the following figures, drawn from successive regular budgets:

	1961–1962	1962–1963	1963–1964
Defense	175.15	235.08	296.00
Police	106.57	113.77	153.77 (estimate)

(in lakhs Nepal rupees; the Nepal rupee is $0.13; one lakh equals 100,000)

Expenditures on social services increased much less rapidly, and in several fields decreases were recorded; expenditure on health, for example, dropped by rupees 3 lakhs in 1962–1963 and declined again, though by a smaller amount, in 1963–1964. Regular budget expenditures, in fact, have increased only slightly in recent years; the 1962–1963 increase over the previous year was only rupees 60 lakhs, or 5.7 per cent of the budget. Expenditure on administration costs stood at rupees 511 lakhs in 1961–1962, but fell in 1962–1963 to rupees 403 lakhs.

The personnel rolls of government have been remarkably stable over the past decade. In 1957 there were 23,774 public employees; of that number 14,148 were registered as peons and orderlies, and 706 were classed as gazetted officers of both administrative and technical grades.[26] By 1964 the total figure was only 24,745, including 1,081 gazetted officers and 13,379 peons.

26. These figures are drawn from the calculations in Walter Fischer, *Personnel Administration in Nepal* (Kathmandu: United Nations, 1958), p. 8.

Throughout the period, the number of non-gazetted administrative and technical officers—the intermediate clerical level—was virtually stationary.

While the personnel force has not grown rapidly, the number of skilled young men and young women in the kingdom has increased quite remarkably, and this increase has been largely a function of the rivalry among foreign aid missions. Tabulations of the Economic Planning Ministry show that approximately 2,900 Nepalese studied outside Nepal on scholarships awarded by foreign aid missions between 1951 and 1964; others, though the number is not known, studied abroad on their own resources or those of programs not supported by government. As of 1964, about seven hundred of the 2,900 total are known to be employed in Nepal; but at least 1,400 who have returned to Nepal are not in the public services and there is no record, either in government or in the aid mission offices, of their present employment, if any. In Nepal, the private sector, other than in agriculture, is not a considerable employer. Approximately seventy of the 2,900 who were supported by foreign aid missions studied in fields which might be identified broadly as "administration."[27] There is no central inventory of the numbers and kinds of skills possessed by persons who have received overseas training. Proposals have failed for an assessment of the kinds of skills that have been acquired and the ways in which they are now being employed. While government has generally welcomed the aid missions' offer of scholarship grants, in a number of fields the production of skill has far outpaced present governmental demand.

(b) *The segmented structure of administration.* Small administrative systems are expected to behave more cohesively than larger and growing systems. Public administration in Nepal, however, is not a single, easily defined entity. Some Nepalese public agencies administer archaic functions inherited intact from the old regime. Others, financed by foreign aid missions, have

27. For extensive data on the 1951–1961 period see *Educational Planning in Nepal and Its Economic Implications*, Draft Report of the UNESCO Mission to Nepal (Kathmandu: United Nations, 1962). This report was prepared by Hugh B. Wood and Bruno Knall.

begun to enunciate development goals and express a concern for change and innovation. In some fields, foreign aid is disbursed directly by the foreign aid agencies, appears in neither regular nor development budgets, and completely bypasses the host country's administration. In certain crucial areas—the land tax being one—the work of administration is in private hands. Elsewhere, a number of topmost positions in the Nepal Civil Service are manned by officers of the Operational Executive and Administrative Personnel (OPEX) program of the United Nations. These executives serve not as advisers but as Nepal government officers responsible to Nepal Civil Service regulations.

Various funds have been established to administer assets and revenues for special purposes. Some are administered and accounted for by public agencies; others, including many public trust funds based on guthi land, are beyond the influence of government. Guthi land is land which does not pay a land revenue tax, but rather a rent based on the productivity of the land; the income is paid to the guthi commissioners and is administered by them for a number of purposes, including the building of temples, schools, orphanages, and old people's homes. The administration of these endowments is subject to abuse; the trusts are not open to public inspection, no accounts are published, and where guthi commissioners are unable to finance their commitments from current revenue, they have appealed, usually with success, to government to make up the deficit. The extent of guthi land is not known and no useful estimate can be made of its value.[28]

More serious separatist tendencies are the byproduct of foreign aid, however necessary that aid may be. Collaboration among donor missions who work in identical fields is not always easy to achieve, and the repercussions of aid mission rivalry are felt in Singha Durbar. Within the first five-year-plan period (1956–1961)[29] foreign aid in the amount of Nepal rupees 383.9 million was received from eleven major donors (Table 1). Strong re-

28. See the description and recommendations of Eric Himsworth, *The Fiscal System of Nepal* (rev. ed.; Kathmandu: United Nations, 1964), pp. 30, 42, 70.
29. The five-year plan was essentially an estimate of public expenditures. See *Draft Five Year Plan: A Synopsis* (Kathmandu: Government of Nepal, 1956).

liance on foreign aid is a feature of the three-year plan (1962–1965), and the number of foreign contributors has increased considerably. Even in small departments, with a high proportion of professional staff and experienced leadership, the work in progress is identified as "U. S." or "Indian," etc., and then by function. Activities of the Forests Department, in the Ministry of Forests and Agriculture, are illustrative of the tendency to fragment along national lines. The fifty-six gazetted officers of that department are led by a UN-OPEX officer, retired from the British Colonial Service, who serves as chief conservator of forests. Three aid missions, other than the United Nations mission, assist the Forests Department; these are the United States Agency for International Development, the Indian Aid Mission, and the

Table 1. *Foreign Aid During the Five Year Plan Period, 1956–1961* (*in Nepal Rupees 100,000*)

Name of country	1956– 1957	1957– 1958	1958– 1959	1959– 1960	1960– 1961[a]	Totals[b]
United States	127.53	484.73	179.51	562.25	869.97	2,223.99
India	145.70	96.05	171.02	184.50	223.55	830.82
U.S.S.R.	—	—	—	—	84.56	84.56
China (People's Republic)	—	—	—	321.35	—	321.35
Great Britain	—	—	—	6.73	30.47	37.20
New Zealand	—	—	—	11.30	10.00	21.30
Australia	—	—	—	—	8.49	8.49
Canada	—	—	—	11.25	—	11.25
Switzerland	—	—	—	19.72	4.09	23.81
Ford Foundation	—	—	—	—	106.55	106.55
United Nations	—	—	—	136.30	33.31	169.61

[a] Estimates only.
[b] During the pre-plan period, foreign aid was given as follows: United States, 24.9 million; India, 70 million.
Source: Progress Report of the First Five Year Plan (Kathmandu: National Planning Council, 1961, p. 6 [in Nepali]).

Swiss Technical Mission. Two of these contribute to the development budget; the third, the Swiss group, acts outside departmental and budgetary lines.[30] The total development budget expenditure for forests in 1962–1963 amounted to Nepal rupees

30. For a general survey of foreign aid in Nepal see Eugene B. Mihaly, *Foreign Aid and Politics in Nepal: A Case Study* (New York, 1965).

37 lakhs and was contributed as follows (in lakhs Nepal rupees): USAID, 20.5; Indian aid, 15.5; Nepal government, 1.5. Both American and Indian aid activities had energetic leadership, and not unexpectedly these generally co-operative aid partners earned inside the gazetted and non-gazetted staff their special ties and associations. Indian aid assistance in forests was aimed at management planning, staff training, and the construction of a forest institute, activities which ran parallel to certain of the American efforts. In other fields of activity, however, including the sensitive areas of communication and transportation, donor groups have found co-operative effort unduly burdensome and have followed wholly separate approaches.

Nowhere is the divided nature of Nepalese administration so apparent as in land administration, where the role of private agents is prominent. Land survey work in Nepal is not new; a survey of the whole country was undertaken about one hundred years ago, and a record was sought of the size of each piece of land, its productive capacity, and the land tax which was payable by each holder. The object of the survey was to compile a register for determining who should pay the land tax and how much they should pay. From time to time new surveys have been made of different areas of the country. The particulars of the surveys were lodged in the local mal adda, the revenue office. When a transfer of land takes place, particulars of this transfer are given to the mal adda, but no attempt seems to have been made to record particulars of transfers in the original registers. On the other hand, the zamindars did and do keep a register, which is jealously guarded from government eyes and which records the tax payable and the person or owner of the land who pays it. Surveys conducted today seek also to give the government the correct particulars of what land is cultivated, its size, and the amount of tax it should be paying. But when such surveys are completed and findings are sent to the mal adda, the master record is not amended, only that of the zamindar, with the result that after a short time the government has no comprehensive record of what land exists, who owns it, and how much tax each person pays. Attempts to compile registers of the information amassed by the current survey have failed; the very foundation of an organized and active central and local land administration has yet to be laid. While there are technical administrative issues involved—matters relating to the training of survey workers, initially—the difficulties are in fact more ideological and political. The assumption of governmental responsibility in land administration has failed, not because of technical gaps, but because programs of minimal governmental responsibility lack political support.

The tendency of government to establish public corporations—some examples being the Royal Nepal Airlines Corporation, the Nepal Industrial Development Corporation, the Nepal Electricity Corporation, the Nepal Bank, Ltd.—beyond the scope of ministerial responsibility has further segmenting effects without at the same time liberating managerial energies in relatively autonomous entities. Most of the public corporations have been led at one time or another by UN-OPEX officers, though such leadership has been at best nominal and the corporation has been absorbed by local cultural landscape. In the language of a Swedish United Nations expert:

On the whole the unfortunate experience of the use of OPEX people as General Managers in different Public Enterprises can be explained. . . . The OPEX man is exercising his authority as General Manager in the same way as in western countries. This is why he has been appointed. However, this is a strange phenomenon with regard to the social structure. Therefore, there is a reaction in order to move him out of the organization or to eliminate his actions. The experience during the last few years indicate that the social structure in this country contains a very strong ability to react against a strange phenomenon.[31]

The OPEX program, begun in 1959, has provided loan or substitute personnel in more than a dozen countries and has received ever-increasing budgetary support from the United Nations. Nepal has received more such operational and executive personnel from the United Nations than has any other country; indeed, this program in Nepal had the personal interest of Dag Hammarskjold. OPEX officers are given executive responsi-

31. Rune Tersman, *Supervision of Public Enterprises in Nepal* (Kathmandu: United Nations, 1963), p. 6.

bilities, but they are also expected to conduct training programs which will enable host country nationals to operate those governmental activities which are assigned temporarily to the international experts. In Nepal OPEX officers have served as managers for the Nepal Bank, Ltd., the Raghupati Jute Mills, and the Royal Nepal Airlines Corporation; as chief officers of the Forests Department, the Basic Survey Department, and the Nepal Electricity Corporation; and as legal assistant to government. OPEX officers in Nepal have been dismissed by the host country, two have died in service, others have experienced severe health problems, and one resigned having found it impossible to harmonize the conflicting purposes of rival aid agencies.

A final segmenting force may be noted, one which responds to the geographic distribution of education in Nepal. Fewer than 2.6 per cent of the children of secondary school age are now enrolled in a school facility; but in the Kathmandu Valley, about 20 per cent are so enrolled.[32] Yet the valley's population is less than half a million; one-twentieth of the country's total. The imbalance in the geographic distribution of education has led to residents of the valley holding a near monopoly over recruitment to the public services. Until 1963 examination for entry to the public services was given only in Kathmandu. While the geography of recruitment may appear to produce solidarity among gazetted officers, it also tends to separate, consciously or otherwise, the interests of the valley from the interests of the country outside the confines of Kathmandu Valley. The physical isolation of Kathmandu Valley from the rest of the country and the discontinuous, often confusing, lines of authority which link Singha Durbar and the districts beyond further contribute to the country's split administrative personality.

(c) *Competing goals in district administration.* Beyond the Kathmandu Valley, the country is organized into thirty-two administrative districts, or ilaka. The valley is divided into three areas—Kathmandu, Lalitpur, and Bhaktapur—each under a magistrate who in turn is supervised by the valley commissioner. The

32. *Educational Planning in Nepal and Its Economic Implications,* p. 37.

thirty-two ilakas comprise about fifty jilla; one or more jilla make up an ilaka. Each jilla is divided into thums (paragannas in the terai), and each thum is made up of a number of villages. The ilakas, the basic administrative district, are grouped into three classes according to their importance (size, population, and revenue being the main criteria); rank of the bada hakim usually corresponds to the class given his ilaka. During the Rana regime, the bada hakim was clearly the leading authority in the ilaka. For the future, however, his supremacy may be tested. The new panchayat ministry—a development budget ministry financed primarily by an external agency, USAID—has organized its field activities into fourteen zones; the fourteen anchal or zonal officers are located in as many ilaka headquarters towns. For these officers the anchaladhi directs the work of seventy-five development blocks.

The historic offices found in each ilaka are:

(1) goswara, the civil administrative office, headed by a bada hakim who reports to the Home Ministry (32 goswara in the country);

(2) mal adda, or land revenue office, reports to the Finance Ministry (77);

(3) adalat (amini in the terai), court, reports its actions to the Law and Justice Ministry (63);

(4) thana, police headquarters, reports to the Home Ministry (68).

Even today the bada hakim is likely to influence in some degree the rulings of the adalat, or court, and he is certain to take an interest in police activities and the collection of land taxes and the disbursement of salaries, the last-named being a function of the mal adda. Most bada hakim are Grade II gazetted officers, excepting only the anchaladhi, the ilaka's ranking officer. The bada hakim is likely, as well, to be better educated than most other officers; in 1964, ten held B.A. degrees. More panchayat development officers, though the bada hakim's junior in rank, will have had foreign aid mission training, including in many cases study outside Nepal.

The duties of the bada hakim are diffused and have never been clearly defined. In one ilaka headquarters, located in a hill and mountain area with a population of 375,000, the bada hakim's directly controlled staff consisted of five clerks and typists, one driver, four horsemen, and eight peons. In one year's time that staff issued licenses (about two thousand licenses for guns and ammunition, three for jeeps, several for radio sets, and a few for touring cinema and plays); received petitions for services (about one hundred); and heard numerous complaints, principally about the boundaries of property. These were the principal items of work.[33] Panchayat development officers, new to the ilaka and linked more directly to an aid mission than to Singha Durbar, have begun to pursue a novel set of aims. They do so with certain advantages, some drawn from superior material resources and some drawn from a far more permissive administrative environment.[34]

Officials of government in Kathmandu are not insensitive to the contrasts which separate the familiar institutional structure and the agencies sponsored by donor countries. In the language of a report of the Economic Planning Ministry, written by its secretary who serves also as foreign aid co-ordinator:

Design of the administrative structure in the districts is of prime importance in the conduct of this experimental program. The crux of the problem is simply that, traditionally, district administration through the Bada Hakim has been concerned largely with the maintenance of law and order, collection of taxes and other routine duties. Now the Panchayat has been created and given a strong economic development orientation. In addition, Zonal Commissioners have been appointed and assigned developmental responsibilities. But there are still many unanswered questions regarding the proper relationship between the district Panchayats, Bada Hakims and Zonal Commissioners.

For example, whereas taxes must be collected and law and order maintained, this can no longer be the central purpose of district

33. S. T. Divers, *District Administration: A Survey of Pokhara District* (Kathmandu: United Nations, 1960); Merrill R. Goodall, *District Administration; Pokhara District Re-Surveyed* (Kathmandu: United Nations, 1963); and Government of Nepal, *Final Report of the Specially Powered Tour Committee* (Kathmandu: Ministry of National Guidance, 1962) (in Nepali).

34. Foreign aid missions learn to move around the highly refined injunctions of two Government of Nepal rule books, *The Financial Handbook* and its companion volume, *The Book of Delegation of Powers*.

administration; yet how much attention must be given to such matters? Similarly, there must be proper and open accounting for expenditure of public funds, whether the funds originate from national, district, or village sources; but who should be responsible for this phasing and execution of the agricultural reorganization plan: In which villages should credit societies be started first?[35]

The questions are as yet unanswered, basically because Nepal, so recently sealed from the rest of the world, has yet to find common ground for both its bada hakim and for the newer and foreign-supported development offices.

Of the three major administrative instrumentalities in Nepal, the Royal Palace is the more influential though the least evident. The façade of the Western state system, which was added after the revolution of 1950–1951, consisted of budgets, economic plans, constitutions, and proposals for administrative reform. The 1951 Interim Government of Nepal Act was written by foreigners; foreign advisers contributed to succeeding budgets and plans; parts of the 1959 Constitution were written by foreigners; indeed, the Economic Planning Ministry itself is underwritten by a foreign foundation, and other nominally Nepalese agencies are linked with members of the foreign aid community.

The arena in which Nepal's administration is to be fashioned extends far beyond Nepal itself. That arena includes a dozen donor countries as well as the United Nations and its specialized agencies. One effect of the presence of these donor groups in the country has been the creation inside the structure of government of new organizations with commitments new to Nepal. These newer entities have been staffed by young men and young women, many of whom have been trained outside Nepal by aid partners. Too much praise cannot be heaped upon many of these young people, some of whom captain entire ministries as senior-most secretary when still in their mid-twenties; they would grace any administrative system in the world. The younger gazetted officers—secretaries, deputy secretaries, assistant secretaries—

---

35. Government of Nepal, *The Economic Affairs Report*, No. 2 (Kathmandu: Ministry of Economic Planning, 1963), I, 18. In No. 1, Vol. I of this excellent series, also issued in 1963, there appeared the first comprehensive catalogue of aid projects under way in the country.

are, however, unusually vulnerable to change in the world outside Singha Durbar, and so also are the organs which they staff. Such agencies have been devised in response to stimuli which are largely external to Nepal. They are not rooted in the Nepalese landscape. They are unsupported by independent Nepalese institutions—not by political party and not by legislative assembly. In such an environment prospects for genuine administrative development are as yet uncertain.

In such a landscape, technical assistance programs in public administration—their characteristic thrust being improved methods and techniques of organization—have had low survival power. The organization and methods offices and the institutes of public administration so far have not been seen as relevant to those few in Nepal who are developmentally oriented, and they have been unnoticed by those who wish and seek no change in the status quo. Where development goals are voiced inside Nepal administration and such goals are likely to be heard with increasing vigor in the immediate future, the foreign specialist in administration will have to relate his contribution to the ends of development. He will have to help prepare the political and administrative base which can advance such goals.

11

Concluding Observations

Ralph Braibanti

Analysis of the bureaucratic systems of India, Pakistan, Burma, Ceylon, and Malaysia, indicates that the apparatus and attitude left by the British has endured for nearly two decades after independence and has shown a remarkable quality of resilience. In none of the states has there been a sharp break with the past, despite political denunciations of the administrative system established under British rule. In both Burma and Malaya, the Japanese military occupation was a more serious break in the continuity of British rule than independence. This might well have been the occasion for abandoning the British pattern and adopting a new one based on indigenous nationalist ideologies. The hiatus of Japanese rule resulted in a decline in elitist exclusivity in both systems, although neither system had carried elitism to quite the same extreme as the ICS in India and later the CSP in Pakistan. While attitudinal change may have been induced by the Japanese occupation, the system which emerged after the Japanese departed showed continuity in structure, behavior, and personnel with the earlier system evolved under British rule. Each of the states has retained an apparatus of discrete cadre entities, although Ceylon has nominally merged two entities into a common administrative service. The dominance of the generalist administrator still prevails, despite some overtures to participation by specialists in all systems. The paramountcy of the secretariat remains in all systems, although it is probably least strong in Malaya and strongest in Pakistan.

The prestige and popularity of government service generally, and of the elite cadre particularly, seems not to have changed very much since before independence, although there are no precisely comparable data to prove this. In Ceylon some 68 per cent of all university graduates in 1962 had taken government positions. In India 9,182 persons applied for the combined Central Superior Services examination in 1961. It is not known what proportion this figure represents of the total number of graduates for that year. In Pakistan about 10 per cent of university graduates take the examinations for the Central Superior Services. These data are not sufficiently comparable to justify generalization; the impression left by field work, however, is that government employment continues to be the occupation of highest prestige, but that in Malaysia, India, and Pakistan trade and commerce are emerging in a competitive role as alternative occupations.

The British physical presence evaporated rather soon after independence in all five major systems. (Nepal is not included in this comparison because there were no British officers in service in Nepal.) Immediately before independence, as Table 1 shows, 52 per cent of the elite cadres were British, the highest proportion (66 per cent) being in Malaya and the lowest (19 per cent) in Ceylon. Table 2 shows that immediately after independence, this proportion was reduced to 22 per cent, with the highest proportion (44 per cent) remaining in Malaya and none remaining in Burma. By 1964, British officers had almost completely disappeared from the scene, only ten out of 3,070 officers (.33 per cent) remaining (Table 3). The connection was cut most sharply in Ceylon, Burma, and India; while in Pakistan, British officers were in key establishment positions for a decade or so after independence. It can be said with some certainty for all five systems that British officers had little if anything to do with formulating government policy after independence, although a few remained on assignment mostly to judicial positions. With the exception of Pakistan, whatever ideological components of the British legacy remained were rediffused, not by British officers themselves, but by British-trained indigenous officers who as the elite cadres staffed all crucial positions.

Table 1. *British Officers of Elite Cadres*[a] *in Service Immediately Before Independence*[b] *in India, Pakistan, Ceylon, Malaya, and Burma*

Country	Number of officers		Totals	Percentage British
	Indigenous	British		
India ⎱ Pakistan⎰	549	608	1,157	52.6
Ceylon	137	32	169	18.9
Malaya	103	202	305	66.2
Burma	64	81	145	55.9
Nepal	Not Applicable			
Totals	853	923	1,776	52.0

[a] The term "elite cadres" refers to the Indian Civil Service (ICS) and its equivalents, Civil Service of Pakistan (CSP), Ceylon Civil Service (CCS), Malayan Civil Service (MCS), and Burma Civil Service (BCS). The Indian Political Service (IPS) is included for Pakistan where twelve indigenous officers and fourteen British officers of that cadre remained and were posted to ICS-type positions. The IPS was originally drawn from the ICS and the army, and its officers served in the Northwest Frontier Province and in the princely states. The Ceylon Civil Service was abolished May 1, 1963, merged with a larger group of officers, and renamed the Unified Administrative Service. The elite cadre in Burma includes members of the ICS, Burma Commission, and its successor, the Burma Civil Service (Class I), in both the Executive and Judicial Branches.

[b] Dates of independence are August 15, 1947, for India and Pakistan; February 4, 1948, for Ceylon; and August 31, 1957, for Malaya. Burma was made independent on January 4, 1948, but the last "normal" year of British rule (prior to Japanese conquest) was 1941.

Sources: For India and Pakistan: comparative analysis of *Combined Civil Lists for India and Burma, Jan.–Mar. 1947,* No. 156 (Lahore, 1947); *Combined Civil List for India, Pakistan and Burma, Jan.–Mar. 1948,* No. 161 (Lahore, 1948). Data cross-checked with senior government officers in India and Pakistan. For Ceylon and Malaya: Chapters 7, 8, and 9, respectively, by Collins, Kearney, and Tilman in this volume. For Malaya, statistics throughout these tables have been tabulated by material published or supplied by the Pensions Division and the Service Division of the Federation Establishment Office. The sources for Malaya may vary by as much as 30 per cent; yet it is impossible to derive all needed information from a single source. An effort has been made to confine specific comparisons to a single source, or if this proved impossible, to make the necessary adjustments of figures to provide comparability. Some inconsistencies are therefore inevitable. For Burma: *Quarterly Civil List for Burma,* No. 287 (*corrected up to 1 October, 1941*) (Rangoon: Government Printing and Stationery, 1941); and G. E. Harvey, *British Rule in Burma: 1824–1942* (London, 1946), p. 31.

In all six states the elite cadres have been the dominant instrument of government, despite the fact, shown by Table 4, that they constituted a mere 3,190 officers out of a total of nearly eleven million government employees in bureaucracies controlling nearly 597 million persons. Just as under British rule a small group of ICS officers were able to control vast populations by means of a carefully devised apparatus, so almost the same proportion of elite cadre are in positions of command today. The elite cadres have not really grown significantly in size since before

Table 2. *British Officers of Elite Cadres*[a] *Remaining in Service Immediately After Independence*[b] *in India, Pakistan, Ceylon, Malaya, and Burma*

| Country | Number of officers | | Totals | Percentage British |
	Indigenous	British		
India	418	33[c]	451	7.3
Pakistan	96	50[c]	146	34.2
Ceylon	137	32	169	18.9
Malaya	162	130	292[d]	44.5
Burma	53[e]	0	53	0.0
Nepal	Not Applicable			
Totals	866	245	1,111	22.1

[a] See note [a], Table 1.
[b] See note [b], Table 1.
[c] This figure, computed from *Combined Civil List for India, Pakistan and Burma, April–June 1949* (Delhi, 1949), is for the number of officers in service as of December, 1948. It is possible that a few more British officers were in service from August, 1947, to December, 1948. Interviews with senior Indian officials reveal that the figure 33 is probably correct for August, 1947, and, if wrong, is wrong by no more than five officers.
[d] This figure is valid as of January 1, 1958, the date closest to independence for which a Staff List is available.
[e] This figure includes five Anglo-Burmans, one of whom was on leave preparatory to retirement.
Sources: For India and Pakistan: comparative analysis of *Combined Civil Lists for India and Burma, Jan.–Mar. 1947,* No. 156; *Combined Civil List for India, Pakistan, and Burma, Jan.–Mar., 1948;* No. 161, and *Combined Civil List for Pakistan, India and Burma, Oct.–Dec. 1949,* No. 168, Parts I, II, III. These computations have been checked by interviews with senior officials in India and Pakistan. For Ceylon and Malaya: chapters by Collins and Tilman in this volume. Figures used for Malaya are those of the Pensions Division, Federal Establishments Office. For Burma: *Union of Burma Civil List,* No. 5 (*corrected up to 1 April, 1948*).

independence, despite the apparent evidence in Table 5. The rate of growth of elite cadres in five states (excluding Nepal) appears to be 181 per cent. But this figure is largely the result of the growth rates for India and Pakistan computed on the basis of the number of officers remaining after division of one system at independence into two sovereign systems. If we assume that India at independence had about 1,157 officers and that Pakistan must have required about four hundred officers to begin a new state, the growth rates would be much more like those of Ceylon, Malaya, and Burma—53 per cent, 14 per cent, and 100 per cent, respectively. While we do not know the growth rate of total government employment (because we do not know the strengths at independence), it can be said with certainty that the elite cadres expanded very little, probably at a lesser proportional rate than did total government employment and population. Despite political diatribes to the contrary, this suggests for all states that

Table 3. *British Officers of Elite Cadres*[a] *in Service in 1964 in India, Pakistan, Ceylon, Malaya, and Burma*

Country	Number of officers			Percentage British
	Indigenous	British	Total	
India	1,971	3	1,974	00.15
Pakistan	428	4	432	00.93
Ceylon[b]	209	0	209	0.00
Malaya	346	3	349	00.86
Burma	106[c]	0	106[d]	0.00
Nepal	Not Applicable			
Totals	3,060	10	3,070	00.33

[a] See note [a], Table 1.

[b] As of May 1, 1963, when the Ceylon Civil Service was abolished.

[c] This figure includes seven Anglo-Burmans, one Anglo-Indian, three Sino-Burmans, three Indo-Burmans, and one Sikh.

[d] Although this figure is derived from a 1960 source, it is improbable that it is significantly different for 1964.

Sources: India: Letter, Ministry of Home Affairs, August 1, 1964. Actual strength as of January 1, 1964. Pakistan: Government of Pakistan, *Gradation List* (*corrected up to January 1, 1964*) (Lahore, 1964). Ceylon: Chapter by Kearney in this volume. Malaya: This figure is an estimate of actual strength by R. O. Tilman based on interviews in Malaya and on the *Malayan Civil List* of July, 1964. Burma: Union of Burma, *Civil List No. 10* (*corrected up to December 31, 1959*). (See note [d].)

Table 4. *Population, Total Government Employment and Elite Cadre Strength in India, Pakistan, Ceylon, Malaya, Burma, and Nepal, 1964*

A Country	B Total government[a] employment	C Elite cadre	D Population[h]	E Percentage (B of D)
India[b]	9,271,000	1,974	449,400,000	2.06
Pakistan[c]	995,000	432	96,500,000	1.03
Ceylon[d]	286,000	209	10,600,000	2.70
Malaya[e]	94,000	349	7,400,000	1.27
Burma[f]	242,000	106	23,200,000	1.04
Nepal[g]	25,000	120	9,756,000	.26
Totals	10,913,000	3,190	596,856,000	1.85

[a] Figures given in column B are estimates. Since standardized data have not been compiled for these countries, careful comparisons based on identical categories of data are not available. The limitations of data and the basis of calculation are described for each country in the notes below. Figures for elite cadre strength are for 1964. Figures for total government employment are as indicated in notes below.

[b] Figures for India are derived from comparative analysis of data given in the *Report of the Commission of Enquiry on Emoluments and Conditions of Service of Central Government Employees 1957–59* (Das Commission) (Delhi, 1960), pp. 8–10; Government of India, Ministry of Labour and Employment, Directorate General of Employment and Training, National Employment Service, *Census of Central Government Employees (as on March 31, 1960)*, p. 4; V. S. Hejmadi and V. A. Panandiker, "The Public Services—Recruitment and Selection," *The Indian Journal of Public Administration*, IX (July–September, 1963), 358; R. K. Trivedi and D. N. Rao, "Growth of Personnel and Civil Expenditure in the Government of India," *Journal of the National Academy of Administration*, VI (April, 1961), 31–87. The figures for the central government are fairly reliable. Figures for employees of the fifteen states have not been collated with the same degree of reliability and are derived entirely from estimates given in the Das Report. The *Census of Central Government Employees* gives the figure 2,250,000 for 1960. This is the base figure used here. The Das Commission Report gave the average annual increase from 1948 to 1957 as 2.5 per cent. Apparently, the actual growth rate was higher, since the census figure of 2,250,000 is greater than the Das figure 1,773,570 by more than 2.5 per cent each year from 1957 through 1960. Assuming an annual increase of 8.3 per cent, the figure is here updated to 2,639,000 for 1962. To this figure, 5,270,000 is added. This is derived from the Das Report (p. 46), which estimates employment of state and local governments (including teachers) at about 4,360,000. Assuming 8.3 per cent annual increase and rounding off the figures, the total comes to 6,632,000 updated to 1962. Hence, the total: 9,271,000. This estimate has been made by R. Braibanti.

[c] Total employment is more difficult to ascertain for Pakistan than for any of the other countries listed in this table. An excellent census exists for the government of West Pakistan—Government of West Pakistan, Planning and Development Department, Bureau of Statistics, *Census of West Pakistan Government Employees 1962* (Lahore, 1963)—but there is none for the central government or for East Pakistan. The census figures for West Pakistan include teachers and railway employees, but not post and telegraph employees, who are central government personnel. Total government employment in West Pakistan, all classes, is 376,521. Unpublished data of the Establishment Division, President's Secretariat, list 122,000 central government employees in 1963, including post and telegraph employees. The total for West Pakistan and the central government is thus 498,521. It is assumed that provincial employment in East Pakistan approximates

the concept of *small* cadres in relation to the total bureaucracy has persisted.

that of West Pakistan. The estimated national total would then be 875,042. This total includes police, teachers, railway, and postal employees, but not those in the armed services. To this should be added an estimated 50,000 employees of government corporations and 32,000 local government employees estimated at four hundred thirty-two for each of seventy-four districts. Allowing for a 4 per cent underestimation, the total would be 995,323. No effort to estimate the annual growth rate from 1959 or retrospectively from the 1963 Census of West Pakistan to 1961 has been made. Thus, the total figure here represents subtotals for 1959 and 1962. This estimate has been prepared by R. Braibanti after consultation with Leon Margosian and J. Maslowski, public administration and statistical advisers, respectively, in the Pakistan Mission of the United States Agency for International Development.

[d] The figure for Ceylon has been computed as follows: *The Statistical Abstract of Ceylon—1960* (Colombo, 1960) shows 245,758 central government employees and teachers in government schools for 1959 (pp. 143–144). Local government employees are not shown for 1959, but 14,618 are listed for 1957 (p. 141). Assuming at least the same number of government employees were in local government in 1959, this totals 260,376. In 1960 the government assumed control of private, state-assisted schools, and teachers of those schools became government employees. *The Statistical Abstract of Ceylon—1960* lists 25,659 teachers in assisted schools in 1957 (p. 139). Assuming at least the same number for 1959, the total number of government employees would approximate 286,035 in 1959. The figures for Ceylon include police, railway employees, postal employees, teachers, and local government workers. They do not include members of the armed services or employees of government corporations. No effort to estimate annual growth through 1961 has been made. This estimate has been made by Robert N. Kearney.

[e] Figures for Malaya have been computed as follows. The base figure, 82,132 employees of the central government posted in the center and in the field, is fairly reliable. It includes police, teachers, and postal employees but does not include railway employees, since railways in Malaya are the responsibility of government corporations. To increase comparability of data, an estimate of 11,800 for railway employees is added. Thus, the total of 93,932 is arrived at. This may be an overestimation of as high as 20 per cent since positions rather than persons are used as the base of computation. The data are based on 1963. No effort has been made to include estimates of annual growth since then. This estimate has been made by R. O. Tilman.

[f] The Burma figures are for 1959–1960 and include employees of government boards and corporations. They are taken from the *Report of the Public Services Enquiry Commission, 1961* (Rangoon, 1961), p. 65. In November, 1963, the Revolutionary Government estimated that more than 300,000 nationals were serving in government departments, boards and corporations, commissions and committees, state and local bodies, and state banks. With the nationalization of retail trade and most other economic activities in the spring of 1964, the number has probably grown considerably. *Forward* (Rangoon: Directorate of Information), November 22, 1963, and March 19, 1964. This estimate has been made by James F. Guyot.

[g] The figure on total employment for Nepal is a rounded-off estimate taken from the 1964 Nepal budget. Elite cadre, defined for Nepal, consists of sixty-eight special class officers and fifty-two first-class officers. In addition, as of January, 1963, there were 251 second-class officers and 710 third-class officers; these latter classes are also technically in the gazetted ranks but should not be regarded as members of the elite cadre. This estimate has been made by Merrill Goodall.

[h] Population for all countries has been taken from United Nations, *Statistical Yearbook* (New York, 1963). The figure for Nepal is taken from the official preliminary census report of 1961. All population figures are rounded off.

With the departure of British officers, those trained by the British constituted the principal matrix for diffusion of British values. In each of the five major systems this group constitutes an elite within an elite, and though there is some tension between post-independence recruits and the "old guard," the old guard is respected and emulated. This relationship has facilitated the diffusion of elite cadre traditions and norms throughout the entire cadre. In Malaya this has been the role of Malay officers of the

Table 5. *Growth in Elite Cadre[a] Strength from Independence[b] to 1964 in India, Pakistan, Ceylon, Malaya, and Burma*

Country[c]	Total actual Strength		Percentage of growth
	At independence	1964	
India	451	1,974	338
Pakistan	146	432	196
Ceylon	137	209	53
Malaya	305	349	14
Burma[d]	53	106	100
Totals	1,092	3,070	181

[a] See note [a], Table 1.
[b] See note [b], Table 1.
[c] Data for Nepal relevant to this table does not exist.
[d] Figure for Burma is estimated from 1960 source. (See note [d], Table 3.)
Sources: Compiled from Tables 3 and 4 in this chapter.

Malay Administrative Service who were trained by British officers of the Malay Civil Service. It is noteworthy that the transmission of British values to these officers was accomplished somewhat differently than it was among ICS officers in India and Pakistan. The senior Malay officers who are now the agents for infusing the system with British norms were educated at Malay College and (after 1929) at Raffles College. These schools were designed to train an elite, and although the instruction was carried on largely by British faculty, it was one step removed from Britain. This appears to have been true in Burma as well, where most of the Burmans entering the BCS(I) were educated either at University

College or Judson College in Rangoon. On the other hand, Indian ICS officers now in India and Pakistan were trained in England at Oxford, Cambridge, or London and also served under British officers in beginning their duties as district officers. It would be interesting to speculate whether British values are held and transmitted in India and Pakistan with a different degree of intensity than in Burma and Malaya. It would appear that the degree of distinctiveness between the "old guard" and new recruits in India and Pakistan is much greater than in Burma and Malaya, and one might conclude that this educational factor is at least one cause. But other variables, such as the more egalitarian social structures of Burma and Malaya, make it difficult to assess precisely the weight of the educational factor.

It is known from data compiled for India and Pakistan that by 1970 the British-trained ICS officers of the elite cadres will not exceed .6 per cent of the total cadre in each country and will probably be even less than that. It is doubtful that any British-trained ICS officers will be left in the cadres by 1980. While such data are not available for Ceylon, Burma, and Malaya, it would be fair to assume the same rate of attrition for British-trained officers in those elite cadres. The decline of direct British influence is somewhat different for Pakistan, where new recruits were sent to England until 1960 for training. Presumably these new recruits will continue to bring British values into the system. It may be, then, that we can expect a firmer attachment to pre-independence ICS traditions in Pakistan than in the other states. But again, there are too many other variables affecting the situation to justify anything more than a cautious suggestion.

The elite cadres in five of the states (no data are available for Nepal) have retained their hold in crucial positions of power at all levels, thus straddling in India, Pakistan, and Malaya what are otherwise somewhat inaccurately regarded as federal systems. Table 6 reveals some marked uniformities as well as differences in assignments within the five systems. In all the systems, from 25 to 30 per cent of the cadres are assigned to district administration. No elite cadre officers are assigned to judicial functions in India, Ceylon, Burma, and Malaya, thus reflecting the fact that judicial and executive functions have been separated in those countries. In Pakistan, where such separation has not occurred, nearly 4 per cent of the cadre is assigned to judicial work. All five countries have deputed officers to diplomatic and related posts abroad, the total being about 2.5 per cent. It is significant to note the uniformity in absorbing the two most important challenges to orthodox bureaucracy, namely, government corporations and community development. Government corporations have absorbed from about 5 to 8 per cent of the cadres, the latter figure being the proportion in Burma. But community development programs have been assigned elite cadre officers only in India, and there only 1.6 per cent. This may very well reflect the strong power orientation of the elite cadre or the vigor of the community development movement and its capacity to preserve a measure of autonomy unaffected by the old-line bureaucracy. The community development movement necessarily relies on persuasive rather than coercive techniques, and its "rice roots" ethos, of course, is antithetical to manifestations of power in the orthodox bureaucracy. On the other hand, the figure for India is not surprising, for the Indian movement is strongest, and the orientation of the elite cadre has probably changed more in India than in the other states. The training pattern is also revealing. We know from sources other than Table 6 that Pakistan pursues a vigorous training program in which about 19 per cent of the elite cadre officers are undergoing training and about 2 per cent are assigned to staff positions in training institutions. India has less than half that number undergoing training, and Ceylon, Malaya, and Burma show none for 1959, 1963, and 1960, respectively. Table 6 seems to indicate that elite cadre officers are scattered in a variety of positions. It also suggests that the distribution is much more even for India and Pakistan, somewhat less even for Burma, and very uneven for Ceylon and Malaya. In the latter two countries, central and district government absorb between 83 and 90 per cent of the cadre strength, and few if any officers seem to be involved in "nation-building" activities. In Burma, the distribution pattern lies somewhere between the pattern for India–Pakistan and Ceylon–Malaya. However, an important caveat should be noted in interpreting the data in Table 6, that is, the figures are for different years. Malayan and Indian data are for 1963, but Pakistan is reported for 1964, Ceylon for 1959, and Burma for 1960. This fact seriously limits the utility of the table to the facts presented for each country for the given year. Comparability for a single year is impossible. On the other hand, it is the impression of the contributing authors to this volume that the percentages for all the countries for 1964 would not vary greatly from the data shown. Nevertheless, it must be reiterated that Table 6 is nothing more than it claims to be, and no rigorously precise comparative conclusions can be derived from it.

In each of the six states (in this instance, Nepal is included) one of the most insistent criticisms against the elite cadres was the sharp disparity in remuneration for comparable work. The origins of this differential are found in the fact that British officers received a higher scale of pay than uncovenanted or indigenous civil servants. As non-British officers entered the elite cadre they were paid on the same scale as their British counterparts. The question of remuneration has probably been the most complex one facing administrative reformers. Each of the six states, except Nepal and Burma, had at least two lengthy committee reports on salaries. Burma had one such inquiry and Nepal had none. These twelve inquiries total some 4,573 pages, comprising 44 per cent of the total bulk of major government reports on administration to 1964.[1] The complexities of the salary system are such that it is virtually impossible to generalize except in the crudest way. Suffice it to say that the highest pre-independence salary typically was received by a full secretary to government who was an elite cadre officer. This salary in most of the states approximated Rs. 4,000 per month, nearly twice the salary of the highest paid

---

1. These reports are listed in Table 8. They are India: Varadachariar and Das reports; Pakistan: Munir and Cornelius reports; Ceylon: Poulier, Christoffelsz, and Perera reports; Malaya: Trusted, Cowgill, Benham, and Himsworth reports; Burma: First Pay Commission Report. It should be said of these reports in general that they constitute some of the finest examples of administrative inquiry found anywhere in the field of public administration. Few Western nations have so exhaustively analyzed economic and theoretical presuppositions underlying salary structure. They are, as a class, outstanding documents.

Table 6. *Categories of Substantive Assignments of Elite Cadre Officers in India (1963), Pakistan (1964), Malaya (1963), Ceylon (1959), and Burma (1960)*[a]

Category[b]	India		Pakistan		Ceylon		Malaya		Burma		Totals[d]	
	No.	Pct.	No.	Pct.	No.	Pct.	No.	Pct.	No.	Pct.	No.	Pct.
Divisional and district administration	514	26.8	108	25.0	62	30.5	78	21.6	29	27.4	791	26.2
Provincial and state secretariat	545	28.4	67	15.5	—	—	60	16.6	3	2.8	675	22.3
Central government secretariat	260	13.5	50	11.6	128	63.1	195	54.0	43	40.6	676	22.4
Under training	142	7.4	81	18.7	—	—	—	—	—	—	223	7.4
Executives of operating nation-building departments	121	6.3	31	7.2	—	—	—	—	2	1.9	154	5.1
Government corporations	107	5.6	19	4.4	7	3.4	4	1.1	9	8.5	146	4.8
Miscellaneous	33	1.7	9	2.1	3	1.5	13	3.6	3	2.8	61	2.0
Diplomatic and other foreign assignments	38	2.0	11	2.5	1	0.5	2	0.6	6	5.7	58	1.9
On leave	18	0.9	11	2.5	—	—	—	—	5	4.7	34	1.1
Community development and co-operatives	31	1.6	—	—	—	—	—	—	—	—	31	1.0
Training staff	15	0.8	9	2.1	—	—	4	1.1	3	2.8	31	1.0
Secretaries to ministers, governors, and presidents	23	1.2	3	0.7	—	—	—	—	2	1.9	28	0.9
Judiciary	—	—	26	6.0	—	—	—	—	—	—	26	0.9
Deputation to other states within the country[c]	20	1.0	—	—	—	—	—	—	—	—	20	0.7
Planning boards (central and state)	13	0.7	5	1.2	—	—	—	—	—	—	18	0.6
Census (central, state, provincial)	18	0.9	—	—	—	—	—	—	—	—	18	0.6
Public service commissions (central, state, provincial)	9	0.5	2	0.5	2	1.0	5	1.4	—	—	18	0.6
University vice-chancellors	10	0.5	—	—	—	—	—	—	—	—	10	0.3
Under suspension	4	0.2	—	—	—	—	—	—	1	0.9	5	0.2
Totals	1,921		432		203		361		106		3,023	

a. Data for Nepal relevant to this table does not exist.

b. Categories have been generalized to render them comparable. Some years are not used for all countries because recency of published civil lists, staff lists and gradation lists varies.

c. This classification refers to officers assigned to one of the fifteen states of India but since no further information is given in the Civil List, it is not known if they are posted in the secretariats of the states or in other assignments.

d. Cadre strength figures are actual posts filled rather than authorized projections.

(New Delhi, 1964), Pakistan: Compiled by S. M. Haider from *Gradation List of the Civil Service of Pakistan*—as of January 1, 1964 (Karachi, 1964). Ceylon: Compiled by Robert N. Kearney from *Ceylon Civil List as of December 31, 1959* (Colombo, 1960). Malaya: Compiled by Robert O. Tilman from Federation of Malaya, *Staff List—1963* (Kuala Lumpur: Government Printing Press, 1962), pp. 2-19. This is based on established posts rather than actual strength; hence, it differs from the figure 349 used in other tables. Burma: Compiled by James F. Guyot from Union of Burma, *Civil List No. 10 (corrected up to 31 December 1960* (Rangoon, 1960).

officials of other, "non-elite" cadres. In each of the states the feeling after independence was much like that expressed in the report of the Perera Commission in Ceylon: "the existence of two sets of officers on different salary levels and with different promotion prospects [had] . . . created . . . a 'caste' system which, besides being a constant source of irritation and discontent, has created a division in an important level of the Public Service."[2] Ceylon responded to this kind of criticism by integrating the CCS with other services and by adjusting salaries. The other countries responded only by making salary adjustments. A crude effort to indicate these differentials is made in Table 7. Again it should be pointed out that the limitations of data which I have attempted to set forth in detail in the notes to Table 7 are serious and that strict comparability is therefore impossible. Further, changes may have been made in some of the states since this information was tabulated. It can be said, with any degree of assurance, only that the sharp disparities in remuneration have been reduced considerably. The Rs. 4,000 monthly salary received by a full secretary in India and Pakistan has been reduced to Rs. 3,500 and Rs. 3,000, respectively. The reduction in disparity cannot be fully appreciated without reference to the over-all disparity which formerly existed. This can be suggested by the following sample figures for India and Pakistan. It is a fairly safe assumption that the disparity was comparable in the other countries as well. In 1939 the highest-paid employee's monthly pay was Rs. 4,000, and the lowest-paid employee received Rs. 14 a month. This is a ratio of 286:1.[3] In 1948 this gap in both countries was reduced to a ratio of about 103:1. In 1965, as Table 7 shows, the ratio was 39:1 in Pakistan and about 64:1 in India. The likelihood is that in India the gap has been further reduced by recent salary changes not included in this table. The gap has been reduced most in Ceylon, where the ratio is 16.66:1, and least in Malaya. None of these ratios between highest- and lowest-paid employees compares favorably with that of the

---

2. *Report of the Salaries and Cadre Commission, 1961,* Part I (Ceylon Sessional Paper III, 1961), p. 161.
3. Pakistan Publications, *Pakistan—1963–64* (Karachi, 1964), p. 26.

Table 7. Comparison[a] of Differentials in Monthly Salaries of Highest Position in Elite Cadres, Highest Paid Stenographer, and Lowest Entrance Salary: India, Pakistan, Ceylon, Malaya, Burma, Nepal, and United States, 1964 and 1965

	A	B	C	D	E
		Monthly salary[b]		Differentials	
Country	Elite cadre	Stenog- rapher	Lowest rank	A-B	A-C
India	Rs. 3,500	Rs. 425	Rs. 55	8.32/1	63.64/1
Pakistan	Rs. 3,000	Rs. 400	Rs. 77	7.50/1	38.96/1
Ceylon	Rs. 2,250	Rs. 300	Rs. 135	6.33/1	38.00/1
Malaya	M$2,270	M$530	M$47.50	4.28/1	47.79/1
Burma	Ks. 1,600	Ks. 300	Ks. 50	5.33/1	32.00/1
Nepal	Rs. 950	Rs. 150	Rs. 45	6.33/1	21.1/1
United States	US$2,042 (GS-18)	US$334 (GS-3)	US$282 (GS-1)	6.11/1	7.24/1

[a] Strict comparability is impossible because of the variables in function and responsibility of the positions compared. For the six Asian states in this table, the positions selected for column A are those of secretary to central government (India and Pakistan) and the equivalent positions of permanent secretary (Ceylon), permanent secretary, Prime Minister's Department (Malaya), and permanent secretary (Burma). This is ordinarily the highest rank which a civil servant may attain and is immediately below the political position of cabinet minister. The position of stenographer is selected to show differential between two positions calling for English language competence and literacy. The stenographer in India, Pakistan, and Ceylon is typically a male secondary school graduate who takes dictation and types. In Malaya, girls sometimes fill these positions. While not of the same social status as an officer of the elite cadre, the stenographer is about halfway up the social and economic scale from the lowest-paid employee (peon or messenger) to the highest secretary (or equivalent). The lowest pay is shown for the lowest rank, variously called peon, daftri, sweeper, or messenger. These positions in India, Pakistan, Ceylon, and Burma are typically held by illiterate or semi-literate, unskilled persons, often underage employees or very old men. In Malaya they are often held by boys who hope to learn typing and English and enter the clerical service. The positions in the United States Civil Service used in this table for comparative reference are those of GS-18, the rank of clerk-typist (GS-3), and the beginning salary of clerks and custodial help (GS-1). Although the social distance between GS-18 and GS-3 is not nearly as great as that between comparable ranks in the Asian states, they are the nearest equivalent ranks.

[b] Only base monthly salary is used here. Retirement benefits, housing, and dearness allowances vary greatly by rank within each system and by assignment within each rank. Hence, these factors cannot be compared. Salaries given are those known to be in effect in 1965, except for Malaya and Burma, where date of source indicates date of validity. Conversion table: one Malay $ equals US$0.33; one Pakistani rupee equals US$0.21; one Indian rupee equals US$0.21; one Ceylonese rupee equals US$0.21; one Burmese kyat equals US$0.21.

Sources: India: Government of India, Report of Commission of Enquiry on Emoluments and Conditions of Service of Central Government Employees— 1957–59 (Das Commission), pp. 76, 206, and letter, Indian Institute of Public Administration, November 20, 1965. Pakistan: Pakistan Publications, Pakistan— 1963–64 (Karachi, 1964), p. 26. Ceylon: Government of Ceylon, Report of the Salaries and Cadre Commission—1961 (Perera Commission), pp. 94, 118, 164,

United States which is 7.24:1. On the other hand, the differentials in the pay of stenographers and secretaries to government is fairly uniform in all six systems. The ratio ranges from 4.28:1 for Malaya to 7.5:1 for Pakistan and compares favorably with the 6.11:1 ratio for the United States. The disparity which continues to exist between the lowest rank and the highest is the inevitable reflection of caste-structured societies in which modes of life are entirely different for these two groups. A moderate reduction in disparity, as between stenographers and the highest-paid officer, is taking place in groups above the lowest classes. Even with sharp disparities reduced, the prestige of the elite cadres remains high in all six states, although the status differential is somewhat less in Nepal, Malaya, and Burma than in the remaining three countries.

Perhaps the most instructive observation to be made about elite cadres in these six systems is their continued existence in concept and structure eighteen years after independence in India, Pakistan, and Burma, and eight years after independence in Malaysia. Even in Ceylon, despite a change in nomenclature, the concept persists. Although adverse criticism has been made of the system in all the states, no state has amalgamated its public services into one common, unified, graded service. Nor have most of the states seriously considered such a prospect. The Pay and Service Commission of 1959 in India, headed by Shri Justice Jagannadha Das, refrained from dealing with the Indian Administrative Service when the Ministry of Finance ruled that the IAS was outside the commission's terms of reference. Asok Chanda and Paul Appleby suggested a unified service, but their suggestion has not found wide acceptance in government circles or even in academic public administration outside government service.[4] The *Indian Journal of Public Administration*, a major source of administrative reform doctrine, has published only two articles on

4. Asok Chanda, *Indian Administration* (London, 1958), p. 127; Paul Appleby's comment appeared in the *Sunday Statesman* (Delhi), April 16, 1961, p. 4.

and letter, Establishment Secretary, Colombo, February 23, 1966. Malaya: Federation of Malaya, *Schemes of Service* (Kuala Lumpur: Government Press, 1956) (with irregularly inserted amendments to 1963), Vols. I and II, *passim*, esp. I, 1–2, 33–34; II, 1–2. Burma: James F. Guyot, interviews and correspondence; Union of Burma, *Civil List No. 10* (Rangoon, 1960).

a unified service.[5] Only one of these articles advocated a unified elite cadre, and this was in response to the first article which argued in favor of keeping the existing fragmented structure. The Perera Commission in Ceylon, although recommending abolition of the CCS, did not suggest a totally unified service. In Malaya the problem has not been systematically dealt with, although it is reported that since Malaysia was formed some thought was given to abolishing the MCS. Although in Burma a merger of Class I and II Services and entrance into the BCS Class I by promotion changed the elite cadre's composition, as it did in Ceylon, the concept of discrete cadres remained. In both India and Pakistan structural change moved in the direction of creating additional cadres, not merging existing segments of the service. In India at least five new all-India services were created: engineering, forestry, health and medical, and an economic service as well as a statistics service were made separate central services. In Pakistan a taxation service and a central information service were created, a separate service for section officers was established, a medical service was set up and then abolished, and proposals were made by government commissions for creation of a judicial service and a scientific service. In both Burma and Pakistan the army was in control for extended periods and might have unified the services by fiat, just as other major reforms were sometimes accomplished. In Pakistan the recommendations of the Cornelius Report relating to change in the structure of the services were not accepted by the government. In both Pakistan and Burma the military elites in control quickly identified themselves with the civil bureaucracy and appeared reluctant to make drastic changes which the civil bureaucracy keenly opposed.

It is pertinent to inquire into the reasons for the basic organization of the fragmented structure of the cadre system and for continuance of the elite cadres in these countries. Members of the elite cadres have been in positions controlling administrative reform and have been understandably less interested in drastic

5. S. Banerji, "A Unified Civil Service," *Indian Journal of Public Administration* IX (April–June, 1963), 189–211. Banerji's argument favoring the existing system is answered in S. Mallick, "A Unified (Central) Civil Service?" *Indian Journal of Public Administration* X (January–March, 1964), 44–57.

structural revision than critics outside the system. The modified adjustments made in India in the admission of large numbers of lateral entrants were probably the consequence of a very serious shortage of officers and the powerful position of Nehru and others who were opposed to ICS attitudes but who did not dare risk overturning the structure. In all the countries here analyzed there seems to have been a natural reluctance to tamper drastically with a functioning system on which the entire operation of the state seemed to depend. Since the discrete entities had woven a complex pattern of allegiances to various ministries, the unification of the services would have involved changes in ministerial organization as well. The existence of separate cadres of government servants at the professional level was more or less articulated to professional organization outside of government. Except for Malaya, the professionalization of medicine, engineering, science, and education has occurred within the bureaucracy rather than outside it. Hence, the separate organization of professionals tended to exert pressures for the same kind of separateness on the various cadres. None of these countries has known any other organizational style of bureaucracy. Even in Pakistan, where American influence has been greatest, contact with a unified service as found in the United States has been limited. Perhaps the most important reason for the continuance of separate cadres is that the discrete entities reflect the caste-structured society of which they are a part and are closely correlated with social status, level of education, and linguistic competence. If this is so, changes in the social order may eventually induce equivalent changes in the present system of a structurally fragmented bureaucracy. Not surprisingly, there does appear to be a positive correlation between the rigidity of hierarchical social strata in the society at large and the rigidity of structure and extent of elitism in the higher bureaucracies. Thus, these attributes appear to be most pronounced in Pakistan where the nature of the system is determined largely by West Pakistani, particularly Punjabis and Pathans. In Malaya and Burma, where these distinctions have been softened considerably, they are softened in the bureaucracy as well.

In all six countries, government service and particularly the elite cadres seem to be continuing to attract a significantly large proportion of university graduates with distinguished academic records. Data on academic attainment is uneven for all countries; hence, no firm comparisons can be made. We know that virtually every recruit in the elite cadre is a university graduate. In Burma 95 per cent are university graduates and almost all have honors degrees. In this respect it cannot be said that they are representative of the larger societies. Fortunately, a fairly close comparison can be made of the examination process for India and Pakistan for 1962. We find for that year that about .09 per cent of university graduates in India and .27 per cent in Pakistan were actually appointed to the IAS and the CSP. The proportion of those who applied for the examination and were appointed to these services was 1.1 per cent for India and 3.1 per cent for Pakistan. Of those who took the written examination, 18.4 per cent passed in India; 33.2 per cent passed in Pakistan. In India, of those passing the examination, 9.3 per cent were appointed; in Pakistan, 10.9 per cent were appointed. It is regrettable that data of this kind are not available for other years and other countries. These limited figures for 1962 quite clearly suggest a very high selectivity in appointments to the elite cadres. It is the general impression of the collaborating authors that such proportions are probably applicable for all years since independence in all five countries (excluding Nepal).

With respect to social background of post-independence recruits into the elite cadres, no sharp discontinuity is noted. Again, we have only limited data—in this instance for Burma, India, and Pakistan—to support this suggestion. The proportions of recruits whose fathers are civil servants are much the same: 51 per cent in Burma, 44 per cent in India, 59 per cent in Pakistan. Income data show a slightly larger proportion of recruits in India from lower-income families than in Pakistan, but the evidence is too sketchy to be certain of this. One significant comparative feature of the new recruits is that the proportion of those who are British-trained is significantly higher in Pakistan than in the remaining five systems. Little is known about the background of new recruits to the elite cadres in the remaining systems. It can be said with certainty of all six systems, however, that there has been no revolutionary displacement of one type of elite by a radically different proletariat elite. We find instead the same type of person, with the same type of education, from more or less the same background joining the elite cadres now as before independence.

One final observation regarding elite cadres seems indicated. In systems which have opened the elite cadres to a significant degree to civil servants promoted from other services, as in Burma, India, and Malaya, or which have absorbed other services in toto, as in Ceylon, animosity toward the elite cadre seems to have significantly diminished. It cannot be said with certainty that this freer access is the principal cause of such change in attitude, for each of these systems has also become extensively politicized. It is probably only in Pakistan, where feelings against the elite cadre continue to run high, that we also find lateral entry of negligible proportions and minimal politicization of the social order.

All six states have been prolific in the preparation of reports on administrative reform. Table 8 shows that they have produced seventy-six major reports totalling 10,208 pages. This is only a portion of the total production, for as the notes to Table 8 indicate, certain categories of reports are not included in that tabulation. Although each of the systems has been productive in this regard, there are important qualitative distinctions not revealed by Table 8. It has already been pointed out that 44 per cent of this reporting has related to salary and service structure rather than to more general problems of administrative reform. Ceylon accounts for about half of the volume of salary and structure reporting (2,113 out of 4,573 pages). Most of the reporting activity in Ceylon (2,113 out of 3,565 pages, or 59 per cent) relates to this subject, which suggests what is already known from field observation, namely, that very little administrative reform or comprehensive planning of reform has taken place in Ceylon. The only major report on broad aspects of administrative reform was completed a year after independence

Table 8. *Major Government Reports*[a] *on Administration for India, Pakistan, Ceylon, Malaya, Nepal, and Burma, 1947–1964*

INDIA[b]

Report of Secretariat Reorganization Committee (Bajpai), 1947*

Report of Reorganization of Machinery of Government (N. Gopalaswamy Ayyangar) 1949, 39 pp.

General Report of Economy Committee (Lalbhai), 1949, 10 pp.

Report of Central Pay Commission (Varadachariar), 1950, 436 pp.

Report on the Efficient Conduct of State Enterprises (A. D. Gorwala), 1951, 34 pp.

Report on Public Administration (A. D. Gorwala), 1951, 66 pp.

Report on the Machinery of Government Improvement of Efficiency (R. A. Gopalaswamy), 1952*

Public Administration in India: Report of a Survey (Paul H. Appleby), 1953, 70 pp.[o]

Note on Changes Necessary in the System of Budgetary and Financial Control and in Other Matters to Eliminate Delays in Execution of Projects (A. K. Chanda), 1954*

Report of Railway Corruption Enquiry Committee (Hriday Nath Kunzru), 1955, 187 pp.

Reexamination of India's Administrative System with Special Reference to Administration of Government's Industrial and Commercial Enterprises (Paul H. Appleby), 1956, 59 pp.

Report of Public Services (Qualifications for Recruitment) Committee (Mudaliar), 1956, 34 pp.

Report of the Commission of Enquiry on Emoluments and Conditions of Service of Central Government Employees (Jagannadha Das), 1959, 640 pp.

Report on Indian and State Administrative Services and Problems of District Administration (V. T. Krishnamachari), 1962, 108 pp.

Report of the Economy Committee, 1963*

Report of the Committee on Prevention of Corruption (K. Santhanam), 1964, 304 pp.

PAKISTAN

Report of Reorganization Committee (Sir Victor Turner), 1947, 4 pp.*

Report of Pakistan Pay Commission (Md. Munir), 1949, 443 pp.

Report of Committee Appointed by the Legislature to Review Government Expenditures (Omar Hayat Khan), 1951, 296 pp.

Financial Enquiry Regarding Allocation of Revenues Between Central and Provincial Governments (Sir Jeremy Raisman), 1952, 86 pp.

Development of Organization and Methods Work (K. S. Jeffries), 1952,* 24 pp.

Report of Committee to Examine Question of Raising Morale of Services (Akhter Husain), 1953,* 57 pp.

Report of Administrative Enquiry Committee (T. Creagh-Coen), 1953, 114 pp.*

Table 8 (*cont.*)

Improvement of Public Administration (Rowland Egger), 1953, 134 pp.°

Reorganization of Pakistan Government for National Development (Bernard Gladieux), 1955, 80 pp.°

Report of Committee to Consider Financial Control over Defence Expenditure (Akhter Husain), 1956,* 133 pp.

Report of Federal Reorganization Committee (G. Ahmed), 1956, 48 pp.

Report of Economy Committee (A. S. M. Akram), 1958, 100 pp.

Report of Administrative Reorganisation Commission (G. Ahmed), 1961, 400 pp.

Report of Committee on Decentralization of Institutions (N. A. Faruqui), 1961, 95 pp.

Report of Pay and Service Commission (A. R. Cornelius), 1962, 300 pp.

Report of Commission on Allocation of Revenues to Central and Provincial Governments (H. A. Majid), 1962, 81 pp.

Report of Standing Organisation Committee on the Reorganisation of the Functions and Structure of the Central Government in the Light of the New Constitution (M. Shoaib), 1962, 101 pp.

CEYLON

Report of the Commission on the Organisation, Staffing, and Operative Methods of Government Departments (Sessional Paper V, 1948), 346 pp.

Detailed Statement of Action Taken on the Report on Organization, Staffing, and Operative Methods in Government Departments (Sessional Paper I, 1951), 50 pp.

Report on the Introduction of an Organization and Methods Division into the Ceylon Public Service (Sessional Paper III, 1951), 55 pp.

Report on the Salaries and Cadres Commission, 1953 (R. S. V. Poulier) (Part I, Sessional Paper XII, 1953; Part II, Sessional Paper XVII, 1953), 595 pp.

Report of the Commission on Local Government (N. K. Choksy) (Sessional Paper XXXIII, 1955), 501 pp.

Report of the Salary Anomalies Commission (A. E. Christoffelsz) (Sessional Paper XXXVII, 1957), 1,024 pp.

Report of the Committee Appointed by the Secretary to the Treasury to Examine and Report on the Classification, Grading, etc. of Labour 1960 (Sessional Paper V, 1962), 196 pp.

Report of the Salaries and Cadre Commission—1961 (W. Perera) (Part I, Sessional Paper III, 1961; Part II, Sessional Paper IV, 1961), 798 pp.

MALAYA°

Public Services Salary Commission of Malaya (Sir H. Trusted), 1947, 175 pp.

Report on the Revision of Salaries in the Public Services of the Federation of Malaya and the Colony of Singapore (J. V. Cowgill), 1949, 156 pp.

Table 8 (*cont.*)

Report of the Special Commission on Salaries in the Federation of Malaya (F. C. Benham), 1950, 28 pp.

Report of the Professional Officers Committee (H. Willan), 1950, 18 pp.

Report to His Excellency the Officer Administering the Government, Sir Donald McGillivray (W. J. Haimes), 1953, 43 pp.

Report of the Committee on the Malayanization of the Government Service (D. Gray), 1954, 124 pp.

Report of the Committee on the Examination of the Superscale Salaries of Division I of the Public Services of the Federation of Malaya and the Colony of Singapore (E. Himsworth), 1954, 41 pp.

Report of a Commission to Enquire into Matters Affecting the Integrity of the Public Services (E. N. Taylor), 1955, 86 pp.

Malayanization of the Public Service: A Statement of Policy, 1956, 8 pp.

Report of the Committee on Malayanization of the Public Service, 1956, 143 pp.

General Circular No. 4 of 1959 (*Organization Within Ministries*), 6 pp.

NEPAL

Report on Administration in Nepal to the Prime Minister (Merrill R. Goodall), 1952, 22 pp.#

Report on the Nepal Administrative Reorganization Committee (N. M. Buch, ICS, and colleagues), 1952, 167 pp.

Report on Reorganization of District Administration in Nepal (Subcommittee of Administrative Reorganization Planning Commission), 1957, 68 pp.

Report of the *Ad Hoc* Advisory Committee Regarding an Institute of Public Administration in Nepal, 1957, 4 pp.

Report of the Committee on the Institute of Public Administration in Nepal, 1957, 6 pp.

Personnel Administration in Nepal (Walter Fischer), 1958, 18 pp.#

Proposal for the Reorganization of the Posts and Telegraphs Services in Nepal (B. Lall), 1958, 44 pp.

Report on the Fiscal System of Nepal (E. Himsworth), 1959, 227 pp.#

District Administration: A Survey of Pokhara District (S. T. Divers), 1960, 13 pp.#

Final Report of the Specially Powered Tour Committee (Ministry of National Guidance), 1962, 45 pp.

Report of the Committee on Administration of His Majesty's Government of Nepal (Premnarsingh Pradhan, Kulsekhar Sharma, Yadunath Khanal, Merrill Goodall), 1962, 10 pp.

District Administration: Pokhara District Re-Surveyed (Merrill Goodall), 1963, 21 pp.#

Development of Public Administration in Nepal, Final Report to the Government of Nepal (Merrill Goodall), 1963, 53 pp.#

Supervision of Public Enterprises in Nepal (Rune Tersman), 1963, 12 pp.#

Table 8 (cont.)

BURMA

Report of the Local Bodies Enquiry Committee (Dr. Maung Set), 1947, 60 pp.

Report of the Pay Commission, 1947, 27 pp.*

The First Interim Report of the Administration Reorganization Committee (U Lun Baw), 1949, 50 pp.

Final Report of the Administration Reorganization Committee (U Lun Baw), 1951, 117 pp.

Report of a Survey on Public Administration in Burma (G. T. Jackson), 1954, 64 pp.#

Report on Public Administration in Burma (F. J. Tickner), 1954,# 10 pp.*

Public Administration in Burma: Progress 1953–1956 (S. T. Divers), 1956, 15 pp.#

Local Government Democratization Program of the Union of Burma (Wendell G. Schaeffer), 1957, 40 pp.°

Public Administration in Burma: 1956–58 (A. S. Pankhurst), 1958, 10 pp.*

Report of the Public Services Enquiry Commission (U Chan Tun Aung), 1961, 189 pp.#

	India	Pakistan	Ceylon	Malaya[c]	Nepal	Burma
Number of reports	16	17	8	11	14	10
Total pages	2,027	2,496	3,565	828	710	582

All six countries: Total number of reports—76   Total number of pages—10,208

[a] Only episodic reports relating to central governments are tabulated here. Annual reports of ministries and departments or of public service commissions are not included. Some seventy-three government reports issued by the fifteen states of India are not included, nor are the eleven reports issued by the two provinces of Pakistan. For Ceylon and Malaya, there are no provincial or state government reports on administration. Reports of parliamentary committees (except the Santhanam Report for India) on administrative matters of the executive branch are not included. For all six countries, central government reports relating to central-local relations are included.

[b] The list of reports for India given in this table differs in important respects from the list in the *Indian Journal of Public Administration*, IX (1963), 581–586. Ephemeral reports (such as those relating to curricula of training institutions) and the Report of the Direct Taxes Administration Enquiry Committee (1960) are omitted from this table.

[c] Reports of Malaya preceding independence in 1957 are included, because during this decade (1947–1957) Malaya faced in a more leisurely fashion the same problems of indigenization and eventual independence confronted rather more suddenly by India, Pakistan, and Ceylon in 1947. Since this comparative table seeks to show the documentary formats used in confronting problems of indigenization and independence, the inclusion of the 1947–1957 decade appears justified.

* Unpublished report: pagination unknown. Unless another estimate has been indicated, the report is estimated at ten pages.

° Prepared under Ford Foundation auspices.

Prepared under United Nations auspices.

in 1948. The situation in Malaya is somewhat the same as in Ceylon. About half of the bulk of the reporting (400 of 828 pages) relates to salaries; the remaining reports deal almost entirely with Malayanization. There have been no major comprehensive plans reported for general administrative reform in Malaya. Again this appears consistent with field observation that very little administrative reform has been planned or has occurred in Malaya. This condition will probably change in a few years, for in the summer of 1965 the Ford Foundation sponsored a study of administrative reform needs in Malaysia.[6] If the experience of similar surveys in India and Pakistan can be an index of activity, it is not unlikely that extensive reform will soon begin in Malaysia. Ceylon and Malaysia seem to be in a category by themselves in the matter of relative lack of activity in administrative reform. In neither of these countries has there been any significant foreign technical assistance in public administration. Malaysia has a highly developed social organization, a sophisticated commercial structure, and a prosperous economy, and Ceylon is not faced with the acute economic problems of India, Pakistan, and Burma. Both countries have had more or less "normal" governments, i.e., martial law has not been declared nor have there been coups d'état accomplished by force. There has been instability of various kinds, and conditions of war in Malaysia with respect to communism, but in neither case has there been total structural or ideological discontinuity with new constitutional polities. These favorable conditions may very well have dulled the awareness of any acute immediate necessity to improve administration drastically. Certainly there have been unstable political conditions, especially in Ceylon, but since in neither country has the military assumed control (as it has in Burma and Pakistan), one of the strongest modernizing influ-

6. This study by John D. Montgomery of Harvard University and Milton J. Esman of the University of Pittsburgh resulted in a 27 page report, published by the Malaysian government: John D. Montgomery and Milton J. Esman, *Development Administration in Malaysia, Report to the Government of Malaysia* (Kuala Lumpur, Malaysia, 1966). The report was favorably received by the Malaysian government and will be followed by the provision of advisory services to that government for a two year period by Harvard University, under contract with the Ford Foundation.

ences which military rule usually brings to bear has been missing.

In India, Pakistan, Burma, and Nepal, extensive reform planning has been carried on and to some extent implemented. The role of foreign technical assistance in this planning appears to be important. In three of the four states where foreign technical assistance was important, its role was advisory rather than operational. Nepal is the exception, with several officers engaged under the United Nations OPEX program holding positions in His Majesty's Government. In Burma there appears to have been an infusion of administrative doctrine from American and Canadian sources, and as a result of the work of the 1961 Public Services Enquiry Commission, from European and Indian sources as well. A major role was played by the United Nations Technical Assistance Programme. Burma was the only country of the six which was influenced also by a private firm of management experts, the Robert R. Nathan organization. This influence was exerted largely through the planning apparatus and continued over a period of eight years. The vigor of reform planning in Burma is matched by similar developments in Pakistan, where, however, the principal influences were the United States Agency for International Development and the Ford Foundation. The major difference between reform developments in these two countries lies in the attention given to the establishment of training programs and institutions. Training was vigorously pursued in Pakistan but was a very minor aspect of reform in Burma. In both Burma and Pakistan a long line of administrative doctrine was consolidated in single major reports appearing in both countries in 1961. These reports (of the Public Services Enquiry Commission in Burma and of the G. Ahmed Committee in Pakistan) capsulated previous reform doctrine and served as the basis for implementation. In India the principal influence in administrative reform was the Ford Foundation; the United States Agency for International Development played a minor role, and United Nations participation was still less important. As in Burma and Pakistan, the planning function was the chief vehicle for the introduction of reform doctrine. Developments in India differed from those in

Burma and Pakistan in that until 1966 there was no single, comprehensive, major inquiry comparable to the 1961 reports for those two countries.[7] To a degree this can be explained by the fact that state governments are more important in India than are units of government below the central government in either Burma or Pakistan, and the major activity in administrative reform in India devolved upon them. Another reason seems to be that India's interest in administrative reform reached its zenith from 1953 to 1956 with publication of the two Appleby reports. Thereafter, interest dwindled, and although vigorous intellectual and research activities in administration were carried on, further governmental attention in the form of comprehensive surveys gave way to more urgent political problems, both internal and international. Finally, large-scale involvement of the Ford Foundation had ceased by 1956, and the United States Agency for Interna-

7. In India a significant development in planning for administrative reform occurred with appointment of the Administrative Reforms Commission on January 5, 1966. (*Gazette of India, Extraordinary*, January 5, 1966, pp. 23–26.) The commission is headed by Morarji Desai, and consists of three other members of Parliament, H. C. Mathur, D. Mookerji (who replaced G. S. Pathak in April 1966), H. V. Kamath, and an ICS officer, V. Shankar. V. V. Chari has been appointed secretary. The responsibilities of the commission are broader than those previously assigned any such commission in India. The terms of reference order the commission to consider (1) machinery of the central government, (2) planning at all levels, (3) centre-state relationships, (4) financial administration, (5) personnel administration, (6) economic administration, (7) state administration, (8) district administration, (9) agricultural administration, (10) redress of citizens' grievances. The Commission appointed 8 study teams (task forces) in May 1966 and plans to appoint twelve more. The Commission is making use of the Indian Institute of Public Administration and has already assigned several studies to the Institute. The Ford Foundation, which helped create the Institute in 1953, is expected to award a grant of $291,500 to the Institute to enable it to engage some 9 foreign and 12 Indian short-term and long-term consultants. To provide continuing help, the India office of the Ford Foundation has added Dr. Edward A. Kielock to its staff as program advisor in public administration. The work of this commission, embracing the totality of India's administrative problems, modelled after the Hoover Commission, including parliamentary membership but responsible to the Ministry of Home Affairs, and utilizing the services of a well-established Indian research organization differs in most of these respects from efforts in the other five states here considered. It is the most ambitious and most complex administrative reform apparatus which has yet appeared on the post-independence scene. Constructed on a base of more than a decade of experience in public administration, it appears to be an impressive means of generating reform throughout India. But its effect on state administration especially, may be difficult to achieve. Several states have already planned administrative reform, the latest being the *Report of the Punjab Administrative Reforms Commission 1964–65* (Chandigahr, 1966). The problem of co-ordinating the disparate administrative competences of 16 states with central government norms may not only affect the success of the total effort but may have important consequences on the nature of India's "federal" system.

tional Development continued to have only slight and peripheral influence in administrative reform. As a consequence there was no continuing foreign impetus to stimulate further reform activity. In Burma and Pakistan the height of interest in reform was reached in the early 1960's; continuing under the aegis of army rule and martial law, this interest was consolidated and implemented with more authoritarian backing than was possible in India. In Nepal reform activity was unusually dynamic, and it is likely that foreign influence there was greater and more effective than in any of the six states. There were 290 foreign advisers in Nepal, a ratio of one for every three Nepalese gazetted officers. The impact here was achieved almost exclusively by the United Nations Technical Assistance Programme, which engaged principally, though not exclusively, American advisers. Just as there is an obvious positive correlation between the extent of foreign aid in public administration and the vigor of administrative reform activity, so is there a positive correlation between reform activity and the establishment of administrative training programs. In Burma and Nepal institutes of public administration were established under the aegis of the United Nations Technical Assistance Programme. India's institute was helped by the Ford Foundation, and Pakistan's three institutes were assisted by the United States Agency for International Development. Ceylon had a training institute originally helped by the United States Agency for International Development, but following the termination of all USAID activity in 1963, the institute ceased operation. Malaysia has no training institute.

An ancillary outcome of administrative reform efforts is the comparative development of research and scholarship in public administration in the six countries. In this respect India surpasses the other states by a very considerable margin. The level and sophistication of scholarship, especially that emanating from the Indian Institute of Public Administration, is clearly of a different order than that of the other nations. Moreover, the accessibility of information and the climate of freedom to criticize government policy and practice make research on administration much easier in India. Finally, the number of foreign scholars embarking on research on administration is proportionately greater in India than in the other five countries. And this relative disparity in research seems to be increasing rather than diminishing. For as research opportunities for both Indians and foreigners expand in India, various internal and external problems have rendered research increasingly difficult in Burma, Pakistan, and Malaysia. In Nepal this condition is not so serious, and in Ceylon it is likely to improve.

The substantive content of administrative reforms which have been planned or put into effect in all six states seems to follow a pattern of both continuity and change. All states except Pakistan have retained the parliamentary system. Central planning is an important part of such reform, being accepted soon after independence; it is most highly developed in Burma, India, and Pakistan. The importance of the district officer remains unchanged and straddles what otherwise approximates a federal system. The secretariat system and the predominance of the generalist remain. Government corporations have been widely used as a means of promoting aspects of economic development. In all five states combined we find a total of at least 297 corporations (India, 178; Pakistan, 36; Ceylon, 35; Burma, 31; Malaya, 17). In none of the systems, however, have the corporations completely escaped the influence of the generalist elite cadres. In Burma, where the control seems to be greatest, secretaries of line ministries also serve in the corporations. In Ceylon corporations also come under close ministerial supervision, and there appears to be little of the autonomy which was envisaged. In India more attention has been given to the role of the corporation in the total government activity than in any of the other countries. The first major scandal involving a corporation, the Mundhra Affair, has directed attention to corporations in India and has strengthened parliamentary and ministerial surveillance over them. Of the six nations discussed in this volume, India is the only one in which we find a mature, logical extension of constitutional doctrine and parliamentary apparatus to encompass the problem of rendering the corporate device accountable and responsible. In the other countries, relationships of the corporations with legislatures and ministries have not been clarified, and in some cases they are not yet recognized as a major problem in constitutional government.

While each of the countries has had a significant rural development movement, in none has there been the severance from the formal bureaucracy which was envisioned. On the contrary, with the possible exception of India, the movements seem to have become absorbed more and more within the bureaucratic ambit. The panchayati raj movement in India has been significant as an arena in which coercive bureaucratic and persuasive, participative norms and behaviors interact. The influence of the latter on the orthodox bureaucracy seems greater than in equivalent community development movements in the other states. This may be helped somewhat by the strength of the dominant mass party apparatus at local levels, which provides a means for articulating and focusing political power through the panchayats and thence into the orthodox bureaucratic structure. The ideological, statutory, and structural strength of panchayati raj seems also to have influenced the elite cadre as well as other elements of the bureaucracy who seem to have accepted their new constructive role of responsibility to elements in society other than themselves. This influence is probably more pronounced in India than in any of the other states.

Perhaps the greatest difference in the administrative development of these six states is in the matter of bureaucratic responsibility. The character of this responsibility seems directly related to the degree of politicization of the social order. Politicization is probably most advanced in India under the dominance of one mass party. Here at every level we find the political process exerting some control over bureaucracy, and there is evidence to suggest that party leaders in the states have some voice even in the posting of IAS officers. The legislative process is also vigorous, and it exerts some control over administration, at least indirectly. Malaysia is clearly not the "administrative state" found in other emerging countries; as in India, the bureaucracy is guided by the political process, and like other elites in society it has come through a process of political socialization. In Burma the measure of political control over bureaucracy which prevailed before 1962 was supplanted by military control after the coup of that year. In Ceylon the bureaucracy appears to be reasonably under the control of the cabinet and Parliament which, in turn, are controlled by quite coherent parties or coalitions. Even the strong trade unions are largely led by parties, and when they act politically (as opposed to seeking simply industrial gains even though the employer is government) they usually act under the control or guidance or in collaboration with parties—most often simply at party direction for party-defined goals. Linguistic and cultural pressure groups, such as the Buddhist and Sinhalese movements, have been largely expressed through political party competition. In Pakistan political control is probably less advanced than in the other states, with the exception of Nepal.

In none of the other states has the judiciary assumed the central position in control of the bureaucracy as it has in Pakistan. The contrast is nicely brought out with respect to Ceylon by two different interpretations of a Privy Council decision in the Nakkuda Ali case. The assumption of such power by the judiciary in Pakistan is probably due in large measure to the absence of other loci of countervailing power which exist in all the other states except Nepal. Thus, the courts have entered a vacuum and in so doing have exerted a control over administrative behavior which temporarily may be more effective than political controls. In India the courts have also developed a substantial corpus of administrative law, and judicial review of administrative discretion has become an important subject of legal research. But there, judicial review functions in a context of other devices of control, much as in Britain and the United States; in consequence, it does not loom as large on the horizon as in Pakistan. This is probably an index of a more symmetrical political development in India than in the other states. Interest groups and other institutions assume some role in the total political process so that no single institution, such as the judiciary, assumes functions somewhat beyond those assumed in older constitutional systems. In Malaya the relatively unimportant role of the judiciary is reflected in the relative unavailability of published court judgments.

Probably the most distinctive factor of control over the bureaucratic system in Ceylon is the strong trade-union movement. This situation is found in none of the other five countries discussed in this volume. More than two-thirds of government servants in Ceylon are members of more than 622 trade unions, the largest of which claims a membership of nearly ten thousand persons. Coupled with this is an absence of restrictions on strikes by government employees, another circumstance not found in the other states. Despite a limitation that strikes not be directed to matters outside service problems, important strikes have been used for external political matters. Although Whitley Councils were introduced in Ceylon, they have not been a successful instrument for the settlement of government employees' grievances. The ecological determinants behind the phenomenal rise of bureaucratic trade unionism in Ceylon have not yet been identified. The Ceylonese bureaucracy has undergone serious dislocations, especially those caused by the language and communal issues. But these dislocations appear to have been no greater than those of Burma, Pakistan, and India; and in none of those countries has trade unionism developed in the same manner as it has in Ceylon. Why was the judiciary not used to meet these demands as in Pakistan, or why did not the political process serve to convert demands into polity as in India? Perhaps the strength of Marxism, the number of parties in relation to population, the relative rigidity of caste lines, and the Tamil-Sinhalese bifurcation of the nation made trade unions the most convenient vehicle for aggregation and articulation of interests. This kind of problem in which the relationship of ecological factors to the development of similar institutions performing somewhat different functions in similar political systems is one of the most challenging in comparative political analysis. The present state of our knowledge allows only tentative suggestions as to a causal relationship.

In Malaysia we find Whitley Councils performing a role roughly analogous to trade unions in Ceylon, the judiciary in Pakistan and, with respect to some bureaucratic behaviors, to the dominant mass party political process in India. In none of the remaining five systems do we find the Whitley Council concept so successful. Approximately one hundred issues are considered each year by the Whitley Council, and agreements are reached in roughly half the cases. Significant service matters are considered, and occasionally, despite a stricture to the contrary, individual cases of grievance are considered by the council. Again it is intriguing to raise the question as to the ecological causal factors behind the rise of Whitleyism in Malaysia but not in the other five states. The reasons may be somewhat easier to identify than the reasons for the vigor of bureaucratic trade unionism in Ceylon. Whitleyism was first introduced in Malaya in 1948 but did not begin to flourish until 1953 as a consequence of the visit of W. J. Haimes and the report he wrote on the subject. Apparently much of the success of the concept is due to Haimes's personal impact. We should probably also note as causes for its adoption the relatively tranquil transition of power in Malaya a decade after the other nations had achieved independence. The longer period of transition under British tutelage and in an economy relatively prosperous and advanced may also have been causal factors.

In none of the six systems studied do we find a significant transfer of the skills and status of bureaucracy to the realm of politics. In Japan, for example, the political process quickly gained in status and intellectual respectability when significant numbers of the elite cadre of bureaucracy ran for political office and were elected. Such transfer of prestige and talent is one of the most effective ways of accelerating politicization of high quality. This has not occurred in these six states in which the factiousness of the political process continues to be held in low esteem. Politicization is most advanced in India, but the high prestige of politics is not due to infusion of that process with bureaucratic skills; rather it is that it developed for long years before independence as an elite rivalling and even exceeding the bureaucracy in prestige.

It is commonly felt by some Western analysts that the bureaucratic systems derivative from the British imperial system are anachronistic and that they have impeded rapid political and economic development. This is an oversimplification. Retrospectively, it is impossible to assess the role of order in development and the role of a particular type of bureaucratic apparatus in both generating and assimilating innovation within the framework of that order. The complexity of the variables suggests the futility, in terms of evidential corroboration, of engaging in retrospective polemics regarding past accomplishments of a bureaucracy when the magnitude of the relevant variables is only partially comprehended and still less understood. Suffice it to say that in none of these six states has the bureaucratic system been abandoned in favor of another system. There has been resilience and adaptability, continuity and change. The change has usually been forced by external pressures, but the response has been made within traditional patterns. This is no small accomplishment for ex-imperial bureaucratic systems which have been buffeted by competing forces in a context of development no longer ideologically hospitable to the concepts of Platonic guardianship, "gentlemanly power," and literary-generalism on which these bureaucracies were so strongly constructed.

Index

Index